The Texas Rangers

# The Texas Rangers

## A Registry and History

Darren L. Ivey

McFarland & Company, Inc., Publishers
*Jefferson, North Carolina*

*The present work is a reprint of the illustrated case bound edition of* The Texas Rangers: A Registry and History, *first published in 2010 by McFarland.*

LIBRARY OF CONGRESS CATALOGUING-IN-PUBLICATION DATA

Ivey, Darren L., 1970–
The Texas Rangers : a registry and history / Darren L. Ivey.
p.     cm.
Includes bibliographical references and index.

ISBN 978-1-4766-7822-1
softcover : acid free paper ∞

1. Texas Rangers—Registers.   2. Texas Rangers—History.
3. Soldiers—Texas—Registers.   4. Police—Texas—Registers.
5. Frontier and pioneer life—Texas.   6. Texas—History, Military.
I. Title.
F391.I94   2019     976.4—dc22     2010004384

British Library cataloguing data are available

© 2010 Darren L. Ivey. All rights reserved

*No part of this book may be reproduced or transmitted in any form or by any means, electronic or mechanical, including photocopying or recording, or by any information storage and retrieval system, without permission in writing from the publisher.*

Front cover images: Frontier Battalion at El Paso and Badge of Ira Aten (courtesy of the Texas Ranger Hall of Fame and Museum, Waco, Texas)

Manufactured in the United States of America

*McFarland & Company, Inc., Publishers
Box 611, Jefferson, North Carolina 28640
www.mcfarlandpub.com*

For Dusti
and our sons
Christopher, Thomas, and Michael

# Table of Contents

*Acknowledgments* ix

*Preface* 1

*Abbreviations* 3

1. For the Common Defense: Rangers in Colonial Tejas (1823–1835) — 7

2. Gained by War: Rangers of the Revolution and Republic (1835–1845) — 14

3. *Los Diablos Tejanos*: Rangers in the U.S.-Mexican War (1846–1848) — 59

4. Rangers of the Old Stamp: The Texas Mounted Volunteers (1848–1861) — 74

5. A Most Desperate Struggle: Rangers in the Civil War (1861–1865) — 100

6. No Surrender, No Prisoners: The Minute Men, the Frontier Forces, and the Frontier Men (1865–1874) — 135

7. A Little Standing Army: Minute Men/Special State Troops/Special Force (1874–1881) — 149

8. Duty Well Performed: The Frontier Battalion (1874–1901) — 157

9. *Los Rinches*: The State Ranger Force (1901–1935) — 173

10. A Fabled Tradition: The Texas Ranger Division (1935–Present) — 190

*Appendix A: Battle Record* 211

*Appendix B: Rangers Who Died in the Line of Duty* 226

*Appendix C: The Texas Ranger Hall of Fame*    246

*Appendix D: Texas Ranger Recipients of the
Department of Public Safety Medal of Valor*    247

*Appendix E: Documents Regarding the Texas Rangers*    250

*Appendix F: The History of the Badge*    308

*Bibliography*    313

*Index*    321

# Acknowledgments

No author, especially one of the non-fiction persuasion, ever writes his book alone. As I researched this subject, that truth was proven time and again. Many people in the great state of Texas generously took the time to lend some of their expertise toward the completion of this book. Among them were Donaly Brice (senior research assistant) and the archives staff at the Texas State Library and Archives Commission, Austin; the reference staff at the Dolph Briscoe Center for American History, the University of Texas at Austin; Senior Captain Ray Coffman, and Captains Gary De Los Santos and H. D. Henderson at Texas Ranger Headquarters, Austin; Christina Stopka (deputy director for operations), Judy Shofner and Christina Smith (research librarians, Texas Ranger Research Center), and Tracie Evans (collections manager) at the Texas Ranger Hall of Fame and Museum, Waco; Mary Jane Harbison (library technician) at Amon Carter Museum, Fort Worth; Dr. Troy Davis (head of the History Department) at Stephen F. Austin State University, Nacogdoches; Jennifer L. Hall and Debi McLoughlin (human resource specialists, Human Resources Bureau) and Lisa Block (public information officer) at the Texas Department of Public Safety, Austin; Lanita Clay (genealogist) and Anita Tufts (archivist/librarian) at the Historical Research Center, Texas Heritage Museum, Hill College, Hillsboro; Patrick Lemelle (programs coordinator–library) at the University of Texas Institute of Texan Cultures, San Antonio; B. C. Lyon (executive director) at the Texas DPS Historical Museum, Austin; and Jerry Brandt of J. Brandt Recognition Ltd., Fort Worth.

Stephen L. Moore, David Paul Smith, Patricia Adkins-Rochette, and Michael R. Thomasson contributed their knowledge and insight into the various eras of Ranger history, and also, in the case of the first two, the publishing process itself.

I am also appreciative of the talented artists who kindly allowed me to reproduce their works. These gentlemen include Bruce Greene (past president of the Cowboy Artists of America), Bruce Marshall (artist of the Sixty-fifth Legislature), Jack Terry (three-time artist for the Former Texas Ranger Foundation), and Jack White (former Official Texas State Artist).

Closer to home, I was aided by the kind folks at the Manhattan, Kansas Public Library, who handled an immense number of interlibrary loan requests for me. They include Melissa Lienemann (interlibrary loan) and Rhonna Hargett, Judi Nichols, Mary Newkirk, Linda Henderson, Sandra Kearns, and Royce Kitts (reference librarians). Kristine Withers (historian/librarian) at the U.S. Cavalry Memorial Research Library, U.S. Cavalry Association,

Fort Riley, provided me with some much needed assistance in tracking down an elusive detail. Eli Martinsen and Katie Franke of the Geographic Information Systems and Spatial Analysis Laboratory, Department of Geography, Kansas State University, created the maps featured throughout the book.

Even closer, I enjoyed the unconditional love and support of my lovely and gracious wife, Dusti. She helped to proof this book, corrected grammar and punctuation mistakes, accompanied me on several memorable trips to Austin and Waco, and offered tremendous aid as my unpaid copy editor and research assistant. Mostly she deserves credit for putting up with me all these years.

Finally, I thank you, dear reader, for spending your valuable time and possibly your hard-earned money in order to read this work. There are legions of books in the Texana genre to be read and I am very grateful you chose mine.

# Preface

This book exists because nowhere among the many fine works concerning the Texas Rangers is there one complete account of every Ranger unit and captain that Texas fielded. Usually for the sake of brevity, authors writing about the Rangers had to choose the men who best epitomized the story they wanted to tell. This tome is intended to fill that void and be a companion to those other books already in print, and the ones yet to come.

While I tried to be as comprehensive as possible, these pages concerning the Texas Rangers are incomplete and, unfortunately, will likely remain so. On October 10, 1855, the office of the Adjutant General was the scene of an apparent arson, allegedly by persons involved in land certificate fraud. This fire destroyed all the muster rolls and other military records compiled since the Revolution. Fortunately, some copies were held by the General Land Office and thus preserved. Then on November 9, 1881, the State Capitol was completely destroyed in another massive fire. Housed within the building was the State Library, which lost numerous volumes and documents.

The maxim that history is written by the victor is certainly true. Another would be that the loser rarely retains abundant records. The National Archives' Confederate service records and the Civil War Ranger Records at the Texas State Library and Archives are both voluminous, but still fragmentary.

When the Ranger Service transferred from the Adjutant General's Department to the Department of Public Safety, they also shifted records covering 1920 to 1935. These mysteriously disappeared sometime after the 1960s. Since the DPS did not have the wherewithal for the historic preservation of its records, it often destroyed closed-case files, obsolete documents, and inactive personnel rosters. One can find more records concerning the Texas Rangers of the nineteenth century than those of the twentieth. Presently, most official records are preserved at the Texas State Library in Austin. The Adjutant General did transfer records dated prior to 1920 that have survived to the State Archives in 1934, with additional transfers in 1962 and 1975. The DPS transferred some Ranger Force records to the Archives in 1978, and a box of newspaper clippings in 1980, but the DPS records for the Rangers from 1935 to the early 1970s are also missing. Some more modern records were transferred by the Texas Ranger Division in 1998. Fortunately, copies of some official and personal papers were often donated to the Texas Ranger Research Center at the Texas Rangers Hall of Fame in Waco. With such an inconsistently documented history, the story of the Texas Rangers is indeed sketchy in places.

One of the first things I had to decide was what defined a Ranger unit. After the formation of the Frontier Battalion and the Special Force in 1874, the definition of Ranger is pretty clear. Before that year, though, the term is more vague. Professor Walter Prescott Webb, the eminent Ranger historian, wrote that the early rangers were "an irregular body; they were mounted; they furnished their own horses and arms; they had no surgeon, no flag, none of the paraphernalia of the regular service. They were distinct from the regular army and also from the militia." Stephen L. Moore, author of the *Savage Frontier* series, described these rangers as a "group of armed men who operated independently from a regular military organization. They were generally self-armed, non-uniformed squads of civilians who patrolled the outer frontiers of a settled area to protect against Indian hostilities."

The rangers of the Republic of Texas (known variously as spies, mounted gunmen, mounted riflemen, minute men, etc.) were found in the regular army, the militia, and the ranging service; they could also be ad hoc volunteers who would gather in times of crisis. Before 1935, the rangers of the State of Texas (known interchangeably as rangers, mounted volunteers, and minute men), as part of either the Union or the Confederacy, were officially state troops.

The responsibilities of the Ranger Service have also changed with the times. They began as citizen-soldiers battling Indians and Mexicans, became frontier/border lawmen from the end of Reconstruction to the end of Prohibition, and then felony investigators for the state Department of Public Safety.

To be included in this book, the pre–1874 unit in question had to be mounted, serve on the frontier (Indian or Mexican), perform ranger-like duties (patrolling, scouting, pursuing, and raiding), be manned by individuals who are universally recognized as rangers (Caldwell, Hays, the McCulloch brothers, Ford, etc.) and be irregular in appearance and attitude. Such criteria are why, for example, the two regiments of "Jack" Hays are included, even though they were in Mexico as United States Volunteers rather than Texas State Troops. They performed essentially the same duties as they did before the war and certainly were a distinctly Texan force. Another example is the men who fought at Plum Creek who were not formally enrolled in Texas' armed forces, even though many had prior and future ranger service.

Once I identified who could be considered a Ranger, I organized them into the appropriate eras of Ranger history. Each time period covered includes a historical note, which is then followed by a register of units, arranged chronologically.

It is my sincere hope that this book will become a much-used reference source in the libraries of many Ranger historians. As time goes on and research continues, possibly more information will become available to complete the story of the legendary Western figures known as the Texas Rangers.

# Abbreviations

| | |
|---|---|
| Adj-Gen. | Adjutant-General |
| BG | Brigadier-General |
| Btn. | Battalion |
| Capt. | Captain |
| CG | Commanding General |
| Col. | Colonel |
| C-in-C | Commander-in-Chief |
| Co. | Company |
| Cpl. | Corporal |
| Det. | Detachment |
| DOW | Died of wounds |
| Front. Dist. | Frontier District |
| Front. Forces | Frontier Forces |
| Front. Men | Frontier Men |
| Front. Reg. | Frontier Regiment |
| GO | General Orders |
| Gov. | Governor |
| KIA | Killed in action |
| Lt. | Lieutenant |
| Lt-Col. | Lieutenant-Colonel |
| Lt-Gov. | Lieutenant-Governor |
| Maj. | Major |
| MG | Major-General |
| MIA | Missing in Action |
| Pvt. | Private |
| Reg. | Regiment |
| Sgt. | Sergeant |
| Sgt-Maj. | Sergeant-Major |
| SO | Special Orders |
| Sqdn. | Squadron |
| Vol. | Volunteer |

*"The Rangers are frequently thrown into positions which require judgment, quick action and undoubted courage. They are frequently required to trail criminals who are known to be without fear, desperate, and with a knowledge of the country as good as that of the ranger. To the credit of the force it can be said that they never refuse to face a danger when duty requires it. The moral effect of their presence in any disturbed district is well known."*
— Adjutant-General Thomas R. Scurry

*"They were a company of sober and brave men. They knew their duty and did it... They had a specie of moral discipline which developed moral courage. They did right because it was right. You might kill them but you could not conquer them."*
— Colonel John S. Ford

# 1

# For the Common Defense: Rangers in Colonial Tejas (1823–1835)

The modern Ranger Service traces its origins from May 5, 1823. On that day *empresario* Stephen F. Austin mustered Lieutenant Moses Morrison and a company of nine volunteers into service. The genesis of this unit was a letter written on January 7, 1823, by John J. Tumlinson, Sr., *alcalde* of the Colorado District, and Robert H. Kuykendall, Sr., commandant of the district's militia, to José Felix Trespalacios, Mexican governor of *Tejas*. Among other items, they requested permission to form a militia company for the protection of the settlements on the lower Colorado and Brazos rivers.

After Morrison, a U.S. Army veteran and the second-in-command of the militia, organized his company, they marched to a creek near the mouth of the Colorado River. They had planned to build a chain of blockhouses and utilize boats to deploy men along the river. Instead, lacking timber for construction, and suitable gunpowder and ammunition for offensive operations, Morrison's men spent most of their three months' service merely trying to survive. By the fall of 1823, the company disbanded without meeting any of its ambitious goals. Historians still debate whether the men of Morrison's company were truly rangers or merely mounted militia.

The Rangers' own belief is based on the address Austin wrote to his colonists concerning the raising of a detachment of "ten men in addition to those employed by the Government [Morrison's company] to act as rangers for the common defense." Austin wrote this address on the back of a proclamation previously penned by the Baron de Bastrop on August 5, 1823. There is no evidence this second body ever took the field, but it does mark the first time the term and concept of "ranger" was documented in Texas.

For many years, the Spanish province of *Tejas* had been subject to an untold number of incursions from belligerent Indian tribes, such as the Comanches, Kiowas, and Apaches, which discouraged settlement of the region. Indeed, the only towns in *Tejas* at the time were San Antonio de Béxar, Nacogdoches, and La Bahía del Espíritu Santo (later renamed Goliad). To erect a buffer zone against Indian pillaging and develop the economic potential of the region, the provincial viceroy approved the granting of twenty thousand acres to three hundred American families with the stipulation they become Spanish citizens and Roman Catholics. After winning independence from Spain in 1821, the new

"A Texas Ranger." This image of an 1840s-era ranger seated on a horse and holding a rifle was reproduced from a wood engraving. His attire and accoutrements more accurately reflect the rangers of the 1830s. The original picture was featured in *Pictorial History of Mexico and the Mexican War* (1848) by John Frost. Courtesy of the Library of Congress, Washington, D.C.

government of Mexico acquiesced to the colonization project and later authorized twenty-five more.

In the fall of the same year, *empresario* Austin established his 15,000-square mile colony along the fertile bottom lands of the Colorado, Brazos, San Jacinto, and San Bernard rivers. After settlers began arriving in sufficient numbers, he located the colonial capital at the new village of San Felipe de Austin in the summer of 1824. The "Old Three Hundred," the first settlers of the colony, welcomed the chance for rich farmland and new opportunities. They were headed by sons and grandsons of the Revolutionary War generation, and many were themselves veterans of General Andrew Jackson's campaigns in the Creek War (1813–1814) and the Battle of New Orleans (1815). These proud and independent-minded Texians (Anglo-American Texans) held personal liberty and property rights as sacrosanct and passionately supported the principles found in the Constitution of the United States. The approximately 2,500 native *Tejanos* (Texans of Spanish and Indian ancestry) welcomed the new immigrants as allies against aggressive Indians and for the capital and enterprise they brought to the region.

But almost immediately, the seeds for future insurrection were sown. The revolutionaries who liberated Mexico from Spain installed a constitutional monarchy that was quickly overthrown. The period afterward was chaotic until the Constitution of 1824 established a federal republic, which created a semblance of order. The seat of government was thousands of miles away in Mexico City and proved unable to properly administer such a distant province. Mexican *soldados* were few and mainly garrisoned at the *presidios* of Béxar and La Bahía. In the absence of central authority, the *Tejanos* became accustomed to a large measure of political autonomy and personal self-reliance. The Texians, many hailing from the Old South, felt little loyalty to the Church of Rome, and often brought their prejudices for darker-skinned ethnicities with them. Although Mexico abolished slavery in 1829, the government turned a blind eye to the holding of slaves, but not the slave trade itself.

Over time, the Old Three Hundred and later settlers, all of whom considered themselves Americans, grew increasingly disillusioned with the Mexican government that had invited them. In 1824, Texas was merged with Coahuila to form the state of *Coahuila y Tejas* with the capital at Saltillo some five hundred miles away. At first, Texas had only one *Tejano* representative in the state legislature, although they did later gain two more seats and a lieutenant governor in Béxar. Mexico City was distracted by the cycle of revolutions and counter-revolutions between *federalistas* (advocates for a constitutional democracy with autonomous states) and *centralistas* (supporters of a strong, autocratic government). The government also imposed trade restrictions on the citizens of Texas, which banned commerce with foreign markets. Since the best and most accessible outlets were in Louisiana, and not in Mexico, the self-sufficient Texians and *Tejanos* simply ignored the bans and the accompanying export duties. The restrictions also kept Texas out of the profitable traffic between the fur trading centers of Taos and Santa Fé and the eager markets of New England and Europe.

In January 1827, the Fredonian Rebellion flared up in Haden Edwards' Nacogdoches colony (established two years before) over perceived injustices in regard to land claims. During this crisis, Captain Abner Kuykendall, commanding perhaps the earliest confirmed company of rangers, was ordered by Stephen Austin to "range" the Old San Antonio Road between the Colorado and Brazos rivers.

Lieutenant-Colonel Austin, in his role as commandant of the colony's militia, commanded numerous companies, including those of captains Jesse Burnam, Amos Rawls, Rawson Alley, William Hall, and Horatio Chriesman. But they seem to have operated as mounted infantry, riding to the scene of battle and then dismounting to fight, and not in the manner typical of rangers. The colonial militia was slow to organize and pursue, ill-armed and under-equipped, and many forays ended in ruined horses and exhausted provisions. Nevertheless, these men took the field; often against hostile tribes such as the Carancahuas (Karankawas), Huacos (Wacos), Caddos, and Tehuacanas (Tawakonis). They

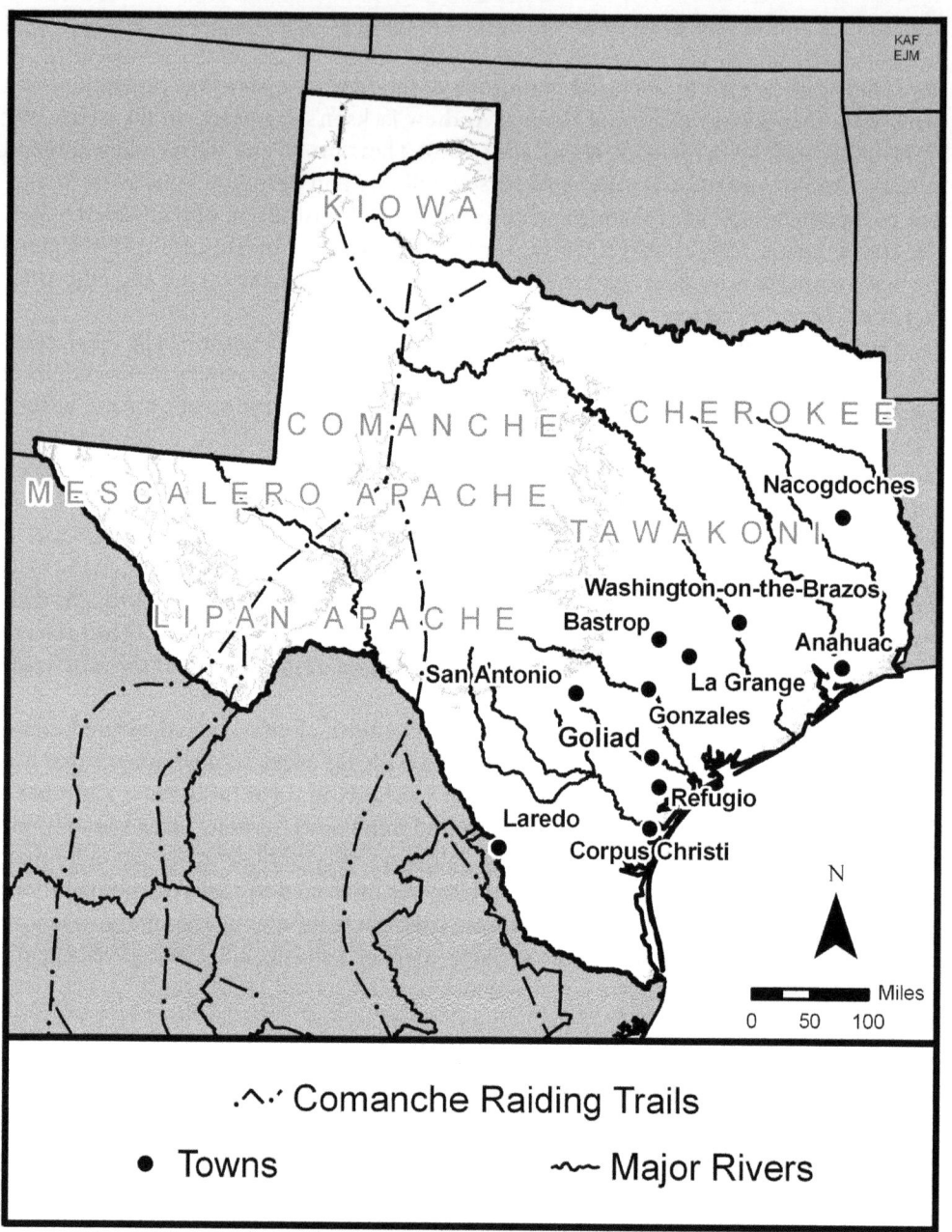

allied with other Indians, including the Wichitas, Lipan Apaches, Coushattas, and especially the Toncahuas (Tonkawas).

Among the battles the colonial militia fought were the June 1823 fight on the Colorado between Robert Kuykendall's company and Karankawa raiders; John J. Tumlinson, Jr.'s, July 1823 engagement with Wacos near present-day Columbus; the September 1824 attack of Randall Jones and twenty-three men on thirty Karankawas on Jones Creek, a tributary of the San Bernard; Aylett C. Buckner's pursuit of Karankawas to their camp near present-day Matagorda in the winter of 1824; Austin's expedition in the spring of 1826 against the Wacos and Tawakonis near the Little Brazos; the attack of Captain James J. Ross and thirty-one men on a Tawakoni camp on Ross' Creek in April 1826; James Tumlinson's rout of a

"Early Rangers" by Bruce Marshall. This watercolor depicts rangers on horseback firing their muskets during a charge. Although until the introduction of revolvers they normally dismounted to fight, the painting accurately depicts the irregular appearance of the rangers. UTSA's Institute of Texan Cultures, No. 073-0173, courtesy of the artist.

Waco war party in present Fayette County in the winter of 1828 and 1829; Abner Kuykendall's August 1829 expedition that engaged a war party of forty to fifty on the Colorado; Kuykendall's September 1829 foray with captains Bartlett Sims and Oliver Jones into the San Saba country; John Ingram's attack on a Karankawa encampment on Live Oak Creek in 1832; and William Oldham and John York's May 1835 fight with the Keechi (Kichai) at their village on Boggy Creek, a tributary of the Trinity.

Also contending with ill-disposed Indians was the Guadalupe River colony of *empresario* Green De Witt, established in April 1825, with its capital at Gonzales. In September 1829, Henry S. Brown commanded his own expedition into the San Saba country, which killed eight or nine Indians in two fights. On April 15, 1835, a thirteen-man trading caravan was massacred by five dozen Comanches on Sandies Creek near Gonzales. Approximately thirty volunteers commanded by Bartlett D. McClure caught fifty of the raiders at the Río Blanco four days later. Among the militia were Mathew Caldwell (prominent ranger captain and Indian fighter), William S. Fisher (future secretary of war), and Alamaron Dickerson (one of the martyrs of the Alamo).

By 1830, the population in Texas consisted of approximately 5,000 *Tejanos*, 11,000 Anglos, and 3,000 slaves. The political situation worsened as the administrations of *presidentes*

Anastasia Bustamante and Antonio López de Santa Anna Perez de Lebron incrementally abandoned federalist principles and concentrated the power of the central government. With the Law of April 6, 1830, Bustamante, along with the general Congress, closed Texas to further Anglo-American immigration, banned commercial trade by non–Mexicans, ceased the issuance of new *empresario* grants, restricted the import of slaves, and garrisoned more *soldados* in the region. Austin did obtain exemptions to the immigration ban and the abolition of slavery, but the other points of the new law resulted in outbursts of protest. *Generalissimo* Santa Anna, the self-styled "Napoléon of the West," declared in 1834 that Mexico was not ready for democracy, although he had been elected president on a Federalist platform the year before. He annulled the constitution of 1824, dissolved Congress and the state legislatures, and ruthlessly crushed a federalist revolt in Zacatecas. To make matters worse, he abolished the states and created departments governed by his own political appointees.

In response, Anglos joined with the *ayuntamientos* (municipal councils) of Béxar, Goliad, San Felipe, and Nacogdoches (with their more cautious *Tejano* majorities) in petitioning for separate statehood for Texas. Both groups initially wanted increased local autonomy and self-determination, but not separation from Mexico. However, beginning in 1832, Texian firebrands began to clamor for complete independence. Fearing eventual annexation by the U.S., Mexico City adamantly opposed statehood for Texas. Friction developed between the Anglo colonists and local Mexican garrisons, which were rumored to be composed of pardoned criminals and other unsavory characters. The flashpoints included Nacogdoches (August 1831), Brazoria (December 1831), Anahuac and Velasco (April–June 1832), and Copano Bay (September 1835).

Through the years, several proposals had been offered to organize ranger companies as part of the colonial militia. Due to political and financial realities, none were followed through until the major settlements began to organize committees of vigilance, safety, and correspondence in May 1835. That year on July 11, Captain Robert M. Coleman, commissioned by the committee of Viesca, was commanding a company of eighteen men on an expedition along the Brazos and was en route to a Tawakoni village near Tehuacana Springs. Some of the estimated one hundred Tawakonis discovered the approaching rangers and, in the subsequent fight, two to four Texians were killed, while the Indians were believed to have sustained a significant number of causalities. Forced to retreat to Parker's Fort on the headwaters of the Navasota River, Coleman returned to Viesca and called for reinforcements. He was joined at Tenoxtitlan by the companies of John H. Moore, Philip H. Coe, George W. Barnett, and Robert McAlpin Williamson. At Fort Parker, they united into a single force commanded by Moore and undertook a second campaign up the Brazos. They found the village at the springs deserted but continued to search the area and killed one Waco Indian.

Many historians consider the men of Coleman's company to be the first official rangers of Texas. Robert Utley, in his book *Lone Star Justice*, described how Coleman became the first ranger captain sanctioned by Texas law. Section III of *An Act Defining the pay of Mounted Riflemen, now and hereafter in the ranging service on the Frontier*, dated December 10, 1836, retroactively encompassed companies under arms since July 1835, including Coleman's.

As John Moore's command returned home, relations between the Texian colonists and the Mexican authorities were about to reach a critical breaking point. Very soon, blood would be shed in the name of constitutional government and personal liberty.

## Historical Register, 1823–1835

*"I wish for peace but am ready for war..."*
— Stephen F. Austin

### MORRISON'S COMPANY
Lieutenant Moses Morrison, Commanding (May 5–Autumn 1823)
*Area of Operations*: Colorado/Mina District of Austin's Colony
  Company raised by colonists with authorization from Gov. J. F. Trespalacios and operated under the orders of the Civil Militia

### AUSTIN'S COMPANY
  Privately authorized and funded by empresario S. F. Austin to augment Morrison's command (August 5, 1823?)— Never organized for service

### KUYKENDALL'S RANGER COMPANY
Captain Abner Kuykendall (January 1827)
*Ranging District*: Between the Brazos and Colorado Rivers along the Old San Antonio Road
  Company operated under the personal orders of Lt-Col. S. F. Austin, commandant of the Civil Militia

## *Moore's Tawakoni Expedition*

### FIELD & STAFF
Colonel John H. Moore (August 1–September 15, 1835)
Lieutenant James C. Neill, Adjutant (July 25–September 12, 1835)

### COLEMAN'S RANGERS
Captain Robert M. Coleman (June 12–August 28, 1835)
  Company operated under the supervision of the Committee of Vigilance, Safety and Correspondence of S. C. Robertson's colony
  First ranger company formally constituted by Texian law (Act of Congress, December 10, 1836— to date from July 1835)

### COE'S RANGERS
Captain Philip H. Coe (July 9–August 31, 1835)

### BARNETT'S COMPANY OF VOLUNTEERS
Captain George W. Barnett (July 20–August 28, 1835)

### MOORE'S/GOHEEN'S VOLUNTEER RANGERS/1ST COMPANY OF VOLUNTEERS
Captain John H. Moore (July 25–31, 1835)
Captain Michael R. Goheen (August 1–September 13, 1835)

### WILLIAMSON'S MOUNTED RIFLEMEN
Captain Robert M. "Three-Legged Willie" Williamson (July 25–September 13, 1835)
*Battalion Ranging District*: Brazos and Trinity Rivers country with headquarters at Fort Sterling/Parker's Fort

# 2

# Gained by War: Rangers of the Revolution and Republic (1835–1845)

By September 29, 1835, the journey toward revolution was nearing completion. On that day, Mexican troops from Béxar arrived in Gonzales to seize the six-pound cannon used for the colonists' defense against Indians. The *soldados*, under orders to avoid a violent confrontation if possible, were met by eighteen armed settlers who refused to surrender the gun. These men, known as the "Old Eighteen," stalled for time until they could be reinforced that evening by volunteers from La Grange, Columbus, and Mina (Bastrop) under the commands of John H. Moore, Joseph W. E. Wallace, Edward Burleson, and Robert Coleman. The gathered insurgents elected Moore commander of the "Army of the People" the following day. The two opposing forces fought a brief skirmish on the morning of October 2 that resulted in no more than two Mexicans killed.

On October 10, while recruits were still assembling in Gonzales, Stephen Austin was elected commander-in-chief of the Texian forces. Two days later, he marched the men for Béxar, but he became too ill to continue in command and was replaced by Edward Burleson on November 24.

Meanwhile, on the political front, delegates were elected on October 5 to attend a general consultation set to meet ten days later, but they lacked a quorum and had to postpone. For the short-term, an impromptu executive committee was established in San Felipe with the necessary powers to act until the Consultation could convene. This body, ironically titled the "Permanent Council," met from October 11 to November 1, and assumed the responsibility for managing Texian affairs. Among other activities, they forwarded supplies and volunteers to the rebel army, commissioned privateers in the Gulf of Mexico, and authorized agents to secure financial assistance abroad. On October 17, delegate Daniel Parker offered a resolution to create three ranging districts to protect the frontier, which was enacted that same day. Silas M. Parker (Daniel's brother), Garrison Greenwood, and Daniel B. Friar were appointed district superintendents and assigned to direct the operations of subordinate company commanders.

By November 1, enough delegates were present for the Consultation to begin deliberations, although they did not achieve a quorum for another three days. On November 6, they authorized a fourth ranging district, and three days later, George W. Davis was commissioned its superintendent. On November 14, the Consultation adjourned and its duties were assumed by the General Council, also at San Felipe.

On November 9 and 24, two articles were enacted specifying a force known as the Corps of Rangers (the first time the term "ranger" was used in legislation), which would replace the ranging districts when its assembly was complete. Rather than Morrison's or Coleman's companies, some historians hold this organization to be the first constituted Ranger Service in Texas. The commanding officer of the new corps held the rank of major and was subordinate to Major-General Samuel Houston, the commander-in-chief of the otherwise non-existent regular army. Each of the three fifty-six-man companies was commanded by a captain and two lieutenants. The rangers, officers and privates alike, received the same pay as their counterparts in the United States dragoons. However, in what became a longstanding ranger tradition, they supplied their own horses, equipment, arms and ammunition, and rations. At all times they had to be prepared to take the field, equipped "with a good and sufficient horse ... [and] with one hundred rounds of powder and ball."

The man appointed to command the Corps of Rangers was Robert M. Williamson, known as "Three-Legged Willie" because of his crippled right leg that was drawn back at the knee and the wooden leg he wore in its place. Williamson, a veteran of Moore's earlier Tawakoni campaign, supervised captains John J. Tumlinson, Jr., William H. Arrington, and Isaac W. Burton. By January 1836, the only company organized and ready for duty was Tumlinson's, who established his post at Hornsby's Station near present-day Austin.

On February 1, representatives were elected to the "Convention of 1836," which convened one month later at Washington-on-the-Brazos. On March 2, the seated delegates wrote and adopted a Declaration of Independence which established the Republic of Texas. Over the next two days, the Convention authorized a battalion of rangers under Colonel Jesse Benton to supplement Major Williamson's corps, and appointed Sam Houston general-in-chief of all Texian regulars, volunteers, and rangers. The delegates also prepared a provisional constitution on March 9 and elected a temporary government on March 16 to serve until the cessation of active hostilities. In the face of the approaching Mexican invasion, the Convention adjourned the following day and the *ad interim* government promptly moved to Harrisburg.

While the nascent rebel governments attempted to guide the political efforts of the Revolution, the insurgency itself was fully under way. Texian troops and Mexican *soldados* clashed at Presidio La Bahía (October 10, 1835), Concepción (October 28), Fort Lipantitlán (November 3), Nueces Crossing (November 4), the "Grass Fight" near Alazán Creek (November 26), the capture of San Antonio de Béxar from the Mexicans (December 5–10), the siege of the Alamo by the Mexicans (February 23–March 6, 1836), San Patricio (February 27), Agua Dulce Creek (March 2), Refugio (March 12–15), Coleto Creek (March 19–20), and the Goliad Massacre (March 27).

Lieutenant George C. Kimbell and twelve men comprising the Gonzales Ranging Company of Mounted Volunteers answered the call for aid from the Alamo defenders. Joined by another twenty Gonzales area residents, the rangers slipped through the Mexican lines in Béxar in the early morning of March 1 and entered the mission. There the "Immortal Thirty-Two" kept their rendezvous with destiny beside Travis, Crockett, Bowie, Dickerson, and the other heroes of the Alamo.

The news of the Alamo's fall sent a wave of panic through the settlements between the Colorado and Brazos rivers. Tumlinson's company was ordered to rendezvous at Bastrop and serve as pickets and rearguard for the chaotic exodus known as the "Runaway Scrape"

(March 14–April 20). The Corps soon splintered as rangers of all ranks left to look to their own families' safety.

Many of them fought with Houston's Texas Army at San Jacinto (April 21), where in approximately eighteen minutes, nine hundred Texians routed 1,300 *soldados* of President Santa Anna's Army of Operations. The Napoléon of the West himself was taken prisoner but later released after signing the two Treaties of Velasco; he recognized the sovereignty of the Republic of Texas and agreed that the international boundary between the two countries would be the Río Grande. The Mexican Supreme Government deposed Santa Anna *in absentia* and repudiated the Treaties, arguing that Santa Anna no longer held authority to represent Mexico and had signed the documents under duress. Texas would continue to define its southern border as the Río Grande, a decision that would have severe repercussions in the years to come.

Swiftly on the heels of victory, the permanent constitution was adopted and elections were held on September 5, 1836. General Houston was chosen as president and Mirabeau B. Lamar as vice-president. Both were sworn into office on October 22 before a joint session of Congress. The issue of the national defense quickly became one of paramount importance in the life of the new republic. Houston's Indian policy was to be one of negotiation and peaceful resolution since "natural reason will teach them the utility of our friendship." His May 5, 1837, address to the First Congress of Texas summed up his position:

> The Indians of the prairies have no local habitations, and, therefore, we can not hope to conquer them by any number of troops....
> Everything will be gained by peace, but nothing will be gained by war.

Vice-President Lamar and the other politicians who favored an aggressive defense policy were a powerful bloc in the Texas government, and the demands of the military budget were a constant drain on the country's treasury. Financial difficulties and the frequent threat of Mexican invasion and Indian depredations proved to be the most serious issues affecting the republic.

Beginning on May 8, 1836, the ranging service was reorganized. The Corps of Rangers was dissolved and Tumlinson and Burton's companies were transferred to Colonel Jesse Benton's regiment. The colonel was involved in building a military road to the Red River and turned acting command over to Lieutenant-Colonel Griffin Bayne. The superintendents and men of the ranging districts completed their enlistments and then disbanded. In late June, Colonel Edward Burleson took command of a six-company ranger battalion along the upper Brazos and Colorado rivers. On August 12, Colonel Robert Coleman was ordered to raise a three-company ranger battalion (later increased to five) under the November 9, 1835 ordinance in order to protect the Colorado River settlements. On September 1, President Houston ordered Major James Smith to muster three companies of fifty-six men each for service between the Brazos and Trinity rivers. In the wake of the controversial November 8 death of a Fort Colorado ranger, the First Congress authorized a 280-man mounted rifle battalion on December 5, 1836, which in effect reorganized Colonel Coleman's regiment. The president relieved Coleman of his command and ordered his arrest on December 19. The new battalion began assembling on December 14 under the leadership of Major William H. Smith, who formally succeeded Coleman on January 9, 1837.

On June 12, the Second Congress approved a corps of six hundred mounted gunmen for six months' service under the command of Colonel Joseph L. Bennett. The new battalion was to be composed of ten companies divided into three divisions. One company of allied Indian spies was to be attached to each division. Captain John Bowyer's Harrisburg County rangers were the first and, as far as can be determined, only company of Bennett's corps to enter the Service.

As a result of wartime behavior, the government decided to disband the unruly volunteers who had won the revolution. Congress authorized the reorganization of the Army of the Republic of Texas on November 30, 1836, but idleness, dissatisfaction with meager rations and poor clothing, and pay in arrears led to a decline in discipline and morale. A dispute over the right to command between generals Albert Sidney Johnston and Felix Huston resulted in a duel on February 7, 1837. After Johnston recovered from the wound he received and assumed command, his stricter discipline and the worsening supply problem led to several incidents of insubordination and mutiny at the posts of Valesco and Camp Preston. Finally, on May 18, President Houston ordered the secretary of war to furlough the entire army, except for six hundred men needed to garrison San Antonio de Béxar and Galveston. The number of furloughed troops and the garrisons were gradually reduced through the expiration of enlistments, additional furloughs, or desertions.

In addition to the ranging service and the regular army, the Republic of Texas also possessed a militia, which included various ranger companies. On December 6, 1836, Congress passed legislation to organize the militia, but without appropriating the necessary funds. The following year, the Second Congress passed the Militia Act of December 18, 1837, which authorized one division divided into four brigades, each commanded by a brigadier-general. Thomas J. Rusk was appointed major-general and commander-in-chief of the militia. Edward Burleson took command of the First Brigade (area west of the Brazos River), Moseley Baker the Second Brigade (between the Trinity and Brazos Rivers, including Liberty County), Kelsey H. Douglass the Third Brigade (between the Trinity and Sabine Rivers), and John H. Dyer the Fourth (between the Sabine and Red Rivers). Hugh McLeod was appointed adjutant and inspector general with the rank of colonel.

While militia rangers contended with hostile Indians on the northern frontier of the Republic, the southern would bring its own set of challenges. Beginning in the 1750s, the Spanish and Mexican governments had distributed the lands between the Nueces River and the Río Grande (also known as the Río Bravo del Norte, or the "Wild River of the North") to wealthy *rancheros*. While each river supported a line of settlements, the *brasada* (brush country of live oak thickets and chaparral) between was reserved for the raising of horses, cattle, sheep, and goats. Overwhelmed by Indian raids, the *rancheros* began departing in 1834, leaving an estimated three million head of livestock behind to run wild. Following the Revolution, the Mexican Supreme Government refused to recognize the independence of Texas but, while steadfastly maintaining the border was the Nueces River, it still withdrew troops to the Río Grande. The region, labeled on period maps as the *Llanos Mesteñas* (Wild Horse Prairie) or *El Desierto Muerto* (the Dead Desert), became the scene of a savage guerrilla war where, for almost ten years, every man was a law unto himself. The violent episodes in the Nueces Strip, as this wild country would become known, would continue for over a century.

From north of the Nueces came Texas "cowboys," mainly discharged soldiers, adventurers, and entrepreneurs, who raided as far south as Matamoros, Guerrero, and Laredo. Between 1838 and 1841, these "cowboys" included numerous men who would later figure in the tale of the Texas Rangers—A. T. Miles, J. C. Neill, John T. Price, W. J. Cairns, James P. Ownby, Ewen Cameron, and Richard Roman, to name a few. Their activities were considered legitimate in Texas only as long as they confined their attentions to Mexican citizens and property. Some did limit themselves to only stealing cattle from Mexicans to sell in Texas and Louisiana, while others were freebooters and murderers who robbed and killed Texians and Mexicans indiscriminately.

From south of the Río Grande came Mexican brigands who raided Texian settlements and merchant caravans as far north as San Antonio, Goliad and Refugio. The marauders were not always *rancheros* or common *bandidos*, but quite often the *federalistas* or *centralistas* battling each other in northern Mexico. The Texian and Mexican governments both publicly sought to suppress raids occurring in the Strip, but they also quietly encouraged their respective countrymen to continue. Indeed, Mexican frontier commanders issued roving commissions to a number of bandit chieftains, including Agatón Quinoñes, Manuel Leal, and Calixto Bravo.

The depredations centered on the vast herds of abandoned livestock at first, but beginning in late 1837, trade developed between San Antonio, Goliad, Victoria, Matagorda, Corpus Christi, and Houston, and settlements in Tamaulipas, Nuevo León, and Coahuila. The Mexicans moved beans, sugar, flour, and leather goods across the Río Grande, while the Texians exported cloth, hardware, and tobacco. These trade items were often smuggled since Mexican authorities capriciously prohibited commerce with its former colony, even while the Texas government encouraged it. The situation in the Strip became even worse when raiders began preying on legitimate merchants, illicit *contrabandistas*, and innocent travelers.

From the northwest came Comanches who, each September for decades, had taken to the war trails that ran from the Arkansas and Red rivers and the *Llano Estacado* (Staked Plains), to merge at the "big spring" in present-day Howard County. One branch continued on to the Horsehead Crossing of the Pecos and Comanche Springs (near present Fort Stockton) where it divided; one part of the trail going into Chihuahua at Presidio, and the other into Coahuila near Boquillas. Another branch left the "big spring" and passed through the *Llanos Mesteñas* before crossing the Río Grande south of Las Moras Spring, where it diverged into eastern Coahuila, Nuevo León, and Tamaulipas. Under the waxing moon (called the "Mexican Moon" by the Comanches and the "Comanche Moon" by the Mexicans), the "Lords of the Southern Plains" hunted for wild mustangs and raided the *haciendas* and *ranchos* for cattle, horses and mules, scalps, slaves, and other spoils.

The five major Comanche bands—the Kotsoteka, the Kwahadi, the Nakoni, the Penateka, and the Yamparika—proved to be the Texians' most implacable foes. Although once tenuously at peace with the colonists, after surveyors and pioneers began encroaching on the *Comanchería* (the Comanche territory that stretched from the *llano* to the Balcones Escarpment and the Cross Timbers, and from the Pecos to the headwaters of the Arkansas River), the Indians included the more accessible Texian settlements in their depredations. Every month for the next forty years, homesteaders and ranchers from the Red River to the Nueces would come to fear the Comanche Moon.

One of the most infamous events occurred on May 19, 1836, when the settlement of Parker's Fort was attacked by a war party of approximately five hundred Comanches and Kiowas. Among the five dead was Silas Parker, who was commanding his ranger district under the October 17 resolution. The five persons captured included Silas' daughter, nine-year-old Cynthia Ann Parker (who would play a role in Ranger history a quarter-century later). Silas' brother James, who commanded a company in the district, survived the massacre and spent the next nine years attempting to recover the captives, including his own daughter and grandson.

2. Gained by War: Rangers of the Revolution and Republic (1835–1845)　　19

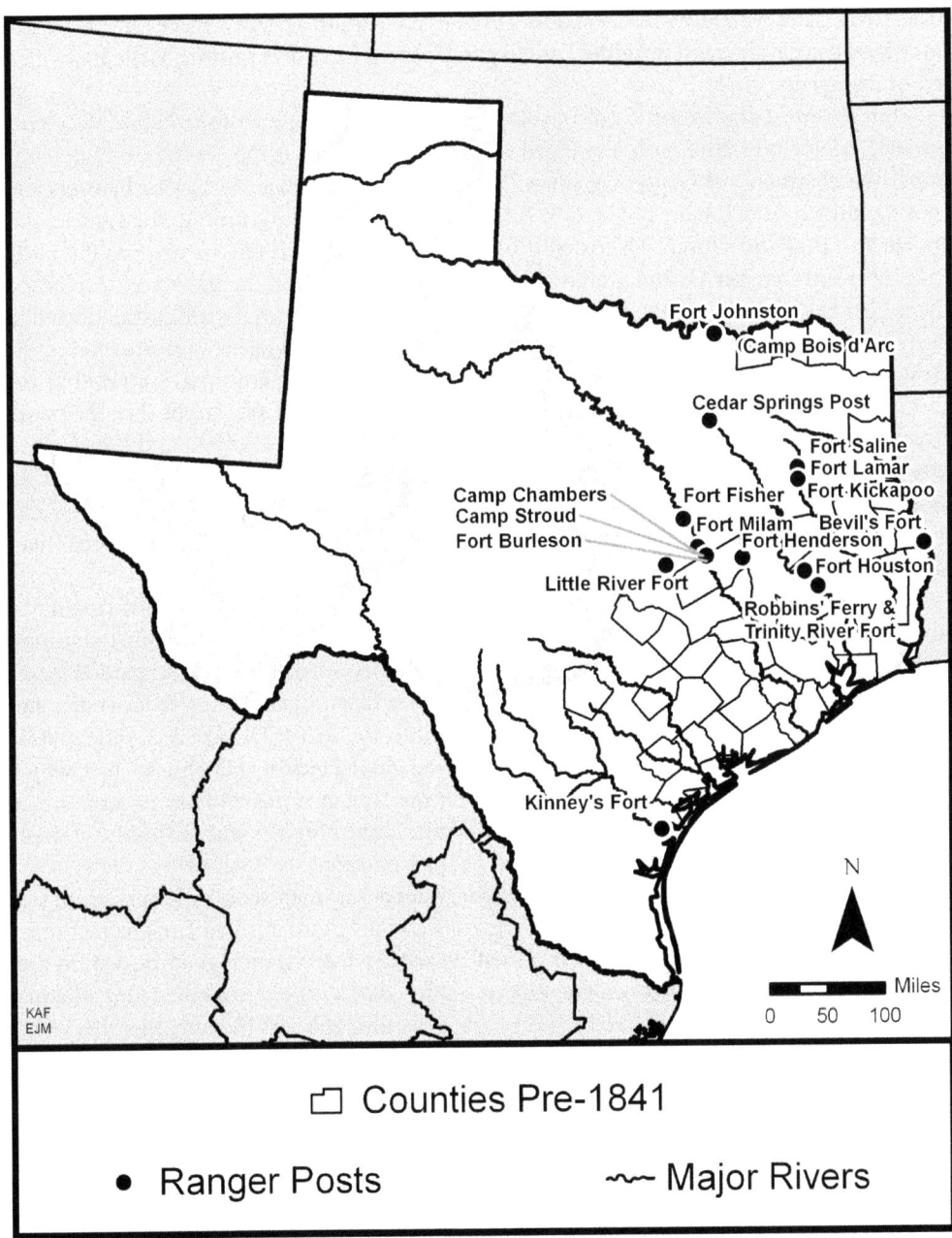

The situation on the frontier was not all one-sided, as the various ranger commands engaged the enemies of the republic on several occasions. On June 3, 1836, Isaac Burton's ranger company seized three Mexican schooners in Copano Bay carrying military supplies worth about $25,000. For this feat, Burton's men were dubbed the "Horse Marines." Acting 1st Lieutenant George B. Erath, leading a thirteen-man detachment, fought approximately one hundred Indians at Elm Creek on January 7, 1837, and lost two rangers killed. The Indians later claimed to have suffered ten causalities. From March 6 to 26, 1837, Captain Erastus "Deaf" Smith and his volunteer spy company conducted a campaign to Laredo to assert Texian sovereignty in the region. On March 17, Smith's twenty-three rangers fought forty Mexican cavalrymen from the Laredo garrison in a forty-five minute battle that killed ten of the enemy.

But the most significant clash in this period was the "Stone Houses Fight." In October 1837, Major William Smith organized what became known as the "Eastland Campaign" under the command of Captain William M. Eastland. Lieutenant A. B. Van Benthuysen, commanding a detachment of Captain John Bowyer's Harrisburg mounted gunmen, was attached to Eastland's force. The expedition departed Fort Smith (also known as the Little River Fort) on October 13, and marched into the country between the Brazos and Colorado rivers. On November 1, while near Pecan Bayou, the campaign split with Eastland leading the majority to Fort Colorado; Van Benthuysen and seventeen rangers continued on to the West Fork of the Trinity River. On November 10, Van Benthuysen's party arrived at the river near three rock formations known as the "Stone Houses." Later in the day, they were attacked by approximately 150 Tawakonis, Kichais, Wacos, and Caddos, and killed up to fifty of the Indians. Four rangers died in the two-hour long, close-quarters battle and six more while falling back into the woods. Losing all their horses and equipment in the escape, the eight surviving rangers retreated on foot and arrived at a settlement on the Sabine River on November 27.

Beginning on January 8, 1838, the Texian government signed numerous treaties of friendship and mutual defense with Cuelgas de Castro's Lipan Apaches against common foes, including the Comanches and the Mexicans. Castro's tribesmen accompanied Texas on several expeditions as scouts and guides, but other Lipan bands living in Coahuila and Nuevo León raided South Texas settlements well into the 1870s. On April 11, the republic also signed a treaty with the Tonkawas under head chief Plácido (Ha-shu-ka-na), which guaranteed the Indians the protected use of their hunting grounds and homes in peaceful coexistence with the whites. Plácido and his warriors served the Texians faithfully on many campaigns and the alliance between the two peoples endured for nearly three decades.

Colonel Henry W. Karnes, commanding a twenty-one-man scouting expedition, was attacked by two hundred Comanches at Arroyo Seco on August 10. The Texians met three mounted charges with alternating platoon volleys in which seven men at a time would fire, while their companions reloaded. The Indians suffered at least twenty killed and an equal number wounded. Karnes received a severe arrow wound and was the only member of his party injured.

On December 10, 1838, Mirabeau Lamar succeeded Houston in the presidency and immediately altered the frontier policies of the republic. President Lamar's vision for the Indians of Texas was one of expulsion or extermination, and his annual address to the Fourth Congress on November 12, 1839 stood in stark contrast to Houston's:

> The white man and the red man cannot dwell in harmony together. Nature forbids it ... pursuing them to their hiding places without mitigation or compassion, until they shall be made to feel that flight from our borders without the hope of return, is preferable to the scourges of war.

In order to fulfill his mandate Lamar clearly required a robust military. The president discharged the remnants of the army on December 16, 1838, and, on December 21, the Third Congress authorized the 1st Regiment of Infantry (also known as the "Frontier Regiment") under Colonel Edward Burleson to be the core of the new Texian army. This fifteen-company force, with a projected strength of 840 men, was to be posted in a permanent line of forts running from the Red River to the Nueces. To oversee the new policy, Lamar appointed the hawkish Albert Sidney Johnston as secretary of war on December 22. Congress also approved the recruitment of eight companies of mounted volunteers on December 29; a company of fifty-six rangers in Gonzales County on January 15, 1839; two more companies of mounted volunteers in Bastrop, Robertson, and Milam counties on January 23; and a two-company corps of rangers in San Patricio, Goliad, and Refugio counties on January 26.

The eight companies authorized on December 29 were intended to compose a regiment. On January 9, 1839, Congress appointed Henry W. Karnes colonel, Devereaux Jerome Woodlief lieutenant-colonel, and William Jefferson Jones major. Only three companies under captains Mark Lewis, James P. Ownby, and Greenberry Harrison were raised, and the first two had to be armed and equipped at public expense as the volunteers could not afford to do so themselves. The Milam County rangers authorized on January 23 were raised by Captain George B. Erath, while two Robertson County ranging companies were commanded by captains Nimrod Doyle and James D. Matthews; all three entered the service on March 8. The Gonzales County rangers were mustered under Captain Mathew Caldwell on March 16.

By January 21, John H. Moore was organizing a campaign to preempt Indian incursions into the Colorado River settlements. His force consisted of Captain William Eastland's company of thirty La Grange volunteers, Captain Noah Smithwick's twenty-five Bastrop County rangers (which were authorized on January 23), and Chief Castro's forty-two Lipan Apache and Plácido's twelve Tonkawa scouts. The column departed La Grange on January 26 and twenty-three days later, after enduring severe winter weather, located a Penateka camp on Wallace (or Spring) Creek in the San Saba River valley. Moore and his men launched a surprise attack on the sleeping Indians the next morning. While sustaining one death themselves, the rangers inflicted an estimated thirty to forty causalities on the enemy. They were soon pressed back by approximately three hundred to five hundred Indians and forced to seek shelter in a nearby ravine. After making several unsuccessful charges and engaging in long-range sniping, the Comanches stole the Texian horse herd before halting their attack. The next day, they allowed the weary rangers to trek on foot the 150 miles to home. Moore's defeat inaugurated a war of attrition against the Indians over the next three years, as the ranging service and the militia participated in numerous pitched battles.

Beginning in late 1836, Mexico pursued an Indo-Mexican alliance aimed at inciting various tribes to rise up against the Texians. For the next several years, the Supreme Government dealt with numerous internal challenges, such as the Federalist War, a French blockade of Vera Cruz, and widespread desertions from military forces in northern Mexico. Unable to field an invasion force to retake the lost province of Texas, commandants of the northern frontier appointed Vicente Córdova and Manuel Flores to serve as agents provocateurs to twelve tribes, including the Delawares, Coshuttas, Choctaws, Cherokees, Kickapoos, Kichai, Chickasaws, Caddos, Wacos, and Tawakonis. The Mexicans promised the Indians the excellent hunting grounds between the Colorado, Brazos, Trinity, and Red rivers in return for their assistance. From August 1838 to May 1839, Mexican and Indian forces under Córdova and Flores engaged Texian militiamen and volunteers in several skirmishes, including at the Kickapoo village north of old Fort Houston (October 16, 1838), Brushy Creek (February 25, 1839), Battle Ground Prairie on Mill Creek (March 29), the Guadalupe River (March 30), and the North San Gabriel River, where Flores was killed (May

17). Córdova was wounded at Battle Ground Prairie and escaped into Mexico, but he would return to bedevil the Texians.

Captured correspondence seemed to indicate the Cherokees were active participants in the Córdova-Flores uprising. Before the alleged discovery, depredations in the area were blamed on "wild Indians." President Lamar ordered Major Baley C. Walters and two spy companies to establish Fort Kickapoo in order to occupy the Neches Saline and observe the Cherokees. Chief Duwa'li Bowles vowed to resist the seizure of the salt plains by force of arms if necessary. Commissioners met with the Cherokees and Shawnees and offered to compensate them for their land improvements, provided the Indians disarm and remove themselves to lands north of the Red River. Bowles refused and 1,100-plus Texian regulars, militiamen, and rangers under the command of General K. H. Douglass marched to the "Cherokee Line," an area defined as the 1.5-million acres north of the Old San Antonio Road, east of the Neches River, and west of the Angelina River extending to the Sabine. The combatants fought at Battle Creek (July 15) and the Neches River (July 16), which resulted in 118 Indians killed, including Bowles, and eight Texians slain and thirty wounded. The retreating Cherokees were pursued by the Texas army, who destroyed villages and crops along the line of march, until most of the tribesmen crossed into Indian Territory (present-day Oklahoma). The Shawnees, observing the fate of Bowles' people, agreed to peacefully depart Texas in October. On December 25, two of the few remaining Cherokee bands were broken by the Frontier Regiment on the Colorado River near its junction with the San Saba. The Cherokee War proved to be the most complete victory of President Lamar's Indian policy.

On November 11, 1839, elections for senior militia officers were held and the results announced on March 7, 1840. Felix Huston became major-general and Alexander Somervell, Edwin Morehouse, James Smith, and Edward H. Tarrant became the commanders of the First, Second, Third, and Fourth Brigades, respectively. Thomas Rusk returned to the commander-in-chief's office on January 16, 1843, and served until June. He was replaced by Sidney Sherman on September 4, who remained in the position until annexation.

Some men, such as Henry Karnes and Noah Smithwick, brokered small steps toward peace between the Penateka Comanche band and the Texians. Unfortunately, any progress was shattered in the Council House Fight of March 19, 1840. Thirty-three Penateka chiefs and warriors, accompanied by thirty-two other Comanches, arrived in San Antonio that day. They brought with them Matilda Lockhart, a sixteen-year-old white girl who had been captured two years before. She claimed that her captors had physically and sexually abused her, and burn scars, coupled with the mutilation of her nose, lent credence to her tale. The Texians were enraged over her physical condition, the Indians' inability (or unwillingness) to bring in fifteen more captives held by other bands, and the Comanche chiefs' arrogance. Convinced the Indians were acting in bad faith, they attempted to take the chiefs into custody. The subsequent fight resulted in twelve Penateka leaders and eighteen warriors dead, as well as three women and two children. The Texians lost seven killed. The Comanches were incensed over the Texians' act of treachery, and slaughtered thirteen of the aforementioned captives. Both sides felt aggrieved and readied themselves for war.

The Great Comanche Raid ensued after the Penatekas traded the Cheyennes and Arapahos immense herds of horses in exchange for firearms, ammunition, kettles, and blankets. Thus equipped and provisioned, six hundred Comanches — including warriors, women, and children — left the *Comanchería* and moved south and east through the open lands between the Guadalupe, San Marcos, and Colorado rivers. On August 6, 1840, the

## 2. Gained by War: Rangers of the Revolution and Republic (1835–1845)

"Captain Hays and Company" by Jack Terry. This painting was commissioned by the Former Texas Rangers Foundation for a fundraiser in August 2002. "Jack" Hays is depicted leading his men past the Alamo in San Antonio on their way to the engagement at Bandera Pass. Courtesy of the artist.

raiding party sacked the Gulf Coast town of Victoria, killed twenty-three people in the area, and made off with over 1,500 horses and mules, two prisoners, and other booty. Two days later, the town of Linnville suffered the same fate, losing five residents killed, 1,000 horses stolen, and four people taken captive.

Several groups of area residents banded together as news of the raid swept the settlements. They were not formally enrolled or mustered into the service of the republic, but were strictly unpaid volunteers. These men did, though, uphold the finest traditions of the Texas Rangers in the coming battles. On August 9, one group of three companies totaling 125 men, under the overall command of Captain John J. Tumlinson, Jr., skirmished with the raiders at Garcitas Creek. Volunteers under the command of captains Mathew Caldwell, Lafayette Ward, and James Bird, and Colonel Burleson composed another group. These latter companies boasted past and future rangers, including Daniel B. Friar, John C. "Jack" Hays, Benjamin and Henry McCulloch, John Henry Brown, and Andrew Jackson Sowell. They rendezvoused near Isham Good's crossing on Plum Creek on August 11, and later the same night were joined by militia general Felix Huston and his staff. The following morning, the question of who would command was decided when Captain Caldwell, one of the most experienced Indian fighters present, graciously offered the honor to General Huston, a man who had never before fought Indians. Huston's two hundred Texians sighted the marauders, who were returning home laden with booty and captives, in a nearby clearing. Huston formed his men into two lines, the right commanded by Burleson and the left by

"Battle of Plum Creek, 1840" by Lee Herring. This oil painting shows the view the rangers had of their enemies at Plum Creek. The Texians pursued a larger force of Comanches to that location and defeated them in the aftermath of the Great Raid. These mounted Indians are poised for a charge in the 1840 battle. UTSA's Institute of Texan Cultures, No. 088-0055; courtesy of Bill Adams.

Caldwell, with a reserve line commanded by Major Thomas Hardeman. In a short time, the Texians engaged the raiders and killed an estimated forty to eighty during a fifteen-mile running fight, but they were unable to save one of the captives.

John Moore's expedition into the Colorado River country dealt another smashing blow to the Comanches, albeit not a fatal one. In the October 24 battle, ninety rangers and seventeen Lipans killed an estimated 140 to 280 Penatekas and took between twenty-seven and thirty-four captive.

The Great Raid and Moore's subsequent action ended the Comanche use of large-scale expeditions for over twenty years. Small incursions of war-parties still continued, but the Comanches learned to treat the Texians more carefully. In turn, the Texians learned the best way to beat the Comanches was to aggressively match them in mounted combat.

At the same time, Texian politics had polarized into partisan anti–Houston and anti–Lamar factions. The Fifth Congress, in session from November 2, 1840 to February 5, 1841, was completely dominated by Houston's supporters. Although Lamar persisted in championing the continued employment of the regular army, his vision of a strong military was doomed. By December 1840, the 1st Infantry had achieved a strength of only 465 men, despite spending over $25,000 for recruiting and payment of land bounties, and was constantly plagued by desertions and overruns in funding. The inducements for prospective recruits could not compete with civilian wages nor compensate for the privations suffered in the service. The regiment stood at five companies stationed along the frontier, which was inadequate to establish any new posts or to counter any offensive operations by Indians or Mexicans. While Lamar was on a medical leave of absence in the United States, the House of Representatives moved to dissolve the army on January 28, 1841. The Senate blocked the adoption of legislation and, in response, the House refused to provide any appropriation for the army's maintenance before adjourning. Without funding, the president, upon his return, was forced to let enlistments expire, and formally disbanded the army on March 24.

At the same time, the depression following the Panic of 1837 in the United States had begun to affect the already struggling Texas economy. Plagued by a depreciated currency (paper money was worth eighteen cents on the dollar) and an inability to secure credit at home or abroad, the country's financial insolvency and the want of a self-sufficient economy severely hampered its ability to defend itself.

With a regular army financially out of the question, Congress again resorted to irregular forces. Legislation enacted on December 26, 1840, authorized three spy companies of fifteen men each under captains John T. Price, Antonio Pérez, and Jack Hays to range the country south of San Antonio and Victoria. Hays and Pérez were active in the Nueces Strip suppressing brigands under captains Agatón Quinoñes and Ignacio García; one instance was when they engaged the Mexicans near Laredo on April 7. The militia continued to field rangers who were involved in Major Mark B. Lewis' expedition to the Nueces, General Edward H. Tarrant's Village Creek and Trinity Expeditions, and General James Smith's Trinity Expedition, among other lesser actions.

On February 4, 1841, Congress authorized the counties of Fannin, Lamar, Red River, Bowie, Paschal, Panola, Harrison, Nacogdoches, Houston, Robertson, Milam, Travis, Bexar, Gonzales, Goliad, Victoria, Refugio, San Patricio, Montgomery, and Bastrop to each raise one company of mounted minute men. They were not called "Rangers," but they were rangers nevertheless. As their title implied, these volunteers were to cease their daily activities at a moment's notice and rush to the scene of the emergency without regard for musters or rules and regulations. Each man equipped himself with "a good substantial horse, bridle, and saddle ... together with a good gun, and one hundred rounds of ammunition." These minute companies were expected to be employed only in times of extreme emergency. Each company consisted of twenty to fifty-six men and, while past companies had served in the field for three to twelve months, these served for less than fifteen consecutive days and the individual minute men for less than four months total. Some were known to have served without pay as needed, while some others were partly reimbursed by their captains. Their operations were supervised by the chief justices of their respective counties, who endorsed muster rolls and pay claims and forwarded them to the secretary of war. Of the twenty counties named in the act, Bastrop, Harrison, and Panola did not form companies, and Bowie and Goliad are unknown to have done so.

Sam Houston, beginning his second presidential term on December 13, 1841, ridiculed his predecessor's policies, including the county minute system, as inefficient and expensive; the minute men often overran appropriations without providing satisfactory service, except in Milam, Robertson, and Béxar counties. At least two captains— James P. Ownby and A. T. Miles— abused their commissions and preyed upon traders in the Nueces Strip. Also, the county chief justices (usually not military experts) often rubber stamped the companies' paperwork and exposed the almost bankrupt treasury to the risks of fraud. Houston still opposed a large, standing military, but realized these companies were the only available means to protect the frontier given the republic's inability to maintain a regular army. The Sixth Congress disagreed and refused to appropriate any new funding. Once again, the financial strain of keeping rangers in the field brought the program to a halt.

Based on his record as a minute and ranger captain, "Devil Jack" Hays became the de facto chief of frontier protection south and west of San Antonio. During Brigadier-General Ráfael Vásquez's offensive in March 1842, Hays' ranging company was the only force on the frontier between San Antonio and the Río Grande. Hays and his one hundred men could only fall back to the Guadalupe and observe the invading force of seven hundred *soldados* as it occupied San Antonio on March 5, then returned to Mexico two days later. Later that same year, Brigadier-General Adrián Woll (a French soldier of fortune in Mexican service) executed a reconnaissance-in-force into Texas, and occupied San Antonio on September 11 with a 1,500-man brigade. Hays joined with Colonel Mathew Caldwell in leading 225 Texian rangers and volunteers against Woll's forces at Salado Creek on September 18. Protected by the creek bed and pecan trees, the Texians sustained one man killed and ten wounded, while Woll's force, exposed on the open prairie, suffered approximately one hundred killed, including Mexican agent Vicente Córdova; and possibly 150 wounded, fifty of whom were said to have died later. At the same time, in a nearby mesquite thicket, the fifty-three volunteers of Nicholas M. Dawson's command marching to reinforce Caldwell were cut off by Mexican troops and surrounded. They lost thirty-five killed and fifteen captured, but two escaped. Laden with plunder and prisoners, Woll withdrew from San Antonio en route to the Río Grande on September 20. Caldwell's army set out in pursuit with Hays' company leading the way. Two days later, the rangers, over a mile in advance of the slower column of volunteers, caught up with the Mexican rearguard at the Arroyo Hondo and boldly attacked an emplaced cannon. They captured the artillery piece and killed five of the gun's crew, but had to fall back in the face of a Mexican infantry counterattack. The Texians broke off their pursuit and the invaders re-crossed the Río Grande on September 29.

The recent incursions enflamed Texian passions and the public demanded the government respond. The president was not confident of a retaliatory expedition's success, but on October 3, Houston ordered General Alexander Somervell to organize volunteers and the militia for the invasion of Mexico. The chief executive left to Somervell the final responsibility of whether to commence, if the general believed the campaign possessed a reasonable chance of success. Jack Hays and his rangers, fresh from their fight at the Arroyo Hondo, were among the first to enlist. With Hays' rangers in the forefront, the Southwestern Army of Operations left San Antonio on November 25 numbering approximately 750 volunteers eager to chastise the enemy, recover prisoners taken during the Woll invasion, and gain glory and plunder for themselves. Almost immediately, the lethargic and indecisive general lost the respect of his men and any semblance of control over them. Twenty men left the column on November 29, much of the expedition disobeyed orders and pillaged Laredo on December 9, and another 187 men left on December 11 after Somervell returned much of the plunder. Somervell and his remaining five hundred men secured the surrender of Guerrero on December 18, but the following day, he recognized the expedition was doomed to fail and ordered the men to disband and return home. Houston, the master politician, had achieved his goals: appeasement of the public demands for retaliation against Mexico, a shift of the blame to another's shoulders, and proof of the futility of prosecuting such an invasion without trained, disciplined troops and adequate supplies and equipment.

Only 189 officers and men obeyed the order to disband, while five captains and 308 rank and file vowed to continue under the command of William S. Fisher. Hays realized the inevitable outcome of continuing and cautioned his men to return with him to San Antonio. Two who did not heed his warnings were Samuel H. Walker and William A. A. "Bigfoot" Wallace. Hays agreed to remain for a few days and assist in crossing the river. The Mier expedition (as it became known) set out on December 20 with a small detachment of rangers under Ben McCulloch leading the way. On December 22, the Texians arrived at the east bank of the Rio Grande opposite Mier, and McCulloch's spies reconnoitered the town. After rangers learned Mexican troops were assembling nearby, Hays warned Fisher against proceeding and urged him to abandon the enterprise. His counsel was ignored and Hays and most of his men returned home to resume their ranger duties. Fisher's column, including Walker and Wallace, crossed the border the following day and entered Mier without opposition. The Texians requisitioned supplies from the town and they waited two days back in Texas for the rations to arrive. On the afternoon of December 25, 261 Texians crossed the Rio Grande and fought the 3,000 Mexican troops now at Mier until the following afternoon. Six hundred Mexicans were killed and two hundred wounded, while thirty Texians were killed or wounded. Hungry and thirsty, their gunpowder nearly exhausted, their discipline all but gone, the Texians surrendered to the Mexican commander.

While Fisher believed he had capitulated under terms of honorable treatment, President Houston later disavowed the men leaving the Mexican government to decide whether they were indeed entitled to prisoner of war status. The captives were marched to Matamoros and to Salado, where 179 men escaped on February 11, 1843; only three were able to reach Texas while the rest were recaptured and returned to Salado. A wrathful President Santa Anna decreed that those who participated in the escape were to be executed, but the order was modified to a decimation of every tenth man. The Texians drew one hundred fifty-nine white or seventeen black beans from an earthen jar, the black beans signifying death. The condemned men were blindfolded and shot at dusk on March 25. Ex-ranger Ewen Cameron (the "bravest of the brave"), leader of the escape attempt, drew a white bean but Santa Anna later personally ordered his execution. The survivors were held at Perote Prison, where a few managed to escape and reach home. Many others died from wounds, disease, and starvation. Sam Walker escaped from Molino del Rey prison in August 1843 and Bigfoot Wallace was liberated in August 1844. The last members of the Mier expedition were repatriated on September 16, 1844.

Up until this time, the standard tactics employed by rangers included dismounting to fight, since they had to recharge their muzzle-loading rifles after every shot (a near-impossible task to perform while on the back of a running horse). Mounted charges, such as the one used at Plum Creek, were rare. The Comanches and Kiowas often maneuvered just outside the effective range of Texian rifles and tried to goad the whites into firing. If an entire complement of rangers discharged a volley at the same time, the Indians were able to dart in with lances and bows and arrows. Texians armed with single-shot horse pistols, swords, or knives stood no chance. As in Colonel Karnes' fight at Arroyo Seco, rangers responded by having a portion of their company shoot, while the others held their fire and covered the men who were reloading.

This changed when the rangers of Hays' company received the new Paterson Colt pistols in 1843. Between 1839 and 1841, the republic had purchased one hundred eighty No. 5 Holster pistols for the navy. They were five-shot .36-caliber weapons with a concealed trigger that protruded when the hammer was cocked. Weighing two pounds twelve ounces, the Paterson used an eighty-three-grain lead ball and a black powder charge of twenty-two grains. To reload, one had to disassemble the pistol into three separate pieces—the grip frame, cylinder, and nine-inch barrel—but, despite the inherent awkwardness, the available firepower of a single ranger was quintupled in one package. This allowed the rangers to employ the mounted charge and meet the Comanches and other horse-riding enemies on their own terms. Due to the rangers' renowned use of the pistol, the Colt would also become known as the "Texas Paterson."

The new weapons were well used in the battle of Walker's Creek. Around June 1, 1844, Hays and his rangers left San Antonio to hunt for a Comanche war party which had been raiding in Bexar County. After they had ranged as far as the Pedernales River, they rode back until they reached the Guadalupe River on June 9. Once more a member of Hays' company, Sam Walker would later describe the ensuing battle:

> ... J. C. Hays with fifteen men fought about eighty Comanche Indians, boldly attacking them upon their own ground, killing and wounding about half their number. Up to this time these daring Indians had always supposed themselves superior to us, man to man, on horse ... the result of this engagement was such as to intimidate them and enable us to treat with them.

This engagement is widely considered to be the first in which "repeating pistols" were used in combat, although an unsubstantiated battle at Bandera Pass is also mentioned. The Comanche chief present at Walker's Creek later complained that the rangers "had a shot for every finger on the hand."

Because of his storied exploits, Hays became the quintessential Ranger captain. Walter P. Webb wrote in *The Texas Rangers: A Century of Frontier Defense*, "...under his leadership the best tradition of the Texas Rangers was established." Robert Utley, in *Lone Star Justice*, opined that "John Coffee Hays resonated through history as the ideal Texas Ranger, the one above all others every Ranger strove to emulate." He built a cadre of men skilled in frontier warfare, which produced extremely competent captains who figured prominently in the Mexican War and beyond.

## Historical Register, 1835–1845

*"What shall we do boys; shall we fight?"*
— Captain Mathew Caldwell

### *Parker's Ranging District*

#### Headquarters
Superintendent Silas M. Parker, Sr. (October 17, 1835–May 19, 1836)

#### Hillhouse's/Seale's Company
Captain Eli Hillhouse (October 23–December 24, 1835)
Captain Eli Seale (December 24, 1835–January 25, 1836)

#### Parker's Company
Captain James W. Parker, Sr. (January 1–May 19, 1836)

#### Head's Company
Captain James A. Head (January 27–April 27, 1836)
District Ranging Area: Between the Brazos and Trinity Rivers with headquarters at Fort Sterling/Parker's Fort
  District operated under the orders of the Permanent Council, the Consultation, the General Council, and the ad interim government

### *Friar's Ranging District*

#### Headquarters
Superintendent Daniel B. Friar (October 17, 1835–February 1, 1836)

### Friar's Mounted Rangers
Captain Daniel B. Friar (November 1, 1835–February 1, 1836)
*District Ranging Area*: Between the Brazos and Colorado Rivers with headquarters at Fort Viesca/Fort Milam
    District operated under the orders of the Permanent Council, the Consultation, the General Council, and the ad interim government

## Greenwood's Ranging District
### Headquarters
Superintendent Garrison Greenwood (October 17, 1835–March or April 1836)

### Sadler's Mounted Rangers/Company No. 10/"Houston Company"
Captain William T. Sadler (January 1–March 16, 1836)
*District Ranging Area*: Between the Trinity and Neches Rivers with headquarters at old Fort Houston on the Trinity
    District operated under the orders of the Permanent Council, the Consultation, the General Council, and the ad interim government

## Davis' Ranging District
### Headquarters
Superintendent George W. Davis (Appointed November 9, 1835)
*District Ranging Area*: Between the Colorado River and Cibolo Creek with headquarters at the Big Spring (the head of the San Marcos River) near Gonzales
    District established by order of the Consultation but no companies were organized for service

## Corps of Rangers
### Headquarters
Major Robert M. "Three-Legged Willie" Williamson (November 28, 1835–April 7, 1836)
Major James Collinsworth (April 7–14?, 1836)

### 1st Company
Captain John J. Tumlinson, Jr. (November 28, 1835–March 17, 1836)
1st Lieutenant George M. Petty, Acting Commander (March 17–May 8, 1836)
*Ranging District*: Colorado River country with headquarters at Hornsby's Station (January), Tumlinson's Fort on Brushy Creek (February), and Bastrop (March)
    Company mustered into service (January 17, 1836) and transferred to Lt-Col. G. Bayne's Division (May 8, 1836)

### 2nd Company
Captain William H. Arrington (Appointed November 28, 1835)
    Company never organized for service

### 3rd Company
Captain Isaac W. Burton (November 28, 1835–May 8, 1836)
*Ranging District*: Robertson's Colony with headquarters at camp on the Sabine River
    Company mustered into service (December 19, 1835) and transferred to Lt-Col. G. Bayne's Division (May 8, 1836)

### Washington Guards
Captain Joseph B. Chance (March 20–June 1, 1836)
    Company mustered into service by Maj. R. M. Williamson at Washington-on-the Brazos (April 7,

1836), assigned to 2nd Regiment of Volunteers, and attached to Baggage and Sick Detail at Camp Harrisburg (April 20–21, 1836)
*Corps Headquarters*: Mina/Bastrop (December); Washington-on-the-Brazos (April); Donoho's Plantation (April)
   Corps operated under the orders of MG S. Houston, C-in-C of the Texas Army

### COMPANY OF RANGERS
Captain Sterling C. Robertson (January 17–February 1836)
Orderly Sergeant Thomas H. Barron, Acting Commander (February 1836)
*Ranging District*: Robertson's Colony with headquarters at the Falls of the Brazos River
   Company organized and mustered into service by empresario S. C. Robertson

### BARRON'S COMPANY
Captain Thomas H. Barron (February–March 16, 1836)
Lieutenant Albert G. Gholson, Commanding (March 16–May 7, 1836)
*Ranging District*: Robertson's Colony/Milam Municipality with headquarters at Tenoxtitlan

### FRANKS' RANGING COMPANY
Captain Louis B. Franks (February 1–April 1, 1836)
*Ranging District*: Brazos and Little Rivers country of Robertson's Colony with headquarters at Ouchaco (Waco village) and the Falls of the Brazos River
   Company operated under the orders of the precinct of Tenoxtitlan

### TOWNSEND'S RANGING COMPANY
Captain Stephen Townsend (February 1–May 12, 1836)
*Ranging District*: Colorado River country of Robertson's Colony with headquarters at the head of Mill Creek
   Company operated under the orders of the General Council

### GONZALES MOUNTED RANGER COMPANY
2nd Lieutenant George C. Kimbell, Commanding (February 23–March 6, 1836)
*Headquarters*: The Alamo, San Antonio de Béxar
   Company operated under the nominal supervision of Maj. R. M. Williamson (February 23, 1836) and the personal orders of Lt-Col. W. B. Travis (March 1, 1836)

### SPY COMPANY
Captain Thomas G. McGehee (February 29–March 20, 1836)
*Ranging District*: Between San Marcos and San Antonio de Béxar
   Company members detached from Capt. J. Billingsley's company of Mina Volunteers, and operated under the supervision of Col. E. Burleson and Maj. R. M. Williamson

### RED RIVER RANGERS/VOLUNTEER COMPANY OF MOUNTED RANGERS
Captain William A. Becknell (April 28–May 28, 1836)
Captain William A. Becknell (July 14–September 13, 1836)
*Ranging District*: Sabine and Trinity Rivers country with headquarters at Clarksville
   Company assigned to 2nd Brigade of Texas Volunteers, Volunteer Auxiliary Corps, Texas Army

## Ranger Regiment/2nd Division of Rangers
### FIELD & STAFF
Colonel Jesse Benton, Sr. (March 3, 1836)
   Col. Benton never formally assumed active command
Lieutenant-Colonel Griffin Bayne, Acting Commander (March 3–June 24, 1836)
Major Isaac W. Burton, Commanding (June 24–September 24, 1836)

### Wilson's Company
Captain William C. Wilson (March 1–June 1, 1836)
*Headquarters*: "Headquarters Battleground" (April 1836)

### Wheelock's Company
Captain E. L. Ripley Wheelock (May 8–August 8, 1836)
  Company attached to 2nd Brigade of Texas Volunteers, Texas Army

### 1st Company
Captain John J. Tumlinson, Jr. (May 8–August 16, 1836)
  Company transferred from Maj. R. M. Williamson's Corps

### 2nd Company ("Horse Marines")
Captain Isaac W. Burton (May 8–June 24, 1836)
Captain Dickinson Putnam (June 24–November 1, 1836)
*Ranging District*: Gulf coast from the Guadalupe River to Mission Bay
  Company transferred from Maj. R. M. Williamson's Corps

### 3rd Company
2nd Lieutenant Samuel Smith (August 21–October 25, 1836)
  Regiment operated under the orders of BG S. Houston and BG T. J. Rusk, C-in-C's of the Texas Army

### Mounted Spy Company/Cavalry Company
Captain William H. Smith (March 16–July 17, 1836)
Captain Thomas Robbins (July 18–August 13, 1836)
1st Lieutenant John H. Dyer, Acting Commander (August 13–September 6, 1836)
Captain John H. Dyer (September 6–November 20, 1836)
*Ranging District*: Colorado, San Jacinto, San Antonio, and Guadalupe Rivers country with headquarters at Beason's Ford (March 1836), Camp Groce's and "Headquarters Battleground" (April 1836), Harrisburg (May 1836), Victoria (June 1836), camp west of San Patricio (August 1836), Placido Rancho and Dimmitt's Landing (September 1836), and Garscata (October 1836); Trinity River country with headquarters at Robbins' Ferry (November 1836)
  Company assigned to 2nd Regiment of Volunteer Infantry as Company "J" (March 16–June 1, 1836) and to Lt-Col. D. M. Fulton's cavalry regiment, 2nd Brigade of Texas Volunteers (June–November 18, 1836)

### Cavalry Company/Mounted Gunmen
Captain John G. W. Pierson (June 30–December 30, 1836)
*Ranging District*: Brazos River country with headquarters at Post Washington
  Company operated under the supervision of the War Department

## Ranging Corps of Mounted Riflemen/1st Division of Rangers

### Field & Staff
Colonel Edward "Ned" Burleson, Sr. (July 1–December 1, 1836)

### Billingsley's Ranging Company
Captain Jesse Billingsley (July 1–October 1, 1836)
*Headquarters*: Bastrop

### McGehee's Rangers
Captain John G. McGehee (July 1–November 20, 1836)
*Headquarters*: Colorado City (Fayette County)

### York's Rangers
Captain John York (July 1–November 20, 1836)
*Headquarters*: Colorado City (Fayette County)

### Hill's Ranging Company
Captain William W. Hill (July 3–October 3, 1836)
*Headquarters*: Bastrop (July); Tenoxtitlan (August)

### Lockhart's Spy Company/Mounted Riflemen
Captain Byrd B. Lockhart, Sr. (July 4–August 16, 1836)
*Headquarters*: San Antonio de Béxar

### Robertson's Rangers
Captain Sterling C. Roberson (July 25–September 11, 1836
Captain Calvin Boales (September 11–November 14, 1836)
*Headquarters*: Tenoxtitlan

### Burleson's Detachment
Colonel Edward "Ned" Burleson, Sr. (November 20–December 1, 1836)
*Corps' Ranging District*: Between the upper Brazos and Colorado Rivers with headquarters at Bastrop
    Corps operated under the orders of BG T. J. Rusk, C-in-C of the Texas Army

### Mounted Volunteer Company
Captain William Scurlock (July 4–October 4, 1836)
*Ranging District*: Between the San Antonio and Guadalupe Rivers with headquarters at Victoria (July 1836) and Coleto Creek (August 1836)
    Company operated under the orders of BG T. J. Rusk, C-in-C of the Texas Army

## *1st Regiment of Rangers/Battalion of Mounted Riflemen*
### Field & Staff
Colonel Robert M. Coleman (August 12, 1836–January 9, 1837)
   *Col. Coleman relieved of command December 14, 1836, becoming effective January 9, 1837*
Major William H. Smith, Commanding (January 9–December 18, 1837)
Captain William M. Eastland, Commanding (December 18, 1837–March 2, 1838)
1st Lieutenant William H. Moore, Commanding (March 2–April 30, 1838)
Major William H. Smith (December 14, 1836–January 9, 1837)
1st Lieutenant Gabriel Long, Quartermaster (December 14, 1836–November 30, 1837)
1st Lieutenant Charles Curtis, Assistant Quartermaster (April 15–October 20, 1837)
Lieutenant Samuel Wolfenberger, Commissary (September 1, 1836–January 21, 1837)
Doctor Alexander Ramsey, Surgeon (December 9, 1836–June 1, 1837)
Doctor Robert Montgomery, Assistant Surgeon (December 16, 1836–May 31, 1837)
Sergeant-Major Azariah G. Moore (August 24, 1836–January 21, 1837)
Quartermaster Sergeant George B. Erath (February 3–April 15, 1837)
Sergeant George B. Erath, Acting Judge Advocate (April 15–October 6, 1837)

### Company A
Captain Alfred P. Walden (August 15–October 5, 1836)
1st Lieutenant Alexander Robbless, Commanding (October 5–December 31, 1836)
Captain Thomas H. Barron (January 1–October 16, 1837)

1st Lieutenant Charles Curtis, Acting Commander (October 20–November 28, 1837)
Captain John L. Lynch (November 28, 1837–February 20, 1838)
1st Lieutenant Charles Curtis, commanding detachment (January 1837)
Acting 1st Lieutenant George B. Erath, commanding detachment (January 6–7, 1837)
*Headquarters*: Camp Coleman (September 1836); Fort Milam with detachment at Little River Fort (January 1837); Fort Fisher (February–March 1837); Fort Milam (May 1837)

## Company B

Captain Thomas H. Barron (September 11–December 31, 1836)
Captain Daniel Monroe (January 1–December 14, 1837)
1st Lieutenant William H. Moore, Commanding (December 14, 1837–April 30, 1838)
Acting 1st Lieutenant George B. Erath, commanding detachment (November–December 1836)
1st Lieutenant Charles Curtis, commanding detachment (December–January 1837)
*Headquarters*: Fort Milam near the Falls of the Brazos River (October 1836) with detachment at Little River Fort/Fort Smith (Erath's det.: November 1836); Tenoxtitlan (December 1836); Little River Fort/Fort Smith (January 1837); Fort Fisher (April 1837); Fort Milam (May 1837); Nashville-on-the-Brazos (September 1837)

## Company C

2nd Lieutenant Benjamin R. Thomas, Commanding (September 20–December 31, 1836)
Captain Micah Andrews (January 1–July 1837)
 *Capt. Andrews continued to be paid as ranger officer through January 5, 1838*
1st Lieutenant Nicholas Wren, Commanding (July 18–October 10, 1837)
2nd Lieutenant Nicholas Wren, commanding detachment (March 1837)
*Headquarters*: Camp Colorado/Fort Colorado (January 1837); New Fort Houston on the Colorado (April 1837)

## Company D

Captain William M. Eastland (January 1, 1837–March 2, 1838)
*Headquarters*: Camp Colorado/Fort Colorado (January 1837); New Fort Houston on the Colorado (April 1837)

## Company E

Captain Lee C. Smith (March 17–September 17, 1837)
1st Lieutenant Joseph Mather, Commanding (September 17–October 1, 1837)
*Headquarters*: Fort Henderson

## Detachment, Harrisburg Mounted Gunmen

1st Lieutenant A. B. Van Benthuysen, Commanding (October–December 8, 1837)
*Headquarters*: Fort Smith (October 1837)
 *Detachment transferred from Col. J. L. Bennett's Regiment for the Eastland Campaign (October 13–November 27, 1837)*
*Regimental Ranging District*: Upper Brazos, Colorado, Guadalupe, and Little Rivers country with headquarters at Camp Coleman/Fort Colorado (September 1836), Fort Smith (March 1837), Fort Fisher (May 1837), and the mouth of Brushy Creek near Nashville-on-the-Brazos (September 1837)
 *Regiment operated under the orders of BG T. J. Rusk, C-in-C of the Texas Army, and BG F. Huston and BG A. S. Johnston, C-in-C's of the Army of the Republic of Texas*

## Smith's/Jewell's Battalion of Mounted Riflemen

### FIELD & STAFF
Major James Smith, Commanding (September 1–October 26, 1836)
Major George W. Jewell, Commanding (October 26–December 31, 1836)
Lieutenant George W. Browning, Post Quartermaster (September 5, 1836–September 29, 1838)
*Headquarters*: Old Fort Houston on the Trinity

### CLAPP'S MOUNTED RANGERS
Captain Elisha Clapp (September 10–December 12, 1836)
*Ranging District*: Between the Brazos and Trinity Rivers with headquarters at Clapp's Blockhouse on Mustang Prairie and detachment at the Trinity River Fort near Robbins' Ferry

### COSTLEY'S MOUNTED RANGERS
Captain Michael Costley (September 11–December 11, 1836)
*Ranging District*: Between the Trinity and Neches Rivers at old Fort Houston on the Trinity

### JEWELL'S COMPANY
Captain George W. Jewell (September 19–October 26, 1836)
Captain Squire Haggard (October 26, 1836–March 19, 1837)
*Ranging District*: Between the Brazos and Trinity Rivers with headquarters at old Fort Houston on the Trinity
> Battalion operated under the orders of BG T. J. Rusk, C-in-C of the Texas Army, and BG F. Huston and BG A. S. Johnston, C-in-C's of the Army of the Republic of Texas

### CAVALRY SPY COMPANY/COMPANY OF VOLUNTEERS
Captain Erastus "Deaf" Smith (December 25, 1836–March 27, 1837)
Captain Nicholas M. Dawson (March 27–May 10, 1837)
*Ranging District*: San Antonio and Medina Rivers country with headquarters at San Antonio de Béxar
> Company assigned to 1st Cavalry Regiment, Army of the Republic of Texas

## Regiment of Mounted Gunmen

### FIELD & STAFF
Colonel Joseph L. Bennett (Nominated June 12, 1837)
Lieutenant-Colonel Alexander Horton (Nominated June 12, 1837)
Major John G. McGhee (Nominated June 12, 1837)

### GALVESTON COUNTY COMPANY
Captain James Perry (Nominated June 12, 1837)

### HARRISBURG MOUNTED GUNMEN
Captain John M. Bowyer (June 18–December 18, 1837)
1st Lieutenant A. B. Van Benthuysen, commanding detachment (October–December 8, 1837)
*Headquarters*: Houston (June 1837) with Van Benthuysen's detachment at Fort Smith (October 1837)
> Lt. Van Benthuysen's detachment attached to Maj. W. H. Smith's Battalion for the Eastland Campaign (October 13–November 27, 1837)

### NACOGDOCHES COUNTY COMPANY
Captain Elisha Clapp (Nominated June 12, 1837)

### St. Augustine Company
Captain John Clark (Nominated June 12, 1837)

### Red River County Company
Captain John R. Craddock (Nominated June 12, 1837)

### Red River County Company
Captain John H. Dyer (Nominated June 12, 1837)

### Milam County Company
Captain James A. Wilkerson (Nominated June 12, 1837)

### Washington County Company
Captain John G. W. Pierson (Nominated June 12, 1837)

### Jasper County Company
Captain Hannibal Good (Nominated June 12, 1837)

### Shelby County Company
Captain George English (Nominated June 12, 1837)
   *Regiment never organized for service*

### Houston Volunteer Guard
Captain Rueben Ross (January 1–April 1, 1838)

*Ranging District*: Medina River country with headquarters at San Antonio
   *Company operated under the supervision of BG A. S. Johnston, C-in-C of the Army of the Republic of Texas*

### Texas Volunteers
Captain A. Jordan

1st Lieutenant Thomas J. Bowen, Acting Commander (April 11–June 11, 1838)
   *Company assigned to 3rd Brigade, Texas Militia*

### Fannin County Volunteer Company of Spies
Captain James R. O'Neal (April 8–September 8, 1838)

*Ranging District*: Fannin County
   *Company assigned to 2nd Regiment, 4th Brigade, Texas Militia*

### Mounted Gunmen/Mounted Volunteer Ranging Company
Captain Jason Wilson (May 27–August 27, 1838)

*Ranging District*: Red River County
   *Company assigned to 1st Regiment, 4th Brigade, Texas Militia*

### Fannin County Mounted Rangers
Captain Claiborne Chisum (June 9–September 9, 1838)

*Ranging District*: Trinity River country
   *Company assigned to 1st Regiment, 4th Brigade, Texas Militia*

### Karnes' 1838 Comanche Expedition
Colonel Henry W. Karnes (August 1838)

*Ranging District*: West of the Medina River with headquarters at San Antonio

### Nacogdoches County Mounted Rangers
Captain Hiram B. Stephens (August 4–September 15, 1838)

*Ranging District*: "Cherokee Line" with headquarters at Nacogdoches
   *Company assigned to 2nd Regiment, 3rd Brigade, Texas Militia for MG T. J. Rusk's Cherokee Nation Expedition (August 9–27, 1838)*

### Mounted Volunteers
Captain James D. Long (August 5–23, 1838)
*Ranging District*: "Cherokee Line" with headquarters at Nacogdoches
    Company assigned to 2nd Regiment, 3rd Brigade, Texas Militia for MG T. J. Rusk's Cherokee Nation Expedition (August 9–27, 1838) and operated under the personal command of Maj. B. C. Walters

### Mounted Company
Captain Lewis Sánchez (August 5–27, 1838)
*Ranging District*: "Cherokee Line" with headquarters at Nacogdoches
    Company assigned to 2nd Regiment, 3rd Brigade, Texas Militia for MG T. J. Rusk's Cherokee Nation Expedition (August 9–27, 1838) and operated under the personal command of Maj. B. C. Walters

## 1st Regiment of Mounted Gunmen/ Battalion of Volunteer Rangers

### Field & Staff
Major Leonard H. Mabbitt, Commanding (September–December 28, 1838)
Amos H. Gates, Commissary (August 30–November 30, 1838)
Lieutenant George W. Browning, Post Quartermaster (September 5, 1836–September 29, 1838)
Doctor William Perry, Surgeon (September–November 7, 1838?)

### Mounted Gunmen (Volunteers)
Captain Champion Blythe (August 30–September 21, 1838)
Captain Squire Brown (September 22–December 28, 1838)

### Houston County Mounted Gunmen
Captain William T. Sadler (September–November 7, 1838)

### Mounted Rangers
Captain Jacob Snively (September 14–December 13, 1838)

### Mounted Riflemen
Captain James Bradshaw (October 10–December 1, 1838)
*Regimental Ranging District*: Houston County from the Trinity River to the Neches River with headquarters at Fort Houston
    Regiment assigned to 3rd Brigade, Texas Militia for MG T. J. Rusk's Cherokee Nation Expedition (August 9–27, 1838) and the Kickapoo War (October 11–21, 1838)

### Mounted Volunteers
Captain Henry W. Augustine (August 8–22, 1838)
*Ranging District*: "Cherokee Line" with headquarters at Nacogdoches
    Company assigned to 1st Regiment, 3rd Brigade, Texas Militia for MG T. J. Rusk's Cherokee Nation Expedition (August 9–27, 1838)

### Spy Company
Captain James H. Durst (August 8–24, 1838)
*Ranging District*: "Cherokee Line" with headquarters at Nacogdoches
    Company assigned to 3rd Brigade, Texas Militia for MG T. J. Rusk's Cherokee Nation Expedition (August 9–27, 1838)

### Mounted Volunteers
Captain George English (August 10–26, 1838)
*Ranging District*: "Cherokee Line" with headquarters at Nacogdoches

Company assigned to 3rd Regiment, 3rd Brigade, Texas Militia for MG T. J. Rusk's Cherokee Nation Expedition (August 9–27, 1838)

### SABINE COUNTY MOUNTED VOLUNTEERS/MOUNTED MILITIA/MOUNTED GUNMEN

Captain David Renfro (August 12–26, 1838)

*Ranging District*: "Cherokee Line" with headquarters at Nacogdoches
Company assigned to 3rd Regiment, 3rd Brigade, Texas Militia for MG T. J. Rusk's Cherokee Nation Expedition (August 9–27, 1838)

### RED RIVER COUNTY RANGERS

Captain Isaac Lyday (September 1, 1838–February 28, 1839)

*Ranging District*: North Sulphur River and Cypress Creek country with headquarters at Fort Lyday/DeKalb
Company assigned to 1st Regiment, 4th Brigade, Texas Militia

### MOUNTED COMPANY

Captain Eli Russell (September 2–November 15, 1838)

*Ranging District*: "Cherokee Line" with headquarters at camp on the Neches Saline
Company assigned to 2nd Regiment, 3rd Brigade, Texas Militia and operated under the personal command of Maj. B. C. Walters

### MOUNTED RIFLEMEN/GUNMEN

Captain Edward H. Tarrant (September 6, 1838–January 7, 1839)

*Ranging District*: Red River country along Texas-Louisiana border (September 1838); Trinity River country with headquarters at camp on the Clear Fork (December 1838)
Company assigned to 4th Brigade, Texas Militia

### FANNIN COUNTY MOUNTED RANGERS

Captain Nathaniel T. Journey (September 13, 1838–March 13, 1839)

*Ranging District*: Trinity River country with headquarters at camp on Bois d'Arc Creek (September) and Camp Journey (January)
Company assigned to 2nd Regiment, 4th Brigade, Texas Militia for the Sloan-Journey Expedition (September 15–21, 1838)

### DETACHMENT OF MOUNTED MEN

Captain James Fisher (September 14–October 3, 1838)

*Ranging District*: "Cherokee Line" with headquarters at camp on the Neches Saline
Detachment assigned to 2nd Regiment, 3rd Brigade, Texas Militia and operated under the personal command of Maj. B. C. Walters

### FANNIN COUNTY RANGERS

Captain Robert Sloan (September 14, 1838–January 14, 1839)

*Ranging District*: Trinity River country with headquarters at camp on Bois d'Arc Creek (September)
Company assigned to 2nd Regiment, 4th Brigade, Texas Militia for the Sloan-Journey Expedition (September 15–21, 1838)

### MOUNTED VOLUNTEERS/SPIES

Captain James Smith (October 7–December 1, 1838)

*Ranging District*: Trinity River to the Sabine River with headquarters at Fort Houston
Company assigned to 3rd Brigade, Texas Militia

### Mounted Volunteers
Captain Joseph Williams (October 9–19, 1838)
*Ranging District*: "Cherokee Line" with headquarters at Fort Houston
  *Company assigned to 2nd Regiment, 3rd Brigade, Texas Militia for the Kickapoo War (October 11–21, 1838)*

### Mounted Volunteers
Captain John M. Durst (October 10–20, 1838)
*Ranging District*: "Cherokee Line" with headquarters at Fort Houston
  *Company assigned to 2nd Regiment, 3rd Brigade, Texas Militia for the Kickapoo War (October 11–21, 1838)*

### Nacogdoches Mounted Volunteers
Captain Robert W. Smith (October 10–21, 1838)
*Ranging District*: "Cherokee Line" with headquarters at Fort Houston
  *Company assigned to 2nd Regiment, 3rd Brigade, Texas Militia for the Kickapoo War (October 11–21, 1838)*

### Mounted Volunteers
Captain George English (October 10, 1838–January 13, 1839)
*Ranging District*: Trinity River to the Sabine River with headquarters at Murchison's Camp
  *Company assigned to 3rd Regiment, 3rd Brigade, Texas Militia*

### Mounted Rangers ("Mustang Hoosiers")
Captain William C. Brookfield (October 12–24, 1838)
*Ranging District*: "Cherokee Line" with headquarters at Fort Houston
  *Company assigned to 2nd Regiment, 3rd Brigade, Texas Militia for the Kickapoo War (October 11–21, 1838)*

### Shelby County Mounted Militia
Captain Richard Haley (October 14, 1838–January 10, 1839)
*Ranging District*: Trinity River to the Sabine River with headquarters at Murchison's Camp
  *Company assigned to 3rd Regiment, 3rd Brigade, Texas Militia*

### Houston County Mounted Riflemen
Captain James E. Box (October 14, 1838–January 14, 1839)
*Ranging District*: "Cherokee Line" with headquarters at Fort Houston
  *Company assigned to 2nd Regiment, 3rd Brigade, Texas Militia for the Kickapoo War (October 11–21, 1838)*

### Mounted Militia/Mounted Gunmen
Captain David Renfro (October 17–November 9, 1838)
*Ranging District*: "Cherokee Line" with headquarters at Nacogdoches
  *Company assigned to 3rd Regiment, 3rd Brigade, Texas Militia*

### Rangers
Captain Madison G. Whitaker (October 30–November 11, 1838)
*Ranging District*: "Cherokee Line" with headquarters at Nacogdoches
  *Company assigned to 3rd Brigade, Texas Militia*

### Sabine County Mounted Militia
Captain William P. Wyche (November 4, 1838–February 4, 1839)
*Ranging District*: Trinity River to the Sabine River with headquarters at Fort Houston
  *Company assigned to 3rd Regiment, 3rd Brigade, Texas Militia*

### HOUSTON COUNTY RANGERS

Captain John Wortham (November 9, 1838–February 8, 1839)
*Ranging District*: Houston County with headquarters at Fort Houston (December), Walker's Station (December), and Fort Houston (January)
 *Company assigned to 3rd Regiment, 3rd Brigade, Texas Militia (November) and Lt-Col. J. Snively's Texas Ranger Staff (January)*

## *Houston Volunteers*

### FIELD & STAFF

Major George W. Bonnell, Commanding (November 7, 1838–January 24, 1839)
James W. Simmons, Quartermaster (November 22–December 22, 1838)
James D. Cocke, Quartermaster (December 21, 1838–February 21, 1839)
Doctor Samuel Pilkington, Surgeon (November 20, 1838–January 12, 1839)

### COMPANY A (MILAM GUARDS)

Captain Joseph Daniels (November 15, 1838–February 15, 1839)
*Headquarters*: Fort Houston (December); Houston (January); New Fort Milam (January)

### COMPANY B (FANNIN RANGERS)

Captain George C. Briscoe (November 16, 1838–January 10, 1839)
*Headquarters*: Old Fort Milam (December)
*Battalion Ranging District*: Brazos River country with headquarters at camp near Spring Creek (November) and camp at the Falls of the Brazos River (December)
 *Command designated 2nd Battalion, 1st Regiment, 2nd Brigade, Texas Militia*

### MOUNTED GUNMEN

Captain John M. Durst (November 17–December 16, 1838)
*Ranging District*: Nacogdoches County with headquarters at Mount Sterling
 *Company assigned to 3rd Brigade, Texas Militia*

### FANNIN COUNTY MOUNTED GUNMEN

Captain John Hart (November 19, 1838–January 1, 1839)
*Ranging District*: Fannin County with headquarters at Fort Inglish
 *Company assigned to 2nd Regiment, 4th Brigade, Texas Militia*

### RED RIVER COUNTY RANGERS

Captain William B. Stout (November 20, 1838–May 26, 1839)
*Ranging District*: North Sulphur River and Cypress Creek country with headquarters at Fort Shelton/Rusk and detachment at Fort Lyday/DeKalb
 *Company assigned to 1st Regiment, 4th Brigade, Texas Militia*

## *Walter's Spy Battalion*

### FIELD & STAFF

Major Baley C. Walters, Commanding (December 1–24, 1838)

### MOUNTED SHAWNEES

Chief (Captain) Panther (November 25–December 20, 1838)
Interpreter Spy Buck, Commanding (December 20, 1838–January 25, 1839)
 *Company transferred to Lt-Col. J. Snively's Texas Ranger Staff (January)*

### MOUNTED RANGERS (INDIANS)

Captain James H. Durst (December 1, 1838–January 25, 1839)

*Company transferred to Lt-Col. J. Snively's Texas Ranger Staff (January)*
*Battalion Ranging District*: "Cherokee Line" with headquarters at Shawnee Town
    *Battalion assigned to 3rd Brigade, Texas Militia*

### Fannin County Volunteers/Mounted Gunmen/ Mounted Rangers

Captain Jesse Stiff (December 1–29, 1838)
1st Lieutenant John P. Simpson, commanding detachment (December 1, 1838–January 14, 1839)
*Ranging District*: Fannin County with headquarters at camp on Pilot's Grove Creek and Simpson's detachment at Fort Saline and Fort Inglish
    *Company assigned to 2nd Regiment, 4th Brigade, Texas Militia*

### Mounted Company

Captain Joseph Ferguson (December 8, 1838–March 8, 1839)
*Ranging District*: Trinity River to the Sabine River with headquarters at Fort Houston
    *Company assigned to 3rd Regiment, 3rd Brigade, Texas Militia*

### Texas Volunteers

Captain William A. Becknell (December 8, 1838–January 9, 1839)
*Ranging District*: Red River County

## Texas Ranger Staff

### Field & Staff

Lieutenant-Colonel Jacob Snively, Commanding (January 6–February 2, 1839)
Peter Tipps, Adjutant (January 6–February 2, 1839)
George Pollett, Commissary (January 3–February 3, 1839)
George W. Jewell, Assistant Commissary (January 6–February 2, 1839)
Doctor John L. Witter, Surgeon (January 6–February 2, 1839)
Sergeant-Major J. G. Grayham (January 6–February 2, 1839)
Albert A. Nelson, Bugler (January 6–February 2, 1839)

### Mounted Rangers

Captain Lewis Sánchez (September 7, 1838–January 27, 1839)

### Mounted Gunmen

Captain James F. Timmins (October 12, 1838–Febuary 6, 1839)

### Houston County Rangers

Captain John Wortham (November 9, 1838–February 8, 1839)
    *Company transferred from 3rd Militia Regiment (January)*

### Mounted Rangers (Indians)

Captain James H. Durst (December 1, 1838–January 25, 1839)
    *Company transferred from Maj. B. C. Walters' Spy Battalion (January)*

### Mounted Shawnees

Interpreter Spy Buck (December 20, 1838–January 25, 1839)
    *Company transferred from Maj. B. C. Walters' Spy Battalion (January)*

### Mounted Rangers

Captain James W. Cleveland (January 6–Febuary 5, 1839)

### MOUNTED RANGERS

Captain James E. Box (January 15–March 25, 1839)
*Staff Ranging District*: "Cherokee Line" with headquarters at Camp Williams and camp on the Neches Saline
    *Ranger Staff assigned to 3rd Brigade, Texas Militia*

## Corps of Rangers

### HEADQUARTERS

Colonel Henry W. Karnes (January 9–July 28, 1839)
Lieutenant-Colonel Devereaux J. Woodlief, Commanding (July 29–September 9, 1839)

## Woodlief's Mounted Volunteer Regiment

### FIELD & STAFF

Lieutenant-Colonel Devereaux J. Woodlief, Commanding (January 9–September 9, 1839)
Major William Jefferson Jones (January 9–September 9, 1839)
William Wirt Adams, Adjutant

### MOUNTED VOLUNTEERS

Captain Mark B. Lewis (March 2–September 9, 1839)
*Ranging District*: Travis County with headquarters at Camp Austin and Bastrop (April 1839); "Cherokee Line" with headquarters at Fort Kickapoo (May–July 1839)
    *Company operated under the personal command of Maj. W. J. Jones (March–May 1839)*

### MOUNTED VOLUNTEERS

Captain James P. Ownby (March 2–September 9, 1839)
*Ranging District*: Travis County with headquarters at Camp Austin and Bastrop (April 1839); "Cherokee Line" with headquarters at Fort Kickapoo (May–July 1839)
    *Company operated under the personal command of Maj. W. J. Jones (March–May 1839)*

### "HOUSTON YAGERS"

Captain John Garrett (April 8–June 10, 1839)
1st Lieutenant John A. Creery, Acting Commander (June 11–August 8, 1839)
*Ranging District*: Travis County with headquarters at Camp Austin
    *Company operated under the personal command of Maj. W. J. Jones (March–May 1839) and assigned to detached duty guarding the capital (May–June 1839)*

### MOUNTED GUNMEN

Captain Greenberry H. Harrison (June 28–August 10, 1839)
    *Company transferred to Maj. B. C. Walters' Mounted Ranger Staff (July)*

### HOUSTON VOLUNTEER COMPANY

Captain John C. Neill (June 1839)
*Ranging District*: Between the Brazos and Colorado Rivers
    *Company assigned to detached duty guarding the frontier*
*Regimental Ranging District*: Bastrop County with headquarters at Camp Austin (April 1839); "Cherokee Line" with headquarters at Fort Kickapoo (May–July 1839)
    *Regiment operated under the personal command of Col. E. Burleson, 1st Infantry Regiment, Army of the Republic of Texas for the Cherokee War (July 15–24, 1839)*

## Karnes' 1839 Comanche Expedition

### FIELD & STAFF

Colonel Henry W. Karnes (June 6–23, 1839)

### Mounted Volunteers
Captain Louis B. Franks (June 6–23, 1839)

### Mounted Volunteers
Captain Juan N. Seguín (June 6–23, 1839)
*Expedition's Ranging District*: Headwaters of the Medina and Hondo Seco Rivers and the Cañon de Uvalde with headquarters at San Antonio
    *Expedition operated under the supervision of President M. Lamar*

### Volunteer Ranging Company
Captain Benjamin F. Bryant (January 14–16, 1839)
1st Lieutenant Ethan A. Stroud, Commanding (January 16, 1839)
*Ranging District*: Brazos River country with headquarters at Bryant's Station
    *Company organized but never formally mustered into service*

### Fannin County Mounted Rangers
Captain Mark R. Roberts (January 14–April 13, 1839)
*Ranging District*: Fannin County with headquarters at Camp Warren
    *Company assigned to 2nd Regiment, 4th Brigade, Texas Militia*

### Houston County Mounted Riflemen/Volunteers
Captain James E. Box (January 15–March 25, 1839)
*Ranging District*: Houston County with headquarters at Fort Houston
    *Company transferred from Lt-Col. J. Snively's Texas Ranger Staff to 2nd Regiment, 3rd Brigade, Texas Militia (February)*

## *Moore's 1839 Comanche Campaign*

### Field & Staff
Major John H. Moore (January 21–February 25, 1839)
William Bugg, Adjutant (January 25–February 25, 1839)

### La Grange Volunteers
Captain William M. Eastland (January 21–February 26, 1839)

### Bastrop Rangers
Captain Noah Smithwick (January 24–February 25, 1839)

### Mounted Lipan Volunteers
Principal Chief Cuelgas de Castro (January 25–February 25, 1839)

### Mounted Tonkawa Volunteers
Captain Plácido (Ha-shu-ka-na) (January 25–February 25, 1839)
*Battalion Ranging District*: San Gabriel, Colorado, and San Saba Rivers country with headquarters at La Grange
    *Campaign operated under the supervision of President M. Lamar*

## *Houston County Ranger Battalion*

### Field & Staff
Major John Wortham, Commanding (February 8–June 1839)

### Houston County Rangers
Captain Solomon Adams (February 8–August 9, 1839)
*Headquarters*: Crockett
    *Company transferred to Maj. B. C. Walters' Mounted Ranger Staff (June)*

### Houston County Rangers
Captain James E. Box (March 26–October 18, 1839)

*Headquarters*: Fort Houston
  Company transferred to Maj. B. C. Walters' Mounted Ranger Staff (June)

*Battalion Ranging District*: Houston County with headquarters at Fort Houston
  Battalion assigned to 3rd Brigade, Texas Militia

## Mounted Texas Rangers Staff

### Field & Staff
Major Baley C. Walters, Commanding (February 14–September 2, 1839)
1st Lieutenant Ira Munson, Adjutant (February 14–September 12, 1839)
Doctor William G. W. Jowers, Surgeon (April 4–September 2, 1839)

### Houston County Company
Captain Balis Edens (February 11–March 1839?)

*Ranging District*: San Pedro Creek country with headquarters at Brown's Fort

### Nacogdoches County Volunteer Rangers
Captain Henry M. Smith (March 1–August 16, 1839)
1st Lieutenant Albert G. Corbin, Acting Commander (August 16–September 2, 1839)

### Houston County Mounted Rangers
Captain James E. Box (March 26–October 18, 1839)
  Company transferred from Maj. J. Wortham's Ranger Battalion (June)

### Houston County Rangers
Captain Solomon Adams (February 8–August 9, 1839)
  Company transferred from Maj. J. Wortham's Ranger Battalion (June)

### Mounted Gunmen
Captain Greenberry H. Harrison (June 28–August 10, 1839)
  Company transferred from Col. H. W. Karnes' Corps of Rangers (July)

### Mounted Volunteers
Captain Benjamin A. Vansickle (July 1–August 5, 1839)

*Mounted Staff Ranging District*: "Cherokee Line" with headquarters at Fort Saline and Fort Kickapoo
  Mounted Ranger Staff temporarily designated as 1st Regiment, 3rd Brigade, Texas Militia for the Cherokee War (July 15–24, 1839)

### Mounted Volunteers
Captain Jacob Burleson (February 24–25, 1839)

*Ranging District*: Colorado River to Battleground, Brushy, and Boggy Creeks country with headquarters at Wilbarger's Fort
  Company merged with Rogers' company and attached to Col. E. Burleson's volunteer command (February 25–26, 1839)

### Mounted Volunteers
Captain James Rogers (February 24–26, 1839)

*Ranging District*: Colorado River to Battleground, Brushy, and Boggy Creeks country with headquarters at Wilbarger's Fort
  Company attached to Col. E. Burleson's volunteer command (February 25–26, 1839)

## Mounted Volunteers

Colonel Edward "Ned" Burleson, Sr. (February 25–26, 1839)
*Ranging District*: Colorado River to Battleground, Brushy, and Boggy Creeks country with headquarters at Bastrop

## Mounted Volunteers

Captain Jesse Billingsley (February 25–27, 1839)
*Ranging District*: Colorado River to Battleground, Brushy, and Boggy Creeks country with headquarters at Bastrop
    *Company attached to Col. E. Burleson's volunteer command (February 25–26, 1839)*

## Gonzales Volunteer Company

Captain Benjamin McCulloch (March 1–2, 1839)
Chief "Captain James Kerr," commanding Tonkawa Indian scouts (March 1–2, 1839)
*Ranging District*: Peach Creek country with headquarters at Gonzales
    *Company organized but never formally mustered into service*

## Milam County Rangers

Captain George B. Erath (March 8–June 8, 1839)
*Ranging District*: Milam County
    *Company operated under the supervision of President M. Lamar and assigned to Robertson County/Milam County Ranger Brigade*

## Robertson County Mounted Rangers

Captain James D. Matthews (March 8–June 8, 1839)
*Ranging District*: Robertson County
    *Company operated under the supervision of President M. Lamar and assigned to Robertson County/Milam County Ranger Brigade*

## Robertson County Volunteer Rangers

Captain Nimrod Doyle (March 8–June 10, 1839)
*Ranging District*: Robertson County
    *Company operated under the supervision of President M. Lamar and assigned to Robertson County/Milam County Ranger Brigade*

## La Grange County Rangers

1st Lieutenant Micah Andrews, Commanding (March 10–June 10, 1839)
1st Lieutenant James O. Rice, commanding detachment (May 17–19, 1839)
*Ranging District*: Colorado and Guadalupe Rivers country with headquarters at Waterloo/Austin
    *Company mustered into the Texas Militia and attached to 1st Infantry Regiment, Army of the Republic of Texas for the Córdova Pursuit (March 25–May 18, 1839)*

## Gonzales County Rangers

Captain Mathew "Old Paint" Caldwell (March 16–June 16, 1839)
1st Lieutenant James Campbell, commanding detachment
*Ranging District*: Guadalupe and Nueces Rivers country with headquarters at camp on the Guadalupe River near Gonzales and Campbell's detachment at Seguín
    *Company assigned to 1st Brigade, Texas Militia for the Córdova Pursuit (March 25–May 18, 1839)*

## Red River and Fannin County Volunteer Company of Rangers/Fannin County Mounted Rangers

Captain John Emberson (March 16–September 16, 1839)

Captain Mark R. Roberts (September 16, 1839–March 16, 1840)
Lieutenant William M. "Buckskin" Williams, commanding detachment (July–September 1839)
*Ranging District*: Red River and Fannin Counties with headquarters at Camp Warren and Williams' "west detachment" at Camp Caldwell
  *Company assigned to 2nd Regiment, 4th Brigade, Texas Militia*

### "Travis Spies"

1st Lieutenant William G. Evans, Commanding (March 20–September 20, 1839)
1st Sergeant William H. Weaver, commanding detachment (May 20–26, 1839)
2nd Corporal Samuel A. Blain, commanding Weaver's detachment (May 26–27, 1839)
*Ranging District*: Brazos River country with headquarters at Fort Milam/Burleson
  *Company organized and mustered into the Texas Militia*

### Mounted Volunteers

Captain Jesse Billingsley (March 27–30, 1839)
*Ranging District*: Colorado and Guadalupe Rivers country with headquarters at Waterloo/Austin
  *Company attached to 1st Infantry Regiment, Army of the Republic of Texas for the Córdova Pursuit (March 25–May 18, 1839)*

### Bird's Rangers (Austin Volunteers)

Captain John Bird (April 24–May 26, 1839)
Captain Nathaniel "Nathan" Brookshire (May 26–July 24, 1839)
*Ranging District*: Brazos and Little Rivers country with headquarters at Fort Milam (April), Fort Smith on the Little River (May), Camp Nashville (May), and Camp Brazos (June)
  *Company organized and mustered into the Texas Militia*

### Bastrop County Rangers

Captain Nelson Merrill (June 10–September 10, 1839)
*Ranging District*: Bastrop and Travis Counties with headquarters at Austin
  *Company organized and mustered into the Texas Militia*

### Mounted Company

Captain Lewis Sánchez (June 16–August 5, 1839)
*Ranging District*: "Cherokee Line" with headquarters at Fort Kickapoo
  *Company assigned to 2nd Regiment, 3rd Brigade, Texas Militia for the Cherokee War (July 15–24, 1839) and operated under the personal command of Maj. B. C. Walters*

### Nacogdoches Mounted Rangers

Captain Alexander Jordan (June 21–August 5, 1839)
*Ranging District*: "Cherokee Line" with headquarters at Fort Kickapoo
  *Company assigned to 2nd Regiment, 3rd Brigade, Texas Militia for the Cherokee War (July 15–24, 1839) and operated under the personal command of Maj. B. C. Walters*

### Sabine County Rangers

Captain John W. Middleton (July 1–August 14, 1839)
*Ranging District*: Sabine River country

### San Augustine County Mounted Rangers

Captain Jacob E. Hamilton (July 22–August 10, 1839)
*Ranging District*: "Cherokee Line" with headquarters at Camp Harris
  *Company assigned to 3rd Brigade, Texas Militia*

### MOUNTED GUNMEN
Captain Joseph L. Bennett (July 28–September 3, 1839)
*Ranging District*: Houston and Robertson Counties with headquarters at Fort Houston
   *Company operated under the supervision of Col. A. S. Johnston, Secretary of War*

### GONZALES RANGING COMPANY
Captain Reuben Ross (July 1–December 15, 1839)
*Ranging District*: San Antonio River country with headquarters at Richmond
   *Company organized and mustered into the Texas Militia, and recruited by Antonio Canales for the Mexican Federalist War (September 30–December 15, 1839)*

### FANNIN COUNTY RANGING COMPANY
Captain Joseph Sowell (August 1–31, 1839)
*Ranging District*: Fannin County with headquarters at Camp Warren
   *Company assigned to 2nd Regiment, 4th Brigade, Texas Militia*

### RED RIVER COUNTY VOLUNTEER MOUNTED RIFLEMEN
Captain James W. Sims (August 2–November 2, 1839)
*Ranging District*: Red River County with headquarters at Clarksville
   *Company assigned to 1st Regiment, 4th Brigade, Texas Militia*

### MOUNTED RANGERS
Captain Joseph Durst (August 15–September 27, 1839)
*Ranging District*: San Antonio Road from Nacogdoches to Fort Lacy with headquarters at Angelina
   *Company assigned to 3rd Brigade, Texas Militia*

### MOUNTED RANGERS/VOLUNTEERS
Captain John William Lane (August 15, 1839–February 16, 1840)
*Ranging District*: Sabine River country
   *Company assigned to 4th Brigade, Texas Militia*

## *1st Regiment of Mounted Gunmen*

### FIELD & STAFF
Colonel John C. Neill (October 5–November 22, 1839)
Lieutenant-Colonel Alexander Somervell (October 5–November 22, 1839)
Major William F. Young (October 5–November 22, 1839)
Benjamin F. Smith, Adjutant (October 5–November 22, 1839)
J. F. Garrett, Commissary (October 5–November 22, 1839)
Harley Price, Assistant Commissary (October 5–November 22, 1839)
Doctor William H. McGee, Surgeon (October 5–November 22, 1839)
Doctor G. D. Long, Assistant Surgeon (October 5–November 22, 1839)
Sergeant-Major John C. Thomas (October 5–November 22, 1839)
Antonio Miller, Musician (October 5–November 22, 1839)

### COMPANY A
Captain Samuel Williams (September 11–December 2, 1839)

### COMPANY B
Captain John P. Gill (September 14–November 22, 1839)

## Company C
Captain Nathaniel H. Carroll (September 15–December 1, 1839)

## Company D
Captain Samuel Davis (September 10–November 27, 1839)

## Company E
Captain William F. Young (September 14–October 4, 1839)
Captain William V. R. Hallund (October 5–November 22, 1839)

## Company F
Captain George W. Long (September 9–November 30, 1839)

## Company G
Captain Henry Reed (October 3–November 22, 1839)

## Jefferson County Artillery Company
2nd Lieutenant Thomas H. Brennan (September 2–December 4, 1839)

## Galveston Mounted Riflemen
Captain William F. Wilson (September 8–November 19, 1839)
Captain Ephraim W. McLean (November 19–December 7, 1839)
*Company detached to Col. H. W. Karnes' Hill Country Expedition (September)*

## Spy Company
Captain John J. Tumlinson, Jr. (October 13–November 22, 1839)
*Regimental Ranging District*: Upper Brazos River country with headquarters at camp on Tinnin's Crossing (October) and camp on Cedar Creek (November)
*Regiment operated under the supervision of the War Department for Col. J. C. Neill's Comanche Expedition (October 9–November 22, 1839)*

## *Karnes' Hill Country Expedition*

### Field & Staff
Colonel Henry W. Karnes (October 20–November 21, 1839)

### San Antonio Mounted Volunteers
Captain José María Gonzales (September 8–November 21, 1839)

### Galveston Mounted Riflemen/Volunteers
Captain William F. Wilson (September 8–November 19, 1839)
Captain Ephraim W. McLean (November 19–December 8, 1839)
*Company detached from 1st Regiment of Mounted Gunmen (September)*
*Expedition's Ranging District*: Guadalupe and San Saba Hills with headquarters at San Antonio
*Expedition operated under the supervision of the War Department*

### Nacogdoches County Rangers
Captain George K. Black (October 22, 1839–Janury 29, 1840)
*Ranging District*: "Cherokee Line" with headquarters at Cook's Fort
*Company assigned to 3rd Brigade, Texas Militia*

### Mounted Volunteer Scouts
Captain Mathew "Old Paint" Caldwell (December 11, 1839–January 12, 1840)
*Ranging District*: San Gabriel, Lampasas, and Colorado Rivers country with headquarters at Camp Caldwell

*Company attached to 1st Infantry Regiment, Army of the Republic of Texas for Col. E. Burleson's Northwestern Campaign (December 16, 1839–January 12, 1840)*

### BOGGY AND TRINITY RANGERS
Captain Thomas N. B. Greer (February 23–May 23, 1840)
*Ranging District*: Navasota and Trinity Rivers country north of the Old San Antonio Road with headquarters at Fort Boggy
*Company assigned to 3rd Brigade, Texas Militia*

### PITKIN GUARDS
Captain John Constantinus Pierce (March 13–June 7, 1840)
Captain Ebenezer B. Nichols (June 8–August 27, 1840)
*Ranging District*: Travis and Béxar Counties with headquarters at Mission San Jose (April–May) and Mission Concepción (June)
*Company assigned to 2nd Brigade, Texas Militia*

### FANNIN COUNTY RANGERS
Captain Daniel R. Jackson (March 28–September 28, 1840)
*Ranging District*: Fannin County with headquarters at Fort Coffee
*Company assigned to 2nd Regiment, 4th Brigade, Texas Militia*

### RANGERS
2nd Lieutenant Moses Wells, Commanding (April 9–July 9, 1840)
*Ranging District*: Colorado River settlements with headquarters at Fort Wells
*Company operated under the supervision of the War Department*

### RED RIVER RANGERS
Captain William B. Stout (May 2–August 2, 1840)
*Ranging District*: Red River County with headquarters at Camp DeKalb (May) and Camp Davis (June)
*Company assigned to 1st Regiment, 4th Brigade, Texas Militia*

### RED RIVER RANGERS
Captain Henry B. Stout (June 10–September 10, 1840)
*Ranging District*: Red River and Lamar Counties with headquarters at Camp Sherman
*Company assigned to 4th Brigade, Texas Militia*

### BORDER GUARDS
Captain James D. Cocke (June 18–August 28, 1840)
*Ranging District*: Travis and Béxar Counties with headquarters at Austin (July) and San Antonio (August)
*Company mustered into service by order of the War Department and operated under the personal orders of Maj. G. T. Howard, 1st Infantry Regiment, Army of the Republic of Texas*

### SPY COMPANY
Captain George B. Erath (July 14–September 20, 1840)
*Ranging District*: Brazos and Bosque Rivers country with headquarters at Little River Fort
*Company operated under the personal orders of MG F. Huston, C-in-C of the Texas Militia*

## Nacogdoches Battalion

### FIELD & STAFF
Major James H. Durst, Commanding (July 20–October 16, 1840)
John F. Graham, Quartermaster (July 20–October 16, 1840)

### Mounted Rangers
Captain Robert Barkley (July 4–October 4, 1840)
Lieutenant Daniel Woodlan, Acting Commander (?–October 4, 1840)

### Mounted Rangers
Captain Adolphus Sterne (July 8–October 16, 1840)
*Battalion Ranging District*: Nacogdoches County with headquarters at Nacogdoches
  *Battalion assigned to 3rd Brigade, Texas Militia*

### Béxar Volunteers
Captain John R. Cunningham (June 25?–July 7, 1840)
*Ranging District*: Between Frio and Leona Rivers with headquarters at San Antonio
  *Company attached to Company "A," 1st Infantry Regiment, Army of the Republic of Texas*

### Lavaca County Volunteers
Captain Adam "Black Adam" Zumwalt (August 6, 1840–?)
*Ranging District*: Lavaca River area of the Big Hill country
  *Company organized but never formally mustered into service*
  *Company merged with Capt. J. J. Tumlinson's command (August 7, 1840) and Col. J. H. Moore's command (August 12, 1840)*

### McCulloch's Gonzales Volunteers
Captain Benjamin McCulloch (August 6–9, 1840)
Lieutenant _____ (August 9, 1840–?)
*Ranging District*: Lavaca River area of the Big Hill country
  *Company organized but never formally mustered into service*
  *Company merged with Capt. J. J. Tumlinson's command (August 7)*

### Tumlinson's Victoria/Cuero Volunteers
Captain John J. Tumlinson, Jr. (August 7, 1840–?)
*Ranging District*: Lavaca and Garcitas Rivers area of the Big Hill country
  *Company organized but never formally mustered into service*
  *Company merged with Col. J. H. Moore's command (August 12)*

### Owen's Texana Volunteers
Captain Clark L. Owen (August 8, 1840–?)
*Ranging District*: Arenosa Creek area of the Big Hill country
  *Company organized but never formally mustered into service*
  *Company merged with Capt. J. J. Tumlinson's command (August 10, 1840) and Col. J. H. Moore's command (August 12, 1840)*

## *Volunteers*

### Field & Staff
Captain Mathew "Old Paint" Caldwell, Commanding (August 11–12, 1840)
Major-General Felix Huston, Commanding (August 12–14, 1840)
Major James Izod, Aide-de-Camp (August 11–14, 1840)
Colonel P. Hansbrough Bell, Volunteer Aide (August 12–14, 1840)
Captain George T. Howard, Volunteer Aide (August 11–14, 1840)
Captain Andrew J. Neill, Volunteer Aide (August 11–14, 1840)
Doctor Caleb S. Brown, Surgeon (August 12–14, 1840)
  *MG F. Huston's staff rendezvoused with Capt. M. Caldwell's command at Plum Creek (August 11)*

### Burleson's Bastrop/Austin Volunteers
Colonel Edward "Ned" Burleson, Sr. (August 11–17, 1840)
Colonel Henry Jones (August 11–17, 1840)
Lieutenant-Colonel Joseph W. E. Wallace (August 11–17, 1840)
Chief Plácido (Ha-shu-ka-na), commanding Tonkawa scouts (August 11–17, 1840)
*Company rendezvoused with MG F. Huston's command at Plum Creek (August 12)*

### Caldwell's Gonzales Volunteers
Captain Mathew "Old Paint" Caldwell (August 5–19, 1840)
*Company rendezvoused at Plum Creek (August 11)*

### Reserves
Major Thomas M. Hardeman, Commanding (August 12–13, 1840)
*Maj. Hardeman rendezvoused with MG F. Huston's command at Plum Creek (August 12)*

### Ward's Lavaca Volunteers
Captain Lafayette Ward (August 8–19, 1840)
*Company rendezvoused with Capt. M. Caldwell's command at Plum Creek (August 11)*

### Bird's Gonzales Volunteers
Captain James Bird (August 10–19, 1840)
*Company rendezvoused with Capt. M. Caldwell's command at Plum Creek (August 11)*
*Command's Ranging District*: Plum Creek country
*Command organized but never formally mustered into service*

### Moore's Fayette County Company
Colonel John H. Moore (August 12, 1840–?)
*Company organized but never formally mustered into service*

## Moore's 1840 Comanche Expedition
### Field & Staff
Major John H. Moore, Commanding (August 20–November 20, 1840)
Smallwood S. B. Fields, Adjutant (October 1–November 20, 1840)
Doctor Henry W. Baylor, Surgeon (October 1–November 20, 1840)

### Fayette County Company
Captain Thomas J. Rabb (September 20–November 20, 1840)

### Colorado County Company
Captain Nicholas M. Dawson (September 20–November 20, 1840)

### Lipan Apache Scout Company
Captain Juan Castro (September 20–November 20, 1840)

### Mounted Detachment
1st Lieutenant Clark L. Owen, Commanding (October 24, 1840)
Expedition Ranging District: Colorado River country with headquarters at La Grange
*Expedition operated under the orders of the War Department (September 20–November 7, 1840)*

### Nichols' Company
Captain Ebenezer B. Nichols (September 25–November 16, 1840)

### Mounted Gunmen
Captain Wesley Askins (October 1–November 20, 1840)

*Ranging District*: Red River County with headquarters at Clarksville
  Company assigned to 4th Brigade, Texas Militia

### MOUNTED RANGERS/VOLUNTEER RANGERS
Captain Jason Wilson (October 24, 1840–January 5, 1841)
*Ranging District*: Red River and Fannin Counties with headquarters at Clarksville
  Company assigned to 1st Regiment, 4th Brigade, Texas Militia

### GONZALES RANGERS/GONZALES VOLUNTEERS
Captain Mathew "Old Paint" Caldwell (September 25–November 16, 1840)
*Ranging District*: Frio, Llano, and Pedernales Rivers country with headquarters at San Antonio
  Company attached to 1st Infantry Regiment, Army of the Republic of Texas for Maj. G. T. Howard's Nueces Expedition (September 29–November 16, 1840)

### COMPANY OF SPIES
Captain George B. Erath (January 1–March 2, 1841)
*Ranging District*: Brazos River country with headquarters at camp on the Falls of the Brazos (January) and Camp Stroud (March)
  Company assigned to 3rd Regiment, 2nd Brigade, Texas Militia for BG E. Morehouse's Brazos Expedition (January 20–March 5, 1841)

### COMPANY OF SPIES
Captain John T. Price (January 3–May 2, 1841)
*Ranging District*: Guadalupe River to Río Grande with headquarters at Victoria (January); Nueces Strip with headquarters at Victoria (April)
  Company operated under the supervision of B. T. Archer, Secretary of War

### COMPANY OF SPIES
Captain John C. "Jack" Hays (January 10–May 10, 1841)
*Ranging District*: Nueces Strip with headquarters at San Antonio
  Company operated under the supervision of B. T. Archer, Secretary of War

### COMPANY OF SPIES
Captain Antonio Pérez (January 20–May 20, 1841)
*Ranging District*: Nueces Strip with headquarters at San Antonio
  Company operated under the supervision of B. T. Archer, Secretary of War

### ROBERTSON COUNTY MOUNTED GUNMEN
Captain Samuel B. Killough (January 20–March 5, 1841)
*Ranging District*: Brazos River country with headquarters at Nashville-on-the Brazos (January) and Camp Franklin (March)
  Company assigned to 3rd Regiment, 2nd Brigade, Texas Militia for BG E. Morehouse's Brazos Expedition (January 20–March 5, 1841)

### MILAM COUNTY MINUTE MEN
Captain George B. Erath (March 9–December 24, 1841)
*Ranging District*: Milam County with headquarters at Nashville-on-the Brazos (April) and Bryant's Station (July)
  Company operated under the supervision of the Chief Justice of Milam County

## Lewis' 1841 Volunteer Expedition
### FIELD & STAFF
Major Mark L. Lewis, Commanding (March 20–June 4, 1841)

Major George T. Howard (March 20–June 4, 1841)
Captain William Bugg, Adjutant (March 20–June 4, 1841)
Joseph H. Rogers, Quartermaster (March 14–June 5, 1841)

### Victoria Company
Captain James Dunn (March 14–June 5, 1841)

### Mounted Riflemen/"Fayette Volunteers"/ "Colorado Volunteers"
Captain Thomas Green (March 20–June 4, 1841)

### Lipan Scouts
Chief Flacco (March 20–June 4, 1841)

### Travis County Spies/Minute Men
Captain George M. Dolson (March 28–December 28, 1841)
1st Lieutenant James W. Newcomb, Acting Commander (April 1–September 6, 1841)
*Ranging District*: Travis County with headquarters at Austin (June–December 1841)
   *Company operated under the supervision of the Chief Justice of Travis County*
*Expedition Ranging District*: Colorado, Concho, San Saba, Llano, and Nueces Rivers country with headquarters at Austin
   *Expedition operated under the supervision of the War Department*

### Robertson County Minute Men
Captain Eli Chandler (March 29–November 5, 1841)
1st Lieutenant William M. Love, commanding detachment (August 3, 1841)
*Ranging District*: Brazos River country with headquarters at Fort Franklin
   *Company operated under the supervision of the Chief Justice of Robertson County*

### Montgomery County Minute Men
Captain Thomas N. B. Greer (April 10–October 7, 1841)
*Ranging District*: Montgomery County
   *Company operated under the supervision of the Chief Justice of Montgomery County*

### Nacogdoches County Minute Men
Captain David Gage (April 12–October 19, 1841)
*Ranging District*: Nacogdoches County with headquarters at Nacogdoches
   *Company operated under the supervision of the Chief Justice of Nacogdoches County and attached to 3rd Regiment, 3rd Brigade, Texas Militia for BG J. Smith's Trinity Expedition (July 10–August 8, 1841)*

### Gonzales Volunteers
Captain Benjamin McCulloch (May 1841)
   *Company organized but never formally mustered into service*

### Lavaca County Minute Men
Captain Adam "Black Adam" Zumwalt (May–December 1841)
*Ranging District*: Lavaca County
   *Company operated under the supervision of the Chief Justice of Lavaca County*

### Red River Volunteers
Captain James Bourland (May 5–30, 1841)
*Ranging District*: Headwaters and west fork of the Trinity River with headquarters at Fort Johnson
   *Company assigned to 4th Brigade, Texas Militia for BG E. H. Tarrant's Village Creek Expedition (May 4–30, 1841)*

### Gonzales County Minute Men
Captain James H. Callahan (May 7–December 20, 1841)
*Ranging District*: Gonzales County with headquarters at Seguín
   *Company operated under the supervision of the Chief Justice of Gonzales County*

### San Patricio County Minute Men
Captain Alanson T. Miles (May 14–June 30, 1841)
*Ranging District*: Nueces River country with headquarters at San Patricio
   *Company operated under the supervision of the Chief Justice of San Patricio County*

### San Patricio Rangers
Captain James P. Ownby (May 18–June 6, 1841)
*Ranging District*: Nueces River country with headquarters at Camp Independence
   *Company members captured and imprisoned by Mexican forces (June 14, 1841–June 14, 1842)*

### Béxar County Minute Men
Captain John C. "Jack" Hays (June 1–October 1, 1841)
Chief Flacco, commanding Lipan Apache and Tonkawa scouts (July 12–August 2, 1841)
*Ranging District*: Nueces River country with headquarters at San Antonio
   *Company operated under the supervision of the Chief Justice of Béxar County*

### Lamar County Minute Men
Captain Mansell W. Matthews (June 1–September 29, 1841)
*Ranging District*: Lamar County with headquarters at Lafayette
   *Company operated under the supervision of the Chief Justice of Lamar County*

### Paschal County Minute Men
Captain Joseph D. Lilly (June 12–November 31, 1841)
2nd Lieutenant Thomas Milligan, commanding detachment (August 24–September 12, 1841)
*Ranging District*: Paschal County with headquarters at Daingerfield
   *Company operated under the supervision of the Chief Justice of Paschal County*

### Houston County Minute Men
Captain William C. Brookfield (June 19–July 1, 1841)
*Ranging District*: Houston County
   *Company operated under the supervision of the Chief Justice of Houston County*

### Company of Spies
Captain John T. Price (June 20–July 2, 1841)
*Ranging District*: Nueces Strip with headquarters at Victoria
   *Company operated under the orders of the War Department*

### Red River County Minute Men
Captain William A. Becknall (June 25, 1841–June 25, 1842)
1st Lieutenant Peter Ringo, commanding detachment (July 1841)
*Ranging District*: Red River County
   *Company operated under the supervision of the Chief Justice of Red River County*

### Victoria County Minute Men
Captain Charles M. Creaner (July–August 1841)
*Ranging District*: Victoria County with headquarters at Victoria
   *Company operated under the supervision of the Chief Justice of Victoria County*

### Mounted Riflemen/Volunteers
Captain John William Lane (July 5–October 5, 1841)
*Ranging District*: Eastern portion of Cross Timbers with headquarters at Fort Inglish
  *Company designated as Company "C," Volunteer Regiment, 4th Brigade, Texas Militia and assigned to BG E. H. Tarrant's Trinity Expedition (July 5–August 11, 1841)*

### Fannin County Minute Men/Rangers
Captain Joseph Sowell (July 6–September 26, 1841)
*Ranging District*: Fannin County with headquarters at Old Warren/Fort Warren
  *Company operated under the supervision of the Chief Justice of Fannin County*

### Houston County Volunteers
Captain John L. Hall (July 10–August 10, 1841)
*Ranging District*: Upper Trinity River country with headquarters at King's Fort
  *Company assigned to 3rd Brigade, Texas Militia for BG J. Smith's Trinity Expedition (July 10–August 8, 1841)*

### San Patricio County Minute Men
Captain Alanson T. Miles (July 12–August 25, 1841)
Captain William J. Cairns (August 29–November 12, 1841)
*Ranging District*: Nueces, Agua Dulce (Sweetwater), and San Fernandez Rivers with headquarters at San Patricio
  *Company operated under the supervision of the Chief Justice of San Patricio County*

### Volunteers
Captain William M. "Buckskin" Williams (July 12–October 12, 1841)
*Ranging District*: Eastern portion of Cross Timbers with headquarters at Fort Inglish
  *Company designated as Company "D," Volunteer Regiment, 4th Brigade, Texas Militia and assigned to BG E. H. Tarrant's Trinity Expedition (July 5–August 11, 1841)*

### Volunteers
Captain John J. Tumlinson, Jr. (July 14–August 25, 1841)

### Mounted Gunmen
Captain Henry B. Stout (July 15–October 15, 1841)
*Ranging District*: Eastern portion of Cross Timbers with headquarters at Fort Inglish
  *Company assigned to Volunteer Regiment, 4th Brigade, Texas Militia for BG E. H. Tarrant's Trinity Expedition (July 5–August 11, 1841)*

### Mounted Volunteers
Captain James P. B. January (August 3–31, 1841)
*Ranging District*: Victoria County with headquarters at Victoria
  *Company operated under the personal orders of B. T. Archer, Secretary of War*

### Lamar County Mounted Gunmen
Captain John Emberson (August 7–29, 1841)
*Ranging District*: Fannin County with headquarters at Fort Inglish
  *Company assigned to 2nd Battalion, 3rd Regiment, 4th Brigade, Texas Militia*

### Bird's Fort Rangers
Captain Alexander W. Webb (September 9, 1841–March 19, 1842)
*Ranging District*: Trinity River country with headquarters at Bird's Fort
  *Company assigned to 2nd Regiment, 4th Brigade, Texas Militia*

### Refugio County Minute Men
Captain John R. Baker (October 25–December 12, 1841)
1st Lieutenant Matthew W. Cody, Acting Commander (November 9–December 12, 1841)
Captain John M. McDaniel (December 16–February 24, 1842)
*Ranging District*: Refugio and Victoria Counties with headquarters at Refugio
    Company operated under the supervision of the Chief Justice of Refugio County

### Western Spy Company
Captain William J. Cairns (November 12, 1841–February 12, 1842)
*Ranging District*: Nueces River country with headquarters at Victoria
    Company operated under the personal orders of Col. P. H. Bell, Adj-Gen. of Texas

### Neill's Ranger Company
Colonel John C. Neill (1842)
*Ranging District*: Upper Trinity River country

### Spy Company/Frontier Rangers
Captain John C. "Jack" Hays (March 10–September 1, 1842)
*Ranging District*: Between San Antonio River and the Río Grande with headquarters at San Antonio
    Company operated under the supervision of G. W. Hockley, Secretary of War and Navy and attached to BG E. Burleson's Texas Volunteers (March 4–April 2, 1842) for the Vásquez Campaign (February 24–March 15, 1842)

### Fannin County Minute Men
Captain Jesse Stiff (March 1–May 19, 1842)
*Ranging District*: Fannin County
    Company operated under the supervision of the Chief Justice of Fannin County

## *Regiment of Volunteers*

### Field & Staff
Colonel Clark L. Owen (March 3–June 6, 1842)
Captain David Murphree, Adjutant (March 6–April 18, 1842)
Richard West, Acting Quartermaster (March 6–June 6, 1842)
1st Lieutenant John A. Rogers, Jr., Assistant Quartermaster (March 6–June 6, 1842)
A. S. McDonald, Assistant Commissary (March 6–June 6, 1842)

### Victoria County Volunteers
Captain John T. Price (March 3–June 6, 1842)

### Matagorda Volunteers
Captain Albert C. Horton (March 6–April 13, 1842)

### Matagorda County Mounted Volunteers
Captain John Rugeley (March 6–April 13, 1842)

### Texana Volunteers
Captain John S. Menefee (March 6–June 6, 1842)

### Victoria County Volunteers
Captain John M. Smith (March 6–June 6, 1842)

### Jackson County Texas Volunteers
Captain Lafayette Ward (March 6–June 6, 1842)

### Columbia Mounted Volunteers
Captain John P. Gill (March 20–June 20, 1842)

### Victoria County Volunteers
Captain William J. E. Heard (March 6–June 6, 1842)
*Regimental Ranging District*: Nueces River country with headquarters at Goliad (March) and Corpus Christi (April)
  *Regiment organized and mustered into the Texas Militia for the Vásquez Campaign (February 24–March 15, 1842)*

### Mounted Gunmen/Company of Spies/ Texas Mounted Volunteers
Captain Ewen Cameron (April 12–August 12, 1842)
*Ranging District*: Victoria County to Nueces County with headquarters at Corpus Christi and Refugio
  *Company attached to Maj. J. J. B. Hoxey's 1st Battalion of Texas Volunteers, Col. J. Davis' Army of Texas Volunteers (May 14–August 23, 1842) for the Canales Campaign (June 24–July 8, 1842)*

### Spy Company/"Corps of Observation"
Captain Ephraim W. McLean (April 9–August 15, 1842)
*Ranging District*: West of Guadalupe River with headquarters at Corpus Christi (April) and Paso del Gobernador (August)
  *Company operated under the supervision of the War Department and attached to Col. J. Davis' Army of Texas Volunteers (May 5, 1842)*

### Company of Cavalry
Captain José Antonio Menchaca (July 1–September 11, 1842)
*Ranging District*: Between the San Antonio River and the Río Grande with headquarters at San Antonio
  *Company operated under the supervision of G. W. Hill, Secretary of War and Marine*

### Burleson's Company
Captain Edward "Ned" Burleson, Sr. (August 5–September 25, 1842)
*Ranging District*: Upper Colorado River country with headquarters at Austin (August 1842); Medina River country (September 1842)

### Matagorda Volunteers
Captain Albert C. Horton (September 12, 1842–?)
  *Company operated under the orders of BG A. Somervell, commanding 1st Brigade, Texas Militia for the Woll Campaign (August 30–September 23, 1842)*

### Béxar Spy Company/Frontier Volunteers
Captain John C. "Jack" Hays (September 13, 1842–January 17, 1843)
*Ranging District*: Between the San Antonio River and the Río Grande with headquarters at San Antonio
  *Company operated under the supervision of G. W. Hill, Secretary of War and Marine, and attached to Col. M. Caldwell's Volunteer Army of Texas (September 17–25, 1842) and BG A. Somervell's Southwestern Army of Operations (November 4, 1842–January 8, 1843)*

### Spy Company
Captain Samuel Bogart (September 25, 1842–January 20, 1843)

*Ranging District*: San Antonio to Guerrero with headquarters at Camp Cooke
  *Company assigned to BG A. Somervell's Southwestern Army of Operations as independent spy company (November 7–29, 1842) and line company in 1st Regiment (November 29–December 19, 1842)*

### COMPANY OF RANGERS/FRONTIER RANGING COMPANY

Captain John C. "Jack" Hays (February 20–November 10, 1843)
*Ranging District*: Bexar, Refugio, Robertson, Milam, Travis, and Goliad Counties with headquarters at San Antonio (February 1843) and camp on the Leona River (July 1843)
  *Company operated under the supervision of G. W. Hill, Secretary of War and Navy*

### FRONTIER RANGING COMPANY/CORPS OF RANGERS

Captain John C. "Jack" Hays (February 25–April 25, 1844)
Captain John C. "Jack" Hays (June 27, 1844–September 28, 1845)
*Ranging District*: Bexar County with headquarters at camp on the Medina River (February 1844) and San Antonio with detachment at camp on the Medina River (July 1845)

### SHELBY COUNTY MOUNTED VOLUNTEERS/MOUNTED MEN

Captain Leonard H. Mabbitt (August 26–November 13, 1844)
*Ranging District*: Shelby County with headquarters at Shelbyville

### CORPS OF CORPUS CHRISTI RANGERS

Captain Henry Clay Davis (November 14, 1844–February 28, 1845)
*Ranging District*: Nueces County with headquarters at the Kinney Rancho and Trading Post

### ROBERTSON COUNTY RANGERS

Lieutenant Thomas I. Smith, Commanding (February 16–September 15, 1845)
*Ranging District*: Between the Brazos and Trinity Rivers with headquarters at Torrey's Trading House (Post No. 2) on Tehuacana Creek and detachments at camps on the Trinity River and Richland Creek
  *Company operated under the personal orders of Capt. J. C. Hays*

### CORPUS CHRISTI CORPS OF RANGERS

Captain P. Hansbrough Bell (February 28–August 28, 1845)
  *Captain Bell simultaneously possessed State and Federal commissions*
*Ranging District*: Nueces County with headquarters at Corpus Christi

### GOLIAD AND REFUGIO RANGER CORPS/VOLUNTEERS/ MOUNTED VOLUNTEERS

Lieutenant John T. Price, Commanding (March 14–August 28, 1845)
*Ranging District*: Goliad and Refugio Counties with headquarters at Goliad
  *Company operated under the personal orders of Capt. J. C. Hays*

### TRAVIS COUNTY RANGERS/AUSTIN RANGERS/ TRAVIS COUNTY RANGER CORPS

Lieutenant Alexander Coleman, Commanding (February 20–June 20, 1845)
Lieutenant David C. Cady, Commanding (June 20–August 20, 1845)
Captain David C. Cady (August 20–October 1, 1845)
*Ranging District*: Travis County with headquarters at Austin
  *Company operated under the personal orders of Capt. J. C. Hays*

### MILAM COUNTY RANGERS

Lieutenant Richard S. Teal, Commanding (March 1–December 5, 1845)

*Ranging District*: Milam County with headquarters at Washington-on-the-Brazos
*Company operated under the personal orders of Capt. J. C. Hays*

### Fannin County Rangers/Fannin County Ranging Corps
Lieutenant John "Jack" McGarrah, Commanding (June 1–September 30, 1845)
*Ranging District*: Red and Trinity Rivers country with headquarters at Dallas

# 3

# *Los Diablos Tejanos*: Rangers in the U.S.-Mexican War (1846–1848)

On April 22, 1844, President John Tyler began the formal process to admit Texas into the Union. After intense political debate, the U.S. Congress passed a *Joint Resolution for Annexing Texas* on February 28, 1845. President Tyler signed the measure into law the following day and the Texas Constitution Convention approved an Ordinance of Annexation on July 4. Acting under orders to provide the prospective state protection from a potentially hostile Mexico, Brigadier-General Zachary Taylor, commanding a "Corps of Observation" at Fort Jesup, Louisiana, marched his troops to Corpus Christi, arriving on July 22. To patrol the frontier, Taylor's force, renamed the "Army of Occupation," was augmented with several ranger companies in federal service commanded by captains P. Hansbrough Bell (a former Texas adjutant general and future governor), John T. Price, Robert Addison "Ad" Gillespie, and David C. Cady.

After Texas was annexed as the twenty-eighth state on December 29, the unresolved question of whether the southern border was the Nueces River or the Rio Grande quickly became an issue. Unable to reach an agreement with the Mexican government, President James K. Polk dispatched General Taylor's army to the Rio Grande on January 13, 1846; a decision Mexico City saw as an unprovoked act of war. Tensions rose even higher when Texas formally transferred sovereignty to the United States on February 19, when Taylor's troops left Corpus Christi on March 8 and arrived on the Rio Grande opposite Matamoros on March 26, and when they built Fort Texas (later renamed Fort Brown). In response, Mexican troops from Matamoros crossed the river on April 25 and ambushed a U.S. dragoon patrol. Stating "American blood has been shed on American soil," Polk used the escalation to obtain a declaration of war from Congress on May 13. Even before formal hostilities were declared, Taylor's 2,200 soldiers defeated a 3,700-man Mexican army at the battles of Palo Alto (May 8) and Resaca de la Palma (May 9); he also won promotion to major-general on June 29. Prominent among the U.S. regulars was a ranger company commanded by Captain Sam Walker.

In these and subsequent battles, newspapers spread the name of the Texas Rangers nationwide and cemented their image in the public consciousness. The Texans were like no other American soldiers in their wild indiscipline, appearance, and fighting style. Ranger units, such as the 1st Texas Mounted Rifles commanded by newly-commissioned Colonel

"Dawn at Monterey" by Bruce Marshall. This watercolor depicts the charge of Hays' Texas Mounted Rifles at the battle of Monterey. The rangers dismounted to advance and engaged in vicious fighting in order to capture Independence Hill. Courtesy of the artist.

Hays, were filled with men hardened by years of conflict with Indians and Mexicans. Many of them were veterans of Hays' ranger companies and included Ben McCulloch, Sam Walker, Thomas Green, "Bigfoot" Wallace, and Ad Gillespie. Officers and enlisted men alike were expert horsemen and able outdoorsmen, and they fought under no flags and wore no uniforms. In the war, General Taylor deployed them as scouts, escorts, and couriers.

The 1st Texas Mounted Rifles was among the American forces at the Battle of Monterey. On September 20, and again the following day, the Texans skirmished with Mexican *lanceros* on the Saltillo Road. They were in the vanguard of Brevet Major-General William J. Worth's 2nd Division in the assault on Federation (September 21) and Independence Hills (September 22). The rangers lost two killed and two wounded in the engagement, and inflicted an undetermined, but presumably heavy, number of causalities upon the defenders. The following day, the rangers, along with the rest of the U.S. offensive, advanced into the city and fought the Mexicans in brutal, house-to-house fighting. On September 24, the commander of Monterey's garrison surrendered the city to General Taylor, who allowed the Mexican force to withdraw from the scene, retaining their arms and ammunition (an eight-week armistice that proved very unpopular in Texas). Regardless of the outcome, the men of the 1st Texas Mounted Rifles played a pivotal role in the city's capture

Unfortunately, the rangers' behavior in their personal deportment and in their relations with Monterey citizens caused Taylor no end of grief. The Texans, independent and proud by nature, were first-class fighting men, but they had little use for military protocol and procedures. Numerous incidents of drunkenness, brawling, shootings and other forms of disorderly conduct caused Taylor to describe them as a "lawless set" and "licentious vandals." Ten years of bitter warfare with Mexico insured the rangers saw the men of Monterey in a far different light than the rest of the American forces. Indeed, those Mexicans who had mistreated the Mier prisoners were often hunted down and summarily executed. The ruthless war the Texans conducted against Mexican *guerrilleros*, and any others who would trifle with them, led a hostile but fearful populace to label them "*los diablos Tejanos*," the Texas devils. Mexican regulars and irregulars also exhibited cruel and savage behavior in attacking and murdering civilian teamsters of U.S. supply trains and solitary or inebriated American soldiers.

While the fighting raged in northern Mexico, settlers in Texas still needed protection from Indian depredations. On May 15, 1846, the Federal Government concluded a treaty with the Comanche, Hainai (Ioni), Ah-mau-dah-ka (Anadarko), Caddo, Lipan, Longwa, Waco, Kichai, Wichita, Tonkawa, and Tawakoni peoples. Despite the agreement, peace still proved elusive on the frontier. From October 1845 to September 1846, Colonel William S. Harney and three companies of the 2nd U.S. Dragoons were garrisoned at San Antonio and Austin to provide security. Prior to leaving San Antonio for the war zone, Harney called for five mounted companies to protect the frontier from Castroville to the forks of the Trinity River. In July 1846, Governor *pro tempore* Albert C. Horton (himself a former ranger captain in the Vásquez campaign) authorized Shapley P. Ross, John J. Grumbles, Thomas I. Smith, Andrew Stapp, and John H. Conner to raise companies for six months' federal service. For three months, the five companies performed their duties in administrative limbo while Governor Horton, Colonel Harney, his successors as San Antonio garrison commander — Lieutenant-Colonel Thomas T. Fauntleroy, Brigadier-General John E. Wool, and Colonel Sylvester Churchill — and General Taylor spent this time mired in a lengthy procedural debate concerning the rangers' employment. The governor proved partially successful and, on September 23, the companies of captains Grumbles and Conner were mustered in, effective their date of enrollment, and immediately mustered out. Captain Ross' men followed suit on October 17. They were then all mustered back into federal service for terms of twelve months. Captains Smith and Stapp remained on the most exposed portion of the frontier and ended their six-month terms without formal status. Two months later, they received pay for their service and expenses.

"Charge of the Texas Rangers" by Bruce Marshall. This watercolor features Hays's Texas rangers conducting a mounted charge against Mexican lancers. The use of Walker Colts and the employment of tactics learned fighting Comanches enabled the rangers to consistently gain victory in the field. UTSA's Institute of Texan Cultures, No. 073-0120; courtesy of the artist.

On April 4, 1847, the companies of Grumbles, Conner, and Ross were grouped together with those of Captain Henry E. McCulloch and Lieutenant E. S. Wyman into a single battalion under Major Thomas Smith. The chain of command for this battalion and subsequent outfits on the frontier was curious in that, officially, the rangers answered to General Taylor through his delegate, the garrison commander in San Antonio. These rangers were just as disdainful of regulations as their comrades in Mexico, though, and continued to report to the governor.

In northern Mexico, General Taylor had been relieved to see the Texans leave for home when their enlistments expired. He did, though, welcome Ben McCulloch's return in January 1847 to lead a spy company for the subsequent campaign. On February 20–21, McCulloch led a scouting party to reconnoiter Mexican positions at La Encarnacíon. He dispatched a report on enemy troop strengths and movements that Taylor put to good use in the February 22–23 battle at La Angostura ("The Narrows") near Buena Vista. Taylor's 4,759 troops were matched against an estimated 20,000 Mexican *soldados* commanded by the Texans' old enemy, *Generalissimo* Santa Anna. After the American victory, Taylor was generous in his praise of McCulloch and his rangers: "The services rendered by Major McCulloch and his men, particularly in reconnoitering the enemy's camp at Encarnacíon, and advising us certainly of his presences there, were of the highest importance." Because the Texans per-

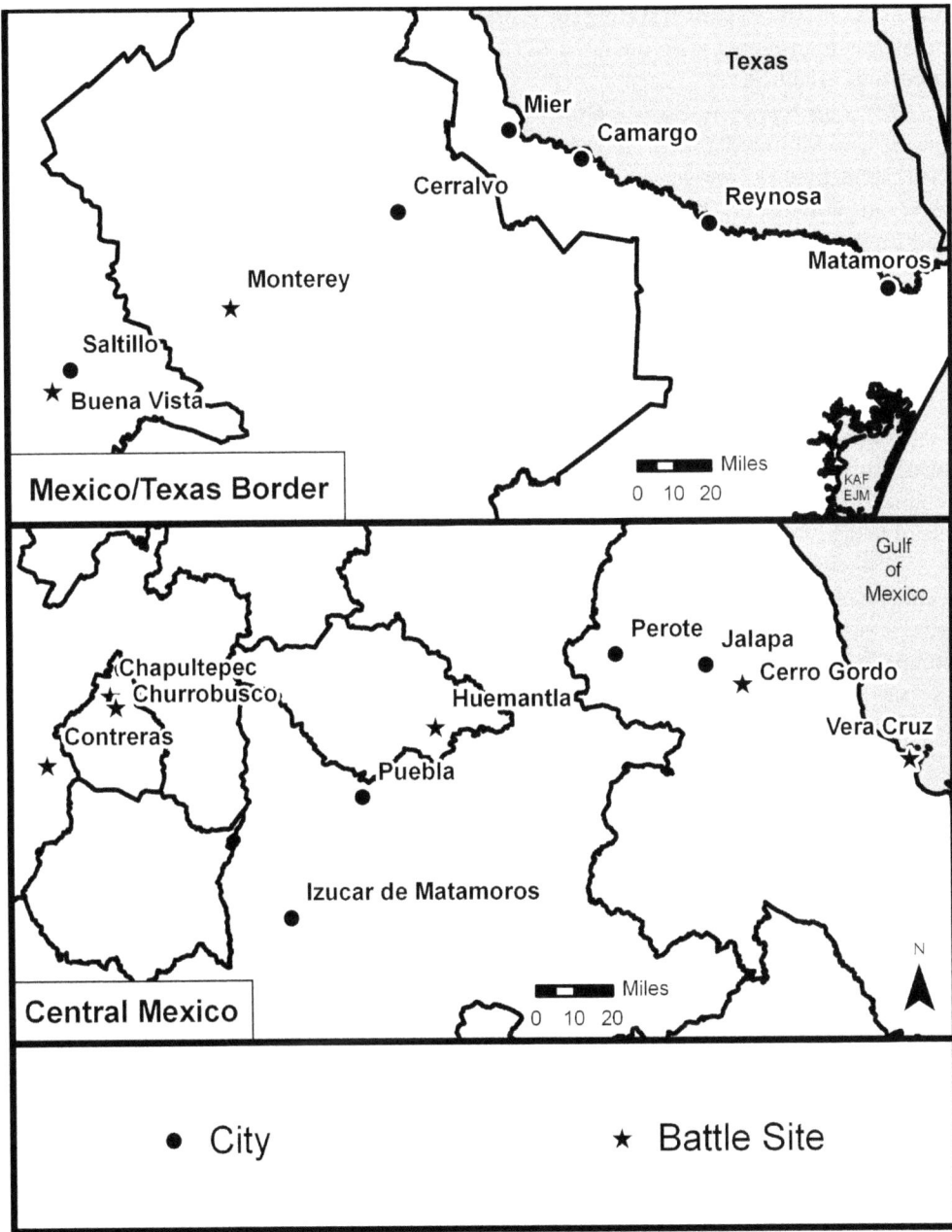

sisted in causing trouble and seldom ended a scouting expedition without killing a Mexican, Taylor wrote the adjutant general on June 16, 1847 to ask "that no more troops ... be sent to this column from the State of Texas."

Other ranger companies besides those of Hays and McCulloch served in northern Mexico. Unfortunately, not all of them acquitted themselves with honor. In February 1847, Captain Mabry B. Gray, a "cowboy" from the Nueces Strip, executed twenty-four male civilians from the town of La Mesa in retaliation for a massacred wagon train. In contrast, the battalion of Majors Mike Chevallie and Walter Lane served well in fighting *guerrilleros* preying on the supply wagons traveling the Camargo-Monterey road. Chief among their opponents was Juan Flores, who operated in the Cerralvo area until he was captured, quickly tried, and executed.

After his service in Hay's regiment, Sam Walker received a commission of captain in the 1st U.S. Mounted Rifles. He was in Maryland on recruiting duty when he decided to visit Samuel Colt's New Jersey factory to discuss the pros and cons of the Paterson pistol. How much of Walker's technical advice was put into practice is disputed, but Colt was publicly appreciative and named his newest model the Walker Colt.

The improvements of the massive Walker Colt over the Paterson model were a bigger, six-shot cylinder that accepted an increased powder charge of sixty grains in each chamber, and fired a .44-caliber 146-grain ball or 128-grain conical bullet. The heavier grips were one-piece walnut with an iron backstrap, a visible trigger was protected by a square-backed guard of brass, and a ramrod was equipped with a hinged lever held in place by a T-spring for reloading without disassembling the weapon (a necessity for mounted gunmen). It had a nine-inch rifled barrel that was part round and part octagonal, an overall length of 15½ inches, and a weight of four pounds nine ounces. The shooter sighted the pistol using a blade located near the end of the barrel and a notch cut in the hammer.

Walker fought a heated battle with the hidebound Army Ordnance Department to sign a contract with Colt and get the pistols into the hands of the troops still fighting in Mexico. He succeeded but only 1,000 were purchased and issued to Walker's own mounted rifle company and Hays' second regiment. The official term for the newly shipped Walker Colts was the "Model of 1847 Army Pistol." Walker wrote that the weapon was "as effective as a common rifle at 100 yards and superior to a musket even at 200." He returned to Mexico and, on October 9, 1847, was killed leading a mounted charge at Huamantla.

At first, the U.S. dragoons and mounted riflemen were armed with Hall Model 1819 .52-caliber breechloading carbines, Springfield Model 1841 .54-caliber muzzleloading rifles, Model 1842 single-shot horse pistols, and Model 1840 heavy cavalry sabers. The valuable lessons the Paterson-armed rangers had learned in fighting the mounted Plains Indians included mobility, superior firepower, and shock action. With the advent of the Walker Colts, the rangers passed on these tactics to the regular cavalry in the years to come.

Colonel Hays and five companies of his second regiment, the 1st Texas Mounted Volunteers, arrived in Central Mexico in October 1847, one month after Mexico City's surrender and four months before the Treaty of Guadalupe Hidalgo formally ended hostilities. Since they were élite partisans themselves, Hays and his men were quickly put to work fighting *guerrillero* bands that prowled Major-General Winfield Scott's 260-mile-long supply and communications line between Vera Cruz and Mexico City. The raiders included those of Padre Caledonio de Jaruata (a Spanish-born priest) in the Vera Cruz area. Hays' regiment was assigned to Brigadier-General Joseph Lane's brigade to conduct counter-guerrilla operations around Puebla, where they engaged Mexican irregulars at Izúcar de Matamoros (November 23) and Galaxa Pass (November 24). The rangers marched to Mexico City in December and again fought Padre Jaruata's *guerrilleros* at San Juan Teotihuacan (January 13) and Zacualtipán (February 25).

As in Monterey, Mexico City's citizens and the rangers clashed. Insults, a stolen handkerchief, a thrown stone, and assaults in back alleys led to several ranger-involved shootings. Private Adam Alsans (a Napoleonic Wars veteran) foolishly wandered alone into the red-light district of the city, known as "Cutthroat," and was mortally wounded by a mob. He died the next day, and that night fifteen to twenty of Allsen's fellow rangers went into the "Cutthroat" quarter seeking vengeance. The number of slain Mexicans was uncertain since relatives recovered many of the corpses from the streets, but the following morning eighty bodies were counted in the city morgue.

Lieutenant-Colonel P. H. Bell and two companies were detached from the 1st Texas Mounted Volunteers in order to protect settlers from Indian ravages. Technically the senior officer on the frontier, Bell would nominally command up to thirteen autonomous companies scattered from the Trinity River in Dallas County to Fredericksburg to San Antonio to Laredo to Corpus Christi.

Once hostilities with Mexico ended, the rangers of Hays' regiment marched to Vera Cruz to be mustered out of service. On about April 25, while encamped near Jalapa, they learned Santa Anna was at nearby San Miguel en route to exile in Jamaica. Several rangers vowed to assassinate the former dictator for his past offenses against Texas. Regimental officers attempted to dissuade the men from such a course, since Santa Anna was protected by a safe conduct pass from General Scott. They argued that to kill their hated foe under these circumstances was the equivalent of murder. When the vengeful rangers remained intent on their decision, the officers reminded them the act would dishonor Texas in the eyes of the world. While willing to sell their lives dearly for their state, the Texans refused to disgrace her name and promptly abandoned the murder plot. Instead, they lined both sides of the road that Santa Anna's procession traveled upon and watched his carriage pass in stony silence. For Hays' rangers, the war in Central Mexico was at an end.

The men of Major Lane's battalion serving with the Army of Occupation in northern Mexico withdrew across the Rio Grande and returned to civilian pursuits. The last rangers in federal service were those of Colonel Bell's regiment on the Texas frontier. Elements of his command remained on station until February 1849.

## Historical Register, 1846–1848

*"The Mexicans are terribly afraid of them."*
— Major-General Ethan Allen Hitchcock

### Bell's Company, Texas Mounted Volunteers
Captain P. Hansbrough Bell (June 28–August 28, 1845)
   *Capt. Bell simultaneously possessed State and Federal commissions*
Ranging District: Nueces County with headquarters at Corpus Christi
   *Company mustered into service as U.S. Volunteers and operated under the orders of HQ, U.S. Army of Occupation*

### Bell's Company, Texas Mounted Volunteers
Captain P. Hansbrough Bell (September 10, 1845–July 6, 1846)
Ranging District: Nueces County with headquarters at Corpus Christi
   *Company mustered into service as U.S. Volunteers and operated under the orders of HQ, U.S. Army of Occupation*

### Robertson County Rangers
Lieutenant Thomas I. Smith, Commanding (September 15–December 16, 1845)
Ranging District: Between the Brazos and Trinity Rivers with headquarters at Torrey's Trading House (Post No. 2) on Tehuacana Creek and detachments at camps on the Trinity River and Richland Creek
   *Company mustered into service as U.S. Volunteers and operated under the personal orders of Maj. J. C. Hays*

### Price's Company, Texas Mounted Volunteers
Captain John T. Price (September 25, 1845–June 15, 1846)
*Ranging District*: Victoria and Goliad Counties with headquarters at Goliad (September 1845); Point Isabel–Fort Texas/Brown line (May 1846)
> *Company mustered into service as U.S. Volunteers and operated under the orders of HQ, U.S. Army of Occupation*

### Field & Staff, Texas Mounted Volunteers
Major John C. "Jack" Hays (September 28, 1845–May 16, 1846)
*Headquarters*: San Antonio
> *Maj. Hays appointed commander of all rangers in federal service on the frontier*

### Bexar Ranging Corps/Gillespie's Company, Texas Mounted Rangers
Captain Robert A. "Ad" Gillespie (September 28, 1845–June 28, 1846)
*Ranging District*: Bexar County with headquarters at San Antonio (September 1845); Carmargo-Matamoros line with headquarters at Matamoros (June 1846)
> *Company mustered into service as U.S. Volunteers and operated under the orders of Maj. J. C. Hays (September 1845) and HQ, U.S. Army of Occupation (June 1846)*

### Cady's Company, Texas Mounted Rangers
Captain David C. Cady (October 1–December 31, 1845)
Captain David C. Cady (April–July 4, 1846)
*Ranging District*: Travis County with headquarters at Austin
> *Company mustered into service as U.S. Volunteers and operated under the orders of HQ, U.S. Army of Occupation*

### Walker's Company, Texas Mounted Rangers
Captain Samuel H. Walker (April 21–June 30, 1846)
Captain Joseph P. Wells (June 30–July 16, 1846)
*Ranging District*: Point Isabel–Matamoros line with headquarters at Fort Texas/Brown
> *Company mustered into service as U.S. Volunteers and operated under the orders of HQ, U.S. Army of Occupation*

### McCulloch's Company, Texas Militia
Captain Benjamin McCulloch (June 13–August 18, 1846)
*Ranging District*: Carmargo-Matamoros line with headquarters at Matamoros
> *Company mustered into service as U.S. Volunteers and operated under the orders of HQ, U.S. Army of Occupation*

## *1st Regiment, Texas Mounted Rifles*
### Field & Staff
Colonel John C. "Jack" Hays (June 24–October 2, 1846)
Lieutenant-Colonel Samuel H. Walker (June 24–October 1, 1846)
Major Michael H. Chevallie (June 24–October 2, 1846)
2nd Lieutenant Charles A. Harper, Adjutant (June 24–October 2, 1846)
1st Lieutenant James M. Alexander, Quartermaster
Lieutenant Richard Roman, Commissary (September 20–October 2, 1846)
Doctor Charles W. Tait, Surgeon (June 24–September 6, 1846)
Doctor Henry W. Baylor, Surgeon (September 6–October 2, 1846)
Doctor Francis McKay, Assistant Surgeon (June 24–October 2, 1846)
Sergeant-Major Morgan L. Payne (June 24–September 10, 1846)
Sergeant-Major Silas B. Hart (September 11–October 2, 1846)

Quartermaster Sergeant A. Bernard (June 24–October 2, 1846)
Francis Bettinger, Bugler

### COMPANY A
Captain Benjamin McCulloch (August 30–September 30, 1846)
  *Company on detached service and operated under the personal orders of MG Z. Taylor, CG of U. S. Army of Occupation (August 30–September 18, 1846)*

### COMPANY B
Captain Christopher B. "Kit" Acklin (June 6–August 1, 1846)
1st Lieutenant Walter P. Lane, Commanding (August 1–September 12, 1846)
Captain Christopher B. "Kit" Acklin (September 12–October 2, 1846)

### COMPANY C
Captain Thomas Green (June 6–October 2, 1846)

### COMPANY D
Captain Samuel L. S. Ballowe (June 19–October 2, 1846)

### COMPANY E
Captain Claibourne C. Herbert (June 7–October 2, 1846)

### COMPANY F
Captain Frank S. Early (June 7–October 2, 1846)

### COMPANY G
Captain James H. Gillespie (June 6–October 2, 1846)

### COMPANY H
Captain Jerome B. McCown (July 13–October 2, 1846)

### COMPANY I
Captain Robert A. "Ad" Gillespie (August 30–September 22, 1846)
1st Lieutenant William A. A. "Bigfoot" Wallace, Commanding (September 22–29, 1846)
  *Company on detached service and operated under the personal orders of MG Z. Taylor, CG of U. S. Army of Occupation (August 30–September 18, 1846)*

### COMPANY K
Captain Eli Chandler (July 18–October 2, 1846)
*Regimental Ranging District*: Matamoros-Monterey line
  *Regiment mustered into service as U.S. Volunteers and operated under the orders of HQ, U.S. Army of Occupation*

### ROSS' COMPANY, TEXAS MOUNTED VOLUNTEERS
Captain Shapley P. Ross (July 20–October 17, 1846)
*Ranging District*: Between the Little and San Gabriel Rivers with headquarters at camp near Bryant's Fort
  *Company retroactively mustered into service as U.S. Volunteers and operated under the personal orders of Lt-Gov. A. C. Horton*

### GRAY'S COMPANY, TEXAS MOUNTED VOLUNTEERS
Captain Mabry B. "Mustang" Gray (July 21, 1846–July 17, 1847)
Lieutenant DeWitt C. Lyons, commanding detachment (March 2–July 17, 1847)
*Ranging District*: Nueces County with headquarters at Corpus Christi (July 1846); Monterey-Camargo line with headquarters at Monterey and Lyons' detachment at Corpus Christi (March 1847)

*Company mustered into service as U.S. Volunteers and operated under the orders of HQ, U.S. Army of Occupation*

### GRUMBLES' COMPANY, TEXAS MOUNTED VOLUNTEERS
Captain John J. Grumbles (July 23–September 23, 1846)
*Ranging District*: Travis County with headquarters at Austin
*Company retroactively mustered into service as U.S. Volunteers (September 23, 1846) and operated under the personal orders of Lt-Gov. A. C. Horton*

### STAPP'S COMPANY, TEXAS MOUNTED VOLUNTEERS
Captain Andrew Stapp (July 24, 1846–February 1, 1847)
*Ranging District*: Trinity River country from Fort Washita to Johnson's Station with headquarters at Elm Station
*Company retroactively mustered into service as U.S. Volunteers and operated under the personal orders of Lt-Gov. A. C. Horton*

### CONNER'S COMPANY, TEXAS MOUNTED VOLUNTEERS
Captain John H. Conner (July 29–September 23, 1846)
*Ranging District*: San Antonio–Laredo line with headquarters at Castroville
*Company retroactively mustered into service as U.S. Volunteers and operated under the personal orders of Lt-Gov. A. C. Horton*

### SMITH'S COMPANY, TEXAS MOUNTED VOLUNTEERS
Captain Thomas I. Smith (August 2, 1846–February 2, 1847)
*Ranging District*: Brazos River country with headquarters at Torrey's Trading House (Post No. 2) on Tehuacana Creek
*Company retroactively mustered into service as U.S. Volunteers and operated under the personal orders of Lt-Gov. A. C. Horton*

### LAMAR'S COMPANY, TEXAS CAVALRY
Captain Mirabeau B. Lamar (October 7, 1846–October 7, 1847)
Captain Mirabeau B. Lamar (October 8, 1847–September 27, 1848)
*Ranging District*: Middle Rio Grande Valley with headquarters at Laredo
*Company mustered into service as U.S. Volunteers and operated under the orders of HQ, U.S. Army of Occupation*

### McCULLOCH'S COMPANY, TEXAS MOUNTED VOLUNTEERS (SPIES)
Major Benjamin McCulloch (January 31–July 31, 1847)
  *Maj. McCulloch appointed army chief of scouts*
*Ranging District*: Saltillo-Encarnacion line with headquarters at Saltillo
*Company mustered into service as U.S. Volunteers and operated under the personal orders of MG Z. Taylor, CG of U. S. Army of Occupation*

## *Chevallie's/Lane's Battalion, Texas Mounted Volunteers*

### FIELD & STAFF
Major Michael H. Chevallie, Commanding (April 25–August 31, 1847)
Captain Walter P. Lane, Acting Commander (August 31–September 27, 1847)
Major Walter P. Lane, Commanding (September 27, 1847–June 30, 1848)
Lieutenant W. S. Murtry, Adjutant
Doctor _____ Roane, Surgeon (?–March 1848)
Sergeant-Major William S. Hughes (November 1, 1847–June 30, 1848)

#### COMPANY A
Captain Walter P. Lane (February 19–September 27, 1847)
1st Lieutenant Governeur H. Nelson, Commanding (September 27–October 19, 1847)
Captain George K. Lewis (October 19, 1847–June 30, 1848)

#### COMPANY B
Captain Robert H. Taylor (February 24, 1847–June 30, 1848)

#### COMPANY C
Captain George W. Adams (March 6, 1847–June 30, 1848)

#### COMPANY D
Captain James B. Reed (May 24, 1847–June 29, 1848)
*Ranging District*: Cerralvo area

#### COMPANY E
Captain Henry W. Baylor (June 17, 1847–June 30, 1848)
*Ranging District*: Cerralvo area
*Battalion Ranging District*: Saltillo-Camargo line with headquarters at Monterey (April 1847) and Saltillo (June 1847)
   Battalion mustered into service as U.S. Volunteers and operated under the orders of HQ, U.S. Army of Occupation

## *Smith's Battalion, Texas Mounted Volunteers*
#### FIELD & STAFF
Major Thomas I. Smith (April 4–August 17, 1847)
Lieutenant James P. Goodall, Adjutant (April 4–August 17, 1847)

#### GRUMBLE'S COMPANY
Captain John J. Grumbles (September 24, 1846–September 23, 1847)
*Ranging District*: Travis County with headquarters at Austin

#### CONNER'S COMPANY
Captain John H. Conner (September 24, 1846–September 25, 1847)
Lieutenant William G. Jett, Acting Commander (March 3–June 30, 1847)
*Ranging District*: San Antonio–Laredo line with headquarters at camp on Arroyo Seco

#### ROSS' COMPANY
Captain Shapley P. Ross (October 18, 1846–October 17, 1847)
*Ranging District*: Between the Little and San Gabriel Rivers with headquarters at camp near Bryant's Station (October 1846); Brazos River country with headquarters at the Waco village (July 1847)

#### MCCULLOCH'S COMPANY
Captain Henry E. McCulloch (October 22, 1846–October 21, 1847)
*Ranging District*: Llano River country with headquarters at camp near the junction of the Colorado and Llano Rivers

#### SMITH'S/WYMAN'S COMPANY
Captain Thomas I. Smith (February 3–April 4, 1847)
1st Lieutenant E. S. Wyman, Commanding (April 4–August 17, 1847)
*Ranging District*: Brazos River country with headquarters at Smith's Station

*Battalion mustered into service as U.S. Volunteers, operated under the supervision of HQ, Post of San Antonio, and under the personal orders of Lt-Gov. A. C. Horton and Gov. J. P. Henderson*

## 1st Regiment, Texas Mounted Volunteers (Six Months)

### FIELD & STAFF
Colonel John C. "Jack" Hays (May 11–June 1847)
Lieutenant-Colonel Charles A. Harper (May 11–June 1847)
Major William H. Bourland (May 11–June 1847)
1st Lieutenant Hugh Hensey, Adjutant (May 11–June 1847)
Sergeant-Major Thomas C. Poe (May 11–June 1847)
Quartermaster Sergeant Henry Smock (May 11–June 1847)

### CLARK'S COMPANY
Captain Thomas W. Clark (May 6–June 5, 1847)

### CRUMP'S COMPANY
Captain William G. Crump (April 30–June 5, 1847)

### GILLET'S COMPANY
Captain James S. Gillet (April 26–June 2, 1847)

### HILL'S COMPANY
Captain Benjamin F. Hill (April 14–June 16, 1847)

### LONG'S COMPANY
Captain John Long (May 3–June 2, 1847)

### MUCKLEROY'S COMPANY
Captain David Muckelroy (April 26–June 4, 1847)

### SIMS' COMPANY
Captain Samuel W. Sims (May 1–June 5, 1847)

### SMITH'S COMPANY
Captain James Smith (May 6–June 4, 1847)

### SNELL'S COMPANY
Captain Martin K. Snell (May 14–June 5, 1847)
*Regiment organized but not mustered into service*

## 1st Regiment, Texas Mounted Volunteers (Twelve Months)

### FIELD & STAFF
Colonel John C. "Jack" Hays (July 10, 1847–July 10, 1848)
Lieutenant-Colonel P. Hansbrough Bell (July 10, 1847–July 10, 1848)
   *Lt-Col. Bell assigned to detached duty as commander, Mounted Regiment of Texian Volunteers (August 11, 1847–July 10, 1848)*
Major Alfred Truitt (October 26, 1847–May 18, 1848)
1st Lieutenant John S. "Rip" Ford, Adjutant (July 7, 1847–July 10, 1848)
Lieutenant Hal G. Runnels, Quartermaster (July 10, 1847–February 16, 1848)
2nd Lieutenant Josiah Pancoast, Commissary of Subsistence
Doctor A. Packer, Surgeon (July 10, 1847–May 18, 1848)
Doctor _____ Tacker, Assistant Surgeon
Reverend Samuel Corley, Chaplain

Sergeant-Major Alexander E. Handley (July 10–October 2, 1847)
Sergeant-Major William M. Hewett (October 2–December 12, 1847)
Sergeant-Major Gilbert Brush (December 13, 1847–May 18, 1848)
H. H. Kinnion, Chief Bugler (July 10–September 1, 1847)
William Self, Chief Bugler (September 1, 1847–January 1, 1848)
Michael Chaffner, Chief Bugler (January 1–July 10, 1848)
Charles B. Daggett, Principal Musician (July 10, 1847–July 10, 1848)

### Company D
Captain Samuel Highsmith (May 10, 1847–May 14, 1848)
 *Company detached to Lt-Col. P. H. Bell's Mounted Regiment of Texian Volunteers (August 11, 1847)*

### Company E
Captain Alfred Truitt (May 12–October 26, 1847)
Captain Chaucer Ashton (October 26–December 14, 1847)
Captain Alexander E. Handley (December 14, 1847–May 1, 1848)

### Company F
Captain Jacob Roberts (May 24, 1847–April 30, 1848)

### Company G
Captain Gabriel M. Armstrong (May 25, 1847–February 29, 1848)
Captain Alfred Evans (March 1–May 1, 1848)

### Company H
Captain James S. Gillett (June 5, 1847–June 15, 1848)
 *Company detached to Lt-Col. P. H. Bell's Mounted Regiment of Texian Volunteers (August 11, 1847)*

### Company I
Captain Isaac Ferguson (June 21, 1847–January 1, 1848)
1st Lieutenant Ephraim M. Daggett, Commanding (January 1–17, 1848)
Captain Ephraim M. Daggett (January 17–May 1, 1848)

### Company K
Captain Stephen Kinsey (July 3–Ocotber 1, 1847)
1st Lieutenant Preston Witt, Commanding (October 1–23, 1847)
Captain Preston Witt (October 23, 1847–April 30, 1848)
*Regimental Ranging District*: Vera Cruz–Mexico City line with headquarters at Vergara (October 1847), Puebla (November 1847), and Mexico City (December 1847)
 *Regiment mustered into service as U.S. Volunteers and operated under the personal orders of BG J. Lane, CO of special brigade, U.S. Army of the Center*

## Mounted Regiment of Texian Volunteers
### Field & Staff
Lieutenant-Colonel P. Hansbrough Bell, Commanding (August 11, 1847–July 10, 1848)
 *Lt-Col. Bell detached from Field & Staff, 1st Regiment, Texas Mounted Volunteers*
Colonel P. Hansbrough Bell (July 11, 1848–February 15, 1849)
Lieutenant-Colonel Middleton T. Johnson (July 11, 1848–February 15, 1849)
Major James S. Gillett (July 11, 1848–February 15, 1849)
Lieutenant James M. W. Hall, Adjutant (July 11, 1848–February 15, 1849)
J. H. Ralston, Assistant Quartermaster
Doctor J. H. Lyons, Surgeon (July 11, 1848–February 15, 1849)

Doctor John Ellis, Assistant Surgeon and Medical Purveyor (July 11, 1848–February 15, 1849)
Sergeant-Major Charles A. Harrison (July 11, 1848–February 15, 1849)

### Company A/Highsmith's Company

Captain Samuel Highsmith (May 10, 1847–December 26, 1848)
*Ranging District*: Llano and San Saba Rivers country with headquarters at Enchanted Rock
    Company detached from 1st Regiment, Texas Mounted Volunteers (August 11, 1847) and attached to J. C. Hays' Texas–El Paso–Chihuahua Expedition (August 22–Decemver 20, 1848)

### Company B/Smith's Company

Captain Middleton T. Johnson (April 5, 1847–July 10, 1848)
1st Lieutenant Joseph M. Smith, Commanding (July 11–August 8, 1848)
Captain Joseph M. Smith (August 8–December 15, 1848)
*Ranging District*: San Antonio area (May 1847); Trinity River country with headquarters at the Waco village (September 1847) and Kaufman Station and detachment at camp on Chambers Creek (1848)

### Company C/Warfield's Company

Captain James S. Gillett (July 5, 1847–July 11, 1848)
1st Lieutenant Hiram Warfield, Commanding (July 11–August 1, 1848)
Captain Hiram Warfield (August 1–December 16, 1848)
1st Lieutenant William Knox, commanding detachment (November 1848)
*Ranging District*: Frio, Medina, Leona, and Sabinal Rivers country with headquarters at Camp Arbuckle and detachment at camp near Woll's Crossing
    Company detached from 1st Regiment, Texas Mounted Volunteers (August 11, 1847)

### Company D/Crump's Company

Captain William G. Crump (September 30, 1847–September 30, 1848)
*Ranging District*: San Antonio–Corpus Christi line

### Company E/Sutton's Company

Captain James S. Sutton (October 20, 1847–October 6, 1848)
Captain James S. Sutton (October 27–December 15, 1848)
*Ranging District*: San Antonio–Corpus Christi line with headquarters at camp on the Nueces River

### Company F/Veatch's Company

Captain John A. Veatch (October 23, 1847–September 20, 1848)
*Ranging District*: Rio Grande country with headquarters at Presidio del Rio Grande (February 1848) and Camp Eagle Pass (May 1848); Leona River country (August 1848)

### Company G/Ross' Company

Captain Shapley P. Ross (November 18, 1847–December 10, 1848)
*Ranging District*: Brazos River country with headquarters at the Waco village and detachment at camp on the Leon River

### Company H/McCulloch's Company

Captain Henry E. McCulloch (October 25, 1847–December 8, 1848)
*Ranging District*: Llano River country with headquarters at McCulloch's Station/Post McCulloch

### COMPANY I/FITZHUGH'S COMPANY

Captain William F. Fitzhugh (February 2, 1847–February 1, 1849)
Lieutenant Alfred Chandler, commanding detachment
*Ranging District*: Trinity River country with headquarters at camp on Elm Creek and Chandler's detachment at camp on Hickory Creek

### COMPANY K/CONNER'S COMPANY

Captain John H. Conner (May 5–December 31, 1848)
*Ranging District*: Between Trinity and Brazos Rivers with headquarters at camp on Richland Creek

### LAMAR'S COMPANY

Captain Mirabeau B. Lamar (February 17–September 27, 1848)
*Ranging District*: Lower Rio Grande Valley with headquarters at Laredo

### ROBERTS' COMPANY

Captain Jacob Roberts (October 24–December 12, 1848)

### HILL'S COMPANY

Captain Benjamin F. Hill (October 27–December 17, 1848)

*Regiment mustered into service as U.S. Volunteers, and operated under the supervision of HQ, Post of San Antonio and under the personal orders of Gov. J. P. Henderson and Gov. G. T. Wood*

# 4

# Rangers of the Old Stamp: The Texas Mounted Volunteers (1848–1861)

Upon annexation, the Federal Government assumed responsibility for the protection of the Texan frontiers. Article XI of the Treaty of Guadalupe Hidalgo also required the United States to interdict Indian incursions into Mexico. The scene had been relatively peaceful during the recent war and remained so for one year afterward. Unfortunately, the Army's twenty-two companies in Texas, totaling 1,000 to 1,400 men, proved unable to halt the rising tide of depredations in 1849, probably because sixteen of those companies were infantry—a poor choice when confronting the finest light cavalry on the continent. Furthermore, the federal troops were stretched thin across three vast lines: the Colorado River, the Rio Grande Valley, and the Nueces River. All of which was coupled with a lack of knowledge concerning Indian-fighting tactics and the terrain and a passive patrol system that responded to raids rather than preempted them.

By the time Texas joined the Union, the line of western settlement had reached the present counties of Cooke, Denton, Tarrant, Ellis, Navarro, McLennan, Bell, Williamson, Travis, Blanco, Gillespie, Kendall, Bexar, and Medina. Between February and December 1849, soldiers of the Eighth Military District (later renamed the Department of Texas) established a chain of forts slightly to the west of the frontier line. These posts included Fort Worth, on the west fork of the Trinity River in Tarrant County; Fort Graham, on the east side of the Brazos in present Hill County; Fort Gates, on the Leon in present Coryell County; Fort Croghan, on Hamilton Creek in present Burnet County; Fort Martin Scott, on the Guadalupe in Gillespie County; Fort Lincoln, on Seco Creek in Medina County; Fort Inge, on the Leona in present Uvalde County; Camp Crawford (later changed to Fort McIntosh), on the Rio Grande near Laredo; and Fort Duncan, on the east side of the Rio Grande near Eagle Pass.

Unfortunately, the Federal Government minimized the crisis, dismissing the reported 171 persons killed, seven wounded, twenty-five captured, and 6,618 animals stolen that year as exaggerations. The secretary of war even went so far as to blame settlers for the unrest. Indeed, Brevet Major-General George M. Brooke, the newly-appointed district commander, hesitated to call up rangers because he feared their presence would ignite a general war with the Indians.

4. Rangers of the Old Stamp: The Texas Mounted Volunteers (1848–1861) 75

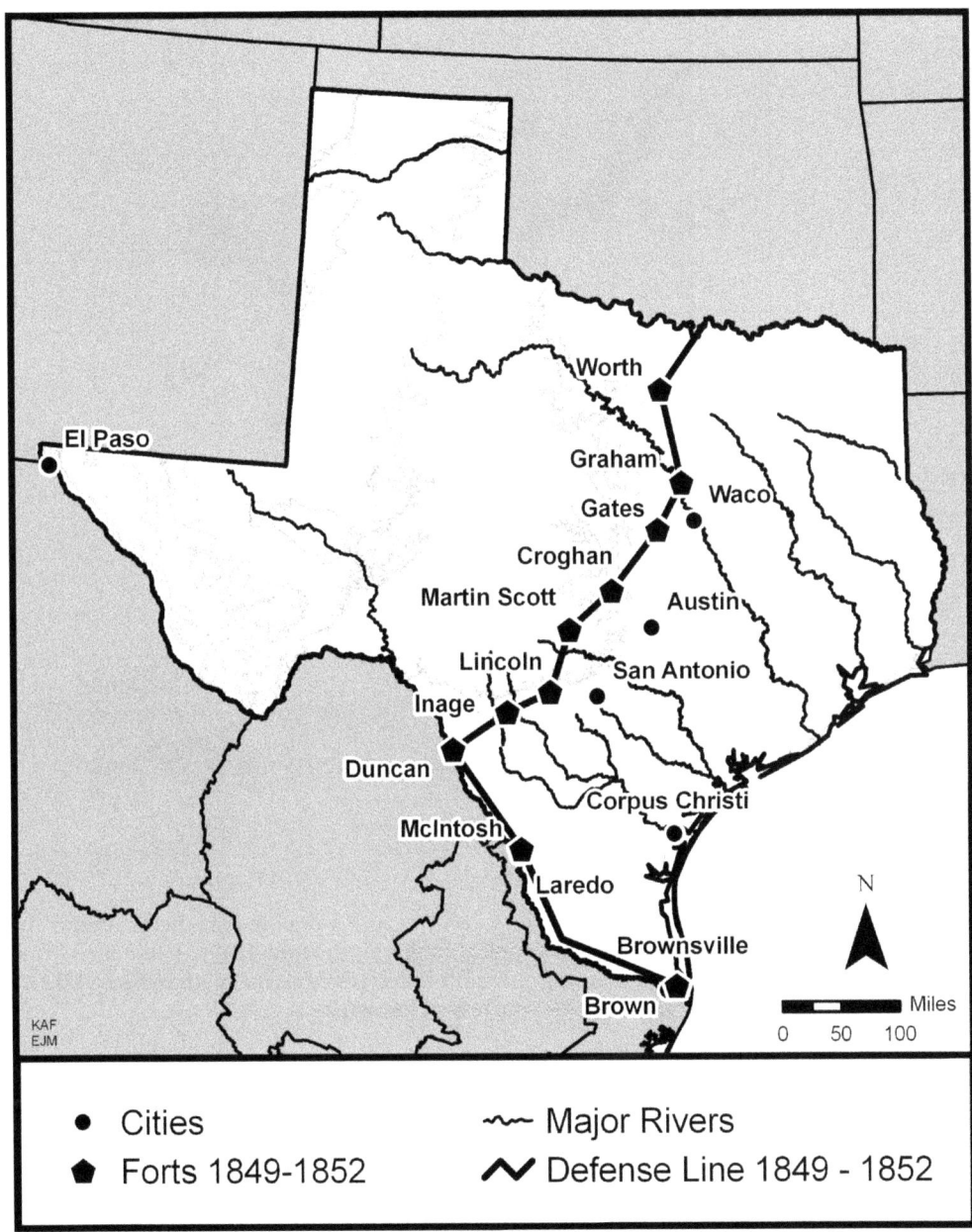

In addition to Indian marauding, most of which occurred between San Antonio and Brownsville until 1857, smuggling across the Rio Grande remained unabated and flourished due to excessive import duties levied by the Mexican Government. American renegades and Mexican *bandidos* continued to infest the region, robbing and killing any unfortunate in their path.

On August 11, 1849, General Brooke requested Governor George T. Wood raise three mounted companies for federal service in South Texas. The *Texas State Gazette* on August 25 named Ford, Gamble (likely John J. Grumbles), and Smock as the new captains. No trace of a Captain Smock can be found in the archival records, and some theorize Henry E.

"Mounted Texas Ranger carrying a Colt Navy revolver and a double-barrelled shotgun" by Bruce Marshall. This watercolor depicts a typical ranger in the mid–1850s. These men often favored shotguns over rifles in the running gunfights that typified clashes with Indians. UTSA's Institute of Texan Cultures, No. 073-0165; courtesy of the artist.

McCulloch commanded this third unit. Eight other companies seem to have been authorized by the State as the Third Legislature passed a joint resolution on January 7, 1850, to reimburse Ben F. Hill, J. M. Smith, Jacob Roberts, John S. Sutton, Shapley P. Ross, Henry McCulloch, Isaac W. Johnson, and Charles Blackwell for services rendered on the frontier; the *Texas State Gazette* reprinted the resolution on March 2, 1850. Only scattered supporting evidence can be found further regarding these gentlemen with the exception of McCulloch, who was quite active in the field later in the year and in 1851. In early 1850, General Brooke called on Governor P. H. Bell for a fourth federalized company and "Bigfoot" Wallace was appointed captain.

A fortunate few of these Indian fighters went into battle armed with revolvers, while the others continued to use old horse pistols and Mississippi rifles. As the years passed, rangers became better armed with the smaller, more practical Colt pistols that replaced the Walkers: the Whitneyville-Hartford Dragoons (known as Transitional Dragoons to modern collectors) produced in late 1847, the First Model Dragoons manufactured from 1848 to 1850, the Second Model from 1850 to 1851, and the Third Model from 1851 to 1861. All of them possessed variations in parts and details, but all were standard in being six-shot, 7½-inch-barreled weapons that discharged a .44-caliber 140-grain ball with a black powder charge of forty to fifty grains, rather than the Walker's sixty. Other common features included a weight of four pounds two ounces, an overall length of 14¾ inches, case hardened and blued finish, one-piece walnut grips, brass backstrap, the addition of a positive latch at the end of the loading lever to prevent it from dropping under recoil, and shorter chambers which, coupled with the reduced powder charge, diminished the occurrence of ruptured cylinders.

For those who desired an even more lightweight weapon, the "Colt Revolving Belt Pistol of Naval Caliber" (or Colt Model 1851 Navy) was an excellent alternative. Originally titled the "New Ranger Size Pistol" to honor Colonel Hays and his men, the Navy Colt was a .36-caliber pistol which weighed two pounds nine ounces. The pistol was equipped with an octagonal 7½-inch barrel, an overall length of fourteen inches, and brass backstraps and trigger guard. The six-shot cylinder fired 83-grain balls backed by twenty-five grains of powder.

After Brooke's death in March 1851, his successor, Brevet Major-General Persifor F. Smith, ordered the construction of a second cordon of outposts about 150 miles west of the first. From north to south, they included Fort Belknap, near the Salt Fork of the Brazos in present Young County; Fort Phantom Hill, on the Clear Fork of the Brazos in present Jones County; Fort Chadbourne, on Oak Creek in present Coke County; Fort McKavett, on the San Saba in present Menard County; Fort Terrett, on the North Fork of the Llano in present Sutton County; Fort Mason, on Post Oak Hill near Comanche and Centennial creeks in present Mason County; and Fort Clark, on Las Moras Creek in Kinney County.

After the federalized companies disbanded, the frontier situation remained grim, especially on the Rio Grande. In response, the governor authorized captains Owen Shaw, G. K. Lewis, and H. Clay Davis to raise ranger companies in the summer of 1852.

By the end of the year, the two lines of defense were completed, and the War Department increased the number of army companies to forty-eight: six of the 2nd Dragoons, eight of the 1st Mounted Rifles, four of the 4th Artillery, and thirty-two of the 1st, 5th, 7th, and 8th Infantry regiments. The new strategy called for the outer chain to be garrisoned by infantry and the inner by cavalry. The infantry was to somehow detect the presence of hostiles, alert the horse soldiers, and seal off escape routes. The cavalry was to pursue the raiders and smash them. The fatal flaw in the plan, which was obvious to veteran Indian fighters, was the fact that foot soldiers lacked the mobility to overtake and engage mounted Indians. Nearly one-quarter of the U.S. Army—some 3,600 troops—was stationed in Texas, and $6 million was being spent annually to protect the frontiers of Texas and New Mexico. Still the Federal Government proved unable to give the citizens the necessary protection.

Much of 1853 was peaceful and, lulled into a false sense of security, the military redeployed troops from the frontier, leaving only two companies of dragoons and four of infantry between the Red and Colorado rivers. Actually, the Indians had only disengaged in order to assess the strengths and weaknesses of the defensive lines. They would return with a vengeance.

Under the terms of annexation, Texas retained title to her public lands for the purpose of selling acreage to pay off the debts of the late Republic. With the adoption of the "Location Bill" of February 6, 1854, the Fifth Legislature set aside twelve leagues of state-owned land so the federal government could settle the Texas tribes in a permanent loca-

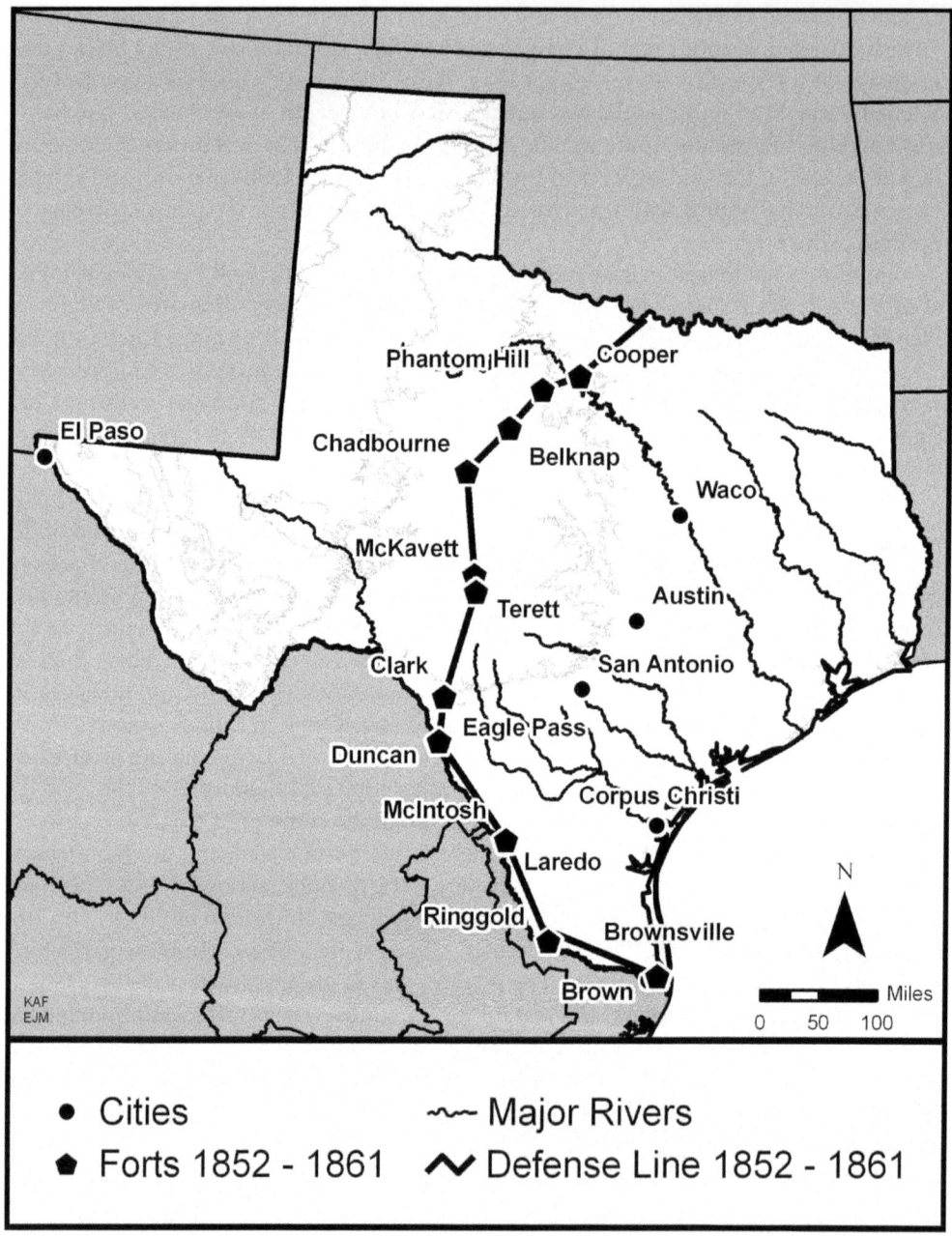

tion. The two sites selected came to be known as the Brazos Reservation (or lower reserve) under Indian agent Shapley P. Ross and the Clear Fork Reservation (or upper reserve or Comanche Reservation) under John R. Baylor. The 37,152-acre Brazos Agency near Fort Belknap was ultimately populated by 1,112 Caddo, Anadarko, Waco, Kichai, Tawakoni, Delaware, and Tonkawa Indians, while the 18,576-acre Comanche Reservation in present Throckmorton County was settled by 557 members of the Penateka band. A large portion of the Comanche nation refused to settle on the reservation and remained beyond the control of the federal government.

In March, the frontier saw a resurgence of depredations in which the Indians avoided the posts manned by dragoons and mounted riflemen and struck the settlements near infantry garrisons. General Smith realized the error of his policy and stationed mounted troops at Belknap, Phantom Hill, Chadbourne, and other posts of the westernmost chain.

On October 9, he also called on Governor Elisha M. Pease for six ranger companies to again augment the regular troops. The Texans were to furnish their own horses, arms, and equipment in accordance with ranger tradition, while the federal government was to provide subsistence and forage, ammunition, and pay. In the end, the War Department reimbursed the rangers for the supplies they had purchased themselves, but Austin had to defray their wages.

On July 5, 1855, Governor Pease selected Captain James H. Callahan (a survivor of the 1836 Goliad Massacre) to raise a ranger company for three months' service. The captain was to counter Lipan Apache, Seminole, and Kickapoo depredations along the Guadalupe and its tributaries in Bexar and Comal counties. The governor warned Callahan he would have to organize the company without the necessary funding; those enlisting would have to support themselves and hope for future reimbursement from the legislature. Despite such handicaps, Callahan was able to muster eighty-five privates instead of the authorized seventy-four, and his rangers met with some success, but the number of Indian attacks increased in Bexar and Medina counties.

Realizing the raids were launched from Coahuila and Chihuahua, Callahan decided in September to mount an unauthorized retaliatory expedition in order to take the fight to the enemy. It has been suggested the incursion was also an unofficial venture to recover runaway slaves from the same region. Nevertheless, he called for reinforcements, and two companies from San Antonio and Seguin were formed under captains William R. Henry and Nat Benton, respectively. Callahan's 110 men crossed the Rio Grande at Eagle Pass on October 1. Two days later, they engaged a combined force of six to seven hundred Mexicans and Indians on the Río Escondido twenty-seven miles inside Mexico. The Texans suffered four men killed and seven wounded, while the enemy lost up to ninety — mostly Indians. The rangers fell back to Piedras Negras, looted and allegedly burned the town, then crossed the river on October 6–7. Following this episode, periodic invasions of Mexico became something of a ranger tradition.

In August 1855, the War Department transferred the dragoons to Kansas Territory to control Sioux unrest on the Platte. The situation began to brighten somewhat in January 1856 when the headquarters of the élite 2nd Cavalry arrived at Fort Mason, and its companies took station along the frontier. The regiment erected new posts over the next several years, including Camp Cooper, on the Clear Fork of the Brazos (near the Comanche Reservation); Camp Colorado, on Jim Ned Creek near the Colorado in Coleman County; Camp Verde, on Verde Creek in Kerr County; Camp Hudson, on San Pedro Creek near Devil's River in Kinney (present Val Verde) County; and Camp Wood, on the Nueces in present Real County.

Regimental commander Colonel Albert Sidney Johnston, the same man who had been a general and secretary of war in the Republic of Texas, instituted an aggressive patrol system that had troopers in the field almost constantly to track Indian war parties and bring them to battle. From 1856 to 1860, the regiment would participate in forty engagements against virulent Indians and Mexicans. Although the 2nd Cavalry achieved an enviable reputation and became the only army regiment universally praised by Texans, its 750 officers and rank and file remained numerically inadequate to the situation at hand.

Throughout the 1850s, the state government requested on numerous occasions that Washington fund a permanent ranger regiment. The State lacked the financial resources and the War Department, of course, refused since to maintain such a force would be admitting that the U.S. Army was incapable of protecting the citizenry. Two decades would have to pass before one finally emerged.

Following the fire which destroyed the adjutant general's office, Governor Pease suspended the position on February 4, 1856, and the department was not reorganized until February 14, 1860. During that time, the state's chief executives would directly supervise ranger companies serving in the field.

The number of Indian raids fell at the end of 1855 and throughout 1856. Consequently, the complement of federal troops in Texas decreased in August 1856, when the mounted rifles were transferred to New Mexico Territory in response to Gila Apache depredations. Again the Comanches had withdrawn, this time to appraise the mettle of the 2nd Cavalry. The following year, attacks occurred in Coryell, Bosque, Erath, Comanche, Stephens, Hamilton, Young, Jack, and Palo Pinto counties. By June 1857, thirty-one army companies were stationed in a 1,300-mile line of posts which stretched from Fort Brown to Fort Duncan to Fort Davis to Fort Belknap. Citing inadequate federal protection, the Seventh Legislature authorized the governor on November 17, 1857, to raise six twenty-man minute detachments to range the frontier between Blanco and Palo Pinto counties.

After failing once again to secure a permanent ranger regiment, Governor Hardin R. Runnels decided to change strategies and mount a punitive expedition to strike deep into the *Comanchería*; the necessary legislation was enacted on January 27, 1858. The next day, the governor appointed "Rip" Ford expedition commander with the rank of senior captain and authority over all state troops in the field. In the spring, Ford organized a force of 101 rangers and 113 Indian auxiliaries from the Brazos Agency; the latter led by ex-ranger Shapley Ross. Ford's command marched to the Canadian River country in Indian Territory and, on May 12, engaged some three hundred Kotsoteka Comanches at Little Robe Creek in the Antelope Hills. The Texas contingent killed the noted chief Po-bish-e-quash-o (called "Iron Jacket" because of the Spanish armor he wore) and seventy-five other warriors, captured three hundred horses, and took eighteen women and children prisoner. The rangers sustained two killed and three wounded. In his official report, Ford stated,

> The conduct of the men of my command was characterized by obedience, patience, and perseverance. They behaved, while under fire, in a gallant and soldier-like manner and I think that they have fully vindicated their right to be recognized as Texas Rangers of the old stamp.

The expedition also demonstrated that well-trained and properly-equipped troops could penetrate the *Comanchería* to pursue and defeat the Comanches on their ground.

The army decided to capitalize on the rangers' success and organized its own campaign, later known as the "Wichita Expedition." On September 15, 1858, Brevet Major Earl Van Dorn and 225 troopers of Companies A, F, H, and K, 2nd Cavalry took the field, along with a fifty-man detachment from Companies C and F, 1st Infantry, and 135 Waco, Tawakoni, Tonkawa, and Caddo auxiliaries under the command of Lawrence Sullivan "Sul" Ross (a future Confederate general and governor of Texas), the son of the Brazos Reservation agent. On October 1, the expedition attacked an encampment of five hundred Penateka Comanches near a village of Wichitas at Rush Springs in the Wichita Mountains. The battleground was broken by ravines and soon shrouded in a dense mixture of morning fog

"We Struck Some Boggy Ground" by Frederic Remington. This wash drawing was featured in Frederic Remington's collection of essays "Crooked Trails" (1898) that ran in *Harper's Monthly*. The illustration portrays "Rip" Ford's attack on the Comanche village at Little Robe Creek in 1858. This engagement, along with the subsequent army campaign, was a decisive action in the continuing war of attrition with the Comanches. Courtesy of the R.W. Norton Art Gallery, Shreveport, LA.

and powder smoke. The one-and-a-half-hour firefight quickly deteriorated into hand-to-hand combat. Captain Ross was praised by Major Van Dorn and no less than General-in-Chief Winfield Scott for his courage and martial ability. First Sergeant John W. Spangler of Company H was singled out in the official report for personally killing six Comanches. A total of fifty-six warriors and two women were killed, another twenty-five were mortally wounded, 120 lodges were destroyed, and three hundred horses were captured. The attackers suffered four killed, one mortally wounded, and twelve wounded, including Van Dorn and "Sul" Ross.

After wintering at Camp Radziminski and scouting the surrounding country, Van Dorn's expedition, now comprised of 427 cavalrymen of Companies A, B, C, F, G, and H, 2nd Cavalry, and fifty-eight Indian scouts, set out on April 30, 1859. They attacked a village on Crooked Creek, a small tributary of the Cimarron River in Kansas Territory, on May 13, whose eighty-odd inhabitants were the same Penatekas who had been at Rush Springs the previous year. Deployed as dismounted skirmishers, the troopers battled the Indians in a rain-soaked ravine of brush and fallen trees. In the end, forty-nine enemy warriors were killed, five wounded, and thirty-two men and five women were taken captive. Van Dorn lost two soldiers killed and thirteen wounded, and two auxiliaries killed and two mortally wounded.

At the same time, while the Brazos and Comanche reservations had been accepted as a viable solution to the frontier problem in 1855, their inhabitants were viewed with outright hostility by early 1859. For the previous three years, raiding parties of Kiowas and northern Comanches had repeatedly struck area settlers and many agitators, including former Comanche Reserve agent Baylor, blamed the reservation Indians. The combination of the reserves being too near the Comanche war-trail to Mexico, Indians leaving the agencies for hunting expeditions or to sometimes join raiding parties, corrupt traders peddling whiskey, and white settlers' general suspicion of all Indians led to the proposed removal of the reservation occupants to north of the Red River. Credible facts suggest Indian raiders and disguised white renegades planted false evidence to incriminate the inhabitants of the two agencies. They were so successful that all Indians found outside the confines of the reservations were considered hostiles to be shot on sight. After several clashes between reservation inhabitants and white volunteers who seemed more interested in seizing the Indians' land and herds, orders for the exodus were issued on June 11, 1859. Escorted by federal troops and Captain John Henry Brown's Bell County rangers, the two groups of Indians crossed the Red River on August 1, and exactly one month later arrived at their new homes at the Wichita Agency in Indian Territory.

One interesting aspect of the episode occurred in the wake of the December 27, 1858, murder of seven innocent Caddos at the hands of a vigilante gang. Captain "Rip" Ford, commanding a ranger company situated between the two reservations, was issued an arrest warrant for seventeen of the killers. Ford emphatically refused to execute the warrant. His reason was not because he agreed the reservation Indians were guilty, as he had publicly declared his belief that the recent pillaging and murders were due to raiders living along the Arkansas River. Instead, Ford held that as a military officer he did not have the authority to directly serve civil process. Heretofore, rangers saw themselves primarily as soldiers and, while they were legally empowered to assist civilian authorities (in this case the county sheriff), they were not peace officers at this time. He was technically correct in interpreting the state statutes, but many thought him morally wrong in refusing to make the arrests.

After the Treaty of Guadalupe Hidalgo ceded the Nueces Strip to the United States in 1848, *Tejanos* living in the Lower Rio Grande Valley found themselves, while numerically superior, second-class citizens. American settlers had moved into the region following the war to raise livestock and exploit the trading opportunities the international boundary offered. The economic and political power passed into the hands of the Anglo merchant and ranching elite, who used the *Tejanos* for their votes in the machine politics of the day. Those of Mexican heritage found themselves at the mercy of the law, which favored the *gringos*. Established *Tejano* landowners often had to defend their decades-old property titles in court and, even if they were successful, they were sometimes swindled by their *norteamericano* attorneys. Such conditions created an atmosphere ripe for war to right these wrongs; all that was needed was someone to light the fuse.

On July 13, 1859, the required spark flared when Juan Nepomuceno "Cheno" Cortina rescued a former employee who was being brutally arrested by the Brownsville city marshal. Cortina shot and wounded the peace officer before escaping into Matamoros, where he was hailed as a champion for oppressed Mexicans. Cortina's mother owned Rancho del Carmen, a 44,000-acre ranch near Santa Rita, and her son, with his own Rancho San José, could have been a member of the dominant local establishment. Indeed, his great-great-grandfather had founded Camargo in 1749 and his great-grandfather had received the 261,275-acre Potrero del Espíritu Santo land grant (which included the future Brownsville townsite) in 1772. Instead, Cortina preferred the rougher company of *rancheros* and *vaqueros*. Despite being under indictment for murder and cattle and horse rustling, he acquired a great deal of political influence as *patrón* to the *campesinos* of Cameron County and was able to deliver the Mexican vote on election days. For Cortina, the encounter with the Brownsville marshal had been a culmination of years of Anglo legal and political abuse against Mexicans.

On September 28, the Lower Valley exploded into violence with the onset of the Cortina War. Having placed his personal enemies on a death list, Cortina and his band of seventy followers crossed the Rio Grande and occupied Brownsville for three hours, looted the town, and killed four of the residents, including the city jailer. Two days later, he issued a *pronunciamiento* justifying his raid as a blow for Mexican rights against a corrupt and racist Anglo establishment. His actions made him the subject of numerous border legends and *corridos* (heroic ballads).

In response, Captain William G. Tobin raised a company of one hundred rangers from Bexar County and marched them to the Rio Grande, arriving on November 10. Three days later, a mob took Cortina's lieutenant, who had been captured some time earlier, and lynched him, possibly with ranger assistance. Soon, other ranger companies began appearing on the scene from Karnes, Live Oak, and Atascosa counties. Tobin then attacked Cortina's camp near Rancho del Carmen, but was repulsed and sent fleeing back to Brownsville.

On November 23, Cortina issued a second *pronunciamiento* in which he expressed confidence that Governor-elect Sam Houston would offer the protection of the law to border Mexicans. He further declared his intention to redress the grievances of dispossessed *Tejanos*. Playing to Mexicans on both sides of the border, he gained both moral and logistical support from officials and citizens of Tamaulipas. He also received implied consent to use Mexican soil for the purpose of mounting forces hostile to the people and property of the United States. Indeed, when Cortina returned from raids loaded with loot, the "Red Robber of the Rio Grande," as he became known, found a ready market for its disposal. From Nuevo León to Tamaulipas to the Nueces River, *peons*, *rancheros*, and *bandidos* either joined the *Cortinistas* or operated independently and began an orgy of rapine and murder. Local vigilantes and rangers retaliated and burned out *Tejanos* suspected of either being sympathetic with or actively involved in the *Cortinista* cause. As Alexander C. Hill wrote Governor Runnels, "Cortinas [sic] is not the only man who is stealing property in this country. There is quite a number engaged in the business trying to place it to Cortinas's [sic] credit...."

On December 5, two companies of the 1st U.S. Infantry, two of the 1st Artillery, and one of the 2nd Cavalry under the overall command of Major Samuel P. Heintzelman arrived at Fort Brown. Nine days later, Heintzelman led a column of 165 regulars and 125 rangers to Cortina's camp at La Ebonal and proceeded to capture it, but the wily revolutionary escaped. Meanwhile, Major "Rip" Ford, appointed by the governor to assume command of the state troops on the border, arrived at Brownsville with fifty-three rangers. Heintzelman's soldiers and the combined Texans then defeated 590 *Cortinistas* at Rio Grande City on December 27, killing at least sixty of the enemy. Even though Runnels had conferred on Ford the rank of major and the command of the state force, the legislation authorizing the troops in service called for an election for the position of commanding officer. Accordingly, Tobin, who desired the command and worked harder in canvassing for it than he had leading his own company, was elected to the post by six votes. Following the election, Ford read his official report of the battle of Rio Grande City to the assembled rangers. He generously praised all the men by name and criticized none. Afterward, he was told that had he read the report before the election, he would have been the one chosen.

Such sentiments were unnecessary, because Major Tobin was ordered on January 12, 1860, to proceed to Brownsville and disband his battalion. On January 20 and February 1, two companies were mustered in with Ford as the senior captain. This force, known as the Rio Grande Squadron, participated in the battles of La Bolsa (February 4) and Rancho La Mesa (March 17), both of which sealed the fate of Cortina's insurrection. Fifteen Americans, eighty Mexican noncombatants, and 151 *Cortinistas* lost their lives in the Cortina War. In the end, the status quo remained unchanged, as hatred for *gringos* remained in the hearts of many border Mexicans and, in the years to come, the Rio Grande valley would again run red with blood.

Despite the removal of the reservation Indians, the frontier from the Red River to the San Saba continued to be ravaged. The local settlers learned too late of the importance of the buffer offered by the two agencies. Indeed, fear of the Comanche Moon heightened as Brown, Lampasas, and San Saba counties experienced a depopulation of their citizens. The year 1860 saw the highest number of ranger companies active in the field since the early 1840s. Newly-inaugurated Governor Houston authorized the formation of three companies under the commands of William C. Dalrymple on December 30, 1859, Edward "Ed" Burleson, Jr., on January 4, 1860, and John H. Conner on January 9. Once organized and mustered into service, the three captains conducted extensive patrols in the most exposed areas, but their men proved too few to counter the constant raiding. In response, on February 13, Houston named lieutenants Robert M. White, John Salmon, and Dixon Walker as the commanders of three twenty-man minute detachments to range Coryell, Hamilton, Comanche, Erath, Eastland, and Palo Pinto counties. On February 21, the governor ordered the chief justices of Montague, Wise, Young, Palo Pinto, Eastland, Erath, Comanche, Bosque, Hamilton, Coryell, Llano, San Saba, Lampasas, Mason, Burnett, Gillespie, Bandera, Kerr, Uvalde, Blanco, Bexar, Medina, and Frio counties to each raise a fifteen-man minute detachment. On March 5, Houston also authorized Captain Peter Tumlinson to raise a forty-eight-man ranger company for service between the Frio River and the Rio Grande. Four days later, the twenty-three county minute companies were mustered into service. With 720 state troops continually patrolling, the frontier settlers were able to enjoy a brief respite. Mindful of the ever-limited treasury, the governor ordered the disbandment of the minute men on May 18, subject to recall.

On March 17, Houston appointed Colonel Middleton T. Johnson (a former officer in P. H. Bell's ranger regiment) his aide-de-camp and commander of a four hundred-man punitive expedition. Johnson's eight companies crossed into Indian Territory on June 23, and ranged as far as the Canadian River in search of belligerent Indians and horse thieves. Organized and fielded at great expense, the campaign was doomed from the start and produced no tangible results. Johnson's weak grasp of command and inadequate logistical planning was compounded by drought-stricken horses and a failure to locate and decisively engage any hostiles. The colonel had even left for Galveston on June 5 to marry, while the column was preparing to move out. Consequently, on August 4, Houston ordered the expedition to disband.

Captain "Sul" Ross, who had led the Indian auxiliaries on the "Wichita Expedition" and commanded one of Johnson's companies, was authorized on September 11 to raise a seventy-man ranger company based near Fort Belknap. Despite Ross' presence in the field, raids increased in Parker, Young, Palo Pinto, Wise, and Jack counties throughout November and into early December. On December 6, Houston appointed Lieutenant James B. "Buck" Barry and a twenty-five-man Bosque County detachment to operate under Ross' overall command, but Barry was not able to muster his men until January 10. Houston also authorized ranger companies under captains A. B. Burleson on December 17, E. W. Rogers on December 26, Thomas L. Harrison and Curtis Mays on January 2, 1861, and J. M. Wright on February 7. On October 10, Houston had appointed William Dalrymple aide-de-camp and commander-in-chief of state troops, with the rank of colonel of cavalry. Dalrymple was ordered to assume personal command of all rangers on the northwestern frontier on December 29. By late February, he was in charge of six companies and based at the old Comanche Reservation.

On December 18, forty of Ross' rangers, along with seventy Palo Pinto volunteers under Captain J. J. "Jack" Cureton and twenty troopers of Company H, 2nd Cavalry under First Sergeant Spangler, engaged Nakoni Comanches on the Pease River that resulted in the death of noted chief Peta Nocona and the "rescue" of Cynthia Ann Parker. Cynthia Ann was the same girl who had been taken in the Parker's Fort Massacre twenty-four years earlier. By this time, she had become completely assimilated into the Comanche society and she died heartbroken four years later in Anderson County, pining for her two sons; one of whom became the last great Comanche war chief Quanah Parker.

## Historical Register, 1849–1861

*"Whip them and then talk of treaties."*
— Colonel John S. Ford

### GOLIAD RANGERS/TEXAS MOUNTED RANGERS

Captain Isaac W. Johnson (July 7–October 20, 1849)
1st Lieutenant R. E. Sutton, Commanding (October 20, 1849–January 7, 1850)
*Ranging District*: Between the San Antonio and Nueces Rivers with headquarters at camp near Goliad
  *Company operated under the supervision of Gov. P. H. Bell*

### TEXAS MOUNTED VOLUNTEERS

Captain Henry E. McCulloch (August 1849–?)
*Ranging District*: Between Goliad and Corpus Christi
  *Company mustered into service as U.S. Volunteers and operated under the orders of Bvt. MG G. M. Brooke, CG of 8th Military District?*

### TEXAS MOUNTED VOLUNTEERS

Captain John J. Grumbles (August 20, 1849–February 26, 1850)
Captain John J. Grumbles (March 2–September 2, 1850)
*Ranging District*: Nueces Strip with headquarters near the Agua Dulce (Sweetwater) River
  *Company mustered into service as U.S. Volunteers and operated under the orders of Bvt. MG G. M. Brooke, CG of 8th Military District*

### FORD'S "OLD RANGER COMPANY"

Captain John S. "Rip" Ford (August 23, 1849–September 23, 1851)
*Ranging District*: Nueces Strip with headquarters at Kinney's Ranch and Trading Post (August 1849), Camp San Antonio Viejo (January 1850), and Los Ojuelos near Laredo (July 1850)

*Company mustered into service as U.S. Volunteers and operated under the orders of Bvt. MG G. M. Brooke, CG of 8th Military District*

## Texas Mounted Volunteers
Captain Jerome B. McCown (October 1849)
*Ranging District*: Medina River country with headquarters near Castroville; Between Leona River and Rio Grande

## Hill's Company
Captain Benjamin F. Hill (January 1850)

## Smith's Company
Captain J. M. Smith (January 1850)

## Robert's Company
Captain Jacob Roberts (January 1850)

## Sutton's Company
Captain John S. Sutton (January 1850)

## Ross' Company
Captain Shapley P. Ross (January 1850)

## Blackwell's Company
Captain Charles Blackwell (January 1850)

## Texas Mounted Volunteers
Captain William A. A. "Bigfoot" Wallace (March 6–September 1850)
*Ranging District*: Nueces Strip
*Company mustered into service as U.S. Volunteers and operated under the orders of Bvt. MG G. M. Brooke, CG of 8th Military District*

## Bagby's Company
Captain James D. Bagby (September 1850)
*Ranging District*: Goliad County

## Texas Mounted Volunteers
Captain Henry E. McCulloch (November 5, 1850–November 4, 1851)
*Ranging District*: Nueces Strip with headquarters at Camp Oakes near Fort Merrill (November 1850); Between the Upper Nueces and the Colorado Rivers with headquarters at Pecan Camp near Fort Martin Scott (June 1851)
*Company mustered into service as U.S. Volunteers and operated under the orders of Bvt. MG G. M. Brooke and Bvt. MG P. F. Smith, CG's of 8th Military District*

## Texas Mounted Volunteers
Captain William A. A. "Bigfoot" Wallace (March 23–May 1851)
*Ranging District*: Leona River country with headquarters at Fort Inge
*Company mustered into service as U.S. Volunteers and operated under the orders of Bvt. MG G. M. Brooke and Bvt. MG P. F. Smith, CG's of 8th Military District*

## Texas Mounted Volunteers/Texas Volunteer Rangers
Captain Owen Shaw (August 18, 1852–February 17, 1853)
*Ranging District*: Lower Rio Grande Valley with headquarters at Camp Bee near Laredo (August 1852), camp on Sauz (Saos) Creek (October 1852), and Camp San Francisco near Laredo (November 1852)
*Company operated under the supervision of Gov. P. H. Bell*

## Texas Mounted Volunteers
Captain Gideon K. "Legs" Lewis (September 14, 1852–March 13, 1853)
*Ranging District*: Lower Rio Grande Valley with headquarters at Brownsville
   *Company operated under the supervision of Gov. P. H. Bell*

## Texas Mounted Volunteers
Captain Henry Clay Davis (September 21–December 12, 1852?)
*Ranging District*: Lower Rio Grande Valley with headquarters at Camp Charco del Monte near Rio Grande City
   *Company operated under the supervision of Gov. P. H. Bell*

## Company A, Texas Mounted Volunteers
Captain Giles S. Boggess (November 2, 1854–March 22, 1855)
*Headquarters*: Fort Chadbourne
   *Company mustered into service as U.S. Volunteers and operated under the supervision of Bvt. Col. C. A. Waite, 5th Infantry (December 23, 1854–March 2, 1855)*

## Company B, Texas Mounted Volunteers
Captain John G. Walker (November 2, 1854–March 31, 1855)
*Headquarters*: Fort Clark
   *Company mustered into service as U.S. Volunteers and operated under the supervision of Bvt. Col. C. A. Waite, 5th Infantry (December 9, 1854–April 2, 1855)*

## Company C, Texas Mounted Volunteers
Captain William R. Henry (November 2, 1854–March 31, 1855)
*Ranging District*: From Rio Grande to the head of the Guadalupe River with headquarters at Fort Clark
   *Company operated under the personal orders of Capt. J. G. Walker and mustered into service as U.S. Volunteers under the supervision of Bvt. Col. C. A. Waite, 5th Infantry (November 29, 1854–April 4, 1855)*

## Company D, Texas Mounted Volunteers
Captain William F. Fitzhugh (November 2, 1854–February 2, 1855)
*Headquarters*: Fort Chadbourne
   *Company operated under the personal orders of Capt. G. S. Boggess and mustered into service as U.S. Volunteers under the supervision of Bvt. Col. C. A. Waite, 5th Infantry (December 24, 1854–March 23, 1855)*

## Company E, Texas Mounted Volunteers
Captain Charles E. Travis (November 2–December 1, 1854)
Captain Charles E. Travis (December 9, 1854–April 1, 1855)
*Headquarters*: Fort Clark
   *Company operated under the personal orders of Capt. J. G. Walker and mustered into service as U.S. Volunteers under the supervision of Bvt. Col. C. A. Waite, 5th Infantry (December 9, 1854–April 1, 1855)*

## Company F, Texas Mounted Volunteers
Captain Patrick H. Rogers (November 8–December 22, 1854)
Captain Patrick H. Rogers (December 24, 1854–March 21, 1855)
*Headquarters*: Fort Clark
   *Company operated under the personal orders of Capt. J. G. Walker and mustered into service as U.S. Volunteers under the supervision of Bvt. Col. C. A. Waite, 5th Infantry (December 24, 1854–March 21, 1855)*

### Texas Rangers/Mounted Rangers
Captain James H. Callahan (July 20–October 19, 1855)
*Ranging District*: Bexar, Medina, Gillespie, and Comal Counties with headquarters at camp near the Blanco River (July 1855) and camp near Bandera (September 1855)
  Company operated under the supervision of Gov. E. M. Pease and attached to the Callahan Expedition (September 15–October 15, 1855)

### Texas Mounted Rangers
Captain Giles S. Boggess (July 20, 1855–March 22, 1856)
  Company operated under the supervision of Gov. E. M. Pease

### Mounted Men/Rangers
Captain Levi English (August 6–November 13, 1855)
*Ranging District*: Western frontier
  Company operated under the supervision of Gov. E. M. Pease

## *Callahan Expedition*

### Field & Staff
Captain James H. Callahan, Senior Captain (September 15–October 15, 1855)

### Texas Rangers/Mounted Rangers
Captain James H. Callahan (July 20–October 19, 1855)
1st Lieutenant Edward "Ed" Burleson, Jr., commanding detachment (September 26–October 15, 1855)

### Texas Rangers/Mounted Rangers
Captain William R. Henry (September 15–October 15, 1855)

### Texas Rangers/Mounted Rangers/Mounted Volunteers
Captain Nathaniel "Nat" Benton (September 15–October 15, 1855)
*Expedition Ranging District*: Rio Grande country south of Eagle Pass and Piedras Negras with Burleson's detachment at camp on the Blanco River
  Expedition operated under the unsanctioned authority of Capt. J. H. Callahan

### Texas Rangers/Mounted Rangers/Mounted Volunteers
Captain Nathaniel "Nat" Benton (October 15, 1855–January 8, 1856)
*Ranging District*: Leona River country
  Company operated under the supervision of Gov. E. M. Pease

### Texas Volunteers
Captain William Tom (October 18–November 15, 1855)
*Ranging District*: Sabinal River country with headquarters at San Antonio
  Company operated under the supervision of Gov. E. M. Pease

### Mounted Texas Rangers/Volunteers
Captain William G. Tobin (October 12–November 15, 1855)
*Headquarters*: San Antonio
  Company operated under the supervision of Gov. E. M. Pease

### Texas Mounted Volunteers
Captain William F. Fitzhugh (January 14–March 11, 1856)
*Headquarters*: McKinney
  Company operated under the supervision of Gov. E. M. Pease

### VOLUNTEER MOUNTED MINUTE MEN
Captain Reading W. Black (January 1–December 31, 1856)
*Ranging District*: Uvalde County
   *Company operated under the supervision of Gov. E. M. Pease*

### MOUNTED VOLUNTEERS/MINUTE MEN
Captain John M. Davenport (March 13, 1856–June 1, 1857)
*Ranging District*: Sabinal River country
   *Company operated under the supervision of Gov. E. M. Pease*

### TEXAS MOUNTED VOLUNTEERS
Captain William R. Henry (April 15–June 21, 1856)
*Ranging District*: From the Rio Grande to the head of the Guadalupe River with headquarters at Fort Clark
   *Company operated under the supervision of Gov. E. M. Pease*

### TEXAS MOUNTED RANGERS/VOLUNTEERS
Captain John W. Sansom (April 16–July 16, 1856)
*Ranging District*: Curey's Creek and Upper Blanco, Guadalupe, and Pedernale Rivers with headquarters at Middle Town
   *Company operated under the supervision of Gov. E. M. Pease*

### TEXAS MOUNTED MILITIA/MOUNTED VOLUNTEERS
Captain Governeur H. Nelson (October 10–December 28, 1857)
*Ranging District*: Karnes County
   *Company operated under the supervision of Gov. E. M. Pease and Gov. H. R. Runnels*

### TEXAS MOUNTED VOLUNTEERS
Lieutenant John H. Conner, Commanding (December 2, 1857–March 2, 1858)
*Ranging District*: Brown and San Saba Counties with headquarters at San Saba
   *Company operated under the supervision of Gov. E. M. Pease and Gov. H. R. Runnels*

### TEXAS MOUNTED RANGERS
Lieutenant Thomas K. Carmack, Commanding (December 14, 1857–March 14, 1858)
*Ranging District*: Erath and Palo Pinto Counties
   *Company operated under the supervision of Gov. E. M. Pease and Gov H. R. Runnels*

### TEXAS MOUNTED VOLUNTEERS
Lieutenant Levi English, Commanding (December 14, 1857–March 14, 1858)
*Ranging District*: Bexar County
   *Company operated under the supervision of Gov. E. M. Pease and Gov. H. R. Runnels*

### TEXAS MOUNTED VOLUNTEERS/MOUNTED MEN
Lieutenant John Seaborn Hodges, Commanding (December 14, 1857–March 14, 1858)
*Ranging District*: Upper Blanco and Guadalupe Rivers country
   *Company operated under the supervision of Gov. E. M. Pease and Gov. H. R. Runnels*

### TEXAS MOUNTED RANGERS/MOUNTED MEN
Lieutenant Thomas C. Frost, Commanding (December 21, 1857–March 21, 1858)
*Ranging District*: Comanche and Coryell Counties with headquarters at Cora and detachment at camp on Ramsey's Creek
   *Company operated under the supervision of Gov. E. M. Pease and Gov. H. R. Runnels*

## Antelope Hills Expedition

### FIELD & STAFF

Senior Captain John S. "Rip" Ford (January 28–August 5, 1858)
  *Capt. Ford appointed commander of all State troops in service*
Doctor Powhatan Jordan, Surgeon

### TEXAS RANGERS

Senior Captain John S. "Rip" Ford (February 8–August 5, 1858)
2nd Lieutenant William A. Pitts, commanding right wing detachment (May 12, 1858)

### TEXAS RANGERS (DETACHMENT)

2nd Lieutenant Allison Nelson, Commanding (January 10–July 10, 1858)
  *Commanded left wing detachment (May 12, 1858)*

### TEXAS RANGERS (DETACHMENT)

Lieutenant James H. Tankersly, Commanding (February 23–August 23, 1858)

### TEXAS RANGERS (DETACHMENT)

Lieutenant William G. Preston, Commanding (April 30–June 30, 1858)

### BRAZOS RESERVATION COMPANY

Captain Shapley P. Ross, Indian Agent (April 22–May 21, 1858)
Jim Linney, captain of the Shawnees and Delawares (April 22–May 21, 1858)
Nid-e-wats, captain of the Tawakonis (April 22–May 21, 1858)
Plácido (Ha-shu-ka-na), chief of the Tonkawas (April 22–May 21, 1858)
Jim Pockmark, captain of the Caddos and Anadarkos (April 22–May 21, 1858)
Shot Arm (Ah-qua-quash), chief of the Wacos (April 22–May 21, 1858)
*Expedition Ranging District*: Brown, Coleman, Palo Pinto, Comanche, Buchanan (present Stephens), and Eastland Counties to the Canadian River country with headquarters at Camp Brown (February 1858) and Camp Runnels (April 1858)
  *Expedition operated under the supervision of Gov. H. R. Runnels (April 22–May 21, 1858)*

### TEXAS MOUNTED RANGERS

Lieutenant William N. P. Marlin, Commanding (February 24–November 15, 1858)
*Ranging District*: Between the Brazos Agency and the Comanche Reserve with headquarters at the Brazos Agency
  *Company operated under the supervision of Gov. H. R. Runnels*

### TEXAS RANGERS/MOUNTED VOLUNTEERS

Lieutenant John Williams, Commanding (May 24, 1858–August 16, 1859)
Sergeant David C. Cowan, commanding detachment (May 24–July 24, 1858)
*Ranging District*: San Saba and Llano Counties with headquarters at San Saba and Cowan's detachment at camp on the "Gold Hunters Trail" near Richland Creek
  *Company operated under the supervision of Gov. H. R. Runnels*

### MOUNTED VOLUNTEERS/1ST AND 2ND DETACHMENTS OF TEXAS MOUNTED RANGERS

Captain James Bourland (October 28, 1858–January 28, 1859)
Captain James Bourland (January 28–April 28, 1859)
*Ranging District*: Between the Trinity and Red Rivers with headquarters at Gainesville
  *Company operated under the supervision of Gov. H. R. Runnels*

## Texas Rangers

Captain John S. "Rip" Ford (November 10, 1858–May 10, 1859)
Orderly Sergeant Sam G. Fiddler, commanding detachment (November 10, 1858–May 10, 1859)
*Ranging District*: Comanche, Buchanan (present Stephens), and Palo Pinto Counties to the Wichita Mountains with headquarters at Camp Leon
   *Company operated under the supervision of Gov. H. R. Runnels*

## Texas/Mounted Rangers

Captain John H. Conner (December 20, 1858–June 10, 1859)
   *Company operated under the supervision of Gov. H. R. Runnels*

## Uvalde County Minute Company

Captain James B. Davenport (February 10–May 17, 1859)
Captain James B. Davenport (October 17, 1859–?)
*Ranging District*: Sabinal and Frio Rivers country with headquarters at Uvalde
   *Company operated under the supervision of Gov. H. R. Runnels*

## Texas Mounted Rangers

Lieutenant William N. P. Marlin, Commanding (February 24–April 4, 1859)
*Ranging District*: Between Brazos Agency and the Comanche Reserve with headquarters at Camp Runnels
   *Company operated under the supervision of Gov. H. R. Runnels*

## Texas Mounted Rangers/Texas Troops/State Troops

Captain John Henry Brown (March 29–May 17, 1859)
*Ranging District*: Bell County with headquarters at Belton
   *Company operated under the supervision of Gov. H. R. Runnels*

## Texas Rangers

Captain William R. Henry (June 19–August 18, 1859)
*Ranging District*: Between the Rio Grande and Guadalupe River
   *Company operated under the supervision of Gov. H. R. Runnels*

## Texas Mounted Rangers/Texas Troops/State Troops

Captain John Henry Brown (June 28–September 12, 1859)
1st Lieutenant J. W. Nowlin, commanding first detachment (July 4–September 1, 1859)
1st Lieutenant Wilson W. White, commanding second detachment (July 4–September 4, 1859)
*Ranging District*: Brazos and Comanche Reservations with headquarters at camp near Caddo Spring
   *Company operated under the supervision of G. B. Erath's Board of Peace Commissioners*

## Lampasas Guards

Captain Hillary Ryan (July 4, 1859–?)
*Ranging District*: Lampasas County

## Texas Mounted Rangers/Kerr County Volunteers

Captain John W. Sansom (August 31–November 30, 1859)
*Ranging District*: Upper Blanco and Guadalupe Rivers country with headquarters at Camy's Creek
   *Company operated under the supervision of Gov. H. R. Runnels*

#### UVALDE RANGERS
Captain Thomas J. Hale (October 1859)
*Ranging District*: Uvalde and Medina Counties with headquarters at Uvalde
  *Company operated under the supervision of Gov. H. R. Runnels*

#### TEXAS RANGERS
Captain John Donelson (November 5–December 10, 1859)
*Ranging District*: Lower Rio Grande Valley with headquarters at Brownsville
  *Company operated under the supervision of Gov. H. R. Runnels*

#### TEXAS RANGERS
Captain Henry W. Berry (November 10–December 20, 1859)
*Ranging District*: Lower Rio Grande Valley with headquarters at Brownsville
  *Company operated under the supervision of Gov. H. R. Runnels*

## *Rio Grande Expedition*

#### HEADQUARTERS
Captain William G. Tobin (October 19–November 17, 1859)
Major John S. "Rip" Ford (November 17, 1859–January 1, 1860)
  *Maj. Ford appointed commander of all State forces on the Rio Grande*
Lieutenant Colin D. McRae, Adjutant (November 25–December 30, 1859)
1st Lieutenant Arthur Pue, Quartermaster (October 19–December 30, 1859)
Doctor Powhatan Jordan, Acting Surgeon (October 19–December 30, 1859)
Quartermaster Sergeant John M. Smith (?–January 1, 1860)

#### TEXAS MOUNTED VOLUNTEERS
Captain William G. Tobin (October 18, 1859–January 1, 1860)

#### TEXAS MOUNTED VOLUNTEERS
Captain G. J. Hampton (November 12, 1859–January 1, 1860)

#### TEXAS MOUNTED VOLUNTEERS
Captain Andrew Herron (November 18, 1859–January 1, 1860)

#### TEXAS RANGERS/VOLUNTEERS
Lieutenant Joseph Walker, Commanding (November 30, 1859–January 20, 1860)

## *{1st} Battalion of Texas Mounted Volunteers*

#### FIELD & STAFF
Major William G. Tobin (January 1–February 10, 1860)
Lieutenant Colin D. McRae, Adjutant (January 1–February 10, 1860)
G. J. Hampton, Quartermaster (December 30, 1859–February 10, 1860)
Doctor Powhatan Jordan, Surgeon (December 30, 1859–February 10, 1860)
Doctor C. R. Combs, Assistant Surgeon (December 30, 1859–February 10, 1860)
Quartermaster Sergeant _____ Harknep

#### TEXAS MOUNTED VOLUNTEERS
Captain John Littleton (January 1–15, 1860)
Major William G. Tobin (January 15–February 10, 1860)

#### MOUNTED VOLUNTEERS
Captain Peter Tumlinson (November 12, 1859–January 20, 1860)

*Expedition Ranging District*: Lower Rio Grande Valley with headquarters at Brownsville and Rio Grande City
    *Expedition operated under the supervision of Gov. H. R. Runnels and Gov. S. Houston*

### DETACHED MOUNTED VOLUNTEERS/TEXAS RANGERS/SPY COMPANY
Orderly Sergeant Alexander C. Hill (December 30, 1859–February 1, 1860)
*Ranging District*: Lower Rio Grande Valley with headquarters at Brownsville
    *Company operated under the personal orders of Gov. S. Houston*

## Rio Grande Squadron

### FIELD & STAFF
Captain John S. "Rip" Ford, Senior Captain (January 20–May 1, 1860)
1st Lieutenant Arthur Pue, Adjutant (February 14–May 16, 1860)
3rd Lieutenant William Howard, Acting Quartermaster (January 20–May 17, 1860)
Doctor John T. Eldridge, Surgeon
    *Listed as serving twenty-six days*
Sergeant-Major James H. Fry (January 20–May 17, 1860)
Quartermaster Sergeant Frank L. Estrange (January 20–May 17, 1860)

### A COMPANY
Captain John S. "Rip" Ford (January 20–May 17, 1860)

### B COMPANY
Captain John Littleton (February 1–May 1, 1860)
*Squadron Ranging District*: Lower Rio Grande Valley with headquarters at Brownsville
    *Squadron operated under the orders of Maj. S. P. Heintzelman, 1st U.S. Infantry, CO of Fort Brown*

### 1ST COMPANY, TEXAS RANGERS/MOUNTED VOLUNTEERS
Captain William C. Dalrymple (January 14–October 13, 1860)
2nd Lieutenant Curtis Mays, commanding detachment (March–August 1860)
*Ranging District*: Young and Cooke Counties between Fish Creek and Big Wichita River with headquarters at Camp Wichita near Liberty Hill and Mays' detachment at camp on Salt Creek (January 1860); Between Red and Canadian Rivers with headquarters at Camp Radziminski (June 1860); Young and Cooke County between Fish Creek and Big Wichita River with headquarters at Camp Wichita near Liberty Hill (August 1860)
    *Company operated under the personal orders of Gov. S. Houston and attached to Col. M. T. Johnson's Mounted Ranger Regiment (May 16–August 20, 1860)*

### RANGERS
Captain H. A. Hamner (January 14, 1860–April 13, 1861)
*Ranging District*: Wise, Parker, Young, Montague, and Jack Counties with headquarters at Jacksboro
    *Company operated under the personal orders of Gov. S. Houston*

### 3RD COMPANY, TEXAS/MOUNTED RANGERS
Captain John H. Conner, Commanding (January 20–May 8, 1860)
1st Lieutenant Washington Hammett, commanding detachment
*Ranging District*: San Saba, Llano, Mason, McCulloch, and Brown Counties with headquarters at Camp Cave and Hammett's detachment at Camp Giles
    *Company operated under the supervision of Gov. S. Houston and the personal orders of Col. M. T. Johnson*

### 2ND COMPANY, TEXAS RANGERS

Captain Edward "Ed" Burleson, Jr. (January 30–September 7, 1860)
*Ranging District*: Nueces River country with headquarters at Camp Blanco (January 1860); Coleman and San Saba Counties with headquarters at Beaver Camp on Home Creek (February 1860); Between Red and Canadian Rivers with headquarters at Camp Radziminski (May 1860); Coleman and San Saba Counties with headquarters at Beaver Camp on Home Creek (August 1860)
*Company operated under the personal orders of Gov. S. Houston and attached to Col. M. T. Johnson's Mounted Ranger Regiment (May 28–July 30, 1860)*

### WISE COUNTY MINUTE MEN

Lieutenant George Isbell, Commanding (?–June 1860)
Ranging District: Wise County
*Company operated under the supervision of the Chief Justice of Wise County*

### MEDINA COUNTY MINUTE MEN

Lieutenant William M. Watkins, Commanding (?–August 12, 1860)
Ranging District: Medina County
*Company operated under the supervision of the Chief Justice of Medina County*

### KERR COUNTY MINUTE MEN

Lieutenant E. A. McFadden, Commanding (?–June 1860)
*Ranging District*: Kerr County
*Company operated under the supervision of the Chief Justice of Kerr County*

### BURNET COUNTY MINUTE MEN

Lieutenant William O'Hair, Commanding (?–June 1860)
*Ranging District*: Burnet County
*Company operated under the supervision of the Chief Justice of Burnet County*

### BELL COUNTY TEXAS RANGERS

1st Lieutenant Robert M. White, Commanding (February 20–June 20, 1860)
*Ranging District*: Hamilton, Comanche, Brown, and Llano Counties with headquarters at Camp Houston
*Company operated under the personal orders of Gov S. Houston*

### BOSQUE COUNTY RANGERS/MOUNTED VOLUNTEERS

Lieutenant Dixon Walker, Commanding (February 25–May 18, 1860)
*Ranging District*: Erath and Bosque Counties with headquarters at camp on Flat Creek near Camp Corner
*Company operated under the personal orders of Gov S. Houston*

### MOUNTED VOLUNTEERS/MOUNTED RANGERS

1st Lieutenant John Salmon, Commanding (February 28–May 21, 1860)
2nd Sergeant John P. Perry, commanding detachment (April 12–May 12, 1860)
Ranging District: Erath County with headquarters at camp on North Palo Pinto Creek and Perry's detachment at camp on Leon River
*Company operated under the personal orders of Gov S. Houston*

### SAN SABA COUNTY MINUTE MEN

Lieutenant William Riley Wood, Commanding (March 5–June 4, 1860)
*Ranging District*: San Saba County with headquarters at San Saba
*Company operated under the supervision of the Chief Justice of San Saba County*

#### Bosque County Minute Men/Texas Rangers (Detachment)
Lieutenant Allison Nelson, Commanding (March 12–May 18, 1860)
*Ranging District*: Bosque County
    Company operated under the supervision of the Chief Justice of Bosque County

#### Coryell County Minute Men (Detachment)
Lieutenant F. W. Fauntleroy, Commanding (March 16–June 16, 1860)
*Ranging District*: Coryell County
    Company operated under the supervision of the Chief Justice of Coryell County

## *Mounted Rangers*

#### Field & Staff
Colonel Middleton T. Johnson (March 17, 1860–January 1, 1861)
    *Col. Johnson appointed commander of all state troops on the northwestern frontier*
Lieutenant-Colonel Joseph M. Smith, Acting Commander (June 5–July 12, 1860)
Lieutenant-Colonel Joseph M. Smith (May 15–October 20, 1860)
Major William F. Fitzhugh (May 15–October 25, 1860)
Lieutenant Richard Ward, Adjutant (May 1–August 20, 1860)
1st Lieutenant B. D. Chenowerth, Adjutant (August 20–September 23, 1860)
2nd Lieutenant William L. Chalmers, Quartermaster (April 14, 1860–January 1, 1861)
Doctor C. M. Peak, Surgeon (April 21–June 5, 1860)
Doctor James H. Swindells, Surgeon (June 5–November 4, 1860)
Sergeant-Major James A. DeCourcy (June 1–October 25, 1860)
Quartermaster Sergeant Alexander Johnston (May 1, 1860–January 1, 1861)

#### McLennan County Rangers
Captain Joseph M. Smith (April 2–May 15, 1860)
Captain Lawrence Sullivan "Sul" Ross (May 18–September 7, 1860)

#### Mounted Rangers/Texas Rangers/Dallas Company
Captain Nicholas H. Darnell (April 14–August 13, 1860)
    *Company attached to regiment (May 16–July 30, 1860)*

#### Texas {Mounted} Rangers
Captain William M. Woods (April 10–October 16, 1860)

#### Texas Mounted Rangers
Captain William F. Fitzhugh (April 14–May 15, 1860)
Captain Gabe S. Fitzhugh (May 15–October 25, 1860)

#### Texas Mounted Rangers/Fort Worth Company
Captain Thomas J. Johnson (April 21–November 10, 1860)

#### Mounted Volunteers/Texas Rangers
Captain William C. Dalrymple (January 14–October 13, 1860)
    *Company attached to regiment (May 16–July 30, 1860)*

#### Texas Rangers
Captain Edward "Ed" Burleson, Jr. (January 30–September 7, 1860)
    *Company attached to regiment (May 28–July 30, 1860)*

#### "Indian Spy Company"
Captain Peter F. Ross (April 6–October 16, 1860)

Chief Plácido (Ha-shu-ka-na), commanding Tonkawa spies (July 1–August 26, 1860)
  *Company attached to regiment (June 1–October 2, 1860)*
*Regimental Ranging District*: From the Clear Fork of the Brazos River to the Canadian River with headquarters at Johnson's Station (March 1860), Fort Belknap (May 1860), Camp Radziminski, Indian Territory (June 1860), Camp Wichita at the Old Wichita Agency, Indian Territory (June 1860), Camp Louise (September 1860), and Fort Belknap (October 1860)
  *Regiment mustered into State service (May 18, 1860), operated under the personal orders of Gov. S. Houston for the Johnson Expedition (May 23–August 4, 1860), and disbanded (August 26, 1860)*

### BELL COUNTY MINUTE MEN/RANGER COMPANY
Lieutenant S. G. Davidson, Commanding (March 20–April 14, 1860)
*Ranging District*: Bell County
  *Company operated under the supervision of the Chief Justice of Bell County*

### MOUNTED VOLUNTEERS
Captain Peter Tumlinson (March 20–June 16, 1860)
*Ranging District*: Sabinal, Uvalde, and Blanco Counties with headquarters at Sabinal
  *Company operated under the personal orders of Gov. S. Houston*

### COMANCHE COUNTY MINUTE MEN/ TEXAS MOUNTED RANGERS (DETACHMENT)
Lieutenant Leonidas "Lon" Price, Commanding (March 20–September 17, 1860)
*Ranging District*: Comanche County with headquarters at Camp Carnes
  *Company operated under the supervision of the Chief Justice of Comanche County*

### HAMILTON COUNTY MINUTE MEN
Lieutenant Frederick B. Gentry, Commanding (March 20–June 21, 1860)
*Ranging District*: Hamilton County
  *Company operated under the supervision of the Chief Justice of Hamilton County*

### LAMPASAS COUNTY MINUTE MEN (DETACHMENT)
Lieutenant Moses Hughes, Commanding (March 21–June 24, 1860)
*Ranging District*: Lampasas County with headquarters at camp near Lampasas
  *Company operated under the supervision of the Chief Justice of Lampasas County*

### GILLESPIE COUNTY MINUTE MEN/DETACHED MOUNTED RANGERS
Lieutenant Erasmus Frandtzen, Commanding (March 24–June 19, 1860)
*Ranging District*: Gillespie County
  *Company operated under the supervision of the Chief Justice of Gillespie County*

### PALO PINTO COUNTY MINUTE COMPANY
Lieutenant Stephen F. Jones, Commanding (March 26–August 29, 1860)
*Ranging District*: Palo Pinto County
  *Company operated under the supervision of the Chief Justice of Palo Pinto County*

### ERATH COUNTY MINUTE MEN/RANGER COMPANY
1st Lieutenant John C. Lowe, Commanding (March 26–December 24, 1860)
*Ranging District*: Erath County with headquarters at Stephenville
  *Company operated under the supervision of the Chief Justice of Erath County*

### YOUNG COUNTY MINUTE MEN (DETACHMENT)
Lieutenant John H. Cochran, Commanding (March 27–May 27, 1860)
*Ranging District*: Young County
  *Company operated under the supervision of the Chief Justice of Young County*

### LLANO COUNTY MINUTE MEN
Lieutenant Gideon P. Cowan, Commanding (March 27–July 13, 1860)
*Ranging District*: Llano County with headquarters at Camp Houston
*Company operated under the supervision of the Chief Justice of Llano County*

### BANDERA COUNTY MINUTE DETACHMENT/TEXAS RANGERS
Lieutenant Robert Ballantyne, Commanding (March 29–July 3, 1860)
*Ranging District*: Bandera County with headquarters at Camp Wehranz
*Company operated under the supervision of the Chief Justice of Bandera County*

### UVALDE COUNTY MINUTE MEN
Lieutenant John Kennedy, Commanding (March 29–July 18, 1860)
Ranging District: Uvalde County
*Company operated under the supervision of the Chief Justice of Uvalde County*

### MASON COUNTY MINUTE DETACHMENT
Lieutenant W. Charles Lewis, Commanding (April 4–June 15, 1860)
*Ranging District*: Mason County with headquarters at Mason
*Company operated under the supervision of the Chief Justice of Mason County*

### TEXAS MOUNTED RANGERS
Captain Aaron B. Burleson (April 4–December 29, 1860)
*Ranging District*: Upper San Saba River country
*Company operated under the personal orders of Gov. S. Houston*

### BEXAR COUNTY MINUTE MEN
Lieutenant James H. Brown, Commanding (April 5–June 6, 1860)
*Ranging District*: Bexar County
*Company operated under the supervision of the Chief Justice of Bexar County*

### MONTAGUE COUNTY MINUTE COMPANY/TEXAS RANGERS
1st Lieutenant John Scanland, Commanding (April 7–June 6, 1860)
*Ranging District*: Montague County with headquarters at camp on Brushy Mound
*Company operated under the supervision of the Chief Justice of Montague County*

### BLANCO COUNTY MINUTE MEN
Lieutenant James M. Patton, Commanding (April 23–June 16, 1860)
*Ranging District*: Blanco County
*Company operated under the supervision of the Chief Justice of Blanco County*

### FRIO COUNTY MINUTE MEN
Lieutenant D. H. Ragsdale, Commanding (April 28–June 8, 1860)
*Ranging District*: Frio County
*Company operated under the supervision of the Chief Justice of Frio County*

### EASTLAND COUNTY MINUTE MEN
Lieutenant William F. Stephens, Commanding (April 30–July 18, 1860)
*Ranging District*: Eastland County
*Company operated under the supervision of the Chief Justice of Eastland County*

### TEXAS RANGERS/MOUNTED RANGERS
Captain Lawrence Sullivan "Sul" Ross (October 4, 1860–February 5, 1861)
3rd Lieutenant David L. Sublett, commanding detachment (October–December 1860)
2nd Lieutenant M. W. Summerville, commanding detachment (November 1860)

*Ranging District*: From the Clear Fork of the Brazos River to the Pease River with headquarters at Elm Creek Station near Fort Belknap
    *Company operated under the personal orders of Gov. S. Houston*

### RED RIVER RANGERS
Captain R. J. Lee (October 27, 1860–?)
*Headquarters*: Rowland

### WEBB'S COMPANY
Captain Milton Webb (December 1860–?)
*Ranging District*: Camp Cooper

### PALO PINTO COUNTY VOLUNTEERS
Captain J. J. "Jack" Cureton (December 5, 1860–?)
*Ranging District*: Pease River country with headquarters at Elm Creek Station near Fort Belknap
    *Company attached to Capt. L. S. Ross' expedition (December 1860)*

### TEXAS RANGERS
Captain Andrew J. Yount (December 8, 1860–?)

## *Texas Mounted Ranger Regiment*

### FIELD & STAFF
Colonel William C. Dalrymple (December 29, 1860–June 22, 1861)
    *Col. Dalrymple appointed to command all state troops on the northwestern frontier*
1st Lieutenant James E. McCord, Adjutant (January 7–May 10, 1861)
1st Lieutenant Jabez L. Brittain, Adjutant (May 11–June 22, 1861)
Captain Joseph Walker, Quartermaster (January 4–June 22, 1861)
Joseph D. Tarish, Commissary of Subsistence (January 20–June 22, 1861)
Doctor J. N. B. Williams, Surgeon (February 25, 1861–?)

### TEXAS MOUNTED RANGERS
Captain Aaron B. Burleson (December 29, 1860–May 9, 1861)
*Ranging District*: Upper San Saba River country

### TEXAS RANGERS
Captain Curtis Mays (January 7–June 22, 1861)
Lieutenant Charles M. Kavenaugh, commanding detachment (February 1861)
*Ranging District*: From the upper San Saba River to Pecan Bayou with headquarters at camp on Hubbard Creek and Kavenaugh's detachment at Pecan Bayou

### TEXAS MOUNTED RANGERS
Captain Thomas L. Harrison (January 10–June 22, 1861)
*Ranging District*: Stephens County with headquarters at camp on Elm Creek (January 1860); Shackelford and Throckmorton Counties with headquarters at camp on the junction of Hubbard Creek and the Clear Fork of the Brazos River (February 1861) and Camp Cooper (February 1861)

### TEXAS RANGERS
Captain Edward W. Rogers (January 28–April 6, 1861)
Captain Edward H. Moore (?–June 22, 1861)
*Ranging District*: Concho and Colorado Rivers country to the Red River with headquarters

at camp on Lost Valley Creek (February 1861), Camp Cooper (February 1861), and camp on Hubbard Creek (April 1861)

### TEXAS RANGERS

Captain David L. Sublett (February 4–May 14, 1861)
*Ranging District*: Throckmorton and Young Counties with headquarters at Elm Creek Station near Fort Belknap

### TEXAS MOUNTED RANGERS

Captain J. M. Wright (March–June 22, 1861)
*Ranging District*: Jack County with headquarters at camp in Lost Valley
*Regimental Ranging District*: Brazos, Wichita, Pease, and Colorado Rivers country with headquarters at camp on Pecan Bayou (January 1861), camps on Hubbard Creek and Old Comanche Reservation near Camp Cooper (February 1861), Camp Cooper (May 1861), and camp near Lampasas (June 1861)
    Regiment operated under the personal orders of Gov. S. Houston and Gov. E. Clark

### BOSQUE COUNTY MOUNTED VOLUNTEERS

1st Lieutenant James B. "Buck" Barry, Commanding (January 10–February 25, 1861)
*Ranging District*: Northwest frontier with headquarters at Flag Mountain on Hubbard Creek
    Company operated under the supervision of Gov S. Houston and the personal orders of Capt. L. S. Ross, and remustered into the Northern District, Provisional Army of Texas (February 25, 1861)

### RANGER COMPANY

Captain Hanna Wood (January 18–February 29, 1861)

### RANGER COMPANY

Lieutenant Christopher Columbus Slaughter, Commanding (January 19–April 23, 1861)
*Ranging District*: Palo Pinto County

# 5

# A Most Desperate Struggle: Rangers in the Civil War (1861–1865)

The conflict of the Civil War caused the Texas Rangers to sink into insignificance as a fighting force.... So much attention was given to the Confederate, and so little to the border, service that it is practically impossible to follow the activities of the so-called Texas Rangers. If the story is ever told, it will be fragmentary, and will not reveal a single character distinguished for his deeds as a Ranger during this period.

So wrote Professor Walter Webb of the rangers in the War Between the States. He was technically correct in his statements—to a point. The story is incomplete because fewer Confederate records were preserved than those of the Union, but it is not impossible to discern what happened in the course of the war. As for the "so-called Texas Rangers," one has to remember there was still no formal organization bearing that name. The men who protected the Indian frontier of Texas during the Civil War operated under the various names of Texas Mounted Rifles, the Frontier Regiment, the Border Regiment, and the Frontier Organization. Even though they were militiamen, minute men, state troops, or Confederate soldiers, they were still rangers performing the same hard service as those in decades past. Overshadowed by the conflict in the east, they gained little in the way of glory as they waged their own war. No decisive battles were fought and, indeed, the most memorable was that of Dove Creek, a dismal failure. With such limitations, no figure was able to reach the prominence in the annals of the Rangers that was enjoyed by Hays or Ford. Rather than dismiss them, one has to remember that they were asked to do what one-fourth of the United States Army had failed to do—end the threat of Indian raids in Texas.

The secession crisis that gripped the nation beginning in October 1860 spread to Austin when, on January 28, 1861, the extralegal Secession Convention met to decide the issue of removing Texas from the Union. Two days later, the convention created a Committee of Public Safety, which usurped the governor's vested military powers. The committee's mandate was to force federal troops from Texas, secure all public property, and provide frontier protection. On February 1, the convention passed an Ordinance of Secession and the legislature voted to submit the ordinance to a popular referendum on February 23. For a time, the state government and the convention pursued separate, conflicting agendas and neither communicated effectively with the other.

On February 5, the committee created three districts commanded by Henry McCulloch, Ben McCulloch, and "Rip" Ford, all of whom were appointed commissioners with the rank of colonel of cavalry in the Provisional Army of Texas. For the next three months, these officers seized military posts all along the frontier, confiscated materiel (quartermaster and commissary stores, arms and ordnance, and medical supplies) worth over $1,500,000, and peacefully secured the evacuation of 3,000 Federal troops from the state. On February 18, departmental commander Brigadier-General David E. Twiggs formally ordered the capitulation of the entire U.S. military establishment in Texas—he was subsequently dismissed for his treasonous act.

Upon learning second-hand of the secession ordinance, Colonel William Dalrymple and three of his ranger companies received the surrender of Camp Cooper in the name of the state government on February 21. Five days later, he left a small detachment at the post under Captain E. W. Rogers and commenced a month-long scout. Henry McCulloch arrived at Camp Cooper on March 7 following his captures of Camp Colorado and Fort Chadbourne. He demanded Rogers surrender the post to the Secession Convention and the captain readily obliged as his men preferred Indian fighting to garrison duty. McCulloch, with his appointment from the Committee of Public Safety, and Dalrymple, with his commission from Governor Houston, possessed equal rank and responsibility for protecting the same territory. A possible conflict between the two was avoided when Dalrymple returned from his scouting expedition and submitted to the authority of the convention. McCulloch was assigned to the overall command of the northwestern frontier and Dalrymple's men were given the sector between Camp Cooper and the Red River to patrol.

All but nineteen of the state's 122 counties ratified the Ordinance of Secession on February 23 by a vote of 46,129 to 14,697. The inability of the Federal Government to secure the borders from Indian raids and Cortina's insurrection was a major reason for the decision. On March 5, Texas formally seceded from the Union and became the seventh state to be admitted into the Confederate States of America. Although personally opposed to secession, Houston bowed to the will of the people, but he refused to swear allegiance to the Confederacy and was deposed on March 16; Lieutenant-Governor Edward Clark replaced him two days later.

After transferring responsibility for frontier protection to the rebel government, Texas was in a unique position in that no other Confederate state had to contend with an Indian menace. Richmond failed to fully appreciate the threat to distant frontier counties. Instead, the Confederate high command preferred to keep its resources along the Red River line and the Gulf coast in preparation for possible Federal invasions. The frontier was often left to fend for itself.

In the initial absence of Confederate support, the state government authorized, on February 7, 1861, one minute company not to exceed forty men for each of thirty-seven frontier counties. The minute men offered a degree of protection until they disbanded on March 1, 1862.

On March 4, Leroy Walker, Confederate Secretary of War, directed Ben McCulloch to raise a mounted rifle regiment of ten companies for frontier defense. Since McCulloch wanted a command fighting the Federals, he declined in favor of his brother, Henry, who was already leading five companies from Camp Colorado. Five additional companies were recruited in Bexar, Travis, Gonzales, Bell, Comanche, Bosque, Rusk, Burleson, and Lamar counties. By mid–April the new regiment was mustered into Confederate service as the 1st

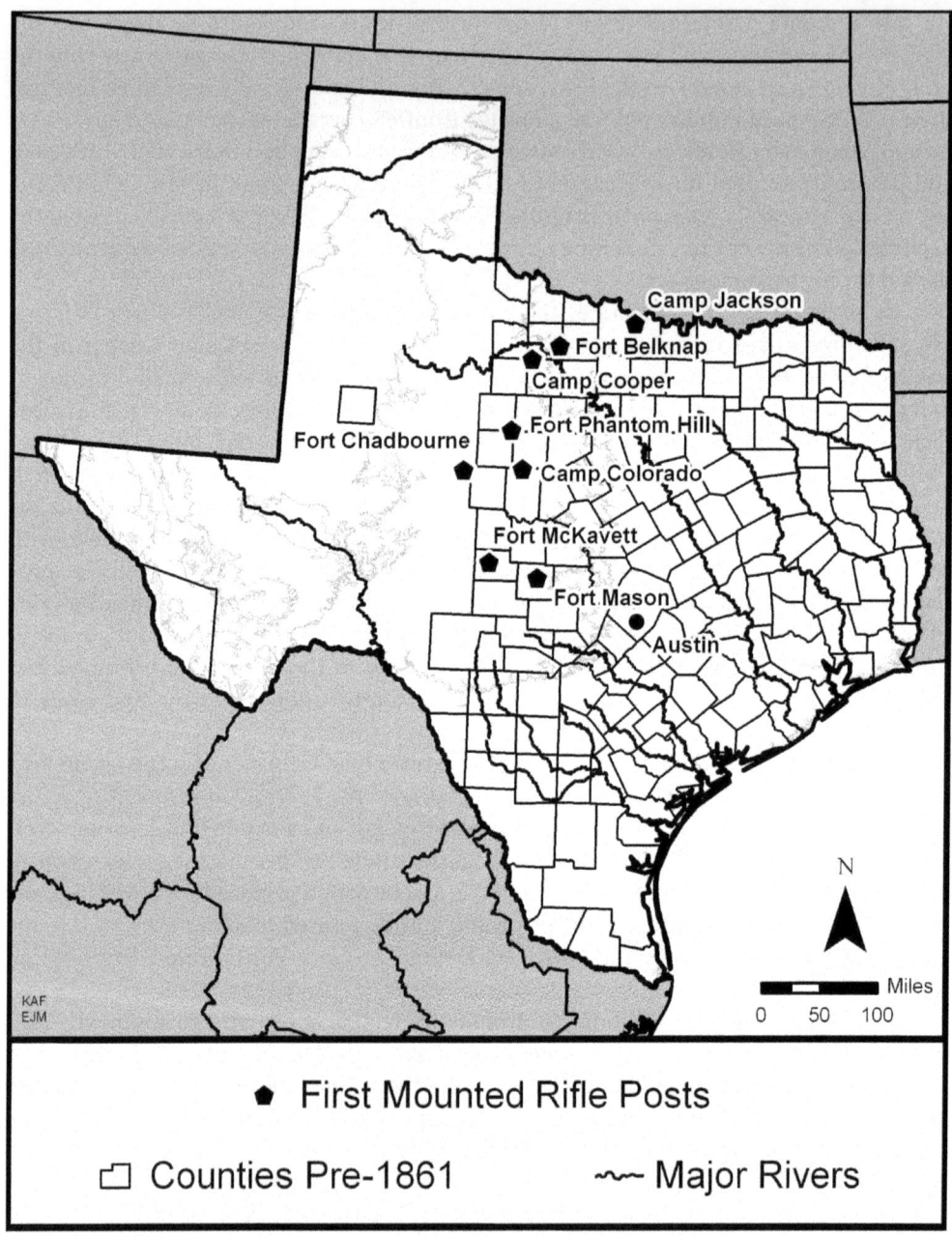

- First Mounted Rifle Posts
- ☐ Counties Pre-1861
- ～ Major Rivers

Regiment, Texas Mounted Rifles. In the election for field officers, McCulloch became colonel, Thomas C. Frost lieutenant-colonel, and Edward Burleson, Jr., major.

The regiment occupied a 400-mile line from Camp Jackson (also known as Red River Station) in Montague County to Fort Belknap in Young County, Camp Cooper in Throckmorton County, Fort Phantom Hill in Jones County, Fort Chadbourne in Cooke (present Runnels) County, Camp Colorado in Coleman (present Mills) County, Camp Concho in Tom Green County, Fort McKavett in Menard County, and Fort Mason in Gillespie (present Mason) County. Throughout the war, the most exposed portion of the frontier was from

5. A Most Desperate Struggle: Rangers in the Civil War (1861–1865) 103

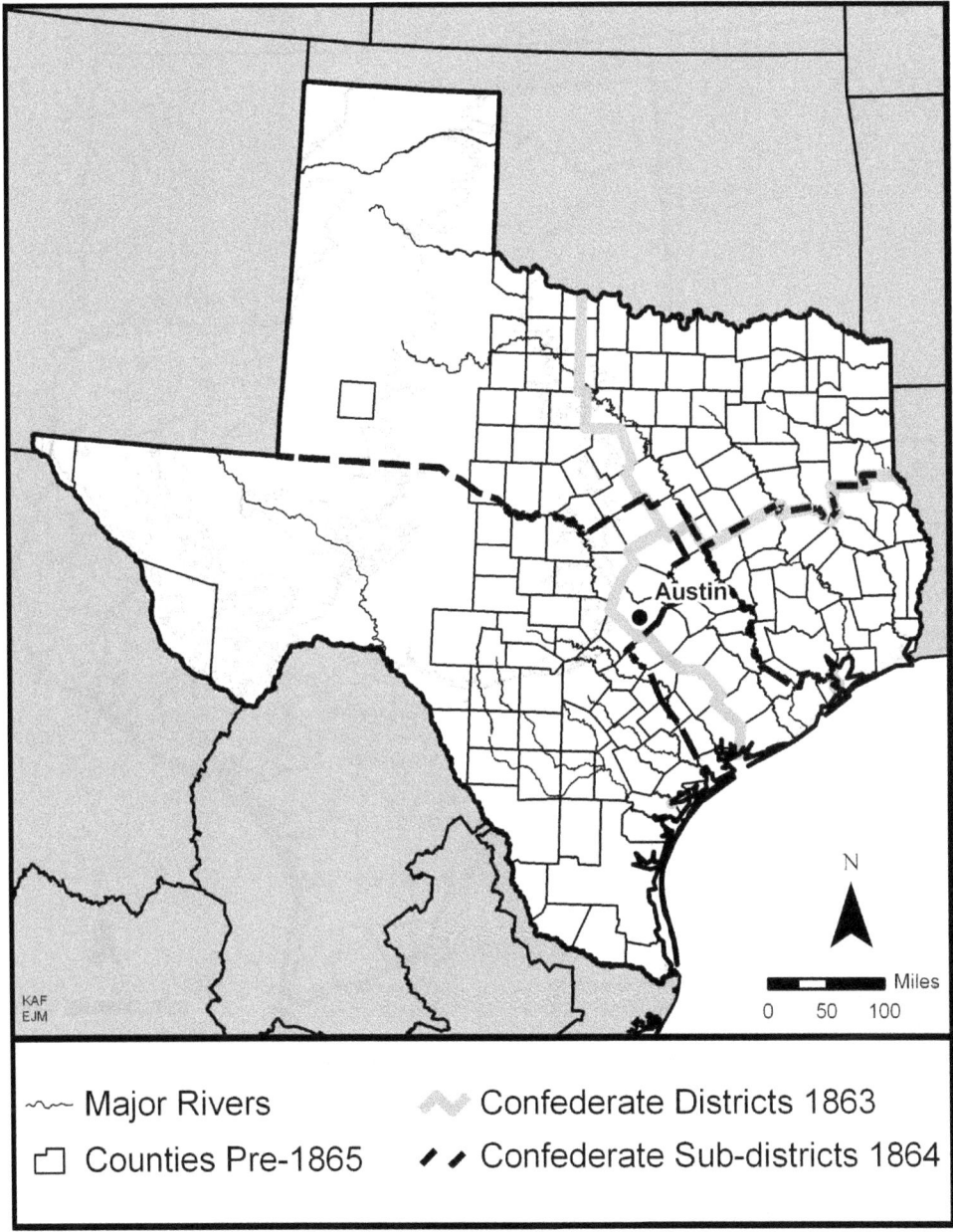

- ~~ Major Rivers
- ☐ Counties Pre-1865
- ~~ Confederate Districts 1863
- ✦✦ Confederate Sub-districts 1864

Cooke County westward through Montague County to Clay County, then southward through Young and Stephens counties to Eastland County. Fort Belknap served as the central bastion for this northwestern line of defense.

McCulloch ordered regular patrols and several expeditions that lasted for two to three weeks into hostile country northwest of the line of companies. Only a few hard-fought skirmishes were waged with no widespread raids by Indians occurring and no major engagements. The goal of the patrols was to intercept and punish raiding parties infiltrating the settlements or as they made their escape afterward. Most engagements were brief and consisted mainly of mounted charges and running fights.

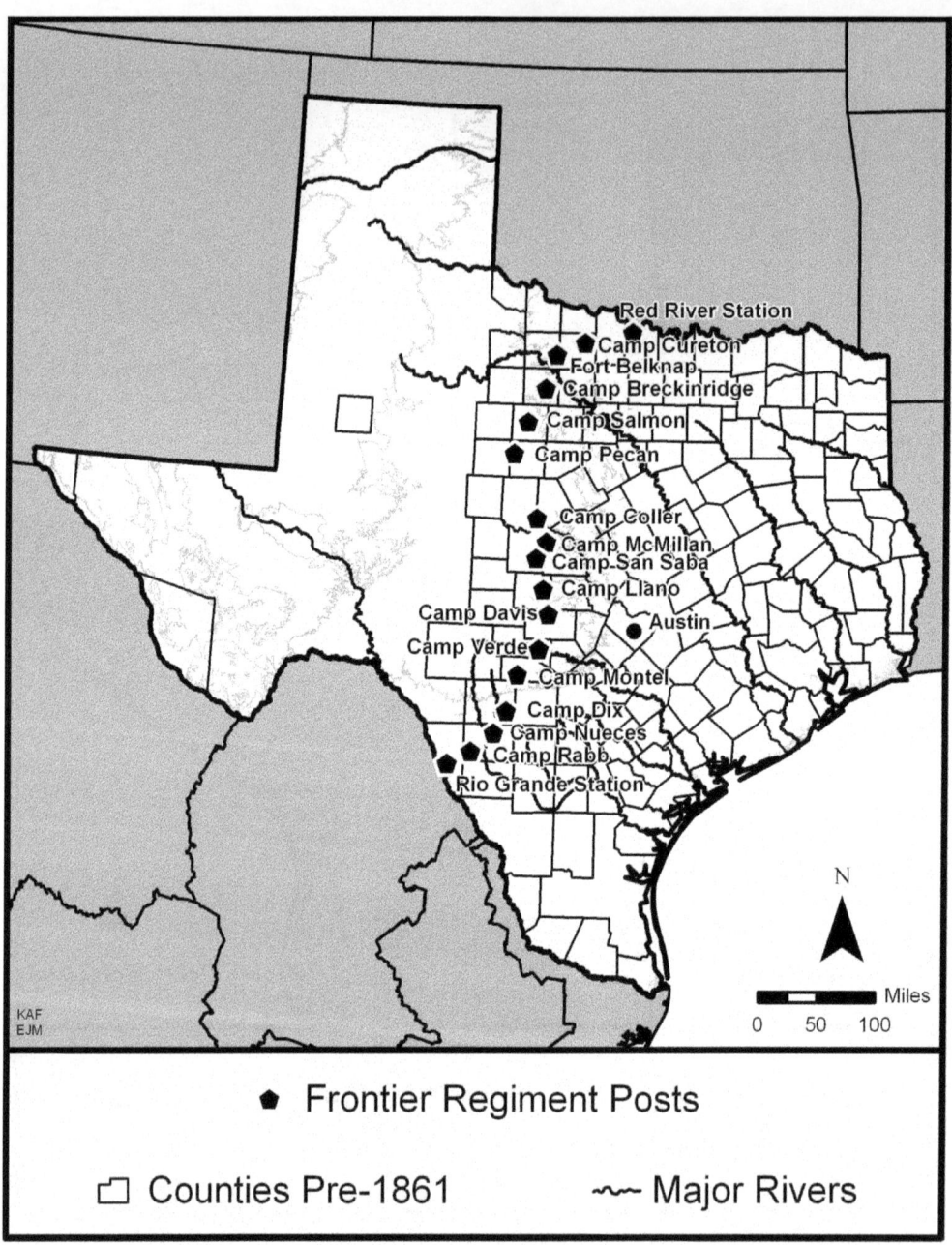

Beginning in September, McCulloch, while technically remaining regimental commander, was assigned to hold the commands of the Confederate Department of Texas, the Western Military District of Texas, and the Sub-Military District of the Rio Grande. In his absence, he named Adjutant William O. Yager and Lieutenant-Colonel Frost as acting commanders of the regiment until the expiration of enlistments in April 1862.

On December 21, 1861, the Ninth Legislature authorized the formation of the Frontier Regiment to replace the 1st Texas Mounted Rifles. The new law called for twelve-month enlistments, and enrolling officers were to raise the first company from Clay, Montague,

Cooke, and Wise counties; the second from Young, Jack, Palo Pinto, and Parker counties; the third from Stephens, Eastland, Erath, and Bosque counties; the fourth from Coryell, Hamilton, Lampasas, Comanche, and Brown counties; the fifth from San Saba, Mason, Llano, and Burnett counties; the sixth from Gillespie, Hays, and Kerr counties; the seventh from Blanco, Bandera, Medina, and Uvalde counties; the eighth from Frio, Atascosa, Live Oak, Karnes, and Bee counties; and the ninth from El Paso and Presidio counties. The tenth company was raised by the governor from McMullen, De Witt, Bexar, Lavaca, Travis, Colorado, Caldwell, Goliad, Fayette, Cameron, Gonzales, Jackson, Tarrant, Burleson, and Victoria counties. Ultimately, the counties of El Paso and Presidio were unable to meet their recruiting commitments and the regiment entered the service with just nine companies.

On January 17, 1862, the Congress in Richmond authorized the secretary of war to muster the Frontier Regiment into Confederate service. This had been the goal of Texas legislatures since the 1850s: a ranger regiment funded and equipped by the national government but under the command and control of the State. However, five days later, President Jefferson Davis vetoed the bill because of the provisions Texas had put into place. The state government wanted the Confederacy to assume the expense of maintaining the unit, but insisted the regiment never be deployed anywhere other than the frontier. Such an arrangement denied the Chief Executive his constitutional authority over troops in the service of the Confederacy. The command also did not adhere to Confederate military regulations, which stated that every regiment was to consist of ten companies. Hence, the men of the Frontier Regiment, 1,050 to 1,200 men strong, remained Texas State Troops. Austin would spend $800,000 to support the regiment in its first ten months of service.

On January 29, 1862, Governor Francis R. Lubbock appointed James M. Norris as colonel of the new regiment, Alfred T. Obenchain lieutenant-colonel, and James E. McCord major. The legislation stipulated that the companies of the Frontier Regiment "shall be stationed in detachments of not less than twenty-five men ... on the outside settlements of the frontier ... from a point on Red River to a point on the Rio Grande." Sixteen camps were established and manned by the regiment: Red River Station (or Camp Brunson) and camps Cureton in Archer County, Belknap in Young County, Breckenridge and Salmon in Stephens County, Pecan in Callahan County, Collier in Brown County, McMillin in San Saba County, San Saba in McCulloch County, Llano in Mason County, Davis in Gillespie County, Verde in Kerr County, Montel in Bandera County, Dix and Nueces in Uvalde County, and Rabb in present Maverick County.

Colonel James E. McCord, the second commander of the Frontier Regiment, had previously served in Ed Burleson's company and as aide-de-camp in Colonel William Dalrymple's regiment. Using his past Indian-fighting experience, he replaced the tactics employed by his predecessor with a more aggressive stance. He ended the war in eastern Texas. McCord Family Collection; courtesy of Michael R. Thomasson and Patricia Adkins-Rochette.

Personally unpopular and lacking experience in Indian fighting, Colonel Norris' tenure quickly proved to be contentious. He dealt with most infractions involving subaltern officers and enlisted men by employing general courts-martial rather than any type of inspirational leadership. He ordered the regiment to conduct patrols, usually of one officer and five privates, from one camp to the next at regular two-day intervals beginning on July 5. The Indians soon discerned the inherent weakness of such a rigid patrol system and quickly moved to take advantage.

Meanwhile, James Bourland, a Mexican War veteran and the provost marshal in Gainesville, was appointed commander of a cavalry battalion in the spring of 1863. The purpose of this outfit was to guard the northern border of Texas and, therefore, was often called the "Border Battalion." The area of operations for Lieutenant-Colonel Bourland encompassed Fort Arbuckle to Fort Cobb to the Wichita Mountains in Indian Territory, plus twelve Texas counties along the Red River. The Federal forces in Kansas and Indian Territory threatened invasion across the state line, and the battalion was directed to counter Union incursions, as well as the menace from renegades, hostile Indians, and deserters. In August 1863, Bourland's battalion was increased to regimental strength and became known as Bourland's Texas Cavalry Regiment, or the "Border Regiment." Two months later, Bourland was promoted to colonel.

Colonel James Bourland served as a ranger captain in the 1840's and 1850's. After the Civil War began, he was provost marshal in Cooke County and was a leading figure in the "Great Hanging" in Gainesville. In 1863, he was appointed to command a cavalry regiment on the Red River frontier and fought Indians, deserters, and renegades. Courtesy of Patricia Adkins-Rochette.

On February 11, 1863, Governor Lubbock once more attempted to transfer the Frontier Regiment to the Confederate army. In accordance with military rules and regulations, he disbanded the men and immediately reorganized them into the ten-company Mounted Regiment, Texas State Troops. Despite the change, most Texans continued to call it by its original name.

President Davis again refused to accept the regiment into Confederate service if the state government continued to insist it remain under Texas control. The Texan leadership, refusing to concede on that crucial point, continued to fund it while exploring other options.

McCord was elected colonel of the new regiment, "Buck" Barry lieutenant-colonel, and W. J. Alexander major. In addition to the original sixteen camps, the detachments of the regiment reoccupied several other posts, including Camps Cooper and Colorado and Forts Phantom Hill, Chadbourne, McKavett, Croghan, and Mason. After assuming command on March 8, Colonel McCord, well aware of the deficiencies of the patrol system, replaced it with more aggressive sweeps of company-strength or greater. He also planned several punitive expeditions into the *Comanchería*, but they were all canceled due to limited funding and manpower. By October 1863, the entire tier of Clay, Palo Pinto, Stephens,

Wise, Montague, Parker, and Jack counties had become depopulated due to the frequency of Indian raids. Unfortunately, in the minds of Confederate commanders, the Indian threat often took second-place to the problem of deserters and renegades that plagued the region.

For the first two years of the war, the Confederate District of Texas was divided into Eastern and Western sub-districts with attention given primarily to the Rio Grande line and the coast. Such an arrangement proved inadequate to administer frontier defense. To help ensure the protection of the northwestern counties, the Northern Sub-District was established on May 30, 1863, with headquarters at Bonham

The 37,000-square mile area of the new sub-district encompassed Clay, Montague, Cooke, Grayson, Fannin, Lamar, Red River, Bowie, Jack, Wise, Denton, Collin, Hunt, Delta, Hopkins, Franklin, Titus, Morris, Cass, Parker, Tarrant, Dallas, Rockwall, Kaufman, Van Zandt, Rains, Wood, Upshur, Marion, Harrison, Somervell, Johnson, Ellis, Smith, Gregg, Hill, Navarro, Henderson, Limestone, Freestone, Anderson, Cherokee, Rusk, and Panola counties; the eastern halves of Wichita, Archer, and Young counties; and Palo Pinto, Hood, Bosque, McLennan, and Falls counties east of the Brazos.

On August 29, Henry McCulloch, now a brigadier-general in the Confederate Army, was assigned to assume command. Governor Lubbock was pleased to have such an experienced officer in charge of the Indian frontier, while Major-General John B. Magruder, commanding the District of Texas, was eager to have McCulloch handle the estimated four to five thousand deserters, draft dodgers, and Unionists in the sector.

Major W. J. Alexander was a company commander in the Frontier Regiment before his promotion to major in 1863. He served mainly on the southern flank of the frontier line until part of the regiment was transferred to eastern Texas. Courtesy of the Historical Research Center, Texas Heritage Museum, Hill College, Hillsboro, TX.

Indeed, eight of the nineteen counties that had opposed secession in 1861 were located in the sub-district. The "Five Corners" area of Collin, Fannin, Hunt, and Grayson counties; the Jernigan Thicket in Hunt, Fannin, and Delta counties; and the brush country of Cooke, Wise, and Denton counties were notorious renegade havens. Over time, McCulloch would be forced to commit one-half of his entire force to the desertion and draft evasion issue. In addition, the command structure he inherited was complicated. General Magruder often stripped McCulloch of the Confederate forces assigned to him and attached them to other commands as the need arose. The sub-district contained most of the Frontier Regiment's area of operations, but they were state troops, rather than Confederate soldiers, and answered to the governor. In addition, the Border Regiment, also a state unit, was attached to the commanding general of Indian Territory until January 1864.

Beginning on December 21, 1863, the sub-district's dispositions were tested by the incursion of three hundred Comanches in what became known as the Cooke County Raid, one of the worst since the Great Comanche Raid twenty-three years earlier. The Indians crossed the Red River east of Red River Station into Montague and Cooke counties and began to murder settlers, steal horses, and plunder and burn homes in a devastating two-day rampage. Captain John T. Rowland of the Frontier Regiment and Captain Samuel P. C. Patton of the Border Regiment, plus a number of civilian volunteers, engaged the Comanches near Cincinnatus Potter's settlement, but the rangers broke and the raiders escaped. Reported losses from the raid were twelve civilians killed, seven wounded, thirteen taken captive, ten homes burned, and numerous horses stolen. McCulloch was left to determine how such a large force of raiders could penetrate the screen of rangers and strike the settlements. Later, he concluded the Comanches had attacked at just the right time and place before a planned rearrangement of the forces in the sub-district could be completed. McCulloch had Bourland's regiment transferred to his command and drew them in closer to the settlements to better coordinate with the Frontier Regiment.

The Tenth Legislature's solution to the Frontier Regiment issue, passed on December 15, 1863, was to establish the Frontier Organization of Texas State Troops and simultaneously transfer the regiment to the Confederacy, effective March 1, 1864. Governor Pendleton Murrah, the Confederate Congress, and President Davis all approved the measure. Meanwhile, the regiment's companies were reorganized into eighty-man units so that two more companies could be formed. These men were formed into the Frontier Battalion under the command of Captain Henry S. Fossett and mustered into service on March 1. Also on this day, the Frontier Regiment was assigned to the Confederate Western Sub-District, while Bourland's Border Regiment was likewise transferred to the Confederate Army and continued to serve in the Northern Sub-District.

The new Frontier Organization act defined the line regarded as the frontier and the fifty-nine organized counties bordering that line. Governor Murrah was authorized to divide these counties into three districts and designate a major of cavalry to command each one. In January 1864, Murrah appointed William Quayle to take charge of the First Frontier District headquartered in Decatur, George B. Erath the Second Frontier District headquartered in Gatesville, and James M. Hunter the Third Frontier District in Fredericksburg. The law also declared that all persons who were actual residents of the frontier counties and liable for military service were to be enrolled into mounted minute companies of twenty-five to sixty-five men. The three majors were to ensure that one-fourth of their men, on a rotating basis, were in service at any one time. By the time of the Frontier Regiment's transfer on March 1, nearly 4,000 men were enlisted in the organization and 1,000 were in the field.

Companies in the Frontier Organization usually numbered between fifty and fifty-five men, often in fifteen-man squads. The minute men were in the field for various lengths of time depending on the mission, the proximity of the enemy, and the availability of supplies, but most squads planned to be on duty for about ten days at a time. While on active service, captains were paid three dollars a day; lieutenants, two dollars and seventy-five cents; sergeants, two dollars and fifty cents; corporals, two dollars and twenty-five cents; and privates, two dollars. Like other ranger forces, they patrolled the frontier line to deter infiltrating raiders or to cut off escape routes prior to engaging them.

On February 2, Colonel McCord and Companies A, B, E, F, I, and K, Frontier Regiment were ordered to concentrate at Camp Verde, Fort Inge, and Fort Duncan prior to being redeployed to the interior to replace troops needed in Louisiana. On May 25, the four remaining companies stationed at Fort Belknap under the command of Lieutenant-Colo-

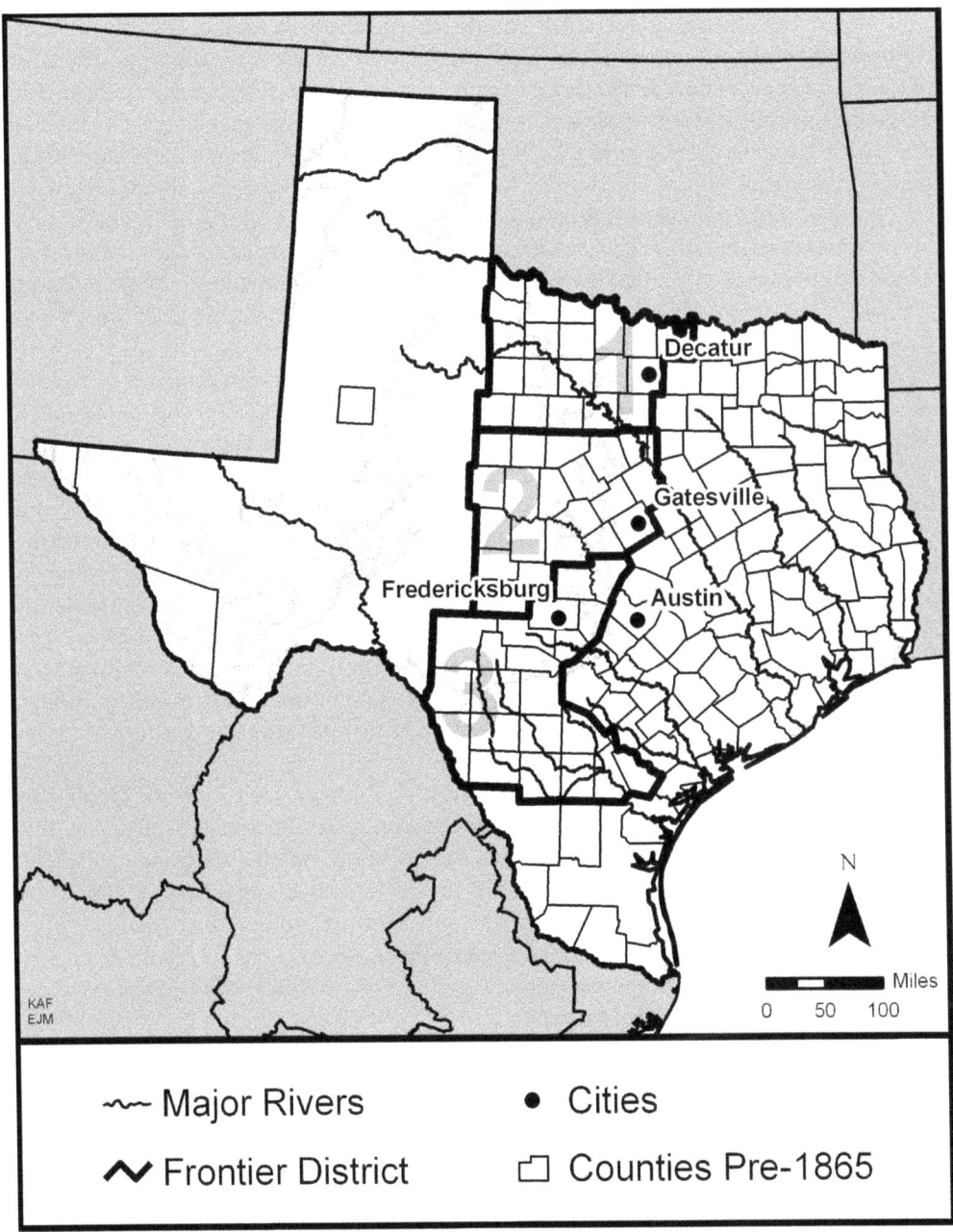

nel Barry were assigned to General McCulloch's sub-district. On August 10, Barry received orders to withdraw Companies C, D, G, and H from the Fort Belknap–Red River line and proceed to Harrisburg. He was then ordered to Hempstead on September 15. Captain Fossett's Frontier Battalion remained at Camps Colorado and San Saba.

Meanwhile, Major Hunter had grown overwhelmed in the administration of the Third Frontier District. He faced an organized resistance to the conscription laws from the local German community (five of the district's twenty counties had opposed secession), heavily-armed gangs of American renegades operating from Mexico, and a series of robberies and murders in Gillespie and Kendall counties perpetrated by members of the Frontier Regiment and his own command. The horse-stealing and murder raids committed by Lipan Apaches became secondary to the threat of rampant lawlessness. The citizens in the district lost confidence in Hunter and pleaded with the governor to make a change. On June 20, 1864, Hunter was replaced by John D. McAdoo, brigadier-general of state troops. Upon assuming command on June 23, McAdoo lost no time in rectifying the situation. He ordered that patrols would no longer operate strictly within their county lines, but would instead cover the areas and routes used by the renegades. By autumn, his men had captured or driven out most of the gangs. Although the various Confederate and state ranger commands were originally established to handle the Indian menace, all along the frontier they were forced to assume the additional (albeit informal) role of peace officers.

Lieutenant Singleton Gilbert, commanding an Eastland County company of the Second District, led twelve to sixteen rangers to a ranch near Ellison Springs on August 9. Alerted to the presence of Indian sign in the area, he encountered a party of thirty to thirty-five Indians. Three separate and differing versions recount the ensuing battle, but in the end Lieutenant Gilbert and one or two of his men were killed, three were wounded, and possibly only one Indian was wounded. Major Erath, commanding the district, commented that the Ellison Springs fight was "a most desperate struggle in which all the bravery of frontier life was brought to bear." His fine words did not take away the bitter sting of defeat, though. What did to a certain degree was when Sergeant A. D. Miller, commanding an eight-man squad of Captain J. W. Curtis' Stephens County company, discovered the very same band of raiders several days later. Without sustaining any casualties themselves, Miller's rangers killed two Indians, wounded three more, and recovered seventy-three horses, seven saddles, and a collection of blankets and bridles.

On September 24, the Northern Sub-District doubled in size to include Hardeman, Wilbarger, Foard, Knox, Baylor, Haskell, Throckmorton, Jones, Shackelford, Stephens, Taylor, Callahan, Eastland, Erath, Runnels east of the Colorado, Coleman, Brown, Comanche, Mills, and Hamilton counties, in addition to its previous territory. General McCulloch now commanded an area equal in size to Maryland and Virginia combined.

Lieutenant-Colonel Barry and his men were ordered to return to Fort Belknap on September 30, but McCord's six companies remained in eastern Texas for the duration of the war, mostly in the Central Sub-District.

Those missing men were sorely needed, as the subsequent Elm Creek Raid proved to be the worst Indian depredation of the Civil War. The raiders unknowingly chose the absolute perfect time for their foray. The Northern Sub-District was without its commander as General McCulloch had taken a two-month leave of absence a few days before. The Border Regiment's defensive line was spread thin to cover the 200-mile gap left by the absence of Barry's Frontier Regiment battalion, which would not arrive from Hempstead until November. The headquarters of the First Frontier District was experiencing a change in command as Major Quayle had resigned effective September 26 due to poor health.

After crossing the Red River and riding down the Brazos Valley during the night of October 12, the raiding party of five hundred to seven hundred Comanches and Kiowas pounced on the small settlements near Fort Belknap the next morning. The worst of the fighting occurred in the area around Elm Creek south of the Brazos. Fourteen Border Regiment rangers under Lieutenant N. Carson engaged three hundred hostiles near George Bragg's ranch. Vastly outnumbered, Carson retreated to Fort Murrah, a civilian stockade built by the order of the governor. While laying siege to the Bragg homestead, the Indian leader was killed and the raiders escaped across the Red River before State or Confederate reinforcements could reach the battlefield. The losses were assessed at five soldiers and seven civilians killed, seven women and children captured, eleven homes burned, and ten thousand head of cattle stolen. Carson reported his detachment killed seven or eight of the raiders and as many as twenty could have been killed at the Bragg ranch. Major Charles L. Roff of the Border Regiment commanded a retaliatory expedition in February 1865, but it could not bring any Indians to battle and was cut short after ten days.

On October 9, 1864, Colonel Bourland was ordered to assume command of all Confederate and state troops in Cooke, Montague, Clay, Archer, Young, Stephens, Palo Pinto, Jack, Parker, Wise, and Denton counties. Brigadier-General James W. Throckmorton succeeded Major Quayle in command of the First Frontier District on December 13. The following month Major John Henry Brown took command of the Third District and General McAdoo assumed overall coordination of the Second and Third Districts.

On December 9, Captain N. W. Gillentine of the Second District discovered the trail of more than five hundred Indians moving southward near the Clear Fork of the Brazos and old Fort Phantom Hill. He immediately sent a message to Lieutenant-Colonel Barry at Fort Belknap informing him of the find. In the report, he stated he found "92 wigwams," an early clue that the mysterious Indians were likely not Comanches or some other nomadic Plains tribe. Undeterred, he rode to Erath County to raise the alarm and gather men. Major Erath was in Austin so his senior captain, Silas Totten, took charge of the operation. Totten assembled 325 state troops from Bosque, Johnson, Comanche, Coryell, and Erath counties and received a request from Captain Fossett to rendezvous at Fort Chadbourne. Instead, he proceeded to the site of the discovery and followed the trail. This decision foreshadowed the lack of coordinated action that would haunt the participants of the coming fight.

On January 7, Totten's column rendezvoused on the Middle Concho with Captain Fossett and fifty rangers of his Frontier Battalion, Lieutenant James R. Giddens and sixty men from Companies D, G, and H of Barry's command, Captain J. J. Cureton and seventeen Stephens County minute men from the First District, and thirty Brown County militiamen commanded by Lieutenant William A. Morton. Scouts had discovered the Indian encampment on the south side of Dove Creek in present Tom Green County the previous day, but did not sufficiently reconnoiter the area. Therefore, they failed to see that the Indians were well-situated in a natural defensive position of brush and timber. The hastily-drawn battle plan called for Totten and some two hundred militiamen to charge the camp across the stream from the north, while Fossett's approximately 170 Confederates would position themselves to the southwest, drive off the horse herd, and assault the Indian position. The two commanders were later criticized for failing to adequately plan and coordinate the attack, distribute orders, form a proper battle line, scout the camp, or otherwise ascertain the identity and intentions of the Indians.

Shortly after nine o'clock on the morning of January 8, the state troops crossed Dove Creek and rushed headlong into a prepared ambush that lasted almost an hour. Battered and bloodied, they then withdrew out of range and remained inactive for the remainder of the battle. The Confederate attack met with some success at first when they easily stampeded the Indians' horses and moved to storm the camp. The opposing forces exchanged a withering fire for nearly six hours before the Texans retired. As they disengaged, Fossett's men inexplicably moved to the north side of the camp, in the face of enemy fire, and were enfiladed by a party of Indians. The Confederates were thrown into confusion and fled northward in a panic, while the Indians continued on their way southward the night after the fight. The Indians' identity, discovered during the battle, was not Comanche, Kiowa, or some other wild band of raiders. Instead, they were Kickapoos merely traveling from their reservation in Kansas to be with others of their tribe in Mexico. The results of this useless debacle were twenty-two state and Confederate troopers killed and nineteen wounded, while the Kickapoo later reported suffering fourteen killed and six wounded. The battle at Dove Creek embittered the Kickapoos, and settlers along the Rio Grande would pay heavily in the years to come.

By February 1865, "Buck" Barry's four companies, Captain Fossett's battalion, the Border Regiment, and the Frontier Organization were all positioned on the northwestern defensive line. Fossett's two companies stationed at Camp Colorado patrolled the extreme left flank, while Barry's battalion ranged the country between Camp Colorado and Fort Belknap and Bourland's regiment protected the right flank from Buffalo Station to Fort Arbuckle in Indian Territory. The companies of the Frontier Organization covered the gaps amidst the Confederate commands. On February 10, Colonel Bourland was assigned to take charge of the northwestern frontier with authority over all C.S. and state troops, while Lieutenant-Colonel John R. Diamond replaced him as regimental commander.

On April 9 and April 26 respectively, the armies of Generals Robert E. Lee and Joseph E. Johnston surrendered, followed by Lieutenant-General Richard Taylor on May 4 and Lieutenant-General Edmund Kirby Smith, commanding the Trans-Mississippi Department (of which Texas was a part), on June 2. Before burning his official papers, General McCulloch issued his last order on June 4, which discharged the Confederate troops in his subdistrict effective May 26. For the next several months, some of the men of the Frontier Organization stayed at their posts and provided a measure of protection until the arrival of Federal troops.

## Historical Register, 1861–1865

*"Be vigilant and watchful and whip the Indians."*
— Brigadier-General Henry E. McCulloch

### Northern District

#### HEADQUARTERS
Colonel Henry E. McCulloch (February 5–March 19, 1861)
Captain Thomas C. Frost, Commanding (March 19–26, 1861)
Lieutenant James H. Price, Assistant Quartermaster and Commissary
Doctor H. L. Little, Surgeon (February 17–May 7, 1861)
  *Post surgeon at Camp Cooper*
Doctor Ransom Tuggle, Surgeon (February 20, 1861–?)
  *Post surgeon at Camp Colorado*

#### FROST'S COMANCHE COUNTY COMPANY
Captain Thomas C. Frost (February 25–May 7, 1861)
*Headquarters*: Camp Colorado

#### BARRY'S BOSQUE COUNTY COMPANY
Captain James B. "Buck" Barry (February 25–May 7, 1861)
*Headquarters*: Camp Cooper

5. *A Most Desperate Struggle: Rangers in the Civil War (1861–1865)*     113

### Holly's Coryell County Company
Captain R. B. Holly (February 25–May 7, 1861)
*Headquarters*: Fort Chabourne

### Hamner's Parker County Company
Captain H. A. Hamner (April 13–May 8, 1861)

### Cowan's San Saba County Company
Lieutenant David C. Cowan (Appointed February 5, 1861)
   *Company never organized for service*

### Texas Rangers
Captain Aaron B. Burleson (December 29, 1860–May 9, 1861)
*Headquarters*: Home Creek midway between Fort Chadbourne and Camp Colorado
   *Company attached to McCulloch's command (March–May 1861)*

### Texas Rangers
Captain Edward M. Alexander (March 12–May 9, 1861)
*Headquarters*: Camp Cooper
*District Ranging Area*: From Fort Chadbourne to the Red River with headquarters at Camp Colorado
   *District mustered into the Provisional Army of Texas (February 5, 1861), operated under the authority of the Committee of Public Safety, and consolidated with the Middle District (February 22, 1861)*

## *Middle District*

### Headquarters
Colonel Benjamin McCulloch (February 5–22, 1861)
Captain W. T. Mechling, Adjutant

### Mounted Rangers
1st Lieutenant James Paul (February 21, 1861–?)
*Ranging District*: Medina County with headquarters at Camp Verde
*District Ranging Area*: Line between Fort McIntosh and Fort Duncan to Fort Chadbourne with headquarters at San Antonio
   *District mustered into the Provisional Army of Texas (February 5, 1861), operated under the authority of the Committee of Public Safety, and consolidated with the Northern District (February 22, 1861)*

## *Southern District*

### Headquarters
Colonel John S. "Rip" Ford (February 5–April 21, 1861)

### Mounted Rangers
Captain John Donelson (February 20–September 20, 1861)
*Headquarters*: Fort Brown

### Texas Mounted Rangers
Captain Mat Nolan (February 23–June 30, 1861)
*Headquarters*: Camp Laguna Seco

### Mounted Rangers
Captain John Littleton
*District Ranging Area*: Rio Grande line from Brownsville to midway between Fort McIntosh and Fort Duncan with headquarters at Fort Brown

District mustered into the Provisional Army of Texas and operated under the authority of the Committee of Public Safety

## 1st Regiment of Texas Volunteers/1st Regiment of Texas Mounted Rifles/1st (McCulloch's) Texas Cavalry

### Field & Staff

Colonel Henry E. McCulloch (March 4, 1861–April 15, 1862)
Lieutenant-Colonel Thomas C. Frost, Acting Commander (January 7, 1861–April 15, 1862)
Lieutenant-Colonel Thomas C. Frost (May 6, 1861–January 7, 1862)
  *Frost elected Lt-Col. (May 6, 1861) and relieved of duty as Capt. (June 8, 1861)*
Major Edward "Ed" Burleson, Jr. (May 6–November 22, 1861)
Major James B. "Buck" Barry (February 22–April 15, 1862)
  *Maj. Barry assumed command of troops at Camp Cooper and Fort Belknap*
1st Lieutenant William O. Yager, Adjutant (April 15–December 18, 1861)
1st Lieutenant Levi W. Goodrich, Acting Adjutant (January 7–April 15, 1862)
Captain Washington L. "Wash" Hill, Acting Quartermaster (March 8, 1861–May 31, 1862)
Lieutenant Hannibal Harris, Assistant Quartermaster
Captain John R. King, Acting Commissary of Subsistence (April 20, 1861–May 31, 1862)
Doctor Henry P. Howard, Acting Surgeon (April 20, 1861–?)
  *Temporary medical officer at San Antonio*
Doctor David McKnight, Surgeon
Doctor Joseph Taylor, Surgeon (July 20–December 1861?)
Doctor Robert B. Harrison, Assistant Surgeon (April 20–December 1861?)
  *Post surgeon at Fort Belknap*
Doctor David P. Smythe, Assistant Surgeon (April 20, 1861–?)
  *Post surgeon at Camp Colorado*
Doctor Patrick H. Johnson, Assistant Surgeon (April 22, 1861–?)
  *Post surgeon*
Doctor Jesse A. Dereson, Assistant Surgeon (May 9, 1861–?)
  *Post surgeon at Fort Chadbourne*
Doctor Ransom Tuggle, Assistant Surgeon (May 12–September 15, 1861)
  *Post surgeon at Camp Colorado*
Doctor Jesse Boring, Assistant Surgeon
Doctor Dickson H. L. Hogg, Acting Assistant Surgeon (April 20–October 1861?)
  *Contract post surgeon at Camp Cooper*
Doctor Robert H. Dryden, Acting Assistant Surgeon
  *Contract surgeon*
Doctor John L. White, Acting Assistant Surgeon
  *Contract post surgeon at Camp Cooper*
Doctor Henry M. Jones, Acting Assistant Surgeon
  *Contract surgeon*
Sergeant-Major William W. Wiggs (May 12, 1861–April 15, 1862)

### Company A

Captain James H. Fry (April 22, 1861–April 15, 1862)
*Headquarters*: San Antonio (April 1861); Concho Junction/Camp Concho (July 1861); Fort McKavett (October 1861); Camp Verde (November 1861–January 1862)

### Company B

Captain William A. Pitts (April 20, 1861–April 15, 1862)
*Headquarters*: San Antonio (April 1861); Camp Colorado (June 1861); Fort Mason (November 1861)

## Company C
Captain William A. Duke (April 20–June 10, 1861)
  *Capt. Duke failed to meet recruiting commitment and company was dropped from regimental rolls*

## Company (D*) C
Captain James B. "Buck" Barry (May 7, 1861–February 22, 1862)
Captain George E. Bushong (March 12–April 15, 1862)
1st Lieutenant Francis H. Combs, commanding detachment
*Headquarters*: Camp Cooper with detachments at camps on Willow Springs and Elm, Paint, and Camp Creeks (May 1861); Fort Mason (January–May 1862)
  *Company designation advanced one letter (June 16, 1861)

## Company (E*) D
Captain William G. Tobin (April 20, 1861–April 15, 1862)
1st Lieutenant Samuel G. Ragsdale, commanding detachment (June 3–September 1861)
*Headquarters*: San Antonio (April 1861) with Ragsdale's detachment at Fort Mason (June–September 1861); Fort Chadbourne (July 1861)
  *Company designation advanced one letter (June 16, 1861)

## Company (F*) E
Captain Governeur H. Nelson (April 20, 1861–April 15, 1862)
*Headquarters*: San Antonio (April 1861) with detachment at Fort Mason (June 1861); Concho Junction/Camp Concho with detachment at Fort Mason (July 1861); Fort McKavett (October 1861)
  *Company designation advanced one letter (June 16, 1861)

## Company (G*) F
Captain Sidney Green Davidson (May 9–June 23, 1861)
1st Lieutenant Matthew J. Kuykendall, Acting Commander (June 23–August 13, 1861)
Captain Robert A. Myers (August 13, 1861–April 15, 1862)
1st Lieutenant Matthew J. Kuykendall, commanding detachment (September 1861)
2nd Lieutenant James S. Bingham, commanding detachment
*Headquarters*: Fort Chadbourne (May 1861) with Kuykendall's detachment at camp on Grape Creek (September 1861); Fort Inge with detachment at Camp Verde (March 1862)
  *Company designation advanced one letter (June 16, 1861)

## Company (H*) G
Captain Thomas C. Frost (May 6–June 8, 1861)
Captain James M. Homsley (June 8, 1861–April 15, 1862)
*Headquarters*: Fort Clark (June 1861); Red River Station/Camp Jackson (July 1861); Camp Colorado (September 1861–February 1862)
  *Company designation advanced one letter (June 16, 1861)

## Company (I*) H
Captain Milton M. Boggess (April 20, 1861–April 15, 1862)
*Headquarters*: San Antonio (April 1861); Fort Phantom Hill (July 1861); Camp Cooper (October–December 1861)
  *Company designation advanced one letter (June 16, 1861)

## Company (K*) I
Captain Travis H. Ashby (April 20, 1861–April 15, 1862)

*Headquarters*: San Antonio (April 1861); Red River Station/Camp Jackson (July 1861); Fort Belknap (September 1861); Camp Colorado (October 1861)
> *Company designation advanced one letter (June 16, 1861)

## COMPANY K
Captain Milton Webb (June 15, 1861–April 15, 1862)
*Headquarters*: Hubbard Creek Station near Camp Cooper (June 1861); Red River Station/Camp Jackson (July 1861); Fort Belknap (September 1861); Camp Colorado (October 1861); Fort Mason (January–May 1862)
*Regimental Ranging District*: Junction of the Big Wichita and the Red Rivers to the Forks of the Concho River to Camp Verde with headquarters at Camp Cooper (April 1861), Camp Colorado (July 1861), and Fort Mason (September 1861–May 1862)
*First Line of Defense Ranging District*: Camp Colorado to Fort McKavett with headquarters at Fort Chadbourne (Lt-Col. Frost, Commanding: June 1861); Fort Phantom Hill to Camp Jackson with headquarters at Camp Jackson (Major Burleson, Commanding: July–November 1861); Camp Cooper to Red River Station with headquarters at Camp Cooper (Major Barry, Commanding: February–April 1862)
> Regiment mustered into C.S. service (April 20, 1861) and completed organization (June 16, 1861)
> Companies A, B, D, E, H, and I mustered out at the expiration of enlistments (April 15, 1862) and Companies C, F, G, and K mustered into 8th Texas Cavalry Battalion (C.S.A.)

## CLAY COUNTY MINUTE MEN
Captain Samuel Green (February 7, 1861–February 1862)
*Ranging District*: Clay County
> Company attached to 21st Militia Brigade

## KERR COUNTY MINUTE MEN
Captain William T. Harbour (February 27–May 27, 1861)
*Ranging District*: Kerr County

## PALO PINTO COUNTY MINUTE MEN
Captain D. B. Cleveland (March 5, 1861–July 27, 1862)
*Ranging District*: Palo Pinto County
> Company attached to 20th Militia Brigade

## MCLENNAN COUNTY MINUTE MEN
Captain George B. Erath (March 8–December 8, 1861)
*Ranging District*: McLennan County

## SAN SABA COUNTY MINUTE MEN/MOUNTED RANGERS
Captain William Riley Wood (March 9–June 9, 1861)
*Ranging District*: San Saba County with headquarters at San Saba
> Company operated under the supervision of the Chief Justice of San Saba County

## TEXAS RANGERS
Captain Ewen Cameron (March 20–June 5, 1861)
*Ranging District*: Gillespie County with headquarters at camp on South Fork of the Llano River

## UVALDE COUNTY MINUTE COMPANY
Captain D. W. C. Rain (March 23–December 14, 1861)
*Ranging District*: Uvalde County

### Mason County Minute Men
Captain Herman R. von Biberstein (March 25, 1861–?)
*Ranging District*: Mason County with headquarters at Mason

### Llano County Minute Men
Captain C. W. Dorsey (April 6–October 2, 1861)
*Ranging District*: Llano County

### Atascosa County Mounted Minute Men
Captain Edward Walker (May 7, 1861–?)
*Ranging District*: Atascosa County with headquarters at Pleasanton

### Texas Rangers
Captain Aaron B. Burleson (May 9, 1861–December 29, 1861)
*Headquarters*: Home Creek midway between Fort Chadbourne and Camp Colorado

### Erath County Minute Men
Captain John J. Keith (May 17–November 17, 1861)
*Ranging District*: Erath County

### Wise County Minute Men
Captain George Birdwell (May 20, 1861–?)
*Ranging District*: Wise County with headquarters at Decatur
    Company attached to 21st Militia Brigade

### Mounted Ranging Company
Captain Hiram W. Cooke (May 24, 1861–?)
*Ranging District*: Coryell County

### Parker County Minute Men
Captain Henry J. Thompson (May 27, 1861–February 14, 1862)
*Ranging District*: Parker County with headquarters at Veal's Station
    Company attached to 20th Militia Brigade

### Coryell County Minute Men
Captain Samuel Friend (June 1861)
*Ranging District*: Coryell County

### Frontier Guards
Captain John Q. O'Neill (June 1, 1861–?)
*Ranging District*: Montague County
    Company assigned to the 21st Militia Brigade

### Comanche County Minute Men
Captain James Cunningham (June 5–September 16, 1861)
*Ranging District*: Comanche County

### Wise County Minute Men/Mounted Rangers
Captain B. P. Earp (June 20, 1861–March 11, 1862)
*Ranging District*: Wise County
    Company attached to 21st Militia Brigade

### Jack County Minute Men/Rangers
Captain Marion D. Tackett (July 17, 1861–March 5, 1862)

*Ranging District*: Jack County with headquarters at Jacksboro
   *Company operated under the supervision of the Chief Justice of Jack County*

### COLEMAN COUNTY MINUTE MEN
Captain James J. Callan (July 27–December 31, 1861)
*Ranging District*: Coleman County with headquarters at camps on the Clear Fork of the Brazos River, Bald Eagle Point, and Moro Mountain

### BROWN COUNTY MINUTE MEN
Captain Abraham K. McCain (July 29, 1861–February 4, 1862)
   *Capt. McCain served as county sheriff (June 6, 1861–August 4, 1862)*
*Ranging District*: Brown County

### BURNET COUNTY MINUTE MEN
Captain Christian Dorbant (August 6–October 3, 1861)
*Ranging District*: Burnet County

### LAMPASAS COUNTY MINUTE MEN
Captain Williamson Jones (September 2, 1861–March 1, 1862)
*Ranging District*: Lampasas County

### ATASCOSA COUNTY MINUTE MEN
Captain Benjamin Slaughter (November 2, 1861–January 20, 1862)
*Ranging District*: Atascosa County

## Frontier Regiment/Mounted Regiment/Frontier Texas Cavalry/ 46th Texas Cavalry Regiment

### FIELD & STAFF
Colonel James M. Norris (January 29, 1862–January 10, 1863)
Lieutenant-Colonel James E. McCord, Acting Commander (January 11–February 11, 1863)
Colonel James E. McCord (February 13, 1863–April 1865?)
Major William J. Alexander, Acting Commander (June 22–August 1864, March 29–April 1865)
Lieutenant-Colonel Alfred J. Obenchain (January 29–August 16, 1862)
Lieutenant-Colonel James E. McCord (August 1862–February 11, 1863)
Lieutenant-Colonel James B. "Buck" Barry (February 13, 1863–May 26, 1865)
Major James E. McCord (January 29–August 1862)
Major James B. "Buck" Barry (September 22, 1862–February 11, 1863)
Major William J. Alexander (February 13, 1863–April 1865?)
1st Lieutenant Hiram W. Cooke, Adjutant
1st Lieutenant Anthony O'Doherty, Adjutant (August 27, 1862–?)
1st Lieutenant Abraham H. See, Adjutant (February 1, 1863–?)
   *Listed variously as A. H. Lee or C. H. Lee*
1st Lieutenant Royal T. Wheeler, Jr., Adjutant (April 1, 1863–?)
1st Lieutenant Abraham H. See, Adjutant (June 20, 1863–April 1865?)
1st Lieutenant Henry Ward, Acting Adjutant (May 21, 1864–February 20, 1865)
   *Lt. Ward assigned to Field & Staff, Lt-Col. J. B. Barry's Battalion*
1st Lieutenant William D. Hord, Acting Adjutant (February 20, 1865–?)
   *Lt. Hord assigned to Field & Staff, Lt-Col. J. B. Barry's Battalion*
Captain W. W. Reynolds, Quartermaster (February 2, 1862–April 1865?)
1st Lewis P. Strong, Assistant Quartermaster (February 20, 1864–?)
   *Post Quartermaster at Camp Belknap*

5. A Most Desperate Struggle: Rangers in the Civil War (1861–1865)    119

Captain Edwin D. Lane, Commissary of Subsistence (February 10, 1862–December 1863)
Captain John H. Prince, Commissary of Subsistence (October 19, 1862–?)
Captain Charles T. Freeman, Acting Commissary of Subsistence (April 20, 1863–?)
Captain W. R. Chase, Acting Commissary of Subsistence (March–April 1865?)
Major John J. Inge, Surgeon (July 1, 1862–March 11, 1863)
Doctor J. R. Worrall, Surgeon (February 29, 1864–January 7, 1865)
Doctor James G. Barbee, Acting Assistant Surgeon (February 29, 1864–April 1865?)
    Contract post surgeon at Camp Llano
Doctor William H. Robinson, Acting Assistant Surgeon (March 29, 1863–February 15, 1865?)
    Contract post surgeon at Fort Belknap
Doctor A. A. Shipp, Assistant Surgeon
    Post surgeon of Camp Verde
Doctor David Ford, Acting Assistant Surgeon
    Contract post surgeon at Camp McCord
Doctor J. M. Young, Acting Assistant Surgeon
    Contract post surgeon at Camp Colorado
Doctor J. G. Weaver, Acting Assistant Surgeon (March 10, 1862–?)
    Contract post surgeon at Camps Salmon and Breckenridge
Doctor Thomas M. Blakemore, Acting Assistant Surgeon (June 20, 1862–?)
    Post surgeon at Camp Dix
Doctor G. Simmerman, Acting Assistant Surgeon (September 1863)
    Contract post surgeon at Camp Dix
Doctor A. Bartley, Assistant Surgeon (October 1863)
    Post surgeon at Camp Cooper
Doctor John L. Hansford, Acting Assistant Surgeon (February 2, 1863–?)
    Contract post surgeon at Camp San Saba
Doctor J. H. Hembree, Acting Assistant Surgeon (June 1–October 1863?)
    Contract post surgeon at Red River Station
Doctor Thomas Stewart, Acting Assistant Surgeon
    Contract post surgeon at Camp Brunson
Doctor J. M. Pound, Assistant Surgeon
    Post surgeon at Camp Davis
Doctor W. J. Smith, Acting Assistant Surgeon (October 1863)
    Contract post surgeon at Camp Salmon
Sergeant-Major James J. Callan (March 24–June 17, 1862)
Sergeant-Major Abraham H. See (August 1, 1862–?)
Sergeant-Major A. M. Lindsey (June 1, 1863–December 8, 1864)
Quartermaster Sergeant D. R. Woods (June 1–July 15, 1862)
Quartermaster Sergeant C. A. Hopkins (August 3, 1862–?)
Quartermaster Sergeant Adolphus G. Luck (July 31, 1863–December 1864?)
    Listed variously as A. G. Leech or A. Y. Luck
Commissary Sergeant W. G. Maynard (August 19, 1863–?)
Ordnance Sergeant _____ McCord (November 1864–April 1865?)
Sergeant Jo F. Galbreath, Bugler (February 2–October 1863?)

### Company A (H*)

Captain Thomas Rabb (January 23, 1862–January 30, 1863)
Captain James M. Hunter (February 7, 1863–February 29, 1864)
Captain William Banta (March 1–August 23, 1864)
    Capt. Banta placed under arrest (April 27, 1864)
Captain Peter O. A. "Alonzo" Rees, Jr. (August 23, 1864–April 1865?)

*Ranging District*: Maverick County with headquarters at Rio Grande Station and detachment at Camp Rabb (April 1862); Gillespie County with headquarters at Camp Davis (December 1862–February 1863); Southern Division with headquarters at Fort Duncan (March 1864); Confederate Western Sub-District with headquarters at Columbus (May 1864) and at camp on Clear Creek near Prairie Point (June 1864); Confederate Eastern Sub-District with headquarters at Camp Gillespie near Harrisburg (August 1864) and Camp Groce near Hempstead (October 1864); Confederate Central Sub-District with headquarters at camp near La Grange (November 1864) and Valesco (April–May 1865)

 *Company assigned to Maj. W. J. Alexander's Southern Division (February 1863) and Col. J. E. McCord's Battalion (May 1864)*

   *Company referred to as Company "H" in SO No. 11 (April 10, 1862), and Company "A" in GO No. 5 (May 30, 1862) and GO No. 7 (April 16, 1863)

## Company B (C*)

Captain John Salmon (March 8–December 19, 1862)
1st Lieutenant William J. Alexander, Acting Commander (December 20–29, 1862)
Captain John Lawhon (December 29, 1862–March 1865?)
*Ranging District*: Stephens and Callahan Counties with headquarters at Camp Breckinridge and detachment at Camp Salmon/Camp McCord (March 1862); Kerr County with headquarters at Camp Verde (May 1863); Southern Division with headquarters at Camp Verde (March 1864); Confederate Western Sub-District with headquarters at Columbus (May 1864) and at camp on Clear Creek near Prairie Point (June 1864); Confederate Eastern Sub-District with headquarters at Camp Gillespie near Harrisburg (August 1864) and Camp Anderson (October 1864); Confederate Central Sub-District with headquarters at camp near La Grange (March–May 1865)

 *Company assigned to Lt-Col. J. B. Barry's Northern Division (March 1863) and Col. J. E. McCord's Battalion (May 1864)*

   *Company referred to as Company "C" in SO No. 4 (March 4, 1862), and Company "B" in GO No. 5 (May 30, 1862) and GO No. 7 (April 16, 1863)

## Company C (A, D*)

Captain Allen Brunson (February 1, 1862–March 16, 1863)
Captain Joseph Ward (March 30–September 6, 1863)
Captain S. G. Thompson (December 18, 1863–May 26, 1865)
2nd Lieutenant W. S. Campbell, commanding detachment (November 1863)
*Ranging District*: Wichita County with headquarters at camp on junction of Big Wichita River and Beaver Creek and detachment at camp near the Big Wichita River (March 1862); Montague and Clay Counties with headquarters at Red River Station and detachment at Camp Brunson (March 1862–June 1863); Northern Division with headquarters at Fort Belknap (March 1864); Confederate Eastern Sub-District with headquarters at Camp Gillespie near Harrisburg (August 1864) and Camp Groce near Hempstead (September 1864); Confederate Northern Sub-District with headquarters at Camp McCord (October 1864–May 1865)

 *Company assigned to Lt-Col. J. B. Barry's Northern Division (March 1863) and Lt-Col. J. B. Barry's Battalion (April 1864)*

   *Company referred to as Company "A" in SO No. 6 (March 7, 1862), Company "C" in GO No. 5 (May 30, 1862), Company "D" in SO No. 44 (July 8, 1862), Company "C" in GO No. 7 (April 16, 1863), Company "D" in June 1864 Company Return, and Company "C" in August 1864 Regimental Return

## Company D (G, B*)

Captain Charles S. de Montel (February 17, 1862–February 9, 1863)
Captain John T. Rowland (May 1, 1863–May 26, 1865)

2nd Lieutenant Ben F. Patton, commanding detachment

*Ranging District*: Kerr and Bandera Counties with headquarters at Camp Verde and Patton's detachment at Camp Montel (March 1862); Montague County with headquarters at Red River Station (December 1862); Northern Division with headquarters at Fort Belknap (March 1864); Confederate Eastern Sub-District with headquarters at Camp Gillespie near Harrisburg (August 1864) and Camp Groce near Hempstead (September 1864); Confederate Northern Sub-District with headquarters at Fort Belknap (October 1864–May 1865)

*Company assigned to Lt-Col. J. B. Barry's Northern Division (March 1863) and Lt-Col. J. B. Barry's Battalion (April 1864)*

*Company referred to as Company "G" in SO No. 2 (February 4, 1862), Company "B" in unnumbered SO (May 18, 1862), Company "D" in GO No. 5 (May 30, 1862) and GO No. 7 (April 16, 1863), Company "G" in May 1864 Company Return, and Company "D" in August 1864 Regimental Return

## Company E

Captain Newton D. McMillin (February 20, 1862–February 2, 1863)

Captain M. B. Loyd (March 14, 1863–April 1865?)

2nd Lieutenant P. S. Oatinan, commanding detachment

*Ranging District*: Mason County with headquarters at Camp Llano (February 1862); San Saba and McCulloch Counties with headquarters at Camp McMillin and Oatinan's detachment at Camp San Saba (May 1862); Callahan County with headquarters at Camp Salmon (March 1863); Confederate Eastern Sub-District with headquarters at Camp Felder (February 1864); Southern Division with headquarters at Fort Inge (March 1864); Confederate Western Sub-District with headquarters at Columbus (May 1864) and at camp on Clear Creek near Prairie Point (June 1864); Confederate Eastern Sub-District with headquarters at Camp Gillespie near Harrisburg (August 1864); Confederate Central Sub-District with headquarters at Camp Felder (October 1864), camp near La Grange (November 1864), and Velasco (April–May 1865)

*Company assigned to Lt-Col. J. B. Barry's Northern Division (March 1863) and Col. J. E. McCord's Battalion (May 1864)*

## Company F

Captain Jacob Kuchler (February 12–March 4, 1862)

*Company dissolved and reorganized by order of Gov. F. R. Lubbock*

Captain Henry T. Davis (March 4, 1862–February 7, 1863)

Captain Hyman T. Edgar (February 14, 1863–April 1865?)

*Ranging District*: Mason and Gillespie Counties with headquarters at Camp Llano and detachment at Camp Davis (March 1862); Uvalde County with headquarters at Camp Dix (February 1863); Southern Division with headquarters at Fort Inge (March 1864); Confederate Western Sub-District with headquarters at Columbus (May 1864) and at camp on Clear Creek near Prairie Point (June 1864); Confederate Eastern Sub-District with headquarters at Camp Gillespie near Harrisburg (August 1864); Confederate Central Sub-District with headquarters at Camp Felder (October 1864), camp near La Grange (November 1864), and Velasco (April–May 1865)

*Company assigned to Maj. W. J. Alexander's Southern Division (February 1863) and Col. J. E. McCord's Battalion (May 1864)*

## Company G (D*)

Captain Frank M. Collier (March 5–June 30, 1862)

*Capt. Collier paid as officer through July 20, 1862*

Captain James J. Callan (June 30, 1862–January 24, 1863)

Captain Newton White (January 2, 1863–May 26, 1865)
Lieutenant J. Campbell, commanding detachment
*Ranging District*: Coleman and Brown Counties with headquarters at Camp Pecan and detachment at Camp Collier (March 1862); Coleman County with headquarters at Camp Colorado (October 1862); Young County with headquarters at Fort Belknap and detachment at camp in Lost Valley (January 1863); Montague County with headquarters at Red River Station (May 1863); Northern Division with headquarters at Fort Belknap (March 1864); Confederate Eastern Sub-District with headquarters at Camp Gillespie near Harrisburg (August 1864) and Camp Groce near Hempstead (September 1864); Confederate Northern Sub-District with headquarters at Camp McCord (October 1864–May 1865)
    *Company assigned to Lt-Col. J. B. Barry's Northern Division (March 1864) and Lt-Col. J. B. Barry's Battalion (July 1864)*

    *Company referred to as Company "D" in SO No. 3 (March 1, 1862), and Company "G" in GO No. 5 (May 30, 1862) and GO No. 7 (April 16, 1863)

## COMPANY H (K*)

Captain John J. Dix (March 6, 1862–February 15, 1863)
Captain Robert M. Whiteside (February 2, 1863–May 26, 1865)
2nd Lieutenant Hyman T. Edgar, commanding detachment
*Ranging District*: Uvalde County with headquarters at Camp Dix and Edgar's detachment at Camp Nueces (April 1862); Throckmorton and Stephens Counties with headquarters at Camp Cooper and detachment at Camp Breckenridge (September 1863); Palo Pinto County with headquarters at Camp Rowland (October 1863); Northern Division with headquarters at Fort Belknap (March 1864); Confederate Eastern Sub-District with headquarters at Camp Gillespie near Harrisburg (August 1864) and Camp Groce near Hempstead (September 1864); Confederate Northern Sub-District with headquarters at Camp McCord (October 1864–May 1865)
    *Company assigned to Lt-Col. J. B. Barry's Northern Division (March 1864) and Lt-Col. J. B. Barry's Battalion (July 1864)*

    *Company reported as Company "K" in SO No. 1 (March 13, 1862), and Company "H" in GO No. 5 (May 30, 1862), SO No. 43 (July 8, 1862) and GO No. 7 (April 16, 1863)

## COMPANY I (B*)

Captain J. J. "Jack" Cureton (March 11–September 25, 1862)
    *Capt. Cureton placed under arrest and court-martialed by order of Lt-Col. Obenchain (June 5, 1862)*
2nd Lieutenant John A. Woolfolk, Acting Commander
Captain William R. Peveler (November 1, 1862–January 31, 1863)
Captain James J. Callan (March 1863–December 11, 1864)
    *Capt. Callan reported as deserter (October 17, 1864)*
Captain Thomas C. Wright (January–April 1865?)
Private John R. "Jack" Wright, commanding detachment (August 1863)
*Ranging District*: Archer and Young Counties with headquarters at Camp Belknap and detachment at Camp Cureton (March 1862); Coleman County with headquarters at Camp Colorado (November 1863); Southern Division with headquarters at Camp Verde (March 1864); Confederate Western Sub-District with headquarters at Columbus (May 1864) and at camp on Clear Creek near Prairie Point (June 1864); Confederate Eastern Sub-District with headquarters at Camp Gillespie near Harrisburg (August 1864) and Camp Anderson (October 1864); Confederate Central Sub-District with headquarters at camp near La Grange (November 1864) and Valesco (April–May 1865)
    *Company assigned to Maj. W. J. Alexander's Southern Division (February 1863) and Col. J. E. McCord's Battalion (May 1864)*

*Company reported as Company "B" in SO No. 5 (March 5, 1862), and Company "I" in GO No. 5 (May 30, 1862) and GO No. 7 (April 16, 1863)

## Company K

Captain William G. O'Brien (December 20, 1862–April 1865?)

*Ranging District*: McCulloch County with headquarters at Camp San Saba (December 1862); Uvalde County with headquarters at Camp Nueces; Confederate Eastern Sub-District with headquarters at Camp Felder (February 1864); Southern Division with headquarters at Fort Duncan (March 1864); Confederate Western Sub-District with headquarters at Columbus (May 1864) and at camp on Clear Creek near Prairie Point (June 1864); Confederate Eastern Sub-District with headquarters at Camp Gillespie near Harrisburg (August 1864) and Camp Groce near Hempstead (October 1864); Confederate Central Sub-District with headquarters at camp near La Grange (November 1864) and Velasco (April–May 1865)

*Company assigned to Maj. W. J. Alexander's Southern Division (February 1863) and Col. J. E. McCord's Battalion (May 1864)*

*Regimental Headquarters*: Camp Collier (February 1862); Camp San Saba (March 1862); Camp Collier (July 1862); Camp Colorado (October 1862); Camp Verde (January 1864); Camp Colorado (March 1864); Columbus (May 1864); camp on Clear Creek near Prairie Point (June 1864); Camp Gillespie near Harrisburg (August 1864); Camp Groce near Hempstead (September 1864); camp near La Grange (November 1864); and Velasco (April–May 1865)

*Northern Division Ranging District*: Camp San Saba to Red River Station with headquarters at Fort Belknap (Lieutenant-Colonel Obenchain, Commanding: April–August 1862); Camp McMillin to Red River Station with headquarters at Fort Belknap (Major Barry, Commanding: November 1862); Camp Colorado to Red River Station with headquarters at Fort Belknap (Lieutenant-Colonel Barry, Commanding: April 1863–May 1864)

*Southern Division Ranging District*: Camp San Saba to Rio Grande Station with headquarters at Camp Verde (Major/Lieutenant-Colonel McCord, Commanding: April 1862); Camp McMillin to Rio Grande Station with headquarters at Camp Verde (Lieutenant-Colonel McCord, Commanding: November 1862–February 1863); Camp Colorado to Rio Grande Station with headquarters at Camp Verde (Major Alexander, Commanding: May 1863–May 1864)

*McCord's Battalion Ranging District*: Confederate Western Sub-District with headquarters at Columbus (May 1864) and at camp on Clear Creek near Prairie Point (June 1864); Confederate Eastern Sub-District with headquarters at Camp Gillespie near Harrisburg (August 1864) and Camp Groce near Hempstead (September 1864); Confederate Central Sub-District with headquarters at camp near La Grange (November 1864) and Velasco (April–May 1865)

*Barry's Battalion Ranging District*: Confederate Northern Sub-District with headquarters at Fort Belknap (May 1864); Confederate Eastern Sub-District with headquarters at Camp Gillespie near Harrisburg (August 1864) and Camp Groce near Hempstead (September 1864); Camp Colorado to Fort Belknap with headquarters at Fort Belknap (Lieutenant-Colonel Barry, Commanding: October 1864–March 1865; Captain Rowland, Acting Commander: April–May 1865; Lieutenant-Colonel Barry, Commanding: May 1865)

*Regiment mustered into State service (March 8, 1862), reorganized (February 11, 1863), and transferred to C.S. service (March 1, 1864)*

*Regiment operated under the orders of HQ, Confederate Western Sub-District of Texas (March 1, 1864)*

*Barry's Battalion operated under the orders of BG H. E. McCulloch, CG of the Confederate Northern Sub-District of Texas (May 25, 1864), HQ, Confederate Western Sub-District of Texas (August 1864), and BG H. E. McCulloch, CG of the Confederate Northern Sub-District of Texas (September 30, 1864)*

Regimental HQ and McCord's Battalion operated under the orders of HQ, Confederate Eastern Sub-District of Texas (August 1864) and HQ, Confederate Central Sub-District of Texas (December 31, 1864)

## "Border Battalion"/Bourland's Texas Cavalry Regiment/ "Border Regiment"

### FIELD & STAFF

Lieutenant-Colonel James Bourland, Commanding (April–October 2, 1863)
Colonel James Bourland (October 2, 1863–May 1865)
    *Col. Bourland appointed commander of the Red River line (October 9, 1864) and the frontier in southern Indian Territory and northern and western Texas (February 10, 1865)*
Lieutenant-Colonel John R. Diamond, Acting Commander (January 19–May 1865)
Lieutenant-Colonel John R. Diamond (May 13, 1864–January 19, 1865)
Major John R. Diamond (March 26–May 13, 1864)
Major Charles L. Roff (May 13, 1864–May 1865)
2nd Lieutenant Henry A. Whaley, Adjutant (August 15, 1863–April 1865?)
Lieutenant James W. S. Merchant, Acting Quartermaster (December 1863)
Captain William C. Twitty, Assistant Quartermaster (March 1864?–February 1865?)
Doctor George L. Scott, Surgeon (March 1864–March 1865?)
Doctor F. L. Cutler, Assistant Surgeon (March 1864–January 1865?)
Sergeant-Major R. H. Franklin (March–August 1864?)
Sergeant-Major W. A. Peter (November 15, 1864–?)
Sergeant-Major J. C. Pearce
Commissary Sergeant Samuel Day (March–September 1864?)
Ordnance Sergeant R. O. (or R. P.) Reeves (March 1864–?)
Ordnance Sergeant Franklin Liedtke (June 7, 1864–March 4, 1865?)
Ordnance Sergeant Charles Hibbert (August 1864?)

### COMPANY A

Captain Charles L. Roff (April 24, 1863–May 13, 1864)
Captain William R. Harrison (June 14, 1864–February 1865?)
*Headquarters*: Camp Arbuckle, Chickasaw Nation (April 1863); Camp Roff, Chickasaw Nation; Camp Simons, Choctaw Nation (March 1864); Camp Nicholson, Choctaw Nation (November 1864); Camp Steele, Chickasaw Nation (January 1865)

### COMPANY B

Captain James J. Diamond (April 28, 1863–November 1864?)
    *Capt. Diamond placed under arrest by order of Col. Bourland and court-martialed*
1st Lieutenant Alexander Boutwell, Acting Commander (?–February 1865?)
*Headquarters*: Gainesville (July 1864); Fort Arbuckle, Chickasaw Nation (August 1864)

### COMPANY C

Captain Andrew J. Nicholson (May 10, 1863–May 1865?)
1st Lieutenant L. P. Moore, Acting Commander (January 20–February 4, 1865)
*Headquarters*: Fort Arbuckle, Chickasaw Nation (October 1863); Camp Nicholson, Choctaw Nation (November 1864)

### COMPANY D

Captain Ambrose B. White (April 28, 1863–May 1864)
    *Capt. White placed under arrest by order of Col. Bourland and court-martialed (May–December 1864?)*
1st Lieutenant William S. Brown, Acting Commander (August 1864)

Captain Ambrose B. White (January 22–May 1865?)

2nd Lieutenant N. Carson, Sr., commanding detachment (July 5–July 18, 1864)

*Headquarters*: Boggy Depot, Choctaw Nation (July 1863); Salt Creek Station (July 1864); Fort Belknap (August 1864); Victoria Peak with Carson's detachment at camp west of Fort Belknap (October 1864); Gainesville (November 1864)

## COMPANY E

Captain F. M. Totty (May 23, 1863–April 1865?)

2nd Lieutenant Jasper S. O'Neal, commanding detachment (January 1865)

*Headquarters*: Gainesville (July 1864); Victoria Peak (August 1864)

## COMPANY F

Captain Samuel F. Mains (October 1863–August 1864?)

1st Lieutenant Jasper F. Hagler, Acting Commander (November 11, 1864–?)

2nd Lieutenant Andrew J. McFarland, Acting Commander

*Headquarters*: Montague (April 1864); Fort Belknap (August 1864); Salt Creek Station (September 1864)

## COMPANY G

Captain Samuel P. C. Patton (March 1–December 28, 1864)
   *Capt. Patton placed under arrest by order of Col. Bourland*

1st Lieutenant James W. Lawler, Acting Commander (January 1865–?)

2nd Lt. J. M. Hamilton, commanding detachment (January 1865)

*Headquarters*: Buffalo Station (July 1864); Gainesville (August 1864); Rock Creek (November 1864) with Hamilton's detachment at Camp Logan (January 1865)

## COMPANY H (I*)

Captain James S. Moore (May–November 1864?)

*Headquarters*: camp on Hubbard Creek (May 1864); camp on Deep Creek (October 1864); Salt Creek Station (November 1864)

*Company reported as Company "H" on August 1864
Regimental Return and Company "I" on November 1864 Return

## COMPANY I (G, H*)

Captain J. B. Anderson (May 1864–August 1864?)
   *Capt. Anderson served as sheriff of Fannin County (August 1, 1864–August 7, 1865)*

1st Lieutenant George W. Patterson, Acting Commander (August 1864)

Captain William M. Bettis, Sr. (September 1864–?)

*Headquarters*: Buffalo Station (July 1864–January 1865)

*Company reported as Company "G" on July 1864 Regimental Return,
Company "I" on August 1864 Return, and Company "H" on November 1864 Return

## COMPANY K (H*)

Captain William C. McKamy (May 9, 1864–January 1865?)

*Headquarters*: Camp Twitty east of Red River Station (June 1864); Camp Point Lookout, Chickasaw Nation (October 1864); Spanish Fort (November 1864); Camp Jim Bourland near Wichita River (January 1865)

*Company reported as Company "H" on July 1864 Regimental Return and
Company "K" on August 1864 Return

*Regimental Ranging District*: Chickasaw and Choctaw Nations in the Confederate District of Indian Territory and Cooke, Montague, Clay, Wichita, Archer, Young, Stephens, Palo Pinto, Jack, Parker, Wise, and Denton Counties in the Confederate Northern Sub-District

of Texas with headquarters at Fort Arbuckle (October 1863), Camp Wichita near Gainesville (January 1864), and Salt Creek Station (January 1865)
>Battalion mustered into State service (early spring 1863), increased to regimental strength (October 2, 1863), and transferred to C.S. service (May 1, 1864)
>Battalion/Regiment operated under the orders of BG H. E. McCulloch, CG of the Confederate Northern Sub-District of Texas (August 23, 1863), HQ, 2nd Brigade, 1st Division, Confederate District of Indian Territory (October 10, 1863), BG R. M. Gano, CG of Texas Cavalry Brigade, Confederate District of Indian Territory (December 26, 1863), and BG H. E. McCulloch, CG of the Confederate Northern Sub-District of Texas (January 19, 1864)

### DOOMAS' CO.
*Company attached to Border Regiment*

### BONE'S COMPANY
Captain John W. Bone (May–October 1864)
*Ranging District*: Confederate Northern Sub-District with headquarters at Camp Grove (August 1864) and camp near Bonham (October 1864)
>*Company attached to Bourland's Border Regiment (May–July 1864)*

### LADIES RANGERS TEXAS CAVALRY COMPANY
Captain John R. Baylor (September–November 1863)
*Headquarters*: Fort Belknap
>*Company operated under the orders of BG H. E. McCulloch, CG of the Confederate Northern Sub-District of Texas (October 6, 1863)*

## *Brush Battalion*

### FIELD & STAFF
Captain John R. Baylor (November 6, 1863–?)
Major John R. Diamond (?–March 26, 1864)
Lieutenant James W. S. Merchant, Quartermaster

### COMPANY
*Ranging District*: Little Wichita River country

### COMPANY
*Ranging District*: Wichita River country

### COMPANY
*Ranging District*: Wichita River country

### COMPANY
*Ranging District*: Near Warren's Trading Post on Cache Creek

### COMPANY
*Ranging District*: Near Warren's Trading Post on Cache Creek
*Battalion Headquarters*: Oxford Lake
>*Battalion operated under the orders of BG H. E. McCulloch, CG of the Confederate Northern Sub-District of Texas*

# Frontier Organization

## *First (or Northern) Frontier District*
### HEADQUARTERS
Major William Quayle, Commanding (January 20–December 13, 1864)

Brigadier-General James W. Throckmorton, Commanding (December 13, 1864–April 1865)
Major John W. Lane, Commanding (May 1–26, 1865)
Major William Quayle (January–March 1865)
Lieutenant J. W. Moore, Adjutant (June 1864)
Captain John P. Hill, Assistant Adjutant General (December 1864–April 1865?)
Captain A. T. Robertson, Quartermaster and Paymaster
Sergeant-Major George Isbell (February 1–October 19, 1864?)
Ordnance Sergeant J. P. Crutchfield (June 1864)
J. L. S. Shuffield, Chief Musician (June 1864)

## COMPANY A
Captain Pleasant Witt (January 27–July 1, 1864)
*Ranging District*: Parker County with headquarters at Weatherford

## COMPANY A
Captain Henry J. Thompson (January 29–April 1, 1864)
    *Capt. Thompson reported as deserter*
Captain T. F. Roberts (April 26–May 31, 1864)
*Ranging District*: Precinct No. 1, Jack County and Clay County with headquarters at Buffalo Springs

## COMPANY A (C)
Captain J. B. Earhart (January 30–June 1, 1864)
Captain J. B. Earhart (?–March 1, 1865?)
*Ranging District*: Wise County with headquarters at Decatur

## COMPANY A
Captain J. H. Dillahunty (January 30–June 29, 1864)
*Ranging District*: Precinct No. 1, Palo Pinto County

## COMPANY A
Captain B. B. Haney (February 1–May 31, 1864)
*Ranging District*: Wise County with headquarters at Decatur

## COMPANY A
Captain William R. Peveler (February 8–June 21, 1864)
*Ranging District*: Precinct No. 1, Young County

## COMPANY A
Captain J. J. "Jack" Cureton (February 19–June 30, 1864)
Captain J. J. "Jack" Cureton (December 1864–January 15, 1865)
*Ranging District*: Stephens County

## COMPANY A
Captain J. P. Guinn (February 23–October 1, 1864)
*Ranging District*: Montague County with headquarters at Montague

## COMPANY B
Captain Jonah S. Culwell (January 29–July 1, 1864)
*Ranging District*: Parker County

## Company B
Captain J. M. Hanks (February 1–June 1, 1864)
*Ranging District*: Wise County with headquarters at Decatur

## Company B
Captain Sevier Shannon (February 1–June 1, 1864)
*Ranging District*: Montague County with headquarters at Montague

## Company B
Captain George B. Pickett (February 1–June 1, 1864)
*Ranging District*: Wise County with headquarters at Decatur

## Company B
Captain John Taylor (February 1–April 15, 1864)
  *Capt. Taylor reported as deserter*
1st Lieutenant J. A. Spear, Commanding (April 15–26, 1864)
Captain E. M. Orrick (April 26–October 1, 1864)
*Ranging District*: Jack County with headquarters at Jacksboro

## Company B
1st Lieutenant Charles Neuhans, Commanding (February 2–July 25, 1864)
*Ranging District*: Precinct No. 2, Young County

## Company C
1st Lieutenant James C. Loving (January 30–June 1, 1864)
*Ranging District*: Palo Pinto County

## Company C
Captain James Graham (January 30–December 31, 1864)
*Ranging District*: Cooke County

## Company C
Captain Joseph Ward (February 1–June 5, 1864)
*Ranging District*: Parker County with headquarters at Weatherford

## Company D
Captain William C. Clayton (September 20, 1863–June 29, 1864)
*Ranging District*: Palo Pinto County with headquarters at Rock Creek Station

## Company D
Captain James M. Luckey (January 29–April 15, 1864)
  *Capt. Luckey arrested and charged with treason (April 19, 1864)*
Captain Monroe Upton (May 7–June 1, 1864)
Captain Monroe Upton (July 1, 1864–?)
*Ranging District*: Precinct No. 1, Parker County with headquarters at Weatherford

## Company D
Captain Cincinnatus Potter (February 5–June 1, 1864)
*Ranging District*: Cooke County

## Company E
Captain David Yeary (March 19–July 1, 1864)
*Ranging District*: Parker County with headquarters at Weatherford

### Shoemake's Company
Captain William H. Shoemake (January 30–June 18, 1864)
*Ranging District*: Wise and Jack Counties with headquarters at Decatur

### Hill's Company
Captain James O. Hill (February 1–May 31, 1864)
*Ranging District*: Cooke County

### Whaley's Company
Captain Thomas F. Whaley (February 1–June 1, 1864)
*Ranging District*: Cooke County

### Johnson's Company
Captain T. J. Johnson (February 1–June 1, 1864)
*Ranging District*: Wise County

### Smith's Company
1st Lieutenant Thomas Smith, Commanding (February 1, 1864–January 1, 1865)
*Ranging District*: Jack County

### Curtis' Company
Captain J. W. Curtis (February 8, 1864–?)
*Ranging District*: Stephens County

### Corning's Company
Captain A. F. Corning
  *Capt. Corning arrested and charged with treason (April 19, 1864)*

### Norton's Company
Captain David O. Norton
  *Capt. Norton arrested and charged with treason (April 19, 1864)*

### Tonkawa Scout Company
Captain W. T. Mosley
Chief Castile (August 1864–?)
*Headquarters*: Fort Belknap
  *Company attached to Frontier Regiment (January 9, 1865)*

### Potter's Battalion
Captain Cincinnatus Potter (February–May 1865)
*Ranging District*: Cooke County
  *Capt. Potter commanded six companies*

### Earhart's Battalion
Captain J. B. Earhart (February–May 1865)
*Ranging District*: Wise County

### Ward's Battalion
Captain Joseph Ward (February–May 1865)
*Ranging District*: Parker County

### Cureton's Battalion
Captain J. J. "Jack" Cureton (February–May 1865)
*Ranging District*: Stephens County

130   THE TEXAS RANGERS

*District Ranging Area*: Cooke, Wise, Jack, Parker, Montague, Young, Palo Pinto, Knox, Baylor, Stephens, Shackelford, Jones, Haskell, Hardeman, Archer, Clay, Throckmorton, Wichita, and Wilbarger Counties with headquarters at Decatur
*District organized and mustered into service as Texas State Troops*

## Second (or Central) Frontier District

### HEADQUARTERS
Major George B. Erath, Commanding (January 6, 1864–June 1865)
1st Lieutenant George F. Adams, Adjutant (February 12–June 1, 1864)

### COMPANY NO. 1
1st Lieutenant Singleton Gilbert (February 9–August 9, 1864)
*Ranging District*: Eastland County with headquarters at Nash Springs

### COMPANY NO. 1
Captain Alf Hunter (1864)
*Ranging District*: Mason County

### COMPANY A
Captain Silas S. Totten (January 23–February 24, 1864)
*Ranging District*: Bosque County

### COMPANY B
Captain J. B. B. Martin (February 1–May 31, 1864)
*Ranging District*: Erath County with headquarters at Stephenville

### COMPANY C
Captain William H. Culver (February 1–May 31, 1864)
Captain William H. Culver (December 1864–January 15, 1865)
*Ranging District*: Erath and Coryell Counties with headquarters at Stephenville

### COMPANY C
Captain W. B. Pace (February 21–June 1, 1864)
Captain W. B. Pace (?–March 17, 1865?)
*Ranging District*: Precincts No. 2 and 3, Lampasas County with headquarters at Lampasas

### COMPANY C
Captain G. W. Haley (May 13–17, 1864)
*Ranging District*: Coryell County

### MCREYNOLDS' COMPANY
Captain J. M. McReynolds (February 1–May 31, 1864)
*Ranging District*: Johnson County with headquarters at Squaw Creek

### SCOTT'S COMPANY
Captain M. J. Scott (February 15–June 1, 1864)
*Ranging District*: Precincts No. 1 and 2, Lampasas County

### MCCAMANT'S SQUAD
1st Lieutenant A. S. McCamant, Commanding (May 9, 1864–?)
*Ranging District*: Erath County

### GILLENTINE'S COMPANY
Captain Nick W. Gillentine (August 8, 1863–January 8, 1865)
*Ranging District*: Erath County with headquarters at Stephenville

### CUNNINGHAM'S COMPANY
Captain James Cunningham (February 6–June 1, 1864)
Captain James Cunningham (December 1864–January 15, 1865)
*Ranging District*: Precincts No. 1, 2, and 3, Comanche County

### BARNES' COMPANY
Captain R. S. "Sam" Barnes (February 1, 1864–January 8, 1865)
*Ranging District*: Bosque County

### BIBBERSTEIN'S COMPANY
Captain Herman R. von Biberstein (1864)
*Ranging District*: Mason and Kimble Counties

### BROWN'S COMPANY
Captain John Henry Brown (February 10–March 8, 1864)
*Ranging District*: San Saba County

### ENGLISH'S COMPANY
Captain James W. English (1864)
*Ranging District*: Johnson County

### GRAHAM'S COMPANY
Captain Gideon "Ged" Graham (January 30–May 31, 1864)
Captain Gideon "Ged" Graham (1864–January 15, 1865)
*Ranging District*: Coryell County

### LANHAM'S COMPANY
Captain B. Lanham (February 5–June 1, 1864)
*Ranging District*: Coryell County

### MOSELEY'S COMPANY
Captain D. H. Moseley (February 5–June 1, 1864)
*Ranging District*: Brown County

### MULLENS' COMPANY
Captain Isaac Mullens (February 1, 1864–?)
*Ranging District*: Coleman and Brown Counties

### PUGH'S COMPANY
Captain E. B. Pugh (February 1–May 31, 1864)
*Ranging District*: Erath County

### RICE'S COMPANY
Captain James M. Rice (February 5–June 1, 1864)
*Ranging District*: Hamilton County

### ROBINSON'S COMPANY
Captain William F. Robinson (1864)
*Ranging District*: Comanche County

### Shipman's Company
Captain J. R. Shipman (February 5–June 1, 1864)
*Ranging District*: Coryell County

### Skaggs' Company
Captain D. Skaggs (February 5–June 1, 1864)
*Ranging District*: Brown County

### Cathey's Company
Captain William H. Cathey (February 1–June 1, 1864)
Captain William H. Cathey (December 1864–January 15, 1865)
*Ranging District*: Johnson County

### McKeen's Company
Lieutenant J. F. McKeen, Commanding
*Ranging District*: Coleman County
*District Ranging Area*: Erath, Bosque, Coryell, Hamilton, Comanche, Brown, Lampasas, San Saba, Mason, Eastland, Coleman, Runnels, Concho, McCulloch, Menard, Kimble, Callahan, and Taylor Counties, and Johnson County west of the Fort Belknap–Fort Graham Road with headquarters at Gatesville
  *District organized and mustered into service as Texas State Troops*

## *Third (or Southern) Frontier District*
### Headquarters
Major James M. Hunter, Commanding (January–June 20, 1864)
Brigadier-General John D. McAdoo, Commanding (June 23, 1864–January 19, 1865)
Major John Henry Brown, Commanding (January 19–May 26, 1865)
Major James M. Hunter (June 23, 1864–January 19, 1865)
2nd Lieutenant Gustav Frasch, Adjutant (April 1, 1864–January 31, 1865)
Major Russell DeArmond, Quartermaster
Captain John R. Franklin, Ordnance Officer (July 13–December 13, 1864?)

### Company No. 1
Captain W. J. Locke (January 27–??, 1864)
*Ranging District*: Gillespie County

### Company No. 4
Captain John Barton (January 27–June 30, 1864)
*Ranging District*: Burnet County with headquarters at Oatmeal

### Company A
Captain William Wahrmund (January 27, 1864–March 20, 1865)
*Ranging District*: Gillespie County

### Company B (II)
Captain L. Schuetze (January 24–February 15, 1864)
Captain E. Krauskopf (February 15–June 1, 1864)
*Ranging District*: Gillespie County

### Company C
Captain Jacob Dearing (April 14–June 1, 1864)
*Ranging District*: Gillespie County

### Company C
Captain William J. Standifer (1864–April 1865)
*Ranging District*: Burnet County

### Herring's Company
1st Lieutenant Curtis Herring, Commanding (April 25–June 1, 1864)
*Ranging District*: McMullen County

### Hudson's Company
1st Lieutenant W. A. Hudson, Commanding (1864)
*Ranging District*: Gillespie County

### Hynes' Company
1st Lieutenant John Hynes, Commanding (February 22, 1864–?)
*Ranging District*: Bee County

### Irving's Company
Captain R. J. Irving (January 30–May 31, 1864)
*Ranging District*: Blanco County

### Farr's Company
1st Lieutenant D. H. Farr, Commanding (February 13–June 1, 1864)
*Ranging District*: Kerr County

### Bittick's Company
Captain G. C. Bittick (January 29–October 1864)
*Ranging District*: Burnet County

### Breazeale's Company
Captain F. Breazeale (February–April 1864)
*Ranging District*: Precincts No. 4, 5, 6, 7, and 8, Llano County

### Dorbandt's Company
Captain Christian Dorbandt (January 24–June 1, 1864)
*Ranging District*: Precincts No. 4, 5, and 6, Burnet County

### Walthersdorff's Company
Captain Albert Walthersdorff (1863–January 1864)
*Ranging District*: Blanco County

### Tom's Company
Captain John Files Tom (February 20–June 1, 1864)
*Ranging District*: Medina and Atascosa Counties

### Gussett's Company
Captain Norwick Gussett (February 23–June 1, 1864)
*Ranging District*: Live Oak County

### Watkins' Company
Captain Theopilus Watkins
*Ranging District*: Uvalde County

### Bourland's Company
Captain James S. Bourland (February 6–March 5, 1864)
*Ranging District*: Llano County

### JONES' COMPANY
Captain William E. Jones (March 1–June 1, 1864)
*Ranging District*: Kendall County

### KING'S COMPANY
1st Lieutenant James P. King, Commanding (February 18, 1864–?)
*Ranging District*: Karnes County west of the San Antonio River

### MAGILL'S COMPANY
Captain James P. Magill (January 28–June 1, 1864)
*Ranging District*: Burnet County

### MITCHELL'S COMPANY
Captain Bladen Mitchell (February 6–May 3, 1864)
*Ranging District*: Bandera County

### ROBBINS' COMPANY
Captain George W. Robbins (March 7–June 1, 1864)
*Ranging District*: Medina County

### WALDRUP'S COMPANY
Lieutenant P. Waldrup, Commanding (January 27, 1864–?)
*Ranging District*: Gillespie County

### WEBER'S SQUAD
1st Lieutenant Augustine Weber, Commanding (March 7, 1864–?)
*Ranging District*: Medina County

### WILLIAMS' COMPANY
Captain R. H. Williams (March 31, 1864–?)
*Ranging District*: Frio County
*District Ranging Area*: Burnet, Kerr, Llano, Gillespie, Blanco, Bandera, Medina, Uvalde, Kendall, Frio, Live Oak, Atascosa, McMullen, Dawson, Maverick, Zavala, Dimmit, La Salle, Edwards, and Kinney Counties, Karnes County southwest of the San Antonio River, and Bee County southwest of the Medina River with headquarters at Fredericksburg
   District organized and mustered into service as Texas State Troops

## Frontier Battalion

### FIELD & STAFF
Captain Henry Fossett, Senior Captain (June 1, 1864–May 26, 1865)
1st Lieutenant Augustus Barry, Adjutant (February 16, 1865–?)

### COMPANY A
Captain Henry Fossett (April 1, 1864–May 26, 1865)
*Headquarters*: Camp Colorado

### COMPANY B
Captain George B. Cooke (April 1, 1864–May 26, 1865)
*Headquarters*: Camp San Saba
   Battalion mustered into C.S. service (March 1, 1864) and operated under the personal orders of Lt-Col. J. B. Barry (October 16, 1864–May 26, 1865)

# 6

# No Surrender, No Prisoners: The Minute Men, the Frontier Forces, and the Frontier Men (1865–1874)

Once the guns fell silent, the Federal Government instituted a process of Reconstruction to gradually readmit the secessionist Southern states into the Union and to protect the new constitutional and legal status of the ex-slaves who were free as a result of the war. In Texas, and throughout the former Confederacy, county and state officials served the people at the pleasure of initially the President and later Congress. The enforcement arm of Reconstruction was the United States Army, which first occupied Texas in late May 1865 with the intent to install and maintain a loyal government and to protect the rights of the Freedmen. While Texas escaped the physical destruction experienced in Virginia or South Carolina, for example, the state was nevertheless in turmoil. Trade and finance were disrupted and citizens were left to deal with political, social, and economic issues brought on by the war. Andrew J. Hamilton, governor from June 17, 1865, to August 9, 1866, faced the ever-present threat of Indian raids, an increase in crime, a fiscal crisis, and a large number of Freedmen (emancipated on June 19) now in the labor force.

Governor James W. Throckmorton (the same who had commanded the First Frontier District) entered office on August 12, 1866. He and federal commanders in Texas quickly found themselves at odds over military interference in civil affairs at the expense of frontier defense. They also quarreled about whether Freedmen and Unionists were being adequately protected under the law. On August 8, 1867, Major-General Philip Sheridan, commanding the Fifth Military District (which encompassed Texas and Louisiana), removed Throckmorton from office as "an impediment to reconstruction"—the only reason necessary to depose an elected official.

Meanwhile, Comanche and Kiowa raids resumed in Comanche, Parker, Bosque, Montague, Clay, Young, Denton, Wise, and Cooke counties. The years 1865 and 1866 saw the highest number of Indian depredations in Texas history; incomplete records documented over 160 civilians killed in Indian attacks, two dozen wounded, more than forty captured, and 30,000 head of cattle and 3,600 horses stolen. Governors Hamilton and Throckmorton responded by ordering several minute companies in Parker, Young, and Wise counties to be raised under the provisions of the frontier defense act of February 7, 1861. The Eleventh Legislature emulated the executives by authorizing a Texas Ranger regiment on Septem-

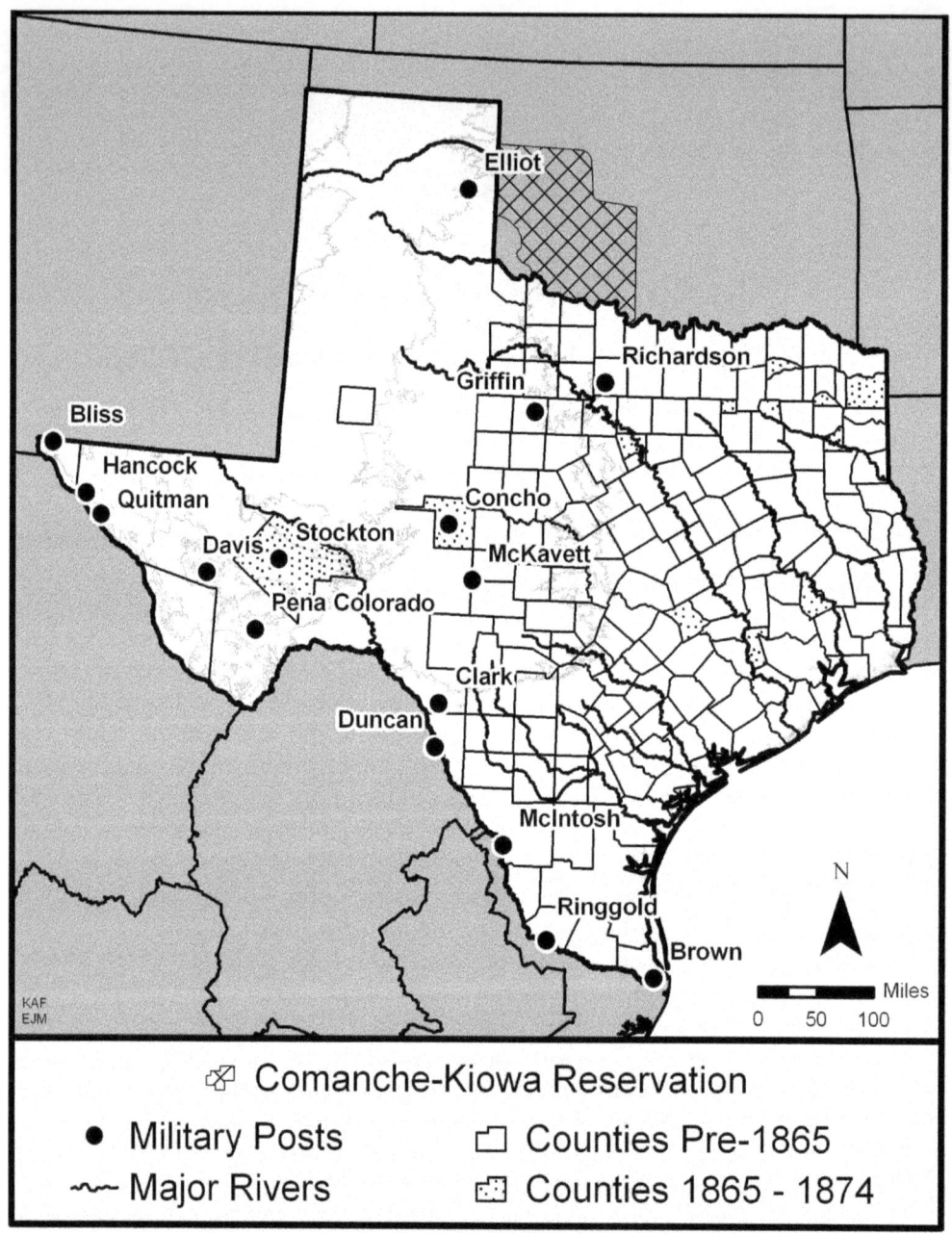

ber 21, 1866 (the first formal use of the term *Texas Rangers* in legislation). Governor Throckmorton appointed Peter Ross colonel, Ed Burleson lieutenant-colonel, and "Buck" Barry major; but before the new regiment could begin to organize, the Fifth Military District ordered all state troops—likely to be formed of ex–Confederates—to disband. This edict included any ranger and militia companies that might patrol the frontier counties. The federal authorities feared they would be used more as a political tool to deter Reconstruction than to fight Indians. Indeed, the Army underestimated the threat from hostile Indians and posted most of the cavalry and infantry companies in the interior counties of the state. The recently arrived commanders knew little of past events in the Texas Indian wars and committed many of the same errors as their predecessors in the 1850s. The garrisons on the frontier, still as undermanned and under-funded as before the war, remained unable to adequately protect settlers.

In addition to retaining Forts McKavett, Clark, and Duncan, the army established a new cordon of frontier posts, including Fort Richardson, on Lost Creek in Jack County; Fort Griffin, on the Clear Fork in present Shackelford County; and Fort Concho, on the junction of the North and Main Concho rivers in present Tom Green County. Beginning in 1867, in order to protect the Trans-Pecos country from Comanche and Mescalero Apache raids, federal troops reoccupied Fort Stockton, at Comanche Springs in present Pecos County; Fort Davis, on Limpia Creek in present Jeff Davis County; and Fort Quitman, on the San Antonio–El Paso road in present Hudspeth County.

Texans in the sixteen years between annexation and secession had repeatedly criticized the federal government for unsuccessfully protecting settlers from Indian inroads. Now they had another objection in that Washington had proceeded to provide the Comanches and Kiowas with a secure base from which to operate. When the Medicine Lodge Treaty was signed on October 21, 1867, both tribes pledged to settle on a reservation in Indian Territory and take up the plow. Members of various religious groups, who were the driving force behind President Ulysses S. Grant's Peace Policy, were appointed Indian agents and special commissioners in the hopes of transforming the nomadic warriors into peaceful farmers. The Society of Friends (Quakers) was given the responsibility for the president's program in Kansas and Indian Territory.

The Peace Policy permitted federal troops to engage hostiles in Texas, but prevented them from crossing the Red River onto the reservation. While the garrison at Fort Sill was responsible for the reservation itself, they could not act in regard to suspected raiders without the approval of the Indian agent (who was a pacifist Quaker). The advocates of the Peace Policy hoped to decrease the number of raids across the Red River, but, in fact, the exact opposite occurred. Instead, the Indians drew their government-supplied rations and other annuity goods while resting between depredations. For instance, on January 5 and 6, 1868, Chief Big Tree and 150–200 Kiowas left the reservation and raided into Cooke County, killing thirteen people and capturing ten women and children; three later escaped and two were ransomed. The Kwahadis under Quanah Parker refused to relocate to the reservation and continued to raid from the *Comanchería*.

While the Comanches and Kiowas made full use of their sanctuary north of the Red River, Lipan Apaches and Kickapoos likewise resided in complete freedom and safety south of the Rio Grande. South Texas, from San Antonio to the border, was beset with Indians who stole horses and cattle, took captives, burned homes, and murdered settlers. Between 1865 and 1867, eighteen people were killed and $30,000 worth of livestock was stolen in Uvalde County alone.

During the late war, ranchers on the unfenced cattle ranges throughout Texas who were serving in the Confederate Army had been forced to leave their stock unattended. Often stray cattle drifted south of the Nueces seeking warmer weather and better grazing and swelled the numbers already there. After the war, the Texas longhorn became a welcome commodity in the East and so began the business of driving steers to the Kansas railheads and beyond. Many of the early trail herds were gathered from the thousands of unbranded and wild cattle, known as "mavericks," roaming the *brasada*. An unwritten rule of the time defined a maverick as an unbranded bovine more than a year old that was not following a branded cow. Any such animal found on one's property or on the open range was considered theirs. Not all subscribed to this custom and, with the value of Texan cattle on the rise, legitimate stock raisers were forced to deal with bands of Anglo and Mexican rustlers, as well as Indian raiders. Often deserters from the Union and Confederate armies, or those involved in the war between the Mexican Republican Army under Benito Juárez and the Imperial forces of Maximilian I and his French masters, the cattle thieves began in September 1865 taking full advantage of the refuge offered by the Rio Grande. They drove the stolen Texan livestock across the river and sold them to wealthy *rancheros*, while Mexican authorities were bribed to ignore the large numbers of animals crossing the border. During Reconstruction and afterward, U.S. policy forbade troops from violating Mexican sovereignty in order to recover stolen property.

The 1869 gubernatorial election, one of the most acrimonious and disgraceful in Texas history, was to have a direct effect on the frontier emergency. Brevet Major-General Joseph J. Reynolds, commanding the Fifth Military District, used his official position and the physical intimidation of his soldiery to skew the results in favor of Edmund J. Davis. Winning by a narrow margin of slightly more than 800 votes, Davis was named provisional governor on January 8, 1870, and inaugurated on April 28. While the new executive was basically an honest man, his Radical Republican administration was riddled with corruption and one of the most controversial in state history. His agenda called for restoring the militia and creating a State Police to provide law enforcement, the expansion of public schools and public works, establishing bureaus of immigration and geology, and the improved protection of the frontier.

The Davis administration, for all its shortcomings, did not neglect this last item on the agenda. In response to the two-front crisis, on June 13, 1870, Governor Davis received authorization from the Twelfth Legislature to muster twenty companies of Texas Rangers into service for twelve months. Each company of the new Frontier Forces was to consist of one captain, one lieutenant, one medical officer, three sergeants, four corporals, one bugler, one farrier, and fifty privates. In accordance with tradition, the rangers provided their own horses, sidearms, and equipment, while the State furnished provisions, ammunition, and forage. For the first time, the State purchased long guns—Winchester Model 1866 .44-caliber lever-action carbines—and issued them to the rangers, with the cost deducted from their first month's pay. Those wages were set at one hundred dollars a month for captains and medical officers, eighty for lieutenants, fifty-four for sergeants, fifty-two for corporals and farriers, and fifty for privates and buglers. While organized according to the rules and regulations of the U.S. Army, the rangers operated under the orders of Colonel James Davidson, adjutant general of Texas. In describing the Reconstruction era, Walter Webb wrote, "For nine years after the Civil War, the Texas Rangers were nonexistent." His statement is at odds with the very existence of the Frontier Forces, who were rangers in every way.

Although the enabling legislation did provide for wages, it did not appropriate funding. To remedy this oversight, the legislature authorized a state bond issue of $750,000 on August 5. These "Frontier Defense Bonds" bore an interest of seven percent and were payable in gold semi-annually. They were to be redeemable in twenty years and payable in forty. The act also levied a property tax, which financed a sinking fund to pay the interest due and to pay two percent of the principal of the bonds at maturity.

Once the issue of financial support was thought settled, the rangers were recruited and mustered into service. The captains were appointed by Governor Davis and had been, for the most part, Union sympathizers during the war. The majority, though, did have prior ranger experience. The number of authorized companies never reached twenty due to limited funds and recruits, but by November 15, fourteen companies were in the field. Soon after, Adjutant General Davidson ordered the reduction of all companies to a total of fifty officers and men.

Secretary of War William W. Belknap responded quickly to the new Frontier Forces and, on July 19, 1870, declared the U.S. Army would continue to have sole responsibility for frontier defense. In defiance of his superiors, General Reynolds, now commanding the Department of Texas, welcomed the presence of more than five hundred rangers on the frontier. He and Davis agreed to ignore the secretary and, in direct violation of the law, placed the rangers under the operational command and control of the department. In the first months of the Frontier Forces, the ranger companies were allowed to draw supplies from military posts. On October 6, Secretary Belknap overruled Reynolds and refused the rangers the use of army stores. Instead, the captains were forced to contract for their own subsistence, further depleting the limited operating budget. For this and other reasons, the governor soon reclaimed the State's control of the Frontier Forces. Later the next year, on February 4, the number of ranger companies was reduced to seven.

Continuing their slow transition from Indian fighters to lawmen, Colonel Davidson ordered the rangers deployed in South Texas to break up the cattle rustling and other depredations. Some of the best captains included John W. Sansom, Henry Jones Richarz, Cesario G. Falcón, and Bland Chamberlain. Sansom at Camp Verde and Richarz at Fort Inge patrolled from the mouth of the Pecos to Laredo against the Kickapoos and Lipans. Captain Falcón in Starr County and Captain Chamberlain in Zapata County with their predominately *Tejano* companies did the same on the lower Rio Grande against Mexican bandits.

Unfortunately, organized rustling in the Nueces Strip would prove hard to eliminate. Due to the indiscretions of Reconstruction authorities and the state politicians they deemed acceptable, there was little public support for law enforcement. Many of the civil officers in the border counties seemed to look the other way and, in truth, some were in business with the rustlers. The state policemen were employed in the interior counties and were too involved in abusing their authority with extortion and the suppression of political opposition to the Davis administration. Such conduct was accepted and, indeed, sponsored by the adjutant general and further eroded Texan respect for the law.

In the Big Bend, the inhabitants of the region had been enduring Indian depredations for more than two centuries. Between March 1865 and January 1867, El Paso County reported that thirty-five Mexican American residents (known as *Paseños*) had been killed and more than 1,200 animals, plus wagons and equipment, had been stolen. Captain Gregorio N. Garcia (a former Mexican soldier and veteran Indian fighter), commanding Company N, was primarily responsible for the local defense.

Meanwhile, on the northwestern frontier, rangers continued their war with the Comanches and Kiowas. One of the hardest-fought battles involved the detachment commanded by Sergeant Edward H. Cobb. Cobb's men were part of Captain David P. Baker's company, which ranged Montague County to patrol the well-used crossings of the Red River. The sergeant was a veteran of the Civil War, but had never been in an engagement with Indians. His men were likewise inexperienced in Indian warfare and, indeed, all but one were raw recruits who had never spilled blood.

In the early morning of February 7, 1871, Cobb received word at his camp on the eastern edge of the Cross Timbers that Indians were raiding along Clear Creek, southeast of

Cobb's position, toward Denton. Cobb, ten of his men, and the messenger immediately set out in pursuit. They rode hard throughout the day, noting that tracks of a second band had joined those of the Indians the Texans were already pursuing. They estimated the combined force totaled at least forty warriors. The rangers caught up with the Indians by late afternoon on Paradise Prairie in Wise County and confirmed them to be Comanches and Kiowas. Upon seeing that their pursuers were fewer in number, the Indians turned and tried to goad the rangers into a fight.

Cobb knew his horses were in no condition to pursue or to retreat, so he had his men assemble at nearby Hickory Creek, then ordered a short gallop. Once out on the prairie, Cobb's men dismounted eighty yards from the nearest Indians and deployed in a loose skirmish line. A. J. Sowell, a ranger who fought in the battle later related, "We were about to play a desperate game.... Well we knew their savage nature, if we were overwhelmed; no surrender; no prisoners taken in this kind of warfare."

The rangers received the first charge and used their Winchester "Yellow Boy" carbines to repulse it and each successive one for about an hour and a half. Cobb then ordered his men to remount and ride for the better defensive position of a nearby knoll. As the Texans withdrew, the Indians darted in and tried to cut off Sowell (nephew of the Plum Creek veteran of the same name) and Gus Hasroot, whose exhausted horses refused to move quickly. The remaining rangers rallied to their comrades' aid and the fighting became desperate and close. Cobb's men shattered two charges and killed the chiefs of the two bands.

As the sun set, the Indians abandoned the field, and the rangers, exhausted and nearly out of ammunition, also left the scene to shelter at the old Keep Ranch house three miles to the east. The Texan casualities consisted of one seriously wounded and several with minor wounds. The Indians were believed to have lost seven killed and an unknown number wounded.

A. J. Sowell, a ranger in the early 1870s, wrote five books, including *Rangers and Pioneers of Texas* (1884). In the portion describing his own service, he detailed the campaign into the Wichita Mountains and the engagement at Paradise Prairie near the Keep Ranch house. Courtesy of the Texas Ranger Hall of Fame and Museum, Waco, TX.

Later the next year, an Indian at Fort Sill talked of the Hickory Creek battle (also known as the Keep Ranch fight). He confirmed the slain Comanche war chief was Oska Horseback (possibly the son of the

Nakoni Comanche chief Horseback), and the other dead leader was Sittanke, the nephew of old Sittanke, the principal chief of the Kiowas.

On May 2, William T. Sherman, commanding general of the U.S. Army, embarked on an inspection tour of the Texas frontier. He and his escort of twenty officers and men crossed Salt Creek Prairie on May 17, approximately eight miles west of Fort Richardson. Their progress was observed by a one hundred-man Kiowa war party waiting in ambush, but the medicine man accompanying the raiders predicted a better prize would soon approach. The unsuspecting soldiers were spared, but the next day a twelve-man wagon train owned by freighting contractor Henry Warren was struck. Eight teamsters were killed, four escaped to Fort Richardson, all ten wagons were burned, and forty-one mules stolen.

The Warren Wagon Train Massacre failed to create any radical change in the Indian Bureau's Peace Policy itself. General Sherman did, though, replace the army's defensive strategy with a program utilizing search and destroy tactics. Colonel Ranald S. Mackenzie, commanding the 4th Cavalry at Fort Richardson, led two expeditions into the *Llano Estacado*, and engaged Kwahadis at Blanco Canyon (October 15, 1871) and Kotsotekas at the North Fork of the Red River (September 29, 1872).

Unfortunately, the Frontier Forces were doomed to a quick end. In June 1871, they exceeded their appropriations and were disbanded. The State, due to its poor credit rating, failed to market the Frontier Defense Bonds that were to fund the program. The returns had been unable to even meet the interest of the bonds. Those held by the Agricultural and Mechanical College (present Texas A&M University) went overdue. In 1874, bonds worth $20,000 were redeemed and canceled. Four years later, another $5,000 in bonds was redeemed and the entire fund was canceled. Once again, prosecution of the Indian wars fell victim to an empty treasury.

On November 25, 1871, the Twelfth Legislature authorized twenty-four minute companies for frontier defense. The rangers again furnished horses, sidearms, and camp equipage, while the state provided rifles, ammunition, and accoutrements, which remained public property. Each company consisted of one lieutenant, two sergeants, two corporals, and fifteen privates. Because of the state's depleted coffers, the new detachments were to serve for ten days a month for twelve months, and only when Indian raids were threatening. While on duty, they received a set wage of two dollars a day. The Minute Men fought in six engagements with Indian raiders in 1872, killing twenty-three and recovering sixty-five stolen horses, while suffering one ranger killed and three wounded.

Between March 1873 and January 1874, twenty-two minute companies were reorganized, with seventeen receiving compensation and five serving without pay. They saw action on nine separate occasions, killing four Indians and recovering 117 horses. They lost one ranger.

The Army struck another blow when Colonel Mackenzie departed Fort Clark and crossed the Rio Grande with Companies A, B, C, E, I, and M, 4th Cavalry, and a twenty-five-man detachment of Seminole-Negro scouts under Lieutenant John L. Bullis. On the morning of May 18, 1873, the soldiers attacked and destroyed three *rancherías* (one Kickapoo, one Lipan, and one Mescalero) near Remolino, killed nineteen Indians, and captured one Lipan chief, forty women and children, and sixty-five horses. One soldier was killed and two were wounded. Due to Mackenzie's foray, residents in South Texas enjoyed a three-year respite from Indian attacks originating in Mexico, although Anglo and Mexican rustlers continued to plague the region.

On November 1, 1873, the governor called up eleven ranger companies for four months' service. The Frontier Men, as they were called, received no appropriations but were promised reimbursement for expenses and wages in some future legislative session. Only eight companies were known to have formed.

Shortly afterward, Governor Davis' time finally ran out. His treasurer was accused of embezzling state funds (although he was later cleared of the charges), too many political blocs were hostile to the administration, the Thirteenth Legislature repealed the State Police act on April 22, 1873, and Adjutant General Davidson absconded with $37,000 from the state treasury and fled to Belgium. Davis ran for re-election and was defeated by Richard Coke on December 2, 1873, by a vote of 85,549 to 42,663. The state supreme court ruled the election unconstitutional and invalidated the results. Davis refused to step down, arguing that he had to abide by the decision of the court. Coke stated his intention to take office regardless of the consequences. Texans publicly ignored the court's decision and federal intervention became Davis's only hope for remaining in office. President Grant refused to involve himself, and Davis reluctantly left office on January 15, 1874, officially marking the end of Reconstruction in Texas.

## Historical Register, 1865–1874

*"Boys, what do you say to a charge?"*
— Sergeant E. H. Cobb

### 1ST PARKER COUNTY MINUTE COMPANY OF TEXAS STATE TROOPS
Captain Lewis Lycurgus "Like" Tackitt (October 20, 1865–June 22, 1866)
*Ranging District*: Parker County with headquarters at Weatherford
    Company operated under the authority of Gov. A. J. Hamilton and under the supervision of the Chief Justice of Parker County

### 2ND PARKER COUNTY MINUTE COMPANY OF TEXAS STATE TROOPS
Captain Harteford Howard (April 26–July 26, 1866)
*Ranging District*: Parker County with headquarters at Weatherford
    Company operated under the authority of Gov. A. J. Hamilton and under the supervision of the Chief Justice of Parker County

### COMPANY OF CITIZEN CAVALRY
Captain Edward "Ed" Burleson, Jr. (July 13–August 4, 1865)
*Ranging District*: Travis County with headquarters at Austin
    Company operated under the authority of Bvt. MG G. Granger, CG of the Department of Texas and under the supervision of Gov. A. J. Hamilton

### WISE COUNTY MINUTE COMPANY
Captain John Teague (October 14–November 7, 1865)
*Ranging District*: Wise County with headquarters at Decatur
    Company operated under the authority of Gov. A. J. Hamilton and under the supervision of the Chief Justice of Wise County

### YOUNG COUNTY MINUTE MEN
Captain William B. Self (January 1–22, 1866)
*Ranging District*: Tarrant County with headquarters at Fort Worth
    Company operated under the authority of Gov. A. J. Hamilton and under the supervision of the Chief Justice of Tarrant County

### Montague County Company of State Troops

Captain John T. Rowland (November 17, 1866–?)
*Company operated under the authority of Gov. J. W. Throckmorton*

### Ranger Company

Captain Andrew J. Yount (November 26, 1866–?)
*Headquarters*: Denton
*Company organized and mustered into service by order of Gov. J. W. Throckmorton*

### Clay County Minute Men

Captain Samuel Green (September 5, 1867–?)
*Ranging District*: Clay County

### Blanco County Minute Men

Captain Alexander "Buck" Roberts (Spring 1870)
*Ranging District*: Blanco and Llano Counties

## *The Frontier Forces*

### Company A

Captain Franklin Jones (August 25–November 12, 1870)
*Ranging District*: Mason County with headquarters at Fort Mason

### Company B

Captain A. H. Cox (September 8, 1870–May 15, 1871)
*Ranging District*: Erath County to the Clear Fork of the Brazos River with headquarters at camp near Fort Griffin (September 1870) and Camp Davidson near Stephenville (November 1870)

### Company C

Captain John W. Sansom (August 25, 1870–May 31, 1871)
*Ranging District*: Kerr, Kendall, Blanco, and Bandera Counties with headquarters at Camp Verde; Fort Griffin (March 1871)

### Company D

Captain John R. Kelso (September 10, 1870–February 2, 1871)
*Ranging District*: Uvalde, Kinney, and Edwards Counties with headquarters at Camp Wood

### Company E

Captain Henry Joseph Richarz (September 9, 1870–June 15, 1871)
*Ranging District*: Uvalde County with headquarters at Fort Inge

### Company F

Captain David P. Baker (November 5, 1870–November 15, 1871)
1st Sergeant Edward H. Cobb, commanding detachment
*Ranging District*: Wise, Montague, and Denton Counties with headquarters at Thompsonville Station and Cobb's detachment at Perryman Station

### Company G (A*)

Captain Cesario G. Falcón (October 8–February 28, 1871)
*Ranging District*: Starr County with headquarters at El Olmito (October 1870) and Rancho Nuevo and detachment at Lomo Blanco (January 1871)

*Company "G" renamed as Company "A" (January 1, 1871)

#### COMPANY H
Captain Bland Chamberlain (November 15, 1870–February 28, 1871)
*Ranging District*: Zapata County with headquarters at Post Davidson

#### COMPANY I
Captain James M. Hunter (September 12, 1870–January 24, 1871)
Lieutenant W. W. Jones, commanding detachment (September 12, 1870–January 24, 1871)
*Ranging District*: Mason County with headquarters at Fort Mason and Jones' detachment at Austin

#### COMPANY K
Captain Jacob M. Harrell (September 16, 1870–February 20, 1871)
*Ranging District*: Lampasas County with headquarters at Camp Russell

#### COMPANY L (G*)
Captain Herman R. von Biberstein (October 10, 1870–April 30, 1871)
*Ranging District*: Gillespie, Menard, and McCulloch Counties with headquarters at Camp Degener (October 1870) and camp on Spring Creek (January 1871)
*Company "L" renamed as Company "G" (January 1, 1871)

#### CAPTAIN N (D*)
Captain Gregorio N. Garcia (August 12, 1870–June 16, 1871)
*Ranging District*: El Paso County with headquarters at San Elizario (August 1870), camp near Fort Quitman (September 1870), San Elizario (November 1870), Dog Canōn, New Mexico Territory (January 1871), and San Elizario (March 1871)
*Company "N" renamed as Company "D" (March 1, 1871)

#### COMPANY O (H*)
Captain Peter Kleid (August 29, 1870–May 31, 1871)
*Ranging District*: Frio and Nueces Canyons country with headquarters at Camp Elm Creek near old Fort Terrett (August 1870) and Camp Rio Frio (March 1871)
*Company "O" renamed as Company "H" (March 1, 1871)

#### COMPANY P
Captain James M. Swisher (August 29, 1870–February 6, 1871)
*Ranging District*: Coleman County with headquarters at camp on Home Creek near Camp Colorado

### *The Minute Men*

#### COMPANY A
Lieutenant James Ingram (January 4–November 17, 1872)
Lieutenant S. B. Gray (April 1–October 1, 1873)
*Ranging District*: Blanco County with headquarters at camp on Round Mountain (January 1872) and Blanco (April 1873)

#### COMPANY B
Lieutenant R. T. Rieger (March 2–September 2, 1872)
Lieutenant George W. Stevens (August 7, 1872–January 2, 1873)
Lieutenant George W. Stevens (September 1–October 31, 1873)
*Ranging District*: Wise County with headquarters at Live Oak

### Company C
Lieutenant Charles A. Patton (February 4 1872–February 4, 1873)
Lieutenant James C. Nowlin (March 1–July 1, 1873)
Lieutenant James C. Nowlin (January 1–February 1, 1874)
*Ranging District*: Kendall County with headquarters at Beorne

### Company D
Lieutenant J. A. Wright (May 25, 1872–June 1, 1873)
Lieutenant W. C. Watkins (September 18, 1873–April 30, 1874)
*Ranging District*: Comanche County with headquarters at camp on Sipe Springs

### Company E
Lieutenant Henry Schwethelm (April 6, 1872–April 10, 1874)
*Ranging District*: Kerr County with headquarters at Comfort

### Company F
Lieutenant J. C. Lacey (April 18–November 25, 1872)
Lieutenant William E. Hudson (December 12, 1872–April 12, 1873)
Lieutenant B. F. Casey (November 21, 1873–April 23, 1874)
*Ranging District*: Gillespie County with headquarters at camp on Spring Creek

### Company G
Lieutenant George H. Adams (June 10, 1872–March 29, 1874)
Sergeant J. J. Carter, Acting Commander (November 1873)
*Ranging District*: Brown County with headquarters at Brownwood

### Company H
Captain Asa Johnson (June 8, 1872–?)
*Ranging District*: Hays County with headquarters at Mountain City

### Company I
Lieutenant J. M. Waide (April 24–November 19, 1872)
Lieutenant J. M. Waide (July 4–6, 1873)
*Ranging District*: Cook County with headquarters at Blocker Station

### Company K
Lieutenant Robert Ballantyne (July 2, 1872–June 20, 1873)
*Ranging District*: Bandera County with headquarters at Bandera

### Company L
Lieutenant John M. Elkins (July 1, 1872–February 1, 1874)
*Ranging District*: Coleman County with headquarters at Camp Colorado

### Company M
Lieutenant George E. Haynie (August 10–November 19, 1872)
Lieutenant A. P. Hall (March 9–August 12, 1873)
Lieutenant E. W. Greenwood (September 12, 1873–March 10, 1874)
*Ranging District*: Lampasas County with headquarters at Lampasas

### Company N
Lieutenant William H. Ledbetter (August 13, 1872–December 11, 1873)
Lieutenant William H. Ledbetter (March 27–April 5, 1874)
*Ranging District*: San Saba County with headquarters at San Saba

## Company O
Lieutenant John Alexander (August 19, 1872–January 16, 1873)
Lieutenant W. H. Sims (March 9–August 13, 1873)
*Ranging District*: Burnet County with headquarters at camps on Underhill Springs (August 1872) and Morgan Creek (March 1873)

## Company P
Lieutenant J. C. Gilliland (August 19, 1872–August 18, 1873)
*Ranging District*: Parker County with headquarters at Cartersville

## Company Q
Lieutenant F. C. Stewart (August 21, 1872–August 9, 1873)
Lieutenant John M. Smith (September 29, 1873–March 29, 1874)
*Ranging District*: Llano County with headquarters at Llano

## Company R
Lieutenant Daniel Hoerster (August 26, 1872–December 20, 1873)
Lieutenant C. C. Smith (December 9, 1873–May 26, 1874)
*Ranging District*: Mason County with headquarters at Mason

## Company S
Lieutenant Newt Atkisson (August 23–October 12, 1872)
Lieutenant J. H. Carothers (October 1, 1873–?)
*Ranging District*: Jack County with headquarters at Keechi

## Company T
Lieutenant D. H. McClure (August 22, 1872–August 12, 1873)
*Ranging District*: Palo Pinto County with headquarters at Palo Pinto

## Company U
Lieutenant John J. Willingham (April 20, 1872–December 21, 1873)
*Ranging District*: Montague County with headquarters at Montague

## Company V
Lieutenant George Haby (September 1, 1872–August 15, 1873)
Sergeant Fred Specht, Acting Commander (July–September 1873)
*Ranging District*: Medina County with headquarters at Castroville

## Company W
Lieutenant J. D. Martinez (October 2, 1872–?)
*Ranging District*: Webb County with headquarters at Laredo

## Company X
Lieutenant Manuel Bau (October 8, 1872–October 8, 1873)
*Ranging District*: Maverick County with headquarters at Eagle Pass

## Company Y
Captain D. A. Bates (October 12, 1872–?)
*Ranging District*: Uvalde County with headquarters at Uvalde

## Company Z
Lieutenant C. M. O'Neal (October 12, 1872–September 30, 1873)
1st Sergeant Stephen P. Keith (October 5–November 20, 1873)

Lieutenant N. Keith (January 18–April 10, 1874)
*Ranging District*: Erath County with headquarters at Dublin

### COMPANY #1
Lieutenant William P. Calloway (May 20–September 5, 1873)
Captain William P. Calloway (September 5, 1873–March 11, 1874)
*Ranging District*: Kerr County with headquarters at Kerrville
*Company members served as volunteers without pay*

### COMPANY #2
Lieutenant George W. Larremore (November 21, 1873–?)
*Ranging District*: Gillespie County with headquarters at Fredericksburg
*Company members served as volunteers without pay*

### COMPANY #3
Captain J. H. Kennedy (January 6, 1873–?)
*Ranging District*: Kinney County with headquarters at Brackett City
*Company members served as volunteers without pay*

### COMPANY #4
Lieutenant John W. Jones (October 6, 1873–March 30, 1874)
*Ranging District*: Callahan County with headquarters at camp near Caddo Peak
*Company members served as volunteers without pay*

### COMPANY #5
Lieutenant P. J. Mires (August 25, 1873–?)
*Ranging District*: Menard County with headquarters at Menardville
*Company members served as volunteers without pay*

### RANGERS/MINUTE MEN
Captain George W. Stevens (November 26, 1873–March 26, 1874)
*Ranging District*: Wise County with headquarters at Camp Sandy

### JACK COUNTY RANGERS/FRONTIER TROOPS
Captain S. W. Eastin (December 3, 1873–April 3, 1874)
*Ranging District*: Jack County with headquarters at Camp Cleveland

### RANGERS
Captain W. C. McAdams (December 13, 1873–April 13, 1874)
*Ranging District*: Palo Pinto County with headquarters at Palo Pinto

### RANGERS/FRONTIER MEN
Captain G. W. Campbell (December 13, 1873–February 13, 1874)
*Ranging District*: Montague County with headquarters at camp on Little Wichita River

### RANGERS
Captain Willis L. Hunter (December 24, 1873–March 24, 1874)
*Ranging District*: Parker County with headquarters at Camp Briscoe

### RANGERS
Captain Andrew C. Tackett (January 6–February 14, 1874)
*Ranging District*: Young County

### RANGERS
Captain John Teague (January 6–February 14, 1874)
*Ranging District*: Wise County

### COMPANY C, BROWN AND SAN SABA RANGERS
Captain J. G. Connell (January 6–March 26, 1874)
*Ranging District*: Brown, San Saba, and McCulloch Counties with headquarters at Brownwood

### RANGERS/FRONTIER MEN
Captain M. R. Green (January 17–February 17, 1874)
*Ranging District*: Erath and Comanche Counties with headquarters at Stephenville

### COMPANY OF VOLUNTEER MINUTE MEN
Lieutenant Henry Schwethelm (November 8, 1874–February 28, 1877)
*Ranging District*: Kerr County with headquarters at Comfort

### YOUNG COUNTY MINUTE MEN
Lieutenant B. F. Kutch (December 1874)
*Ranging District*: Young County

# 7

# A Little Standing Army: Minute Men/Special State Troops/ Special Force (1874–1881)

The end of Reconstruction and the return of the Democratic Party to power in the statehouse ushered in a new era for the Texas Rangers. The crime rate had risen sharply in the last few years with Mexican banditti crossing the Rio Grande to commit rapine and murder, feudists lynching and assassinating their neighbors, highwaymen and rustlers preying on stage lines and isolated ranches, and renegade Indians ravaging the frontier settlements. The consequences of Reconstruction were realized as citizens felt little or no respect for the law and settled their own differences, usually with violence. One special case was the Sutton-Taylor feud of De Witt County, which began in Clinton on December 25, 1868, over the questionable sale of horses. Each side would muster more than one hundred fighting men and the civil authorities proved either too timid to act or actively supported the Sutton faction.

The state was in debt and the effects of the Panic of 1873 were evident. In spite of the fiscal situation, Governor Coke and the Fourteenth Legislature knew the breakdown in law and order had to be curbed. In an act dated April 10, 1874, the legislature appropriated $300,000 to a frontier defense fund and authorized two distinct formations with explicit missions. The endemic Indian violence was answered with the creation of a permanent Ranger battalion which would address the shortcomings of temporary organizations, but the legislature also wanted to avoid the excesses of another State Police. To this end, the first eighteen sections of the act provided for minute companies serving three to twelve month enlistments to deal with "marauding or thieving parties." Section 28 vested these men with the powers of peace officers, and they were required to execute criminal processes and arrest any offender of state laws. Three of these emergency detachments were fielded in Webb, El Paso, and Nueces counties. Known variously as Frontier Men, Minute Men, or Rangers, two were composed of twenty-five men and the third of fifty men, but all were commanded by lieutenants.

In July, another company was raised under the legislation to quell the murder and larceny raging in DeWitt County. To command the new outfit, the governor appointed Leander H. McNelly, an ex–Confederate captain of scouts and former state policeman. Despite his past affiliation with the State Police, his forthright conduct while a member of that hated

"Leander McNelly" by Jack White. McNelly was a Confederate officer and Texas State Police captain before he became commander of the Special State Troops. While suffering from tuberculosis, he was active in the Lower Rio Grande Valley and engaged Mexican bandits numerous times. On one occasion he instigated an international incident while recovering stolen livestock. He was later inducted into the Texas Ranger Hall of Fame. Courtesy of the artist.

organization, coupled with his distinguished war record, more than qualified him to handle the situation. Additionally, the governor believed McNelly, as a resident of Washington County, would conduct himself impartially as he had no vested interest in the feud. The new command was mustered into service as Company A, Washington County Volunteer Militia.

Similar to whether Morrison's, Coleman's, or Williamson's units could each claim the title of the first Texas Rangers, McNelly's status as a Ranger captain is disputed. Some base their pedantic argument on the fact his companies never legally bore the designation of "Ranger." Others point to the act of 1874 which established the same type of minute companies that had been standard for decades—companies long accepted as rangers.

Although he was slowly dying from advanced tuberculosis, Captain McNelly and his forty minute men helped bring an temporary peace to DeWitt and adjoining counties by the force of his own personality as much as his State commission. Their recurring presence would be required for several years afterward as the violence repeatedly flared.

Although his work was unfinished in De Witt County, McNelly was ordered into the Nueces Strip in April 1875 to combat the rampant cattle rustling still occurring there. Following the border war of 1859 and 1860, Juan Cortina had remained in Mexico and received citizenship. He served both the *Imperialista* and *Juarista* causes as a general of brigade, before becoming an acting military governor of Tamaulipas, commander of the Line of the Bravo, *alcalde* of Matamoros, and a leading *caudillo* (politico-military strongman) in the region. Although raiding had occurred for years, beginning in 1871, Cortina orchestrated a marked increase in the theft of Texas cattle from Rio Grande City to Brownsville and as far north as Corpus Christi. An estimated five thousand head were driven across the Rio Grande each month. Using some of the rustled herds to stock four of his twenty ranches, the general also became the principal supplier of stolen beef throughout Tamaulipas and Nuevo León and even Cuba.

McNelly's company arrived at Brownsville and the captain promptly disbanded the numerous vigilante gangs that were arbitrarily executing Mexicans suspected of cattle theft. He then established an intelligence network to locate the rustler bands; he even infiltrated a spy into Cortina's headquarters. On June 12, 1875, at the old Mexican War battleground of Palo Alto, the captain and twenty-two Rangers caught a party of sixteen *Cortinistas* en route to the border with three hundred head of stolen stock. They killed fifteen of the bandits with a loss of one of their own.

The Mexican government bowed to diplomatic pressure (and the threat of American gunboats on the Rio Grande) from Washington and placed Cortina under house arrest in July 1875. Unfortunately for Texas ranchers on the border, others stood ready to take his place. The *caudillo* was released the following year, but after dabbling in revolutionary politics, Cortina was imprisoned in Mexico City. He died in Atzcapozalco on October 30, 1894.

The crisis in the *brasada* called for ruthless methods and McNelly proved more than willing to employ them when necessary. He adopted the use of *la ley de fuga* ("the law of flight"), the Spanish custom that empowered law officers to shoot desperadoes "resisting arrest" or prisoners allegedly attempting to escape. This practice became known as the "Ranger Conviction" and was used to eliminate the worst of the outlaws rather than attempt to capture them. He also sanctioned the application of harsh interrogation techniques to extract information from prisoners and bribed several bandits to betray their partners in crime. For these and other reasons, Mexicans from Brownsville to Laredo would long remember L. H. McNelly.

To arm McNelly's men, the State purchased Sharps Model 1865 .50-caliber carbines, with the cost deducted from the Rangers' first pay. The adjutant general furnished the well-known, rugged and inexpensive Sharps for both McNelly's Rangers and the Frontier Battalion of Major John B. Jones. The carbine was a single-shot, breech-loading weapon with a falling block, a weight of eight pounds, a thirty-inch octagonal barrel, and an overall length of forty-seven inches. For the second time in history, the State provided ammunition for the Rangers' use. The carbines were originally manufactured utilizing linen cartridges and percussion caps, but they were later converted to fire metallic ammunition. The .50-70 Government center-fire cartridge used a 450-grain bullet propelled by seventy grains of black powder that could down a bull buffalo at six hundred yards. "Each Ranger was a little standing army in himself," as Lieutenant L. B. Wright described the available arsenal years later.

Later, the State provided the Sharps Model 1874 carbine, which possessed similar specifications to the earlier model. The newer rifle was chambered for the .45-70 Government cartridge using a 405-grain bullet backed by seventy grains of powder.

In April 1876, the Rangers received thirty Winchester Model 1873s from Captain Richard King, owner of the famed Santa Gertrudis Ranch, as a token of thanks for the recovery of stolen cattle. Later, the State would replace the Sharps with Winchesters and provide ammunition for not only the rifles, but the other weapon most associated with the West: the Colt Peacemaker.

The "Colt New Model Army Metallic Cartridge Revolving Pistol" (known today in all its versions as the Single Action Army) was factory produced as a solid-frame pistol with a 7½-inch barrel, blued and case hardened finish, oil-stained walnut grips, cartridge ejection mechanism, and the same single-action design that had been a mainstay for the previous twenty-five years. Adopted by the Army Ordnance Department as the "Army Model of 1873" or the "Cavalry Model," it assumed its "Peacemaker" moniker the following year. After government and foreign orders were met, the pistols were offered to the domestic market and available in the West by 1876. To say it proved extremely popular is something of an understatement. The initial ammunition was a center-fire .45 Long Colt cartridge using a 230-grain round-nose bullet with a powder charge of forty grains. The company began to market a "Civilian Model" in the late 1870s featuring a 4¾-inch barrel, which became a favorite choice of gunfighters on both sides of the law. In 1878, the "Frontier Model" utilizing the .44-40 Winchester Center Fire cartridge was offered for use in conjunction with the Winchester rifle. From 1895 to 1903, the "Artillery Model" with a 5½-inch barrel was produced.

The Rangers would need reliable firearms once McNelly, weary of having to stop at the Rio Grande while in hot pursuit of rustlers, precipitated the international incident known as the "Las Cuevas War." Knowingly violating international law, the captain crossed the river in the early morning of November 19, 1875 to attack Rancho Las Cuevas, the headquarters of bandit chieftain General Juan Flores Salinas, and recover rustled stock. Tragically, the Rangers were guided to the wrong ranch, where they killed over a dozen *vaqueros* before the mistake was realized. McNelly then led his twenty-six men to nearby Las Cuevas and engaged a large force of Mexican regulars, who had been alerted by the earlier fighting. Flores gathered twenty-five henchmen and moved to cut the Texans off from the river. The Rangers withdrew to the border where, reinforced by forty U.S. cavalry troopers, they repulsed a charge made by Flores' horsemen, killing the general in the process. Even after more than two hundred bandits and soldiers began forming near his position, McNelly brazenly refused to cross over to Texas, and demanded the stolen cattle be brought to him ... or else. After lengthy negotiations, punctuated with intimidating promises, McNelly returned to the United States on November 21 with sixty-five head of stolen cattle. The Federal Government did have to pay damages to Mexico, but McNelly was lionized in Texas for his actions.

The Washington County company was mustered out on June 25, 1876, and reorganized as Special State Troops the following day. By November of that year, they were being used as roving troubleshooters from San Antonio to Eagle Pass to Brownsville to Corpus Christi. By January 1877, McNelly's health had worsened, his State-paid medical bills had mounted, and finally the governor felt forced to make a change in leadership. His choice was Jesse "Lee" Hall, a former deputy sheriff and master-at-arms of the Fifteenth Legislature, who had been with the Rangers since August 1876. Captain Leander H. McNelly died at his Washington County farm on September 4, 1877, at the age of thirty-three.

Lieutenant Hall, as McNelly's second-in-command and heir assumptive, had returned to De Witt County in December 1876. The grand jury reconvened for the first time in several years with 150 indictments on the docket, but witnesses were being intimidated or murdered. The Rangers guarded the jurors and, armed with over thirty warrants, including seven for murder, arrested the suspects. As time went by, more of the county's residents, sick of the killing, would find the wherewithal to aid the Rangers in restoring order

## 7. A Little Standing Army (1874–1881)

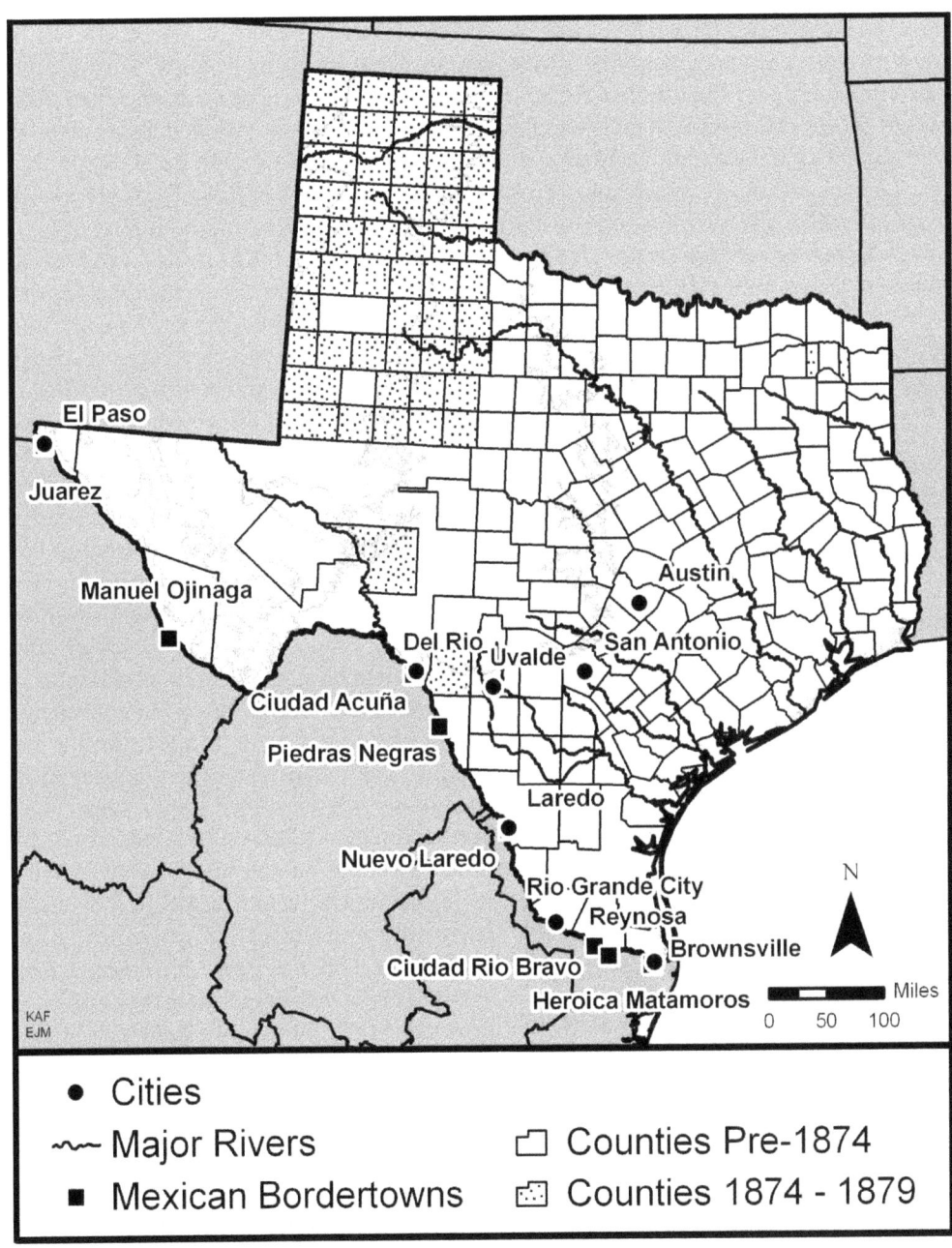

to the area. The violence stopped but the feud continued in the courts for another two decades. Hall went on to lead the company for three years as they rode the chaparral plains, bringing numerous rustlers, bank and stagecoach robbers, and murderers to justice.

One significant event during Hall's tenure was the apprehension of infamous mankiller John Wesley Hardin. The most dangerous gunman in Texas was ironically the son of a Methodist circuit preacher. He was rumored to have killed up to fifty men, although Bill O'Neal, in the *Encyclopedia of Western Gunfighters*, reckoned the total at eleven or twelve in nineteen documented gunfights in Texas, Indian Territory, and Kansas. After escaping from the Gonzales County jail in November 1872, Hardin joined his Clements cousins in De Witt County as a member of the Taylor faction. Texas finally had enough when Hardin killed Brown County Deputy Sheriff Charles Webb in Comanche. The State offered a $4,000 reward for his capture and delivery to the Travis County jail. Hardin fled Texas with his wife and infant daughter and settled in Pensacola, Florida, posing as "John H. Swain, Jr."

Lieutenant John B. Armstrong, remembered as "McNelly's Bulldog," was recovering from an accidentally self-inflicted gunshot wound in the early spring and summer of 1877. In July, he requested the governor give him the special assignment of hunting down Hardin. Aided by Dallas police detective John R. "Jack" Duncan, Armstrong tracked the fugitive from Gonzales to Montgomery, Alabama and finally to Pensacola. On August 23, Armstrong, along with local officers, boarded a train that Hardin and several of his friends were on. The county sheriff and his deputy seized Hardin's arms as Armstrong rushed forward. Spotting Armstrong's long-barreled Colt .45, Hardin exclaimed, "Texas, by God!" and struggled to free himself. The killer got a hand on his own pistol, but the weapon became tangled in his suspenders. One of Hardin's companions, Jim Mann, pulled his gun and fired several shots at Armstrong but missed. Armstrong returned fire and hit Mann, who jumped through the window and collapsed on the platform dead. Armstrong then demanded Hardin's surrender, but he replied, "Shoot and be damned, I'd rather die than be arrested." Instead, Armstrong slammed his gun barrel over the outlaw's head and ended his resistance. After several legal issues were resolved which involved the governors of Alabama and Texas, Armstrong and Duncan escorted Hardin to the Travis County jail, arriving on August 28. In September, a jury in Comanche found the gunfighter guilty of second-degree murder and sentenced him to twenty-five years at Huntsville State Penitentiary. While in prison, he studied law and, following his parole in February 1894, became a practicing attorney in El Paso. Hardin soon fell back into his old habits and was murdered by outlaw turned constable John Selman on August 19, 1895.

John B. Armstrong served under McNelly and "Lee" Hall as a sergeant and lieutenant. "McNelly's Bulldog," as he was known, was instrumental in capturing notorious gunfighter John Wesley Hardin in Florida. He was later inducted into the Texas Ranger Hall of Fame. Courtesy of the Texas Ranger Hall of Fame and Museum, Waco, TX.

Another notorious Texas desperado Hall dealt with was John King Fisher, "the king of the Strip." A successful rancher on Pendencia Creek near Eagle Pass, the flamboyant Fisher was nevertheless wanted in several counties for rustling and murder. His ranch provided safe haven for scores of outlaws and held hundreds of cattle stolen in Texas and Mexico. Backed by his own gang of cutthroats, Fisher exerted a great deal of influence in Dimmit and Maverick Counties, where intimidated local authorities and terrorized citizens proved unwilling to testify against him. The trail leading to his ranch bore the sign, "This is King Fisher's road. Take the other."

McNelly had arrested Fisher and members of his gang in June 1876, but the gunman was released on a $20,000 bond and remained unindicted by four successive grand juries. Beginning in May 1877, Hall guided several grand juries into returning twenty-one indictments for first-degree murder, cattle rustling, horse theft, and other offenses. The captain repeatedly arrested Fisher, who was often denied bail and incarcerated in San Antonio, Castroville, and Uvalde jails to await trial. His attorney successfully defended him in court, but the endless legal battles and extended jail time seemed to have encouraged Fisher to go straight. By 1881, he was cleared of all charges and appointed a deputy sheriff of Uvalde County. After serving one year as acting sheriff, he decided to run for the office in the upcoming election. Instead, he was murdered in San Antonio's Vaudeville Variety Theater on March 11, 1884.

Anglo outlaws were not the only concern as the Las Cuevas affair had not ended the issue of Mexican depredations. Over 1,400 head of Texas cattle were lost to rustlers in December 1875 alone; also Lipan and Mescalero raids recommenced in the spring of 1876. From May 1876 to October 1877, Lieutenant-Colonel William R. "Pecos Bill" Shafter, commanding the 24th Infantry at Fort Duncan, and Lieutenant John Bullis at Fort Clark crossed into Coahuila on numerous occasions to punish Indian raiders; one significant engagement was at a Lipan *ranchería* near Zarragosa on July 30, 1876. On June 1, 1877, President Rutherford B. Hayes authorized U.S. troops to cross the border in hot pursuit without seeking the permission of Mexican authorities. Such a formal violation of Mexican sovereignty seriously chilled relations between the two countries. On June 12, 1878, Colonel Ranald Mackenzie and Lieutenant-Colonel Shafter again invaded Mexico, this time for a symbolic show of force. The column was comprised of eight troops of the 4th Cavalry, three battalions of the 24th and 25th Infantry regiments, three batteries of artillery, Lieutenant Bullis' Seminole-Negro scouts, and a supply train of forty wagons. Mackenzie twice bloodlessly humbled Mexican forces sent to block his advance before returning to Texas on June 21. After being humiliated by this most recent incursion, the new regime of *presidente* Porfirio Díaz consolidated its control over the country and aggressively suppressed the raiding from the Mexican side of the Rio Grande. With Mexico at last committed to policing its northern frontier, President Hayes rescinded his hot pursuit order on February 24, 1880.

As always, financial limitations set by the legislature effected operations in the field. The appropriation of $40,000 for the year 1878 was exhausted by the autumn and additional monies would not be forthcoming. Despite pleas from a multitude of citizens in South Texas, Hall was forced to discharge twelve men between August 31 and November 1, leaving him with a force of eighteen Rangers. By this time, monthly salaries were set at one hundred and sixty-six dollars for the captain, one hundred and thirty-three dollars for the lieutenant, fifty dollars for the two sergeants, and forty dollars for the privates.

On August 1, 1879, the Special State Troops were renamed the Special Force, and the following year Captain Thomas L. Oglesby took command. Finally, in March 1881, the Special Force was reorganized as Company F of the Frontier Battalion.

# Historical Register, 1874–1881

*"I'll never send you into a battle, I'll lead you."*
— Captain L. H. McNelly

### El Paso County Frontier Men/Company "25"
Lieutenant/Captain Telesforro Montes (May 27, 1874–November 27, 1876)
*Ranging District*: El Paso County with headquarters at San Elizario
    Company transferred to the supervision of HQ, Frontier Battalion (November 1874)

### Webb County Frontier Men
Lieutenant Refugio Benavides (June 13–December 13, 1874)
*Ranging District*: Webb County with headquarters at Laredo

### Nueces and Rio Grande Frontier Men
Captain Warren Wallace (June 29–September 29, 1874)
*Ranging District*: Nueces Strip with headquarters at Concepcion

### Company A, Washington County Volunteer Militia
Captain Leander H. McNelly (July 14, 1874–May 31, 1876)
*Ranging District*: De Witt County with headquarters at Clinton (July 1874); Nueces Strip with headquarters at Rancho Las Rucias near Edinburg (April 1875), Santa María (June 1875), Retama (December 1875), Laguna de Las Flores (February 1876), Fort Ewell (May 1876), and Oakville (May 1876)
    Company operated under the supervision of the Adjutant General's office

### Special State Troops/Special Force
Captain Leander H. McNelly (July 26, 1876–January 31, 1877)
2nd Lieutenant Jesse L. "Lee" (Red) Hall, Commanding (February 1–March 31, 1877)
1st Lieutenant Jesse L. "Lee" (Red) Hall, Commanding (April 1–November 30, 1877)
Captain Jesse L. "Lee" (Red) Hall (December 1, 1877–February 29, 1880)
Captain Thomas L. Oglesby (March 1, 1880–February 28, 1881)
*Ranging District*: South Texas with headquarters at Oakville (July 1876), San Antonio (October 1876), Goliad (February 1877), Clinton (March 1877), Austin (April 1877), Eagle Pass and Castroville (May 1877), Cuero (May 1877), Eagle Pass (August 1877), Rio Grande City (August 1877), Corpus Christi (December 1877), camp near San Antonio (March 1878), Victoria (May 1878), Collins Station (August 1878), Corps Christi (December 1878), and San Diego (August 1879) and *detachments* at Carrizo Springs (May 1876), Carrizo Springs (Armstrong's detachment: August 1876), San Patricio (Armstrong's detachment: August–September 1876), Goliad (Hall's detachment: August–November 1876), Oakville (Hall's detachment: October 1876), Clinton (Hall's detachment: December 1876), Refugio and San Patricio (February 1877), Dog Town (Hall's detachment: February 1877), Clinton (Armstrong's detachment: April 1877), Oakville (April 1877), Goliad (Deeg's detachment: April 1877), Beeville (Parrott's detachment: April 1877), Banquette and San Diego (December 1877), Cuero (Armstrong's detachment: August 1878), Live Oak (Rudd's detachment: August 1878), Fort Ewell (Oglesby's detachment: May 1879), Cuero (Hall's detachment: September 1879), San Diego (Hall's detachment: October 1879), Santa Maria (Rudd's detachment: November 1879), Nueces Canyon (McMurry's detachment: January 1881), and Schulenburg (J. McNelly's detachment: January 1881)
    Company operated under the supervision of the Adjutant General's office and reorganized as Company F, Frontier Battalion (March 1881)

### Kerr County Volunteer Militia Company
Captain J. R. Merritt
Ranging District: Kerr County

# 8

# Duty Well Performed: The Frontier Battalion (1874–1901)

The modern Texas Rangers trace the lineage of their current organization directly from the Frontier Battalion. In the past, ranger companies had been raised for a set period of time, or for a definite crisis, and then disbanded. For the first time in Texas history, the Frontier Battalion would, despite turn-over in personnel, provide continuity that had been heretofore lacking in frontier defense. Long a tradition in the state, the Texas Rangers would now become an institution. Section 19 of the act of 1874 provided for this standing formation in the form of the "battalion of mounted men"—they were not called "Rangers" in the legislation and "Frontier Battalion" would be only an administrative appellation. The transition from Indian fighters to law enforcers was nearly complete, as the act also formally invested battalion members with the powers of peace officers.

Raised in May 1874, the Frontier Battalion was commanded by Major John B. Jones, a former Confederate officer. He reported to the adjutant general and, through him, to the governor. Like Jack Hays, Jones differed from the traditional mold of the Ranger commander. Short and of slight build, he abstained from drinking or smoking, was well-groomed, was forty years old at the time of his appointment (twice the age of most of his men), and was a strict disciplinarian. Overseeing the entire western frontier from the Red River to the Nueces, the major combined the necessary martial spirit with executive and administrative aptitude. Preferring to command in person rather from his Austin office, Jones, accompanied by a thirty-man escort detachment, undertook a regular circuit of the line of companies in order to ascertain the efficiency of the men and the conditions in the field.

The new battalion was authorized six companies of seventy-five Rangers each. The company commanders continued to personally appoint their men for twelve-month enlistments, although a Ranger could readily obtain an early discharge if he so desired. Unlike other lawmen in the state, the rank and file of the battalion was not required to post a surety bond in order to obtain their appointments; instead, they received their commissions directly from the governor through their officers. As always, the Rangers provided their own horses, sidearms, and gear, but the State supplied ammunition, forage, camp equipment, and a carbine, although the cost of the latter was still deducted from the first month's pay. The battalion commander received one hundred and twenty-five dollars per month; captains, one hundred dollars; lieutenants, seventy-five dollars; sergeants, fifty dollars; corporals and privates, forty dollars. At this point, there was still no standard mode of dress or an official badge. The officers were supplied with warrants of authority to act as their official credentials, while the enlisted men received descriptive lists as their identification. The adjutant general's office published General Order No. 2 which described the type of men required, "As it is expected that this force will be kept actively employed during their term of service, only sound young men without families and with good horses will be received. Persons under indictment or of known bad character or habitual drunkards will be rejected."

The ongoing war of attrition between the Comanche and Kiowa tribes and the Texans was nearing its climax that same year. For some time, the Federal Government had defaulted on its obligations as stipulated by the Medicine Lodge Treaty. Rations that were to be issued to the reservations monthly were consistently inadequate or failed to arrive, gangs of gunrunners and whiskey smugglers ran rampant, and white horse thieves from both Kansas and Texas preyed on the Indian herds. In 1872, scores of buffalo hunters descended on the Plains and began to slaughter the bison by the millions for their hides, which were fashioned as coats and robes for the Eastern market. The carcasses of the slain animals were left to rot in the sun. The Comanches and Kiowas, who could not depend on government rations and saw their alternate source of subsistence being decimated, were forced to wage an all-out war for survival; they were joined in increasing numbers by Southern Cheyenne and southern Arapaho bands.

From June 27 to July 1, 1874, several hundred Comanches and Cheyennes attacked a camp of twenty-eight hide-hunters at Adobe Walls on the North Canadian River in the Staked Plains. They killed three of the hunters outside the building, but could not break through to the remainder. The heavy rifles of the hunters wreaked havoc on the tribesmen and forced them to break off their attack. The Indians, unsuccessful in siege warfare, returned to the use of murder raids, but the attack on Adobe Walls also ended the Peace Policy. Congress passed legislation that temporarily transferred the Indian Bureau to the War Department. The army was further authorized to prepare for total war.

Concurrently, on July 12, while following an Indian trail, Major Jones, with twenty-five Rangers from his escort detachment and eleven men from Company B, engaged a war party of up to 150 Comanches and Kiowas in Lost Valley. The advance guard of the inexperienced Rangers was duped into riding into an ambush on the valley floor, but Jones held the remainder in a good defensive position further uphill. The Rangers used their Sharps rifles to great effect, easily outranging the Indians' lighter weapons. After several failed attempts to draw the Rangers out into the open, the Indians withdrew taking their dead and wounded with them.

The coup de grâce came courtesy of the United States Army when they initiated the Red River War on July 25. The objective of the campaign was to once and for all subjugate or annihilate the recalcitrant bands taking refuge in the *Comanchería*. Colonel Nelson A. Miles commanded a northern column from Fort Dodge, Kansas, consisting of four companies of his 5th Infantry and eight troops of the 6th Cavalry, an artillery element (one Parrott ten-pound cannon and two ten-barrel Gatling guns), and two detachments of civilian and Delaware Indian scouts; all of which worked in conjunction with a western column under Major William R. Price from Fort Union, New Mexico Territory, composed of four troops of his 8th Cavalry, two howitzers, and Navajo scouts. Three separate columns striking from the south and east were led by Colonel Ranald Mackenzie from Fort Concho,

8. Duty Well Performed: The Frontier Battalion (1874–1901) 159

"Ranger Escort West of the Pecos" by Tom Lea. This oil painting was created for Texas Governor John Connally in 1965. The artwork depicts Captain G. W. Baylor's forty-two day journey to join his company in El Paso and also features Sergeant J. B. Gillett (right). The painting was used as the cover art for the second edition of Walter Prescott Webb's groundbreaking book *The Texas Rangers: A Century of Frontier Defense*. Courtesy of the State Preservation Board, Austin, TX; Accession ID: CHA 1989.751; Photographer: Eric Beggs, 8/21/97; post conservation.

who commanded eight troops of his 4th Cavalry, four companies of the 10th Infantry and one of the 11th, and thirty civilian and Seminole, Lipan, and Tonkawa Indian scouts; by Lieutenant-Colonel George P. Buell from Fort Griffin, with two companies of his 11th Infantry, and four troops of the 9th Cavalry and two troops of the 10th; and by Lieutenant-Colonel John W. "Black Jack" Davidson from Fort Sill, leading six troops of his 10th Cavalry, three companies of the 11th Infantry, a mountain howitzer section, and a company of Indian scouts. The forty-six companies of regulars and five detachments of assorted auxiliaries faced 1,800 Southern Cheyennes, 2,000 Comanches, and 1,000 Kiowas, of whom a total of 1,200 were fighting men.

Elements of Miles' 744-man column engaged the hostiles near Mulberry Creek, a tributary of the Prairie Dog Town Fork of the Red River, and along Tule Canyon (August 27–31); at the Lyman Wagon Train Battle near the Washita River (September 10–14); near Gageby Creek (September 12); and in the Buffalo Wallow Fight (September 12).

Mackenzie led his 471-man column northward along the eastern edge of the *Llano Estacado* and, on September 26–27, skirmished with 250 Comanches at Tule Canyon. Companies A, D, E, F, H, I, K, and L, 4th Cavalry delivered the decisive blow of the campaign at Palo Duro Canyon on September 28, when they routed a large force of Kotsoteka and

Kwahadi Comanches, Kiowas, and Cheyennes. Although the Indians lost only three warriors before they escaped, their winter food stores, lodges, and camp equipment were all destroyed. The following day, Mackenzie ordered the destruction of the Indian herd of over 1,000 horses.

The various columns prowled the region destroying deserted camps, pursuing fleeing Indians, and participating in numerous small actions, until they went into winter quarters in December and January. Throughout the spring of 1875, various bands of once-defiant Indians submitted to reservation authorities. The last holdouts, four hundred Kwahadi Comanches under Quanah Parker, surrendered to Mackenzie at Fort Sill on June 2, 1875.

During the Red River War, which was an exclusively military operation, the Rangers were achieving their own successes. By September 30, 1874, the Frontier Battalion had fought in sixteen engagements, in which they killed twenty-four Indians and wounded ten more. They had also arrested twenty-eight outlaws, killed three cattle rustlers, and recovered one kidnapped Mexican boy, twenty-eight stolen horses and 1,000 head of rustled cattle. The contributions of the battalion in its first year led to an increased respect for the law, missing since the days of Reconstruction.

The Frontier Battalion, McNelly's Rangers, and the three Frontier Men detachments, as well as several militia companies that had assisted civil authorities, all drew against the frontier defense fund. By the fall of 1874, the year's appropriation for the fund was dwindling and, to forestall disbandment, the governor ordered the reduction of the battalion on November 25 from 470 men to 200. On December 9, Companies A, B, C, D, and E were decreased to one lieutenant, two sergeants, three corporals, and twenty-five privates. Company F was downgraded to one captain, one lieutenant, three sergeants, three corporals, and thirty-seven privates. Also, the monthly wage for privates was cut to thirty dollars. Throughout its existence, the strength of the battalion would continue to fluctuate according to the monies available, as reduction in force was deemed preferable to demobilization.

In addition to the celebrated Colt Peacemaker, the Rangers were armed with the Winchester Model 1873. As discussed in the previous chapter, the State purchased Sharps carbines for the Frontier Battalion just as the Winchester '73 was being made available. They elected to provide the Sharps because of its well-known reliability (while the Winchester was yet untested) and a belief that men would waste ammunition with a repeating rifle. This theory was held by the army, which advised the state adjutant general's office in its weapon choices. Many of the Rangers disagreed and purchased lever-action rifles and corresponding cartridges with their own money. By the early 1880s, the State was purchasing the Winchester '73 for the Rangers to buy at cost and supplying the ammunition. "The Gun That Won the West" was offered in two versions: the rifle with a twenty-four-inch octagonal barrel and a magazine capacity of fifteen rounds, and the carbine with a twenty-inch round barrel and a magazine capacity of twelve rounds. Among the standard features were blued finish, iron frames, and case-hardened levers, hammers, and buttplates. The weapon utilized .44-40 Winchester Center Fire ammunition, which was basically a pistol cartridge consisting of a .44-caliber 200-grain bullet and a powder charge of forty grains. While underpowered, the rifle proved to be extremely popular on the frontier and overseas.

Another novel weapon in the Ranger arsenal was the *List of Fugitives from Justice* published from 1878 to 1900. Distributed by the Adjutant General's Department, this booklet (also known as "the Book of Knaves," "the Ranger's Bible," or "the Crime Book") indexed the names and descriptions of thousands of wanted men and women by county and also alphabetically.

Using their armament, the Frontier Battalion experienced hard and varied service in the last years of the 19th century, which secured their place in American history. On February 18, 1875, the Mason County War (also known as the "Hoodoo War") commenced over the stealing and killing of cattle. While widely believed to be strictly a conflict between German settlers and Anglo-American residents, a combination of several causes, including a powerful lawless element, simmering hatreds between Unionist and secessionist factions, private vendettas, and political corruption, contributed to the turmoil. Nine murders in quick succession prompted Governor Coke to dispatch Major Jones and detachments from Companies A and D to restore order. Arrests were made but, although more than fifteen men were slain, only one feudist was convicted since county authorities (including the sheriff) were embroiled in the fighting. The Rangers, in addition to halting the lawlessness which spread to Llano, Burnet, Gillespie, Kimble, and Menard counties, had to track down one of their own. Scott Cooley, formerly of Company D, had sworn vengeance after the murder of a close friend by nightriders. Three Rangers received honorable discharges when they expressed an unwillingness to pursue their former comrade, who incidentally was never captured. By 1882, the ringleaders of the factions had either died, dispersed to other locales, or settled down to an uneasy peace.

Cattle rustling, a by-product of the Mason County troubles, reigned supreme in Kimble County by the spring of 1877; so much so that even county officials were involved. Judge William A. Blackburn of the Seventeenth Judicial District was unable to hold court due to widespread corruption and violence. To counter the outlaws' mastery of the area, Major Jones initiated the famous Kimble County Clean-Up on April 19. As Robert Utley wrote in *Lone Star Justice*, "Jones' cleanup of Kimble County was a masterpiece of careful planning, solid intelligence, organization, secrecy, rapid movement, and decisive action." He and fifty men from three companies swept through the county, arrested every suspicious person they found and took them into Junction, the county seat. After about five days, forty-one fugitives had been taken into custody without incident. Protected by Rangers, Judge Blackburn and the district attorney convened the grand jury, which handed down twenty-five indictments. Among those named were the sheriff and the county judge. Many outlaws not caught in Jones' net departed the county bound for the Pecos country, New Mexico, or Arizona. Few were tried or convicted and Rangers would periodically return to the county, but the stranglehold the rustlers had enjoyed was broken.

Lampasas County became the next flashpoint as the Horrell-Higgins Feud erupted. John P. C. "Pink" Higgins, a known hardcase, came to believe his neighbors Thomas and Martin Horrell were rustling Higgins cattle. The Horrells were equally dangerous men who had gunned down four state policemen in Lampasas' Matador Saloon in March 1873. Four years later, on January 22, Pink killed Merritt Horrell, Tom and Mart's brother, in the very same establishment. Anticipating retaliation, he then led his men to ambush the two surviving Horrell brothers on March 20; both survived the attack, though. On June 7, the two gangs met in the streets of Lampasas and one man from each group was killed in the resulting shootout. The local citizenry had enough and the Rangers were called in. Major Jones, backed by fifteen men, arrested the leaders of both families and proceeded to mediate a settlement to the feud. Soon, the two factions signed a pledge declaring hostilities to be at an end.

The El Paso Salt War came to be a sore subject in the history of the Texas Rangers. Beginning in 1872, attorney Charles H. Howard acquired ownership of huge salt deposits at the foot of the Guadalupe Mountains, one hundred miles north and east of El Paso. The local Mexican community along both sides of the Rio Grande was incensed since the salt was traditionally considered a public resource and not a private financial concern. Two years later, Howard was elected district judge and abused his authority in a political rivalry with state representative Louis Cardis, the champion of the *Paseño* electorate. After his life was threatened, Howard killed Cardis in an El Paso store on October 10, 1877. The victim's constituents demanded justice, but local law officers (all of them Anglos) were reluctant to arrest a sitting judge. Major Jones, upon his arrival, ignored local politics and arrested Howard on a charge of murder. He then organized a twenty-man detachment of Company C to keep the peace and appointed John B. Tays detachment commander with the rank of second lieutenant. With the new Rangers in place and order seemingly restored, Jones returned to Austin. For years afterward, many wished he had stayed.

Sometime around December 1, enraged Mexicans crossed the Rio Grande and murdered two of Howard's associates. The judge, free on bond, and several of his cronies sought the protection of Detachment C in San Elizario. The emerging mob, some two to three hundred in number, demanded the surrender of Howard and, after it was refused, laid siege to the Rangers' headquarters. After five days of sporadic fighting, Howard submitted to the Mexicans under a pledge of safe conduct. Tays and his men followed suit — the first and last time an officer of the Texas Rangers ever capitulated — and were disarmed. Despite the promises made by the mob's leaders, Howard and two others were put up against a wall and executed. Tays and his men, stripped of their weapons, were allowed to leave unharmed and the mob proceeded to ransack the town.

In its quarter-century of service, the Frontier Battalion brought more than 3,000 Texas desperados to justice. None seemed to have captured the public's imagination as did Sam Bass. After squandering his cowhand's wages in unsuccessful gambling, Bass, an Indiana native turned Texan, began to hold up stagecoaches and trains in Nebraska, the latter becoming his specialty. Returning to Texas in 1878, he organized an outlaw gang and robbed two stagecoaches and four trains. The general public resented the large and powerful railroads, and Bass became something of a Robin Hood–like folk hero. The Rangers vowed to capture Bass and nearly succeeded on several occasions, but he proved elusive. The Rangers did arrest James Murphy, one of Bass' associates, and turned him into their informant. In the summer of 1878, the spy informed Jones that the Bass gang was planning to rob the bank in Round Rock. On July 19, the major and Rangers Richard C. "Dick" Ware, Chris Connor, and George Harrell confronted the four bank robbers (one of whom was the turncoat Murphy) in the streets of Round Rock. The four lawmen killed Seaborn Barnes and mortally wounded Sam Bass; Murphy surrendered and was later pardoned, and the fourth man was never captured.

Despite the results of the Red River War, and the construction of Fort Elliot on Sweetwater Creek in present Wheeler County in June 1875, warlike Comanches and Kiowas were still a source of concern. The Indians remained confined to the reservation at Fort Sill, but small bands of warriors were allowed to hunt outside the agency's boundaries. Armed with government-supplied rifles and ammunition, these Indians, especially glory-seeking young braves, sometimes returned to their old ways and raided the settlements. On July 1, 1879, on the North Concho, Corporal Y. Douglass' detachment of Company B fought what proved to be the last engagement between the Texas Rangers and the Comanches. Despite being a tactically inconclusive skirmish that resulted in one Ranger casualty, with this action, the terror of the Comanche Moon was ended forever.

The Rangers' last Indian fight on Texas soil occurred in the Sierra Diablo range in present Hudspeth County. After attacking a stagecoach in Quitman Canyon and killing the driver and a passenger, a ragged band of Mescalero Apaches — twelve warriors, four women, and four children — took refuge in the mountains. On the morning of January 29, 1881, Captain George W. Baylor's Company A and Lieutenant C. L. Nevill's Company E located and attacked the raiders' camp. The twenty-five Rangers killed four braves, two women, and two children, while wounding most of the others. One woman and two children were captured. The survivors scattered into the rocks, but wounds, the lack of food or blankets, and the bitter cold almost certainly sealed their fate.

According to the Adjutant General's Department, the Texas Rangers participated in thirty-two engagements with hostile Indians from 1874 to 1881, killing eighty-two, wounding twelve, and capturing four. With the threat of Indian depredations eliminated, the role of the Frontier Battalion permanently changed to that of a mounted constabulary.

On February 8, 1879, Major Jones was appointed adjutant general and, even after assuming his new office, continued to supervise the battalion. He died on July 19, 1881, at the age of forty-seven, following surgery for an abscess on his liver. First as battalion commander and later as adjutant general, he proved vital to the resurgence of the Texas Rangers and left his mark on the organization's traditions, discipline, standards, and administration. He provided stability by keeping men in the field in the midst of financial struggles, sometimes reduced in numbers but always ready for duty. Built on the foundation of his leadership, the institution of the Ranger Service has endured, through times both bright and dark, into the twenty-first century.

By 1883, the frontier was disappearing and previously unsettled land was becoming available for stock-raising or farming. The development of barbed wire enabled landowners to assert their property rights and allowed for the stricter control of livestock breeding. Unfortunately, access to public roads, land, and water sources was often denied to "nesters" (farmers who squatted on some remote corner of a ranch) and "free grazing" cattlemen, who maintained the range should be available to all. The traditional cattle industry was changed as barbed wire spelled the end of the multi-county roundup, the trail drive, and the Texas longhorn. The presence of sheep herds also added to the brewing conflict, due to the commonly held belief that sheep grazing destroyed the pasturage for cattle. Local cattle barons in Hamilton, Archer, Clay, Jack, and Coleman counties had their fences targeted on both public land and private property. The cattlemen retaliated by destroying the livestock and holdings of suspected fence cutters. The Frontier Battalion was caught in the middle since public opinion was against wealthy stockmen who used the wire to the detriment of homesteaders and small ranchers. Although the Rangers made several arrests, fence cutters often had the tacit support of local officers, and most cases were dismissed or ended with charges not filed. Ordered to obtain a conviction, several Rangers were sent undercover to gather the necessary evidence or catch the offenders in the act. One such operative was Corporal Ira Aten of Company D, who was attempting to apprehend fence cutters in Lampasas, Brown, and Navarro counties. At last, discouraged and frustrated at the lack of progress, he developed the novel idea of mounting a dynamite bomb on a fence line which would detonate if the wire was cut or torn down; he even instructed local ranchers in the proper technique. Aten was ordered to cease his plan and return to his company, but word of the bombs spread and the frequency of fence cutting decreased for a time.

Sometime in the mid–1880s, in response to yet another budget crisis, Adjutant General Wilburn H. King, Jones' successor, established the position of Special Ranger. Those chosen as such received no wages but were allowed to carry firearms and clothed in all the

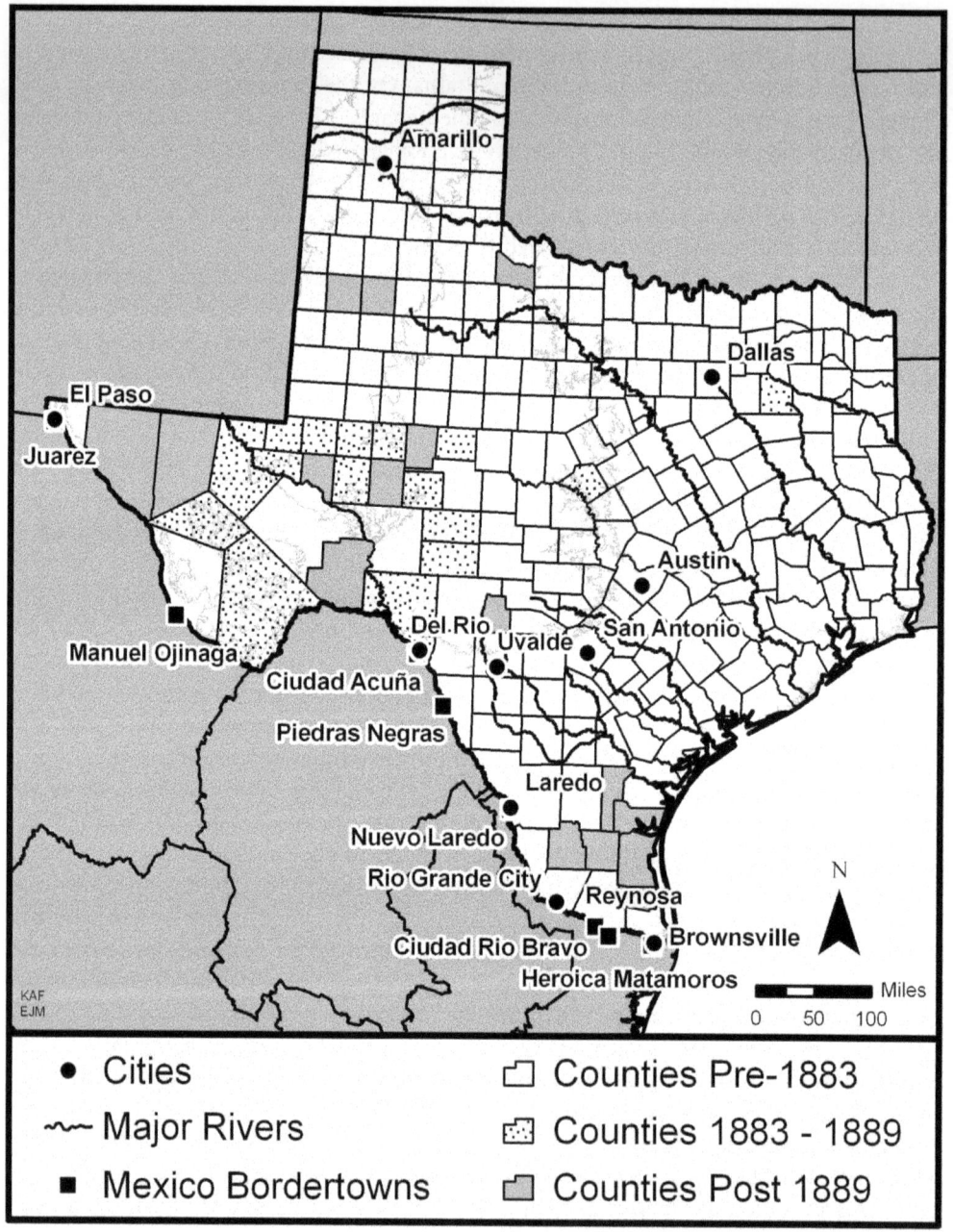

authority of regular Rangers. These appointments were often held by local or federal peace officers, cattlemen's association inspectors, former lawmen, or ranchers far from the protection of the law. Although originally created to serve the law enforcement needs of Texas without incurring additional expense to the state, the position was sometimes held by political appointees who protected their influential patrons' interests more than those of ordinary citizens.

From May 1874 to November 30, 1889, the battalion fought in fifty-six engagements with Indians or outlaws, killed sixty-nine criminals, and wounded twenty-seven more.

Rangers conducted 4,870 scouts and 759 escorts, and traveled over 500,000 miles in the performance of their duties. They investigated 512 homicides and 1,669 cases of stock theft, and captured seventy-seven outlaws, 130 escaped prisoners, and thirteen bandits.

As the new century approached, the Rangers intercepted Mexican *bandidos* from across the Rio Grande; maintained law and order in Big Bend mining towns; contended with cattle rustlers, and bank and train robbers, especially in the Big Bend and the Panhandle; pursued *mescalleros* (bootleggers dealing in mescal, the preferred border liquor of the time) and other smugglers along the border; quelled the Fort Bend County War, the Reece-Townsend feud, and other private conflicts; broke up the Buzzard's Water Hole vigilante "mob" in San Saba County; kept order during railroad and mine labor strikes; and at times protected blacks from white lynch mobs.

On September 30, 1891, another in the long series of disturbances along the Rio Grande occurred with the "Garza War." For the third time that year, Catarino Erasmo Garza Rodriguez, the Mexican-born editor of the Eagle Pass *El Libre Pensador*, unsuccessfully attempted to overthrow the government of Porfirio Díaz. Beginning in December, four troops of the 3rd U.S. Cavalry, one company of the 18th Infantry, two federal marshals, and Rangers from Companies E and F patrolled the Lower Valley in order to enforce state criminal statutes and federal neutrality laws. Part revolutionary patriots and part border ruffians, the *Garzistas* clashed with the Anglo peace officers on several occasions, until Garza himself left the country in January 1892 and the last of his followers were dispersed in May.

Sometime around the turn of the century, the men of the Frontier Battalion, either individually or by company, began replacing their Winchester '73s with Winchester Model 1894s chambered in .30 Winchester Center Fire (.30-30 Winchester). The most famous and best-selling high-powered rifle in U.S. history, its standard features included black walnut stocks, blued finish, dovetail front and open rear sights, and a weight of approximately six to seven pounds. The rifles possessed twenty-six-inch octagonal or round nickel-steel barrels, an overall length of 43¾ inches, and a magazine capacity of eight rounds, while the carbines had twenty-inch round barrels and a six-round capacity. The early ammunition was 160- to 170-grain "metal patched" bullets propelled by thirty grains of a revolutionary new smokeless powder.

In February 1896, nearly the entire battalion was sent to El Paso to prevent the Robert Fitzsimmons–Peter Maher world title bout from occurring on Texas soil. The boxing match was controversial because the Twenty-fourth Legislature had prohibited prizefighting in the state the year before, and Governor Charles A. Culberson was determined that the law be enforced. The fight's promoters were finally forced to stage the match on a sandbar in the Rio Grande near Langtry. In his official report following the incident, dated February 27, Adjutant General Woodford H. Mabry wrote:

> I wish to express my approbation for the intelligent and efficient manner in which Captains Brooks, McDonald, Hughes and Rogers executed every order and performed every duty. The Rangers conducted themselves in such a manner as to reflect additional credit upon the name of a ranger — already a synonym for courage and duty well performed.
>
> They were active in the performance of every duty, quiet and orderly in manner, determined in mien, fearless and vigilant on duty; they naturally incur the displeasure of lawbreakers everywhere.

As early as 1882, some legislators questioned the need for the Frontier Battalion, especially once the frontier ceased to exist, the Indian threat ended, and the standard of local law enforcement improved. The conduct that Mabry praised was indicative of the Rangers'

TEXAS RANGERS.

"Texas Rangers" by Frederic Remington. This lithograph, which depicts members of the Frontier Battalion on a scout, was featured in Frederic Remington's collection of essays "Crooked Trails" (1898) that ran in *Harper's Monthly*. Contrary to the popular image of the lone-wolf lawman, the Rangers of this era usually worked in detachments or as a whole company, and were accompanied with the equipage needed for extended duty in the field. Private Collection / Peter Newark American Pictures / The Bridgeman Art Library.

actions in the 1890s, which kept the disbandment of the battalion from being seriously considered for a few more years. The "Four Great Captains"—James A. Brooks, William J. McDonald, John R. Hughes, and John H. Rogers—provided superb leadership and elevated the Rangers to legendary status.

The death knell of the Frontier Battalion was sounded in May 1900 when a criminal defense attorney studied the act which had established the force in 1874. He specifically noticed a legal technicality in Section 28:

> Each officer of the battalion ... shall have all the powers of a peace officer, and it shall be his duty to execute all criminal processes directed to him, and make arrests under capias [writ] properly issued, of any and all parties charged with offense against the laws of this State.

The lawyer argued that the law gave arrest powers to only commissioned officers, such as captains and lieutenants, so the rank and file (approximately ninety-five percent of the force) who apprehended lawbreakers was subject to prosecution for false imprisonment.

The original framers of the law, of course, meant all members of the battalion, in the role of peace officers, were to possess arrest powers. The matter ended up on the desk of Governor Joseph D. Sayers, who deferred to Attorney General Thomas S. Smith. On May 26, 1900, the attorney general ruled that only commissioned officers of the Frontier Battalion possessed the powers of peace officers, including the authority to make arrests. In one stroke, nearly every capture made since May 1874 had been rendered illegal.

Thus, the Frontier Battalion, which had shielded the state for over twenty-five years, was doomed. A renewed and concerted effort to abolish the Texas Rangers was launched, mostly by the friends and families of those who had been arrested in years past. They were stymied by the continual call for the Rangers' assistance throughout the state. The governor, not wanting to lose such a valuable resource, directed his attorney general to render a second opinion, which allowed a temporary Frontier Battalion to remain in place until the legislature could amend the defective law. This provisional body, operating from June 1, 1900, to July 8, 1901, was composed of six companies, each manned by one captain, two lieutenants, and one private. The officers were the only Rangers authorized to make arrests, although the privates could assist them. The "Four Captains," who were all natural leaders of exceptional initiative, moral and physical courage, intelligence, and judgment proved essential in maintaining the capabilities and the traditions of the Texas Rangers and ensuring their continued existence into the 20th century.

## Historical Register, 1874–1901

*"Nothing will do any good here but a first class killing..."*
— Sergeant Ira Aten

### Headquarters

Major John B. Jones, Commanding (May 2, 1874–January 24, 1879)
  *Command authority transferred to the office of the Adjutant General (February 8, 1879)*
Major George W. Baylor, Acting Commander (March 6–July 15, 1884)
Captain A. P. Blocker, Quartermaster (May 7–16 1874)
Captain Martin M. Kenney, Quartermaster and Paymaster (May 16, 1874–March 16, 1875)
Captain Cornelius V. "Neal" Coldwell, Quartermaster (May 9, 1879–December 31, 1882)
Captain John O. Johnson, Quartermaster (January 1, 1883–October 15, 1885)
Captain Lamartine P. "Lam" Sieker, Quartermaster (October 15, 1885–February 1, 1893)
Captain George A. Wheatley, Quartermaster (February 1, 1893–December 31, 1895)
Captain W. H. Owen, Quartermaster (January 1, 1896–December 31, 1898)
Captain Lamartine P. "Lam" Sieker, Quartermaster (April 11, 1899–July 8, 1901)
2nd Lieutenant J. Thomas Wilson, commanding escort detachment (July–December 1874?)
Doctor S. G. Nicholson, Surgeon (June 9, 1874–December 1, 1876)
  *Battalion operated under the supervision of the Adjutant General's office*

### Company A

Captain John R. Waller (May 25–October 4, 1874)
1st Lieutenant James W. Millican, Commanding (October 5–December 23, 1874)
2nd Lieutenant J. Thomas Wilson, Commanding (December 23, 1874–April 30, 1875)
  *Company "A" disbanded (May 1875) and reorganized as Maj. J. B. Jones' escort (September 1875)*
1st Lieutenant Ira Long, Commanding (September 1, 1875–August 31, 1876)
1st Lieutenant J. M. Denton, Commanding (September 1–November 30, 1876)

Captain Cornelius V. "Neal" Coldwell (December 1, 1876–August 31, 1878)
1st Lieutenant G. B. Broadwater, Commanding (September 1, 1878–February 28, 1879)
1st Sergeant Thomas L. Oglesby, Acting Commander (March 1–July 31, 1879)
   Company "A" disbanded (August 1879–September 1880)
Captain George W. Baylor (September 1, 1880–April 15, 1885)
   Company "A" disbanded (April 1885–June 1900)
1st Lieutenant Harry B. Dubose, Commanding (June 1, 1900–July 8, 1901)
1st Lieutenant James W. Millican, commanding detachment (May 25–September 26, 1874)
Sergeant Nelson O. "Mage" Reynolds, commanding detachment (July 27–August 9, 1877)
*Ranging District*: Erath, Comanche, Eastland, Callahan, Brown, Coleman, and Stephens Counties with headquarters at camp on Sandy Creek (May 1874), camp on Lodge Creek (December 1874), and Comanche; Mason County with headquarters at Mason (September 1875–January 1876); Lower Rio Grande Valley with headquarters at Ringgold Barracks (September 1876); Frio, Callahan, Kimble, and Kerr Counties with headquarters at camp on the headwaters of the Guadalupe River (1876), Junction (April 1877), Camp Hubbard, and camp on Elm Creek (December 1877); El Paso and Presidio Counties with headquarters at Ysleta (September 1880–April 1885) and detachments at Toyah in Reeves County (1883) and the Texas and Pacific Railroad line (1883); Val Verde County with headquarters at Comstock (June 1900–July 1901)

## Company B

Captain George W. Stevens (May 5, 1874–August 31, 1875)
1st Sergeant C. H. Hamilton, Acting Commander (September 1–November 30, 1875)
1st Lieutenant G. W. Campbell, Commanding (December 1, 1875–February 29, 1876)
2nd Lieutenant C. H. Hamilton, Commanding (March 1–August 31, 1876)
1st Lieutenant G. W. Campbell, Commanding (September 1, 1876–May 18, 1878)
Sergeant J. E. Van Riper, Acting Commander (May 19–31, 1878)
Captain Junius "June" Peak (June 1, 1878–February 29, 1880)
Lieutenant Ira Long, Commanding (March 1–November 30, 1880)
Captain Bryan Marsh (December 1, 1880–August 31, 1881)
Captain Samuel A. McMurry (September 1, 1881–November 30, 1890)
Captain William J. "Bill" McDonald (December 1, 1890–July 8, 1901)
2nd Lieutenant Ira Long, commanding detachment (August 31, 1874–May 31, 1875)
Lieutenant Junius "June" Peak, commanding detachment (April 17–June 1, 1878)
Sergeant Richard C. "Dick" Ware, commanding detachment (July 1880–January 1881)
1st Sergeant W. John L. Sullivan, commanding detachment (June 1896–March 1897)
*Ranging District*: Young, Wise, Parker, Palo Pinto, Jack, Throckmorton, and Young Counties with headquarters near Fort Belknap (May 1874), camp on Salt Creek near Graham (July 1874), camp on Flat Top Mountain (July 1874), camp on Raines Spring near Jacksboro (September 1874), and camp on the Brazos River (September 1876) and detachment in Mason County (Long's detachment: November 1874); Kerr, Bandera, Medina, Frio, and Dimmit Counties with headquarters at Camp Hubbard (December 1876), Camp Vinton (June 1877), camp on Elm Creek (December 1877), Camp Vinton (July 1878), and Camp Carrizo Springs (July 1879) and detachment in Lampasas County (September 1877); Taylor and Runnels Counties with headquarters at Buffalo Gap (February 1879); Concho River country with headquarters at Fort Concho (May 1879); Mitchell and Howard Counties with headquarters at Hackberry Springs (February 1880), Colorado City (January 1881), and Big Spring (August 1884) and detachments at Swenson's Pasture in Travis County (Ware's detachment: July 1880), Midland (1883–1884), Big Spring (1883–1884), Abilene (1883–

1884), Vernon in Wilbarger County (1883), and Wichita Falls in Wichita County (1883); Wichita and Wilbarger Counties with headquarters at Wichita Falls (May 1885) and Harrold (November 1885) and detachment at Fort Worth in Tarrant County (April 1886); Panhandle country with headquarters at Quanah (November 1886) and detachment at Thurber in Erath County (1887); Erath and Palo Pinto Counties with headquarters at Thurber (February 1889) and detachment in San Saba County (1889); Panhandle country with headquarters at Amarillo (August 1889), Quanah (May 1890), Amarillo (August 1890), Quanah (February 1891), Amarillo (May 1892), Quanah (June 1893), Amarillo (August 1893), Quanah (December 1893), and Amarillo (February 1894) with detachments at Regency (Sullivan's detachment: June–November 1896), San Saba (Sullivan's detachment: November 1896–March 1897, McDonald's detachment: March–November 1897), El Paso and Langtry (February 1896), Hartley (1897), San Saba (February 1898), Spofford Junction (May 1898), Memphis (August 1898), Columbus (March 1899), Athens (1899), and Orange (September 1899); Hall County (1900); Orange County with headquarters at Orange (1900); Hardeman County (September 1900)

## Company C

Captain E. F. Ikard (May 5–August 31, 1874)
2nd Lieutenant L. P. Beavert, Commanding (September 1–December 29, 1874)
1st Lieutenant L. P. Beavert, Commanding (December 29, 1874–February 28, 1875)
   *Company "C" disbanded (March 1875–October 1876)*
Captain John C. Sparks (October 1, 1876–November 30, 1877)
1st Lieutenant George W. Arrington, Commanding (November 30, 1877–April 30, 1879)
Captain George W. Arrington (May 1, 1879–August 31, 1882)
Lieutenant John Hoffar, Commanding (September 1, 1882–August 31, 1883)
Lieutenant George H. Schmitt (September 1–December 1, 1883)
Captain George H. Schmitt (December 1, 1883–November 30, 1888)
   *Company "C" disbanded (December 1888–June 1900)*
1st Lieutenant William J. McCauley, Commanding (June 1–November 30, 1900)
2nd Lieutenant John B. Tays, commanding detachment (November 10, 1877–March 31, 1878)
2nd Lieutenant James A. Tays, commanding detachment (April 1, 1878–December 31, 1879)
1st Sergeant Marcus H. Ludwick, commanding detachment (January 1–September 5, 1879)
1st Lieutenant George W. Baylor, commanding detachment (August 1, 1879–September 1, 1880)
   *Lt. Baylor assumed formal command effective September 15, 1879 and Detachment "C" renamed as Company "A" (September 1, 1880)*

*Ranging District*: Young, Archer, Clay, and Jack Counties with headquarters at Camp Eureka (May 1874); Llano County with headquarters at Llano (October 1876); Lampasas County with headquarters at Lampasas (March–May 1877) with detachment at San Elizario and Ysleta (J. B. Tays' detachment: November 1877–March 1878, J. A. Tays' detachment: April–December 1878, Ludwick's detachment: January–September 1879, Baylor's detachment: May 1879–August 1880); Coleman County with headquarters at Pecan Springs (November 1877); Panhandle country with headquarters at Camp Loma Vista near Fort Griffin (July 1878), Mobeetie (June 1879), Camp Roberts (September 1879), and Mobeetie (August 1882); Gray County (February 1883); Greer-Collingsworth Counties line (November 1883); Wilbarger County with headquarters at Wichita Falls and detachment at Vernon (February 1884); Frio, La Salle, Duval, Webb, and Starr Counties with headquarters at Pearsall (December 1885), Cotulla (January 1886), Laredo (May 1886), Rio Grande City (November 1886), Pena (December 1886), and Cotulla (January 1887) and detachment at Fort

Worth in Tarrant County (April 1886); Brown County with headquarters at Brownwood and detachment at Sellman's Ranch (February 1887); Karnes County with headquarters at Helena (August 1887); Bee Counties (November 1887); Tom Green County with headquarters at San Angelo (June–November 1900)

## Company D

Captain Cicero Rufus "Rufe" Perry (May 5–December 9, 1874)
2nd Lieutenant Daniel W. Roberts, Commanding (December 10, 1874–August 31, 1876)
2nd Lieutenant Frank M. Moore, Commanding (September 1, 1876–August 31, 1877)
Captain Daniel W. Roberts (September 1, 1877–August 31, 1881)
1st Sergeant Lamartine P. "Lam" Sieker, Acting Commander (September 1–31, 1881)
1st Lieutenant Lamartine P. "Lam" Sieker, Commanding (October 1, 1881–August 31, 1882)
Captain Lamartine P. "Lam" Sieker (September 1, 1882–October 15, 1885)
1st Lieutenant Frank D. Jones, Commanding (October 15, 1885–February 28, 1886)
Captain Frank D. Jones (March 1, 1886–June 30, 1893)
Captain John R. Hughes (July 4, 1893–July 8, 1901)
2nd Lieutenant Daniel W. Roberts, commanding detachment (September 1, 1874–February 28, 1875)
Sergeant Nelson O. "Mage" Reynolds, commanding detachment (September 1875)
Sergeant Edward A. Sieker, Jr., commanding detachment (May 30–August 25, 1880)
Sergeant Rush G. Kimball, commanding detachment (October 1880)
Sergeant Charles H. Fusselman, commanding detachment (October 1889)
1st Sergeant Ira Aten, commanding detachment (July–August 1889)
*Ranging District*: Coleman, Menard, and Mason Counties with headquarters at camp on Elm Creek (May 1874), camp at Post Oak Springs (July 1874), camp at Little Saline Creek (November 1874), camp at Mud Creek (December 1874), and Camp Las Moras near Menardville (June 1875) and detachment at Mason (Roberts' detachment: September 1874–February 1875); Uvalde, Zavala, Webb, and Dimmit Counties with headquarters at camp near Laredo and detachments at Carrizo Springs and Roma (September 1876); Kimble County with headquarters at Bear Creek (April 1877); Uvalde County with headquarters at camp on Sabinal River (October 1877); Menard and Kimble Counties with headquarters at Menardville (1878), Camp McCulloch (April 1879), and Fort McKavett (May 1879); Trans-Pecos country with headquarters at Fort Davis (E. Sieker's detachment: May–August 1880; Company D: August 1880); Menard and Kimble Counties with headquarters at camp near Campbell (December 1880) and camp near Junction (September 1881); Rio Grande Valley from Pecos River to Starr County with headquarters at Camp King, Uvalde County (1882) and Uvalde (1884); Menard County with headquarters at camp on Pegleg Crossing of the San Saba River and "Fort Iceberg" near Menardville (1886); Edwards County with headquarters at Barksdale and detachment at Camp Wood (Aten's detachment: 1886); McCulloch County with headquarters at Brady City (March 1887); Starr and Duval Counties with headquarters at Rio Grande City (September 1887); Uvalde County with headquarters at Uvalde (February 1889) and detachment at Alpine (Fusselman's detachment: February 1889–April 1890); Fort Bend County with headquarters at Richmond (Company D: June 1889, Atens's detachment: July–August 1889); La Salle County with headquarters at Cotulla (February 1890); El Paso, Presidio, Brewster, Jeff Davis, Reeves, and Pecos Counties with headquarters at Camp Hogg near Alpine (May 1890), Marathon (1892), Langtry (April 1893), and Ysleta (June 1893) and detachments at Alpine (June 1893) and El Paso and Langtry (February 1896)

## COMPANY E

Captain William J. "Jeff" Maltby (May 5–August 31, 1874)
2nd Lieutenant B. F. Best, Commanding (August 31–October 2, 1874)
1st Lieutenant B. F. Best, Commanding (October 2–December 12, 1874)
1st Lieutenant B. S. Foster, Commanding (December 12, 1874–May 31, 1877)
Sergeant D. M. Whelan, Acting Commander (June 1–August 31, 1877)
2nd Lieutenant Nelson O. "Mage" Reynolds, Commanding (September 1, 1877–February 28, 1879)
1st Sergeant Charles L. Nevill, Acting Commander (February 28–August 31, 1879)
2nd Lieutenant Charles L. Nevill, Commanding (September 1, 1879–August 31, 1881)
Captain Charles L. Nevill (August 31, 1881–November 25, 1882)
1st Lieutenant J. T. Gillespie, Commanding (December 1, 1882–November 30, 1883)
Captain J. T. Gillespie (December 1, 1883–April 15, 1887)
   *Company "E" disbanded (April 1887–June 1891)*
Captain James S. McNeel, Sr. (June 1, 1891–December 31, 1892)
Captain John H. Rogers (January 1, 1893–July 8, 1901)
Sergeant L. Arnett, commanding detachment (August 31–December 12, 1874)
1st Sergeant J. T. Gillespie, commanding detachment (September 1–November 30, 1882)
*Ranging District*: Coleman County with headquarters at camp on the head of Home Creek (May 1874); Duval and Hidalgo Counties with headquarters at Concepcion (August–December 1874); Coleman and Callahan Counties with headquarters at camp on Home Creek (June 1876) and camp on Jim Ned Creek (September 1876); Kimble County with headquarters at Camp Steele (April 1877); Lampasas County (July 1877); Austin (September 1877); Kimble, Menard, Mason, and Kerr Counties with headquarters at camp on Bear Creek (October 1877); Burnet, San Saba, Llano, and Lampasas Counties with headquarters at Camp Burnet (May 1878), camp near San Saba River (July 1878), Camp Stockbridge (September 1878), and Camp Simpson (October 1878) and detachment at Austin (Wilson's detachment: September 1878); Kerr County with headquarters at Camp Contrary (November 1878), Dowdy Ranch (January 1879), and Camp Swenson (May 1879); Pecos and Presidio Counties with headquarters at Fort Davis (June 1880) and Camp Mousquie Cañon (September 1880); Uvalde County with headquarters at Camp King (May 1883); Trans-Pecos country with headquarters at Camp Burgess near Murphysville (September 1883); Brown County with headquarters at Brownwood (May 1884); Taylor County with headquarters at Abilene (1884) and Camp Elm (January 1885); Trans-Pecos country with headquarters at Camp Johnson (March 1885), Toyah (August 1885), and Murphysville (May 1886); Nueces, Starr, Harris, Menard, Kimble, La Salle, Bexar, Washington, Tom Green, Medina, Caldwell, Duval, Encinal, Webb, and Val Verde Counties with headquarters at Camp Mabry near Alice (June 1891), Cotulla (July 1898), Comstock (October 1899), and Laredo (November 1900) and detachments at Realitos (September 1891), Ringgold Barracks (December 1891), Alice (February 1892), El Paso and Langtry (February 1896), Laredo (March 1899), Wharton County (April 1899), Columbus (June 1899), Orange in Orange County (August–September 1899), Del Rio (Dubose's detachment: September–November 1899), Del Rio (January 1900), Hempstead (November 1900), and Marathon in Brewster County (December 1900)

## COMPANY F

Captain Cornelius V. "Neal" Coldwell (June 4, 1874–August 31, 1876)
1st Lieutenant Patrick Dolan, Commanding (September 1, 1876–November 30, 1877)

Captain Patrick Dolan (December 1, 1877–April 30, 1879)
1st Sergeant Richard Jones, Acting Commander (March 1–May 31, 1879)
 *Company "F" disbanded (June 1879–March 1881)*
Captain Thomas L. Oglesby (March 1, 1881–November 25, 1882)
Lieutenant Charles B. McKinney, Commanding (December 1, 1882–March 1, 1883)
Sergeant William L. Rudd, Acting Commander (March 1–April 31, 1883)
Lieutenant Joseph Shely, Commanding (May 1, 1883–March 1, 1884)
Captain Joseph Shely (March 1, 1884–May 31, 1885)
1st Lieutenant William Scott, Commanding (June 1, 1885–February 28, 1886)
Captain William Scott (March 1, 1886–February 29, 1888)
1st Lieutenant James A. Brooks, Commanding (March 1, 1888–February 28, 1889)
Captain James A. Brooks (March 1, 1889–July 8, 1901)

*Ranging District*: Kerr and Edwards Counties with headquarters at camp on Silver Creek (June 1874); Nueces County with headquarters at Corpus Christi (September 1874); Kerr County with headquarters at Camp Menite (May 1875); Menard County with headquarters at camp on San Saba River (September 1876); Nueces Canyon country with headquarters at Camp Wood (October 1877); Duval, Webb, Atascosa, La Salle, Zavala, Maverick, McMullen, Frio, Karnes, De Witt, Dimmit, Kinney, Bandera, Uvalde, Tom Green, Edwards, and Chambers Counties with headquarters at San Diego (March 1881), camp near Iuka (August 1881), Carrizo Springs (1881), Cotulla (May 1882), and Uvalde (May 1885) and detachments at Cotulla (McKinney's detachment: April 1881), Fort Ewell (Rudd's detachment: July 1881), Uvalde (1882), Cuero (January 1883), Frio County (Morris' detachment: January 1883), Rio Grande City (Rudd's detachment: 1883), Anahuac (August 1884), and Carrizo Springs (Farrow's detachment: January 1885); Wilbarger, Hardeman, and Childress Counties with headquarters at Vernon (October 1885) and detachment at Alavarado in Tarrant County (April 1886); Sabine County with headquarters at Hemphill (July 1886); Brown, McCulloch, Concho, and Lampasas Counties with headquarters at Brownwood (September 1886); Sabine and San Augustine Counties with headquarters at Hemphill (March 1887); Parker, Eastland, Brown, and Callahan Counties with headquarters near Weatherford (May 1887) and Cisco (June 1887) and detachment at Brownwood (August 1887); Runnels, Tom Green, Mills, San Saba, and Edwards Counties with headquarters at Ballinger (August 1887), camp on Concho River near San Angelo (November 1887), and Ballinger (March 1888) and detachments at San Angelo (Rogers' detachment: October 1887) and Mullin (March 1888); La Salle, Val Verde, Uvalde, Bandera, Frio, Bee, Karnes, De Witt, Dimmitt, Kerr, Kimble, Encinal, Webb, Duval, Nueces, Hidalgo, Cameron, Starr, Zavala, Waller, Harrison, Wharton, Matagorda, Bastrop, San Augustine, Karnes, and Galveston Counties with headquarters at Kerrville (June 1888), Rio Grande City (October 1888), Edinburg (January 1890) Cotulla (May 1890), Realitos (June 1892), Cotulla (June 1893), Laredo (April 1898), Alice (May 1898), and Cotulla (June 1899) and detachments at Laredo (October 1888–January 1889), Santa María (October 1889–January 1890), Rio Grande City (January 1890), Encinal (May 1890), Rio Grande City (January 1892), El Paso and Langtry (February 1896), in Reeves County (August 1896), Brownsville (May 1898), and Brownsville and Hebbronville (June 1899)

# 9

## *Los Rinches*: The State Ranger Force (1901–1935)

On July 9, 1901, the new Ranger Force was organized "for the purpose of protecting the frontier against marauding or thieving parties, and for the suppression of lawlessness and crime throughout the State." The personnel included one quartermaster with the rank of captain and four companies of mounted men. Each company was authorized one captain, one sergeant, and twenty privates, but again budgetary constraints would determine the field strength. The company commanders and the quartermaster were appointed by the adjutant general, with gubernatorial approval, for two-year terms, and served at the executive's pleasure. The captains, in turn, continued to recruit their own men, and Section 11 of the new legislation granted all personnel the authority to make arrests and execute criminal processes throughout the state. The monthly wages for captains were one hundred dollars, fifty dollars for sergeants, and forty dollars for privates.

For the first decade of the 20th century, the State Rangers performed routine law enforcement — pursuing rustlers and *mescalleros*, keeping order at elections and court sessions, and enforcing gambling laws and local option liquor ordinances — in support of local officers.

Between September 1, 1902, and August 31, 1904, the Ranger Force traveled a total of 225,557 miles in the discharge of their duties, in which they conducted 630 scouts, made 768 arrests for all offenses (including seventy for murder), recovered 579 head of stolen livestock, killed three criminals in four engagements, and suffered one Ranger killed and one wounded.

The new century began on a positive note with the "Rules and Regulations Governing Company C Ranger Force" circulated by Captain J. H. Rogers in 1906:

1. Men, upon entering the service, are required to procure a good outfit consisting of horse, saddle, Winchester, six-shooter, rope, and bedding. It shall be maintained in good order continuously as long as they remain in the service.
2. Each Ranger is required to perform his full amount of camp duty, such as cooking, herding horses and any and all of the regular routine camp work. This must be strictly observed and any complaint substantiated shall be sufficient grounds for a dismissal from the service.
3. Each member of the Ranger force is expected to look out for and care for and take interest in the preservation of all State property; and especially the pack saddle, pack blankets and pack

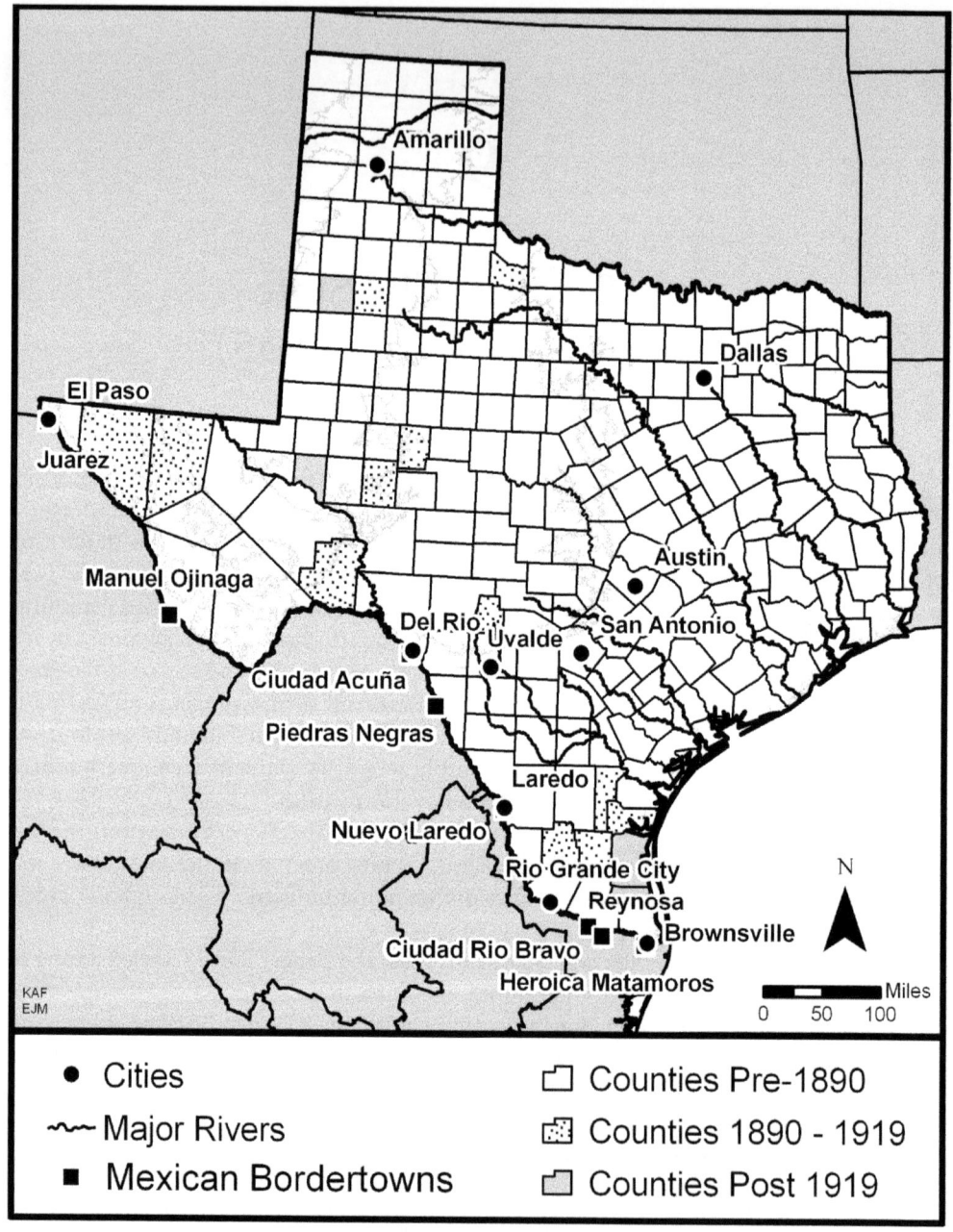

rope must be kept hanging together and not be molested by the men for their own use in any way, but in some designated place understood by the men it must be kept so that it may be readily found any time even of a dark night when we might be leaving in haste.
4. Men are expected to keep their quarters, at least, in a reasonably clean and neat condition. No one need even apply for a position in this company that is not sober, honest and of a good moral character.

Captain Rogers' rules were just one example of the leadership of the "Four Captains" and the code of conduct followed by the Rangers, which enabled them to maintain their reputation for high standards. Unfortunately, the Rangers' ethics and integrity would be sorely challenged in the years to come.

The Mexican Revolution began on November 20, 1910, when Francisco I. Madero rose up against the autocratic rule of President Porfirío Díaz. Although Díaz was forced from office on May 25, 1911, the conflict continued intermittently over the next nine years as numerous revolutionary factions vied for power. Madero was overthrown in a February 18, 1913, coup d'état engineered by General Victoriano Huerta, who was himself deposed by Venustiano Carranza on July 15, 1914. During the decade the various insurgencies raged, Rangers patrolled the 1,200-mile border in order to neutralize Mexican revolutionaries, arms smugglers, and bandits who crossed the Rio Grande to procure livestock, munitions, materiel, and specie. On February 3, 1913, Governor Oscar B. Colquitt wrote Captain Hughes in El Paso, "... I instruct you and your men to keep them [the Mexican raiders] off of Texas territory if possible, and if they invade the State let them understand they do so at the risk of their lives." Some of the bloodiest and most brutal fighting in Ranger history was waged during the revolution. This was truly their darkest hour.

Even as the Rio Grande country simmered with revolutionary unrest, Rangers were still needed elsewhere. Throughout the state, they contended with thieves and killers, race riots, lynch mobs, railroad labor strikes, potentially explosive trials, bitterly-fought elections, and personal and political feuds.

Governor Colquitt, who took office in January 1911, assumed the prerogative of personally appointing Ranger captains, a responsibility traditionally delegated to the adjutants general. Indeed, Colquitt and his successors bypassed the chain of command and issued orders directly to Ranger captains. The quality of the Ranger Force declined as the governors perpetuated a spoils system in the appointment process. Often they, rather than the captains, personally selected recruits for purposes of patronage or political reward rather than for experience or competence. The "Four Captains" would be gone by 1915 and the leaders that remained did not measure up to the standards of the past. The politicization of the Service brought an influx of unqualified appointees, a number of who would later commit widespread abuses of their authority, especially against those of Mexican heritage.

The Ranger Force was reduced to three companies on September 30, 1910, and to two companies totaling thirteen men on February 1, 1911. On October 1, the Rangers were again expanded to three companies, each consisting of one captain, one sergeant, and twelve privates. Later in the month, a fourth was authorized consisting of just one captain, who acted as an undercover detective. The actual size of the force fluctuated every two years thereafter as the governor and the legislature debated the size of appropriations. In light of the financial situation, Colquitt also increased the number of Special Ranger commissions.

The meager wages of the State Rangers often could not attract or retain the caliber of individuals desired, since most competent officers invariably sought better-paying employment with county sheriffs, cattlemen's associations, railroads, or the federal customs and immigration services. Some good men did periodically return out of a sense of duty or a love for the Ranger life. Because a number of them were regularly in and out of the force, there was little opportunity for continuity. They were also compelled to depend on free railroad passes or their own horses for transportation.

Following the October 1911 reorganization, the Rangers began to phase out the Winchester '94s and the Colt Single Action Army (SAA) pistols that had been standard for years. The Winchester was replaced by another of its family, the Model 1895. The U.S. Army had offered a contract for a new rifle in 1895 that would utilize the powerful, spitzer bullets of the .30-40 Krag cartridge (also known as the ".30 Army" or ".30 Government"). Departing from the tubular magazine of its earlier lever-actions, Winchester fabricated the Model '95 as the first to utilize an innovative non-detachable "box magazine." Unfortunately, the rifle selected by the Ordnance Board was the Krag-Jørgensen developed in Norway.

Despite the Army's rejection, the Winchester design became a favorite among many civilians and peace officers in the Southwest. The rifles were forty-five inches overall with a barrel length of twenty-eight inches, while the barrels of the carbines were twenty-two inches. The weapons possessed oil-finished, straight-grain walnut stocks and a five-round magazine capacity, and weighed approximately eight pounds. Most rifles were fitted with open tangent rear sights and unprotected blade front sights. The First Models had flat sides, a rounded top and breech bolt, and a one-piece lever. The Second Model changed to a fluted receiver to reduce weight and a two-piece lever. The two calibers most commonly used by the Rangers were the .30-40 Krag and the .30-06 Springfield. The rimmed .30-40 cartridge consisted of a .30-caliber 220-grain softpoint bullet with lead core and cupro-nickel jacket, which was propelled by forty grains of smokeless powder. Capable of long-range shots up to 1,100 yards, the original military .30-06 ammunition ("Ball Cartridge, caliber .30, Model of 1906") consisted of a flat base, cupro-nickel jacket, short casing, and high-velocity 150-grain spitzer bullet driven by fifty grains of pyrocellulose powder.

The Colt SAA six-shooters slowly gave way to another Colt product, the Model 1911 and its successor, the Model 1911A-1. In 1892, the U.S. Army had replaced their Cavalry Model .45 pistols with Colt .38-caliber revolvers, but they proved unreliable and underpowered in the Philippine Insurrection (1899–1903). Army Ordnance went through a lengthy battle between 1904 and 1911 to get an improved, more modern sidearm into the hands of the troops. In an ironic twist to Samuel Walker's fight to get the Walker Colt accepted, the U.S. Cavalry balked at the thought of a semi-automatic pistol being adopted rather than the traditional revolver. Of course, the Ordnance Board won the day and the Government Model 1911 was placed into service. The pistol was 8½ inches overall with a five-inch barrel, weighed thirty-nine ounces, and had a seven-round magazine capacity. It used .45-caliber Automatic Colt Pistol (ACP) cartridges, which grew to include a wide spectrum of ammunition ranging from 185-grain hollowpoint to 230-grain full-metal-jacketed military hardball. In June 1926, the military adopted an improved Colt pistol which was designated the Model 1911A-1. The new pistol featured a lengthened grip safety tang, arched mainspring housing, fully checkered grips, and a manually operated slide lock to prevent accidental firing. Other modifications included improved rifling, shortened trigger and hammer spur, and widened front sight. The U.S. Armed Forces retired the 1911A-1 in 1985, but it currently remains in use with several law enforcement agencies, including the Los Angeles Police Department SWAT team and the Texas Rangers.

Topnotch weapons would be sorely needed as diplomatic relations between the United States and Mexico deteriorated in the wake of the "Tampico Affair" of April 9, 1914, when American sailors were detained by soldiers loyal to Huerta. Washington found the formal Mexican apology unsatisfactory and U.S. Marines were ordered to occupy Vera Cruz from April 21 to November 23, 1914.

The situation on the border was strained to the breaking point when the *"Plan de San Diego"* was first detected on January 24, 1915. The Plan was a revolutionary manifesto that called for Mexicans on both sides of the Rio Grande to rise up on February 20 and exterminate every male *norteamericano* over the age of sixteen, excluding old men, in Texas, New Mexico, Colorado, Arizona, and California. This would allow the five states to be transformed into an independent republic that would be annexed by Mexico when appropriate. Indian lands in the Southwest would be returned to their former owners and African Americans would receive their own republic from the former states of Oklahoma, Kansas, Nebraska, South Dakota, Wyoming, and Utah.

With the revelation of the Plan, the long-simmering tensions in the Lower Valley exploded into a clash of cultures. The Anglo Texans, especially those who arrived after the introduction of the railroad in 1904, were already traditionally distrustful and disdainful of their Hispanic neighbors. Despite the fact the February 20 uprising failed to take place, overnight every person of Mexican heritage was considered part of a possible terrorist conspiracy. In turn, the Latin community of the valley, both Mexican and Hispanic, which had composed ninety-five percent of the population prior to 1904, bore old grudges dating back to the 1840s, including generations of Anglo political corruption, discrimination, and the loss of land titles. They remembered the deeds of Cameron, Hays, Gray, Callahan, Ford, McNelly, and others. The Hispanic term for the Rangers, "*los rinches,*" carried the connotation of a racist and brutal Anglo peace officer who used the law for his own ends. The term came to mean any *gringo* lawman, whether a Ranger or not.

The "Bandit War" began in early July 1915 and occurred in Cameron, Hidalgo, Willacy, Starr, Brooks, Zapata, Duval, and Webb counties. Despite the name, most of the Mexicans involved in this conflict were guerrilla insurgents, called *Sediciosos* (Seditionists), fighting in support of the Plan of San Diego. Unlike the apolitical brigands and freebooters who took advantage of the uprising, the *Sediciosos* targeted members of the Anglo establishment and its infrastructure — railroad bridges, automobiles, telegraph and telephone lines, stores and ranches, water pumping plants, and irrigation systems. Indeed, Charles H. Harris III and Louis R. Sadler presented compelling evidence in their book, *The Texas Rangers and the Mexican Revolution*, suggesting President Carranza might have sponsored the Plan for his own political goals.

Hurt politically and financially, cattle barons and other powerful figures in the Valley demanded action. Governor James E. "Farmer Jim" Ferguson, elected to office in November 1914, responded by calling on Henry Lee Ransom to help combat the *Sediciosos*. Undoubtedly a ruthless, cold-blooded killer, Ransom was a veteran of the Philippine Insurrection and a career lawman. While a special officer for the mayor of Houston in 1910, he had murdered a criminal defense attorney, but was acquitted on a plea of self-defense. Given a virtual hunting license by the governor, he was appointed captain of Company D on July 20, 1915, and began recruiting a complement of ex–prison farm guards.

Under the rules of engagement, the federal troops on the lower Rio Grande were prohibited from crossing the border, so they garrisoned ranches and towns while the State Rangers and local officers took the lead in the pursuit of the guerrillas.

On August 8, *Sediciosos* attacked the headquarters of the Norias division of the King Ranch and were repulsed by an eight-man detachment of Troop C, 12th U.S. Cavalry and eight civilians. The *insurrectos* lost at least five killed and two wounded. Shortly after the skirmish, Rangers under Ransom and Captain J. Monroe Fox arrived on the scene, where they tortured a captive to death for information. The next morning, Fox and two other riders posed for pictures taken by Brownsville photographer Robert Runyon. The photographs, erroneously dated October 8, portrayed the three mounted with their lariats around four dead bodies. After the pictures were published in various newspapers, they brewed up a firestorm of protest among the Hispanic population, further strengthening the Plan of San Diego movement, and tarnishing the reputation of the Ranger Force.

This photograph was one of at least nine taken by Brownsville photographer Robert Runyon the day after the Norias Bandit Raid on August 8, 1915. For years, Runyon chronicled the events of the Lower Rio Grande Valley, including the Mexican Revolution and the Bandit War. Once published in newspapers, the Norias photographs worsened an already tense situation. Courtesy of the Runyon (Robert) Photograph Collection, No. RUN00096, Dolph Briscoe Center for American History, UT–Austin.

Unfortunately, Ransom, Fox, and their ilk did not stop with desecrating the dead. Their offenses would go on to include the unlawful use of authority, political partisanship, drunkenness, assault, torture, lynchings, and prisoner abuse. They established a "blacklist" and began an indiscriminate purge (known locally as "evaporations") of any Mexican or Hispanic suspected of actively participating in the depredations, aiding and abetting the *Sediciosos*, or simply sympathizing with their position. Any of these "suspicious" Mexicans were dealt with using the "Ranger Conviction." Those trying to stay off the blacklist also faced death from the insurgents, who would not tolerate any Mexican not aiding the cause. The population of the Lower Valley declined by more than half because of the summary executions or a mass exodus away from the killing zone. While more than twenty Anglos were murdered by *bandidos* and *insurrectos* along the border between 1914 and 1919, approximately one hundred to three hundred persons of Mexican descent were thought to have been killed in that same time frame; it is unlikely that all were guilty of criminal offenses against the laws of Texas. In fairness, local officers and vigilante groups were also active, and Anglo citizens either condoned or ignored their activities. Furthermore, not all State Rangers were involved in the "evaporations," but enough participated to stain the Service's honor.

On October 19, 1915, Venustiano Carranza obtained grudging diplomatic recognition of his administration from President Woodrow Wilson. This action by the United States angered Francisco "Pancho" Villa, a rival of Carranza's in the ongoing revolutionary struggle, who had hoped to receive American support himself. Intent on punishing the Wilson Administration and discrediting Carranza, Villa raided Columbus, New Mexico on March 9, 1916, killing ten soldiers and eight civilians, while losing over a hundred of his own partisans to death or wounds. His attack brought the two countries to the brink of war. The United States responded on March 15 by sending the 10,000-man Punitive Expedition, Brigadier-General John J. "Black Jack" Pershing commanding, into Chihuahua to pursue Villa. The Ranger Force itself was not involved in the campaign, which ended on February 7, 1917, but several ex–Rangers did participate as civilian employees. Washington and Mexico City alike had no desire for war, but the incursions into the U.S. and the presence of American troops on Mexican soil gave both governments cause for hostilities.

On June 17, 1916, the rules of engagement changed when U.S. cavalry troopers from Fort Brown were ordered to pursue raiders back across the border, where they skirmished with Mexican soldiers. In response, the local Mexican commander gave assurances that no more raids would take place from his district. The next day, President Wilson mobilized the entire National Guard and dispatched 112,000 troops from fourteen different states to the Rio Grande. The Bandit War was at an end.

While American and Mexican contingents dueled across the Rio Grande, the First World War was raging in Europe. Throughout the majority of the conflict, the United States officially pursued a neutral course. By January 1917, the German Empire, desperate to cut the British supply line to North America, decided to resume submarine attacks on merchant shipping in the Atlantic, regardless of nationality; a policy they feared would bring the U.S. into the fighting on the side of the Allies. The Imperial Foreign Secretary in Berlin dispatched a coded message (known as the "Zimmerman Telegram") to the German ambassadors in Washington and Mexico City. The cable proposed a German-Mexican military alliance if the U.S. appeared ready to enter the war. Germany was to offer Mexico financial support in reclaiming Texas, New Mexico, and Arizona. President Carranza ultimately rejected the German entreaty as unfeasible, but the telegram had been deciphered by British cryptographers and its contents subsequently shared with President Wilson. The damage to U.S.-Mexican relations was done. Congress responded to the revelation by declaring war on Germany on April 6, 1917.

Even as American soldiers prepared for the battlefields of Europe, the House of Representatives of the Thirty-fifth Legislature voted, on August 18, 1917, to impeach Governor Ferguson for misappropriation and embezzlement of state funds and failure to enforce banking laws. Indeed, Ferguson's tenure would far surpass E. J. Davis' administration as the most corrupt in Texas history. The Senate found him guilty on September 24 and Lieutenant-Governor William P. Hobby succeeded Ferguson in office. The most important item on the new executive's agenda was his own upcoming election for a full term. To that end, he exceeded his predecessors in politicizing the State Rangers. During his tenure, Ferguson had expanded the force to six companies totaling seventy-three men and issued approximately three hundred Special Ranger commissions. Hobby surpassed the former governor and enlarged the Service to a total of ten companies. The only qualification for new or veteran Rangers became the possession of political connections. He discharged Ferguson's Special Rangers (many of whom were guilty of accepting bribes and embezzling state funds) and appointed four hundred of his own supporters.

After the commencement of hostilities, legislation was introduced creating a "Ranger Home Guard" to deter expected German subversion, propaganda, and espionage along the Rio Grande. The bill was passed on May 25, signed into law on October 15, and became effective December 28. Under this act, Hobby increased the number of companies to eleven (eight of which were stationed on the border) with a projected total force of 175 men, which offered him the chance to offer even more political patronage. The governor went even further and sponsored the "Hobby Loyalty Act" which, on March 4, 1918, rendered illegal any dissenting action or speech concerning U.S. involvement in the war. The Loyalty Secret Service Department was established under the provisions of the Ranger Home Guard Act. Three Loyalty Rangers were assigned to each of the state's 252 counties to enforce the Loyalty Act. Captain William M. Hanson, a Hobby political operative and an enthusiastic empire builder, was placed in charge of the department and responsible for tracking revolutionary and subversive activities, pursuing fugitive draft evaders, preventing armed incursions from Mexico, and handling confidential assignments. Quite often the only loyalty he insured was to Hobby's election campaign.

The last hot spot of the decade was the Big Bend country. The Mexican state of Chihuahua was a haven for smugglers, revolutionaries, and *bandidos*, while the Trans-Pecos counties of Texas possessed their own share of rustlers and renegades. State Rangers, cavalry troopers, and federal customs inspectors, such as ex–Ranger Joe Sitter, dealt with them all. On December 25, 1917, the Presidio County ranch of Lucas C. Brite, one of the largest in the Big Bend, was attacked by approximately thirty bandits who murdered three people and looted the store and post office. The raiders escaped into Mexico, but not before encountering two separate army patrols that killed at least ten bandits and recovered much of the stolen property. Ranger Captain Fox believed the nearby village of Porvenir was a center for bandit activity and its inhabitants were guilty of aiding the Brite raiders. Fox ordered Private Bud Weaver and seven other Rangers to the village to exact retribution. None of the eight were veteran Rangers or professional lawmen, and were indicative of the waning standards of the Force. Weaver and his men entered Porvenir about midnight on January 28, 1918, for the purported purpose of searching for firearms and bandits. Instead, they herded the male villagers out of town a quarter mile and executed fifteen of them. The Rangers reported that an ambush had occurred and the villagers were simply caught in the crossfire. The soldiers who had reluctantly accompanied the Rangers and provided perimeter security reported a massacre. Fox and the eight men were discharged from the Service.

With the end of the Great War, the approximately 460 Special Rangers had their commissions revoked on January 14, 1919, and the Loyalty Rangers followed suit the next month. To meet the conditions of post-war Texas, three companies were disbanded and at least twenty-seven regular Rangers received honorable discharges in the first three months of the year.

On January 15, José Tomás Canales, a state representative from Brownsville, introduced House Bill No. 5, which listed measures to reform the Ranger Force. He filed nineteen separate charges of irregularities and called for a massive reorganization of the Service. In the political maneuvering over the bill, the force's defenders called for a legislative inquiry into Ranger abuses. They also wanted to investigate Canales' motivations for his bill. Following the joint committee hearings, which convened from January 31 to February 13, and legislative debate, which revealed misconduct but exonerated the governor, adjutant general, and Ranger commanders, a substitute version of HB No. 5 was signed into law on March 19. The Ranger Force was reduced to four companies, each composed of a captain, a sergeant, and fifteen privates. In addition, the Thirty-sixth Legislature authorized a quartermaster with the rank of captain, and a headquarters company of six men in Austin under the command of a senior captain. The Rangers were offered more competitive salaries—one hundred and fifty dollars per month for captains, one hundred dollars for sergeants, and ninety for privates—in order to attract "men of high moral character." As a result, the quality of the Rangers improved during the early 1920s, especially under the leadership of able captains, such as William L. Wright, Roy W. Aldrich, Tom R. Hickman, and Francis A. "Frank" Hamer.

The Mexican Revolution ended after Carranza was assassinated on May 20, 1920, and Pancho Villa laid down his arms on July 29. Between November 10, 1910, and September 30, 1919, 785 Americans had been "killed, wounded, or outraged" and the border country had suffered $50 million in property damage.

"The Ranger Code" by Bruce Green. This oil painting was commissioned by the Texas Ranger Association Foundation in 2006 in order to honor the heritage of the Texas Rangers. The artist depicts Captain J. H. Rogers reading his company's code of conduct to his assembled men. The rules detailed the captain's expectations for professional competence and moral behavior from the rangers under his command. Courtesy of the artist.

Even as the conflict was reaching a conclusion, the endemic violence along the Rio Grande was about to resume as the Rangers faced their next challenge. On January 29, 1919, Congress ratified the Eighteenth Amendment prohibiting "the manufacture, sale, or transportation of intoxicating liquors," the Volstead Act, which defined the alcohol cited and banned its consumption, was passed on October 28, and National Prohibition became the law of the land on January 16, 1920. Since 1837, the laws of supply and demand had insured that cross-border smuggling occurred with the only difference being the commodity in question—arms and ammunition, black-market clothing and foodstuffs, illegal immigrants, duty-free mescal—and the direction it was taken. The "Noble Experiment" would prove to be a godsend to the *contrabandistas*. After the new laws were enacted, various distilleries and breweries moved their entire operations to Mexico and the Caribbean. The illicit profits from liquor smuggling (or "rumrunning") were just too lucrative for distillers and border runners alike to ignore. The pack mules of Rio Grande smugglers (known as *tequileros* and "horsebackers") were each able to carry eighty bottles of mescal, tequila, or whiskey. A sixty-cent tequila bottle in Mexico brought fifteen dollars in San Antonio, while mescal worth fifty cents a quart was sold for up to ten dollars. The towns of San Diego in Duval County, San Ygnacio in Zapata County, Roma, LaGrulla, and Rio Grande City in Starr County, Del Rio, Laredo, and El Paso became major points of entry for liquor smuggling from Mexico, as did Galveston for rumrunning from Cuba, British Honduras, and the Bahamas. In addition to violating federal Prohibition laws, *tequileros* defied state criminal statutes by cutting pasture fences to facilitate their movement and indiscriminately murdering witnesses. They also broke state sanitation laws since their horses and mules often carried fever ticks which infected Texas livestock. Shootouts between law officers (including county sheriffs, State Rangers, mounted customs inspectors, U.S. marshals, and federal prohibition agents) and the *tequileros* were all too common in South Texas and the Big Bend.

During the "Roaring Twenties," moonshiners, bootleggers, and speakeasy owners flourished throughout the state. Normally law-abiding young citizens, eager to forget the horrors of the war, and shed the traditions and Victorian morals of their elders, routinely flouted the unpopular law. Despite the Herculean efforts of Rangers, such as Marvin "Red" Burton, the plethora of illegal distilleries in North and East Texas producing moonshine and "Choc" beer was a problem that could never be adequately dealt with. Too many local law officers either ignored them as not worth the effort, or were bribed to let them continue. Other Rangers kept busy raiding and closing "gin joints" and elite gambling clubs in San Antonio, Dallas/Fort Worth, Corpus Christi, Galveston, and Houston, usually to have them quickly reopened due to widespread corruption in municipal governments. Even after the Twenty-first Amendment repealed Prohibition on December 15, 1933, Rangers continued to enforce state liquor laws until they too were rescinded on August 24, 1935.

Even while they enforced Prohibition, the Rangers were active in other matters across the state. Captain Aldrich and three others were ordered to the Galveston wharves on May 13, 1920, to help keep order during a labor strike. Following the declaration of martial law on June 7, an emergency company under Captain C. J. Blackwell was sent in on September 30 to take over police duties. Rangers from Headquarters Company and Companies B and C were ordered to Red River, Gregg, Cass, Bowie, Shelby, and Milam counties in June 1921 to quell the East Texas "tick war." In October 1921 and again two years later, Rangers gathered sufficient evidence of Ku Klux Klan ("the Invisible Empire") violence, but rarely were they able to secure convictions. On July 23, 1922, Governor Pat M. Neff sent nearly the entire Ranger Force to Denison to handle a railroad employee strike. Three days later, he declared martial law and dispatched 473 National Guardsmen to the scene, where they stayed until the occupation ended on October 21. The governor proceeded to use the Rangers in fifteen other railroad towns, and augmented the Service with 450 "Railroad Rangers" who were often hastily recruited troublemakers. In Denison, none of the three hundred people arrested during the strike were prosecuted for an offense, and the real trouble spots of the state were left unattended.

Oil production began in Texas with the Spindletop strike near Beaumont in January 1901, and at first occurred primarily on the Gulf Coast. Then, on October 25, 1917, a well in the town of Ranger hit a gusher and the oil industry expanded into North and Central Texas and the Panhandle. These bonanzas brought untold wealth and prosperity to the state, but they often occurred in small ranching or railroad towns overwhelmed by the rushes of wildcatters, roughnecks, land agents, speculators, and laborers. The criminal element, including hijackers, prostitutes, gamblers, bootleggers, con men, and drug peddlers, quickly followed. The Rangers targeted lawless oil towns such as Batson, Ranger, Mexia, Borger, Desdemona, Wink, and Kilgore, sometimes more than once. Often lacking jail space, they shackled their prisoners to a "trotline," a heavy chain secured to a tree or floor beam, which became a standard tool in the boomtown cleanups. Many times, the Rangers were unable to gain cooperation from county judges, prosecutors, or lawmen who were tools of underworld syndicates. The effects of their work were brought home in August 1921 when state legislators, allied with corrupt oil town officials, cut the budget by $50,000 so the Rangers' numbers never exceeded fifty.

Miriam A. "Ma" Ferguson, wife of the former governor (who was himself barred from holding political office), was victorious in the November 1924 gubernatorial election. She acted as a figurehead for her husband who was now able to govern without legal restraint. Together they accepted bribes in exchange for the granting of more than 3,000 pardons and paroles, and facilitated state road contracts to political supporters. The threat of her own impeachment was raised, although that proved to be a failure. The co-governors again used the Rangers as a political tool for dispensing patronage. On February 20, 1925, the Fergusons reduced the five companies of the Ranger Force to a total of twenty-eight men. They were used primarily on the Rio Grande and prohibited from operating in the interior counties unless specifically requested by local officers. Captains Wright, Gray, and Hamer resigned only to be replaced by others unsuited for law enforcement, including J. Monroe Fox of Porvenir infamy. The biggest challenges facing the Rangers during the Ferguson administration was the sudden surge of bank robberies in North Texas, the vast number of liquor stills in East Texas, and organized cattle rustling in South and West Texas.

Daniel J. Moody, Jr., elected governor in 1926 and 1928, reversed the Ranger policies of the Fergusons and even sponsored a salary increase — two hundred and twenty-five dollars per month for captains, one hundred and seventy-five for sergeants, and one hundred and fifty for privates. The force was authorized a complement of fifty men again, but the legislature was forced to cut the budget, and appropriations never allowed more than the previous thirty. The Rangers had to again depend on free railroad passes or their own automobiles — with a fifty dollar monthly allowance for maintenance per company. Frank Hamer, Will Wright, and, most unexpectedly, John H. Rogers (one of the "Four Great Captains") returned, William W. Sterling was appointed a captain, and the Ferguson appointees were discharged. Under a supportive governor, the Ranger Force again became an effective organization.

Governor Ross S. Sterling, who took office in January 1931, wanted to continue the Rangers' recent record of success. To this end, he appointed Captain William Sterling (no relation to the governor) to the post of adjutant general on January 22. General Sterling left the National Guard to its own devices and concentrated exclusively upon the Rangers. He was determined to preserve the Service as an institution honored and respected by local officers and the public. He increased the annual travel allotments to $15,360 and paid particular attention to recruitment and promotion practices, the latter based on merit, and competitive salaries. He administered through a cadre of highly experienced and qualified captains. Several former Rangers opined that the men under Governor Sterling were the best officers ever assembled up to that time.

In 1932, Governor Sterling ran for re-election and was opposed by "Ma" Ferguson. Remembering the previous Ferguson administrations, General Sterling and most of the Ranger Force actively campaigned for the incumbent. After the governor lost the race due to massive voter fraud, the adjutant general and some Rangers resigned rather than serve under Mrs. Ferguson. The remainder were discharged the day after she took office. To replace them, she and her husband issued thirty-nine regular and 2,344 special commissions to individuals whose only necessary prerequisite was political loyalty to the administration. The latter included newspaper editors, bankers, retail liquor dealers, and nightclub bouncers who were given arrest powers and the right to carry a firearm. Such a blatant spoils system brought scorn from many in the public and media. The Forty-third Legislature supported the new co-executives by slashing the operating budget by approximately forty-seven percent and the monthly salaries to one hundred and fifty dollars for captains, one hundred and thirty for sergeants, and one hundred and fifteen for privates. They further reduced the regular force to a total of six captains, one sergeant, and twenty-five privates. The new appointees, who were inexperienced, undermanned, underpaid, incompetently led, and poorly trained and equipped, proved unable to adequately cope with the crime wave sweeping the state. Indeed, some were involved in their own misconduct, ranging from embezzlement to extortion to murder.

Although no longer in the Service, Frank Hamer once again reminded the public of the stuff real Rangers were made of. As special investigator for the Texas Prison System, he, along with ex–Ranger Manny Gault and a posse of Texas and Louisiana lawmen, tracked Clyde Barrow and Bonnie Parker for 103 days. The manhunters finally ambushed and killed the pair near Gibsland, Louisiana on May 23, 1934.

The state of law and order in Texas and the possibility of reform was a major issue in the 1934 gubernatorial race. James V. Allred was elected governor based on campaign promises of improved law enforcement, specifically for the Rangers. His tenure would herald a new era of much needed overhaul and modernization.

## Historical Register, 1901–1935

*"Mean as Hell. Had to kill him."*
— Private Nat B. "Kiowa" Jones

### HEADQUARTERS
Captain Lamartine P. "Lam" Sieker, Quartermaster (July 8, 1901–1905)
Captain James T. Stockton, Quartermaster (February 1–September 1, 1917)
Captain Harry M. Johnston, Quartermaster (November 15, 1917–February 13, 1919)
 *Capt. Johnston suspended from duty (February 7–13, 1919)*
Captain William M. Hanson, Special Investigator/Inspector (January 31, 1918–June 20, 1919)
 *Capt. Hanson appointed commander of all Ranger field activities from office in San Antonio*
Captain Roy W. Aldrich, Quartermaster (February 13–June 20, 1919)
Sergeant P. A. Cardwell, Assistant Quartermaster (November 12, 1917–January 1918?)
Headquarters: Camp Mabry in Austin with detachment at Ranger (Hanson's detachment: January 1919)
 *Ranger Force operated under the supervision of the Adjutant General's Department*

### HEADQUARTERS COMPANY
Senior Captain William M. Hanson (June 20–September 4, 1919)
Senior Captain Joe B. Brooks (October 1, 1919–February 15, 1921)
Senior Captain Roy C. Nichols (March 15, 1921–January 1, 1922)
Senior Captain Francis A. "Frank" Hamer (January 1, 1922–June 30, 1925)
Senior Captain Thomas R. "Tom" Hickman (July 1, 1925–May 1, 1927)
Senior Captain Francis A. "Frank" Hamer (May 1, 1927–November 1, 1932)
 *Capt. Hamer retained ranger commission through February 1, 1933*
Senior Captain Thomas R. "Tom" Hickman (November 1, 1932–January 18, 1933)
Senior Captain D. Estill "Cap" Hamer (January 19, 1933–January 23, 1935)
Senior Captain Thomas R. "Tom" Hickman (January 23–August 10, 1935)
Captain Roy W. Aldrich, Quartermaster (June 20, 1919–January 31, 1931)
Captain Charles O. Moore, Quartermaster (February 1, 1931–January 18, 1933)
Captain Roy W. Aldrich, Quartermaster (January 18, 1933–August 10, 1935)
Captain Richard C. "Red" Hawkins, Unattached (February 19–August 10, 1935)

Reverend Doctor (Captain) Pierre Bernard Hill, Chaplain (October 19, 1928–December 30, 1931)
Private E. B. McMordle, commanding detachment (August–November 1928)
*Headquarters*: Camp Mabry in Austin with detachments at Desdemona (Aldrich's detachment: April 1920), Wichita Falls (Aldrich's detachment: October 1920), Breckenridge (Aldrich's detachment: December 1920), Cameron (June 1921), Mount Pleasant (October 1921), Mexia (Hamer's detachment: January 1922), Childress and Amarillo (Hamer's detachment: July 1922–January 1923), Corpus Christi (Hamer's detachment: October 1922), Borger (Hickman's detachment: April 1927), Gatesville (McMordle's detachment: August–November 1928), Borger (Hamer's detachment: September 1929), and Sherman (Hamer's detachment: May 1930).

## COMPANY A

Captain James A. Brooks (July 9, 1901–November 15, 1906)
Sergeant J. D. Dunaway, Acting Commander (November 16–December 31, 1906)
Captain Francis N. "Frank" Johnson (January 28, 1907–September 30, 1910)
   *Company "A" disbanded (October 1910–February 1911)*
Captain John R. Hughes (February 1, 1911–January 31, 1915)
Captain John J. Sanders (February 1, 1915–March 4, 1919)
   *Capt. Sanders suspended from duty (February 6, 1919)*
   *Company "A" disbanded (March–June 1919)*
Captain Jerry Gray (June 20, 1919–April 30, 1925)
Captain J. Monroe Fox (June 6, 1925–March 31, 1927)
Captain William L. "Will" (Bud) Wright (May 15, 1927–January 18, 1933)
Captain Jefferson Eagle "Jeff" Vaughan (January 19, 1933–January 24, 1935)
Sergeant Sid Kelso, Acting Commander (?–August 10, 1935)
*Headquarters*: Alice (July 1901) with detachment at Brownsville (January 1902); Laredo (March 1903) with detachments at Batson (January–November 1904) and Moonshine Hill (January 1905); Colorado City (July 1905); Weatherford (January 1908); Amarillo (August 1908–January 1909); Harlingen with detachments at Falfurrias, Rio Grande City, Brownsville, and San Benito (January 1910); Ysleta with detachments at Fort Hancock, Valentine (February 1911), Terlingua, and Austin (January 1912); El Paso (May 1912); Brownsville (Hughes' detachment: July–August 1912); San Antonio (November 1912); Ysleta with detachments at El Paso, Marfa, Valentine, Hebbronville, Dickens, and Fort Stockton (January 1913), and Uvalde and Raymondville (April 1914); Del Rio (February 1915) with detachments at Carrizo Springs, Hebbronville, Alice, Pharr, San Benito, and Rio Grande City (May 1915); Laredo (July 1915); Norias with detachments at Del Rio and San Angelo (August 1915); Alice (October 1915); Marfa (June 1919); Presidio (January 1920) with detachment at Palestine (July 1922–January 1923); Marfa (July 1925); McCamey (February 1928); Fort Stockton (August 1928); Marfa (January 1932) with detachment at Kilgore (August 1932).

## COMPANY B

Captain William J. "Bill" McDonald (July 9, 1901–January 16, 1907)
Sergeant William J. McCauley, Acting Commander (January 16–31, 1907)
Captain Tom M. Ross (February 1, 1907–February 28, 1910)
Captain Marvin E. Bailey (March 1, 1910–February 1, 1911)
Captain John J. Sanders (February 1, 1911–February 1, 1915)
Captain J. Monroe Fox (February 1, 1915–June 8, 1918)
   *Company "B" disbanded (June–September 1918)*

Captain Jerry Gray (September 10, 1918–June 20, 1919)
Captain Charles F. Stevens (June 20, 1919–February 3, 1920)
  *Company "B" disbanded (February 1920–February 1921)*
Captain Thomas R. "Tom" Hickman (February 15, 1921–June 15, 1925)
Captain David E. Lindsey (July 4, 1925–March 31, 1927)
Captain William W. Sterling (April 15–May 1, 1927)
Captain Thomas R. "Tom" Hickman (May 1, 1927–January 18, 1933)
Captain Harry T. Odneal (January 19, 1933–April 28, 1934)
Captain Leon P. Hannah (May 1, 1934–January 24, 1935)
Captain Fred L. McDaniel (January 25–August 10, 1935)
*Headquarters*: Amarillo with detachments at Colorado City (July 1901) and Port Arthur (March 1902); Fort Hancock (December 1902) with detachment at Eagle Pass (September 1903); Alice (1903) with detachments at Kittrell's Cut-off (December 1903), Groveton (January 1904), Edna (October 1905, May 1906), Harlingen, Brownsville (August 1906), and Rio Grande City (November 1906); Trinity (May 1907); Alice (August 1908); Amarillo (January 1909); Ysleta (November 1909); Marfa with detachments at Shafter and Comstock (April 1910); San Benito with detachment at Brownsville (September 1910); Harlingen (March 1911); Kenedy with detachments at Del Rio and Laredo (March 1911); Del Rio with detachments at Comstock, Eagle Pass, and Laredo (January 1912), Sinton (January 1913), Brownsville (Sander's detachment: April 1912), El Paso (Sander's detachment: May–July 1912), and Brownsville (Sander's detachment: October–November 1912); Ysleta (January 1913) with detachments at Laredo (Hines' detachment: February 1913) and Shafter (July 1913); Laredo with detachments at Sanderson, Shafter, and Palafox (December 1913), and Block & Ford Ranch and Carrizo Springs (April 1914); Del Rio (July 1914); Valentine with detachments at Fabens and Marfa (February 1915); Brownsville (August 1915); Marfa with detachment at Sierra Blanca (September 1915); Ysleta (June 1919); Wichita Falls (1919); Fort Worth (February 1921) with detachments at Clarksville, Longview, Atlanta, and New Boston (June 1921–May 1922), Waco and Wichita Falls (October 1921), Mexia (January 1922), Presidio (May 1922), Denison (June 1922), Sherman (July 1922) and Waco; Denison (January 1923); Corpus Christi (April 1923) with detachments at Glen Rose (Burton's detachment: August 1923) and Corsicana (Burton's detachment: February 1924); Fort McKavett (February 1924); Waco (August 1924); Del Rio (July 1925); Fort Worth (April 1927) with detachments at Borger (Sterling's detachment: April 1927), Dallas (Gonzaullas' detachment: August 1928), Borger (August 1928), Borger (Hickman's detachment: June 1929), Shamrock (Gonzaullas' detachment: July 1930), Sherman (Hickman's detachment: May 1930), Kilgore (Gonzaullas' detachment: February 1931), Gladewater and Henderson (March 1931), Denison (Hickman's detachment: July 1931), and "Proration Hill" near Kilgore (August 1931)

## Company C

Captain John H. Rogers (July 9, 1901–January 31, 1911)
  *Company "C" disbanded (February–September 1911)*
Captain William "Australian Billy" Smith (September 1–October 5, 1911)
Captain J. Monroe Fox (October 5, 1911–February 1, 1915)
Captain Edward H. Smith (February 1, 1915–January 21, 1917)
  *Company "C" disbanded (January–July 1917)*
Captain Henry L. Ransom (July 19, 1917–April 1, 1918)
Sergeant Sam McKenzie, Acting Commander (April 2, 1918–March 31, 1919)
Captain William M. Ryan (June 20, 1919–February 10, 1921)

Captain Aaron W. Cunningham (February 15–August 31, 1921)
Captain Francis A. "Frank" Hamer (September 21, 1921–January 1, 1922)
Captain Roy C. Nichols (January 1, 1922–March 31, 1927)
Captain John H. Rogers (May 15, 1927–November 11, 1930)
Captain Light Townsend (February 1, 1931–May 10, 1932)
Captain J. B. Wheatley (May 18, 1932–January 16, 1933)
Captain E. H. Hammond (January 19, 1933–August 31, 1934)
Captain George H. Johnson (September 1, 1934–January 18, 1935)
Captain James W. McCormick (January 25–August 10, 1935)

*Headquarters*: Laredo (July 1901); Colorado City with detachments at Amarillo and Fort Hancock (December 1902), Plemons (January 1903), Thurber (September 1903), and Plemons (October 1903); Alpine with detachment at Fort Hancock (May 1905); Austin (May 1907); Laredo (October 1910); Sam Fordyce with detachment at Harlingen (October 1911); Brownsville (November 1911) with detachments at Rio Grande City, San Fordyce, and Harlingen (January 1912); San Angelo (October 1912); Falfurrias (November 1912); Austin (January 1913); Abilene (1914); Austin (March 1915); Harlingen with detachment at Edinburg (1917); Sweetwater (January 1918); Laredo (June 1919); Del Rio (February 1921) with detachments at Center (June 1921) and Marshall (July 1922); Marshall (April 1923) with detachments at Lufkin (February 1924) and Borger (October 1926); Del Rio (May 1927) with detachment at Mariscal (August 1928) and Kilgore (March 1931); Houston (January 1933) with detachment at Kilgore (September 1934); San Augustine (January 1935)

## COMPANY D

Captain John R. Hughes (July 9, 1901–February 1, 1911)
  *Company "D" disbanded (February–October 1911)*
Captain William "Australian Billy" Smith (October 5, 1911–August 1912)
  *Company "D" disbanded (August 1912–January 1915)*
Captain Edward H. Smith (January 19–February 1, 1915)
  *Company "D" disbanded (February–July 1915)*
Captain Henry L. Ransom (July 20, 1915–February 1, 1917)
  *Company "D" disbanded (February–May 1917)*
Captain Jerry Gray (May 28–August 20, 1918)
Captain Joseph L. Anders (August 20, 1918–June 20, 1919)
Captain William M. Hanson, Acting Commander (January 30–May 19, 1919)
Captain William L. "Will" (Bud) Wright (June 20, 1919–April 1, 1925)
Captain William M. Ryan (June 16, 1925–February 2, 1927)
Captain Francis A. "Frank" Hamer (February 2–April 31, 1927)
Captain William W. Sterling (May 1, 1927–November 1930)
Captain Albert R. Mace (November 17, 1930–January 18, 1933)
Captain James Robbins (January 19, 1933–January 24, 1935)
Captain William W. "Bill" McMurrey (January 25–August 10, 1935)

*Headquarters*: El Paso (July 1901) with detachment at Alice (October 1902); Alice (July 1903) with detachment at Rio Grande City (November 1906); Marfa (July 1907); Ysleta (September 1908); Amarillo with detachments at Colorado City, Marlin, Post City, Coahoma, and Brownsville (November 1909); Ysleta (1910); Galveston, Taylor, Georgetown, San Antonio, and El Paso (October 1911–July 1912); Brownwood (August 1912); Harlingen with detachments at Brownsville, E. A. Sterling Ranch near Monte Christo, Hebbronville, and Floresville (July 1915); Pharr (May 1916); Austin (May 1917); Marfa (June 1918); Austin

(August 1918); Brownsville with detachments at Marathon, Mercedes, Mission, Rio Grande City and Glenn Springs (June 1919), Rio Grande City (March 1920), Hebbronville (March 1920), Weslaco (October 1921), Cleburne (July 1922), Floresville (October 1922), Mission (December 1923), and Donna and Rio Grande City (May 1925); Hebbronville (February 1927) with detachments at Borger (Hamer's detachment: April 1927), Laredo (April 1927), and Raymondville (August 1928); Falfurrias (September 1928) with detachments at El Campo (May 1929), Del Rio (November 1930), Fort Worth (March 1931), Kilgore (Mace's detachment: March 1931), "Proration Hill" near Kilgore (August 1931), and San Antonio (January 1933); Falfurrias (January 1933); San Angelo (May 1933); Uvalde (January 1934); and Hebbronville (January 1935)

### COMPANY E
Captain W. L. Barler (April 24, 1917–March 19, 1919)
Captain Joseph L. Anders (June 20, 1919–February 15, 1921)
    *Company "E" disbanded (February 1921–September 1923)*
Captain Berk C. Baldwin (September 1, 1923–February 21, 1925)
*Headquarters*: Del Rio (August 1917) with detachments at Indio Cattle Company Ranch near Eagle Pass (Barler's detachment: December 1917), Comstock (January 1918), and Langtry (January 1918); Eagle Pass (August 1918); Marathon (June 1919–February 1921); San Antonio (September 1923–February 1925)

### COMPANY F
Captain Carroll Bates (August 22, 1917–August 31, 1918)
Captain William W. Taylor (September 1–December 31, 1918)
    *Company "F" disbanded (January–July 1919)*
Captain Will W. Davis (July 1, 1919–February 10, 1921)
*Headquarters*: Marathon (December 1917) with detachments at Santa Helena and Mariposa (April 1918); Brownsville (August 1918) with detachment at Ranger (March 1919); Del Rio (June 1919)

### COMPANY G
Captain Charles F. Stevens (November 17, 1917–June 20, 1919)
    *Capt. Stevens suspended from duty (February 11–May 19, 1919)*
Captain Joseph L. Anders, Acting Commander (February 11–May 19, 1919)
*Headquarters*: Edinburg with detachments at Harlingen, Raymondville, El Ebano, and Hidalgo (December 1917); Mercedes with detachments at Harlingen, Raymondville, El Ebano, and Hidalgo (January 1918), and Piper Plantation, La Paloma, Santa María, and Mission (July 1918); Sanderson (August 1918); Del Rio (August 1918); Marathon (August–December 1918); and Ysleta (June 1919)

### COMPANY H
Captain Roy W. Aldrich (December 1, 1917–February 13, 1919)
*Headquarters*: Austin

### COMPANY I
Captain William M. Ryan (November 28, 1917–June 20, 1919)
*Headquarters*: Laredo

### COMPANY K
Captain William L. "Will" (Bud) Wright (January 1, 1918–June 20, 1919)
*Headquarters*: Laredo (January 1918) with detachments at Santa María (September–November 1918) and Mission (April–June 1919)

## COMPANY L
Captain Will W. Davis (December 8, 1917–March 21, 1919)
*Headquarters*: Ysleta with detachments at Fabens and Clint

## COMPANY M
Captain K. F. Cunningham (December 10, 1917–February 7, 1919)
  *Capt. Cunningham suspended from duty (June 1918)*
Sergeant Lon L. Willis, Acting Commander (June–September 30, 1918)
Captain Lon L. Willis (October 1, 1918–March 10, 1919)
  *Company "M" disbanded (March–May 1919)*
Captain Woody T. Townsend (May 19–June 20, 1919)
*Headquarters*: Eagle Pass with detachments at Indio Cattle Company Ranch and Val Verde Irrigation Company (January 1918); Del Rio (August 1918)

## COMPANY N (HUDSPETH SCOUTS)
Captain Dan G. Knight (April 16–August 31, 1918)
*Ranging District*: Presidio County with headquarters at Valentine

## EMERGENCY COMPANY #1
Captain Charles J. Blackwell (October 1, 1920–February 15, 1921)
Captain Joe B. Brooks (February 15, 1921–February 15, 1923)
*Headquarters*: Galveston (October 1920) with detachment at Ranger (December 1920–February 1921)

## EMERGENCY COMPANY #2
Captain Thomas R. "Tom" Hickman (November 22, 1920–February 15, 1921)
*Ranging District*: Stephens, Eastland, and Wichita Counties with headquarters at Breckenridge

## COMPANY A VOLUNTEERS (SPECIAL RANGERS)
Captain James B. Murrah (December 1, 1917–January 15, 1919)
*Headquarters*: Comstock

## COMPANY B VOLUNTEERS (SPECIAL RANGERS)
Captain J. C. Rawlings (November 22, 1917–February 14, 1918)
*Headquarters*: Plainview

## COMPANY C VOLUNTEERS (SPECIAL RANGERS)
Captain Eugene Buck (December 27, 1917–January 15, 1919)
*Headquarters*: Indio Cattle Company Ranch

## LOYALTY SECRET SERVICE DEPARTMENT
Captain William M. Hanson (June 1918–February 1919)
*Headquarters*: San Antonio

# 10

# A Fabled Tradition: The Texas Ranger Division (1935–Present)

Shortly after taking office, Governor Allred implemented his program to reform law enforcement in the state. On January 23, 1935, he began by discharging all but three of the regular and special Ferguson Rangers. He then commissioned thirty-six new appointees, eleven of whom had prior Ranger experience. On May 8, the Forty-fourth Legislature established the Texas Department of Public Safety (DPS), an umbrella organization that would administer and control the Headquarters Division, the Highway Patrol, and the Texas Rangers. One of the branches of the Headquarters Division was the Bureau of Intelligence, which boasted a cutting-edge scientific laboratory that gathered and analyzed crime-scene evidence. The Rangers were formally transferred from the adjutant general's office to the DPS on August 10. The traditional company structure remained (a Headquarters Company of a senior captain, one sergeant, and four privates, and four companies of one captain, one sergeant, and fifteen privates each), but recruitment and promotion practices were changed. The new qualifications for applicants were that they had to be between thirty and forty-five years of age, at least five feet eight inches in height, and in good physical and mental condition. Commissions were bestowed upon the recommendation of a Ranger captain and the approval of the DPS director. After acceptance, the recruits received training in various aspects of criminology including fingerprinting, communications, ballistics, recordkeeping, and, of course, firearms usage. Promotion was based on seniority and performance. Monthly salary schedules were set at $154.50 for captains, $136.50 for sergeants, and $120.75 for privates. Although there were no educational requirements, each Ranger had to be literate enough to submit a weekly report of his activities. The number of Special Rangers was limited by law to three hundred.

Overseen by a three-person Public Safety Commission, the director and assistant director supervised the operations and administration of the DPS. The senior leadership of the department was at first heavily composed of Highway Patrol personnel, and many of the Rangers feared the Service would be overshadowed or replaced by "a bunch of motorcycle jockeys." Retired Ranger H. Joaquin Jackson wrote in his memoir *One Ranger* that the "Romantics saw this move as the final blow to a fabled tradition, the death of the legend." Professor Walter Webb voiced just such a belief when he wrote, "It is safe to say that as time goes on the functions of the un-uniformed Texas Rangers will gradually slip away and that those of the Highway Patrol will increase." While some expected the Rangers to fade away into history, many Texas sheriffs feared the new department would encroach upon their prerogative as the chief law officers of their counties.

Although the burgeoning relationship between the Rangers, the DPS administration, and the state's 254 sheriffs was at times rocky, the Rangers survived and became an integral component of the state law enforcement community, without usurping the authority of the county officers. Much of this was due to Colonel Homer Garrison, Jr., who was appointed DPS director on September 27, 1938.

Over the next thirty years, the Garrison Rangers became the criminal investigative arm of the DPS, while the Highway Patrol assumed the traditional role of uniformed state troopers. Technically freed from political interference by the advent of the DPS, a Ranger commission became a career rather than an appointment subject to political whim as in the past. They became internationally recognized law enforcement officers, bolstered by modern training and techniques, and inspired by a century of tradition and pride. Garrison, a staunch supporter of the Ranger mythos, became *ex officio* chief of the Texas Rangers and ordered company commanders to report directly to him. He upgraded the crime lab, developed better training methods, gradually established a communications system for closer coordination between Rangers, highway patrolmen, and local law enforcement, and tirelessly advocated for increased appropriations and manpower. Not since the days of John B. Jones had the Rangers served under such a beloved leader. Ranger Jackson described the affection and respect Garrison reciprocated, "Col. Garrison loved to swear in new Rangers. He knew that badge stood for something — something hard won by blood, grit, courage, and a gun."

The Rangers numbered forty-five men in 1941, fifty-one in 1947, and sixty-two in 1961. They added a sixth company in 1957. Each company headquarters office was assigned a specific geographic district of the state's 267,000 square miles and supervised Rangers who were stationed in various communities throughout their area. Each Ranger had responsibility for a minimum of two to three counties; some were assigned to even larger sectors. In 1946, the salary of a Ranger captain was two hundred and fifty dollars per month; sergeants, two hundred dollars; and privates, one hundred and seventy-five.

Their mandate remained the same as in years past: the elimination of social violence (insurrection and riots), the enforcement of state criminal statutes, the investigation of major crimes, and the apprehension of fugitives. They enjoyed close cooperation with county and municipal law enforcement and were readily summoned when local peace officers experienced an exceptionally dangerous criminal or situation. In the 1930s, they deterred gangsters in East Texas, and pursued smugglers and stock thieves in South and West Texas. In World War II, in addition to their regular duties, they tracked down deserters, recaptured escaped prisoners of war, and assisted the civil defense in protecting electrical generating plants, dams, factories, and other industries from possible sabotage. After the war, the Rangers conducted raids on illegal gambling establishments in Fort Worth, San Antonio, Corpus Christi, Houston, and Galveston. They also returned to strike duty in Paris in 1941, Corpus Christi in 1947, and the Lone Star Steel plant in Daingerfield in 1957 and again in 1968–1969 (the second was the longest and most violent labor dispute in Texas history). Gambling and strikes were regarded as distractions from their true mission of criminal investigation, as was the suppression of slant hole drilling of "hot oil." One notable investigation was Captain Manuel T. "Lone Wolf" Gonzaullas' tireless but unsuccessful

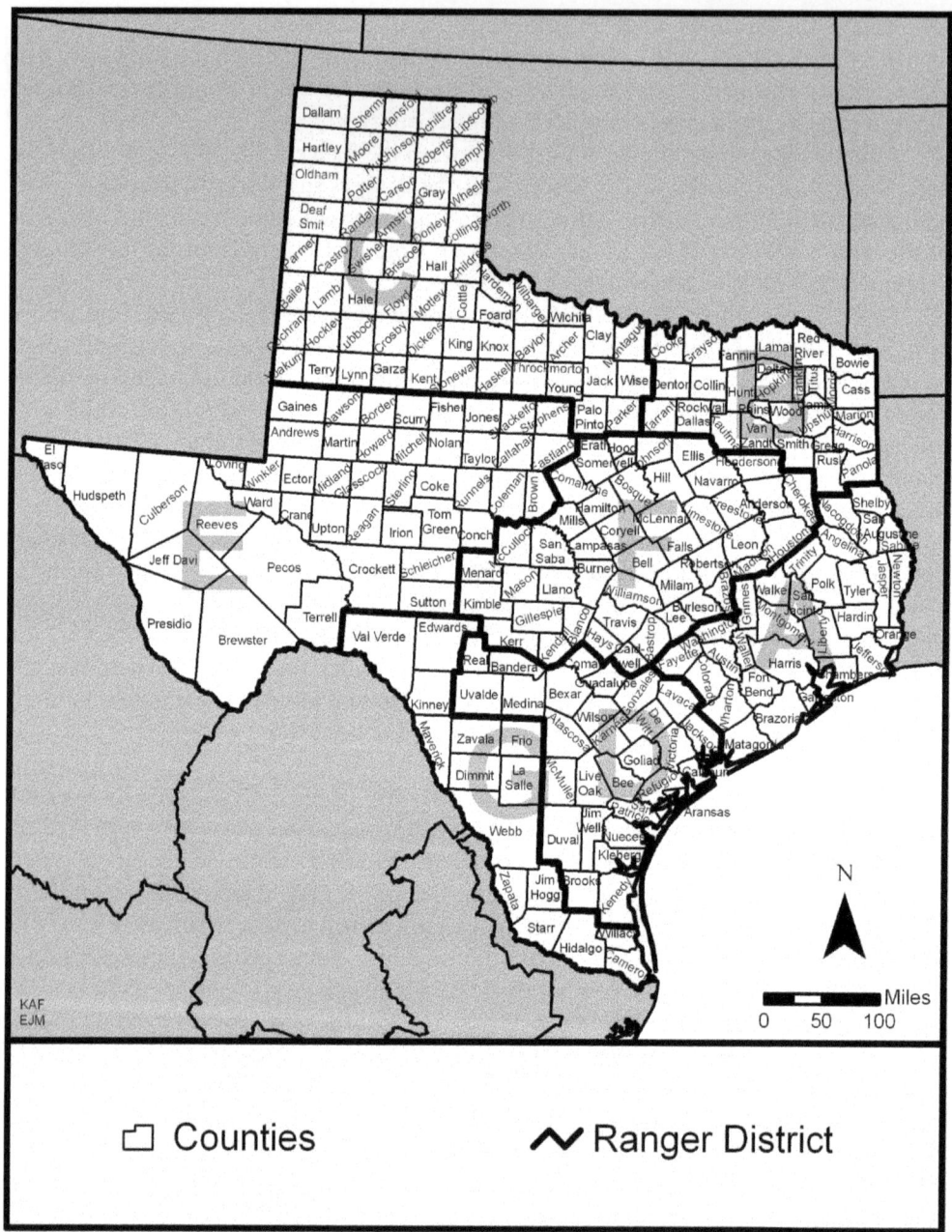

pursuit of the "Phantom Killer," a serial murderer who committed five homicides in Texarkana in early 1946.

Texas enjoyed a rapid increase in urbanization, industry, and population in the postwar boom. The Rangers' caseload increased in that they worked 255 cases in 1936 and 16,701 in 1956.

The Rangers resumed their exalted status during the Garrison era, which had been missing since prior to the "Bandit War" years. Exceptional captains such as Hardy B. Purvis and John J. "Johnny" Klevenhagen and Rangers like Zeno Smith and Edgar D. "Ed" Gooding ensured that excellence and professionalism was again achieved and maintained. One example of the new Texas Ranger was Captain Robert A. "Bob" Crowder of Company B who, on April 14, 1955, single-handedly ended a hostage situation at the maximum-security unit of Rusk State Hospital without firing a shot. Crowder's successor, Captain E. J. Banks, along with Johnny Klevenhagen, permanently ended the murderous careers of gangsters Gene Paul Norris (the "smiling killer") and William Carl "Silent Bill" Humphrey on April 29, 1957.

By 1955, the need for additional modernization became recognized, as thirteen separate divisions and bureaus, including the Rangers and the Highway Patrol, were directly answering to Colonel Garrison; a number well beyond the accepted span of control. An independent study recommended the DPS field apparatus be split into six regional commands headed by majors who would each supervise his region's uniformed services and supplemental forensic lab. One Ranger company was to be assigned to each commander. Colonel Garrison approved the study, and legislation enacted on September 1, 1957, allowed him to implement the reorganization. The new chain of command quickly proved unworkable and Ranger captains were once more reporting to the director effective January 1, 1958.

A Garrison Ranger, Zeno A. Smith joined the organization in 1935. It was in San Antonio that he made his reputation as a law officer to be feared and respected. When he retired in 1969, the Texas Legislature passed a resolution urging the DPS to retain him on the force. He returned to law enforcement as a deputy sheriff in Wilson County before his death in 1972. Courtesy of the Texas Ranger Hall of Fame and Museum, Waco, TX.

In the 1960s, the Rangers' response to the civil rights movement in Texas again had many questioning their necessity. Their traditional attitudes and hard-nosed approach to law enforcement clashed with the forces of social change. The counterculture, the Civil Rights Act of 1964, and the U.S. Supreme Court's 1966 *Miranda v. Arizona* decision all impacted on the Rangers' methods. One practice the new legal and political landscape ended was the "East Texas Merry-Go-Round." The Go Round was the tactic of hiding suspects (especially drug addicts needing a fix) from their attorneys by moving them from one county jail to another until confessions could be obtained and charges readied for filing.

The Mexican American population continued to regard them as *los rinches*, with a history of mistrust stretching back to the 1840s. After World War I, Hispanics had organized to provide themselves the benefits of the American Dream. They formed several groups that sought integration into mainstream society by the use of legal action. Victories included the elimination of school segregation, the white primary, and the poll tax. Despite such gains, their movement grew more activist and militant in the 1960s. They worked to get lower-class Hispanics to the voting booths instead of the courtrooms. These "Chicanos," as they called themselves, aggressively confronted Anglo officials and threatened massive, possibly violent, protests.

Captain Alfred Y. Allee, Sr., a Ranger since 1931 and a noted captain since 1947, was vilified in the 1970s as an example of all that was wrong with the Rangers. During *la Huelga* ("the Strike"), the 1966–1967 United Farm Workers strike in Starr County, Captain Allee and his Company D Rangers served arrest warrants on *Huelgistas* for trespassing, unlawful assembly, illegal picketing, impersonating an officer, and interfering with an arrest. The U.S. Commission on Human Rights and its Texas Advisory Committee, both composed of people sympathetic to the workers' plight, accused the Rangers of two instances of brutality in apprehending *Huelgistas*. After the strike ended, a movement to abolish the Texas Rangers was initiated but ultimately failed. The Farm Workers union went on to file a federal class-action lawsuit against Allee, a number of his Rangers, and several local law officers. The conclusion of *Medrano v. Allee* had to wait for a Supreme Court decision in 1976. The law officers basically received a slap on the wrist since the laws they had enforced had already been found unconstitutional and stricken from the books. The most important conclusion for the Rangers was the fact that working a strike was, for them, a no-win proposition.

Chicano militant José Angel Gutierrez of Crystal City was the leader of the nonprofit organization Mexican American Youth Organization (MAYO). He helped to found the political party La Raza Unida in Zavala County and managed candidates in the elections of 1970 and 1972. In both contests, Rangers were on hand to observe and keep order; only once were the proceedings marred by violence. The school board elections of 1973 and 1974 were more turbulent, with speakers shouted down and teachers and students intimidated and assaulted. Gutierrez himself was elected county judge in the 1974 general election and used his new authority to benefit his La Raza followers (in accordance with traditional Texas politics). The party collapsed in 1978 after several years of infighting and charges of corruption. In 1969, Arturo "Rudy" Rodriguez was the first Hispanic promoted to the Rangers in the DPS era, and since the 1970s, numerous Hispanic Rangers, such as Ramiro "Ray" Martinez, have served the people of Texas with honor and distinction. In December 2008, Captain Antonio Leal was appointed the newest chief of the Ranger Division. He was the first Hispanic and the youngest man to obtain that position.

After Colonel Garrison died on May 5, 1968, the Public Safety Commission again reorganized the Ranger force. Wilson E. Speir, Garrison's successor, oversaw an expansion to seventy-three Rangers in 1969, eighty-two in 1971, eighty-eight in 1974, and ninety-four a year later. Early in 1968, the Ranger Service was subordinated to a criminal law enforcement (CLE) division of the DPS along with the narcotics, intelligence, and motor vehicle theft services. The individual company commanders now reported to the new division chief, rather than the DPS director. The position of senior captain was revived in November 1969 to exercise direct supervision over the field companies, while still answering to the CLE chief. Revised guidelines required a recruit to be between thirty and fifty years in age, have at least eight years of law enforcement experience, including two with the DPS, and possess forty to sixty hours of college credit. The state began offering better salaries, together with such benefits as longevity pay, hospitalization insurance, and a paid life-insurance policy. The commissioners also lowered the mandatory retirement age from seventy years old to sixty-five, an unpopular ruling that forced out eight Garrison Rangers. After 1971, applicants had to successfully complete a written examination and oral interview boards in order to receive a commission.

The new generation of captains, such as Jack Dean and Robert K. "Bob" Mitchell (known as "the captain's captain"), and Rangers, such as Glenn Elliott (called "the Ranger's Ranger") and Tolliver "Tol" Dawson, continued to build on the traditions of the Garrison era. The training requirements were increased so that Rangers had to attend at least forty hours of in-service instruction every two years; most exceeded that requisite. Despite increasing caseloads, the applicant list for Ranger service grew to an average of two hundred candidates vying for one vacancy.

A recurring challenge the Rangers dealt with was the taking of hostages. On July 24, 1974, Captain James F. "Pete" Rogers of Company A, Captain G. W. Burks of Company B, and members of their respective companies were called to Huntsville State Penitentiary to assist in a hostage situation. Three inmates had taken approximately twenty-one people prisoner and demanded freedom. The eleven-day crisis was resolved with a desperate rescue attempt that left two hostages and two of the hostage-takers dead and one captive gravely wounded. Beginning on January 11, 1985, and continuing for three days, Captain Bob Mitchell and his Company F Rangers, along with county officers and Federal Bureau of Investigation agents, effected the rescue of a thirteen-year-old girl from five kidnappers in Alvarado. On August 28–29, 1985, Captain Mitchell and his men, including Sergeant Bob Prince acting as the negotiator, peacefully defused a hostage standoff in Meridian. Two years later, on January 22, 1987, Captain Mitchell again dealt with a hostage situation when a two-year-old girl was kidnapped in Llano County. Rangers Stanley Guffey and Johnnie Aycock were primarily responsible for the girl's successful rescue, but, tragically, Ranger Guffey lost his life in the ensuing gunbattle. The two were awarded the DPS Medal of Valor and Guffey was inducted into the Ranger Hall of Fame.

Controversy again dogged the Rangers after Ranger Phil Ryan of Company C arrested Henry Lee Lucas in June 1983. Charging him with the illegal possession of a firearm, officers actually wanted to interview Lucas concerning the disappearance of an elderly woman. He readily confessed to killing her and, as time went on, to as many as six hundred others (including his own mother), but his statements were problematic since he was also an opportunistic liar. Many of the homicides he would divulge were allegedly committed with

After service as a military policeman, Glenn Elliott joined the Highway Patrol in 1949. He pinned on a Texas Ranger badge in 1961 and wore it proudly until his retirement in 1987. Afterward, he remained busy in Ranger-related activities and co-authored two books. In 2008, he was honored by his friends and colleagues with an exhibit at the Texas Ranger Hall of Fame and Museum detailing his illustrious career. Courtesy of the Texas Ranger Hall of Fame and Museum, Waco, TX.

his equally loathsome transvestite lover Ottis Toole, a serial arsonist and the murderer of six-year-old Adam Walsh. For the next two years, homicide investigators from eighteen states and the District of Columbia interviewed Lucas in the hopes of closing some of their cold cases. Sometimes he detailed aspects of the crimes that were unknown to the general public, while other times he gave contradictory and obviously erroneous information — usually before recanting his confession. In retrospect, he was simply playing a game for his own amusement. The resulting media frenzy led many to declare all of Lucas' confessions a hoax, embarrassed the Rangers, and encouraged several ambitious politicians to use the fiasco for their own ends. Ultimately, Lucas was convicted of eleven murders, while some believed him responsible for twenty to forty. Since he died in prison of heart failure in March 2001, and his 3,000 confessions obfuscated the issue, the true number will never be known.

In late February 1993, the federal Bureau of Alcohol, Tobacco, and Firearms (ATF) moved to execute search warrants at the Mount Carmel compound of the Branch Davidian sect near Waco. Since June 1992, the ATF had been investigating David Koresh and his Davidians for federal weapons violations. Apostate sect members and the media had stirred public emotions by portraying the Davidians as a cult who practiced brainwashing, pedophilia, polygamy, and drug abuse. On February 28, 1993, the ATF raid was launched, but proved to be a debacle which left four federal agents dead and twenty wounded. The Davidians lost six killed and an unknown number wounded. The assistance of the Rangers was not desired at the time of the raid (fortunately for them), but afterward the ATF requested that Captain Bob Prince of Company F investigate the deaths of the federal agents. Prince, and later Captain David Byrnes of Company B, conducted interviews of raid witnesses and participants while the standoff continued. In order to provide federal grand jury testimony, the investigating Rangers were sworn in as deputy U.S. marshals. They often ran afoul of the FBI, who had taken command of the scene and proceeded to live up to their reputation for arrogance and high-handedness toward state and local law enforcement ("uncooperative and unprofessional," as Captain Byrnes labeled them). Following weeks of psychological warfare tactics and inconclusive negotiations, the FBI ordered an assault on April 19, which ended when the compound erupted into flames and seventy-six men, women, and children died from gunshot wounds, smoke inhalation, or collapsing concrete walls. The FBI promptly turned incident command over to the Rangers, who could at last enter the seventy-seven-acre crime scene and process the remaining physical evidence. They went on to serve as prosecution witnesses in the federal trial in Waco, which charged eleven Davidian survivors with conspiracy to murder federal officers, attempted murder of federal officers, aiding and abetting the murder of federal officers, four counts of murdering federal officers, and possession of illegal firearms. The basic questions of responsibility for the ignition source of the fire and the appropriateness of the tactics employed were never answered to the satisfaction of all involved. The entire episode brought discredit to every major participant (FBI, ATF, and even the U.S. attorney general), except the Texas Rangers.

Four years later, the Rangers again faced a dissident group in a potentially disastrous standoff. Richard McLaren was the leader of an eight-member faction of the Republic of Texas (ROT) militia group, which refused to acknowledge the United States' annexation of Texas and proclaimed the state actually remained an independent republic. McLaren styled himself as ambassador and general counsel of the provisional government of the ROT and his "embassy" (an old horse trailer and attached wooden lean-to) was in the Davis

Mountain resort area of Jeff Davis County. On April 27, 1997, a member of McLaren's group was arrested for traffic and firearms violations, and the movement responded by storming a neighbor's house and taking the married residents hostage. The kidnapped neighbors had been keeping the county sheriff apprised of McLaren's activities, which made them a target for the group. Captain Barry Caver of Company E was called in and he became incident commander with tactical authority over more than three hundred local, state, and federal officers. When the standoff began, Captain Caver had been the commander of Company E for about six months. At thirty-nine years old, he was the youngest Ranger captain in the history of the Department of Public Safety. He quickly obtained the release of the captives in return for the hostage-takers and the member originally arrested being allowed to return to the "embassy." He then patiently set out to effect the surrender of McLaren and his cohorts. After seven days, he successfully did so by signing a "cease-fire" agreement and by treating the militia members with dignity and respect — something they seemed to crave more than their stated anti-government goals. Two of the militants escaped into the rough country of Jeff Davis County; one was killed resisting arrest and the other was apprehended four months later in Sam Houston State Park near Huntsville. The surviving members were charged with aggravated kidnapping and attempted capital murder. Following the trial, McLaren received life imprisonment, three others received ninety-nine years, and one fifty years.

Another case was the 1999 investigation conducted by Sergeant Matt Cawthon, Bellmead police detective Tom Noble, and U.S. Postal Inspector Bob Adams that broke up a pedophile and child-pornography ring in Waco and Bellmead. That same year, Rangers Andrew "Drew" Carter, Brian Taylor, and David Maxwell and DPS investigator Mark Moorhead collaborated in apprehending "Railway Killer" Angel Maturino Resendez (aka Rafael Resendez Ramírez).

Meanwhile, several bureaucratic actions brought some welcome changes to the Service — and some not-so-welcome. On September 1, 1988, Lee Roy Young, Jr., a fifteen-year DPS veteran, was appointed to be the first black Texas Ranger in the modern era. He was joined by Earl Ray Pearson in January 1989 (who became senior captain in May 2004) and Jesse Mack in July 1994. By 1989, the "working title" of Ranger private was equivalent to

A Southwest Texas State University (now Texas State University) graduate, Sergeant William M. "Matt" Cawthon joined the Highway Patrol in 1982. After transferring to the Criminal Intelligence Service in 1989, he was promoted to the Texas Rangers in 1992. He was named a National Police Officer of the Year in 1999 after closing an investigation into a child pornography ring in Bellmead. Cawthon retired in 2009. Courtesy of the Texas Ranger Hall of Fame and Museum, Waco, TX.

the "payroll title" (salary grade) of uniformed sergeants elsewhere in the DPS, as was that of Ranger sergeants to DPS lieutenants. In order to comply with new state and federal wage and labor guidelines, the DPS changed the title of field Rangers from private to sergeant, and that of the first-line supervisors from sergeant to lieutenant. In 1993, Ranger Leo Hickman, then sixty-five years old, asked for an exemption from the mandatory retirement policy; his request resulted in the age limit being abolished altogether.

On September 1, 1993, the Texas Rangers were removed from the auspices of the CLE chief and again became an operating division. As such, the senior captain once more reported to the director of the DPS. That same month, the Seventy-third Legislature again increased salaries and benefits and also enlarged the overall size of the division to ninety-nine Rangers, including two women. Bowing to political pressure, the DPS had promoted sergeants Cheryl Steadman and Marrie García Aldridge to Rangers, but their new male colleagues expressed concern over their perceived lack of qualifications. The new change was contentious and was a public relations fiasco for the organization. Indeed, several veteran Rangers quietly resigned over the decision. Sergeant Steadman also quit and, along with a potential recruit, lodged sexual harassment and discrimination complaints against Senior Captain Maurice Cook. The two women's allegations were dismissed but the division publicly mishandled the episode. Marrie Aldridge and Christine Nix, who was commissioned in 1994, served without further controversy; Sergeant Nix in Company F until her retirement in 2004, and Sergeant Aldridge in Company D until hers in 2008. In the latter year, DPS sergeants Wende Wakeman and Laura Simmons and Trooper Melba Molina were promoted to the Rangers and assigned to Companies A, B, and G respectively.

In the early morning of December 31, 1999, a knife-wielding man broke into the double-wide mobile home of Terry and Crystal Harris in the Guajia Bay subdivision of Del Rio. Once inside, the intruder proceeded to the bedroom of thirteen-year-old Kaylene "Katy" Harris. There he woke the sleeping girl and began to sexually molest her. Katy's struggles to free herself roused her ten-year-old friend Krystal Surles, who was sleeping in the same room. The assailant inflicted eighteen fatal knife wounds on Katy before he turned on Krystal and slit her throat. He then left through the front door, sparing the four others sleeping in the trailer. Fortunately, although suffering a severed windpipe and grazed carotid artery that was literally a millimeter away from ending her life, Krystal survived the attack.

After her successful surgery, Krystal provided a detailed witness statement that aided Ranger Johnny Allen and Val Verde County Sheriff's investigators in obtaining an arrest warrant only two days after the crime. They took into custody Tommy Lynn Sells, a family acquaintance and frequent visitor to the Harris home. In his initial interview, Sells showed investigators the face of true evil when he calmly confessed to a shocking series of rapes and homicides across the country—nearly twenty killings, including those of nine children, in thirteen states. Remembering the Henry Lee Lucas fiasco, the Rangers and the FBI were cautious with Sells' statements, only accepting those they could corroborate with independently-obtained evidence. For over two decades, Sells, an alcoholic drug abuser with a childhood history of neglect and sexual abuse, was a petty criminal who managed to escape justice due to his transitory lifestyle. He was constantly on the move and did not possess a driver's license, checking account, credit cards, or other means to create a paper trail. After his arrest, he was diagnosed as a psychopath and sexual predator who raped, mutilated, and killed adolescent girls and petite women—usually lonely single mothers. The males he confessed to slaying were usually witnesses or were killed in the commission of other crimes.

In September 2000, Sells was tried for the capital murder of Kaylene Harris, and Krystal Surles was the prosecution's chief witness. In her emotional but resolute testimony, she positively identified Sells as the killer. Once the case was sent to the jury, they deliberated for two hours before returning a verdict of guilty and sentencing him to death. Sells was placed on Death Row at the Polunsky Unit in Livingston, but Texas law automatically grants an appeal process in capital cases. In August 2003, he pled guilty to the murder of a young girl in San Antonio in exchange for the death penalty being waived. Authorities have been able to link Sells to the quadruple homicide of an entire family in Ina, Illinois, and the murders of a young girl in Lexington, Kentucky, and a woman in Lockport, New York; he is also the only suspect in three killings in Missouri. His execution was finally set for May 17, 2006, but stayed due to questions concerning his mental capacity. A new date has not been set.

One true mystery the Ranger Division worked began in rural Brown County in October 2003. Three years previously, Stephen and Deena Roberts had purchased an A-frame style house six miles southeast of the town of Bangs. They were planning a home renovation project in the unused second story. While inspecting the work area, Deena noticed a small door built into the back of a closet. Peering into the crawl space behind the door, she found a plastic trash bag. Upon opening the bag, she discovered a paper sack holding the wrapped mummified body of a newborn child. The Roberts immediately notified the Brown County Sheriff's Department and, after ascertaining the corpse was indeed human, the responding deputies called in Ranger Nick Hanna of Company E. Investigators decided to send the remains and the two bags to the Travis County Medical Examiner's Office in Austin for analysis. There the case became even more bizarre when medical examiners discovered plastic sacks inside the larger trash bag containing the skeletal remains of two additional infants. Treating the deaths as homicides, Ranger Hanna and the sheriff's office were left to solve a cold case with virtually no evidence beyond the bodies. They agreed to first determine the identity of the newborns and then establish a timeline of the house's various occupants, every one of whom was considered a suspect.

A search of missing person reports and hospital records was unsuccessful in achieving their first goal. The Brown County courthouse yielded better results when investigators located a 1987 building permit issued to James Bowling, a local electrical engineer, who had constructed the A-frame. He lived there with his wife, Doris, daughters Traci Ann and Constance, and son Eddie. After James died in 1999, and Doris in 2000, the three siblings put the house on the market and each moved to various parts of the state. The dwelling stood vacant for five months until the Roberts family purchased it in July 2000.

Stephen and Deena volunteered to provide DNA samples in order to be ruled out as suspects. Traci Ann and Constance Bowling were located in San Angelo and Texarkana respectively, where they each expressed shock and disbelief upon hearing of the discovery. They also agreed to provide samples. Their brother, Eddie, was reportedly living in the Corpus Christi area but his exact whereabouts remain unknown. After checking all available records and conducting numerous interviews, Ranger Hanna and the sheriff's investigators were forced to depend on whatever physical evidence forensic scientists could extract from the infants' remains. The bodies were minutely examined to establish the cause and time of death, gender, age, and if they were related. The various bags they were found in were analyzed for fingerprints and trace evidence (hairs and fibers). In 2007, the bodies were concluded to be between thirty and forty years old, further substantiated by a wedding gift card, dated 1959 and addressed to the Bowlings, which was found inside the trash bag.

More importantly, based on the DNA samples, pathologists determined the infants were the natural siblings of the Bowling daughters, who had no prior knowledge of the babies' existence. Doris Bowling had reportedly suffered a miscarriage decades before her death, and investigators speculate the newborns were the result of that failed pregnancy. The exact causes of death were never determined and the reason why James and Doris kept the bodies rather than giving them a proper burial continues to be a mystery. As long as Eddie Bowling was missing and thus not cleared as a suspect, the case officially remained open. Presently, the Ranger Headquarters classifies the current status as "suspended," and they were not able to release any information.

On September 1, 2001, the Seventy-seventh Legislature authorized the establishment of the Unsolved Crimes Investigation Team (UCIT). Commanded by the Headquarters Captain, who was stationed in Austin, the entire unit was based in San Antonio alongside Company D. The UCIT was responsible for conducting investigations of unsolved homicides and suspected serial criminal activity throughout the state. To save costs and increase productivity, the UCIT was dispersed on January 1, 2008, and one sergeant was assigned to each field company to work up cold cases and major crimes in that company's geographic area. On the same day, the Ranger Division established a seventh company to enhance criminal investigative support on the border. In addition, Joint Operations Intelligence Centers at El Paso, Fort Davis, and Del Rio were organized under three staff lieutenants to coordinate federal, state, and local law enforcement efforts along the entire Rio Grande and better ensure border security.

In the first years as part of the DPS, the Texas Rangers were issued Colt Model 1911A-1 .45 pistols and Winchester '94 .30-30 rifles. Later, they would acquire automatic weapons, such as Thompson .45-caliber submachine guns, which increased their chances in gunbattles with similarly-armed gangsters. Rangers had to provide their own vehicles, horses, and saddles, although the DPS furnished horse trailers and reimbursed the Rangers for automobile mileage. After Colonel Garrison's death, the Rangers were armed with Smith & Wesson Model 19 or Model 586 .357 Magnum revolvers, Remington Model 1100 twelve-gauge shotguns, and Remington Model 742 .30-06 rifles. They could carry personally-owned weapons as long as they regularly qualified with them.

Although they continued to have no official uniform, they did for a time wear "adopted clothing," which consisted of a silver-colored Stetson, Western-style tan gabardine pants and brush jacket, white shirt with tie, and black boots.

Presently, active-duty Texas Rangers are furnished with State-issued transportation (sedan or four-wheel drive) in addition to helicopters, airplanes, armored personnel carriers and horses. Stored throughout their vehicles are electronic equipment (Dell notebook computer, Sony digital camera, Motorola Saber III portable radio, Marantz PM0201 tape recorder, Sony micro cassette recorder, cellular phone and charger, video camera, and copier); cameras, optics, and illumination (Canon F1 camera, camera tripod, Bushnell binoculars, flashlight, and Mela Beam hand spotlight); restraints (Smith and Wesson handcuffs, leg irons, transport belt, and belt rig with buckle); and various kits and tools (fingerprint kit, first aid kit, tool box, evidence kit, web gear, and bolt cutters). They are issued a raid jacket, coveralls, parka jacket, and Battle Dress Uniforms (military-style fatigues). The "adopted clothing" regulation was abolished in 1974. Instead, Rangers receive a clothing allowance of one hundred dollars a month and, since there is still no standard uniform, choices conform to personal preference with Western-style remaining prominent — white hats, belts with hand-crafted nickel-silver buckles, and cowboy boots are the customary fashion. The service badge is traditionally fabricated from a Mexican *cinco peso* coin in gold for captains and silver for lieutenants and sergeants.

Rangers are permitted to carry any sidearm they wish as long as they qualify on a semi-annual basis. Most choose the department-issue SIG Sauer P-226 .357 SIG semi-automatic pistol or a version of the Model 1911A-1 .45 ACP. The SIG Sauer is a double-action handgun that is 7.7 inches long overall with a barrel length of 4.4 inches and a weight of twenty-nine ounces. The pistol features an alloy frame, stainless-steel slide, black Nitron finish, black polymer grips, and a ten- or twelve-round magazine capacity. The DPS authorizes Rangers to use Speer Gold Dot 125-grain jacketed hollowpoint ammunition in .357 SIG and Remington Golden Sabre 230-grain jacketed hollowpoints in .45 ACP.

For more than twenty years, the Rangers employed the Ruger Mini-14 .223 Remington semi-automatic rifle, but in 2006 they began to replace the Rugers with the Bushmaster Firearms M4A3 .223 carbine. The new weapon is 34¾ inches long with the stock fully extended and has a barrel length of sixteen inches. It is equipped with a thirty-round magazine and a six-position, collapsible stock for use as a 400-meter precision weapon or for close-quarters battle. Possessing dual iron sights, the M4 is also mounted with a Picatinny rail system to allow for a variety of optics including an EOTech holographic sighting system, tactical flashlight with pressure switch, infrared illumination, or telescopic scope. For the M4, the Rangers use Winchester Ranger 64-grain Power-Point ammunition. They are also issued on a limited basis the Remington Model 870 twelve-gauge shotgun and Federal or Remington 000 buckshot and rifled slugs. Other defensive gear includes a gas mask, Level Four body armor, ASP baton, and Kevlar helmet.

In 1987, the median age of the Rangers was approximately forty-five years. The average Ranger had completed forty-two hours of college instruction, with twenty-eight Rangers holding college degrees (including two with Master's degrees). By 2007 the average age was forty-seven and the average amount of college credit had increased to 117 hours. Fourteen Rangers possessed Associate's degrees, forty-one Rangers held Bachelor's degrees, and three had Master's degrees.

The modern Texas Ranger Division performs a variety of traditional criminal investigations involving homicide, robbery, sexual assault, missing persons, burglary, theft, questionable deaths, and unidentified bodies. They also work specialized cases such as fraud (including bank fraud), theft by credit card and computer-generated counterfeit checks, misuse of criminal history information, misconduct and corruption of public officials, threats against the governor and other state and federal officials, and parental abductions.

According to the Ranger Headquarters staff, in 2008, a total of 4,624 investigations resulted in 1,517 felony arrests and 190 misdemeanor arrests. The Texas Rangers served 834 warrants, 454 search warrants, and 248 subpoenas, and obtained 3,263 witness statements and 671 confessions to criminal activity. They recovered stolen property valued at $2,305,645 and seized contraband assessed at $1,703,006. Their work resulted in 1,701 convictions that were punished by four death sentences, fifty-nine life sentences, various prison terms totaling 7,457 years, and $6,482,942 in fines and restitution.

As of January 1, 2008, the Texas Ranger Division has an authorized strength of 134 commissioned Rangers, one forensic artist, one fiscal analyst, and a support staff of twenty-four civilians. By December of that year, the number of sworn officers on duty stood at 125: ninety-eight Caucasian males, four African American males, nineteen Hispanic males, one American Indian male, two Caucasian females, and one Hispanic female. The chief (with the rank of senior captain), assistant chief (with the rank of captain), the headquar-

Company D of the Texas Rangers, 2006, posing in front of the Rio Grande. Courtesy of the Texas Ranger Hall of Fame and Museum, Waco, TX.

ters captain, and the headquarters lieutenant are assigned to Ranger Headquarters in Austin. Company A based in Houston is composed of one captain, two lieutenants, and eighteen ranger sergeants; Company B in Garland has one captain, two lieutenants, and seventeen ranger sergeants; Company C in Lubbock one captain, two lieutenants, and fourteen ranger sergeants; Company D in San Antonio one captain, two lieutenants, and fourteen ranger sergeants; Company E in Midland one captain, two lieutenants, and fifteen ranger sergeants; Company F in Waco one captain, two lieutenants, and twenty ranger sergeants; and Company G in McAllen one captain, two lieutenants, and eleven ranger sergeants.

## Historical Register, 1935–Present

*"They were men who could not be stampeded."*
— Colonel Homer Garrison, Jr.

### HEADQUARTERS COMPANY/RANGER HEADQUARTERS (COMPANY H)

Senior Captain Thomas R. "Tom" Hickman (September 1–November 12, 1935)
  *Capt. Hickman appointed HQ Company commander (August 10, 1935)*
Senior Captain James W. McCormick (November 12, 1935–June 25, 1936)
  *Command authority transferred to the office of the DPS Director (July 30, 1936–May 7, 1968)*
Captain Fred C. Olson, HQ Company commander (September 1, 1945–March 3, 1953)
Captain Clinton T. "Clint" Peoples, HQ Company commander (July 1, 1953–August 31, 1957)
Captain Robert A. "Bob" Crowder, Acting Chief (October 1, 1956–August 31, 1957)
Senior Captain Clinton T. "Clint" Peoples (November 1, 1969–March 31, 1974)
  *Command authority transferred to the office of the senior captain (November 1, 1969–Present)*
Senior Captain William D. "Bill" Wilson (April 1, 1974–January 1, 1985)
Senior Captain H. R. "Lefty" Block (February 1, 1985–June 30, 1992)
Senior Captain Maurice C. Cook, Chief (July 1, 1992–August 31, 1996)
  *Title of "Chief of the Texas Rangers" instituted October 1, 1993*
Senior Captain Bruce M. Casteel, Chief (September 1, 1996–August 31, 2001)
Senior Captain Charlie J. Havrda, Chief (September 1, 2001–April 21, 2004)
Senior Captain Earl R. Pearson, Chief (May 1, 2004–August 31, 2005)
Senior Captain Raymond L. "Ray" Coffman, Chief (September 1, 2005–October 31, 2008)
Senior Captain Antonio "Tony" Leal, III, Chief/Assistant Director (December 10, 2008–Present)
  *Assistant Director for Texas Ranger Division (July 30, 2009)*
Captain William D. "Bill" Wilson, Assistant Supervisor (September 1, 1971–March 31, 1974)

Captain James L. "Skippy" Rundell, Assistant Supervisor (July 1, 1974–August 31, 1981)
Captain H. R. "Lefty" Block, Assistant Supervisor (September 1, 1981–January 31, 1985)
Captain Maurice C. Cook, Assistant Supervisor (February 1, 1985–June 30, 1992)
Captain Bruce M. Casteel, Assistant Commander/Assistant Chief (July 1, 1992–August 1, 1996)
   Title of Assistant Commander revised as Assistant Chief (October 1, 1993)
Captain George E. "Gene" Powell, Assistant Chief (August 5, 1996–August 31, 2001)
Captain Earl R. Pearson, Assistant Chief (September 5, 2001–May 1, 2004)
Captain Raymond L. "Ray" Coffman, Assistant Chief (May 4, 2004–August 31, 2005)
Captain James L. "Jim" Miller, Assistant Chief (September 1, 2005–August 31, 2008)
Captain Gerardo J. "Gary" De Los Santos, Assistant Chief (September 1–December 31, 2008)
Captain Levy C. Wilson, Assistant Chief (December 31, 2008–Present)
   *Capt. Wilson promoted to Headquarters (December 31, 2008) and relinquished command of Co. "A" (May 1, 2009)*
Captain Roy W. Aldrich, Quartermaster (August 10, 1935–September 1, 1939)
Captain Charles R. "Charlie" Brune, HQ Captain (September 1, 1998–August 31, 2002)
Captain Gerardo J. "Gary" De Los Santos, HQ Captain (November 1, 2005–August 31, 2007)
Captain H. D. "Dino" Henderson, HQ Captain (September 1, 2007–August 31, 2009)
Captain Robert J. "Bob" Bullock, HQ Captain (September 1, 2009–Present)
   *Capt. Bullock promoted to Headquarters while retaining command of Company "A"*
*Previous Duty stations*: Pleasanton (March 1945); La Grange, Waco, Killeen, Kerrville, San Antonio, Smithville, and Comanche (March 1953)
*Previous Ranger District*: Lampasas, Coryell, Llano, Burnet, Williamson, Bell, Milam, Robertson, Burleson, Lee, Fayette, Bastrop, Caldwell, Comal, Hays, Travis, Kendall, Blanco, Gillespie, Kerr, Real, Bandera, Medina, Bexar, Guadalupe, Wilson, Karnes, and Atascosa Counties with *duty stations* at Pleasanton, Kerrville, and La Grange and *headquarters office* at Austin (September 1948)
*Previous Ranger District*: Travis, Hays, Bastrop, and Caldwell counties with headquarters at Austin (August 1992)
*Headquarters*: Austin (June 1997)
   *Division operated under the supervision of the Texas Department of Public Safety*

## Company A

Captain James W. McCormick (August 10–November 12, 1935)
Private Dan Hines, Acting Commander (December 10, 1935–June 1, 1936?)
Captain Hardy B. Purvis, Jr. (1936–December 31, 1956)
Captain John J. "Johnny" Klevenhagan, Sr. (January 1, 1957–November 26, 1958)
Captain Eddie L. Oliver (December 8, 1958–December 31, 1971)
Captain James F. "Pete" Rogers (January 1, 1972–February 2, 1978)
Captain Grady Sessums (March 2, 1978–February 28, 1982)
Captain Dan H. North (March 1, 1982–August 1, 1986)
Captain Bob G. Prince (September 1, 1986–June 31, 1992)
Captain W. D. Vickers (August 1, 1992–September 1, 1996)
Captain Earl R. Pearson (November 1, 1996–September 5, 2001)
Captain Cleatis R. "Clete" Buckaloo (October 1, 2001–May 6, 2004)
Captain James L. "Jim" Miller (May 7, 2004–August 31, 2005)
Captain Antonio "Tony" Leal, III (October 1, 2005–December 10, 2008)
Captain Levy C. Wilson (December 10, 2008–April 30, 2009)
Captain Robert J. "Bob" Bullock (May 1, 2009–Present)
*Previous Headquarters Office*: Lufkin (August 1935); Houston

*Previous Duty Stations*: San Augustine (August 1935–September 1939)
*Previous Ranger District*: Leon, Houston, Cherokee, Rusk, Panola, Nacogdoches, Shelby, San Augustine, Angelina, Sabine, Newton, Jasper, Tyler, Polk, Trinity, Madison, Brazos, Grimes, Walker, Montgomery, San Jacinto, Liberty, Hardin, Orange, Jefferson, Chambers, Galveston, Harris, Waller, Austin, Washington, Gonzales, Lavaca, Colorado, Wharton, Fort Bend, Brazoria, Matagorda, Jackson, Victoria, De Witt, Goliad, Refugio, Calhoun, and Aransas Counties with *duty stations* at Victoria, San Augustine, and Center and *headquarters office* at Houston (September 1948)
*Previous Duty Stations*: Huntsville, Woodville, Lufkin, San Augustine, and Burton (March 1958)
*Previous Ranger District*: Nacogdoches, Shelby, Angelina, San Augustine, Sabine, Trinity, Polk, Tyler, Jasper, Newton, Walker, San Jacinto, Grimes, Montgomery, Liberty, Hardin, Orange, Washington, Waller, Harris, Chambers, Jefferson, Austin, Fort Bend, Brazoria, Fayette, Colorado, Wharton, and Matagorda Counties with *headquarters office* at Houston (September 1968)
*Present Ranger District*: Nacogdoches, Shelby, Angelina, San Augustine, Sabine, Trinity, Polk, Tyler, Jasper, Newton, Walker, San Jacinto, Grimes, Montgomery, Liberty, Hardin, Orange, Washington, Waller, Harris, Chambers, Jefferson, Austin, Fort Bend, Brazoria, Fayette, Colorado, Wharton, and Matagorda Counties with *duty stations* at Nacogdoches, Lufkin, Livingston, Jasper, Huntsville, Conroe, Liberty, Brenham, Beaumont, Bellville, Richmond, Texas City, and Bay City and *headquarters office* at Houston (August 1992)

## Company B

Captain Fred L. McDaniel (August 10, 1935–August 31, 1937)
Captain Seabren O. Hamm (November 1, 1937–October 7, 1938)
Captain Royal B. Phillips (October 13, 1938–February 26, 1940)
Captain Manuel T. "Lone Wolf" Gonzaullas (February 27, 1940–July 31, 1951)
Captain Robert A. "Bob" Crowder (August 1, 1951–September 31, 1956)
Sergeant E. J. "Jay" Banks, Acting Commander (October 1, 1956–August 31, 1957)
Captain E. J. "Jay" Banks (September 1, 1957–March 10, 1960)
Captain Robert A. "Bob" Crowder (March 15, 1960–August 31, 1969)
Captain William D. "Bill" Wilson (September 1, 1969–August 1, 1971)
Captain G. W. Burks (September 1, 1971–August 31, 1986)
Captain James A. Wright (September 1, 1986–October 31, 1991)
Captain David A. Byrnes (December 1, 1991–August 31, 1996)
Captain W. D. Vickers (September 1, 1996–June 30, 2002)
Captain Richard H. Sweaney (September 1, 2002–August 31, 2008)
Captain Alvin A. "Al" Alexis (September 1, 2008–Present)
*Previous Headquarters Offices*: Fort Worth (August 1935); Wichita Falls (December 1935); Dallas (November 1937)
*Previous duty stations*: Fort Worth and Lubbock (December 1935)
*Previous Ranger District*: Wilbarger, Wichita, Clay, Montague, Cooke, Grayson, Fannin, Lamar, Red River, Bowie, Cass, Morris, Camp, Titus, Franklin, Hopkins, Hunt, Collin, Denton, Wise, Jack, Young, Throckmorton, Baylor, Archer, Delta, Shackelford, Stephens, Palo Pinto, Parker, Tarrant, Dallas, Rockwall, Kaufman, Van Zandt, Rains, Wood, Upshur, Marion, Harrison, Gregg, Smith, Henderson, Anderson, Freestone, Navarro, Ellis, Johnson, Hill, Limestone, Falls, McLennan, Bosque, Somervell, Hood, Erath, Eastland, and Callahan Counties with *duty stations* at Clarksville, Tyler, Waco, Vernon, Gainesville, Graham, Greenville, and Stephenville and *headquarters office* at Dallas (September 1948)

*Previous Duty Stations*: Mount Pleasant, Forney, Bonham, Tyler, Gainesville, and Marshall (March 1958)

*Previous Ranger District*: Cooke, Grayson, Fannin, Lamar, Red River, Bowie, Denton, Collin, Hunt, Delta, Hopkins, Franklin, Titus, Camp, Morris, Cass, Tarrant, Dallas, Rockwall, Kaufman, Rains, Van Zandt, Wood, Upshur, Gregg, Marion, Harrison, Smith, Rusk, and Panola Counties with *headquarters office* at Dallas (September 1968)

*Present Ranger District*: Cooke, Grayson, Fannin, Lamar, Red River, Bowie, Denton, Collin, Hunt, Delta, Hopkins, Franklin, Titus, Camp, Morris, Cass, Tarrant, Dallas, Rockwall, Kaufman, Rains, Van Zandt, Wood, Upshur, Gregg, Marion, Harrison, Smith, Rusk, and Panola Counties with *duty stations* at Sherman, Texarkana, McKinney, Greenville, Mount Pleasant, Hurst, Longview, and Tyler and *headquarters office* at Garland (August 1992)

## COMPANY C

Captain Richard C. Hawkins (August 10, 1935–August 31, 1939)
Captain Benjamin M. "Manny" Gault (September 1, 1939–December 4, 1947)
Captain Robert A. "Bob" Crowder (December 9, 1947–July 31, 1951)
Captain Raymond Waters (August 1, 1951–January 31, 1967)
Captain Frank J. Probst (December 1, 1967–August 31, 1968)
Captain James M. "Jim" Ray (September 16, 1968–June 21, 1969)
Captain James F. "Pete" Rogers (September 1, 1969–December 31, 1971)
Captain James L. "Skippy" Rundell (January 1, 1972–June 30, 1974)
Captain Walter Werner (July 1, 1974–August 31, 1981)
Captain Charles Moore, Jr. (September 1, 1981–April 30, 1988)
Captain Bruce M. Casteel (May 1, 1988–June 30, 1992)
Captain Joe F. Wilie (August 1, 1992–October 31, 1993)
Captain Carl F. Weathers (November 1, 1993–August 31, 2002)
Captain James L. "Jim" Miller (September 1, 2002–May 6, 2004)
Captain Gerardo J. "Gary" De Los Santos (May 7, 2004–August 31, 2005)
Captain Randy Prince (September 1, 2005–Present)

*Previous Headquarters Office*: San Angelo (December 1935); Lubbock (1946)

*Previous Duty Stations*: Uvalde and Alpine (December 1935)

*Previous Ranger District*: Dallam, Sherman, Hansford, Ochiltree, Lipscomb, Hemphill, Roberts, Hutchinson, Moore, Hartley, Oldham, Potter, Carson, Gray, Wheeler, Collingsworth, Donley, Armstrong, Randall, Deaf Smith, Parmer, Castro, Swisher, Briscoe, Hall, Childress, Hardeman, Foard, Cottle, Motley, Floyd, Hale, Lamb, Bailey, Cochran, Hockley, Lubbock, Crosby, Dickens, King, Knox, Haskell, Stonewall, Kent, Garza, Lynn, Terry, Yoakum, Gaines, Dawson, Borden, Scurry, Fisher, Jones, Taylor, Nolan, Mitchell, Howard, Martin, and Andrews Counties with *duty stations* at Abilene, Amarillo, and Lamesa and *headquarters office* at Lubbock (September 1948)

*Previous Duty Stations*: Vernon, Jacksboro, Memphis, and Amarillo (March 1958)

*Previous Ranger District*: Dallam, Sherman, Hansford, Ochiltree, Lipscomb, Hartley, Moore, Hutchinson, Roberts, Hemphill, Oldham, Potter, Carson, Gray, Wheeler, Deaf Smith, Randall, Armstrong, Donley, Collingsworth, Parmer, Castro, Swisher, Briscoe, Hall, Childress, Hardeman, Bailey, Lamb, Hale, Floyd, Motley, Cottle, Foard, Wilbarger, Wichita, Cochran, Hockley, Lubbock, Crosby, Dickens, King, Knox, Baylor, Archer, Clay, Montague, Yoakum, Terry, Lynn, Garza, Kent, Stonewall, Haskell, Throckmorton, Young, Jack, Wise, Palo Pinto, and Parker Counties with *headquarters office* at Lubbock (September 1968)

*Present Ranger District*: Dallam, Sherman, Hansford, Ochiltree, Lipscomb, Hartley, Moore, Hutchinson, Roberts, Hemphill, Oldham, Potter, Carson, Gray, Wheeler, Deaf Smith, Randall, Armstrong, Donley, Collingsworth, Parmer, Castro, Swisher, Briscoe, Hall, Childress, Hardeman, Bailey, Lamb, Hale, Floyd, Motley, Cottle, Foard, Wilbarger, Wichita, Cochran, Hockley, Lubbock, Crosby, Dickens, King, Knox, Baylor, Archer, Clay, Montague, Yoakum, Terry, Lynn, Garza, Kent, Stonewall, Haskell, Throckmorton, Young, Jack, Wise, Palo Pinto, and Parker Counties with *duty stations* at Dumas, Pampa, Amarillo, Hereford, Childress, Wichita Falls, Brownfield, Graham, Decatur, Mineral Wells and *headquarters office* at Lubbock (August 1992)

## COMPANY D

Captain William W. "Bill" McMurrey (August 10, 1935–January 1, 1940)
Captain Seabren O. Hamm (January 1, 1940–May 31, 1943)
Captain Gully Cowsert, Sr. (June 1, 1943–December 31, 1944)
Captain Stephen Ernest Best, Sr. (January 1, 1945–August 1, 1947)
Sergeant Alfred Y. Allee, Sr., Acting Commander (August 1–October 31, 1947)
Captain Alfred Y. Allee, Sr. (November 1, 1947–September 30, 1970)
Captain John M. Wood (October 1, 1970–October 31, 1978)
Captain Jack O. Dean (November 1, 1978–August 31, 1993)
Captain Charlie J. Havrda (September 1, 1993–August 31, 2001)
Captain Raymond L. "Ray" Coffman (September 1, 2001–May 4, 2004)
Captain Cleatis R. "Clete" Buckaloo (May 7, 2004–August 31, 2007)
Captain Gerardo J. "Gary" De Los Santos (September 1, 2007–August 31, 2008)
Captain Henry L. "Hank" Whitman, Jr. (September 1, 2008–Present)
*Previous Headquarters Offices*: Hebbronville (August 1935); Del Rio (January 1940); Junction (June 1943); Alice (May 1944); Raymondville (January 1945); Falfurrias (1945); Kingsville (April 1947); Harlingen (August 1947)
*Previous Ranger District*: Kinney, Uvalde, Maverick, Zavalla, Frio, Dimmit, La Salle, McMullen, Live Oak, Bee, Webb, Duval, Jim Wells, San Patricio, Nueces, Kleberg, Zapata, Jim Hogg, Brooks, Kenedy, Starr, Hidalgo, Willacy, and Cameron Counties with *duty stations* at Crystal City, Falfurrias, Corpus Christi, Uvalde, Harlingen, and Alice and *headquarters office* at Carrizo Springs (September 1948)
*Previous Headquarters Office*: Corpus Christi (March 1958)
*Previous Duty Stations*: Uvalde, Victoria, Harlingen, Kingsville, Eastwood, San Antonio, and Cotulla (March 1958)
*Previous Ranger District*: Bandera, Comal, Guadalupe, Gonzales, De Witt, Lavaca, Victoria, Jackson, Calhoun, Uvalde, Medina, Bexar, Wilson, Karnes, Goliad, Refugio, Aransas, Zavala, Frio, Atascosa, Dimmit, La Salle, McMullen, Live Oak, Bee, Webb, Duval, Jim Wells, San Patricio, Nueces, Kleberg, Zapata, Jim Hogg, Brooks, Kenedy, Starr, Hidalgo, Willacy, and Cameron Counties with *duty stations* at Seguin, Uvalde, Pearsall, Jourdanton, Victoria, Laredo, Sinton, San Antonio, Kingsville, McAllen, Harlingen, and Brownsville and *headquarters office* at Corpus Christi (September 1968)
*Previous Ranger District*: Real, Bandera, Comal, Guadalupe, Gonzales, De Witt, Lavaca, Victoria, Jackson, Calhoun, Uvalde, Medina, Bexar, Wilson, Karnes, Goliad, Refugio, Aransas, Maverick, Zavala, Frio, Atascosa, Dimmit, La Salle, McMullen, Live Oak, Bee, Webb, Duval, Jim Wells, San Patricio, Nueces, Kleberg, Zapata, Jim Hogg, Brooks, Kenedy, Starr, Hidalgo, Willacy, and Cameron Counties (August 1992)
*Previous Ranger District*: Real, Bandera, Comal, Hays, Guadalupe, Caldwell, Gonzales, De Witt,

Lavaca, Victoria, Jackson, Calhoun, Uvalde, Medina, Bexar, Wilson, Karnes, Goliad, Refugio, Aransas, Maverick, Frio, Atascosa, La Salle, McMullen, Live Oak, Bee, Duval, San Patricio, Nueces, Kleberg, Brooks, Kenedy, Maverick, Webb, Zavala, Dimmit, Zapata, Jim Hogg, Starr, Hidalgo, Willacy, and Cameron Counties (June 1997)

*Present Ranger District*: Real, Bandera, Comal, Hays, Guadalupe, Caldwell, Gonzales, De Witt, Lavaca, Victoria, Jackson, Calhoun, Uvalde, Medina, Bexar, Wilson, Karnes, Goliad, Refugio, Aransas, Maverick, Frio, Atascosa, La Salle, McMullen, Live Oak, Bee, Duval, San Patricio, Nueces, Kleberg, Brooks, and Kenedy Counties with *duty stations* at Floresville, Jourdanton, Corpus Christi, Seguin, Beeville, Kingsville, Uvalde, and Sinton and *headquarters office* at San Antonio (January 2008)

## COMPANY E

Captain James W. McCormick (June 25, 1936–May 31, 1938)
?
Captain Stephen Ernest Best, Sr. (September 1, 1941–January 1, 1945)
Captain Gully Cowsert, Sr. (January 1, 1945–December 1, 1957)
Captain Frank J. Probst (January 1, 1958–November 31, 1967)
Captain James F. Riddle (December 1, 1967–January 22, 1975)
Captain J. P. Lynch (April 1, 1975–August 31, 1982)
Captain Maurice C. Cook (September 1, 1982–January 31, 1985)
Captain George E. "Gene" Powell (February 1, 1985–August 5, 1996)
Captain Barry K. Caver (November 1, 1996–June 30, 2008)
Captain Levy C. Wilson (July 1–September 31, 2008)
Captain Jerry Byrne, Jr. (October 1, 2008–Present)

*Previous Headquarters Office*: Wichita Falls (July 1936); San Angelo (September 1942); Junction (1945)

*Previous Duty Stations*: Pecos, Sanderson, Rocksprings, Sweetwater, Sierra Blanca, and Sonora (January 1948)

*Previous Ranger District*: Comanche, Brown, Coleman, Runnels, Coke, Sterling, Glasscock, Midland, Ector, Winkler, Loving, Reeves, Culberson, Hudspeth, El Paso, Jeff Davis, Presidio, Brewster, Pecos, Ward, Crane, Upton, Reagan, Irion, Tom Green, Concho, McCulloch, San Saba, Miles, Hamilton, Mason, Menard, Kimble, Edwards, Sutton, Schleicher, Val Verde, Crockett, and Terrell counties with *duty stations* at San Angelo, Brownwood, Sierra Blanca, Rocksprings, Alpine, Pecos, and Sanderson and *headquarters office* at Junction (September 1948)

*Previous Headquarters Office*: Midland (March 1958)

*Previous Duty Stations*: Sweetwater, Sanderson, Sierra Blanca, Sonora, San Angelo, Pecos, and Rocksprings (March 1958)

*Previous Ranger District*: Gaines, Dawson, Borden, Scurry, Fisher, Jones, Shackelford, Stephens, Andrews, Martin, Howard, Mitchell, Nolan, Taylor, Callahan, Eastland, El Paso, Hudspeth, Culberson, Reeves, Loving, Winkler, Ector, Midland, Glasscock, Sterling, Coke, Runnels, Coleman, Brown, Ward, Crane, Upton, Reagan, Irion, Tom Green, Concho, Jeff Davis, Pecos, Crockett, Schleicher, Sutton, Presidio, Brewster, Terrell, Val Verde, Edwards, Kinney, and Maverick Counties (September 1968)

*Previous Ranger District*: Gaines, Dawson, Borden, Scurry, Fisher, Jones, Shackelford, Stephens, Andrews, Martin, Howard, Mitchell, Nolan, Taylor, Callahan, Eastland, El Paso, Hudspeth, Culberson, Reeves, Loving, Winkler, Ector, Midland, Glasscock, Sterling, Coke, Runnels, Coleman, Brown, Ward, Crane, Upton, Reagan, Irion, Tom Green, Concho, Jeff

Davis, Pecos, Crockett, Schleicher, Sutton, Presidio, Brewster, Terrell, Val Verde, Edwards, Kinney, and Maverick Counties (August 1992)

*Previous Ranger District*: Gaines, Dawson, Borden, Scurry, Fisher, Jones, Shackelford, Stephens, Andrews, Martin, Howard, Mitchell, Nolan, Taylor, Callahan, Eastland, El Paso, Hudspeth, Culberson, Reeves, Loving, Winkler, Ector, Midland, Glasscock, Sterling, Coke, Runnels, Coleman, Brown, Ward, Crane, Upton, Reagan, Irion, Tom Green, Concho, Jeff Davis, Pecos, Crockett, Schleicher, Sutton, Presidio, Brewster, Terrell, Val Verde, Edwards, and Kinney Counties with *stations* at Snyder, Abilene, El Paso, Brownwood, San Angelo, Fort Stockton, Alpine, and Del Rio and *headquarters office* at Midland (June 1997)

*Present Ranger District*: Gaines, Dawson, Borden, Scurry, Fisher, Jones, Shackelford, Stephens, Andrews, Martin, Howard, Mitchell, Nolan, Taylor, Callahan, Eastland, El Paso, Hudspeth, Culberson, Reeves, Loving, Winkler, Ector, Midland, Glasscock, Sterling, Coke, Runnels, Coleman, Brown, Ward, Crane, Upton, Reagan, Irion, Tom Green, Concho, Jeff Davis, Pecos, Crockett, Schleicher, Sutton, Presidio, Brewster, and Terrell Counties with *duty stations* at Snyder, Abilene, El Paso, Brownwood, San Angelo, Fort Stockton, Alpine, and Del Rio and *headquarters office* at Midland (January 2008)

## Company F

Captain Clinton T. "Clint" Peoples (September 1, 1957–September 31, 1969)
Captain E. G. "Butch" Albers, Jr. (November 1, 1969–August 31, 1974)
Captain Robert K. "Bob" Mitchell (September 1, 1974–June 30, 1992)
Captain Bob G. Prince (July 1, 1992–September 30, 1993)
Captain Joe F. Wilie (November 1, 1993–August 31, 1995)
Captain Kirby W. Dendy (November 1, 1995–Present)

*Previous Ranger District*: Erath, Hood, Somervell, Johnson, Ellis, Henderson, Brown, Coleman, Comanche, Hamilton, Bosque, Hill, Navarro, Anderson, Cherokee, Mills, Coryell, McLennan, Limestone, Freestone, Concho, McCulloch, San Saba, Lampasas, Bell, Falls, Robertson, Leon, Madison, Houston, Menard, Mason, Llano, Burnet, Williamson, Milam, Burleson, Brazos, Kimble, Gillespie, Blanco, Travis, Bastrop, Lee, Hays, Caldwell, Kerr, Kendall, and Bandera Counties with *duty stations* at Belton, Fairfield, Mason, Stephenville, Killeen, and Austin and *headquarters office* at Waco (September 1957)

*Previous Ranger District*: Erath, Hood, Somervell, Johnson, Ellis, Henderson, Brown, Coleman, Comanche, Hamilton, Bosque, Hill, Navarro, Anderson, Cherokee, Mills, Coryell, McLennan, Limestone, Freestone, Concho, McCulloch, San Saba, Lampasas, Bell, Falls, Robertson, Leon, Madison, Houston, Menard, Mason, Llano, Burnet, Williamson, Milam, Burleson, Brazos, Kimble, Gillespie, Blanco, Travis, Bastrop, Lee, Hays, Caldwell, Kerr, Kendall, and Bandera Counties with *duty station* at San Marcos and *headquarters office* at Waco (September 1968)

*Previous Ranger District*: Erath, Hood, Somervell, Johnson, Ellis, Henderson, Comanche, Hamilton, Bosque, Hill, Navarro, Anderson, Cherokee, Mills, Coryell, McLennan, Limestone, Freestone, McCulloch, San Saba, Lampasas, Bell, Falls, Robertson, Leon, Madison, Houston, Menard, Mason, Llano, Burnet, Williamson, Milam, Burleson, Brazos, Kimble, Gillespie, Blanco, Lee, Kerr, Kendall, and Bandera Counties with *headquarters office* at Waco (August 1992)

*Present Ranger District*: Erath, Hood, Somervell, Johnson, Ellis, Henderson, Comanche, Hamilton, Bosque, Hill, Avarro, Anderson, Cherokee, Mills, Coryell, McLennan, Limestone, Freestone, McCulloch, San Saba, Lampasas, Bell, Falls, Robertson, Leon, Madison, Houston, Menard, Mason, Llano, Burnet, Williamson, Milam, Burleson, Brazos, Kimble, Gillespie, Blanco, Travis, Hays, Caldwell, Bastrop, Lee, Kerr, and Kendall Counties with *duty stations* at Stephenville, Cleburne, Athens, Palestine, Brady, Lampasas, Temple, Centerville, Llano, Austin, Bastrop, and Kerrville and *headquarters office* at Waco (June 1997)

## COMPANY G

Captain Skylor D. Hearn (January 1, 2008–Present)

*Ranger District*: Val Verde, Edwards, Kinney, Maverick, Webb, Zavala, Dimmit, Zapata, Jim Hogg, Starr, Hidalgo, Willacy, and Cameron Counties with *duty stations* at Laredo, Del Rio, Brownsville, Rio Grande City, Victoria, and Pearsall and *headquarters office* at McAllen (January 2008)

## UNSOLVED CRIMES INVESTIGATION UNIT

Lieutenant Gerardo J. "Gary" De Los Santos (October 1, 2001–March 30, 2003)
Lieutenant Antonio "Tony" Leal, III (April 1, 2003–August 31, 2005)
Captain Gerardo J. "Gary" De Los Santos (September 1, 2005–August 31, 2007)
Captain H. D. "Dino" Henderson (September 1, 2007–Present)

*Ranger District*: Statewide jurisdiction with headquarters office at San Antonio (October 2001) and Austin (January 2008)

# Appendix A: Battle Record

| Site of Battle | Date | Unit(s) Involved |
|---|---|---|
| Tawakoni village near Tehuacana Springs and the Brazos River, Texas | July 11, 1835 | Capt. R. M. Coleman's Co. |
| Waco village near the Trinity River, Texas | August 1835 | Col. J. H. Moore's Expedition |
| Near the Brazos River, Texas | September 1, 1835 | Capt. M. R. Goheen's Co., Capt. R. M. Williamson's Co., Moore's Expedition |
| Mill Creek, Texas | December 1835 | Maj. R. M. Williamson's det., Ranging Corps |
| Walnut Creek near the Guadalupe River, Texas | January 20, 1836 | Capt. J. J. Tumlinson's Co., Ranging Corps |
| The Alamo, San Antonio de Béxar, Texas | March 6, 1836 | Lt. G. C. Kimbell's Co. |
| Parker's Fort, Texas | May 19, 1836 | Supt. S. M. Parker; Capt. J. W. Parker's Co. |
| Capano Bay, Gulf of Mexico, Texas | June 3, 1836 | Capt. I. W. Burton's Co., Ranging Corps |
| Near Gonzales, Texas | July 1, 1836 | Capt. T. Robbins' Co. |
| Between the Yegua and Little Rivers, Texas | August 1836 | Capt. W. W. Hill's Co. |
| Coleto Creek near Victoria, Texas | August 22, 1836 | Capt. J. G. W. Pierson's Co. |
| Elm Creek on the Brazos River, Texas | January 7, 1837 | Lt. G. B. Erath's Det., Co. A, Btn. Mtd. Rifles |
| Near Little River, Texas | January 7, 1837 | Lt. C. Curtis' Det., Co. B, Btn. Mtd. Rifles |
| Trinity River near new Fort Houston, Texas | January 28, 1837 | Pvts. A. Anglin, D. and E. W. Faulkenberry, B. W. Douthit, J. S. Hunter, and C. C. Anderson (Haggard's Co., Jewell's Btn.) |
| Colorado River near new Fort Houston, Texas | March 1837 | Lt. N. Wren's Det., Co. C, Btn. Mtd. Rifles |
| Near Laredo, Texas | March 17, 1837 | Capt. E. Smith's Co. |
| Near San Antonio, Texas | May 1837 | Pvt. J. C. Hays' Det., E. Smith's Co. |
| Post Oak Springs, Texas | May 6, 1837 | Det. B., Btn. Mtd. Rifles |
| Perry Creek, Texas | May 27, 1837 | Pvt. J. Coryell's Det A, Btn. Mtd. Rifles |
| Ruan Bayou, Texas | November 1837 | Co. D, Btn. Mtd. Rifles |

| Site of Battle | Date | Unit(s) Involved |
|---|---|---|
| Near the Forks of the Brazos River, Texas | November 3, 1837 | Lt. A. B. Van Benthuysen's Det., Bowyer's Co. |
| "Stone Houses Fight" near the head-waters of the West Fork of the Trinity River, Texas | November 10, 1837 | Lt. A. B. Van Benthuysen's Det., Bowyer's Co. |
| Arroyo Seco, Texas | August 10, 1838 | Col. H. W. Karnes' 1838 Expedition |
| ? | October 3, 1838 | Maj. L. H. Mabbitt's Btn. |
| East of Fort Houston, Texas | October 12, 1838 | Maj. L. H. Mabbitt's Btn. |
| Kickapoo Creek, Texas | October 16, 1838 | Maj. L. H. Mabbitt's Btn.; Maj. B. C. Walter's Mtd. Rangers Staff |
| Near Morgan's Point and the Brazos River, Texas | January 16, 1839 | Capt. B. F. Bryant's Co. |
| Wallace's Creek near the junction of Colorado and San Saba Rivers, Texas | February 14, 1839 | Maj. J. H. Moore's 1839 Expedition |
| Brushy Creek, Texas | February 25, 1839 | Col. E. Burleson's Co.; Capt. J. Burleson's Co.; Capt. J. Rogers' Co.; and Capt. J. Billingsley's Co. |
| Peach Creek, Texas | March 2, 1839 | Capt. B. McCulloch's Co. |
| Mill Creek near Guadalupe River, Texas (Battleground Prairie) | March 29, 1839 | Lt. M. Andrews' Co.; Capt. J. Billingsley's Co. |
| Young's Ford, Texas | March 30, 1839 | Pvts. J. M. Day, T. R. Nichols, J. W. Nichols, D. N. Poore, and D. Reynolds (Caldwell's Co.) |
| North Fork of the San Gabriel River, Texas | May 17, 1839 | Lt. J. O. Rice's Det., Andrews' Co. |
| Bird's Creek, Texas (Near Fort Smith on the Little River) | May 26, 1839 | Capt. J. Bird's Co.; Sgt. W. H. Weaver's Det., Evan's Co. |
| Sabinal Canyon, Texas | June 10, 1839 | Capt. J. N. Seguín's Co., Karnes' 1839 Expedition |
| Battle Creek, Texas | July 15, 1839 | Maj. L. H. Mabbitt's Btn.; Lt-Col. D. J. Woodlief's Reg. |
| Neches River, Texas | July 16, 1839 | Maj. L. H. Mabbitt's Btn.; Lt-Col. D. J. Woodlief's Reg. |
| Anadarko village on the Brazos River, Texas | October 25, 1839 | 1st Mtd. Gunmen |
| Comanche village near the Pedernales River, Texas | November 1, 1839 | Col. H. W. Karnes' Hill Country Expedition |
| Clear Fork of the Trinity River near Comanche Peak, Texas | November 5, 1839 | 1st Mtd. Gunmen |
| Richland Creek, Texas | November 11, 1839 | 1st Mtd. Gunmen |
| Cherokee village near junction of the Colorado and San Saba Rivers, Texas | December 25, 1839 | Capt. M. Caldwell's Co. |
| West of Leona, Texas near the Rio Frio and the Presidio Rio Grande Road | July 4, 1840 | Capt. J. R. Cunningham's Co. |
| Carmargo, Mexico | July 6, 1840 | Capt. E. Cameron's Co. |
| Garcitas Creek, Texas | August 9, 1840 | Capt. A. Zumwalt's Co.; Capt. B. McCulloch's Co.; Capt. J. J. Tumlinson's Co. |
| Plum Creek, Texas | August 12, 1840 | MG F. Huston/Capt. M. Caldwell's Btn. |
| Red Fork of the Colorado River, Texas | October 24, 1840 | Maj. J. H. Moore's 1840 Expedition |
| Near the Pedernales River, Texas | March 30, 1841 | Capt. G. M. Dolson's Co. |

## Battle Record

| Site of Battle | Date | Unit(s) Involved |
|---|---|---|
| Near Laredo, Texas | April 7, 1841 | Capt. J. C. Hays' Co.; Capt. A. Pérez Co. |
| Near Pecan Creek, Texas | April 21, 1841 | Capt. E. Chandler's Co. |
| Johnson's Fork of the Llano River, Texas | May 1841 | Capt. B. McCulloch's Co. |
| Near the Trinity River, Texas | May 2, 1841 | Capt. J. Bourland's Co. |
| Between the San Saba and Llano Rivers, Texas | May 20, 1841 | Capt. W. Bugg's det., Lewis' Expedition |
| Nueces River Valley, Texas | May 21, 1841 | Capt. T. Green's Co., Lewis' Expedition |
| Nueces River, Texas | May 21, 1841 | Maj. M. L. Lewis' Expedition |
| Village Creek, Texas | May 24, 1841 | Capt. J. Bourland's Co. |
| Near Trinity River, Texas | June 4, 1841 | Capt. D. Gage's Co. |
| East of Trinity River, Texas | June 4, 1841 | Capt. D. Gage's Co. |
| Cross Timbers, Texas | June 9, 1841 | Capt. E. Chandler's Co. |
| Sabinal Canyon, Texas | June 24, 1841 | Capt. J. C. Hays' Co. |
| Bandera Pass, Texas<br>*Existence of battle debated by historians* | July 1841 | Capt. J. C. Hays' Co. |
| Cañon de Uvalde, Texas | July 1, 1841 | Capt. J. C. Hays' Co. |
| Leona River, Texas | July 1, 1841 | Capt. M. Green's Det. |
| Near the Río Frio, Texas | July 19, 1841 | Capt. J. C. Hays' Co. |
| Enchanted Rock, Texas<br>*Existence of battle debated by historians* | August 1841 | Capt. J. C. Hays |
| Cross Timbers, Texas | August 3, 1841 | Capt. G. B. Erath's Co.; Lt. W. M. Love's det., Chandler's Co. |
| Cross Timbers on the Brazos River, Texas | August 5, 1841 | Capt. E. Chandler's Co.; Capt. G. B. Erath's Co. |
| Near Franklin, Texas | August 22, 1841 | Pvt. G. W. Heard's det., Chandler's Co. |
| Nueces River, Texas | September 8, 1841 | Capt. W. J. Cairns' Co. |
| Elm Fork of the Trinity River, Texas | December 1841 | R. Sloan's det., Red River militiamen |
| Near Corpus Christi, Texas | December 1841 | Capt. W. J. Cairns' Co. |
| East of Elm Creek, Texas | December 25, 1841 | Capt. A. W. Webb's Co. |
| Near San Antonio, Texas | February 1842 | Capt. J. C. Hays |
| Near the Nueces River, Texas | March 11, 1842 | Capt. J. C. Hays' Co. |
| Nueces River near San Patricio, Texas | March 14, 1842 | Capt. W. J. Cairns' Co. |
| Lipantitlán, Texas | July 7, 1842 | Capt. E. Cameron's Co. |
| Salado Creek, Texas | September 18, 1842 | Capt. J. C. Hays' Co.; Capt. E. Cameron's Co. |
| Arroyo Hondo, Texas | September 22, 1842 | Capt. J. C. Hays' Co. |
| Near the Llano River, Texas | 1843 | Capt. J. C. Hays' Co. |
| Near the Medina River, Texas | August 1843 | Capt. J. C. Hays' Co. |
| Rio Frio, Texas | November 1843 | Capt. J. C. Hays' Co. |
| Nueces Canyon, Texas | April 1, 1844 | Capt. J. C. Hays' Co. |
| Sister's Creek, Texas | May 31, 1844 | Capt. J. C. Hays' Co. |
| Walker Creek, Texas | June 8, 1844 | Capt. J. C. Hays' Co. |
| Walker Creek, Texas | June 10, 1844 | Capt. J. C. Hays' Co. |
| Near Corpus Christi, Texas | June 1844 | Capt. H. C. Davis' Co. |

## Appendix A

| Site of Battle | Date | Unit(s) Involved |
|---|---|---|
| Agua Dulce (Sweetwater), Texas | July 1844 | Capt. J. C. Hays' Co. |
| Turkey Creek, Texas | August 1844 | Det., Capt. J. C. Hays' Co. |
| Near Llano River, Texas | February 1846? | Capt. J. C. Hays' Co. |
| Paint Rock, Texas | March 1846 | Capt. J. C. Hays' Co. |
| Near Point Isabel, Texas | April 28, 1846 | Capt. S. H. Walker's Co. |
| Near Point Isabel, Texas | May 2, 1846 | Capt. S. H. Walker's Co. |
| Palo Alto Prairie, Texas | May 7, 1846 | Capt. S. H. Walker's Co. |
| Resaca de la Palma, Texas | May 9, 1846 | Capt. S. H. Walker's Co. |
| San Juan River, Mexico | August 1846 | Lt-Col. S. H. Walker's det., 1st Mtd. Rifles |
| Near Camargo, Mexico | August 1846 | Lt-Col. S. H. Walker's det., 1st Mtd. Rifles |
| Punta Aguda, Mexico | August 12, 1846 | Co. A, 1st Mtd. Rifles |
| Near Ramos, Mexico | September 14, 1846 | Co. A, 1st Mtd. Rifles |
| China, Mexico | September 15, 1846 | Co. H, 1st Mtd. Rifles |
| Near Monterey, Mexico | September 1846 | 1st Mtd. Rifles |
| Saltillo Road, Mexico | September 20, 1846 | 1st Mtd. Rifles |
| Monterey, Mexico | September 21–23, 1846 | 1st Mtd. Rifles |
| Near Encarnacion, Mexico | February 18, 1847 | Capt. B. McCulloch's Co. |
| Saltillo-Agua Nueva Road, Mexico | February 22, 1847 | Capt. B. McCulloch's Co. |
| Buena Vista, Mexico | February 23, 1847 | Capt. B. McCulloch's Co. |
| Monterey, Mexico | February 1847 | Co. E, Chevallie's Btn. |
| La Mesa Rancho, Mexico | February 1847 | Capt. M. B. Gray's Co. |
| Concepcion, Mexico | March 25, 1847 | Co. A, Chevallie's Btn. |
| Lake Parras, Mexico | April 1847 | Co. C, Chevallie's Btn. |
| Papagallos, Mexico | July 29, 1847 | Co. D, Chevallie's Btn. |
| Monterey, Mexico | August 13, 1847 | Cos. C and E, Chevallie's Btn. |
| Llano River, Texas | August 1847 | Co. D, 1st Mtd Rifles |
| Los Tablas, Mexico | August 5, 1847 | Co. E, Chevallie's Btn. |
| Rancho Sablas, Mexico | ? | Co. E, Chevallie's Btn. |
| Encontalla, Mexico | ? | Chevallie's Btn. |
| Puebla, Mexico | ? | 1st Mtd. Vols. |
| Camargo, Mexico | September 8, 1847 | Co. D, Lane's Btn. |
| Hacienda de San Juan, Mexico | October 1847 | Co. E, 1st Mtd. Vols. |
| Near Vergara, Mexico | October 1847 | Co. E, 1st Mtd. Vols. |
| Near Medelin, Mexico | October 1847 | Co. F, 1st Mtd. Vols. |
| Monterey, Mexico | October 16, 1847 | Co. D, Lane's Btn. |
| Near Santa Fe, Mexico | October 17, 1847 | Det., 1st Mtd. Vols. |
| Agua Fria, Mexico | November 2, 1847 | Co. D, Lane's Btn. |
| Between Ramos and Capadero, Mexico | November 7, 1847 | Co. D, Lane's Btn. |
| Agua Noche, Mexico | November 21, 1847 | Co. A, Lane's Btn. |
| La Encantada, Mexico | ? | Lane's Btn. |
| Izúcar de Matamoros, Mexico | November 22, 1847 | 1st Mtd. Vols. |
| Galaxa Pass, Mexico | November 24, 1847 | 1st Mtd. Vols. |
| Parras, Mexico | December 1847 | Co. A, Lane's Btn. |

| Site of Battle | Date | Unit(s) Involved |
|---|---|---|
| Agua Noche, Mexico | December 15, 1847 | Cos. A and C, Lane's Btn. |
| Between Mexico City and San Angel, Mexico | January 1848 | Co. I, 1st Mtd. Vols. |
| San Juan Teotihuacan, Mexico | January 13, 1848 | F & S and Co. I, 1st Mtd. Vols. |
| "Cutthroat," Mexico City, Mexico | February 14, 1848 | 1st Mtd. Vols. |
| Zacualtipán, Mexico | February 25, 1848 | 1st Mtd. Vols. |
| Near Llano River, Texas | March 15, 1848 | Capt. S. Highsmith's Co., Bell's Reg. |
| Despoblade, Mexico | March 30, 1848 | Co. I, 1st Mtd. Vols. |
| Rio Frio, Mexico | April 1848 | 1st Mtd. Vols. |
| San Carlos, Mexico | April 1848 | 1st Mtd. Vols. |
| Pedernales River, Texas | April 1848 | Co. D, 1st Mtd. Vols. |
| Concepción, Mexico | May 25, 1848 | Lane's Btn. |
| Sabinal River, Texas | August 29, 1848 | Det., Capt. H. Warfield's Co., Bell's Reg. |
| Leona River, Texas | September 4, 1848 | Det., Capt. H. Warfield's Co., Bell's Reg. |
| Sabinal Canyon, Texas | November 12, 1848 | Lt. W. Knox's det., Warfield's Co., Bell's Reg. |
| Near the Comanche Crossing of the Nueces River, Texas | May 12, 1850 | Capt. J. S. Ford's Co. |
| Near Fort Merrill, Texas | May 26, 1850 | Capt. J. S. Ford's Co. |
| Agua Dulce (Sweetwater) Creek near Fort Merrill, Texas | May 29, 1850 | Capt. J. S. Ford's Co. |
| Benavides Ranch near Laredo, Texas | June 1850 | Lt. A. J. Walker's det., Ford's Co. |
| San Antonio Viejo, Texas | June 1850 | Lt. M. B. Highsmith's det., Ford's Co. |
| Santa Gertrudis, Texas | June 1850 | Pvts. D.C. Sullivan, J. L. Wilbarger, and A. D. Neal (Ford's Co.) |
| Nueces River, Texas | July 15, 1850 | Capt. W. A. A. Wallace's Co. |
| Near the San Saba River, Texas | November 1850 | Capt. H. E. McCulloch's Co. |
| Between Medio Creek and Aransas River, Texas | December 26, 1850 | Lt. J. R. King's det., H. E. McCulloch's Co. |
| Todas Santos Creek, Texas | ? | Capt. W. A. A. Wallace's Co. |
| Arroyo Gato, Texas | January 25, 1851 | Lt. A. J. Walker's det., Ford's Co. |
| San Antonio-Laredo Road near Nueces River, Texas | January 27, 1851 | Lt. E. Burleson's det., Ford's Co. |
| San Saba River, Texas | September 15, 1851 | Capt. H. E. McCulloch's Co. |
| Arroyo San Roque near the Nueces River, Texas | September 17, 1852 | Capt. O. Shaw's Co. |
| Bandera County, Texas | August 1855 | Capt. J. H. Callahan's Co. |
| Bandera County, Texas | September 7, 1855 | Capt. J. H. Callahan's Co. |
| Río Escondido, Mexico | October 3, 1855 | Capt. J. H. Callahan's Expedition |
| Piedras Negras, Mexico | October 7, 1855 | Capt. J. H. Callahan's Expedition |
| Leona River near Fort Inge, Texas | June 9, 1856 | Capt. J. M. Davenport's Co. |
| Little Robe Creek near the Canadian River, Indian Territory | May 12, 1858 | Capt. J. S. Ford's Expedition |

## APPENDIX A

| Site of Battle | Date | Unit(s) Involved |
|---|---|---|
| Near Richland Springs, Texas | November 1858 | Pvts. J. M. Brown, W. J. Cathey, H. G. Farrar, N. A. Taylor, S. S. and B. F. Gholson, J. Meyers, R. C. Williams, S. J. Kemp, and R. Petit (Capt. J. Williams' Co.) |
| Hamilton County, Texas | December 19, 1858 | Lt. N. D. McMillan's det., Williams' Co. |
| Near Comanche Reservation, Texas | July 24, 1859 | Lt. J. W. Nowlin's 1st Det., Brown's Co. |
| Palo Alto Prairie, Cameron County, Texas | November 21, 1859 | Lt. J. Littleton's det., Tobin's Co. |
| Near Rancho del Carmen, Cameron County, Texas | November 22, 1859 | Capt. W G. Tobin's Co.; Capt. H. W. Berry's Co. |
| Rancho La Ebonal, Cameron County, Texas | December 14, 1859 | Capt. W G. Tobin's Co. |
| Rio Grande City, Texas | December 26, 1859 | Capt. J. S. Ford's Co.; Capt. W G. Tobin's Co. |
| Yellow Wolf Creek near the Colorado River, Texas | 1860 | Capt. J. J. Cureton's Co. |
| Rancho La Bolsa, Mexico | February 4, 1860 | Rio Grande Sqdn.; Capt. W G. Tobin's Co. |
| Rancho La Mesa, Mexico | March 17, 1860 | Rio Grande Sqdn. |
| Rancho Maguey, Mexico | March 19, 1860 | Rio Grande Sqdn. |
| Pease River, Texas | December 17, 1860 | Capt. L. S. Ross' Co. |
| South Elm Creek, Throckmorton County, Texas | February 25, 1861 | Capt. T. L. Harrison's Co. |
| Near Jacksboro, Texas | Spring 1861 | Jack County Minute Men |
| Between the Pease River and the Prairie Dog Town Fork of the Red River, Texas | June 23, 1861 | Lt-Col. Frost's Det. D and F, 1st Mtd. Rifles |
| Little Wichita River near Camps Cooper and Jackson, Texas | June 26, 1861 | Cpl. T. J. Ercanbrack's Det. C, 1st Mtd. Rifles |
| Little Wichita River, Texas | July 29, 1861 | Det. C, 1st Mtd. Rifles |
| Cedar Brake, Coleman County, Texas | July 29, 1861 | Capt. J. J. Callan's Minute Men |
| Coleman County, Texas | October 5, 1861 | Capt. J. J. Callan's Minute Men |
| Near Camp Colorado on the Pease (or Peosi) River, Texas | November 1, 1861 | Capt. J. B. Barry's Det. C and Capt. M. M. Boggess' Det. H, 1st Mtd. Rifles |
| Wichita River, Texas | February 16, 1862 | Det. I, 1st Mtd. Rifles |
| San Saba River, Texas | April 2, 1862 | Det. E, Front. Reg. |
| Headwaters of the San Saba River, Texas | April 9, 1862 | Co. C, 1st Mtd. Rifles |
| Between Camp Collier and Pecan Bayou, Texas | April 14, 1862 | Lt. W. F. Robinson's det., Front. Reg. |
| Near Santa Anna Gap, Texas | December 24 or 25, 1862 | Lt. J. Chandler's or J. Sparks' Det. G, Front. Reg. |
| Head of Perdenales and James Rivers, Texas | February 1863 | Lt. P. O. A. Reese's Det. A, Front. Reg. |
| House Mountain, Llano County, Texas | February 1863 | Co. A, Front. Reg. |
| Clay County, Texas | February 16, 1863 | Lt. C. Lindsay's Det. C, Front. Reg. |
| Clear Fork of the Brazos River, Texas | July 24, 1863 | Capt. M. B. Loyd's Det. E, Front. Reg. |

| Site of Battle | Date | Unit(s) Involved |
|---|---|---|
| Coleman County, Texas | July 25, 1863 | Lt. T. C. Wright's Det. I, Front. Reg. |
| Near Paint Creek, Texas | July 26, 1863 | Det. E and H, Front. Reg. |
| Santa Anna Mountains, Texas | July 30, 1863 | Sgt. \_\_\_\_\_'s det., Front. Reg. |
| Blanket Creek, Texas | July 31, 1863 | Lt. J. H. Chrisman's Det. I, Front. Reg. |
| Near Buffalo Gap, Texas | August 29, 1863 | Lt. T. C. Wright's Det. I, Front. Reg. |
| Near the Red River, Montague County, Texas | October 1863 | Capt. F. M. Totty's Det. E, Border Reg.; Det. G, Front. Reg. |
| Near Murphy's Station, Jack County, Texas | October 1863 | Pvt. A. B. Smith's Det. C, Front. Reg. |
| Webber Falls, I.T. | October 12, 1863 | Border Reg. |
| Between Lost Valley and Fort Belknap, Texas | Fall 1863 | Det. G, Front. Reg. |
| Near Beaver Creek and Big Wichita River, Texas | November 17, 1863 | Lt. W. S. Campbell's Det. C, Front. Reg. |
| Fort Gibson, I.T. | December 16, 1863 | Border Reg. |
| Potter's Settlement, Cooke County, Texas | December 23, 1863 | Co. G, Front. Reg.; Co. G, Border Reg. |
| Cooke County, Texas | December 25, 1863 | Front. Reg. |
| Denton County, Texas | January 21, 1864 | Border Reg. |
| Hondo River, Texas | May 8, 1864 | Front. Reg. |
| Stephens County, Texas | August 1864 | Sgt. A. D. Miller's det., Curtis' Co., 2nd Front. Dist. |
| Ellison Springs, Eastland County, Texas | August 9, 1864 | Co. No. 1, 2nd Front. Dist. |
| Near Jacksboro, Texas | August 18, 1864 | Det., 1st Front. Dist. |
| Beans Creek, Texas | September 3, 1864 | Pvts. P. P. (or J.) Brown, A. Coker, T. R. Simpson, & D. S. Howell (Co. H, Border Reg.) |
| Salt Creek Prairie, Young County, Texas | September 13, 1864 | 2nd Lt. W. R. Peveler's Det. G, Front. Reg. |
| Bragg Ranch, Young County, Texas | October 13, 1864 | Lt. N. Carson's Det. D, Border Reg. |
| Camp Roff, Indian Territory | January 6, 1865 | Sgt. J. C. Jones' Det. G, Border Reg. |
| Montague County, Texas | January 7, 1865 | Lt. J. S. O'Neal's Det. E, Border Reg. |
| Dove Creek, Texas | January 8, 1865 | Front. Btn.; Co. D, G, and H, Front. Reg.; Cureton's Co., 1st Front. Dist.; Gillintine's Co., Cunningham's Co., Barnes' Co., Graham's Co., Culver's Co., Cathey's Co., 2nd Front. Dist. |
| Sabinal Canyon, Texas | ? | Lt. B. Patton's Det. G, Front. Reg. |
| Near Springtown, Texas | June 29, 1866 | 2nd Parker County Co. |
| Near Leona River, Texas | December 5, 1870 | Dr. S. E. Woodbridge's Det. E, Front. Forces |
| Blanco Creek, Texas | December 6, 1870 | Pvts. W. Richarz and J. R. Riff (Co. E, Front. Forces) |

## Appendix A

| Site of Battle | Date | Unit(s) Involved |
|---|---|---|
| ? | January 23, 1871 | Co. P, Front. Forces |
| Paradise Prairie, Wise County, Texas | February 7, 1871 | Sgt. E. H. Cobb's Det. F, Front. Forces |
| Starr County, Texas | April 21, 1871 | Co. G, Front. Forces |
| Palo Pinto County, Texas | May 4, 1871 | Sgt. R. V. Parker's Det. B, Front. Forces |
| ? | August 17, 1872 | Co. I, Minute Men |
| Coleman County, Texas | September 24, 1873 | Sgt. B. F. Beck's Det. L, Minute Men |
| Coleman County, Texas | January 24, 1874 | Lt. J. M. Elkins' Det. L, Minute Men |
| Palo Pinto County, Texas | January 29, 1874 | Palo Pinto County Rangers |
| Brown County, Texas | March 27, 1874 | Sgt. J. J. Carter's Det. G, Minute Men |
| Near Red River, Texas | May 7, 1874 | Capt. E. F. Ikard's Det. C |
| Comanche County, Texas | May 30, 1874 | Capt. J. R. Waller's Det. A |
| Comanche County, Texas | June 9, 1874 | Lt. J. W. Millican's Det. A |
| Big Wichita River, Archer County, Texas | July 9, 1874 | Cpl. J. W. Newman's Det. B |
| Lost Valley, Jack County, Texas | July 10, 1874 | Co. C, Kendall County Minute Men |
| Lost Valley, Jack County, Texas | July 12, 1874 | Maj. J. B. Jones' escort and Co. B |
| Clear Fork of the Brazos River, Texas | July 25, 1874 | Pvt. M. T. Israel's Det. F |
| Coleman County, Texas | October 3, 1874 | Sgt. M. T. Israel's Det. F |
| Near Clinton, Texas | August 6, 1874 | Det. A, Washington County Vol. Mil. |
| El Paso County, Texas | September 15, 1874 | El Paso County Co. |
| Shackelford County, Texas | November 17, 1874 | Lt. J. W. Millican's Det. A |
| Near Brownwood, Texas | November 18, 1874 | Lt. B. F. Best's Det. E |
| Mason County, Texas | November 21, 1874 | Lt. D. W. Roberts' Det. D; Lt. L. P. Beavert's det., Maj. J. B. Jones' escort |
| Between the South Concho and Pecos Rivers, Texas | November 23, 1874 | Co. D |
| Young County, Texas | December 1, 1874 | Young County Minute Men |
| Kerr County, Texas | February 24, 1875 | Kerr County Minute Men |
| Fredericksburg road, Mason County, Texas | February 18, 1875 | Lt. D. W. Roberts (Co. D) |
| Rock Creek, Lost Valley, Jack County, Texas | May 8, 1875 | Maj. J. B. Jones' escort and Lt. I. Long's Det. B |
| Palo Alto Prairie, Cameron County, Texas | June 12, 1875 | Co. A, Washington County Vol. Mil. |
| Big Lake, Texas | August 25, 1875 | Lt. D. W. Roberts' Det. D |
| Guadalupe Mountains, Texas | September 1875 | El Paso County Co. |
| Eagle Mountains, Texas | November 13?, 1875 | El Paso County Co. |
| Rancho Cachattus (or Las Cucharas), Tamaulipas, Mexico | November 19, 1875 | Co. A, Washington County Vol. Mil. |
| Las Cuevas, Tamaulipas, Mexico | November 19, 1875 | Co. A, Washington County Vol. Mil. |
| Las Cuevas crossing of the Rio Grande, Tamaulipas, Mexico | November 19, 1875 | Co. A, Washington County Vol. Mil. |

| Site of Battle | Date | Unit(s) Involved |
|---|---|---|
| Near Little Devil's River, Texas | December 1875 | Lt. C. V. Coldwell's Det. F |
| Rincón de Perro Ranch, Cameron County, Texas | December 28, 1875 | Lt. T. C. Robinson's Det. A, Washington County Vol. Mil. |
| Kerr County, Texas | January 1876 | _____ Watson's det., Kerr County Minute Men |
| Kerr County, Texas | January 15, 1876 | Cpl. — Watson's det, Kerr County Minute Men |
| Dog Cañon, New Mexico Territory | April 18, 1876 | El Paso County Co. |
| El Sabinito Rancho, Zapata County, Texas | May 17, 1876 | Co. A, Washington County Vol. Mil. |
| Near Colorado River, Texas | July 11, 1876 | Lt. B. S. Foster's Det. E |
| Espinoza Lake near Carrizo Springs, Texas | October 1, 1876 | Sgt. J. B. Armstrong's det., Spec. State Troops |
| Whaley Ranch, Dimmit County, Texas | October 1, 1876 | Cpl. M. H. Williams' det., Spec. State Troops |
| Mayfield Ranch, Wilson County, Texas | December 7, 1876 | Sgt. J. B. Armstrong and Pvt. T. W. Deggs (Spec. State Troops) |
| Near San Antonio, Texas | December 20, 1876 | Cpl. M. H. Williams' det., Spec. State Troops |
| Potter Ranch, Menard County, Texas | January 18, 1877 | Cpl. J. B. Gillett's Det. E |
| Hays County, Texas | February 2, 1877 | Pvt. W. T. Davis' det., Spec. State Troops |
| Devil's River, Texas | March 25, 1877 | Lt. P. Dolan's Det. F |
| Near Nuevo Laredo, Mexico | April 1877? | Capt. D. W. Roberts' Det. D |
| Pensacola, Florida | August 23, 1877 | 2nd Lt. J. B. Armstrong (Spec. State Troops) |
| Middle Oak Creek, Texas | September 15, 1877 | Pvt. T. M. Sparks (Co. C) |
| San Elizario, Texas | December 13–16, 1877 | Lt. J. B. Tays' Det. C |
| Little Saline Creek, Menard County, Texas | December 25, 1877 | Det. E |
| Near Fort McKavett, Texas | January 2, 1878 | Co. A |
| Llano River, Menard County, Texas | February 1878 | Lt. N. O. Reynolds' Det. E |
| Llano River, Kimble County, Texas | Spring 1878 | Lt. N. O. Reynolds' Det. E |
| Salt Creek, Wise County, Texas | June 13, 1878 | Capt. J. Peak's Det. B |
| Round Rock, Texas | July 19, 1878 | Maj. J. B. Jones (HQ) and Pvts. R. C. Ware, C. R. Connor, and G. Harrell (Co. E) |
| Las Cornudas, El Paso County, Texas | August 10, 1878 | Lt. J. B. Tays' Det. C |
| Near the Pease River, Texas | January 15, 1879 | Co. C |
| Kimble County, Texas | Spring 1879 | Det. D |
| ? | June 11, 1879 | Co. B |
| Five Wells, Texas | June 12, 1879 | Co. B |
| Head of the North Concho River, Texas | June 28–29, 1879 | Cpl. Y. Douglas' Det. B |
| Head of the North Concho River, Texas | July 1, 1879 | Cpl. Y. Douglas' Det. B |
| Near Dublin Farm, Menard County, Texas | August 1879 | Cpl. H. T. Ashburn's Det. D |
| Sierra Bentano near Guadalupe, Mexico | October 6, 1879 | Lt. G. W. Baylor's Det. C |

## APPENDIX A

| Site of Battle | Date | Unit(s) Involved |
|---|---|---|
| Wolfe City, Atascosa County, Texas | November 1879 | Capt. J. L. Hall's det., Spec. Force |
| El Sauz Division, King Ranch, Willacy County, Texas | February 26, 1880 | Cpl. C. B. McKinney and Pvt. W. O. Tompkins (Spec. Force) |
| Sauz Creek, La Salle County, Texas | March 29, 1880 | Cpl. C. B. McKinney (Spec. Force) |
| Presidio Del Norte, Texas | July 3, 1880 | Sgt. E. A. Sieker's Det. D; Sgt. L. B. Caruthers (Co. E) |
| Near Pope's Wells and the Horsehead Crossing of the Pecos River Texas | October 8, 1880 | Sgt. R. G. Kimball's Det. D |
| Sierra Diablo, Texas | January 29, 1881 | Co. A and E |
| Colorado City, Texas | May 16, 1881 | Cpl. J. M. Sedberry, Pvts. J. D. Milton and L. B. Wells (Co. B) |
| Eagle Pass, Texas | Spring 1882 | Pvts. L. S. Delony and S. Adams |
| Ranger, Texas | April 20, 1882 | Cpl. J. McNelly's Det. B |
| Toyah, Texas | July 18, 1883 | Three unknown Rangers |
| Gonzales, Texas | January 1, 1884 | 2nd Lt. W. L. Rudd (Co. F) |
| San Angelo-Abeline stage road, Texas | February 4, 1884 | Sgt. L. S. Turnbo (Co. A) |
| Wichita Falls, Texas | March 27, 1884 | Capt. G. H. Schmitt's Det. C |
| On Rio Grande, Texas | May 1884 | Det. D |
| Near Cotulla, Texas | May 9, 1884 | Pvts. S. V. Edwards & A. L. Shely (Co. F) |
| Near Mexan Springs, Texas | June 5, 1884 | Cpl. C. H. Fusselman (Co. D) |
| Near Uvalde, Texas | June 29, 1884 | Det. D |
| Green Lake, Texas | July 28, 1884 | Cpl. P. C. Baird's Det. D |
| Near San Ambrosia Creek, Maverick County, Texas | May 31, 1885 | Cpl. B. D. Lindsey, Pvts. C. W. Griffin, F. E. Sieker, I. Aten, and B. C. Riley (Co. D) |
| Toyah, Texas | August 18, 1885 | 1st Sgt. L. F. Cartwright, Cpl. W. S. Hughes, Pvts. F. W. DeJarnette and T. P. Nigh (Co. E) |
| Alex, Indian Territory | May 19, 1886 | Sgt. J. A. Brooks & Pvt. H. Putz (Co. F) |
| Baugh Ranch, Brown County, Texas | November 9, 1886 | Capt. W. A. Scott, Sgt. J. A. Brooks, Pvts. J. Carmichael, W. Treadwell, and J. H. Rogers (Co. F) and I. Aten (Co. D) |
| Twohig, Texas | January 17, 1887 | Capt. G. H. Schmitt, Sgt. A. C. Grimes and Pvt. J. W. Durbin (Co. C) |
| On the Sabine River near Hemphill, Texas | March 31, 1887 | Capt. W. Scott, Sgt. J. A. Brooks, Pvts. J. H. Rogers, W. Treadwell, J. Carmichael, and J. H. Moore (Co. F) |
| Burnet-Williamson county line, Texas | April 1887 | Cpl. I. Aten (Co. D) |
| Liberty Hill, Texas | June 1887 | Cpl. I. Aten (Co. D) |
| Texas Panhandle | July 1887 | Cpl. I. Aten (Co. D) |
| San Angelo, Texas | October 5, 1887 | Cpl. J. H. Rogers and unknown Ranger (Co. F) |
| Sabine County, Texas | October 25, 1887 | Unknown Rangers |
| Mitchell County, Texas | March 6, 1888 | Cpl. J. H. Rogers (Co. F) |

| Site of Battle | Date | Unit(s) Involved |
|---|---|---|
| Shafter, Texas | 1889 | Cpl. J. R. Hughes and Pvt. A. V. Oden (Co. D) |
| Maxan Springs, near Marathon, Texas | June 5, 1889 | Cpl. C. H. Fusselman (Co. D) |
| Richmond, Texas | August 16, 1889 | Sgt. I. Aten, Pvts. A. McNabb and F. L. Schmid (Co. D) |
| Near Vance, Texas | December 25, 1889 | Cpl. J. R. Hughes, Pvts. C. G. Aten and B. L. Outlaw (Co. D) |
| Franklin Mountains, Texas | April 17, 1890 | Sgt. C. H. Fusselman (Co. D) |
| Shafter, Texas | August 4, 1890 | Pvt. J. F. Gravis (Co. D) |
| Glass Mountains near Marathon, Texas | January 31, 1891 | Pvts. J. M. Putman and T. T. Cook (Co. D) |
| Realitos, Texas | September 1891 | Det. E |
| Encinal County, Texas | September 26, 1891 | Pvts. J. Natus & T. Harris (Co. F) |
| Near Howard's Well, Texas | October 10, 1891 | Co. D |
| La Granjenita Ranch, Starr County, Texas | December 29, 1891 | Det. E |
| La Havana Ranch, Starr County, Texas | January 6, 1892 | Co. E and Co. F |
| Near Shafter, Texas | January 12, 1892 | Cpl. J. R. Hughes and Pvt. A. V. Oden (Co. D) |
| Lower Rio Grande Valley, Texas | March 20, 1892 | Co. E |
| Near Bennett Ranch, Starr County, Texas | March 22, 1892 | Co. E |
| Lower Rio Grande Valley, Texas | March 26, 1892 | Pvt. D. L. Musgrave (Co. F) |
| Lower Rio Grande Valley, Texas | March 30, 1892 | Sgt. J. H. Rogers (Co. F) |
| Near Caudalorio, Presidio County, Texas | June 22, 1892 | Cpl. J. R. Hughes, Pvts. A. V. Oden and J. M. Putman (Co. D) |
| Live Oak County, Texas | November 22, 1892 | Pvts. G. Bigford and C. L. Rogers (Co. F) |
| Beeville, Texas | 1893 | Pvt. C. L. Rogers and unknown Ranger (Co. E) |
| Tres Jacales, "Pirate Island," Mexico | June 29, 1893 | Co. D |
| Langtry, Texas | July 22, 1893 | Sgt. D. L. Musgrave and Pvt. R. C. Lewis (Co. F) |
| Quanah, Texas | December 9, 1893 | Capt. W. J. McDonald (Co. B) |
| El Paso, Texas | April 5, 1894 | Pvt. J. W. McKidrict (Co. D) |
| Near Bellevue, Clay County, Texas | November 17, 1894 | Sgt. W. J. L. Sullivan, Pvts. W. J. McCauley, J. M. Wise, D. Neely, J. Harwell, and B. D. McClure (Co. B) |
| Greer County, Texas | December 28, 1895 | Sgt. W. J. L. Sullivan, Pvts. W. J. McCauley, B. D. McClure, J. Harwell, and L. Queen, and Special Ranger B. Hardin (Co. B) |
| Bajitas, Texas | March 1896 | Capt. J. R. Hughes' Det. D |
| Reeves County, Texas | August 16, 1896 | Sgt. L. F. Cartwright (Co. F) |
| Nogalitos Pass, Davis Mountains, Texas | September 28, 1896 | Capt. J. R. Hughes, Sgt. T. T. Cook, and Pvt. R. E. Bryant (Co. D) |
| Uvalde County, Texas | July 7, 1897 | Pvt. J. W. Moore (Co. F) |
| Socorro, New Mexico Territory | August 20, 1898 | Pvt. E. St. Leon (Co. D) |
| San Saba, Texas | November 3, 1898 | Pvt. D. S. Barker (Co. B) |

| Site of Battle | Date | Unit(s) Involved |
|---|---|---|
| Laredo, Texas | March 20, 1899 | Capt. J. H. Rogers, Sgt. H. G. Dubose, Pvts. A. Y. Old, C. Taylor, W. L. Wright, W. A. Old, and Special Rangers T. Ragland and O. N. Wright (Co. E) |
| Sonora, Texas | November 8, 1899 | Sgt. H. G. Dubose's Det. E |
| Orange County, Texas | December 21, 1899 | Pvt. T. L. Fuller (Co. B) |
| Smither Ranch, Duval County, Texas | March 21, 1900 | Sgt. W. B. Bates' Det. F |
| Well's Pasture, Texas | September 9, 1900 | Co. A |
| Orange, Texas | October 15, 1900 | Lt. T. L. Fuller (Co. B) |
| Cotulla, Texas | October 24, 1900 | Lt. W. L. Wright (Co. E) |
| Palito Blanco, Texas | August 19, 1901 | Sgt. A. Y. Baker and Pvt. A. W. Livingston (Co. A) |
| Hidalgo County, Texas | December 31, 1901 | Pvts. F. Layton and H. Wallis (Co. A) |
| El Sauz Ranch, Cameron County, Texas | May 16, 1902 | Sgt. A. Y. Baker's Det. A |
| Near Brownsville, Texas | September 9, 1902 | Sgt. A. Y. Baker and Pvts. J. A. Miller and E. Robuck (Co. A) |
| Near Brownsville, Texas | October 3, 1902 | Sgts. A. Y. Baker (Co. A) |
| El Paso, Texas | December 1903 | Pvt. J. B. Bean (Co. B) |
| Polk County, Texas | January 1904 | Capt. W. J. McDonald (Co. B) |
| Los Hermanos Ranch, Webb County, Texas | January 1904 | Pvt. L. Tumlinson (Co. A) |
| Halff Ranch, Gaines County, Texas | July 17, 1904 | Capt. J. H. Rogers (Co. C) |
| Near Terlingua, Texas | September 13, 1905 | Pvt. T. J. Goff (Co. C) |
| Between Sam Fordyce and Rio Grande City, Texas | | November 8, 1906   Co. B |
| Near Del Rio, Texas | December 1, 1906 | Capt. J. H. Rogers, Pvts. F. A. Hamer and R. M. Hudson (Co. C) |
| Weatherford, Texas | February 4, 1908 | Pvt. H. White (Co. A) |
| Amarillo, Texas | January 6, 1909 | Co. A |
| Trinity County, Texas | September 5, 1909 | Capt. J. H. Rogers, Pvts. G. White, M. E. Bailey, and H. Avriett (Co. C) |
| Harlingen, Texas | May 28, 1910 | Pvt. G. T. Jones (Co. A) |
| Navasota, Texas | July 17, 1910 | Pvt. H. Avriett (Co. C) |
| Near Navasota, Texas | July 18, 1910 | Pvt. H. Avriett (Co. C) |
| Near San Benito, Texas | July 31, 1910 | Pvts. Q. B. Carnes and J. P. N. Craighead (Co. D) |
| San Benito, Texas | October 1, 1910 | Pvt. J. P. N. Craighead (Co. D) |
| Calero, Texas | October 11, 1911 | Pvt. H. L. Roberson (Co. A) |
| Brownsville, Texas | November 10, 1912 | Capt. J. J. Sanders, Pvts. R. C. Hawkins and J. J. Jenkins (Co. B) |
| Pirate Island, Texas | January 29, 1913 | Pvts. C. R. Moore and C. H. Webster (Co. A) |
| Near Marfa, Texas | April 1, 1913 | Pvts. J. E. Vaughan and (Co. B) |
| Near El Paso, Texas | April 22, 1913 | Pvt. G. S. Russell (Co. A) |
| Near El Paso, Texas | June 23, 1913 | Co. A |
| Near Marathon, Texas | June 14, 1913 | Pvts. R. E. Speed and R. C. Hawkins (Co. B) |

| Site of Battle | Date | Unit(s) Involved |
|---|---|---|
| Ysleta, Texas | April 25, 1914 | Pvt. G. C. Webb (Co. A) |
| Marfa, Texas | July 2, 1914 | Sgt. H. L. Roberson and Pvt. I. W. Cline (Co. A) |
| Near Boquillas, Texas | May 1915 | Pvt. W. F. Bates (Co. B) |
| Near Norias, Texas | May 22, 1915 | Pvts. J. B. Brooks and W. T. Moseley (Co. A) |
| Pilares Canyon, Texas | May 24, 1915 | Pvts. H. C. Trollinger, E. B. Hulen and A. P. Cummings (Co. B) |
| Pilares, Texas | June 1915 | Pvts. A. P. Cummings and S. M. Jester (Co. B) |
| Fabens, Texas | June 7, 1915 | Pvts. R. L. Burdett and C. P. Beall (Co. B) |
| Paso Real on the Arroyo Colorado, Texas | August 7, 1915 | Capt. H. L. Ransom, Sgt. J. L. Anders, Pvts. C. W Price and J. Taylor (Co. D) |
| Norias Division, King Ranch, Willacy County, Texas | August 29, 1915 | Unknown Ranger (Co. A) |
| Madero Crossing, Hidalgo County, Texas | September 4, 1915 | Sgt. J. L. Anders' Det. D |
| McAllen Ranch, Hidalgo County, Texas | September 24, 1915 | Capt. H. L. Ransom's Det. D |
| Tandy Station, Cameron County, Texas | October 19, 1915 | Capt. H. L. Ransom's Det. D |
| Pilares Canyon, Texas | May 24, 1916 | Det. B |
| Near Fabens, Texas | July 1916 | Pvts. J. B. Swift and W. B. Sands (Co. B) |
| Del Rio, Texas | September 9, 1916 | Pvt. W. L. Barler (Co. C) |
| El Paso, Texas | September 21, 1916 | Pvt. W. B. Sands (Co. B) |
| Sweetwater, Texas | October 1, 1917 | Sgt. F. A. Hamer (Co. C) |
| Candelaria Rim, Brite Ranch, Presidio County, Texas | December 25, 1917 | Det. B |
| San José, Mexico | December 30, 1917 | Co. M |
| Brite Ranch, Texas | January 28, 1918 | Pvt. A. H. Woelber (Co. B) |
| Porvenir, Texas | January 28, 1918 | Pvt. B. Weaver's Det. B |
| El Pourveni, Texas | March 1918 | Co. B |
| El Javali Ranch, Starr County, Texas | March 8, 1918 | Capt. W. L. Wright, Pvts. S. S. Hutchison, T. N. Pullin, W. C. Wells, M. Wells, and J. P. Perkins (Co. K) |
| Near Fabens, Texas | March 23, 1918 | Pvts. T. E. P. Perkins, F. A. Black, and B. L. Pennington (Co. L) |
| Near Rio Grande in Chihuahua, Mexico | April 3, 1918 | Co. F |
| Rio Grande near Santa Helena, Texas | April 4, 1918 | Co. F |
| Santa Helena, Texas | April 7, 1918 | Co. F |
| Tomate Bend near Fort Brown, Texas | August 21, 1918 | Pvt. J. R. Shaw and unknown Ranger (Co. G) |
| Piper Plantation, Texas | August 24, 1918 | Det. G |
| Los Saenz Ranch near Rio Grande City, Texas | October 6, 1918 | Sgt. J. J. Edds (Co. K) |
| Tomate Bend near Fort Brown, Texas | October 10, 1918 | Capt. W. W. Taylor, Sgt. D. Timberlake and Pvt. F. A. Hamer (Co. F) |

| Site of Battle | Date | Unit(s) Involved |
|---|---|---|
| Near Anaya Ranch, Texas | November 7, 1918 | Pvt. T. E. P. Perkins (Co. L) and Special Ranger J. T. Place |
| Calero, Texas | December 2, 1918 | Pvt. H. L. Roberson (Co. A) |
| Ranger, Texas | December 20, 1918 | Pvts. J. R. Bloxman and J. B. Nalls (Co. C) |
| Near Austin, Texas | February 7, 1919 | Capt K. F. Cunningham (Co. M) and Pvt. B. C. Veale (Co. D) |
| Brownsville, Texas | June 1919 | Capt. W. L. Wright |
| Crestonia, Texas | December 9, 1919 | Co. I |
| Near Presidio, Texas | January 1920 | Pvts. P. F. Dyches and B. H. Woodland (Co. A) |
| Near Redford (Polvo), Texas | March 30, 1920 | Pvt. E. B. McClure (Co. A) |
| Rio Grande between Comstock and Del Rio, Texas | May 10, 1920 | Pvt. N. B. Jones (Co. F) |
| Near Concepcion, Texas | September 21, 1920 | Co. D |
| Ranger, Texas | November 24, 1920 | Pvts. M. N. Koonsman and M. T. Gonzaullas (HQ Co.) |
| Near Uvalde, Texas | December 12, 1920 | Co. F |
| Bradley's Corner, Texas | January 5, 1921 | Pvt. J. W. McCormick (HQ Co.) |
| Near Laredo, Texas | January 6, 1921 | Capt. W. W. Ryan's Det. C |
| Rio Grande in La Salle County, Texas | September 1921 | Sgt. J. J. Edds and Pvt. J. Pérez (Co. D) |
| Colorado Chiquita, Texas | November 17, 1921 | Capt. W. L. Wright's Det. D |
| Brunei, Texas | November 18, 1921 | Capt. W. L. Wright's Det. D |
| Barreneña Ranch, Duval County, Texas | November 22, 1921 | Capt. W. L. Wright's Det. D |
| Polvo, Texas | December 25, 1921 | Co. A |
| Mexia, Texas | January 7, 1922 | Capt. T. R. Hickman's Det. B |
| Near Laredo, Texas | November 18, 1922 | Capt. W. L. Wright's Det. D |
| Las Animas Ranch, Jim Hogg County, Texas | December 18, 1922 | Capt. W. L. Wright's Det. D |
| Freeman-Hampton, Texas | July 21, 1923 | Pvt. M. N. Koonsman (Co. B) |
| Near Glen Rose, Texas | August 26, 1923 | Pvt. M. Burton (Co. B) |
| Near Boquillas, Texas | May 14, 1924 | Pvts. J. A. Miller and R. Miller (Co. A) |
| Duval County, Texas | November 15, 1924 | Capt. W. L. Wright's Det. D |
| Near Hebbronville, Texas | July 5, 1925 | Capt. W. W. Ryan's Det. D |
| Dallas, Texas | August 13, 1925 | Pvt. M. T. Gonzaullas (Co. B) |
| Near Marshall, Texas | December 29, 1925 | Pvts. H. D. Glasscock and C. M. Ezell (Co. C) |
| Clarksville, Texas | September 9, 1926 | Capt. T. R. Hickman (HQ Co.) |
| Lower Rio Grande Valley | January 1926 | Pvts. J. W. Sadler and J. W. Smith (Co. D) |
| Near South Bend, Texas | December 27, 1927 | Pvt. C. Bradford (Co. B) |
| Grayson County, Texas | April 19, 1928 | Special Ranger T. S. Willard |
| Gladewater, Texas | July 7, 1931 | Pvt. D. L. McDuffie (Co. C) |
| Near New London, Texas | September 2, 1931 | Pvt. T. Tarver (Co. A) |
| Austin, Texas | July 3, 1933 | Pvt. W. S. Byars (HQ Co.) |
| Waco, Texas | July 11, 1933 | Co. C |
| Near Marfa, Texas | August 1934 | Pvt. W. F. Hale (Co. A) |

| Site of Battle | Date | Unit(s) Involved |
|---|---|---|
| Gladewater, Texas | January 25, 1943 | Capt. M. T. Gonzaullas, Rangers R. Oldham and R. L. Badgett (Co. B) |
| Houston, Texas | June 1943 | Rangers J. J. Klevenhagen and E. Oliver (Co. A) |
| Galveston, Texas | Late 1945 | Ranger J. J. Klevenhagen (Co. A) |
| Near Burkburnett, Texas | January 27, 1948 | Ranger J. Geer (Co. B) |
| Brazos River near Ramsey State Prison Farm, Brazoria County, Texas | ? | Ranger J. J. Klevenhagen (Co. A) |
| Limestone County, Texas | May 15, 1955 | Capt. C. T. Peoples (HQ Co.), Capt. R. A. Crowder and Ranger J. L. Rogers (Co. B) |
| Green Mountain near Yegua Creek, Burleson County, Texas | July 7, 1956 | Capt. J. J. Klevenhagen (Co. A) |
| Groesbeck, Texas | March 31, 1957 | Capt. C. T. Peoples (HQ Co.) and Capt. J. J. Klevenhagen (Co. A) |
| Walnut Creek near Springtown, Texas | April 29, 1957 | Capt. J. J. Klevenhagen (Co. A) and Capt. E. J. Banks (Co. B) |
| Waco, Texas | May 3, 1958 | Capt. C. T. Peoples (Co. F) |
| Houston, Texas | May 23, 1962 | Ranger E. D. Gooding (Co. A) |
| Catarina, Texas | December 6, 1967 | Ranger R. C. Favor (Co. D) |
| Highway 259 near Daingerfield, Texas | October 22, 1968 | Capt. R. A. Crowder and Ranger R. K. Mitchell (Co. B) |
| Carrizo Springs, Texas | April 3, 1969 | Capt. A. Y. Allee, Sr., Rangers H. J. Jackson, T. Dawson (Co. D), and A. Y. Allee, Jr. (Co. A) |
| Atascosa County, Texas | ? | Sgt. H. R. Block, Rangers D. H. North, G. B. Krueger, G. Kea and H. J. Jackson (Co. D) |
| Rio Bravo, Texas | ? | Ranger W. Russell (Co. D) |
| Alpine, Texas | ? | Ranger H. J. Jackson (Co. D) |
| ? | ? | Ranger J. Harrison (Co. D) |
| Dallas, Texas | December 20, 1970 | Rangers G. Elliott, R. K. Mitchell, R. M. Arnold, and M. V. Womack (Co. B) |
| Near Pittsburgh, Texas | June 15, 1971 | Ranger R. M. Arnold (Co. B) |
| Southlake, Texas | October 14, 1971 | Ranger T. E. Arnold (Co. B) |
| Huntsville State Penitentiary, Walker County, Texas | August 2, 1974 | Capt. J. F. Rogers and Sgt. J. Krumnow (Co. A), Capt. G. W. Burks (Co. B), et. al. |
| Argyle, Texas | February 21, 1978 | Ranger B. P. Doherty (Co. B) |
| Wichita Falls, Texas | May 19, 1983 | Sgt. W. R. Gerth (Co. C) |
| Near Mount Pleasant, Texas | January 13, 1985 | Rangers J. E. Ray and J. F. Wilie (Co. F) |
| Saltillo, Texas | January 13, 1985 | Rangers H. P. Alfred, J. L. Waldrip, and J. Dendy (Co. F) |
| Horseshoe Bay, Texas | February 22, 1987 | Sgts. S. K. Guffey and J. E. Aycock (Co. F) |
| Waco, Texas | September 11, 1995 | Sgt. W. M. Cawthon (Co. F) |
| Davis Mountains, Texas | May 5, 1997 | Sgt. G. Kea (Co. E) |
| Sulphur Springs, Texas | January 6, 1998 | Sgt. D. V. Rhea (Co. B) |

# Appendix B: Rangers Who Died in the Line of Duty

## For the Common Defense: Rangers of Colonial Tejas

| Name/Rank/Unit | Date | Site of Death |
|---|---|---|
| Hornsby, Moses S., Pvt. (Goheen's Co., Moore's 1835 Expedition)<br>*Killed by friendly fire* | September 1, 1835 | Near the Brazos River, Texas |
| Williams, John, Pvt. (Coleman's Co.) | July 11, 1835 | Tawakoni village near Tehuacana Springs and the Brazos River, Texas |

## Gained by War: Rangers of the Revolution and Republic

| Name/Rank/Unit | Date | Site of Death |
|---|---|---|
| Anderson, Joseph S., Pvt. (Lewis' Co.) | July 15, 1839 | Battle Creek, Texas |
| Bailey, Jesse, Pvt. (Co. B, Smith's Btn) | May 6, 1837 | Post Oak Springs, Texas |
| Baker, Isaac G., Pvt. (Kimbell's Co.) | March 6, 1836 | The Alamo, San Antonio de Béxar, Texas |
| Barton, Hale, Pvt. (Bryant's Co.) | January 16, 1839 | Near Morgan's Point, Texas |
| Bird, John, Capt (Bird's Co.) | May 26, 1839 | Bird's Creek, Texas |
| Blair, Jesse, Pvt. (Bowyer's Co.) | November 10, 1837 | "Stone Houses Fight" near the headwaters of the West Fork of the Trinity River, Texas |
| Bostwick, Alexander, Pvt. | November 10, 1837 | "Stone Houses Fight" near the headwaters of the West Fork of the Trinity River, Texas |
| Bullock, Julius, Pvt. (Brown's Co.) | October 12, 1838 | East of Fort Houston, Texas |
| Cain, John, Pvt. (Kimbell's Co.) | March 6, 1836 | The Alamo, SanAntonio de Béxar, Texas |
| Carpenter, John W., Pvt. (Brown's Co.) | October 12, 1838 | East of Fort Houston, Texas |
| Childers, Francis, Pvt. (Co. A, Btn. Mtd. Rifles) | January 7, 1837 | Elm Creek on the Brazos River, Texas |
| Christian, James, Pvt. (Bowyer's Co.) | November 10, 1837 | "Stone Houses Fight" near the headwaters of the West Fork of the Trinity River, Texas |
| Clark, David, Pvt. (Co. A, Btn. Mtd. Rifles) | January 7, 1837 | Elm Creek on the Brazos River, |

| Name/Rank/Unit | Date | Site of Death |
|---|---|---|
| | | Texas |
| Clubb, David (or Samuel), Pvt. (Sloan's det., Red River militiamen) | December 1841 | Elm Fork of the Trinity River, Texas |
| Cooper, Joseph, Pvt. (Bowyer's Co.) | November 10, 1837 | "Stone Houses Fight" near the headwaters of the West Fork of the Trinity River, Texas |
| Coryell, James, Pvt. (Co. A, Btn. Mtd. Rifles) | May 27, 1836 | Near Perry's Creek, Texas |
| Cottle, George W., Pvt. (Kimbell's Co.) | March 6, 1836 | The Alamo, San Antonio de Béxar, Texas |
| Crane, John, Pvt. (Harrison's Co.) | July 15, 1839 | Battle Creek, Texas |
| Crowson, Henry P., Pvt. (Harrison's Co.) DOW | July 15, 1839 | Battle Creek, Texas |
| Cullins, Aaron, Pvt. (Co. B, Btn. Mtd. Rifles) | May 6, 1837 | Post Oak Springs, Texas |
| Cummings, David P., Pvt. (Kimbell's Co.) | March 6, 1836 | The Alamo, San Antonio de Béxar, Texas |
| Darst, Jacob C., Pvt. (Kimbell's Co.) | March 6, 1836 | The Alamo, San Antonio de Béxar, Texas |
| Davis, John, Pvt. (Kimbell's Co.) | March 6, 1836 | The Alamo, San Antonio de Béxar, Texas |
| Daymon, Squire, Pvt. (Kimbell's Co.) | March 6, 1836 | The Alamo, San Antonio de Béxar, Texas |
| Dearduff, William, Pvt. (Kimbell's Co.) | March 6, 1836 | The Alamo, San Antonio de Béxar, Texas |
| Denton, John B., Pvt. (Bourland's Co.) | May 24, 1841 | Village Creek, Texas |
| Despallier, Charles, Pvt. (Kimbell's Co.) | March 6, 1836 | The Alamo, San Antonio de Béxar, Texas |
| Dorsey, L., Vol. (Bryant's Co.) | January 16, 1839 | Near Morgan's Point, Texas |
| Duvalt, Andrew, Pvt. (Kimbell's Co.) | March 6, 1836 | The Alamo, San Antonio de Béxar, Texas |
| Earle, John J., Pvt. (Co. G, 1st Mtd. Gunmen) | November 11, 1839 | Richland Creek, Texas |
| Eaton, Alfred P. Vol. (Bryant's Co.) | January 16, 1839 | Near Morgan's Point, Texas |
| Ewing, John, Pvt. (Harrison's Co., Mabbitt's Btn.) DOW | July 16, 1839 | Neches River, Texas |
| Farmer, David M., Pvt. (Co. B, Btn. Mtd. Rifles) | May 6, 1837 | Post Oak Springs, Texas |
| Fishbaugh, William, Pvt. (Kimbell's Co.) | March 6, 1836 | The Alamo, San Antonio de Béxar, Texas |
| Flanders, John, Pvt. (Kimbell's Co.) | March 6, 1836 | The Alamo, San Antonio de Béxar, Texas |
| Floyd, Dolphin W., Pvt. (Kimbell's Co.) | March 6, 1836 | The Alamo, San Antonio de Béxar, Texas |
| Fohr, Peter, Pvt. (Hays' Co.) | June 8, 1844 | Walker Creek, Texas |
| Fullerton, William, Vol. (Bryant's Co.) | January 16, 1839 | Near Morgan's Point, Texas |
| Fuqua, Galba, Pvt. (Kimbell's Co.) | March 6, 1836 | The Alamo, San Antonio de Béxar, Texas |
| Garvin, John E., Pvt. (Kimbell's Co.) | March 6, 1836 | The Alamo, San Antonio de Béxar, Texas |
| Gaston, John E., Pvt. (Kimbell's Co.) | March 6, 1836 | The Alamo, San Antonio de Béxar, |

## Appendix B

| Name/Rank/Unit | Date | Site of Death |
|---|---|---|
| | | Texas |
| Gay, Thomas, Pvt. (Evan's Co.) | June 26, 1839 | Bird's Creek, Texas |
| George, James, Pvt. (Kimbell's Co.) | March 6, 1836 | The Alamo, San Antonio de Béxar, Texas |
| Haigwood, Henry, Vol. (Bryant's Co.) | January 16, 1839 | Near Morgan's Point, Texas |
| Hall, H. M. C., Pvt. (Bird's Co.)<br>*DOW inflicted June 26, 1839 — died at Fort Smith* | June 27, 1839 | Bird's Creek, Texas |
| Hall, James, Pvt. (Bradshaw's Co., Mabbitt's Btn.)<br>*DOW inflicted October 16, 1838-died at Fort Houston* | December 17, 1838 | Kickapoo Creek, Texas |
| Harrell, Garrett, Pvt. (Rabb's Co.)<br>*Choked to death* | October 19, 1840 | Camp Rabb, Texas |
| Heard, George W., Pvt. (Chandler's Co.) | August 22, 1841 | Near Franklin, Texas |
| Hughes, John, Vol. (Co. B, Btn. Mtd. Rifles) | May 6, 1837 | Post Oak Springs, Texas |
| Jackson, Thomas, Pvt. (Kimbell's Co.) | March 6, 1836 | The Alamo, San Antonio de Béxar, Texas |
| Jett, Stephen, Pvt. (Hays' Co.) | September 18, 1842 | Salado Creek, Texas |
| Joslen, James, Pvt. (Bowyer's Co.) | November 10, 1837 | Stone Houses Fight" near the headwaters of the West Fork of the Trinity River, Texas |
| Kellogg, John B., Pvt. (Kimbell's Co.) | March 6, 1836 | The Alamo, San Antonio de Béxar, Texas |
| Kent, Andrew, Pvt. (Kimbell's Co.) | March 6, 1836 | The Alamo, San Antonio de Béxar, Texas |
| Kimbell, George C., Lt. (Kimbell's Co.) | March 6, 1836 | The Alamo, San Antonio de Béxar, Texas |
| King, William P., Pvt. (Kimbell's Co.) | March 6, 1836 | The Alamo, San Antonio de Béxar, Texas |
| Lindley, Jonathan L., Pvt. (Kimbell's Co.) | March 6, 1836 | The Alamo, San Antonio de Béxar, Texas |
| Lynch, John L., Vol. (Caldwell's Co.) | December 25, 1839 | Cherokee village near the junction of the Colorado and San Saba Rivers, Texas |
| McCoy, Jesse, Pvt. (Kimbell's Co.) | March 6, 1836 | The Alamo, San Antonio de Béxar, Texas |
| McGrew, G. Washington, Vol. (Bryant's Co.) | January 16, 1839 | Near Morgan's Point, Texas |
| McPherson, James, Pvt. (Cairns' Co.)<br>*Drowned* | September 8, 1841 | Nueces River, Texas |
| Marlin, William N. P., Vol. (Bryant's Co.)<br>*DOW* | January 16, 1839 | Near Morgan's Point, Texas |
| Martin, Joseph S., Pvt. (Moore's Co.)<br>*DOW — died a few weeks later* | February 14, 1839 | Wallace's Creek, Texas |
| Martin, Philip, Pvt. (Co. C, Btn. Mtd. Rifles) | March 1837 | Colorado River near new Fort Houston, Texas |
| Miles, Alfred L., 2nd Lt. (Bowyer's Co.) | November 10, 1837 | "Stone Houses Fight" near the headwaters of the West Fork of the Trinity River, Texas |
| Miller, Thomas R., Pvt. (Kimbell's Co.) | March 6, 1836 | The Alamo, San Antonio de Béxar, Texas |

| Name/Rank/Unit | Date | Site of Death |
|---|---|---|
| Millsaps, Isaac, Pvt. (Kimbell's Co.) | March 6, 1836 | The Alamo, San Antonio de Béxar, Texas |
| Mindiola, Marino, Pvt. (Gonzales' Co., Karnes' Exped.)<br>*DOW inflicted in accidental shooting (October 22, 1839)* | October 28, 1839 | Near Guadalupe River, Texas |
| Morales, Pedro F., Pvt. (Seguin's Co.)<br>*DOW inflicted in accidental shooting* | June 18, 1839 | Near the Rio Frio, Texas |
| Mordica, Benjamin H., Vol. (Tumlinson's Co.) | August 9, 1840 | Garcitas Creek, Texas |
| Mott, _____, Pvt. (Hays' Co.) | June 8, 1844 | Walker Creek, Texas |
| Nash, Jesse E., Pvt. (Bird's Co.) | June 26, 1839 | Bird's Creek, Texas |
| Neal, Claiborne, Vol. (Co. B, Btn. Mtd. Rifles) | May 6, 1837 | Post Oak Springs, Texas |
| Neggan, George, Pvt. (Kimbell's Co.) | March 6, 1836 | The Alamo, San Antonio de Béxar, Texas |
| Nicholson, Westley, Pvt. (Bowyer's Co.) | November 10, 1837 | "Stone Houses Fight" near the headwaters of the West Fork of the Trinity River, Texas |
| Nicholson, William, Pvt. (Bowyer's Co.) | November 10, 1837 | "Stone Houses Fight" near the headwaters of the West Fork of the Trinity River, Texas |
| "Paddy," Pvt. (Hays' Co.) | April 1, 1844 | Nueces Canyon, Texas |
| Parker, Benjamin, Pvt. (Parker's Co.) | May 19, 1836 | Parker's Fort, Texas |
| Parker, Silas M., Supt. (Parker's Dist.) | May 19, 1836 | Parker's Fort, Texas |
| Plummer, Jacob, Vol. (Bryant's Co.) | January 16, 1839 | Near Morgan's Point, Texas |
| Powers, Andrew J., Vol. (Bryant's Co.) | January 16, 1839 | Near Morgan's Point, Texas |
| Rattan, Wade H., Pvt. (Webb's Co.) | December 25, 1841 | East of Elm Fork, Texas |
| Robinett, _____, Pvt. (Pierson's Co.) | August 22, 1836 | Coleto Creek near Victoria, Texas |
| Robinson, Thomas J., Pvt. (Pierson's Co.) | August 22, 1836 | Coleto Creek near Victoria, Texas |
| Sanders, William, Dr. (Bowyer's Co.) | November 10, 1837 | "Stone Houses Fight" near the headwaters of the West Fork of the Trinity River, Texas |
| Sauls, Charles, Vol. (Bryant's Co.)<br>*DOW* | January 16, 1839 | Near Morgan's Point, Texas |
| Scheuster, Lewis P., Pvt. (Bowyer's Co.) | November 10, 183 | "Stone Houses Fight" near the headwaters of the West Fork of the Trinity River, Texas |
| Scott, Thomas M., Pvt. (Brown's Co.) | October 12, 1838 | East of Fort Houston, Texas |
| Sewell, Marcus L., Pvt. (Kimbell's Co.) | March 6, 1836 | The Alamo, San Antonio de Béxar, Texas |
| Sisty, William R., Corp. (Wilson's Co., Karnes' Exped.) | October 26, 1839 | Near Guadalupe River, Texas |
| Slein, John, Pvt. (Hays' Co.) | July 24, 1841 | Sabinal Canyon, Texas |
| Smith, Abram T., Pvt. (Erath's Co.) | August 3, 1841 | Cross Timbers, Texas |
| Stein, John, Pvt. (Hays' Co.)<br>*DOW inflicted July 1, 1841* | July 2, 1841 | Cañon de Uvalde, Texas |
| Summers, William E., Pvt. (Kimbell's Co.) | March 6, 1836 | The Alamo, San Antonio de Béxar, Texas |
| Thompson, John S., Pvt. (Smith's Co., Mabbitt's Btn.) | July 16, 1839 | Neches River, Texas |

| Name/Rank/Unit | Date | Site of Death |
|---|---|---|
| Thompson, Jonathan, Pvt. (Mtd. Rangers) *DOW inflicted in accidental discharge of a musket* | February 27, 1839 | ? |
| Tumlinson, George W., Pvt. (Kimbell's Co.) | March 6, 1836 | The Alamo, San Antonio de Béxar, Texas |
| Ward, Cyrus L., Vol. (Bryant's Co.) | January 16, 1839 | Near Morgan's Point, Texas |
| Weaver, William H., 1st Sgt. (Evan's Co.) | June 26, 1839 | Bird's Creek, Texas |
| Webb, Andrew J., Vol. (Bryant's Co.) | January 16, 1839 | Near Morgan's Point, Texas |
| Whepler, Phillip, Pvt. (Co. G, 1st Mtd. Gunmen) | November 11, 1839 | Richland Creek, Texas |
| White, Robert, Pvt. (Kimbell's Co.) | March 6, 1836 | The Alamo, San Antonio de Béxar, Texas |
| Wilson, John, Pvt. (Brown's Co.) | October 12, 1838 | East of Fort Houston, Texas |
| Wolf [deWolf], Gottip, Pvt. (Border Guards) | August 12, 1840 | Plum Creek, Texas |
| Wright, Claiborne, Pvt. (Kimbell's Co.) | March 6, 1836 | The Alamo, San Antonio de Béxar, Texas |

## *Los Diablos Tejanos*: Rangers in the U.S.-Mexican War

| Name/Rank/Unit | Date | Site of Death |
|---|---|---|
| Abbott, Benjamin F., Pvt. (Co. K, 1st Mtd. Vols.) | December 18, 1847 | Mexico |
| Allen, William W., Cpl. (Co. I, 1st Mtd. Vols.) | November 28, 1847 | National Bridge, Mexico |
| Allison, Walter C., Pvt. (Co. A, Chevallie's Btn.) | June 20, 1847 | Monterey, Mexico |
| Alsans, Adam, Pvt. (Co. F, 1st Mtd. Vols.) *DOW inflicted February 12, 1848 — died at Mexico City* | February 13, 1848 | Mexico City, Mexico |
| Alston, Fielding, Pvt. (B. McCulloch's Co.) | March 22, 1847 | ? |
| Anderson, William H. (B. McCulloch's Co.) | February 23, 1847 | Buena Vista, Mexico |
| Ashton, Chaucer, Capt. (Co. E, 1st Mtd. Vols.) | December 14, 1847 | Mexico City, Mexico |
| Austin, W. J. D., Bugler (Co. E, 1st Mtd. Rifles) | September 21, 1846 | Monterey, Mexico |
| Banton, John D., Pvt. (Co. G, 1st Mtd. Rifles) | September 9, 1846 | China, Mexico |
| Barber, William, Pvt. (Co. D, 1st Mtd. Vols.) | January 1, 1848 | Enchanted Rock, Texas |
| Barrow, James C., Pvt. (Co. K, 1st Mtd. Vols.) | December 23, 1847 | Mexico |
| Barton, Lewis, Pvt. (Co. E, Chevallie's Btn.) | August 13, 1847 | Monterey, Mexico |
| Bartrane, John, Pvt. (Fitzhugh's Co., Bell's Reg.) | January 2, 1848 | ? |
| Bell, William H., Pvt. (Co. A, Lane's Btn.) | November 21, 1847 | Agua Noche, Mexico |
| Bird, James, Pvt. (Co. F, 1st Mtd. Vols.) | March 10, 1848 | Mexico City, Mexico |
| Blackwell, James, Pvt. (Smith's Co., Bell's Reg.) | October 11, 1848 | Kaufman Station, Texas |
| Borgas, John, Pvt. (Co. I, 1st Mtd. Vols.) | January 15, 1848 | Mexico City, Mexico |
| Brookfield, Walter, Pvt. (Co. F, 1st Mtd. Vols.) | January 4, 1848 | ? |

| Name/Rank/Unit | Date | Site of Death |
|---|---|---|
| Brooks, Augustus, Pvt. (Gray's Co.) | February 3, 1847 | Corpus Christi, Texas |
| Brown, Edward, Pvt. (Lamar's Co.) | January 1, 1847 | ? |
| Browning, J. E., Pvt. (Co. C, Chevallie's Btn.) | April 20, 1847 | China, Mexico |
| Buchanan, John, Pvt. (Co. H, 1st Mtd. Rifles)<br>*MIA — presumed killed* | September 15, 1846 | Near China, Mexico |
| Burt, Harrison, Pvt. (Lamar's Co.) | December 25, 1847 | Laredo, Texas |
| Butler, Charles, Pvt. (Co. D, Lane's Btn.) | September 28, 1847 | Monterey, Mexico |
| Byers, Benjamin F., Pvt. (Co. A, Chevallie's Btn.) | August 15, 1847 | Saltillo, Mexico |
| Calvert, James, Pvt. (Co. D, 1st Mtd. Vols.) | November 15, 1847 | Enchanted Rock, Texas |
| Campbell, Charles A., Pvt. (Co. I, 1st Mtd. Vols.) | January 20, 1848 | Mexico City, Mexico |
| Carder, Christian C., Pvt. (Co. K, 1st Mtd. Vols.) | December 28, 1847 | Mexico City, Mexico |
| Carder, Elijah, Pvt. (Co. K, 1st Mtd. Vols.) | December 26, 1847 | Mexico City, Mexico |
| Cargile, I. D., Pvt. (Co. C, Chevallie's Btn.) | August 13, 1847 | Monterey, Mexico |
| Chambliss, Simon, Pvt. (H. E. McCulloch's Co., Smith's Btn.) | January 5, 1847 | San Antonio, Texas |
| Chandler, Benjamin T., Pvt. (Grumble's Co., Smith's Btn.)<br>*Died on march to the Rio Grande* | April 24, 1847 | ? |
| Chano, A., Pvt. (Lamar's Co.) | March 3, 1847 | ? |
| Cherry, Henry G., Pvt. (Co. A, Chevallie's Btn.) | June 15, 1847 | Castanuela, Mexico |
| Clark, R., Pvt. (Lamar's Co.) | December 19, 1847 | ? |
| Connell, Richard, Pvt. (Grumble's Co., Smith's Btn.) | February 4, 1847 | Near Austin, Texas |
| Connor, William, Pvt. (Highsmith's Co., Bell's Reg.) | June 7, 1848 | Camp Llano, Texas |
| Conway, Samuel D., Pvt. (Co. C, Lane's Btn.) | January 14, 1848 | Camargo, Mexico |
| Cooke, C. T. C., Pvt. (Co. C, Lane's Btn.) | September 18, 1847 | Saltillo, Mexico |
| Coonrod, Stephen, Pvt. (Co. K, 1st Mtd. Vols.) | January 24, 1848 | San Angel, Mexico |
| Coonrod, William J., Pvt. (Johnson's Co., Bell's Reg.) | September 8, 1847 | Waco Village Station, Texas |
| Corlew, Alney M., 1st Sgt. (Co. B, Chevallie's Btn.) | June 29, 1847 | La Encantada, Mexico |
| Corrigan, James, Pvt. (Co. E, Chevallie's Btn.)<br>*Assassinated* | February 12, 1847 | Monterey, Mexico |
| Couzens, Thomas, Lt. (Co. H, 1st Mtd. Vols.)<br>*DOW inflicted in battle with Indians — died at Laredo* | January 11, 1848 | Near Laredo, Texas |
| Cox, Abner, Pvt. (Co. B, Chevallie's Btn.) | August 16, 1847 | Saltillo, Mexico |
| Cox, H. M., Cpl. (Crump's Co., Bell's Reg.) | May 16, 1848 | Camp Medina, Texas |
| Cox, Jesse, Pvt. (Co. B, Lane's Btn.) | June 13, 1848 | Monterey, Mexico |
| Crabtree, Job, Pvt. (Co. C, Chevallie's Btn.)<br>*Drowned* | April 1, 1847 | Rio Grande River |

| Name/Rank/Unit | Date | Site of Death |
|---|---|---|
| Crayton, James, Pvt. (Grumble's Co., Smith's Btn.) | January 4, 1847 | Laredo, Texas |
| Cummings, Wiley, Pvt. (Gray's Co.) | February 10, 1847 | Guadalupe River, Texas |
| Cundiff, Charles E., Pvt. (Johnson's Co., Bell's Reg.) | September 20, 1847 | Waco Village Station, Texas |
| Cummings, Wiley, Pvt. (Mabry's Co.) | February 10, 1847 | Guadalupe River, Texas |
| Darnell, Dewitt C., Pvt. (Johnson's Co., Bell's Reg.) | September 26, 1847 | Waco Village Station, Texas |
| Davidson, Jesse J., Pvt. (Co. K, 1st Mtd. Vols.) | January 24, 1848 | Mexico City, Mexico |
| Deckert, John, Pvt. (Sutton's Co., Bell's Reg.) *Accidentally killed* | February 11, 1848 | Camp Nueces, Texas |
| DeMay, Charles, Pvt. (Fitzhugh's Co., Bell's Reg.) | January 5, 1849 | Hickory Creek Station, Texas |
| Dial, Asa, Pvt. (Co. E, 1st Mtd. Vols.) | February 18, 1848 | Mexico City, Mexico |
| Dier, Wesley, Pvt. (Warfield's Co., Bell's Reg.) | November 12, 1848 | Sabinal Canyon, Texas |
| Dressler, Charles F., Pvt. (Co. G, 1st Mtd. Vols.) | November 23, 1847 | Puebla, Mexico |
| Duffinger, George, Pvt. (Co. G, 1st Mtd. Vols.) | December 11, 1847 | ? |
| Eastland, C. C., Pvt. (Co. F, 1st Mtd. Vols.) | December 23, 1847 | Mexico City, Mexico |
| Edwards, John H., Pvt. (Co. A, Chevallie's Btn.) | August 16, 1847 | Saltillo, Mexico |
| English, William T., Pvt. (Co. E, 1st Mtd. Vols.) | January 23, 1848 | Mexico City, Mexico |
| Erath, Anthony, Pvt. (Conner's Co., Smith's Btn.) | June 8, 1847 | Monterey, Mexico |
| Field, Henry H., Pvt. (Co. E, Chevallie's Btn.) | August 5, 1847 | Los Tablas, Mexico |
| Fink, Leopold, Pvt. (Co. F, 1st Mtd. Vols.) *Accidentally shot and killed* | August 10 or September 8 or 9 or 30, 1848 | Mier, Mexico |
| Fink, Napoleon Pvt. (Co. F, 1st Mtd. Vols.) | August 31, 1847 | ? |
| Fisher, Israel P. (Co. E, Chevallie's Btn.) | August 5, 1847 | Los Tablas, Mexico |
| Flanagan, Joshua, Cpl. (Conner's Co., Smith's Btn.) | May 5, 1847 | Monterey, Mexico |
| Floyd, William F., Pvt. (H. E. McCulloch's Co., Smith's Btn.) | January 10, 1847 | Monclova, Mexico |
| Ford, Silas, Pvt. (Co. D, Lane's Btn.) *Assassinated* | September 8, 1847 | Camargo, Mexico |
| Foster, James, Pvt. (Co. G, 1st Mtd. Vols.) | January 10, 1848 | Tacubaya, Mexico |
| French, Hiram, Bugler (Co. I, 1st Mtd. Vols.) | March 10, 1848 | Mexico |
| Fulcher, Solomon F., Pvt. (Ross' Co., Smith's Btn.) | January 31, 1847 | Austin, Texas |
| Fullerton, John M., Cpl. (Co. K, 1st Mtd. Rifles) | September 21, 1846 | Monterey, Mexico |
| Gaither, Carlos S., Lt. (Co. G, 1st Mtd. Vols.) | December 1, 1847 | Jalapa, Mexico |

| Name/Rank/Unit | Date | Site of Death |
|---|---|---|
| Gilam, Dudley, Pvt. (Co. B, Chevallie's Btn.) | June 26, 1847 | Saltillo, Mexico |
| Gilbert, Richard S., Pvt. (Co. H, 1st Mtd. Vols.) | December 18, 1847 | ? |
| Gillespie, Robert A., Capt. (Co I, 1st Mtd. Rifles) *DOW inflicted September 22, 1846 — died at Monterey* | September 23, 1846 | Monterey, Mexico |
| Gooch, William J. (Co. E, Chevallie's Btn.) | August 5, 1847 | Los Tablas, Mexico |
| Gorhmly, James S., Pvt. (Co. A, Chevallie's Btn.) | October 17, 1847 | Saltillo, Mexico |
| Graves, William, Pvt. (Co. E, 1st Mtd. Vols.) | December 26, 1847 | Mexico City, Mexico |
| Green, Jamson, Pvt. (Lamar's Co.) | December 31, 1847 | Laredo, Texas |
| Gregg, Ellis, Pvt. (Ross' Co., Smith's Btn.) | April 16 or 18, 1847 | San Patricio, Texas |
| Greggory, J. B., Pvt. (Co. E, 1st Mtd. Vols.) | January 3, 1848 | Puebla, Mexico |
| Gregory, Thomas W., Pvt. (Co. I, 1st Mtd. Vols.) | January 12, 1848 | Jalapa, Mexico |
| Griffin, John, Pvt. (Co. C, Chevallie's Btn.) | June 1, 1847 | China, Mexico |
| Griffin, Joseph, Pvt. (Co. E, 1st Mtd. Vols.) | December 26, 1847 | Puebla, Mexico |
| Gunter, R. H., Pvt. (H. E. McCulloch's Co., Smith's Btn.) | June 27, 1847 | Rio Grande River |
| Guthrie, W. A., Pvt. (Sutton's Co., Bell's Btn.) | April 24, 1848 | San Patricio, Texas |
| Hack, Isaac, Pvt. (Warfield's Co., Bell's Reg.) | August 29, 1848 | Sabinal River, Texas |
| Hall, John, Pvt. (Co. E, Chevallie's Btn.) | August 5, 1847 | Los Tablas, Mexico |
| Halton, Reuben B., Pvt. (Johnson's Co., Bell's Reg.) | March 10, 1848 | Waco Village Station, Texas |
| Hardaway, James M., Bvt. Lt. (Co. D, Chevallie's Btn.) | July 29, 1847 | Papagallos, Mexico |
| Harney, John, Pvt. (Conner's Co., Smith's Btn.) | June 12, 1847 | Pedernales, Texas |
| Harris, E., Pvt. (Walker's Co.) | April 28, 1846 | Point Isabel, Texas |
| Harrison, W. B., Pvt. (Sutton's Co., Bell's Reg.) *Killed in private affray* | August 17, 1848 | San Patricio, Texas |
| Hart, Henry A. (Gray's Co.) | May 1, 1847 | Camargo, Mexico |
| Hart, James, Pvt. (Co. G, 1st Mtd. Vols.) | December 15, 1847 | Puebla, Mexico |
| Hastings, H. H., Pvt. (Walker's Co.) | April 28, 1846 | Point Isabel, Texas |
| Hawes, Prince B., Pvt. (Co. E, 1st Mtd. Vols.) | December 13, 1847 | Mexico City, Mexico |
| Herrill, Charles W., Pvt. (Co. K, 1st Mtd. Vols.) | ? | Puebla, Mexico |
| Herrill, William, Bugler (Co. K, 1st Mtd. Vols.) | ? | Puebla, Mexico |
| Hewett, Ezekiel T., Pvt. (Co. E, 1st Mtd. Vols.) | January 31, 1848 | Mexico City, Mexico |
| Higgins, Peter, Pvt. (Co. A, Lane's Btn.) | May 25, 1848 | Concepción, Mexico |
| Holmes, Peter W., Pvt. (Co. A, Lane's Btn.) *Assassinated* | October 6 or November 5, 1847 | Monterey, Mexico |

APPENDIX B

| Name/Rank/Unit | Date | Site of Death |
|---|---|---|
| Holmork, Ansburry, Sgt. (Crump's Co., Bell's Reg.) | January 2, 1848 | San Antonio, Texas |
| Hord, William I., Pvt. (Co. E, Chevallie's Btn.) | July 27, 1847 | Monterey, Mexico |
| Horne, Jacob M., Pvt. (Co. E, 1st Mtd. Vols.) | February 25, 1848 | Zacualtipán, Mexico |
| Hosly, David V., Pvt. (Co. K, 1st Mtd. Rifles) | September 28, 1846 | Monterey, Mexico |
| Hudson, David, Pvt. (Ross' Co., Smith's Btn.) | January 10, 1847 | Austin, Texas |
| Hudson, William, Pvt. (Co. C, Lane's Btn.) | September 3, 1847 | Saltillo, Mexico |
| Jennings, Henry L., Pvt. (Co. H, 1st Mtd. Vols.) | November 10, 1847 | Laredo, Texas |
| Jobe, James L., Pvt. (Co. D, 1st Mtd. Vols.) | January 6 or 25, 1848 | Enchanted Rock, Texas |
| Johnson, Nathaniel, Pvt. (Co. G, 1st Mtd. Vols.) | January 10, 1848 | Tacubaya, Mexico |
| Johnston, Joshua W., Pvt. (Johnson's Co., Bell's Reg.) | September 30, 1847 | Waco Village Station, Texas |
| Jones, John A., Pvt. (Crump's Co., Bell's Reg.) | June 23, 1848 | Sulphur Springs, Texas |
| Juthan, Pope, Pvt. (Co. G, 1st Mtd. Vols.) | November 20, 1847 | Vera Cruz, Mexico |
| Keese, William W., Pvt. (H. E. McCulloch's Co., Smith's Btn.) | April 15, 1847 | San Antonio, Texas |
| Kinnion, H. H., Pvt. (Co. G, 1st Mtd. Vols.) | December 12, 1847 | Mexico City, Mexico |
| Knight, Richard, Pvt. (Co. B, Chevallie's Btn.) | April 18, 1847 | Camargo, Mexico |
| Koch, Henry, Pvt. (Conner's Co., Smith's Btn.) | April 18, 1847 | Castroville, Texas |
| Lamb, Mark, Pvt. (Co. B, Lane's Btn.) | March 26, 1848 | Saltillo, Mexico |
| Latharp, Oliver, Pvt. (Co. E, 1st Mtd. Vols.) | April 18, 1848 | Mexico City, Mexico |
| Layne, William, Pvt. (Co. G, 1st Mtd. Vols.) | January 11 or 12, 1848 | Tacubaya, Mexico |
| Lincecum, Lycurgus, Pvt. (Co. G, 1st Mtd. Vols.) | December 22, 1847 | Mexico City, Mexico |
| Loyd, Elijah, Pvt. (Conner's Co., Smith's Btn.) | June 18, 1847 | Cerralvo, Mexico |
| Lyon, Henry P., Pvt. (Co. H, 1st Mtd. Rifles) *MIA — presumed killed* | September 15, 1846 | Near China, Mexico |
| McCaleb, William B., Pvt. (Co. G, 1st Mtd. Vols.) | January 9, 1848 | Puebla, Mexico |
| McCarty, Daniel, Pvt. (Co. D, 1st Mtd. Rifles) | September 23, 1846 | Monterey, Mexico |
| McCommas, Burk, Pvt. (Co. K, 1st Mtd. Vols.) | December 26, 1847 | Mexico City, Mexico |
| McCommas, Stephen B., Cpl. (Co. K, 1st Mtd. Vols.) | December 12, 1847 | Mexico City, Mexico |
| McConnell, David D., Pvt. (Co. G, 1st Mtd. Vols.) | January 9, 1848 | Mexico City, Mexico |

| Name/Rank/Unit | Date | Site of Death |
|---|---|---|
| McGinnis, James, Pvt. (Co. F, 1st Mtd. Vols.) | October 9, 1847 | Near the Rio Grande, Mexico |
| McKay, Francis, Pvt. (Co. A, Lane's Reg.) | November 11, 1847 | Parras, Mexico |
| McKinney, John, Pvt. (Fitzhugh's Co., Bell's Reg.) | November 26, 1847 | ? |
| McPhail, Robert, Pvt. (Co. B, Chevallie's Btn.) | June 6, 1847 | Monterey, Mexico |
| Malpass, William, Pt. (Co. F, 1st Mtd. Vols.) | November 24, 1847 | Galaxa Pass, Mexico |
| Mangum, Nathaniel H., Pvt. (Warfield's Co., Bell's Reg.) *DOW inflicted in Lipan Apache skirmish (September 4, 1848) — died at Camp Leon* | September 5, 1848 | Leona River, Texas |
| Manning, Richard P., Pvt. (Co. I, 1st Mtd. Vols.) | January 30, 1848 | Mexico City, Mexico |
| Masters, James, Pvt. (Fitzhugh's Co., Bell's Reg.) | February 7, 1849 | Hickory Creek Station, Texas |
| Mathews, Olin, Pvt. (Co. A, Lane's Btn.) | March 29, 1848 | Mazafull [Mazaprul], Mexico |
| Merram, Edgar, Pvt. (Co. G, 1st Mtd. Vols.) | January 10, 1848 | Tacubaya, Mexico |
| Miller, John, Pvt. (Co. I, 1st Mtd. Vols.) | March 27, 1848 | Perote, Mexico |
| Milligan, Little, Pvt. (Gray's Co.) | November 30, 1846 | Corpus Christi, Texas |
| Mills, M. J., Pvt. (Wyman's Co., Smith's Btn.) | July 26, 1847 | Smith's Station, Texas |
| Mimms, Jefferson, Pvt. (Gray's Co.) | April 1, 1847 | Monterey, Mexico |
| Moniere, Daniel M., Pvt. (Co. I, 1st Mtd. Vols.) | December 30, 1847, or January 2, 1848 | Mexico City, Mexico |
| Montgomery, A. D., Pvt. (Co. F, 1st Mtd. Vols.) | March 15, 1848 | Mexico City, Mexico |
| Moore, Elisha H., Pvt. (Co. I, 1st Mtd. Vols.) | February 2, 1848 | Mexico City, Mexico |
| Moore, William, Pvt. (Co. G, 1st Mtd. Vols.) | January 12, 1848 | Tacubaya, Mexico |
| Morton, Russian, Pvt. (Co. K, 1st Mtd. Vols.) | December 22, 1847 | Mexico City, Mexico |
| Murphy, Benjamin W., Pvt. (H. E. McCulloch's Co., Smith's Btn.) *Died en route to Mexico from accidental shooting* | December 2, 1846 | ? |
| Neil, Perry, Pvt. (Ross' Co., Smith's Btn.) | January 21, 1847 | San Gabriel, Texas |
| Newton, James R., Pvt. (Co. K, 1st Mtd. Vols.) | December 26, 1847 | Mexico City, Mexico |
| Nichols, William, Pvt. (Co. I, 1st Mtd. Vols.) | January 1, 1848 | Mexico City, Mexico |
| Nolan, Christian, Pvt. (Co. K, 1st Mtd. Vols.) | January 25, 1848 | Puebla, Mexico |
| Oatte, Charles (Co. E, Chevallie's Btn.) *Assassinated* | August 13, 1847 | Monterey, Mexico |
| O'Bryant, C. P., Pvt. (Stapp's Co.) | September 18, 1846 | Elm Station, Texas |
| O'Hair, Michael, Pvt. (Johnson's Co., Bell's Reg.) *Drowned in Mountain Creek* | June 9, 1848 | Near Kaufman Station, Texas |
| O'Neal, William, Pvt. (Sutton's Co., Bell's Reg.) | August 29, 1848 | Corpus Christi, Texas |

## Appendix B

| Name/Rank/Unit | Date | Site of Death |
|---|---|---|
| Owens, Patrick, Pvt. (Co. D, Lane's Btn.) | October 16, 1847 | Monterey, Mexico |
| Parmer, Fletcher, Pvt. (Co. I, 1st Mtd. Vols.) | ? | Jalapa, Mexico |
| Pelham, Thomas E., Pvt. (Fitzhugh's Co., Bell's Reg.) | July 12, 1848 | Hickory Creek Station, Texas |
| Peltz, Otto, Pvt. (Co. A, Lane's Btn.) | November 28, 1847 | Parras, Mexico |
| Pendergrass, Nathaniel D., Pvt. (Warfield's Co., Bell's Reg.) | September 6, 1848 | Camp Leon, Texas |
| Phrene, Otto, Pvt. (Co. G, 1st Mtd. Vols.) | January 1, 1848 | ? |
| Preston, David, Pvt. (Co. E, Chevallie's Btn.) | August 5, 1847 | Los Tablas, Mexico |
| Pritchett, Edley, Pvt. (Fitzhugh's Co., Bell's Reg.) | July 1, 1848 | Hickory Creek Station, Texas |
| Prostoski, Joseph, Pvt. (Walker's Co.) | April 28, 1846 | Point Isabel, Texas |
| Radcliffe, Edward S., 1st Sgt. (Walker's Co.) | April 28, 1846 | Point Isabel, Texas |
| Rainbolt, John P., Pvt. (Co. H, 1st Mtd. Vols.) *Accidentally killed* | August 21, 1847 | Camp Arbuckle, Texas |
| Ratton, Littleton, Pvt. (Co. H, 1st Mtd. Vols.) | December 18, 1847 | ? |
| Reed, Thompson, Lt. (Co. H, 1st Mtd. Vols.) | ? | Camp Arbuckle, Texas |
| Rhew, William, Pvt. (Conner's Co., Smith's Btn.) | December 18, 1846 | San Antonio, Texas |
| Robbins, John R., Pvt. (Co. E, 1st Mtd. Vols.) | December 20, 1847 | Mexico City, Mexico |
| Roberts, James, Pvt. (Co. F, 1st Mtd. Vols.) | January 29, 1848 | Mexico City, Mexico |
| Roberts, Joseph, Pvt. (Fitzhugh's Co., Bell's Reg.) | January 3, 1848 | ? |
| Roberts, Thomas, Pvt. (Ross' Co., Smith's Btn.) | January 17, 1847 | San Gabriel, Texas |
| Robinson, J., Pvt. (Walker's Co.) | April 28, 1846 | Point Isabel, Texas |
| Romaine, William C., Pvt. (Co. K, 1st Mtd. Vols.) | ? | Puebla, Mexico |
| Ross, Angus, Pvt. (Grumble's Co., Smith's Btn.) | February 18, 1847 | Near Austin, Texas |
| Runnolds, B. F., Pvt. (Crump's Co., Bell's Reg.) *Killed in private affray* | December 11 or 14, 1847 | Camp Medina, Texas |
| Sanders, Joseph D., Pvt. (Co. G, 1st Mtd. Vols.) | September 30, 1847 | Vergara, Mexico |
| Sellers, Isaac, Pvt. (Co. F, 1st Mtd. Vols.) | January 4 or February 12, 1848 | Mexico City, Mexico |
| Sessum, Jacob, Pvt. (Co. E, 1st Mtd. Vols.) | January 1, 1848 | Jalapa, Mexico |
| Sevier, Charles, Pvt. (Co. C, Chevallie's Btn.) | April 1, 1847 | Camargo, Mexico |
| Shackhart, Adolph, Pvt. (Co. F, 1st Mtd. Vols.) | March 6, 1848 | Puebla, Mexico |
| Shahan, William P., Pvt. (Co. K, 1st Mtd. Vols.) | December 9, 1847 | Perote, Mexico |

| Name/Rank/Unit | Date | Site of Death |
|---|---|---|
| Shields, James M., Pvt. (Co. I, 1st Mtd. Vols.) | January 14, 1848 | Jalapa, Mexico |
| Shoemaker, David H., Pvt. (Co. E, Chevallie's Btn.) | August 5, 1847 | Los Tablas, Mexico |
| Shults, Robert, Pvt. (Co. F, 1st Mtd. Vols.) | October 20 or 25, 1848 | Brazos Santiago, Texas |
| Simons, Thomas, Pvt. (Gray's Co.) | May 1, 1847 | Monterey, Mexico |
| Sish, Alfred, Pvt. (Co. E, 1st Mtd. Vols.) | January 30, 1848 | Mexico City, Mexico |
| Smith, Ben P., Lt. (Co. F, 1st Mtd. Vols.) | January 29, 1848 | Mexico |
| Smith, Elisha, Cpl., (Fitzhugh's Co., Bell's Btn.) | October 2, 1847 | ? |
| Smith, Focke H., Pvt. (Conner's Co., Smith's Btn.) | March 18, 1847 | Camargo, Texas |
| Smith, Francis M., Pvt. (Fitzhugh's Co., Bell's Btn.) | December 20, 1847 | ? |
| Snee, James, Pvt. (H. E. McCulloch's Co., Bell's Btn.) | April 21, 1848 | McCulloch's Station, Texas |
| Soleus, Charles B., Cpl. (Conner's Co., Smith's Btn.) | February 18, 1847 | Nueces River, Texas |
| Steen, Richard, Pvt. (Co. K, 1st Mtd. Vols.) | January 16, 1848 | San Angel, Mexico |
| Stiff, James M., Pvt. (Fitzhugh's Co., Bell's Btn.) | September 9, 1847 | ? |
| Stockman, Reason P., Pvt. (Co. I, 1st Mtd. Vols.) | January 14, 1848 | Mexico |
| Stone, James, Pvt. (Co. I, 1st Mtd. Vols.) | January 7, 1848 | Mexico City, Mexico |
| Story, Ephraim, Pvt. (Co. E, 1st Mtd. Vols.) | January 25, 1848 | Mexico City, Mexico |
| Struhan, A., Pvt. (Co. F, 1st Mtd. Vols.) | February 29, 1848 | Mexico City, Mexico |
| Sutton, Charles F., Pvt. (Co. G, 1st Mtd. Vols.) | February 25 or 27, 1848 | Mexico City, Mexico |
| Talbot, William, Pvt. (Co. B, Chevallie's Btn.) | June 30, 1847 | Monterey, Mexico |
| Tanner, Harris T., Pvt. (Co. G, 1st Mtd. Vols.) | January 12, 1848 | Tacubaya, Mexico |
| Temple, William B., Pvt. (Co. G, 1st Mtd. Vols.) | January 12, 1848 | Tacubaya, Mexico |
| Thomas, Herman S., Pvt. (Co. A, 1st Mtd. Rifles)<br>*DOW inflicted on September 22, 1846 — died at Monterey* | September 23, 1846 | Monterey, Mexico |
| Thomas, Jefferson, Pvt. (Co. I, 1st Mtd. Vols.) | January 17, 1848 | Mexico City, Mexico |
| Thomas, Robert, Pvt. (Co. I, 1st Mtd. Vols.) | January 4, 1848 | Mexico |
| Thompson, David, Pvt. (Lamar's Co.) | December 19, 1847 | Laredo, Texas |
| Tidwell, Peter, Pvt. (Johnson's Co., Bell's Reg.) | August 4, 1847 | Austin, Texas |
| Tolbert, John F., Pvt. (Conner's Co., Bell's Reg.)<br>*Killed in private affray* | December 17, 1848 | Brazos River, Texas |
| Trammel, Benjamin, Pvt. (Grumble's Co., Smith's Btn.) | December 20, 1846 | Austin, Texas |

APPENDIX B

| Name/Rank/Unit | Date | Site of Death |
|---|---|---|
| Trimmer, Beverly, Pvt. (Ross' Co., Bell's Reg.) | July 17, 1848 | Bosque Station, Texas |
| Tufts, Charles W., Pvt. (Co. H, 1st Mtd. Rifles) *MIA — presumed killed* | September 15, 1846 | Near China, Mexico |
| Tumlinson, Josiah, Pvt. (H. E. McCulloch's Co., Smith's Btn.) | December 3, 1846 | San Marcos, Texas |
| Turley, Elisha, Pvt. (H. E. McCulloch's Co., Bell's Reg.) | July 11, 1848 | McCulloch's Station, Texas |
| Vanslike, Andrew H., Pvt. (Co. K, 1st Mtd. Vols.) | ? | Puebla, Mexico |
| Vatch, T. J., Pvt. (Co. F, 1st Mtd. Vols.) | January 4, 1848 | Mexico City, Mexico |
| Vaughan, Richard, 1st Sgt. (Cady's Co.) | June 4, 1846 | ? |
| Vernon, Thomas, Pvt. (Co. C, Lane's Btn.) | May 21, 1848 | Parras, Mexico |
| Vining, W. W., Pvt. (Co. C, Chevallie's Btn.) | April 23, 1847 | Monterey, Mexico |
| Vinson, Milton, Pvt. (Co. K, 1st Mtd. Vols.) | ? | Puebla, Mexico |
| Viveon, Thacker, Pvt. (Crump's Co., Bell's Reg.) | January 30, 1848 | San Antonio, Texas |
| Wade, Peter F., Pvt. (Co. A, Chevallie's Btn.) | July 3, 1847 | Saltillo, Mexico |
| Warnell, John, Pvt. (Co. G, 1st Mtd. Vols.) | February 27, 1848 | Tacubaya, Mexico |
| Warring, Thomas, Pvt. (Ross' Co., Smith's Btn.) | February 13, 1847 | San Antonio, Texas |
| Waters, Robert G., Pvt. (B. McCulloch's Co.) | August 6, 1846 | Matamoros, Mexico |
| Waters, William, Pvt. (Walker's Co.) | April 28, 1846 | Point Isabel, Texas |
| Weatherford, John, Pvt. (Warfield's Co., Bell's Reg.) | August 12, 1848 | Camp Arbuckle, Texas |
| Webster, Booker, Pvt. (Co. F, 1st Mtd. Vols.) | January 16, 1848 | Mexico City, Mexico |
| Wells, Joseph, Pvt. (Sutton's Co., Bell's Reg.) | December 22, 1847 | Camp Nueces, Texas |
| West, Jackson, Pvt. (Co. E, 1st Mtd. Vols.) | December 12, 1847 | Mexico City, Mexico |
| West, William, 1st Sgt. (Co. E, Lane's Btn.) | October 24, 1847 | Monterey, Mexico |
| Wethers, James W., Pvt. (Fitzhugh's Co., Bell's Reg.) | July 27, 1848 | Hickory Creek Station, Texas |
| White, Joseph S., 1st Sgt. (Co. B, 1st Mtd. Rifles) | September 13, 1846 | China, Mexico |
| Willhyte, William, Pvt. (Co. K, 1st Mtd. Vols.) | February 16, 1848 | San Angel, Mexico |
| Williams, Thomas, Pvt. (Co. H, 1st Mtd. Vols.) | March 31, 1848 | Camp Arbuckle, Texas |
| Willingham, Eli, Pvt. (Ross' Co., Smith's Btn.) | January 20, 1847 | Independence, Texas |
| Wilson, Samuel, Pvt. (Co. I, 1st Mtd. Vols.) | ? | Jalapa, Mexico |
| Wilson, William A., Pvt. (Co. I, 1st Mtd. Vols.) | February 23, 1848 | Mexico City, Mexico |
| Wolfscroner, Augustus, Pvt. (Co. G, 1st Mtd. Vols.) | January 6 or 8, 1848 | Jalapa, Mexico |

| Name/Rank/Unit | Date | Site of Death |
|---|---|---|
| Wright, George W., Pvt. (Co. I, 1st Mtd. Vols.) | January 6, 1848 | Jalapa, Mexico |

## Rangers of the Old Stamp: The Texas Mounted Volunteers

| Name/Rank/Unit | Date | Site of Death |
|---|---|---|
| Barton, Samuel Baker, Pvt. (Ford's Co.) | January 27, 1851 | San Antonio-Laredo Road near Nueces River, Texas |
| Clopton, William H., Pvt. (Callahan's Co.) | October 3, 1855 | Río Escondido, Mexico |
| Drennan, Thomas, Sgt. (H. E. McCulloch's Co.)<br>  *Died of disease* | June 16, 1851 | ? |
| Earbee, William, Pvt. (Ford's Co.)<br>  *Accidentally shot* | May 5, 1858 | ? |
| Estes, Smith, Pvt. (Brown's Co.)<br>  *Died of disease* | July 15, 1859 | Camp Estes, Texas |
| Fox, John, Pvt. (Tobin's Co.) | November 21, 1859 | Near Brownsville, Texas |
| Gillespie, William, Pvt. (Ford's Co.)<br>  *DOW inflicted May 29, 1850* | May 29, 1850 | Agua Dulce (Sweetwater) Creek near Fort Merrill, Texas |
| Grier, Thomas, Pvt. (Tobin's Co.) | November 21, 1859 | Palo Alto Prairie, Cameron County, Texas |
| Herman, David, Pvt. (Tobin's Co.) | December 14, 1859 | La Ebonal, Cameron County, Texas |
| Holland, H. K., Pvt. (Benton's Co.) | October 3, 1855 | Río Escondido, Mexico |
| Jackson, Samuel, Lt. (Tobin's Co.)<br>  *Thrown from and struck by carriage* | November 13, 1859 | Brownsville, Texas |
| Johnson, Isaac W., Capt. (Goliad Rangers)<br>  *Killed in private affray* | October 20, 1849 | Goliad County, Texas |
| Jones, Willis E., Pvt. (Henry's Co.) | October 3, 1855 | Río Escondido, Mexico |
| Lackey, William, Pvt. (Ford's Co.) | January 27, 1851 | San Antonio-Laredo Road near Nueces River, Texas |
| Lane, James, Pvt. (Cureton's Co.)<br>  *DOW nine days later at Fort Belknap, Texas* | 1860 | Yellow Wolf Creek near the Colorado River, Texas |
| McKay, William, Pvt. (Tobin's Co.) | November 21, 1859 | Palo Alto Prairie, Cameron County, Texas |
| Mallet, Nicholas R., Pvt. (Tobin's Co.) | November 21, 1859 | Palo Alto Prairie, Cameron County, Texas |
| Martinez, Tiophilo, Pvt. (Dalrymple's Co.) | September 10, 1860 | Belknap, Texas |
| Nickles, Robert, Pvt. (Ford's Co.) | May 12, 1858 | Little Robe Creek near the Canadian River, I.T. |
| Reed, John A., Pvt. (Goliad Rangers)<br>  *Drowned* | January 1, 1850 | San Antonio River, Texas |
| Smith, Augustus, Pvt. (Callahan's Co.) | October 3, 1855 | Río Escondido, Mexico |
| Sullivan, D. C. "Doc," Pvt. (Ford's Co.) | June 1850 | Santa Gertrudis, Texas |
| Thompson, Jonathan, Pvt. (Bourland's Co.)<br>  *Accidentally shot* | March 1859 | Cooke County, Texas |
| Wilbarger, John L., Pvt. (Ford's Co.) | June 1850 | Santa Gertrudis, Texas |
| Willis, Henry J., Pvt. (H. E. McCulloch's Co.) | September 15, 1851 | San Saba River, Texas |

| Name/Rank/Unit | Date | Site of Death |
|---|---|---|
| Woodruff, Fountain B., Pvt. (Ford's Co.) | February 4, 1860 | Rancho La Bolsa, Mexico |
| Unknown Ranger (Ford's Co.) | January 25, 1851 | Arroyo Gato, Texas |
| Unknown Waco Indian, Pvt. (S. P. Ross' Co.) | May 12, 1858 | Little Robe Creek near the Canadian River, I.T. |

## A Most Deperate Struggle: Rangers in the Civil War

| Name/Rank/Unit | Date | Site of Death |
|---|---|---|
| Barnes, R. S. "Sam," Capt. (Barnes' Co., 2nd Front. Dist.) | January 8, 1865 | Dove Creek, Texas |
| Bible, Noah, Pvt. (Barnes' Co., 2nd Front. Dist.) | January 8, 1865 | Dove Creek, Texas |
| Birdwell, Thomas G., Pvt. (Co. C, Front. Reg.) | February 16, 1863 | Clay County, Texas |
| Blue, Erastus, Pvt. (Co. D, Border Reg.) | October 13, 1864 | Bragg Ranch, Young County, Texas |
| Burke, John, Pvt. (Gillintine's Co., 2nd Front. Dist.) | January 8, 1865 | Dove Creek, Texas |
| Collins, _____, Sgt. (Co. H, Front. Reg.) | July 26, 1863 | Near Paint Creek, Texas |
| Connelly, Harrison R. "Tips," Pvt. (Co. C, 1st Mtd. Rifles) | July 29, 1861 | Near Little Wichita River, Texas |
| Cox, M., Pvt. (Cunningham's Co., 2nd Front. Dist.) | January 8, 1865 | Dove Creek, Texas |
| Culver, William H., Capt. (Culver's Co., 2nd Front. Dist.) | January 8, 1865 | Dove Creek, Texas |
| Davidson, Sidney Green, Capt. (Co. F, 1st Mtd. Rifles) | June 23, 1861 | Between the Pease River and the Prairie Dog Town Fork of the Red River, Texas |
| Dyer, Jake B., Pvt. (Co. G, Front Reg.) *DOW between January 8–15, 1865* | January 8, 1865 | Dove Creek, Texas |
| Epperson, G. M., Cpl. (Co. A, Fossett's Btn) | January 8, 1865 | Dove Creek, Texas |
| Everett, Albert E., Pvt. (Barnes' Co., 2nd Front. Dist.) | January 8, 1865 | Dove Creek, Texas |
| Ford, _____, Sgt. (Co. G, 1st Mtd. Rifles) | October 8, 1861 | Camp Jackson, Texas |
| Giddens, James R., Lt. (Co. D, Front Reg.) *DOW between January 8–15, 1865* | January 8, 1865 | Dove Creek, Texas |
| Gilbert, Singleton, Lt. (Co. No. 1, 2nd Front. Dist.) | August 9, 1864 | Ellison Springs, Eastland County, Texas |
| Gillintine, John O., Pvt. (Gillintine's Co., 2nd Front. Dist.) | January 8, 1865 | Dove Creek, Texas |
| Gillintine, Nick W., Capt. (Gillintine's Co., 2nd Front. Dist.) *DOW between January 8–15, 1865* | January 8, 1865 | Dove Creek, Texas |
| Gillintine, William M., Pvt. (Gillintine's Co., 2nd Front. Dist.) *DOW inflicted January 8, 1865* | 1867 or 1868 | Dove Creek, Texas |
| Gipson, Francis, Pvt., (Graham's Co., 2nd Front. Dist.) | January 8, 1865 | Dove Creek, Texas |
| Graves, Ransom, Pvt. (Smith's Co., 1st Front. Dist.) *Murdered by Border Reg. troops* | April 25, 1864 | Cooke or Fannin County, Texas |

## Rangers Who Died in the Line of Duty

| Name/Rank/Unit | Date | Site of Death |
|---|---|---|
| Harris, George, Pvt. (Graham's Co., 2nd Front. Dist.) | January 8, 1865 | Dove Creek, Texas |
| Jones, James, Pvt. (Co. K, Border Reg.) *Died of "brain fever"* | September 5, 1864 | Spanish Fort, Texas |
| Jones, Sim, Sgt. (Co. D, Border Reg.) | October 13, 1864 | Bragg Ranch, Young County, Texas |
| Kegans, Benjamin H., Pvt. (Co. C, 1st Mtd. Rifles) | December 16, 1861 | Camp Cooper, Texas |
| Kelly, William B., Pvt. (Co. C, 1st Mtd. Rifles) | June 26, 1861 | Little Wichita River near Camps Cooper and Jackson, Texas |
| Latham, B. D., Lt. (Graham's Co., 2nd Front. Dist.) | January 8, 1865 | Dove Creek, Texas |
| Love, W. M., Sgt. (Graham's Co., 2nd Front. Dist.) | January 8, 1865 | Dove Creek, Texas |
| Lynn, Jerome C. "Bud," Pvt. (Co. C, 1st Mtd. Rifles) | July 29, 1861 | Little Wichita River, Texas |
| McCarty, Andrew J., Pvt. (Co. D, 1st Mtd. Rifles) | June 23, 1861 | Between the Pease River and the Prairie Dog Town Fork of the Red River, Texas |
| McCarver, W. P., Pvt. (Co. G, 1st Mtd Rifles) *Died from Bilious fever* | September 27, 1861 | Camp Colorado, Texas |
| McFarland, James D., Lt. (Co. H, 1st Mtd Rifles) | August 5, 1861 | ? |
| McKee, James, Pvt. (Co. C, 1st Mtd. Rifles) *DOW inflicted July 26, 1861* | July 27, 1861 | Little Wichita River near Camps Cooper and Jackson, Texas |
| Mabray, James S., Pvt. (2nd Front. Dist.) *DOW between January 8–15, 1865* | January 8, 1865 | Dove Creek, Texas |
| Maroney, P. Nelson, Pvt. (Graham's Co., 2nd Front. Dist.) | January 8, 1865 | Dove Creek, Texas |
| Maupin, Perry, Pvt. (Hill's Co., 1st Front. Dist.) | March 25, 1864 | Cooke County, Texas |
| Maxwell, R. H., Pvt. (Orrick's Co., 1st Front. Dist.) | March 15, 1864 | Jack County, Texas |
| Mayes, James N., Pvt. (Co. C, 1st TX. Mtd. Rifles) *Died of typhoid fever* | September 23, 1861 | Camp Cooper, Texas |
| Neatherey, Robert, Pvt. (Co. D, Texas Border Reg.) | October 13, 1864 | Bragg Ranch, Young County, |
| Owen, Solomon H., Pvt. (Co. C, 1st TX. Mtd. Rifles) | October 23, 1861 | Camp Cooper, Texas |
| Parker, Tom, Pvt. (Cunningham's Co., 2nd Front. Dist.) | January 8, 1865 | Dove Creek, Texas |
| Peveler, William R., Lt. (Co. G, Front. Reg.) *DOW inflicted September 13, 1864–died at Flag Springs* | September 22, 1864 | Salt Creek Prairie, Young County, Texas |
| Sageser, J. A., Pvt. (Hill's Co., 1st Front. Dist.) | March 25, 1864 | Cooke County, Texas |
| Snodgrass, Henry I., Pvt. (Co. D, Border Reg.) | October 13, 1864 | Bragg Ranch, Young County, Texas |

| Name/Rank/Unit | Date | Site of Death |
|---|---|---|
| Steene, John D., Pvt. (Barnes' Co., 2nd Front. Dist.) | January 8, 1865 | Dove Creek, Texas |
| Still, Washington, Pvt. (Hank's Co., 1st Front. Dist.)<br>*Hanged* | April 28, 1864 | Wise County, Texas |
| Strong, J. R., Pvt. (Cureton's Co., 1st Front. Dist.) | May 6, 1864 | Stephens County, Texas |
| Stuart, J., Sgt. (Cathey's Co., 2nd Front. Dist.) | January 8, 1865 | Dove Creek, Texas |
| Walker, J. G., Pvt. (Co. D, Young Border Reg.) | October 13, 1864 | Bragg Ranch, County, Texas |
| Weatherby, Thomas C., Pvt. (Co. C, 1st Mtd. Rifles) | July 29, 1861 | Little Wichita River, Texas |
| Willis, S. M., Pvt. (Co. A, Fossett's Btn.)<br>*Died in fall from horse* | April 4, 1865 | Camp Colorado, Texas |
| Wray, S. M., Pvt. (Barnes' Co., 2nd Front. Dist.) | January 8, 1865 | Dove Creek, Texas |
| Wylie, W. L., Pvt. (Co. A, Fossett's Btn) | January 8, 1865 | Dove Creek, Texas |
| Young, Harve F., Pvt. (Co. D, Border Reg.) | July 14, 1864 | Gainesville, Texas |
| Unknown Ranger (Co. E, Front. Reg.) | July 24, 1863 | Clear Fork of the Brazos River, Texas |
| Unknown Ranger (Co. E, Border Reg.) | October 1863 | Montague County near the Red River, Texas |
| Unknown Ranger (Co. G, Front. Reg.) | December 23, 1863 | Potter's Settlement, Cooke County, Texas |
| Unknown Ranger (Co. G, Front. Reg.) | December 23, 1863 | Potter's Settlement, Cooke County, Texas |
| Unknown Ranger (Co. G, Front. Reg.) | December 23, 1863 | Potter's Settlement, Cooke County, Texas |
| Unknown Ranger (Co. G, Front. Reg.) | December 23, 1863 | Potter's Settlement, Cooke County, Texas |
| Unknown Ranger (Co. No. 1, 2nd Front. Dist.) | August 9, 1864 | Ellison Springs, Eastland County, Texas |

## No Surrender, No Prisoners: The Minute Men, the Frontier Forces, and the Frontier Men

| Name/Rank/Unit | Date | Site of Death |
|---|---|---|
| Biediger, Lorenz, Pvt. (Co. E, Front. Forces) | December 5, 1870 | Near Leona River, Texas |
| Clark, Alvin A., Pvt. (2nd Parker County Co.) | June 29, 1866 | Near Springtown, Texas |
| Goodlet, Patrick, Pvt. (Co. B, Front. Forces)<br>*Died of pneumonia* | February 11, 1871 | Erath County, Texas |
| Holmes Frank, Pvt. (Co. B, Front. Forces)<br>*Murdered by fellow ranger* | November 3, 1870 | Fort Griffin, Texas |
| Jones, Henry, Pvt. (Co. C, Kendall County Minute Men)<br>*DOW inflicted July 10, 1874* | July 12, 1874 | Lost Valley, Jack County, Texas |
| Osgood, Joseph F., Pvt. (Front. Men) | 1874 | ? |
| Richarz, Walter, Pvt. (Co. E, Front. Forces) | December 6, 1870 | Blanco Creek, Texas |

| Name/Rank/Unit | Date | Site of Death |
|---|---|---|
| Riff, Joseph R., Pvt. (Co. E, Front. Forces) | December 6, 1870 | Blanco Creek, Texas |
| Swift, Albert M., Pvt. (Co. F, Front. Forces)<br>*Died of illness* | December 27, 1870 | Fort Griffin, Texas |

## A Little Standing Army: Minute Men/Special State Troops/Special Force

| Name/Rank/Unit | Date | Site of Death |
|---|---|---|
| Smith, L. Berry "Sonny," Pvt. (Co. A, Washington County Vol. Mil.) | June 12, 1875 | Palo Alto Prairie, Texas |

## Duty Well Performed: The Frontier Battalion

| Name/Rank/Unit | Date | Site of Death |
|---|---|---|
| Anglin, William B., Pvt. (Co. B) | July 1, 1879 | Head of the North Concho River, Texas |
| Bailey, David W. H., Pvt. (Co. B) | July 12, 1874 | Lost Valley, Jack County, Texas |
| Bingham, George R. "Red," Pvt. (Co. D) | July 3, 1880 | Near Presidio Del Norte, Texas |
| Bohannon, William M., Pvt. (Co. C)<br>*Died of typhoid fever while on a scout* | July 2, 1885 | Pearsall, Texas |
| Doaty, Robert. E., Pvt. (Co. E) | March 22, 1892 | Near Bennett Ranch, Starr County, Texas |
| Fuller, Thomas L., Lt. (Co. B) | October 15, 1900 | Orange, Texas |
| Fusselman, Charles H., Sgt. (Co. D) | April 17, 1890 | Franklin Mountains, Texas |
| Glass, William A., Pvt. (Co. B) | July 12, 1874 | Lost Valley, Jack County, Texas |
| Gravis, John F., Pvt. (Co. D) | August 4, 1890 | Shafter, Texas |
| Hooker, W. L., Pvt. (Co. F)<br>*Drowned in river* | August 28, 1894 | Nueces River, Texas |
| Jones, Frank D., Capt. (Co. D) | June 29, 1893 | Tres Jacales, "Pirate Island," Mexico |
| McBride, John E., Sgt. (Co. C) | December 17, 1877 | San Elizario, Texas |
| McCarty, Timothy J., Pvt. (Co. A) | January 2, 1878 | Near Fort McKavett, Texas |
| McKidrict, Joseph W., Pvt. (Co. D) | April 5, 1894 | El Paso, Texas |
| Moore, James H., Pvt. (Co. F) | March 31, 1887 | On the Sabine River near Hemphill, Texas |
| Mortimer, C. E., Sgt (Co. C) | December 13, 1877 | San Elizario, Texas |
| Nigh, Thomas P., Pvt. (Co. F) | August 16, 1896 | Reeves County, Texas |
| Ruzin, A. A., Pvt. (Co. C) | August 10, 1878 | Las Cornudas, El Paso County, Texas |
| St. Leon, Ernest, Pvt. (Co. D)<br>*DOW inflicted August 20, 1898–died in El Paso* | August 31, 1898 | Socorro, New Mexico Territory |
| Schmid, Frank L., Jr., Pvt. (Co. D)<br>*DOW inflicted August 16, 1889–died in Austin* | June 17, 1893 | Richmond, Texas |
| Sieker, Frank E., Pvt. (Co. D) | May 31, 1885 | Near San Ambrosia Creek, Maverick County, Texas |
| Warren, Benjamin G., Pvt. (Co. E)<br>*Assassinated* | February 10, 1885 | Sweetwater, Texas |
| Wood, J. G., Pvt. (Co. C)<br>*Died of illness* | May 13, 1885 | Fredericksburg, Texas |

| Name/Rank/Unit | Date | Site of Death |
|---|---|---|
| Woods, J. W., Pvt. (Co. E) *Disappeared while working undercover* | November 30, 1893 | Menard County, Texas |

## *Los Rinches*: The State Ranger Force

| Name/Rank/Unit | Date | Site of Death |
|---|---|---|
| Alsobrook, William M., Pvt. (Co. I) *DOW inflicted December 8, 1919 — died in Laredo* | December 9, 1919 | Crestonia, Texas |
| Buchanan, Joseph B., Pvt. (Co. A) | December 25, 1921 | Polvo, Texas |
| Burdett, Robert Lee, Pvt. (Co. B) | June 7, 1915 | Fabens, Texas |
| Carnes, Quirl Bailey, Pvt. (Co. D) | July 31, 1910 | Near San Benito, Texas |
| Goff, Thomas J., Pvt. (Co. C) *DOW inflicted September 13, 1905* | September 14, 1905 | Near Terlingua, Texas |
| Goodrich. O. W., Pvt. (Co. B) | February 11, 1916 | Valentine, Texas |
| Hulen, Eugene B., Pvt. (Co. B) | May 24, 1916 | Pilares Canyon, Texas |
| Hunt, Robert E., Pvt. (Co. L) *Died of Spanish Influenza* | October 15, 1918 | El Paso, Texas |
| Hyde, Thomas C., Pvt. (Co. L) *Died of amoebic dysentery* | April 30, 1918 | Clint, Texas |
| McDuffie, Dan L., Pvt. (Co. B) | July 7, 1931 | Gladewater, Texas |
| Moran, John A., Pvt. (Co. A) *Died of pneumonia* | December 12, 1910 | Alice, Texas |
| Pennington, Ben L., Pvt. (Co. L) *Died of Spanish Influenza* | October 12, 1918 | El Paso, Texas |
| Perkins, T. E. P., Pvt. (Co. L) | November 7, 1918 | Near Anaya Ranch, Texas |
| Ransom, Henry L., Capt. (Co C) | April 1, 1918 | Sweetwater, Texas |
| Robuck, W. Emmett, Pvt. (Co. A) | September 9, 1902 | Near Brownsville, Texas |
| Russell, Grover Scott, Pvt. (Co. A) *Murdered in ambush* | June 23, 1913 | Near El Paso, Texas |
| Sadler, Leonard T., Pvt. (Co G) *Killed accidentally* | September 15, 1918 | Devil's River, Texas |
| Shaw, Joe R., Pvt. (Co G) | August 21, 1918 | Tomate Bend near Fort Brown, Texas |
| Sherman, S. F., Pvt. (Co. A) *Struck by train* | November 7, 1922 | Palestine, Texas |
| Stillwell, William B., Pvt. (Co. F) | April 3, 1918 | Near Rio Grande in Chihuahua, Mexico |
| Thomas, H. M. "Doc," Pvt. (Co. A) | January 6, 1909 | Amarillo, Texas |
| Timberlake, Delbert "Tim," Sgt. (Co. F) *DOW inflicted October 10, 1918 — died in Brownsville* | October 11, 1918 | Tomate Bend near Fort Brown, Texas |
| Turner, H. R., Pvt. (Co. C) *Died of heart attack* | July 11, 1933 | Waco, Texas |
| Veale, Bert C., Pvt. (Co. D) *Murdered by Capt. K. F. Cunningham* | February 7, 1919 | Near Austin, Texas |
| White, Emmett, Pvt. (Co. C) *Struck by oil field truck on "Pistol Hill"* | August 8, 1933 | Near Kilgore, Texas |
| White, Homer, Pvt. (Co. A) | February 4, 1908 | Weatherford, Texas |
| White, John Dudley, Sr., Pvt. (Co. B) | July 12, 1918 | Near Broaddus, Texas |
| Willard, Timothy S., Special Ranger | April 19, 1928 | Grayson County, Texas |

## A Fabled Tradition: The Texas Ranger Division

| Name/Rank/Unit | Date | Site of Death |
|---|---|---|
| Doherty, Bobby Paul, Ranger (Co. B) | February 20, 1978 | Argyle, Texas |
| Guffey, Stanley Keith, Sgt. (Co. F) | January 22, 1987 | Horseshoe Bay, Texas |
| Nordyke, Clarence R., Sgt. (Co. E)<br>*Died in automobile accident* | July 18, 1955 | Near Mertzon, Texas |
| White, H. A., Ranger (Co. A)<br>*Died in automobile/train collision* | December 8, 1961 | Near Richmond, Texas |

# Appendix C:
# The Texas Ranger Hall of Fame

*(Inductees Listed with Their Highest Rank Held in the Ranger Service)*

| | |
|---|---|
| Stephen F. Austin | Captain John R. Hughes |
| 1st Lieutenant John B. Armstrong | Major John B. Jones |
| Sergeant Ira Aten | Captain John J. Klevenhagen, Sr. |
| Captain George W. Baylor | Captain Benjamin McCulloch |
| Captain James A. Brooks | Captain William J. McDonald |
| Ranger Martin Burton | Captain Leander H. McNelly |
| Captain Robert A. Crowder | Captain Bryan Marsh |
| Ranger Bobby Paul Doherty | Ranger Charles E. Miller |
| Major John S. Ford | Senior Captain Clinton T. Peoples |
| Sergeant James B. Gillett | Captain James E. Riddles |
| Captain Manuel T. Gonzaullas | Captain John H. Rogers |
| Sergeant Stanley Keith Guffey | Captain Lawrence S. Ross |
| Captain Jesse L. Hall | Captain Samuel H. Walker |
| Senior Captain Francis A. Hamer | Captain William A. A. Wallace |
| Captain John C. Hays | Captain William L. Wright |
| Senior Captain Thomas R. Hickman | |

# Appendix D: Texas Ranger Recipients of the Department of Public Safety Medal of Valor

"The Medal of Valor is the highest award presented by the Texas Department of Public Safety. It may be issued to any member of the Department who intelligently distinguishes himself conspicuously by gallantry and intrepidity at the risk of his or her own life. The deed performed must have been by voluntary act and of personal bravery or self-sacrifice so conspicuous as to distinguish clearly the individual for gallantry and intrepidity above his or her comrades and must have involved risk of life, known to the member before performing the act. It must be the type of deed which, if left undone, would not subject him to any justifiable criticism. The act must be far above and beyond the normal call of duty."—Department of Public Safety description

### Texas Ranger Sgt. William R. Gerth
Awarded May 23, 1983

"*Awarded in recognition of the gallant manner in which he risked his own life to preserve that of a fellow law enforcement officer.*

*Ranger William R. Gerth, on May 19, 1983, in Wichita Falls, Texas, responded to a police department radio broadcast advising that an alleged bank robber was traveling on Sisk Road in that City. Ranger Gerth observed the suspect vehicle and requested backup support from a DPS trooper. As the trooper joined pursuit, the suspect vehicle came to an abrupt stop. The robbery suspect exited his vehicle and immediately opened fire with an automatic weapon on the trooper causing minor lacerations and pinning the trooper inside his vehicle. As the armed suspect approached the trooper's vehicle, Ranger Gerth became involved in an exchange of gunfire with the suspect, which resulted in the suspect being killed. As a result of Gerth's positive, timely, and gallant actions, the life of the DPS trooper was spared.*"

### Texas Ranger Sgt. Stanley Keith Guffey
Posthumously Awarded February 10, 1987

"*Awarded in recognition of the gallant and courageous manner in which he effected the rescue of a kidnapped child being held for ransom at the expense of his life.*

*Texas Ranger Stanley Keith Guffey, along with another Texas Ranger, on January 22, 1987, in Llano County, Texas, volunteered to be the arrest and rescue team in a high-risk tactical operation. It had been determined that a kidnapper holding a two-year-old girl for ransom could not be permitted to depart a designated ransom-exchange area with the kidnapped child, as it was believed he would attempt to murder her. He had claimed to have murdered a second victim, which claim was subsequently determined to be true. Ranger Guffey, along with his fellow Ranger, concealed himself in an automobile that was to be delivered to the kidnapper at the exchange point. The subject appeared and, rather than releasing the child, placed her and the ransom money in the vehicle where he was confronted by the Rangers, who identified themselves in an effort to effect his surrender and avoid bloodshed. The kidnapper commenced firing and, in an ensuing exchange of gunfire between the Rangers and the suspect, the suspect was killed and Ranger Guffey was mortally wounded. These heroic actions rescued the kidnapped victim from certain death. Ranger Guffey's dedication to duty, his concern for human life, and gallantry and courage exhibited while fulfilling the responsibilities of his chosen life role brought much credit to himself, his family, and to the cause of law enforcement."*

## Texas Ranger Sgt. John E. Aycock
First Award February 10, 1987

"Awarded in recognition of the gallant and courageous manner in which he effected the rescue of a kidnapped child being held for ransom at the risk of his own life.

*Texas Ranger John E. Aycock, along with Texas Ranger Stanley Keith Guffey, on January 22, 1987, in Llano County, Texas, volunteered to be the arrest and rescue team in a high-risk tactical operation. It had been determined that a kidnapper holding a two-year-old-girl for ransom could not be permitted to depart a designated ransom-exchange area with the kidnapped child, as it was believed he would attempt to murder her. He had claimed to have murdered a second victim, which claim was subsequently determined to be true. Ranger Aycock, along with his fellow Ranger, concealed himself in an automobile that was to be delivered to the kidnapper at the exchange point. The subject appeared and, rather than releasing the child, placed her and the ransom money in the vehicle where he was confronted by the Rangers, who identified themselves in an effort to effect his surrender and avoid bloodshed. The kidnapper commenced firing and, in an ensuing exchange of gunfire between the Rangers and the suspect, the suspect was killed and Ranger Guffey was mortally wounded. These heroic actions rescued the kidnapped victim from certain death. Ranger Aycock's dedication to duty, his concern for human life, and gallantry and courage exhibited while fulfilling the responsibilities of his chosen life role brought much credit to himself and to the cause of law enforcement."*

## Texas Ranger Sgt. John E. Aycock
Second Award September 1, 1995

"Awarded in recognition of his valorous performance and extraordinary skill exhibited during the successful conclusion of a life-threatening hostage situation.

Sergeant Aycock was involved as a "hostage negotiator" during a situation where an individual was holding a 14-month-old child at gunpoint and law enforcement officials in a standoff in a field in rural Mills County. The individual had kidnapped the child earlier in the day, firing a 12-gauge shotgun through a door of a residence threatening to kill the child's mother. A high-speed chase ensued and the individual's stolen vehicle was disabled. Continuously threatening the life of the child, the individual indicated that he might attempt suicide. Over approximately a four hour period, Sgt. Aycock at great personal risk, exhibited extraordinary courage, skill, and judgment in negotiating with the individual and finally successfully rescued the child and arrested the individual. His performance exemplifies the high standards of the Ranger Division and reflects credit upon him, the Texas Department of Public Safety, and the law enforcement profession."

## Texas Ranger Sgt. Danny V. Rhea
Awarded March 9, 1998

"*Awarded in recognition of his valorous and professional response exhibited during a crisis situation where he faced a deranged individual holding what was believed to be an explosive device in a Texas Department of Public Safety building.*

*On January 6, 1998, Ranger Sergeant Danny V. Rhea assisted Trooper Cody Sanders and Trooper George K. Harris in dealing with a man who was carrying what was identified as a bomb at the Sulphur Springs Texas Department of Public Safety office. The man told Trooper Harris to evacuate the building because he was going to blow himself up. The building was evacuated and the officers negotiated with the man for almost an hour believing he was holding an explosive device and intended to detonate the device. The man eventually displayed a handgun and pointed it at Trooper Harris. Ranger Sergeant Rhea then fired one shot, fatally wounding the man. Ranger Sergeant Rhea's courage, decisive action, and dedication to duty in this tense and volatile situation bring great credit to him, the Texas Department of Public Safety, and the profession of law enforcement.*"

# Appendix E: Documents Regarding the Texas Rangers

Various letters and pieces of legislation are featured in this appendix because they reflect the evolution of the Ranger Service. The growth of the organization from a tradition of ad hoc units of frontiersmen to an institution of professional law enforcement officers can be found in the following pages.

---

### John Tumlinson & Robert Kuykendall to Governor Trespalacios District of Colorado 7th January 1823

His Excellency the Commandant General of Texas
Sir

In obedience to Verbal Orders given us by your commissioner Baron De Bastrop we made an Exploration to the Sea Coast our party was fourteen strong all mounted on reaching [illegible] Eight Leagues above the landing of the bay we found that the Indians had been at that place a few days before we reached it in considerable force and had burned all the little huts but one & that one they had set fire to but it did not take almost all of the property that had been stored at this place was either destroyed or carried off from there we proceeded on to Wilsons Camp (Mr Wilson being with us) on the Trespalacios river where we found the most of his property safe some had been taken off by unknown hands but no appearance of Indian Signs. The Weather being Wet and the country very flat & full of water we found it would be useful to attempt to leave the coast as well as from the weakness of our party and the bad condition of our horses & being well convinced that nothing Effectual could be done without boats and force at any time as there will have to be a force on the Water at the same time to act with a land force from this place we returned in three days to [illegible] Camp where we discovered that the Indians had spies out as there was fresh horse signs at or near the camp and the evening before and the day there were several fires or signals on the west of the Colorado those signals extended for almost ten leagues from one extreme to the other.

We are of opinion that if your Excellency would give the permission that we could raise fifteen hardy expert young men who are expert with the rifle by Enlistment for the same pay that the troops of the Empire receive & with this number and an addition of ten of your troops we have no doubt but the coast could be protected in such a manner that settlers could land with safety in our waters. There would be an other advantage in having of a number of our people to help to guard the Post they generally are very Expert with tools and would in a short time be able to build safe defensive Blockhouses as well as Small Boats we are confident that no Effectual Expedition can be made against those Indians with out boats & if they could be provided our Militia would as soon as the ground would Support horses and the grassed Earth become firm turn out in Mass & divide their forces part by land and part by water & not to return until those [illegible] Should be brought to a sense of their true interests our people who would be enlisted in the service could be discharged at the end of six or nine months we don't believe that they would be willing to leave more that nine months as it is all of their intentions to make farms and [plant?] another year. There can be a plentitude of corn procured about twelve or fifteen Leagues above where the Blockhouses we expect would be wanted this corn would not cost more than from two & a half Bits per [illegible] and Beef could be had in these Settlements at six Dollars per 100 lbs so there would be but little inconvenience in procuring these supplies.

Subject Matter of this letter

[mostly illegible apology for letter]
John Tumlinson, alcalde
Robert Kuykendall, Captain

P.S. If your Excellency can not with convenience forward an answer to this letter immediately that Mr Brotherton the Bearer of this will immediately return with your answer

Lieutenant Moses Morrison of this district is willing to take the charge of Commander of the troops We consider him very capable of such a charge knowing that he would spare no pains or trouble to have blockhouses immediately built as well as the necessary boats We know that his judgment in both of these is good as he has been in the United States Service on the Upper Mississippi frontier and is well acquainted in the manner that both ought to be constructed. a few days before we made the Expedition to the Coast some of our neighbors were at the Lower landing at the mouth of this river & reported that the Indians had completely carried every thing off from there We hope Your Excellency will as soon as convenient advise us of the [illegible]

---

### Governor Trespalacios to Tumlinson & Kuykendall

This is in response to the two letters dated the 7th instant that Your Excellencies sent to me by Mr. Brotherton. I must say to Your Excellencies that I am not at all opposed to the proposal that includes enlisting fifteen men and a commander for guarding the coast, also for constructing sturdy blockhouses and for constructing small boats.

I received an order from the Commandant General in his last letter telling me that if the Indians continue their depredations I am to go after them and either destroy them altogether or subdue them in as fair and equitable a way as possible. However I want to bring to the attention of Your Excellencies that those troops that are enlisted for this exercise should not receive the same pay as veteran troops whose duties have included a variety of operations for which the new recruits are not being enlisted. Therefore it is essential that Your Excellencies tell me how you want to handle this particular assignment. At the same time, please also send me an estimate of the cost of the blockhouses and of the small boats.

Two soldiers who deserted are imprisoned under suspicion of being the ones who killed Thomas Rogers and a foreigner who were found on the Colorado River. By courier I am sending you one of the two carbines that were found on them, and hope that if there is such a thing as conscientiousness, the gun will be returned to me via Nelson and the others. They might know the four Spaniards who were in the company of the foreigner at the Colorado River, and they could act as witnesses against them.

The individuals hired by the Judge, as couriers shouldn't be excluded from these duties for the duration of their term, since guarding the inhabitants of this area is essential. I hope to be able to meet with you in this area in the spring.

May God bless and protect Your Excellencies for many years.

Jose Felix Trespalacios

Bexar, January 31, 1822 (1823)
The Honorable Judges Tumlinson and Robert Kuykendall
The Colorado River

---

## John Tumlinson & Robert Kuykendall to Governor Trespalacios
### District of Colorado Province of Texas, 5 March 1823

To His Excellency Jose Felix Trespalacios Govt Gen of the Province

We the Civil Judge [illegible] desire to [illegible] to you Honor that the Result of your Letter under date 30th January last by Mr. Brotherton was well pleasing to us and the american Settlers generally as it Evinced a disposition in the Govt to grant us that protection we so much need.

And in Answer to that part of the Letter where your Excellency observing that the fifteen men to be Enlisted by the Americans cannot expect to receive the same pay as the Spanish soldiers in as much as they will not be in active service. We beg leave to observe, that we have taken all due pains to know the opinion, of the Settlers generally on this head & find that but one opinion appears to prevail, to wit —

That good & Efficient Men cannot be raised for a less Sum than $24 [illegible] they to furnish themselves with clothing & provisions but they further Say — that they will build such Blockhouses as may be deemed necessary & sufficient for their Safety & protection & to answer present purposes at their own Expense and will do all in their power to give general satisfaction —

We now have dispatched the bearer Lieut. Moses Morrison to your Excellency, We beg leave to recommend him as a young man of worth & bravery & who has been Selected as a proper person to take Command of the little Garrison now Contemplated, to be Established at the Bay. He will communicate to you the particulars of the late depredations committed by the Indians on three of our young men who were ascending the River with a Canoe laden with Corn & on Sunday 23 last were attacked by the Savages, two of them to wit John Alley & H W Law were killed by them John Clark badly wounded & of the affairs of Brotherton, being robbed and wounded on the 24th we have written to your Excellency & stated with what promptness & success we proceeded against the Savages on the 25th last. We hope & trust that when your Excellency takes into consideration the busy season of the years and the disturbed and distracted state of [illegible] Settlement. At present many remaining in doubt whether to plant their ground after having prepared it for Corn or to move back to the U States with their families. We have used our best endeavours to quiet their minds until the return of bearers from S Antonio not doubting that your Excellency will grant us the aid and assistance so absolutely necessary for the safety & protection of our infant settlement.

As it Respects the building of boats which your Excellency desires to know the cost of, we are not at present able to ascertain the Expense of not having the size or description of the kind best suited or required and not having materials here suitable for such purposes but are of opinion they could be obtained on easier terms and with more facility at N Orleans.

With regard to the Murder of Rogers, and the Stranger with him by four Spaniards we beg leave to observe that the Rifle found in possession of the Spaniards & sent on here by the hands of Brotherton for examination, is well known by many of the inhabitants here as the property of the late Rogers [illegible] & by the bearer Lieut Morrison who is now accompanied by James Neilson, who goes with the Rifle as witness against the prisoners.— and further we would observe that the Stranger Murdered in Co. With Rogers we have ascertained to be a young man of Merit by the name of Hines, who resided for sometime with Col. Pettus on the Brazos and who unfortunately fell in completely with the four Spaniards on the route tho he being a stranger to them & considered them as guides and protectors to [illegible] & S Antonio where he was going with a quantity of Buttons, one Gold and two Silver Watches for disposal of—

We are much pleased with the Idea of Serving your Excellency at our Settlement the present Spring and will do all in our power to make you as Comfortable as our poor abilities will allow.— and pray the lord always to have you in the holy Keeping

John Tumlinson<br>Robert Kuykendall

PS we herewith send a list of the Names of the Inhabitants of our settlement Their occupation & observing at same time that those are yet some not yet returned and will be forwarded in due time

---

## AUSTIN'S ADDRESS TO COLONISTS

[August 5, 1823?]*

Since the commencement of this Colony no labor or expense has been spared on my part towards its organization benefit and security — And I shall always be ready and willing to risk my health, my property or my life for the common advantage of those who have embarked with me in this enterprise. As proof of the reality of this declaration I have determined to augment at my own private expense the company of men which was raised by order of the late Govr Trespalacios for the defense of the Colony against hostile Indians. I therefore by these presents give public notice that I will employ ten men in addition to those employed by the Governt to act as rangers for the common defense. The said ten men will form a part of Lieut. Moses Morrisons Company and the whole will be subject to my orders. The wages I will give the said ten men is fifteen Dollars a month payable in property, they finding themselves— Those who wish to be employed will apply to me without delay.

---

### *Journal of the Permanent Council.*

Council Room Oct 17, 1835.

*On motion of Mr. Parker of Nacogdoches the following resolutions were adopted:*

*Resolved*, That Silas M. Parker be and is hereby authorized and required to impl[o]y and superintend the conduct and proceedings of twenty five rangers whose business shall be to range and guard the frontiers between the Brazos and Trinity rivers, and that Garrison Green-

---

*Written on the reverse of Bastrop's proclamation of August 5.

wood be and is hereby authorized and required to impl[o]y and superintend the proceedings and conduct of ten rangers on the East side of the Trinity River — and that D. B. Friar be and is hereby authorized and required to impl[o]y and superintend the conduct and Proceedings of twenty five Rangers Whose business it shall be to range between the Brazos and Colorado Rivers and that each of those superintendents have a right To engage to each ranger that [is] employed one dollar and twenty five cents per day until the convention make other arrangements and to draw on the council or the executive established by the Convention from time to time for such sums of money as is necessary to defray expenses accompanying each draft by account of expenditures.

On motion a committee of five men appointed on the subject of the above resolutions.

Whereupon the following persons were nominated by the Chair said committee Daniel Parker, Alexander Thompson, A. G. Perry, J. G. W. Pierson, William Pettus

On motion of Mr. Perry the house adjourned to wait the report of the Committee appointed by the Chair on Mr. Parker's Resolution.

Saturday 3 o'clock the council met in pursuant to adjournment.

Mr. Perry from Viesca Chairman of the Committee to whom were referred the resolution of Mr. Parker on the subject of a line of rangers on the frontiers made the following report:

The committee to whom were referred the resolution of Daniel Parker adopted by the genl council of Texas for the establishment of a line of Rangers from the Colorado to the Nazish [Neches] River have had the matters and things referred to them under consideration and beg leave to report that in their opinion that the superintendents of the rangers from the Colorado to the Brazos and from the Brazos to the Trinity should make their place of rendezvous at the Ouaco [Waco] village on the Brazos River, that the superintendent of the rangers on the East side of the Trinity River make his place of rendezvous at the town of Houston that the said superintendents have full power and authority to call and contract with men and for ammunition and provisions agreeable to said resolutions and draw on the genl council or executive hereafter appointed for pay — making an exhibition of his accounts for the same that said Superintendents should be Vigilant in carrying said resolutions into effect on being notified of said resolutions that said companies when assembled at their places of rendezvous shall elect their officers whose duty it shall be to report to the superintendents every fifteen days their proceedings who shall report the same to the genl council or executive as the case may be at least very thirty days by express the expenses of which shall be paid out of the public funds of Texas that the companies ranging from the Colorado to the Brazos and from the Brazos to the Trinity shall rendezvous at the Ouaco Village very fifteen days unless prevented by engagement with or in pursuit of the Indians that said companies shall unite when ever in the opinion of their officers it shall from the situation of the country become necessary that said officers be particular not to interfere with friendly tribes of Indians on our borders that said superintendents shall watch over the conduct of the officers and report accordingly and see that full justice is done to the bounds assigned them.

A. G. Perry Chm
Daniel Parker
Alexander Thompson
J. G. W. Pierson
William Pettus

Which on motion of Mr. Perry was adopted

## Journals of the Consultation

SAN FELIPE DE AUSTIN, Nov. 7th, 1835.
TWO O'CLOCK P.M.

Mr. Clements offered the following resolution:

*Resolved*, That the route of the rangers who are employed, or may be employed, to protect our frontier, shall be extended from the Colorado river, their present limits, to the settlements on the Guadalupe river, &c.; and that a proportionate number of men be appointed for that purpose, equal to that employed on the balance of the frontier,

Which, on motion of Mr. Perry, was laid on the table one day.

HENRY MILLARD, *Chairman*.

R. R. ROYAL, *Secretary*.

---

## Journals of the Consultation

SAN FELIPE DE AUSTIN, Nov. 9th, 1835.
NINE O'CLOCK A.M.

Mr. Parker from the committee to whom was referred the resolution of Mr. Clements respecting the rangers, made report, which was read and adopted, as follows:

The committee to whom was referred the resolution of Mr. Clements, on the subject of a line of rangers from the Neches river to the Colorado, has had the same under consideration, and beg leave to report the following resolution:

*Resolved*, That we recognize the acts of the general council on that subject, sufficient for the present emergency. That said line of rangers be extended from the Colorado river to the Cibollo, with a company of twenty rangers from the superintendence of G. W. Davis, who shall be governed by the same resolutions and instructions of the other superintendent heretofore given; and that the said G. W. Davis, make his place of rendezvous at the place known by the big spring or head of St. Mark's [San Marcos] river.

From the information before your committee, they recommend that the acts of Silas M. Parker, in the organization of rangers under his superintendence, before they reached the proper place of rendezvous, be recognized; and that the said S. M. Parker be authorized to add ten more men to their company, by and under the former authority and rules.

DANIEL PARKER, *Chairman*.

---

## Ordinances and Decrees of the Consultation, Provisional Government of Texas

*Ordinances and Decrees*
OF THE MILITARY
Article IX

There shall be a corps of Rangers under the command of a major, to consist of one hundred and fifty men, to be divided into three or more detachments, and which shall compose a battalion under the commander-in-chief, when in the field.

(Signed) JAMES W. ROBINSON
Lieut. Gov. and ex-officio President of the General Council
Attest, P. B. DEXTER, Secretary of the General Council
Approved, 19th Nov. 1835

HENRY SMITH, Governor.
C. B. STEWART, Secretary to the Executive and Recording Clerk.

## Ordinances and Decrees of the Consultation, Provisional Government of Texas

*Ordinances and Decrees*
OF THE MILITARY
*An Ordinance and Decree to establish and organize a Corps of Rangers.*

Be it ordained and decreed, and it is hereby ordained and decreed by the General Council of the Provisional Government of Texas, That there shall be, and there is hereby created and established a Corps of Rangers, which shall consist of three companies of fifty-six men each, with one Captain, one Lieutenant, one second Lieutenant for each company; and there shall be one Major to command the said companies, who shall be subject to the orders and direction of the Commander-in-Chief of the Regular Army.

SEC. 2. *Be it further ordained and decreed, &c.*, That the privates of said Corps shall be enrolled for one year, and shall receive, as a full compensation for pay, rations, clothing and horse service, one dollar and twenty-five cents per day for themselves and service of their horses; and the said privates shall be, and they are hereby required to be always ready armed and equipped, and supplied with one hundred rounds of powder and ball, and to have always ready for active service, a good and sufficient horse, properly accoutred and equipped with saddle, bridle and blanket, at their own expense; and in default thereof, the captain or commanding officer of the said company to which said private belongs, shall cause a horse to be purchased for said private and charge him with the same, in the settlement of his quarterly accounts.

SEC. 3. *Be it further ordained and decreed, &c.*, That the officer of the said Corps, in addition to the per diem compensation of the privates in the Corps of Rangers, shall receive the same pay as the officers of the same rank and grade in the Regiment of Dragoons in the Army of the United States of America.

Passed at San Felipe de Austin, Nov. 24, 1835.

(Signed) JAMES W. ROBINSON,
Lieut. Gov. and ex-officio Pres't of G. C.

P. B. DEXTER,
Sec'y of the Gen. Council.
Approved, Nov. 26, 1835.

HENRY SMITH,
Governor.

CHARLES B. STEWART,
Executive Secretary.

## Laws of the Republic of Texas.
AN ACT,
**To protect the Frontier.**

SEC. 1. Be it enacted by the senate and house of representatives of the republic of Texas, in congress assembled, That the president be, and he is hereby required to raise, with as little delay as possible, a battalion of mounted riflemen, to consist of two hundred and eighty men, for the protection of the frontier, to be officered in like manner as the balance of the army.

SEC. 2. Be it further enacted, That the term of service of said corps shall be for twelve months or upwards, and each man shall be bound to furnish himself with a suitable, serviceable horse, a good rifle, and one brace of pistols, if they can be procured; and no one shall be allowed to enter said corps without first submitting his horse, arms, and equipments, to the inspection of an officer specially appointed by the inspector general of the army, who shall certify that such man, horse, and equipments are fit for the service.

SEC. 3. Be it further enacted, That the pay, emoluments, and bounty of said corps shall be the same as that provided for other corps of the army, with this addition, that the sum of fifteen dollars per month be allowed for the furnishing of the horses and arms.

SEC. 4. Be it further enacted, That the president be, and he is hereby authorized to order out, for the protection of the frontier, such number of the militia as the exigencies of the case may require.

SEC. 5. Be it further enacted, That it shall be the duty of the president to cause to be erected such block houses, forts, and trading houses, as in his judgment may be necessary to prevent Indian depredation.

SEC. 6. Be it further enacted, That the president have full power, when in his opinion the exigencies of the country may require it, to order said corps to any other point than the frontier, or to the main army.

SEC. 7. Be it further enacted, That it shall be the duty of the president to enter such negotiations and treaties as in his opinion may secure peace to the frontiers; and that he have power to appoint agents to reside amongst the Indians, and that he be authorized to distribute amongst the different tribes such presents as her may deem necessary, not to exceed in amount twenty thousand dollars.

SEC. 8. Be it further enacted, That the said corps shall be under the same rules, regulations, and restrictions of the regular army of the republic; and should any officer or soldier be found guilty of a willful neglect of duty or disobedience of the order of his superiors, he shall be subject to the usual pains and penalties inflicted on officers and soldiers in the regular army for like offenses.

SEC. 9. Be it further enacted, That should a larger force be necessary, the president shall be authorized to extend the number so as not to exceed one regiment, of five hundred and sixty men, rank and file.

IRA INGRAM,
Speaker of the house of representatives.
RICHARD ELLIS,
President pro tem. of the senate.

Approved, December 5, 1836.

SAM HOUSTON

## Laws of the Republic of Texas.
### AN ACT
Defining the pay of Mounted Riflemen, now and hereafter in the ranging service on the Frontier.

SEC. 1. Be it enacted by the senate and house of representatives of the republic of Texas, in congress assembled, That each and every mounted rifleman, who has entered the ranging service, and not otherwise provided for, be, and is hereby entitled to twenty-five dollars per month as pay, and the same bounty of land as other volunteers in the field.

SEC. 2. Be it further enacted, That the pay of officers in the above service shall be as follows: a captain shall be entitled to receive seventy-five dollars per month, a first lieutenant shall receive sixty dollars per month, a second lieutenant, fifty dollars per month, and the orderly sergeant, forty dollars per month; the said officers shall also be entitled to the same bounties of land as officers of the same grade and rank in the volunteer army.

SEC. 3. And be it further enacted, That all officers and soldiers, who have been actually engaged in the ranging service since July 1835 shall be included in this act, and shall receive pay for the time he is in service.

IRA INGRAM,
Speaker of the house of representatives.
RICHARD ELLIS,
President pro tem. of the senate.

Approved, December 10, 1836.

SAM HOUSTON

---

## Laws of the Republic of Texas.
### AN ACT
### For the better protection of the northern frontier.

SEC. 1. Be it enacted by the Senate and House of Representatives of the republic of Texas, in Congress assembled, That a corps of mounted gun men, consisting of six hundred mounted men, rank and file, shall be raised by voluntary enlistment, for a term of six months, dating from the time of rendezvous, and officered in the following manner, viz: one colonel, one Lieutenant-Colonel, one major, ten captains, ten first and second lieutenants; all of whom shall be appointed by the president, by and with the advice and consent of the senate.

SEC. 2. Be it further enacted, That each officer and private shall furnish himself with substantial horse, well shod all round, and extra shoeing nails, a good gun, two hundred rounds of ammunition, and all other necessary equipment, provisions, &c., except beef.

SEC. 3. Be it further enacted, That the officers shall receive the same pay as is fixed in the corresponding rank in the ranging service; and the privates twenty-five dollars per month, and the officers and men a bounty of six hundred and forty acres each.

SEC. 4. Be it further enacted, That when spoils are taken from the enemy, the commanding officer shall have the same divided equally amongst officers and men.

SEC. 5. Be it further enacted, That the corps shall be divided into three divisions, to rendezvous at such times and places as may be directed by the president.

SEC. 6. Be it further enacted, That a quarter master appointed by the president, shall attend each division, whose duty it shall be to purchase beef at the expense of the government for the supply of said troops.

SEC. 7. Be it further enacted, That each six men shall furnish themselves with a packhorse.

SEC. 8. Be it further enacted, That if practicable, there shall be attached to each division one company of spies, composed of Shawnees, Cherokees, Delewares, or of other friendly Indians, who shall be supplied with provisions, and shall receive such pay as may be agreed upon between them and the president, which shall be paid in goods.

SEC. 9. Be it further enacted, That when any officer or soldier shall disobey orders, or shall behave in an ungentlemanly or unsoldierlike manner, if an officer, the president shall have the power to discharge him dishonorably, and report the same to the senate; and if a non-commissioned officer or private, in like manner to give him a dishonorable discharge; and in all cases of dishonorable dismissal the individual shall forfeit all right to pay and bounty land; and it shall be the duty of the president, in conformity with the provisions of this section, to discharge all officers and soldiers in the service who disobey orders.

SEC. 10. Be it further enacted, That the president shall have the power to appoint an inspector, or inspectors, whose duty it shall be to report all delinquents to the president, who on such information shall exercise the powers of dismissal embraced in the preceding section.

SEC. 11. Be it further enacted, That the president shall have the power of discharging them at an earlier period than six months, if he should deem it expedient.

B. T. ARCHER,
Speaker of the house of representatives.
JESSE GRIMES,
President pro tem. of the senate.

Approved, June 12, 1837.

SAM HOUSTON

---

## Laws of the Republic of Texas.
### AN ACT
### Entitled an Act for the further Protection of the Frontier against the Comanche and other Indians.

Sec. 1. Be it enacted by the Senate and House of Representatives of the Republic of Texas in Congress assembled, That the President be, and he is hereby authorized to accept of the service of eight Companies of Mounted Volunteers, to consist of one Captain, one First and Second Lieutenant, three Sergeants, and fifty-three Privates, each for the term of six months, to be placed on the same footing as regards monthly pay as Mounted Riflemen in the Ranging Service, agreeably to an Act passed December the tenth, one thousand eight hundred and thirty-six.

Sec. 2. Be it further enacted, That the said Companies shall constitute one Regiment, to be commanded by one Colonel, one Lieutenant Colonel, and one Major, to be appointed by the President.

Sec. 3. Be it further enacted, That for the purpose of carrying into effect the provision of this act, the sum of seventy-five thousand dollars is hereby appropriated, and the President is authorized to issue of the promissory noted of the Government such an amount as will be required for immediate purposes.

Sec. 4. Be it further enacted, That the President shall have power to use the troops contemplated in this Act offensively or defensively, as in his opinion the interest of the country may require.

JOHN M. HANSFORD,
Speaker of the House of Representatives.
S. H. EVERITT,
President pro tem. of the Senate.

Approved, December 29, 1838.

MIRABEAU B. LAMAR

## Laws of the Republic of Texas.
### AN ACT
#### Entitled an Act for the Protection of a portion of the Frontier.

Sec. 1. Be it enacted by the Senate and House of Representatives of the Republic of Texas in Congress assembled, That the sum of five thousand dollars be, and the same is hereby appropriated for the purpose of raising and supporting a Company of fifty-six Rangers for three months, to be commanded by Captain John Wortham, whose duty it shall be to range on the frontier of Houston, or any frontier Counties, and to protect the settlements; which said sum shall be at the disposition of the President.

Sec. 2. Be it further enacted, That it shall be the duty of the Captain of the Company herein created, to report at least every two weeks to Brigadier General K. H. Douglass, and keep him advised of his movements.

JOHN M. HANSFORD,
Speaker of the House of Representatives.
S. H. EVERITT,
President pro tem. of the Senate.

Approved, January 1, 1839.

MIRABEAU B. LAMAR

---

## Laws of the Republic of Texas.
### AN ACT
#### To authorize the raising of a company of fifty-six men for the ranging service.

Sec. 1. Be it enacted by the Senate and House of Representatives of the Republic of Texas in Congress assembled, That the sum of five thousand dollars be, and the same is hereby appropriated for the purpose of raising and supporting a company of fifty-six men, to act as rangers for three months, to be commanded by such person as the President may appoint by and with the consent of the Senate, whose duty it shall be to range on the frontier of Gonzales county, and protect the settlements; which said sum shall be at the disposition of the president.

Sec. 2. Be it further enacted, That it shall be the duty of the captain of the company herein created, to report to the secretary of war and to the Brigadier General of the first brigade, and keep them advised of his movements.

JOHN M. HANSFORD,
Speaker of the House of Representatives.
DAVID G. BURNET,
President of the Senate.

Approved, January 15, 1839.

MIRABEAU B. LAMAR

---

## Laws of the Republic of Texas.
### AN ACT
#### To provide for the raising of three Companies of Mounted Volunteers for frontier service against the hostile Indians.

Sec. 1. Be it enacted by the Senate and House of Representatives of the Republic of Texas in Congress assembled, That the President be, and he is hereby authorized to accept the services of three companies of mounted volunteers for immediate active service, on the frontiers of Bastrop, Robertson, and Milam counties, for the term of six months, unless sooner discharged, to be mounted and armed and equipped at their own expense, each company to consist of one captain, one first lieutenant, one second lieutenant, three sergeants and fifty-three privates; the men composing each company will elect the officers of the company, and the officers and men of said companies will elect a major to command them.

Sec. 2. Be it further resolved, That the said companies shall be allowed the same pay, except the bounty of land, as is granted by the law defining the pay of mounted riflemen in the ranging service, approved 10th December, 1836.

Sec. 3. Be it further resolved, That upon the receipt of the final muster rolls at the War Department, after the discharge of said companies, the President be authorized to order their payment out of any money that may be in the treasury not otherwise appropriated.

JOHN M. HANSFORD,
Speaker of the House of Representatives.
DAVID G. BURNET,
President of the Senate.

Approved, January 23, 1839.

MIRABEAU B. LAMAR

## Laws of the Republic of Texas.
### AN ACT
**Entitled an act for the raising of certain Troops therein named.**

Sec. 1. Be it enacted by the Senate and House of Representatives of the Republic of Texas in Congress assembled, That a corps of rangers, to consist of two companies of fifty-six men each be, and hereby created for the protection of the counties of San Patricio, Goliad and Refugio.

Sec. 2. Be it further enacted, That said corps shall be established by voluntary enrollment, for the term of six months, to be commanded by officers appointed by the President; that the President be required to report such appointments to the next Congress within ten days after its session.

Sec. 3. Be it further enacted, That the pay of each private, and non-commissioned officer, shall be twenty-five dollars per month, the horses, arms, and other equipage, being furnished in all cases by the individuals.

Sec. 4. Be it further enacted, That the sum of fifteen hundred dollars is hereby appropriated for carrying into effect the object of the foregoing sections of this act, and the secretary of the treasury is hereby required to issue that amount of the promissory notes of the Government for that purpose.

JOHN M. HANSFORD,
Speaker of the House of Representatives.
DAVID G. BURNET,
President of the Senate.

Approved, January 26, 1839.

MIRABEAU B. LAMAR

## Laws of the Republic of Texas.
### AN ACT
#### To raise a Company of Mounted Gunmen to called the "Fannin Guards."

Sec. 1. Be it enacted by the Senate and House of Representatives of the Republic of Texas in Congress assembled, That so soon as any number of the citizens of Fannin county, not less than fifty-three nor more than eighty-five in number, shall equip themselves with good serviceable horses, saddles, bridles and other necessary riding apparatus, with a rifle gun and sufficient supply of powder and ball, and a good belt knife for each man, they shall have the right to elect one captain, one first and second lieutenant, and shall be known as the "Fannin Guards." The captain so elected shall have the right, and it is hereby made the duty of such captain to report such company to the commandant of the 4th brigade of militia, whose duty it shall be to give to such captain orders, under which he shall act, until; he shall have received orders from the Secretary of War, whose duty it shall be to make out and forward orders to such captain, with the commissions for the officers of such company, and it shall be the duty of such company to be constantly employed in active service, for which they shall furnish all the necessary rations and provisions without aid of a Quarter-master; Provided however, That no pay for services nor rations of any description shall be allowed said company, except for the time they are in actual service, and that they shall receive one dollar and twenty-five cents per day, for privates, and the officers to be paid in the same proportion.

DAVID S. KAUFMAN,
Speaker of the House of Representatives.
DAVID G. BURNET,
President of the Senate.

Approved, 4th February, 1839.

MIRABEAU B. LAMAR

---

## Laws of the Republic of Texas.
### JOINT RESOLUTION
#### Authorizing the President to employ three Spy Companies for the Western Frontier.

Sec. 1. Resolved by the Senate and House of Representatives of the Republic of Texas in Congress assembled, That the President be, and he is hereby authorized to appoint and commission, three persons to raise fifteen men each, to act as Spies upon the Western and North Western Frontier of this Republic, for the space of four months, unless the President shall think their services can be dispensed with in a shorter period.

Sec. 2. Be it further enacted, That this resolution be in force and to take effect from and after its passage.

DAVID S. KAUFMAN,
Speaker of the House of Representatives.
ANSON JONES,
President pro tem. of the Senate.

Approved, December 26th, 1840.

DAVID G. BURNET

## Laws of the Republic of Texas.
### AN ACT
### To encourage Frontier Protection.

Sec. 1. Be it enacted by the Senate and House of Representatives of the Republic of Texas, in Congress assembled, That the settlers on the frontier borders of each one of the counties of Fannin, Lamar, Red River, Bowie, Paschal, Panola, Harrison, Nacogdoches, Houston, Robertson, Milam, Travis, Bexar, Gonzales, Goliad, Victoria, Refugio, San Patricio, Montgomery, and Bastrop, may organize themselves into volunteer companies of not less than twenty nor more than fifty-six men, rank and file; provided, only one company shall be raised in each county.

Sec. 2. Be it further enacted, That each company when raised, may assemble at the most convenient place in the county, for the purpose of electing their officers: which election shall be conducted by some acting justice of the peace, whose certificate of the same, together with a correct muster roll of the company, shall be forwarded by the captain elect, to the chief justice of the county, who, upon the reception of such returns from the captain, will approve and forward the same to the Secretary of War.

Sec. 3. Be it further enacted, That said companies shall hold themselves in readiness as minute men, for the purpose of affording a ready and active protection to the frontier settlements: the members of said companies shall at all times be prepared with a good substantial horse, bridle, and saddle, with other necessary accoutrements, together with a good gun, and one hundred rounds of ammunition; and in addition to this, when called into service, such number of rations as the captain may direct.

Sec. 4. Be it further enacted, That the captains shall have full command of their companies, and ample authority to enforce all orders in accordance with the rules and articles of war; said companies shall not be called into active service, unless the settlements are threatened with extraordinary danger; and in all cases when the company is called out, the captain shall keep a muster of the members present in the expedition, noting the length of time in service, and on his return, shall make return thereof to the chief justice of the county, to be approved and forwarded to the Secretary of War.

Sec. 5. Be it further enacted, That the members of said companies, from the date of their enrollment to the date of their discharge, shall be exempted from performing any kind of militia duty, from working on roads or public highways, from paying a state, county, and corporation poll tax, and the tax assessed by law upon one saddle horse.

Sec. 6. Be it further enacted, That the captains of said companies may, when they deem it prudent, detail from their companies, a number of spies, not more than five, to act upon the frontier of their several counties.

Sec. 7. Be it further enacted, That when service shall be rendered by the whole, or a part of any one said companies, the captain shall make out a muster roll of the same, and certify that it is correct, and in strict accordance with this act, and forward the same to the chief justice of the county, which, by him, if approved, shall be forwarded to the Secretary of War, upon which muster roll, if certifies and approved as above, each individual rendering such service, shall receive one dollar per day in par funds, or its equivalent; provided, that the members of said companies, shall not receive pay on any expeditions for a longer period than fifteen days; and on the several expeditions within one year after their organization, shall not receive pay for a longer period than four months in the aggregate, excepting the spies for every year thereafter; and so long as this act remains in force, the said companies shall be paid according to the same rates as herein provided for the first year.

Sec. 8. Be it further enacted, That the chief justice of any of said companies, shall not approve any muster roll returned to him under the provisions of this act, unless he believes the same be just, and that the safety of the county strictly required the service which is therein purported to have been rendered.

Sec. 9. Be it further enacted, That this act be in force and take effect from after its passage.

DAVID S. KAUFMAN,
Speaker of the House of Representatives.
ANSON JONES,
President pro tem. of the Senate.

Approved February 4th, 1841.

DAVID G. BURNET

---

*Laws of the Republic of Texas.*
JOINT RESOLUTION
For the protection of the Southern Frontier

Sec. 1. Be it resolved by the Senate and House of Representatives of the State of Texas in Congress assembled, That the President be, and he is hereby authorized to employ one company of mounted men, to act as rangers, on the southern frontier, on such terms as he may deem most beneficial to the public interest.

Approved, 29th January 1842.

---

*Laws of the Republic of Texas.*
JOINT RESOLUTION
For frontier protection

Section 1. Resolved by the Senate and House of Representatives of the Republic of Texas in Congress assembled, That the President be, and he is hereby authorized and required to accept the services of one company of volunteers for the purpose of ranging on the frontier, on the rivers Trinity and Navasoto; provided, they equip themselves, at their own expense, for a tour of not less than two months; and that the sum of two hundred and fifty dollars be, and the same is hereby, appropriated, of the twenty thousand dollars, heretofore made for frontier protection; which shall be applied to the purchase of supplies for said company; which amount shall be drawn and receipted for by the Captain in command; — and that the President be also allowed to raise two companies, to range on the South-Western frontier, and the sum of two thousand dollars be, and is hereby, appropriated out of the appropriation of twenty thousand dollars for frontier protection, for their maintenance.

Sec. 2. Be it further resolved, That this Joint Resolution take effect from and after its passage.

Approved July 23rd, 1842.

---

*Laws of the Republic of Texas.*
AN ACT
To authorize the President to accept the services of one company of mounted men, to act as spies on the South Western frontier.

Section 1. Be it enacted by the Senate and House of Representatives of the Republic of Texas in Congress assembled, That the President be, and he is hereby authorized to accept of the service of one company of mounted men, to act as spies on the South Western frontier, until the provisions of an act, entitled "an act to provide for the protection of the Western and South Western frontier and for other purposes," can be carried into effect.

Sec. 2. Be it further enacted, That the sum of five hundred dollars be, and is hereby appropriated to carry out the provisions of this bill.

Sec. 3. Be it further enacted, That this act takes effect from and after its passage.
Approved, 16th, Jan., 1843.

---

## Laws of the Republic of Texas.
### AN ACT
#### Authorizing John C. Hays to raise a Company of Mounted Gunmen, to act as Rangers, on the Western and South-Western Frontier.

Section 1. Be it enacted by the Senate and House of Representatives of the Republic of Texas in Congress assembled, That John C. Hays is hereby authorized to raise one company of mounted gunmen, which company shall consist of one Captain, one Lieutenant, and forty privates, and that the said John C. Hays shall command the same, and the said lieutenant, shall be elected by the members composing said company; the said company shall be organized by the first day of February, A. D. one thousand eight hundred and forty-four, or as soon thereafter as practicable, and so soon as organized and reported, shall be received by the President, for the services herein expressed.

Sec. 2. Be it further enacted, That each man admitted into the service of said company, shall be well mounted and well armed, at their own expense.

Sec. 3. Be it further enacted, That the said company shall range on the Western and South-Western frontier, from the county of Bexar to the county of Refugio, and westward, as the public interest may require.

Sec. 4. Be it further enacted, That the Captain of said company shall receive the sum of seventy-five dollars, per month; the Lieutenant the sum of fifty dollars per month; and each private the sum of thirty dollars per month, while in actual service; and that each member of said company shall receive pay for his services, at the expiration of every two months; and the Captain of said company is, hereby, made the disbursing officer, on his giving bond and security, to the amount of five thousand dollars, for the faithful performance of his duty.

Sec. 5. Be it further enacted, That the Secretary of War and Marine be, and he is hereby authorized to draw on the Treasurer every two months, in advance, in favor of the disbursing officer of said company, for such sum, as will meet the expenses, as estimated for rations and forage, and that the sum of seven thousand one hundred and forty-one dollars and sixteen cents be, and the same is hereby, appropriated, to carry into effect the provisions of this act.

Sec. 6. Be it further enacted, That the said company, shall be enrolled for the term of four months from the time of organization, and that the President be, and he is hereby, authorized and required to retain the services of said company for a longer term, should he in his judgment or opinion, believe the public interest or safety requires it, and in such event, a sum sufficient is, hereby, appropriated to carry the same into effect, according to. the estimate, terms, and provisions, of the foregoing recited act.

Sec. 7. Be it further enacted, That this act shall take effect, from and after its passage.
Approved, January 23d, 1844.

## Laws of the Republic of Texas.
## AN ACT
### For the Protection of the Frontier

Section 1. Be it enacted by the Senate and House of Representatives of the Republic of Texas in Congress assembled, That the President is hereby authorized and required, to appoint Captain John C. Hays to organize and command the following detachments of troops, for the protection of the frontier, viz: For Robertson and Milam counties, two detachments, each to be commanded by a Lieutenant, and to consist of ten men: for the protection of Travis county, a detachment of fifteen men, to be commanded by a Lieutenant: for the county of Bexar, a detachment of one Lieutenant and thirty men, to be commanded by Captain Hays in person: and for the counties of Refugio and Goliad, a detachment of fifteen men, to be commanded by a Lieutenant, whose pay shall be as follows: Captain, seventy-five dollars per month; Lieutenant, thirty dollars; Privates, twenty dollars, and who shall be furnished with ammunition, forage, and subsistence, horse-shoeing, and medicines, by the Government: Provided, the same shall not exceed the sum of ten dollars per month for each person.

Sec. 2. Be it further enacted, That as soon as the above detachments shall be organized and reported, it shall be the duty of the President to cause the Officers to be commissioned, with instructions to scour the frontiers of their respective counties, protect them from incursions, and when concentrated in emergencies, to be under the command of Captain Hays. Each commander of a detachment, shall be the disbursing officer for the same, and shall be competent to make his return to the Secretary of War and Marine, and shall receive from the Secretary of the Treasury the money due for pay, subsistence, forage and ammunition, horse-shoeing and medicines, and disburse the same under bonds of three thousand dollars for the faithful performance of the duty.

Sec. 3. Be it further enacted, That the sum of three thousand dollars is hereby appropriated, to carry out the above provisions.

Sec. 4. Be it further enacted, That Henry L, Kinney, be, and he is hereby authorized to raise and organize one Company of forty armed men, with one Captain and one Lieutenant, for the purpose of protecting the settlements at Corpus Christi and its vicinity; and the President, so soon as they are organized and reported, shall receive them into the service, and issue the requisite commissions.

Sec. 5. Be it further enacted, That when the said H. L. Kinney has given his bond and security of five thousand dollars, conditioned for its faithful application, the Secretary of the Treasury shall cause the sums necessary for the pay, subsistence, forage and ammunition of the said Company, to be paid over quarterly to the said H. L. Kinney, to be disbursed by him; and the sum of fifteen thousand dollars is hereby appropriated for that purpose.

Sec. 6. Be it further enacted, That the Auditor is hereby required to audit the accounts of H. L. Kinney, for the amount due of the pay and other contingent expenses of the Company now in service at Corpus Christi, under the order of the President, from the twenty-eighth November, eighteen hundred and forty-five; and that the Secretary of the Treasury pay over the aforesaid amount to said Kinney, which sum shall be deducted from the appropriation in this Act, for the protection of Corpus Christi.

Sec. 7. Be it further enacted, That should any circumstances transpire that might render unnecessary the longer continuance in service of any portion of the forces herein authorized to be raised the President is authorized to disband the same.

Sec. 8. Be it further enacted, That the said H. L. Kinney, shall never receive compensation for the services herein authorized, and the armed forces thus employed, shall be subject to the rules and articles of war; and that this Act shall take effect from and after its passage.

Approved, February 1st, 1845.

---

Orders No. 53}

Headquarters, 8th Department
San Antonio, August 11th, 1849

1. In consequence of the repeated and continued depredations of the Indians, the commanding general has determined to make a requisition on his Excellency Gov. George T. Wood, of Texas, for three mounted companies of Rangers, 78 strong in the aggregate.

2. The general depot for these troops will be at Corpus Christi, and they are intended to operate thro' the Southwestern frontier of this State, viz: from Goliad to Corpus Christi, and thence to the Rio Grande, ranging the whole country, more particularly where the Indians are supposed to be marauding.

3. The quarter master, subsistence and ordinance officers respectively, will take immediate steps for supplying the necessary transportation (either in wagons or pack mules), camp equipage, subsistence for 6 months, rifles and pistols, equipments and ammunition for 9 officers and 225 men, at the point designated above.

4. Brevet Major Babbitt, A. Q. M., will employ an agent for his and the subsistence department, who will also take charge of and issue the arms, equipments and ammunition, under such instructions as he may receive from the ordinance officer at these headquarters.

By order of Bvt Major Gen'l Brooke,
Geo. Deas
Ass't Adj't Gen'l.

---

Orders No. 57}

Headquarters, 8th Department
San Antonio, August 19th, 1849

1. The Commanding Gen'l having received notice from the Executive of this state, that two companies of mounted volunteers will be in readiness, at Austin, to be mustered into the service of the United States, on Thursday the 23rd inst, Bvt Brig Gen'l Harney will please designate an officer for the execution of that duty, at the time and place specified.

2. The term of service is to be, for six months, unless sooner discharged by order of the President of the United States. The organization of each company will be as follows: one Captain, one 1st Lieut., one 2nd Lieut., four Sergeants, four Corporals, two buglers, two farriers and blacksmiths, and sixty four privates; and in accordance with the regulations, each man is to provide himself with a horse, saddle, saddle blanket, bridle, halter and "lariat." The mustering officer will govern himself by the "Instructions" published by the War Dept. June 12th, 1848, particularly paragraphs 98, 99 and 100, and will reject all men and horses that may appear to be incapable of performing the duties and service incident to an active Indian Campaign. If blank forms for Muster Rolls cannot be procured, they must be made on large folio paper.

3. Under the belief that the volunteers lately called out by the State, and operating near Corpus Christi, would principally compose the present force required, the necessary arms, equipment, ammunition and camp equipage, has been forwarded to that place, where they will be issued by the agent appointed for that purpose.

4. As soon as the Muster is completed the two companies will be put "en route" for this

point, by Bvt Brig Gen'l Harney, with orders to report to the General Commanding, for special instructions. The necessary subsistence will be issued at Austin.

5. If the place of rendezvous for the remaining company of volunteers called for, be selected by the Executive, in the vicinity of Austin, Gen'l Harney will cause it to be mustered into the service in the manner prescribed for the others—if below San Antonio, the Mustering officer will be designated from this post.

The Commanding Gen'l in thus calling for the services of volunteers, in preference to making a requisition for an additional number of regular troops, pays a just tribute to the favorable consideration in which the Texas Ranger is held, for the performance of the harassing and arduous duties of a frontier soldier. The General feels confident that the well earned fame of the hardy sons of Texas will, in their coming sphere of action, be well sustained, by a rigorous prosecution of their campaign, and hopes, that long ere their term of service shall have expired, we shall no longer be annoyed by the presence, within our settlements, of the audacious and marauding savage.

By order of Bvt Major Gen'l Brooke,
Geo. Deas
Ass't Adj't Gen'l.

---

### Laws of the State of Texas
### CHAPTER XXXII
### An Act relative to the payment of certain Volunteer Companies for services rendered on the Western Frontier of the State of Texas.

Whereas, in the opinion of his Excellency, the Governor of this State, emergencies have existed which required the services of mounted volunteers on our border country; and whereas, to meet said emergencies, the Governor has called into service from time to time the following companies, commanded respectively by Captain Ben. F. Hill, J. M. Smith, Jacob Roberts, John S. Sutton, Shapley P. Ross, Henry E. McCulloch, Isaac W. Johnson, and Charles Blackwell; and whereas, the said companies promptly responded to the calls above referred to, and by their zeal and activity, answered the ends for which they were called, in stopping the further progress of murder and bloodshed by the ruthless savages who infested our frontier, and whose acts of violence and barbarity are now too fresh in the memory of every Texian to need recapitulation; and whereas, the services here alluded to, seem not to be recognized by the Government of the United States, which leaves the officers and men comprised in said companies totally without remedy to pay for the meritorious services rendered the State by them as aforesaid; and believing that said companies have a right to look to the Legislature of the State for relief, and believing their claim for pay to be just and meritorious, and that the United States Government will not hesitate to reimburse the State the amount hereby assumed; therefore,

Section 1. Be it resolved by the Legislature of the State of Texas, That the officers, non-commissioned officers, musicians and privates of said companies are entitled to the same pay, mileage and emoluments which they would have received had they been called into service by the United States Government, according to the dates of said service on file in the office of the Adjutant-General of the State.

Sec. 2. Be it further resolved, That the State of Texas assume, and will pay to the officers, non-commissioned officers, musicians and privates, or their heirs and legal representatives, the true amounts due them respectively, for the services rendered the State by them as aforesaid, as well as the foraging and subsisting of said companies, or so many of the same as have not already been paid.

Sec. 3. Be it further resolved, That the Governor is hereby authorized and required to appoint some suitable person or agent of the State, to collect together all the muster rolls, pay rolls, accounts, vouchers and other evidences of services rendered, and expenditures incurred, by any and all persons of this State for the protection of the frontier from Indian depredations, since the annexation of Texas to the American Union, which have not heretofore been liquidated by the General Government.

Sec. 4. Be it further resolved, That said agent shall make out complete and correct duplicate muster and pay rolls of all and each of said companies; and also, duplicate accounts of all the expenses incurred, whether by the State or citizens thereof, for the subsistence and maintenance of said forces, which have been raised for protecting the State from Indian invasion and depredations, exhibiting the authority for the same in each case; whether the troops, as raised, were mustered into the service of the United States or the State of Texas: The whole in the form required for liquidation by the laws of the United States and the regulations of the War Department, one copy of each of which he shall deposite in the Adjutant-General's office in this State, and the other retain himself, for the purposes hereinafter set forth.

Sec. 5. Be it further resolved, That said agent shall proceed with such rolls, accounts, vouchers and other evidence of services rendered and expenses incurred, fully made out and properly authenticated, in accordance with the united States army regulations, to the City of Washington, and present them to the proper officers of the Government for settlement, and take such advice, and adopt such measures, in conjunction with our Senators and Representatives in Congress, as will secure the prompt payment of said claims.

Sec. 6. Be it further resolved, That said agent shall receive as compensation for the services required of him, five per cent. on the amount which he may procure to be paid as provided in the fifth section: Provided, that said compensation of five per cent. be deducted from, and paid out of the amount so obtained from the United States Government; And moreover provided, that the sum of fifteen hundred dollars be, and the same is hereby appropriated out of any money in the State Treasury not otherwise or previously appropriated, to defray the expenses of said agent in discharging the duties herein assigned him; which amount of fifteen hundred dollars shall, in the event of a collection of the demands of the State, against the United States Government, be refunded by him, the said agent, in the manner hereinafter provided, to the State, out of the per centage allowed him by the provisions of this resolution.

Sec. 7. Be it further resolved, That it shall be the duty of said agent, in the event he obtains from the United States Government the amount claimed by the State, or any portion thereof, to proceed forthwith to the seat of government of the State with the same, and make a deposit thereof with the State Treasurer, in the same manner that other public moneys are paid into said Treasury, and on the same receipts and vouchers.

Sec. 8. Be it further resolved, That it shall be made the duty of the Governor, and he is hereby required to cause said agent, before entering on his duties, to make and execute to the Governor of the State of Texas, and his successors in office, a good and sufficient bond, with two or more satisfactory and solvent securities, conditioned for the well and faithful performance of all duties required of him, which shall not be void on the first recovery, but liable to be sued on from time to time by the party or parties interested, until the whole amount thereof is recovered.

Sec. 9. Be it further resolved, That it shall be the duty of the Treasurer of the State to disburse the moneys so deposited by said agent to him, upon the application of the parties entitled to the same, their heirs or legal representatives, assignees or attorneys in fact, upon their producing evidence of their right to the same, from the Adjutant-General of the State, that the corresponding service was performed by the party claiming, or in right of whom it is made.

Sec. 10. Be it further resolved, That the accompanying memorial of the Legislature of the State of Texas to the Honorable the Senate and House of Representatives of the Congress of the United States, upon the subject of expenses incurred by the State in providing a military defence upon the frontier in the years 1848 and 1849, is hereby approved and adopted, together with the accompanying report of the Adjutant-General of the State, setting forth the time the several companies were mustered into service, and the time of their discharge from the same, with the estimated amounts due each company respectively.

Sec. 11. Be it further resolved, That the Clerk of the House of Representatives of the State of Texas be, and he is hereby required to make out a complete and certified copy of the report of the chairman of the Military committee, to whom was referred so much [of the Governor's message] as related to the payment of the companies of mounted volunteers, recently mustered into service for frontier protection, as well as this joint resolution, together with the memorial and report of the Adjutant-General above referred to; and it shall be his duty to deliver the same to his Excellency, the Governor of the State of Texas, to be by him forwarded, as contemplated in this joint resolution, to the Congress of the United States, with such directions, statements and views as to him may seem right and proper.

Sec. 12. Be it further resolved, That these joint resolutions take effect and be in force from and after their passage.

Approved, January 7, 1850.

---

## *Joint Resolutions.*
## CHAPTER 2.
### Joint Resolution authorizing the Governor to raise and muster into the service of the State mounted men for the protection of the frontier

Whereas, Many of our fellow citizens are suffering in life and property from the depredations of hostile bands of Indians, on the extreme frontier of the State; And Whereas, the limited number of mounted Federal troops, at present stationed on our borders, are inadequate to afford protection. Therefore,

Be it Resolved by the Legislature of the State of Texas, That the Governor be, and he is hereby authorized to order out mounted volunteers, not to exceed one hundred in number, to be divided into two or more companies, as he may think proper, to be armed and equipped as he may direct, and placed upon such portions of the frontier as he may consider best for the interest of the country; said company or companies to be mustered into the service for the term of three months, and such as much longer as the Governor may think necessary.

Be it further Resolved, That the sum of twenty thousand dollars, or so much thereof as may be necessary, be appropriated out of any money in the Treasury not other otherwise appropriated, to defray the expenses of said company or companies; and that the pay and allowances of the troops so called into service; shall not exceed that allowed to mounted volunteers during the Mexican war; and that these resolutions take effect from their passage.

Approved, November 17, 1857.

## Laws of the State of Texas.
### CHAPTER 65.
### An Act for the better protection of the Frontier.

Section 1. Be it enacted by the Legislature of the State of Texas: That the Governor is hereby authorized and required to call into service one hundred mounted volunteers, in addition to the force now in service, for the term of six months, unless sooner discharged, and all said force may be continued in service for any length of time, if the safety of the frontier require it.

Sec. 2. That the Governor may appoint a person experienced in such service, with the rank of Senior Captain, to command all the forces of the State so enrolled, and superintend the protection of the frontier.

Sec. 3. That the Governor shall direct the organization and equipment of all the forces on the frontier, and make such regulations as are necessary and most expedient for the protection of the frontier, and the officers and men shall be allowed such pay and emoluments as mounted men are allowed in like service of the United States; and he shall also be authorized to appoint a person to act as Quarter-master, and Pay-master to facilitate operations, who shall give sufficient bonds and security to be approved by the Governor.

Sec. 4. That the Volunteers raised in Bosque county, since first of January 1858, may be accepted as a portion of the force to be raised by this act, and allowed pay from the date at which they entered service.

Sec. 5. That whenever an efficient force shall be placed on the frontier by the Government of the United States, all the men raised by the State shall be discharged.

Sec. 6. That in the event of a continuation of hostilities by the Indians, and the failure of the Federal Government to protect the frontier, the Governor is authorized to call out any number of men, and to carry on active and offensive operations against all Indians at war.

Sec. 7. That the sum of seventy thousand dollars is hereby appropriated out of any money in the Treasury to carry out the provisions of this act, and that this act take effect from and after it passage.

Approved January 27, 1858.

---

## Laws of the State of Texas.
### CHAPTER 1.
### Joint Resolution.

Resolved, That the Governor be authorized to call out such a number of volunteers to quell the insurrection or invasion of Cortinas and followers on the Rio Grande as may be necessary, and, in case the Governor should deem it necessary to call out volunteers under the provisions of this joint resolution, then, that those citizens of Texas, who have already left their homes with this object, shall be adopted into the public service from the time they left their homes, or so many of them as choose to volunteer, and that said volunteers elect their commissioned officers, and be retained in service till the object for which they are called out shall be accomplished, and that said volunteers receive like pay as the same troops in the U.S. service; that this joint resolution take effect and be in force from and after its passage.

Approved November 18th, 1859.

## Laws of the State of Texas.
### CHAPTER 11.
### An Act for the Protection of the Frontier.

Whereas, a state of hostilities exists between the people of the State of Texas and various Indian tribes who inhabit the unsettled portions of the State and adjacent territory — bands of said Indians having at times within the last three years invaded our settlements, murdered our people, and carried off or destroyed their property, so that the frontier settlements are receding before the invaders, and our frontier counties in danger of depopulation:

And whereas, the Federal Government, whose duty it is primarily to protect the State from such hostilities, has not efficiently afforded such protection:

And whereas, we are continually in such imminent danger of being invaded by said Indians tribes, as will not admit of delay:

Therefore,

Section 1. Be it enacted by the Legislature of the State of Texas: That the Governor of the State be, and he is hereby authorized to raise and muster into the service of the State, a regiment of mounted men, if so many be necessary, consisting of ten companies, or such smaller number as he shall deem sufficient to afford efficient protection to the entire frontier; and one-half of said force, at least, shall be immediately, upon their organization, placed on the frontier, in such manner as to act as spies and minute men, for the protection and defense of the settlements, as the Governor may think proper. Each company shall be composed of eighty-three men, rank and file, to be enlisted for the term of twelve months, unless sooner discharged; to be re-enlisted for another term of twelve months, or others taken in their place, at the expiration of the first term of service. The officers of each company to be elected by the men composing the same.

Sec. 2. For the command of the whole of said force the members shall elect a Colonel, Lieut. Colonel and a Major; and each company shall have one Captain, three Lieutenants, four Sergeants and four Corporals, and one Surgeon; and there shall be selected from each company one of the Lieutenants, to act as Quartermaster and Commissary for said company, with the rank of Second Lieutenant; and when two or more companies are acting together, said Lieutenants shall be acting as the commanding officers may direct, as Quartermasters, or Commissaries, or Adjutants; and there shall also be appointed from among the men, such non-commissioned staff as may be necessary.

Sec. 3. Said officers and men shall provide themselves wit arms, horses, and all accoutrements and camp equipage; and shall be furnished at the expense of the State in provision, ammunitions, medicines and forage for horses where practicable; and shall receive for their services the following sums: The Colonel, one hundred and eighty dollars per month; the Lieutenant-Colonel, one hundred and fifty dollars per month; the Major, one hundred and twenty-five dollars per month; the Captains, one hundred dollars per month; the First Lieutenants, seventy-five dollars per month; the Second Lieutenants, sixty dollars per month; Sergeants, four dollars per month in addition to pay of privates; and Corporals, three dollars in addition to pay of privates; and privates shall receive twenty-five dollars per month; and commissioned staff officers shall be allowed twenty dollars per month extra to the pay of their rank, and non-commissioned staff officers eight dollars per month in addition to the pay of privates; the Surgeon shall be entitled to one hundred and twenty dollars per month, and shall furnish his instruments, but be furnished with medicines.

Sec. 4. The said force shall be employed in ranging and scouting on the frontier, from the most eligible point on the Rio Grande to Red River; and their operations shall be entirely under the control of the Governor, who shall appoint their proper places of rendezvous, and deposit, and direct all arrangements necessary to carry out the intention of this act; and said force shall be subject to the rules and regulations of the army of the United States; and when in the opinion of the Governor, their further services are not necessary, may be reduced or disbanded, or if provisions shall be made by the Governments of the United States to accept the said, in whole or in part, for the protection of the frontier of Texas, it shall be turned over for that purpose.

Sec. 5. That this force shall be raised in such manner as the Governor may direct, from any portion of the State; and, when mustered into service, shall take such position on the frontier as they shall be ordered by the Governor, and shall operate during the time they are in the service of the State under the order of the Governor.

Sec. 6. That this act take effect from its passage.

Approved January 2d, 1860.

---

## *Laws of the State of Texas.*
### CHAPTER X.
### An Act to provide for the protection of the Frontier of the State of Texas.

Section 1. Be it enacted by the Legislature of the State of Texas, That the counties of Montague, Jack, Clay, Wise, Young, Parker, Palo Pinto, Johnson, Erath, McLennan, Comanche, Hamilton, Bosque, Coryell, Bell, Lampasas, Brown, San Saba, Llano, Burnet, Gillespie, Bandera, Frio, Uvalde, Mason, Medina, Atascosa, Live Oak, Nueces, Starr, Hidalgo, Cameron, Zapata, Webb, El Paso, Blanco and Kerr, and that all unorganized counties be attached as for Judicial purposes—may each organize a company of Minute Men not to exceed forty in number, (rank and file.)

Sec. 2. That each member of such company, shall be required to keep himself furnished with a suitable horse, gun, navy revolver, at least one hundred rounds of ammunition, ten days provisions, and all necessary equipments, to be ready at any moment when called on to take the field.

Sec. 3. That said Minute Men shall be exempt from poll tax, militia, road, and jury duty, and when in actual service, shall be entitled to one dollar and fifty cents a day, covering all their claims against the State.

Sec. 4. That each company shall be entitled to one Captain, and if numbering twenty men, and less than twenty-eight men to one Lieutenant, and if numbering over twenty-eight men to two Lieutenants, and each company shall be entitled to one Sergeant and one Corporal for every ten men in said company.

Sec. 5. The Chief Justice or County Court, of each county above mentioned, shall cause said men to be enrolled and organized the same by holding elections, and when organized the Captain of each company, shall return a muster-roll certified to by the Chief Justice or County Court of their respective counties, to the Governor of the State, and another copy to the Comptroller.

Sec. 6. The Captain of each company, when engaged in actual service, or business for the company or service, shall be entitled to two dollars and fifty cents per day; and Lieutenants, when similarly engaged, to two dollars per day. No other allowances shall be made to officers or men but the amount stated as "per diem" in this act.

Sec. 7. From each company, a number of spies not exceeding ten men, and one commissioned officer, may be kept in constant service as scouts, and when considered necessary, the officer in command may call out part of the whole of the company, but no larger number than ten men shall at any one time be entitled to more than twelve days pay, and whenever a call is made, the officer commanding, shall make a correct report of the number of days served by each man, which report shall be certified to by the Chief Justice or the County Court of the county to which such company belongs; that the call was justifiable or necessary from the notice or alarm, which report shall be forwarded immediately by the principal officer to the Governor, with regular reports to be made at least once in every three months.

Sec. 8. The Governor shall have the power to direct that the number of spies may be reduced in any county, or the services of the whole number suspended, but the company shall nevertheless retain its organization, and hold itself in readiness for duty whenever the circumstances require it.

Sec. 9. The men called out under the provisions of this act, shall, when in actual service, be governed by the rules and articles of war governing the army of the United States, whenever applicable, and when not in actual service, by such by-laws and regulations as they may make, not being inconsistent with the Constitution or laws of this State.

Sec. 10. That this act take effect and be in force from and after its passage.

Passed February 7, 1861.

## *Ordinances.*
### No. 14.— AN ORDINANCE.
**To provide in part for the Military Defence of the State of Texas.**

Section 1. Be it ordained by the People of the State of Texas in Convention assembled, That there shall be immediately raised and mustered into the service of the State of Texas, a regiment of mounted volunteers, consisting of ten companies, and each company shall consist of one hundred men, rank and file, to be enrolled for twelve months, unless sooner discharged by the Governor. The commissioned officers of each company to be elected by the men, the non-commissioned officers to be appointed by the Captains.

Sec. 2. That for the command of said regiment there shall be elected by this Convention a Colonel, a Lieutenant-Colonel, and a Major, and appointed by said Colonel an Adjutant, a Quartermaster, a Commissary, a Regimental Surgeon, each with the rank of Captain, and such other officers and employees as the service may require, and as may be allowed by the laws, rules and regulations governing the army of the Confederate States of America; and for each of said companies there shall be elected as aforesaid, a Captain, a first Lieutenant, a second Lieutenant, and a Surgeon; and appointed by the Captains four Sergeants, four Corporals and a Bugler.

Sec. 3. That there shall be appointed by the Governor an enrolling officer for each of said companies, who shall enroll the men and assist at their organization; and, after said organization, the rolls shall be delivered to the Captains, who shall immediately return certified muster rolls to the Colonel. The companies shall be mustered into the service under the directions and by such officers as may be appointed by the Colonel for that purpose, and it shall be the special duty of the Colonel to superintend the arming and equipment of the men, in order that they may be brought into active service with as little delay as possible.

Sec. 4. That the officers and men shall provide themselves with suitable horses and accoutrements, and if any soldier prefers to furnish his own arms he shall be permitted to do so, provided the arms furnished are adapted to the service, of which the mustering-in officer shall determine; and there shall be allowed to each soldier who furnishes his own arms, one dollar per month additional pay, said officers and men shall be furnished, armed and equipped at the expense of the State, except their horses, accoutrements and clothing, and shall receive for their services the same pay that is allowed for service of the same character by the Confederate States of America.

Sec. 5. That said regiment shall be employed for the defence of the frontier of Texas, and in the prosecution of active campaigns into the Indian country; and should the Confederate States adopt and accept said regiment as a part of their military force, then and in that case said regiment shall be subject to its orders and laws; and while said force remains in the service of Texas it shall be governed by the laws, rules and regulations governing the army of the Confederate States of America.

Sec. 6. That while said regiment remains in the service of the State of Texas, the officer commanding the same shall report to the Governor of the State of Texas; but if accepted by the Confederate States of America, the commanding officer shall report as may be required by the laws of the Confederate States.

Sec. 7. That such portion of the public property now belonging to the State of Texas, whether the same may consist of arms, munitions of war, army stores, transportation, or any other thing which may be needful or necessary to the service, shall be and is hereby appropriated for the use of said force, and shall be delivered to such officers or persons as may be authorized to demand and receive the same, upon the requisition of the proper officer for the purpose aforesaid.

Sec. 8. That the volunteer force now in the service of the State of Texas, shall be received as a part of the force hereby provided, upon their compliance with the provisions of this ordinance.

Sec. 9. That the Governor of the State of Texas shall commission all the officers created by this ordinance, who are by law required to be commissioned; and each of said officers shall, before entering upon the duties of his office, take the oath of office prescribed by this Convention for all State officers; and every disbursing officer herein provided for shall enter into bond payable to the State of Texas in such sums as may be required by the Treasurer and Comptroller of the State of Texas, and to be approved by them.

Sec. 10. Be it further ordained, that this ordinance shall be and remain in full force and effect until otherwise provided by act of the Legislature of Texas, or by act of the Congress of the Confederate States.

Adopted in convention, at Austin, on the 18th day of March, A.D. 1861.

---

### *Laws of the State of Texas.*
### CHAPTER XVI.
#### An Act to provide for the protection of the Frontier of the State of Texas.

Section 1. Be it enacted by the Legislature of the State of Texas, That there shall be raised a regiment of Rangers for the protection of the Northern and Western Frontier of the State of Texas, to consist of ten companies, to be raised as hereinafter prescribed, to be officered according to the rules and regulations of the Confederate States army, and the number of officers and privates, their pay and emoluments, shall be the same as in similar service in the Confederate States army.

Sec. 2. Said men shall furnish themselves with arms, horses and accoutrements, and shall be enrolled for a term not less than twelve months, unless sooner discharged; and at the expiration of their term of service others shall be enrolled to supply their places.

Sec. 3. The requisite number of men for said regiment shall be raised in the frontier counties, to wit: One company shall be raised in the counties of Clay, Montague, Cooke and Wise; one company shall be raised in the counties of Young, Jack, Palo Pinto and Parker; one company from the counties of Stephens, Eastland, Erath and Bosque; one company from the counties of Coryell, Hamilton, Lampasas, Comanche and Brown; one company from the counties from the counties of San Saba, Mason, Llano and Burnet; one company from the counties of Blanco, Bandera, Medina and Bee; one company from the counties of Frio, Atascosa, Live Oak, Karnes and Bee; one company from the counties of El Paso and Presidio; and one company may be raised in any section of the State the Governor may direct. And, provided, that the unorganized counties shall furnish men with the counties to which they are attached for judicial purposes, and every county named in this section shall have the privilege to furnish its proportion of men, in preference to all other applications; and when any company cannot be furnished with the requisite number of men from the counties named in this act, then the deficiency may be supplied from the nearest adjoining counties not named in this act.

Sec. 4. Said troops shall be stationed in detachments of not less than twenty-five men. When the requisite number of men shall have entered this service, and shall take their stations on the outside settlements of the frontier, as nearly as practicable in a direct line from a point on Red River to a point on the Rio Grande river, and thence down said river to its mouth, to be selected by the commanding officer, and the commanding officer shall select the posts at the direction of the Governor, in accordance with this act; and such stations shall be, if practicable, about twenty-five miles distant from other, or so near each other that scouts pass over the ground between two stations once every day. And further, that the companies, or parts of companies, shall be stationed on that part of the frontier in which they have been enrolled, and that the posts on Red River shall be supplied with additional force of not less than twenty-five men; and the company to be raised in any part of the State, shall be in readiness to report to any part of the line the Governor or commanding officer may think necessary.

Sec. 5. That the Governor is required, immediately after the passage of this act, to commission competent persons, one for every company and district, as set forth in this act, to enroll the number of men for a company, and when at least sixty-four men shall been enrolled, they shall organize by holding elections for company officers, and the Captain elected shall return a muster-roll, and make such other reports as may required by the Governor, to the Adjutant-General's department, and shall, as soon as ordered by the Governor, repair to the frontier, and perform duty on the plan laid down in this act, until otherwise directed by the Governor or superior officer.

Sec. 6. The Governor shall have power to appoint the field officers, as well as all other disbursing officers, pertaining to said regiment.

Sec. 7. The troops raised under and by virtue of this act shall be subject to the rules and regulations of the Confederate States army, but shall always be subject to the authorities of the State of Texas for frontier service, and shall not be removed beyond the limits of the State of Texas; and that it shall be the duty of the Governor to enclose of his act to the Secretary of War, and to each of our Representatives in Congress, urging the acceptance of said regiment in the service of the Confederate States, as in lieu of one of the regiments now upon said frontier, as the effective and economical mode of frontier protection.

Sec. 8. That no portion of said troops shall become a charge against the State until organized, as required by the fifth section of this act, and placed under orders.

Sec. 9. That an act to provide for the protection of the frontier of the State of Texas, passed February 7th, 1861, be and the same is hereby repealed, from and after the first day of March next.

Sec. 10. The Governor shall have power to disband said regiment whenever in his judgment the services shall no longer be necessary for frontier protection, should the same not be accepted by the Confederate Government, under the provisions of this act.

Sec. 11. That this act take effect and be in force from and after its passage.

Approved December 21st, 1861.

---

## Laws of the State of Texas.
### CHAPTER XXV.
### An Act to provide for the defence of the Frontier, and repealing certain provisions of An Act entitled "An Act to provide for the protection of the Frontier," approved December 21, 1861.

Whereas, under the provisions of "An Act to provide for the protections of the Frontier of the State of Texas," approved December 21st, 1861, a regiment, composed of nine companies of cavalry, was organized and sworn into the service of the State of Texas for the term of twelve months: And, whereas, by the provisions of the seventh section of said act, the Governor was required to urge the acceptance of said regiment in the service of the Confederate States for the purpose of frontier protection: And, whereas, by reasons of the provisions of said act, and the organization of said regiment being inconsistent with the army regulations of the Confederate States, said regiment was not received into the service of the said Confederate States: And, whereas, to meet a provision of said army regulations, that each regiment shall be composed of ten companies, the Governor disbanded said regiment, and on the 11th day of February, 1863, of the same material, completed the organization of another regiment composed of ten companies, denominated "the Mounted Regiment of Texas State Troops," and mustered the same into the service of the State of Texas, under the command of Colonel James E. McCord, for the term of three years or during the war: Therefore,

Sec. 1. Be it enacted by the Legislature of the State of Texas, That said mounted regiment of Texas State Troops, organized and commanded as aforesaid, be, and the same is hereby recognized and acknowledged as the Frontier Regiment, contemplated to be raised by the act of this Legislature aforesaid, subject to the provisions of said act, except as may be herein otherwise provided, and that the sum of eight hundred thousand dollars, ($800,000) or so much thereof as may be necessary, be, and the same is hereby appropriated for the pay and support of said regiment for the term of twelve months from the said 11th day of February, 1863, or until further action of the Legislature of this State.

Sec. 2. That the Governor be, and he is hereby authorized to transfer said regiment to the service of the Confederate States: Provided such transfer can be made upon the condition, and with the express understanding that said regiment, shall be retained and remain upon the Indian frontier of the State of Texas, for its protection; in which event said regiment shall be subject solely to the military authorities of the Confederate States, and no further charge for the pay or support thereof shall thereafter accrue against the State of Texas, but in the event no transfer of said regiment is made under the provisions of this act, said regiment shall remain upon said frontier for the full term of twelve months from the said February 11th, 1863, or until otherwise provided by law.

Sec. 3. That so much of the "Act to provide for the protection of the frontier of the State of Texas," approved December 21st, 1863, or of any act, as conflicts with the provisions of this act, are hereby repealed, and that this act take effect from and after its passage.

Approved March 6, 1863.

## Laws of the State of Texas.
## CHAPTER LXVII.
### An Act to Provide for the Protection of the Frontier, and turning over the Frontier Regiment to Confederate States Service.

Section 1. Be it enacted by the Legislature of the State of Texas, That all persons able to do military service, who are at the passage of this act bona fide citizens of the following line of counties, and all counties lying north and west of said line, to wit: Cook, Wise, Parker, that part of Johnson west of the Belknap and Fort Graham road, Bosque, Coryell, Lampasas, Burnett, Blanco, Bandera, Medina, Kendall, Atascosa, Live Oak, McMullen, La Salle, Dimmit, and Maverick, shall be enrolled and organized into companies, not less than twenty-five nor more than sixty-five men, rank and file.

Sec. 2. That it shall be the duty of the Governor, immediately after the passage of this act, to cause the counties designated in the preceding section to be divided into three districts, as nearly equal in territory and population as may be; in each of which districts he shall appoint a suitable person, with the rank and pay of major of Cavalry, who shall be the ranking officer of the district to which he is appointed, and which officer, and with the control of the companies when organized, and the defense of the same, as provided herein, and under such other regulations as the Governor may prescribe.

Sec. 3. That the commissioned officers of each company, of fifty men or more, shall consist of one Captain and two Lieutenants; if less than fifty men, two Lieutenants. The non-commissioned officers shall consist of one Sergeant and one Corporal for every ten men.

Sec. 4. That each member of a company shall be required to keep himself furnished with a suitable horse, gun, and ten days provisions, and all necessary equipments, [including ammunition.]

Sec. 5. That no person who is not a actual resident, in good faith, of the frontier districts herein specified at the passage of this act, shall be a member of the organization provided for by this act; and it shall be the duty of captains of companies, and of the commanding officers of the several districts, to exclude non-residents of the frontier districts from membership in said organizations, and, in case of doubt, strict and full proof under oath shall be required, to the satisfaction of the officer.

Sec. 6. That the companies organized under the provisions of this act, shall be required to keep at least one-fourth of their number in the field in actual service, making equal divisions of time; and the officers commanding districts shall have the power and authority to order out the whole force, under such restrictions, regulations and requirements as the Governor may devise for the control and management of the organization herein provided for.

Sec. 7. That every officer and private of each of said companies shall, before entering upon duty, be required to take an oath before some one authorized by law to administer oaths, that he will use his best endeavors to arrest, and deliver to the nearest Confederate States authorities, every person reported or known to him to be a deserter, either from the State or Confederate States army, and also all persons from the interior counties who are avoiding conscription or draft service.

Sec. 8. That the pay of officers and privates, while engaged in actual service as provided in the sixth section of this act, shall be as follows, to wit: Captains, three dollars per day; lieutenants, two dollars and seventy-five cents per day; sergeants, two dollars and fifty cents per day; corporals, two dollars and twenty-five cents per day; and privates, two dollars per day; and no other pay or allowances shall be made to officers or privates than the per diem as above provided.

Sec. 9. That any officer or private willfully failing or refusing to perform his duty, or guilty of any other offense, shall be reported by one of the commissioned officers of his company to the district officer, whose duty it shall be to order the sitting of a Court Martial, to consist of not less than three nor more than five commissioned officers, who shall proceed to hear the evidence, and shall acquit or convict, as the merits of the case may demand; and, in case of conviction, the Court may assess such punishment as is prescribed by the rules, regulations, and articles of war, for the army of the Confederate States: Provided, if any person convicted of a minor offense be of conscript age, hw may, at the discretion of the Court, be delivered to the nearest officer of the Confederate States for service on the army of the Confederate States.

Sec. 10. That it shall be the duty of the Governor to appoint such person or persons, as he may choose, to draw from the proper authorities of the State the fund appropriated for the pay of the men organized under this act. Such persons or persons, so appointed, to give bond or security for the faithful performance of the duties required of them. The payments to be made to the men as often as once in every four months.

Sec. 11. That it shall be the duty of the Adjutant General to furnish the companies organized under this act, with the necessary amount of ammunition, upon proper requisitions made by the commanders of the several districts.

Sec. 12. That the Governor shall, upon the completion of the foregoing organization, turn over the Frontier Regiment, with all its equipments, to the Confederate States service: Provided, the Confederate Commander will account to the State for all property so turned over at its proper value; otherwise the Governor shall make such disposition of said property as shall best subserve the interest of the State; any law conflicting with this provision be and the same is hereby repealed.

Sec. 13. That the Governor shall cause to be made such other regulations, for the government and control of the organizations herein provided for, as he may deem necessary, to the end that the force so provided shall be made as effectual as possible to defend the frontier; and should Confederate troops be kept on the frontier, and in the event that the enemy should invade any portion of the State near the frontier, the Governor shall have the power to order the commanders of such districts, as may be contiguous to the sense of danger, to take the whole or part of their respective forces and participate in repelling the enemy; but in no event are such forces to be kept away from their own proper field of operations for a larger time than one month, unless such forces are used against an Indian enemy.

Sec. 14. That this act take effect and be in force from and after its passage.

Approved December 15th, 1863.

---

## *Laws of the State of Texas.*
### CHAPTER XXV.
### An Act supplementary to "An Act to provide for the protection of the Frontier, and turning over the Frontier Regiment to the Confederate States service." Approved December 15, 1863.

Section 1. Be it enacted by the Legislature of the State of Texas, That the Governor of the State shall cause to be enrolled into the companies already organized within the Frontier Districts, all persons between the ages of seventeen and eighteen years of age.

Sec. 2. That should the Confederate military authorities authorize the withdrawal of the reserve corps from field and camps, and the persons in the State composing the reserve corps, be allowed such authority to return to their homes, either permanently or temporarily, the

Governor shall direct the same course to be pursued towards persons of like age in the frontier organization; provided, such persons shall hold themselves in readiness to repair to their respective companies when ordered.

Sec. 3. That, in each of the Frontier Districts there shall be organized, under the direction of the Governor, a provost guard, to consist of not exceeding two companies of sixty-four men each, rank and file, for constant duty. That the companies so organized, shall be armed by the State, and shall be placed on the same footing as to pay, rations and everything else as Confederate States troops.

Sec. 4. That the pay of officers and privates of this organization, except that of the provost guards, while engaged in actual service, shall be the same as provided for in the act to which this is supplementary.

Sec. 5. That fractions of companies of less than twenty-five men may be attached to and become parts of companies hereafter organized, and so much of the act, to which this is supplemental, as restricts companies to sixty-four men rank and file, is hereby repealed.

Sec. 6. That the Governor cause to be furnished to the commanding officer of the Frontier Districts such stationary, camp and garrison equipage, and transportation as may be actually necessary

Sec. 7. That in addition to the oath heretofore required, the officers and men of this organization shall swear allegiance to the Confederate and States Governments, to obey the Constitutions and laws thereof, and to obey the orders of their superior officers.

Sec. 8. That in the event of an invasion, by the enemy, of any part of the frontier or of any portion of the State contiguous thereto, the Governor shall have authority to order out the entire force of this organization or any part thereof, for such length of time as he may judge necessary, to aid in repelling such invasion. In the event any such contingency should occur, and extraordinary expenditure be incurred, the same shall be paid out of the general appropriation made by the First Session of the Tenth Legislature for the defence of the State.

Sec. 9. That whenever the Governor deems it proper, he shall assign to duty within the limits of the Frontier District such of the State Brigadier-Generals as may be necessary, to make more efficient the frontier organization. When any such officer is assigned to duty, he shall make his Headquarters within the limits of his command, at such point as will keep him in direct communication with all the forces of the frontier.

Sec. 10. This act shall be in force from its passage.

Approved May 31st, 1864.

## *Laws of the State of Texas.*
## CHAPTER XII.
### An Act to provide for the Protection of the Frontier of the State of Texas.

Section 1. Be it enacted by the Legislature of the State of Texas, That there may be raised three battalions of Texas Rangers for the protection of the northern and western frontier of the State of Texas, to consist of ten companies, giving to two battalions three, and to one battalion four companies, to be raised as hereinafter prescribed, and to consist of one captain, two lieutenants, four sergeants, four corporals, one bugler, one farrier and eighty-seven privates each. The field and staff officers to consist of one colonel, one Lieutenant-Colonel, and one major, one assistant adjutant general, with the rank of captain, one adjutant with the rank of lieutenant, one assistant quartermaster and commissary with the rank of captain, and two assistant quartermasters and commissaries with the rank of first lieutenant, one surgeon with the rank of major, and three assistant surgeons with the rank of captains, entitled to pay as follows, to wit: The colonel shall receive two hundred dollars per month, Lieutenant-Colonel one hundred and fifty dollars per month, the major one hundred and forty dollars per month, captains one hundred and twenty-five dollars per month, lieutenants ninety dollars per month, first sergeants, thirty-eight dollars per month, sergeants, thirty-four dollars per month, corporals, bugler, and farriers, thirty-three dollars per month, and privates, thirty dollars per month; Provided, the pay of all officers and men, shall be in currency, and further that the pay herein provided shall be full compensation in lieu of all other pay and commutation for clothing for officers and men.

Sec. 2. Said men shall furnish themselves with horses, arms and accoutrements, and shall be furnished with ammunition, and shall be enlisted for twelve months unless sooner discharged.

Sec. 3. The requisite number of men for said battalions, shall be raised if possible in the counties of Cook, Denton, Montague, Clay, Jack, Wise, Young, Parker, Tarrant, Palo Pinto, Johnson, Hill, Erath, Comanche, Hamilton, Bosque, Coryell, Lampasas, Brown, San Saba, McCulloch, Mason, Menard, Llano, Williamson, Burnet, Blanco, Comal, Kendall, Gillespie, Kerr, Bandera, Uvalde, Frio, Medina, Atascosa and such other counties as border on the above line of companies of said regiment; Provided, that the Governor may receive three companies of said regiment from other counties not specified.

Sec. 4. That the Governor be authorized immediately after the passage of this Act, to commission competent persons, one for every company, to enroll the number of men for a company; and when at least sixty-four men shall be enrolled, they shall organize, by holding an election for company officers, and the captain elected shall return a muster roll, and such other reports as may be required by the Governor to the Adjutant General's Department, and hold his company in readiness to take the field, in obedience to orders from the Governor or superior officer.

Sec. 5. The Governor shall have power to appoint the field and staff officers, together with all disbursing officers of each battalion, and shall have power to remove from office any of the field or staff officers for neglect of duty, incompetency or disobedience of orders, and furloughs and leaves of absence shall be granted under rules and regulations prescribed by him.

Sec. 6. The troops raised under by virtue of this Act, shall be governed by the rules and regulations of the army of the United States, but shall always be subject to the authority of the State of Texas for frontier service, and shall not be removed beyond the limits of the State of Texas, (except for the purpose of following and chastising marauding bands of Indians wherever found,) and it shall be the duty of the Governor to forward a copy of this Act to the Secretary of War, urging the acceptance of said battalions for frontier protection.

Sec. 7. That no portion of said troops shall become a charge against the State of Texas until organized as required by the fourth section of this Act, and placed under orders.

Sec. 8. That the quartermaster and commissary of said regiment be authorized under instructions from the Governor to contract for the following transportation for the regiment, viz: One six mule team and wagon, together with such number of pack animals and accoutrements as the colonel with the Governor's approval, may require for each battalion as transportation for the troops, and one two horse wagon and two mules for the field and staff of each battalion. The supplies are to be delivered by contractors at the place designated by the commanding officer, who shall give information to the quartermaster and commissary at what point and at what time the supplies must be delivered, and all supplies purchase by the quartermaster must be of good quality; and his accounts or certificates shall be examined and allowed by the commanding officer in the field before the same shall become binding as a claim against the State; Provided, that the office of assistant quartermaster and commissary, within the meaning of this Act, is but one office, and is to be held but by one person.

Sec. 9. That the Governor shall have power to disband said battalions or any portion of them whenever, in his judgement, their services may no longer be necessary for frontier protection, and may thereafter call into the service and recognize such companies and battalions whenever the condition of the frontier may require it, provided it shall not be for a longer period than twelve months, and should the same not be accepted by the united States Government under the provisions of this Act.

Sec. 10. The present Legislature shall make all necessary appropriations, and provide means to enable the Executive of this State to carry out the provisions of this act.

Sec. 11. That the acts to provide for the protection of the frontier, passed February 7th, 1861, and December 24th, 1861, be and the same are hereby repealed.

Sec. 12. This Act to take effect and be in force from and after its passage.

Approved September 21, 1866.

---

## *Laws of the State of Texas.*
## CHAPTER V.
### An Act to provide for the protection of the frontier.

Section 1. Be it enacted by the Legislature of the State of Texas, That the Governor of the State be and is hereby authorized to raise and muster into the service of the State, for the protection of the northern and western Frontier, twenty companies of Texas Rangers, to be raised as hereinafter prescribed, and to consist of one captain, one lieutenant, one medical officer, three sergeants, four corporals, one bugler, one farrier and fifty privates, each entitled to pay as follows, to wit: The captain and medical officers to receive one hundred dollars per month; lieutenants eighty dollars per month; sergeants fifty-four dollars per month; corporals and farriers fifty-two dollars per month; privates and buglers fifty dollars per month; and the pay herein provided shall be full compensation in lieu of all other pay and communication for clothing for both officers and men.

Sec. 2. That the requisite number of officers and men for said companies shall be raised, if possible, in the Frontier counties of the State.

Sec. 3. That the Governor is required, immediately after the passage of this act, to appoint competent persons as captains of companies to enroll, as set forth in this act, the requisite number of men for the companies, and when as many as fifty men shall be enrolled for any one company, said company shall proceed to organize by holding an election for lieutenant, after which the captain so previously appointed shall return the muster roll, together with a full report of the condition of the company, to the Governor, who shall thereupon commission the officers of said company, supply said company as, under the provisions of this act, he may deem proper and necessary, and order them upon duty in accordance with the provisions of this act.

Sec. 4. Said men shall be furnished by the State with the most effective and approved breech-loading cavalry arms; and for this purpose the Governor is hereby authorized, on the passage of this act, to contract in behalf of the State for fifteen hundred stand of arms, together with a full supply of ammunition, each company, on its organization to be supplied with its full quota of arms and ammunition, the same so furnished to be all of the same make and caliber, and each member of the company to be furnished with the arm to be used by him at the price the same shall cost the State, which sum shall be retained out of the first moneys due him.

Sec. 5. That each member of said company shall be required to furnish himself with a suitable horse, six-shooter pistol, (army size) and all necessary accoutrements and camp equipage, the same to be passed upon and approved by the enrolling officer before enlistment; and such member at any time fail to keep himself furnished as required above, then the officer in command shall be authorized and required to purchase the articles of which he may be deficient and charge the cost of the same to the person for whom the same shall be provided; provided, that all horses killed in action shall be replaced at the cost of the State, and the cost of horses so killed in action shall be determined by a board of officers, to be composed of the captain, one lieutenant and medical officer of the company to which such animals belonged.

Sec. 6. That said officers and men shall be furnished at the expense of the State with provisions and ammunition and forage for horse when practicable.

Sec. 7. That the men shall be enrolled for the term of twelve months, unless sooner discharged, and at the expiration of their term of service others shall be enrolled to supply their places, in case the Governor deems such action necessary for the protection of the Frontier.

Sec. 8. That no enlisted man shall be discharged from the service without special order from the Governor, nor shall any members of said company dispose of or exchange their horses or arms without the consent of the commanding officer of the company while in the service of the State.

Sec. 9. That the Governor of the State shall be required to divide into convenient districts the several Frontier counties of the State, and that all officers shall take rank, when acting together, according to seniority and date of commission.

Sec. 10. That the commanders of companies, when acting independently, shall use their own judgment and discretion as to the manner of their operations, selecting as their base the most unprotected and exposed settlements in their respective districts, and shall keep weekly communication at least.

Sec. 11. That the troops raised under and by virtue of this act, shall be governed by the rules and regulations of the army of the United States so far as the same may be applicable, but shall always be and remain subject to the authority of the State of Texas for Frontier service.

Sec. 12. That the Governor shall designate the ranking officer of each district, who shall be the senior officer of said district; and in order to secure the effective co-operation of the several companies, said officer shall be given a general supervising authority over the companies of his district, and shall have authority when, in his opinion, the public defense shall require it, to concentrate the whole or any portion of the force within his district for the purpose of following and chastising any marauding bands of hostile Indians, or for 5the purpose of carrying out any other measures that may contribute to the better security of the frontier. Said several companies to be as thoroughly subject to the authority of said senior officer in said district (when such officer deems proper to exercise such general authority) as they would have been under a regular battalion organization.

Sec. 13. That the entire force raised under the provisions of this act shall be at all times under and subject to the orders of the Governor, and shall be exempt from all militia or other service; and that the Governor shall direct all the arrangements necessary to carry out the intentions of this act, with full power to remove any officer or agent for incompetency, neglect of duty or disobedience of orders.

Sec. 14. That the Governor, in case he deems it necessary at any time to make a campaign against the Indians, may nominate the officer to take command of such expedition, assigning him to the command of the whole or any part of said forces, without regard to previous rank or date of commission; he may also assign any officers to any special duty or service; may convene courts martial for the trails of officers and men, and findings whereof shall be approved by him before being carried into effect.

Sec. 15. That the Governor shall appoint a paymaster, whose duty it shall be to draw from the proper authorities the necessary funds for the purchase of supplies, and for the payment of officers and men, and to disburse the same; payment to be made to officers and men at least once in three months. Said officer to rank as captain, and to receive as pay one hundred and forty dollars per month. Said officer shall also give good and efficient bond to the Governor for the faithful discharge of his duties.

Sec. 16. That the Governor shall be authorized to appoint a special agent or agents, who shall give bond and security for the faithful discharge of their duties; which said agents shall be authorized to purchase all necessary pack mules, to be furnished each company for transportation purposes; to purchase all necessary supplies, to be delivered by contractors at the places designated by the commanding officers of companies, and all accounts and certificates of such agents shall be examined and allowed by commanding officers of companies before the same shall become binding as a claim against the State.

Sec. 17. That the Governor shall have power to disband said companies or any portion thereof when, in his opinion, their services shall no longer be necessary for Frontier protection.

Sec. 18. That the present Legislature shall make all necessary appropriations to enable the Executive to carry out the provisions of this act.

Sec. 19. That no portion of said troops shall become a charge against the State until organized and placed under orders.

Sec. 20. That this act take effect and be in force from and after its passage.
Approved June 13, 1870.

## *Laws of the State of Texas.*
## CHAPTER XLII.
### An Act to muster into service minute men for the protection of the frontiers.

Section 1. Be it enacted by the Legislature of the State of Texas, That there shall be mustered into the service of the State, twenty-four companies of minute men, for the protection of the frontier from the raids of the Indians and other marauding parties. The term of service to be for twelve months from the day of general muster; each company to consist of one lieutenant, to be elected by the company, two sergeants, two corporals and fifteen men, to be stationed in each of the following counties, to wit: Montague, Cook, Wise, Jack, Parker, Palo Pinto, Erath, Comanche, Brown, San Saba, Hamilton, Lampasas, Burnet, Llano, Mason, Gillespie, Blanco, Kerr, Kendall, Medina, Uvalde, Maverick and Webb.

Sec. 2. That the minute companies, organized by virtue of this act, shall at all times hold themselves in readiness to meet and repel an Indian raid, or depredations on the frontier counties of the State.

Sec. 3. That it shall be the duty of the Governor of the State, to see that the minute companies are provided with arms and ammunition suitable to this service.

Sec. 4. That the minute companies, shall not be called into the field at any other time than in this act is provided, unless the officer in command shall receive notice that there is, or unless there is a strong probability of a Indian or other marauding raid, or unless he shall receive notice from the officer commanding an adjoining post; that his services are required in the field.

Sec. 5. That the minute companies shall receive the sum of two dollars per diem, for the time actually taken in the field in guarding the frontier; but the time shall in no case exceed ten days in any one calendar month; and no person shall be entered as of any of the said minute men, unless he is an inhabitant of the county, or the county adjoining.

Sec. 6. That the officer in command of a minute company shall keep up his communications with the minute companies adjoining, and he shall be allowed to expend not more than thirty dollars per month in this service; but he shall not receive pay, unless he shall present vouchers for the amount, per month, expended in this service, therein specifying the party performing service, and the nature thereof; and no money shall be paid from the Treasury of the State unless proper vouchers are had.

Sec. 7. That the pay of the minute companies organized by virtue of this act shall come out of the balance (after paying off the ranger companies now in service) of the money now in the hands of the Governor, the proceeds of the hypothecation of the bonds issued for the frontier defence by an act, approved August 5, 1870, and should there be a balance remaining of the said money after paying off said ranger companies, and the minute men organized by virtue of this act, for twelve months service, then the remainder of the moneys if any, shall be paid over by the Governor into the State Treasury, to be applied to the frontier protection of the frontier.

Sec. 8. That every minute man shall provide himself with a good and sufficient horse, such as the officer in command of company shall accept as suitable for the service, and if any minute man's horse shall be killed, prematurely disabled, or unavoidably lost in action, the same shall be paid for by the State; the amount to be accessed by the three highest officers in command not interested in the award: that the commanding officer in charge shall make a monthly report to the Governor of the State, of his command, and the nature of the services performed.

Sec. 9. That should marauding companies or Indians succeed in seizing any property of the frontier citizens, the same on identification, shall be delivered up to the owners free of all charge; and should there be any cost incurred in taking charge thereof, the cost shall be borne by the State. But should there be now owner found for property taken, the same shall be divided amongst the captors, share and share alike.

Approved November 25, 1871.

---

### *Laws of the State of Texas.*
### CHAPTER LXVII.
#### An Act to amend the first section of an Act entitled "An Act to muster into service Minute Men for the protection of the Frontiers," approved November 25th, 1871.

Section 1. Be it enacted by the Legislature of the State of Texas, That the first section of an act entitled "An act to muster into service minute men for the protection of the frontiers," approved November 25th, 1871, to be and the same is hereby amended so as to hereafter read as follows: Section 1. Be it enacted by the Legislature of the State of Texas, That whenever satisfactory evidence is furnished to the Governor that any frontier county in this State is suffering from the raids of Indians or other marauding bands, it shall be the duty of the Governor to cause to be mustered into the service of the State, for the protection of such county from raids of such bands of Indians or other marauding parties, a company of minute men; the term of service of such company to be for twelve months; each company to consist of one lieutenant, two sergeants, two corporals and fifteen men.

Sec. 2. That this act take effect and be in force from and after its passage.

Approved June 2d, 1873.

---

*Laws of the State of Texas.*
## CHAPTER LXVII.
### An Act to Provide for the Protection of the Frontier of the State of Texas against the invasion of hostile Indians, Mexicans, or other marauding or thieving parties.

Section 1. Be it enacted by the Legislature of the State of Texas, That upon satisfactory evidence being furnished the Governor of this State that hostile Indians, Mexicans, or other marauding or thieving parties are depredating upon the lives or property of the citizens of any county or counties upon the frontier of this State, the Governor is hereby required, and shall organize or cause the same to be done, one company of not less than twenty-five, nor more than seventy-five men, for each county that may be so infested; provided, the whole number of men shall not exceed seven hundred and fifty.

Sec. 2. That said companies shall be raised from the county and surrounding counties on the frontier, designated by Governor.

Sec. 3. That no company shall be mustered into the service of this State, under the provisions of this act, for a longer period of time than twelve, nor shorter period than three months.

Sec. 4. The commissioned officers of each company of fifty men or more shall consist of one captain, one first lieutenant and one second lieutenant; of less than fifty men, one first lieutenant and one second lieutenant. The non-commissioned officers for each company shall consist of one sergeant and one corporal for every ten men.

Sec. 5. That the commanding officers of the companies shall purchase all necessary rations and forage hereinafter provided for, and shall give the person from whom such purchases shall be made a certificate of purchase, stating the amount, kind, quality and price of articles furnished, to which shall be attached an affidavit, signed by the officer and the person from whom the purchase may have been made. Said affidavit shall be as follows: That the claim or account is accurate and just, and that the price charged is not above the market value of the article at the time and place where sold, and that said articles were actually used or consumed by said company.

Sec. 6. In the event any commanding officer shall purchase a greater amount of rations or forage than is hereinafter allowed, the paymaster shall deduct the excess thereof from his pay.

Sec. 7. That the commanding officer of each company mustered into service under the provisions of this act, shall forward to the Adjutant General of the State, on the last day of each month, a pay-roll showing the amount due each member of his command; which pay-roll shall be certified to by the commanding officer. And it is hereby made the duty of the Comptroller to draw his warrant upon the Treasurer in favor of each officer, non-commissioned officer and private in the command, separately, for the amount due on each one as set forth in the pay-roll, which warrants shall be forwarded by the Adjutant General to the commanding officer of the company, to be delivered to the men of his command, and said warrants may be paid by the sheriff of the county in which the command was raised or is in service, out of any funds in his hands belonging to the State, and all transfer of warrants by officers or men shall be certified to before some civil officer authorized to administer oaths, and when so transferred they shall be payable at the treasury of the State upon presentation.

Sec. 8. Each member of such company organized under the provisions of this act shall be required to furnish himself with a suitable horse, and one six-shooting pistol (army size) blankets, clothing and camp equipage: the horse shall be valued by the enrolling officer hereinafter provided for, and two other disinterested persons, who shall be sworn to make a true and fair valuation of the same; and should any horse or horses be killed or permanently disabled whilst in action, the paymaster shall pay the owner of the same the appraised value thereof, upon an affidavit made to that effect by the owner of the horse and a member of the company, upon the certificate of the commanding officer of the company, that the facts set forth in said affidavit are true; and no member of any company shall dispose of or exchange his horse or arms whilst in the service of the State, without the consent of the commanding officer of his company.

Sec. 9. The State shall furnish all necessary ammunition, and each officer and private an improved breach-loading cavalry gun at cost; the guns furnished each company to be of the same kind and calibre, the price of which shall be deducted from the first money due the company; provided, that any member may furnish his own gun if of the same kind, calibre and good condition.

Sec. 10. The presiding justice of each of the counties in which it may be necessary to organize a company, shall be the enrolling officer for such county, whose duty it shall be to organize and muster into service the company of such county, and return the muster rolls of the company to the Adjutant General. And should any county not organized require a company under the provisions of this act, then the presiding justice of the county to which said unorganized county is attached for judicial purposes, shall organize and muster into service the company of such unorganized county in the same way and manner as prescribed by this section for the company of his own county.

Sec. 11. The commanding officer of any company, in case of emergency, shall have the right to call to his assistance the companies from the adjoining counties; provided, that not more than one-half of the men of any company shall be forced to leave their county. And when the troops are so called together, the ranking officer present shall take the command of all the troops, and shall hold them together so long as the emergency exists.

Sec. 12. The Governor shall designate the seniority of the commissioned officers of same grade created by this act.

Sec. 13. The amount of rations and forage shall not exceed the following, to-wit: For each man's daily allowance, three-fourths pound bacon, or one and one-half pounds fresh beef; one and one-fourth pounds flour or corn meal; and for every fifty men, seven and one-half pounds beans or peas, five pounds rice, ten pounds green coffee, ten pounds sugar, one-half gallon vinegar, one-half pound candles, one pound soap, two pounds salt, two ounces black pepper, fifteen pounds potatoes. The forage for each horse shall not exceed twelve pounds corn or oats per day, two ounces salt per week.

Sec. 14. Upon the organization of any company under the provisions of this act, the officers shall be elected by the members composing the same, and all vacancies shall be filled by election.

Sec. 15. The pay of officers and privates shall be as follows: For captains, ($100) one hundred dollars; lieutenants, ($75) seventy-five dollars each; sergeants, ($50) fifty dollars each; for all other non-commissioned officers, ($40) forty dollars each, and privates ($40) forty dollars each per month, for every month of actual service.

Sec. 16. The Governor, when he may deem it necessary, shall appoint a surgeon for one or more companies, whose pay shall not exceed one hundred dollars per month, and all necessary medicines to be furnished him by the State.

Sec. 17. The troops raised under the provisions of 'this act shall be governed by the rules and regulations of the United States army, so far as the same may be applicable, but shall always be and remain subject to the authority of the State of Texas, for the protection of the frontier.

Sec. 18. The Adjutant General shall cause to be made such other regulations for the government and control of the organization herein provided for as he may deem necessary, to the end that the force so provided shall be as effective as possible.

Sec. 19. That in addition to the force herein provided for, the Governor be and he is hereby authorized to organize a battalion of mounted men, to consist of six companies, of seventy-five men each. The commissioned officers shall be one major, who shall command the battalion, and one captain and two lieutenants for each company, and one quartermaster. The battalion and company officers shall be appointed by the Governor, and shall be removed at his pleasure.

Sec. 20. The pay of the officers and men shall be as follows: major, ($125), one hundred and twenty-five dollars; captains ($100), one hundred dollars each; lieutenants ($75), seventy-five dollars each; sergeants ($50), fifty dollars each; for all other non-commissioned officers ($40), forty dollars each; privates ($40), forty dollars each, per month; and nothing shall be paid by way of commutation.

Sec. 21. The Governor shall appoint a quartermaster for this force, who shall discharge the duties of a quartermaster, commissary and paymaster, and shall rank and receive the pay of a captain, and give such bond as the Governor may require for the faithful performance of his duties.

Sec. 22. That the officers and men of this force shall be paid quarterly.

Sec. 23. That this force is not designed as a standing force, but shall always be under the command of the Governor, to be operated by his direction in such manner, in such detachments, and in such localities as the Governor may direct; and the same shall be disbanded and reorganized, or reassembled, from time to time, as in his judgment the exigencies of the frontier may demand.

Sec. 24. Each soldier and officer shall furnish his own horse, and, unless the same is killed in battle, shall not be paid for by the State.

Sec. 25. The Governor is hereby authorized to keep this force in the field as long as in his judgment there may be a necessity for such a force, and soldiers who may volunteer in such service shall do so for such term not to exceed four years, subject to disbandment and re-assemblage by order of the Governor.

Sec. 26. Whenever, in the opinion of the Governor, this force shall be insufficient to protect the frontier, he shall be authorized to call out the minute men, or any part thereof, hereinbefore provided for, which said force is hereby declared to be auxiliary and supplemental to the battalion of mounted men authorized by this act.

Sec. 27. The State shall furnish necessary ammunition, and to each officer and private of this battalion an improved breech-loading cavalry gun, at cost; the guns furnished to be of the same kind and calibre, the price of which shall be deducted from the first money due the battalion.

Sec. 28. Each officer of the battalion and of the companies of minute men herein provided for, shall have all the powers of a peace officer, and it shall be his duty to execute all criminal processes directed to him, and make arrests under *capias* properly issued, of any and all parties charged with offense against the laws of this State.

Sec. 29. That the Governor of the State is authorized to disband all troops now in the service of the State for frontier protection, as soon as practicable, and that they be allowed to retain all arms furnished by the State at the same price that the same were furnished to the State.

Sec. 30. That an act entitled "An Act to provide for the protection of the frontier," approved June 13, 1870, also an act entitled "An Act to muster into service mounted men for the protection of the frontier , approved November 25, 1871; also an act entitled "An Act to amend the first section of an act entitled 'An Act to muster into service minute men for the protection of the frontier,' approved November 28, 1871," approved June 2, 1873, and all other laws and parts of laws heretofore enacted on the same subject, be and the same are hereby repealed.

Sec. 31. The Governor and the Adjutant General are hereby authorized and empowered to make all additional regulations not contrary to the laws of this State, which are necessary to carry out the provisions of this act.

Sec. 32. That this act take effect and be in force from and after its passage.

Approved April 10, 1874.

---

## Laws of the State of Texas.
### CHAPTER LVI.
### An Act to suppress lawlessness and crime in certain parts of the State, and to make an appropriation therefor.

Whereas, In several counties in the Western part of the State the people are being depredated on, in person and property, by bands of criminal and lawless men too strong to be suppressed by the civil authorities unaided, and by bandits and robbers from Mexico; therefore, for the purpose of maintaining law and order, and giving security to that section against foreign invasion and domestic disturbance, and, for that purpose, to aid the civil authorities.

Section 1. Be it enacted by the Legislature of the State of Texas, That the Governor is hereby authorized and required to immediately organize a company of fifty men, rank and file, to-wit Forty-two privates, four sergeants, and four corporals; and, in addition, thereto, there shall be one captain, one first lieutenant, and one second lieutenant; and, in the aggregate, said company shall consist of fifty-three men, noncommissioned officers, and privates.

Sec. 2. That said company shall be mustered into the service of the State of Texas for the period of six calendar months, or longer should the Governor deem it necessary, in such manner as the Adjutant General may designate. Each officer, non-commissioned officer, and private thereof, shall furnish his own horse, saddle, bridle, rope, clothing, etc., for the entire term of service, and replace any or all of said articles, should it become necessary so to do.

Sec. 3. That the State of Texas shall furnish said company with arms, ammunition, camp and garrison equipage, and rations of subsistence for the men, and forage for the horses, and with transportation necessary to move said supplies. The arms shall be issued and charge to the men, and, in case any of said arms shall be lost through neglect, or by disobedience of orders, the value thereof shall be charged upon the roll as a stoppage against the party losing the same; but in no case, shall arms lost in the discharge of duty be so charged.

Sec. 4. The members of said company shall be allowed the following pay, to-wit: The captain one hundred and sixty-six dollars per month; the first lieutenant, one hundred and thirty-three dollars per month;; the second lieutenant, one hundred and twenty-five dollars per month; the sergeants, fifty dollars each per month; the corporals, forty dollars each per month; and the privates, forty dollars each per month. The payments shall be made at such time and in such manner as the Adjutant General of the State may prescribe.

Sec. 5. That said company shall be governed by the rules and regulations of the army of the United States and the articles of war, as far as the same may be applicable, and by such orders, rules and regulations as may be prescribed from time, to time by the Governor and the Adjutant General of this State.

Sec. 6. That the officers, non-commissioned officers, and privates of said company shall be clothed with the powers of peace officers, and shall aid the civil authorities in the execution of the laws. They shall have authority to make arrests, and, in such cases, they shall be governed by laws regulating and defining the powers and the duties of Sheriffs when in discharge of these duties, take an oath before some authority legally authorized to administer the same, that each of them will faithfully perform his duties in accordance with law. In order to arrest and bring to justice men who have banded together for the purpose of committing robbery or other felons, and to prevent the execution of the laws, the officers, non-commissioned officers, and privates of said company, may accept the services of such citizens as shall volunteer to aid them; but while so engaged, such citizens shall not receive pay from the State for their services.

Sec. 7. When said company, or any member or members thereof, shall arrest any person or persons charged with the commission of a criminal offense or offenses, they shall convey said person or persons to the county or counties where he or they stand charged with the commission of an offense, and shall deliver him or them to the proper officer, taking his receipt thereof; and all necessary expenses thus incurred shall be paid by the State.

Sec. 8. That the sum of forty thousand dollars, or much thereof as may be necessary, be, and the same is hereby appropriated out of any moneys in the Treasury not otherwise appropriated, to carry out the objects of this act.

Sec. 9. That the fact of the existence of bands of lawless men in counties of this State, of their having prevented the execution of the laws, and placed the good people in various counties in continual fear of the commission of outrages upon their persons and property, constitutes a public necessity and emergency that this act take effect and it is hereby declared that the same go into effect and be in force from and after its passage.

Approved July 22, 1876.

Takes effect from its passage.

---

## *Laws of the State of Texas.*
## CHAPTER CXXIII.
**An Act to suppress lawlessness and crime and to organize a force for that purpose.**

Whereas, It is credibly reported that in several counties in the western and southwestern part of the state, the people are being depredated on in person and property by bands of criminal and lawless men too strong to be suppressed by the civil authorities unaided, and by bandits and robbers from Mexico; therefore, for the purpose of maintaining law and order and giving security to that section against foreign invasion and domestic disturbance and to aid the civil authorities.

Section 1. Be it enacted by the Legislature of the State of Texas, That the governor is hereby authorized to immediately organize a company of twenty-five men rank and file to wit: Twenty-one privates, two sergeants and two corporals, and in addition thereto there shall be one captain and one first lieutenant and in the aggregate said company shall consist of twenty-seven men, officers and non-commissioned officers and privates.

Sec. 2. That said company shall be mustered into the service of the State of Texas for the period of twelve calendar months, or longer or shorter, and may be disbanded when they are no longer needed, should the governor deem it necessary, in such manner as the adjutant general may direct. Each officer, non-commissioned and private thereof, shall furnish his own horse, saddle, bridle, rope, clothing, etc., for the entire term of service, and replace any or all of said articles, should it become necessary so to do.

Sec. 3. That the State of Texas shall furnish said company with arms, ammunition, camp and garrison equipage, and rations of subsistence for the men and forage for the horses, and with transportation necessary to move said supplies. The arms shall be issued and charged to the men, and in case any of said arms shall be lost through neglect or by disobedience of orders, the value thereof shall be charged upon the rolls as a stoppage against the party losing the same; but in no case shall arms lost in the discharge of duty be so charged.

Sec. 4. The members of said company shall be allowed the following pay, to wit: The captain, one hundred and twenty-five dollars per month; the first lieutenant, one hundred dollars per month; the sergeants, corporals and privates, thirty dollars each per month. The payments shall be made at such times and in such manner as the adjutant general of the state may prescribe.

Sec. 5. That said company shall be governed by the rules and regulations of the army of the United States, and the articles of war, so far as the same may be applicable, and by such orders, rules and regulations as may be prescribed from time to time by the governor and the adjutant general of this state.

Sec. 6. That the officers, non-commissioned officers and privates of said company shall be clothed with the powers of peace officers, and shall aid the civil authorities in the execution of the laws. They shall have authority to make arrests, and in such cases they shall be governed by the laws regulating and defining the powers and duties of sheriffs when in the discharge of similar duties. They shall, before entering upon the discharge of these duties, take an oath before some authority legally authorized to administer the same, that each of them will faithfully perform his duties in accordance with law. In order to arrest and bring to justice men who have banded together for the purpose of committing robbery or other felonies, and to prevent the execution of the laws the officers, non-commissioned officers, and privates of said company may accept the services of such citizens as shall volunteer to aid them, but while so engaged such citizens shall receive no pay from the state for their services.

Sec. 7. When said company or any member or members thereof shall arrest any person charged with the commission of a criminal offense or offenses, they shall convey such person or persons to the county or counties where he or they stand charged with the commission of an offense, and shall deliver him or them to the proper officer, taking his receipt therefor, and all necessary expenses thus incurred shall be paid by the state.

Sec. 8. That the officers and members of all military companies organized for the protection of the frontier, or for the suppression of lawlessness and crime in this state, shall receive pay for services in accordance with the rate established by section four of this act.

Sec. 9. That the fact of the existence of bands of lawless men in counties in this state, of their having prevented the execution of laws, and placed the good people in various counties in continual fear of the commission of outrages upon their persons and property, constitute a public necessity and emergency that this act take effect and be in force from and after its passage, and it is so enacted.

Approved April 22, A. D. 1879.
Takes effect ninety days after adjournment.

---

## GENERAL LAWS OF TEXAS.
### Ranger Force — Organization of.

H. B. No. 52.]  CHAPTER XXXIV.

An Act to provide for the organization of a "Ranger Force" for the protection of the frontier against marauding and thieving parties, and for the suppression of lawlessness and crime throughout the State; to prescribe the duties and powers of members of such force, and to regulate their compensation.

SECTION 1. *Be it enacted by the Legislature of the State of Texas*: That the Governor be and is hereby authorized to organize a force to be known as the "Ranger Force," for the purpose of protecting the frontier against marauding or thieving parties, and for the suppression of lawlessness and crime throughout the State.

SEC. 2. The "Ranger Force" shall consist of not to exceed four separate companies of mounted men, each company to consist of not to exceed one captain, one first sergeant and twenty privates, and one quartermaster for the entire force. The captains of companies and the quartermaster shall be appointed by the Governor, and shall be removed at his pleasure; unless sooner so removed by the Governor, they shall serve for two years and until their successors are appointed and qualified.

SEC. 3. The pay of officers and men shall be as follows: Captains, one hundred ($100) dollars each, per month: sergeants, fifty ($50) dollars each, per month; and privates forty ($40) dollars each, per month. The payments shall be made at such times and in such manner as the Adjutant General of the State may prescribe.

SEC. 4. The Governor shall appoint a quartermaster for this force, who shall discharge the duties of quartermaster, commissary and paymaster, and shall rank and receive the pay of a captain.

SEC. 5. That this force shall always be under the command of the Governor, to be operated by his direction in such manner, in such detachments and in such localities as the Governor may direct.

SEC. 6. The Governor is hereby authorized to keep this force, or so much thereof as he may deem necessary, in the field as long as in his judgment, there may be necessity for such a force; and men who may volunteer in such service shall do so for such term not to exceed two years, subject to disbandment in whole or in part at any time, and reassemblage or reorganization of the whole force, or such portion thereof as may be deemed necessary by order of the Governor.

SEC. 7. That the quartermaster, or if so directed by the Adjutant General, company commanders shall purchase all supplies hereinafter provided for, and shall make a certificate on the voucher of the party or parties from whom the supplies and (sic) purchased, to the effect that "the account is correct and just, and the articles purchased were at the lowest market prices."

SEC. 8. Each officer, non-commissioned officer and private of said force shall furnish himself with a suitable horse, horse equipment, clothing, etc.; provided, that if his horse is killed in action it shall be paid for by the State at a fair market value at the time when killed.

SEC. 9. That the State shall furnish each member of said force with one improved carbine and pistol at cost, the price of which shall be deducted from the first money due such officer or man, and shall furnish said force with rations of subsistence, camp equipage and ammunition for the officers and men, and also forage for horses.

SEC. 10. The amount of rations and forage shall not exceed the following, to wit: For each man's daily allowance, twelve ounces bacon or twenty ounces beef, twenty ounces of flour or corn meal, two and two-fifths ounces of beans or peas, one and three-fifths ounces of rice, three and one-fifth ounces of coffee, three and one-fifth ounces of sugar, one-sixth gill of vinegar or pickles, one-sixth ounce candles, one-third ounce of soap, two-thirds of an ounce of salt, one-twenty-fourth of an ounce of pepper, four and four-fifths ounces of potatoes, sixteen twenty-fifths of an ounce of baking powder. The forage for each horse shall not exceed twelve pounds of corn or oats, and fourteen pounds of hay per day, and two ounces of salt per week; provided, that when in case of emergency the members of said force are employed in such duty that it Is impracticable to furnish the rations herein provided for, each member of said force so employed shall be allowed for his necessary actual expenses for such subsistence not to exceed one dollar and fifty cents ($1.50) per day; and provided further, that when it becomes necessary to move the members of said force from one place to another by railroad, the actual necessary expenses of such transportation shall be paid.

SEC. 11. The officers, non-commissioned officers and privates of this force shall be clothed with all the powers of peace officers, and shall aid the regular civil authorities in the execution of the laws. They shall have authority to make arrests, and to execute process in criminal cases, and in such cases they shall be governed by law regulating and defining the powers and duties of sheriffs when in discharge of similar duties; except that they shall have the power, and shall be authorized to make arrests and to execute all process in criminal cases in any county in the State. They shall, before entering on the discharge of these duties, take an oath before some authority legally authorized to administer the same, that each of them will faithfully perform his duties in accordance with law. In order to arrest and bring to justice men who have banded together for the purpose of committing robbery or other felonies, and to prevent the execution of the laws, the officers, noncommissioned officers and privates of said force may accept the services of such citizens as shall volunteer to aid them, but while so engaged such citizen shall not receive pay from the State for such services.

SEC. 12. When said force, or any member or members thereof, shall arrest any person charged with the commission of a criminal offense, they shall forthwith convey said person to the county where he or they stand charged with the commission of an offense, and shall deliver him or them to the proper officer, taking his receipt, therefore, and all necessary expenses thus incurred will paid by the State.

SEC. 13. The Governor and Adjutant General shall cause to be made such regulations for the government and control of the organization herein provided for, and for the enlistment and employment of non-commissioned officers and privates, as they may doom necessary, to the end that the force so provided shall be as effective as possible.

SEC. 14. All laws and parts of laws, both general and special, in conflict with the provisions of this act, are hereby repealed.

SEC. 15. The fact that the Revised Statutes are indefinite; and that a defect exists, in that the privates of said force have no authority to execute criminal process, creates an emergency and an imperative public necessity that the constitutional rule requiring bills to be read on three several days be suspended, and that this act take effect and be in force from and after its passage, and it is so enacted.

[Note.— The enrolled bill shows that the foregoing act passed the House of Representatives, no vote given, and passed the Senate by two-thirds vote, yeas 23, nays 3.]

Approved March 29, 1901.
Takes effect 90 days after adjournment.

---

## GENERAL LAWS OF TEXAS.
## RANGER HOME GUARD.

S. B. No. 28.] CHAPTER 36.

An Act to provide for the organization of a Ranger Home Guard for the protection of the frontier against marauding and thieving parties, foreign foes, or any enemy of the State of Texas, or the government of the United States, and for the suppression of lawlessness and crime throughout the State, or to suppress any invasion from an alien enemy of this State, or any State of the United States of America; to prescribe duties and powers of members of such force; to regulate their compensation; and declaring an emergency.

*Be it enacted by the Legislature of the State of Texas*:

Section 1. That the Governor be and he is hereby authorized to organize a force to be known as the Ranger Home Guard for the purpose of protecting the frontier against marauding and thieving parties, and other lawlessness or any invasion by any foreign foe or alien enemy.

Section 2. The Ranger Home Guard of this State shall consist of not to exceed one thousand men, to be selected and appointed by the Governor, or under his direction, and all officers of said force necessary for the commandeering, equipping, and regulating of the said force shall be appointed by the Governor; and any officer or member of said force shall be removed at the pleasure of the Governor and shall serve for a period of three years, unless sooner removed by the Governor.

Section 3. The pay of officers and men in said force be as follows; Captain One Hundred and Twenty-Five Dollars ($125.00) per month, Sergeants Sixty Dollars ($60.00) per month, Privates Fifty Dollars ($50.00) per month. The payment shall be made at such times and in such manner as the Adjutant General of the State or the Governor may prescribe, and it is further provided that the Governor may appoint captains and other officers who may serve without pay, or cost to the State, except their immediate traveling expenses and food for themselves and horses when transferred from their home to some other part of the State, under orders from competent authority.

Section 4. The State shall furnish each member of said force with one carbine and pistol at cost, the price of which will be deducted from the first money due such officer per man, and shall furnish said force with rations of subsistence, medicines and medical attendance, camp equipage and ammunition for the officers and men, and also forage for the horses. The State shall pay funeral expenses of member of the Ranger Home Guard dying in the service, and it is further provided that any person who may desire to join said force and who shall be appointed by the Governor, and who shall stipulate that are serving without pay, except as herein provided, may furnish his own carbine and pistol and shall be permitted to furnish his own horse or other means of transportation which may be acceptable to the captain of nay company in he desires to enlist.

Section 5. The amount of rations and forage shall be that now or hereafter prescribed in the United States army regulations to be furnished by the State of Texas, provided that when it is impracticable to furnish rations in kind they may be commuted at not to exceed the rate of two dollars per man per day for such period.

Section 6. It is hereby agreed and understood that this is a separate and distinct act passed at this time to cover a period of such time as the Governor of this State may deem necessary no to exceed three years from the taking effect of this Act, and it is cumulative of an act passed by the Twenty-seventh Legislature providing for the organization of the Ranger Home Guard, and does not in any wise repeal said act passed by the Twenty-seventh Legislature except as to Section 3 of said Act relative to pay, rations and forage of officers and privates of the present Ranger Home Guard, and in that respect it is amendatory of said section providing for the payment of the salaries, rations and forage of said officers, and all officers and privates, of the present Ranger Home Guard are hereby from and after the taking effect of this Act placed on the same salaries, rations and forage as provided for in this Act, and in other respect this Act is cumulative of the present law governing the Ranger Home Guard in this State.

Section 7. The sum of Two Hundred and Fifty Thousand Dollars ($250,000.00) or so much as may be necessary, is hereby appropriated out of the funds in the State Treasury not otherwise appropriated for the payment of the salaries, expenses or other necessary things incidental to the organization of said force, as herein provided.

Section 8. The fact that this government, of which this State is a part, is now engaged in a war with the Imperial German Government, and the further fact that we have something like eight hundred miles of border to be protected, and that the citizenship of this State and the property of said citizenship should be protected during the period of said war from any foreign foe or marauder or invader creates an emergency and an imperative public necessity that the constitutional rule requiring bills to be read on three several days be suspended, and it is hereby suspended, and this Act shall take effect from and after its passage, and it is so enacted.

Approved May 25, 1917.

Take effect 90 days after adjournment.

---

## GENERAL LAWS.
## PROVIDING FOR THE REORGANIZATION OF
## THE STATE RANGER FORCE FOR THE PROTECTION OF
## THE FRONTIER AND SUPPRESSION OF LAWLESSNESS
## THROUGHOUT THE STATE.

H. B. No. 5.]  CHAPTER 144.

An Act to amend Title 116, the Revised Civil Statutes of the State of Texas including Articles 6754 6755, 6756, 6757, 6758, 6759, 6760, 6761, 6762, 6763, 6764, 6f65, 6766 be amended and Article 6767 added thereto, said Act providing for the organization of a ranger force for the protecting of the frontier against marauders or thieving parties; for the suppression of lawlessness and crime throughout the State; to prescribe the duties and powers of members of such force; to regulate their compensation; and declaring an emergency.

*Be it enacted by the Legislature of the State of Texas:*

SECTION 1. Title 116 of the Revised Civil Statutes of the State of Texas including Articles 6754, 6755, 6756, 6757, 6758, 6759Y 6760, 6761, 6762, 6763, 6764, 6765, 6766 be amended and Article 6767 be added thereto so that they will hereafter read as follows:

Article 6754. The ranger force authorized to be organized by the Governor is for the purpose of protecting the frontier against marauding or thieving parties, and for the suppression of lawlessness and crime throughout the State, and to aid in the enforcement of the laws of the State.

Article 6755. The ranger force shall consist of not to exceed one headquarters company and four companies of mounted men, except in cases of emergency, when the Governor shall have authority to increase the force to meet extraordinary conditions.

The headquarters company shall consist of one captain, who shall be designated the senior captain of the force, one sergeant, and not to exceed four privates.

Each separate mounted company shall consist of not to exceed one captain, one sergeant and fifteen privates. The captains and the quartermaster shall be appointed by the Governor and shall be removed at his pleasure; unless so removed by the Governor they shall serve for two years and until their successors are appointed and qualified.

The enlisted men and non-commissioned officers of each company shall be appointed by the Governor, acting by and through the Adjutant General, who shall pass upon the qualifications of such men, and so far as practicable shall make such appointment upon the recommendation of the captain, under whom such men are to serve. The enlisted men and non-commissioned officers shall serve for two years, unless sooner removed by the Governor or the Adjutant General for cause.

Article 6756. The pay of officers and men shall be as follows: Captains $150.00 each per month; sergeants $100.00 each per month and privates $90.00 each per month, except as herein otherwise provided. The payment shall be made monthly at such times and in such manner as the Adjutant General of the State may prescribe.

The officers and enlisted men on the ranger force shall receive in addition to their regular salary an increase of five per cent after the first two years of continuous service and five per cent for each additional year not to exceed in all twenty per cent of their salary as above provided. For the violation or breach of such rules and revelations for the governing of the ranger force as may be prescribed by the Adjutant General and approved by the Governor, officers and enlisted men shall forfeit their right to participate in the increase or longevity pay, or any portion thereof provided for herein.

Article 6757. The Governor shall appoint a quartermaster for the ranger force, who shall discharge the duties of a quartermaster, commissary and paymaster, and shall have the rank and pay of a captain.

Article 6758. This force shall always be under the command of the Governor; to be operated under his direction in such manner, in such detachments, and in such localities as the Governor may direct, acting by and through the Adjutant General.

Article 6759. The Governor is authorized to keep this force, or so much thereof as he may deem necessary in the field as long as in his judgment there may be necessity for such a force; and men who may be enlisted in such service shall do so for such term not to exceed two, years subject to disbandment in whole or in part at any time and reassemblage or reorganization of the whole force, or such portion thereof as may be deemed necessary by order of the Governor.

Article 6760. The quartermaster when directed by the Adjutant General shall purchase all supplies for the ranger force, and shall make a certificate on the voucher of the party or parties from whom the supplies are purchased to the fact that the account is correct and just, and the articles purchased were at the lowest market prices.

Article 6761. Members to Furnish Equipment, etc. Each officer, non-commissioned officer and private of said force shall furnish himself with a suitable horse, horse equipment, clothing, etc.; provided, that if his horse is killed in action it shall be paid for by the State at a fair market value at the time when killed.

Article 6762. Arms and Equipment. The State shall furnish each member of said force with one improved carbine and pistol at cost, the price of which shall be deducted from the first money due such officer or man, and shall furnish said force with rations of subsistence, camp equipage and ammunition for the officers and men, and also forage for horses.

Article 6763. In addition to the pay allotted to each officer and man of this force, they shall be allowed not to exceed $30.00 per month for subsistence when at their station, and when on duty outside of his district each member of said force shall be allowed his actual necessary expenses for subsistence and quarters, to be paid on a sworn account showing the actual amount expended, not to exceed $3.00 per day. In addition thereto each member shall be allowed his actual railroad expenses when traveling under orders.

Provided further, that when any company of said force furnishes motor transportation without expense to the State, they shall be allowed $50.00 per month per company for repairs and upkeep for said motor vehicle.

Article 6764. Clothed with Powers of Peace Officers.—The officers, non-commissioned officers and privates of this force shall be clothed with all the powers of peace officers, and shall aid the regular civil authorities in the execution of the laws. They shall have authority to make arrests, and to execute process in criminal cases, and in such cases they shall be governed by law regulating and defining the powers and duties of sheriffs when in discharge of similar duties; except that they shall have the power and shall be authorized to make arrests and to execute all process in criminal cases in any county in the State. They shall, before entering on the discharge of these duties, take an oath before some authority legally authorized to administer the same, that each of them will faithfully perform his duties in accordance with law. In order to arrest and bring to Justice men who have banded together for the purpose of committing robbery, or other felonies, and to prevent the execution of the laws, the officers, non-commissioned officers and privates of said force may accept the services of such citizens as shall volunteer to aid them; but while so engaged such citizens shall not receive pay from the State for such services.

Article 6765. When said force, or any member or members thereof, shall arrest any person charged with the commission of a criminal offense, they shall forthwith convey said person to the county where he or they stand charged with the commission of an offense and shall deliver him or them to the proper officer, taking his receipt therefore: and all necessary expenses thus incurred will be paid by the State.

Article 6766. The Governor and Adjutant General shall cause to be made such regulations for the government and control of the organization herein provided for, for the enlistment and employment of non-commissioned officers and privates as they may deem necessary to the end that the force so provided or shall be as effective as possible; provided that when any complaint is made to the Adjutant General charging any ranger with misconduct or violation of the law, the Adjutant General will have the right to institute proceedings before any magistrate in the county where the offense is alleged been committed. Upon application of the Adjutant General said magistrate shall issue process for witnesses to appear and testify under oath, which testimony shall be reduced to writing by a stenographer and transmitted by the court to the Adjutant General, who shall take such action as the facts warrant. The cost of such proceedings including fee of $3.00 of the magistrate and fifteen cents for each one hundred words of testimony so taken and transcribed shall be paid by the Comptroller of Public Accounts upon approval by the Adjutant General out of funds appropriated for enforcement of law.

Provided further, that it shall be the duty of any citizen who knows of any such misconduct or violation of the law on the part of any member of the ranger force to at once notify the Adjutant General in writing of misconduct, and it shall be the duty of the Adjutant General to at once conduct such examination and to take such action thereon as the facts make necessary, and he shall without delay submit all of such evidence and his actions thereon to the Governor for his approval or disapproval.

Article 6766a. All officers and men selected under this Act shall be men of good moral character, shall furnish satisfactory evidence thereof, sober, of sound judgment and shall conform to such qualifications as the Governor shall prescribe for appointment, and all applications for appointment to the ranger force shall be made to the Governor, who shall pass upon the qualifications of each applicant for a position on such force. Provided, however, that no person shall be appointed to the ranger force who is not a citizen of the United States and of Texas, and preference shall always be given to discharged soldiers holding certificates of honorable discharge from the United States Army.

SEC. 2. The fact that there is now no sufficient law prescribing the duties, pay and qualifications of State Rangers creates an emergency and an imperative public necessity requiring that the constitutional rule requiring bills to be read on three several days be suspended; and that this Act take effect and be in force from and after its passage, and it is so enacted.

[Note.— H. B. No. 5 passed the House of Representatives on March 8, 1919, by a vote, yeas 95, nays 5; and passed the Senate with amendments on March 17, 1919, by a vote, yeas 27, nays 1; the House concurred in the Senate amendments on March 17, 1919, but no vote given.]

Approved March 31, 1919.

Becomes effective 90 days after adjournment.

---

## FORTY-FOURTH LEGISLATURE — REGULAR SESSION.
## GENERAL LAWS.
## CREATING DEPARTMENT OF PUBLIC SAFETY OF THE STATE OF TEXAS AND PUBLIC SAFETY COMMISSION.

S. B. No. 146.]                     CHAPTER 181.

An Act to create the Department of Public Safety of the State of Texas; and the Public Safety Commission; providing for the appointment of members of the Public Safety Commission and for the organization of the Commission and of the Department; and fixing the expense allowance of the Commissioners; providing for the appointment of a Director of the Department of Public Safety Commission and an Assistant Director and prescribing the duties and powers of the Director of the Public Safety Commission; providing for the appointment, promotion and discharge of all officers and employees of the Department of Public Safety; providing for the number of rangers that may be appointed by the Department of Public Safety; providing for the transfer of the Texas Ranger force from the Adjutant General's Department to the Department of Public Safety; providing for the appointment of special rangers not to exceed three hundred; providing that no more than ten special ranger commissions may be issued to any person, firm or corporation except in emergencies; prescribing the duties of special rangers that are appointed by the Commission; providing for an increase of twenty-six privates in the Sate Highway Motor patrol; providing for the transfer of the State Highway Motor Patrol of Texas from the State Highway Department to the Department of Public Safety; creating divisions and bureaus within the said Department; defining the powers, duties and functions of the Commission and the Department, and its various divisions, rangers, motor patrol, and bureaus and co-ordinating them; providing for the cooperation of the State owned educational institutions, and all State officers and departments, and all county and municipal law enforcement officers and agencies with the Department; providing personnel, buildings, quarters, equipment, and appropriations for the Department; fixing the terms of office, methods of appointment, promotion, reduction, suspension and discharge of the officers and employees of the Department; providing for the transfer of pending business and the transfer of funds; providing for the Governor of the State of Texas to command the Department in times of public emergency; providing for the issuance of commissions of all law enforcement members of the Department; repealing all laws and parts of laws in conflict herewith, and appropriating moneys to put this Act into force and effect; declaring the rule that the remainder of the Act shall not be affected by the unconstitutionality or invalidity of any part thereof; and for other purposes, and declaring an emergency.

*Be it enacted by the Legislature of the Ste of Texas:*
SECTION 1. CREATION OF THE DEPARTMENT OF PUBLIC SAFETY: There is hereby created a Department of Public Safety of the State of Texas, hereinafter designated as "the Department," in which is vested the enforcement of the laws protecting the public safety and providing for the prevention and detection of crime. The Department shall have its principal office and headquarters in the City of Austin, where all of its records shall be kept.

SEC. 2. CREATION OF THE PUBLIC SAFETY COMMISSION: The control of the Department is hereby vested in the Public Safety Commission, hereinafter designated as "the Commission," which Commission shall consist of three citizens of this State. The Governor shall, within thirty days after this Act shall take effect, appoint the members of the Commission by and with the advice and consent of the Senate to hold office until December 31, 1935, and they shall constitute the Public Safety Commission; and on the 1st day of January, 1936, the Governor shall appoint one member to hold office for two years, one for four years, and one for six years, and at the end of every two years thereafter, the Governor shall in like manner, by and with the advice and consent of the Senate of the State of Texas, appoint one citizen of Texas as the successor of the member of the Commission whose term shall expire in that year, to serve as such member of six years and until his successor is appointed and qualified. The Commission shall elect annually one member of the Commission to serve as chairman thereof. Two members of the Commission shall constitute a quorum. In the event of a vacancy occurring on said Commission, the Governor shall appoint a new member of the Commission to fill the said vacancy for such unexpired term, such appointment to be subject to the advice and consent of the Senate of the State of Texas, at the next session thereof. The members of the Commission shall be elected because of their peculiar qualifications fitting them for these positions. In the appointment of the members of the Commission, the following qualifications among others shall be observed: Knowledge of laws; experience in the enforcement of law; honesty, integrity; education, training and executive ability. They shall serve without compensation, but shall be entitled to receive Ten ($10.00) Dollars per day as an expense account and necessary mileage in the performance of their duties, such expense allowance shall not exceed Five Hundred ($500.00) Dollars annually for each member.

SEC. 3. ORGANIZATION OF THE COMMISSION: The Commission shall meet at such time and places as they may provide for by rules or as the chairman or any two members may call.

SEC. 4. DUTIES AND POWERS OF THE COMMISSION:
(1) The Commission shall formulate plans and policies for the enforcement of the criminal laws and of the traffic and safety laws of the State, the prevention of crime, the detection

and apprehension of violators of the laws, and for the education of the citizens of the State In the promotion of public safety and law observance.

(2) It shall organize the Department and supervise its operation; it shall establish grades and positions for the Department, and for each grade and position it shall designate the authority and responsibility within the limits of this Act. For each such grade and position so established, the Commission shall set standards of qualifications and shall fix prerequisites of training, education and experience, and shall make necessary rules and regulations for the appointment, promotion, reduction, suspension and discharge of all employees after hearings before the said Commission; that any officer or employee of the said Department who shall be discharged shall upon application to the Commission be entitled to a public hearing before said Commission and the Commission shall determine whether such discharge shall be affirmed or set aside. All persons inducted into the service of the Department shall be considered on probation for the first six months and at any time during such period they may be discharged if found to be unsuitable for the work by the Director, with the advice and consent of the Commission, and, if so discharged, such persons shall not be entitled to the public hearing hereinabove provided for.

(3) The Commission shall establish and make public proclamation of all rules and regulations for the conduct of the work of the Department as may be deemed necessary and as may not be inconsistent with the provisions of this Act or of the laws of the State.

(4) The Commission shall maintain records of all proceedings and official orders.

(5) The Commission shall biennially submit a report of its work to the Governor, and the Legislature, with its recommendations and those of the Public Safety Director. A quarterly statement containing an itemized list of all moneys received, and from what sources received, and all moneys expended and for what purposes expended, shall be prepared by the Director sworn to and filed in the records of the Department and a copy shall be sent to the Governor.

SEC. 5. The Commission shall appoint a Public Safety Director hereinafter designated as the "Director," who shall be a citizen of this State and who shall hold his position until removed by the Commission. The Commission shall also appoint an Assistant Director who shall perform such duties as may be designated by the Director. The Director and Assistant Director shall be selected on the basis of training, experience, and qualifications for said positions, and shall have at least five (5) years experience, preferably police or public administration. The Director and Assistant Director shall draw annual salaries as fixed by the Legislature not to exceed Four Thousand Two Hundred ($4,200.00) Dollars, and the Assistant Director shall receive an annual salary not to exceed Three Thousand ($3,000.00) Dollars, said salaries to be paid monthly. The Director shall be directly responsible to the Commission for the conduct of all the affairs of the Department.

SEC. 6. DUTIES AND POWERS OF THE DIRECTOR:

(1) The Director shall act with the Commission in an advisory capacity, without vote, and shall quarterly, annually and biennially submit to the Commission detailed reports of the operation of the Department and statements of its expenditures.

(2) He shall be the executive officer of the Department, and subject to the approval of the Commission and to the provisions of this Act, he shall have authority to appoint, promote, reduce, suspend and discharge all officers and employees of the Department. He shall issue and sign requisition as provided by law for the purchase of supplies for the office and officers of the Department, suitable uniforms, arms and equipment; and make such rules and regulations, subject to the approval of the Commission, as are deemed necessary for the control of the Department.

SEC. 7. AUTHORITY TO ISSUE COMMISSIONS: The Director, under the direction of the Commission, shall issue commissions as law enforcement officers to all members of the Texas Rangers, to all members of the Texas Highway Patrol, and to such other officers of the Department as may be employed by the said Department.

SEC. 8. APPOINTMENT OF DIVISION AND BUREAU CHIEFS: The Senior Captain of the Texas Rangers shall be Chief of the Bureau of Intelligence; the Chief of the Highway Motor patrol shall be the Chief of the Bureau of Communications; the Assistant Director of the Department of Public Safety shall be the Chief of the Bureau of Education; the Chief of the Bureau of Identification and Records shall be appointed by the Director of the Department of Public Safety with consent of the Commission.

SEC. 9. APPOINTMENT, PROMOTIONS, AND DISCHARGES:

(1) The appointment and promotion of all officers and employees shall be made on the basis of merit, to be determined by examinations under the rules and regulations of the Commission which shall be taken into consideration the age, physical condition, experience and education of the applicant. All persons who have applications on file for nay position in the Department shall be given reasonable written notice of the place and time where said examinations are to be held.

(2) All applications for positions in the Department shall be citizens of the United States of America, and shall have been bona fide residents of the State of Texas for a period of not less than one year immediately prior to the filing of the application. No applicant for a position in the Department shall be questioned at any time as to his religious faith or beliefs, or as to his political affiliations. No person in the Department shall contribute any money or other thing of value for political purposes, nor shall any person in the Department engage in political activities or campaign for or against any candidate for any public office in this State. Any person violating any provision of this subsection shall forfeit his position with the Department.

(3) No officer or employee of the Department shall be discharged without just cause. The Director shall determine whether or not the officer or the employee be discharged; and in case he is ordered discharged, he shall have the right to appeal to the Commissioners; during such appeal, he shall be suspended without pay.

(4) The chiefs of the several Divisions and Bureaus, after due investigation, shall once each six months make report to the Commission of the efficiency of each employee within such Divisions or bureau. These reports shall be kept in the permanent files of the Commission, and shall be given proper consideration in all matters of promotion and discharge.

SEC. 10. DEPARTMENT DIVISIONS: The Department shall be composed of three divisions; i.e. (a) The Texas Rangers; (b) The Texas Highway Patrol; and (c) The Headquarters Division, and such other divisions as the Commission may deem necessary.

SEC. 11. THE TEXAS RANGERS:

(1) The Texas Ranger Force and its personnel, property, equipment and records, now a part of the Adjutant General's Department of the State of Texas, are hereby transferred to and placed under the jurisdiction of the Department of Public Safety, and are hereby designated as the Texas Rangers, and as such, constitute the above mentioned division of the Department.

(2) The Texas Rangers shall consist of one headquarters company and not to exceed two companies of mounted men, except in cases of emergency when the Commission, with the consent of the Governor, shall have the authority to increase the force to meet extraordinary conditions.

The headquarters company shall consist of one captain, who shall be designated as the senior captain of the Texas Rangers, and who shall be the executive officer and in command of that division; one sergeant, and not to exceed four privates and one stenographer.

Each separate mounted company shall consist of not to exceed one captain, one sergeant, and fifteen privates.

There shall be a quartermaster for the division, who shall discharge the duties of quartermaster, commissary and pay-master, and who shall have the rank and pay of captain.

(3) The Compensation of the officers shall be such as allowed by the Legislature.

(4) The officers shall be clothed with all the powers of peace officers, and shall aid in the execution of the laws.

They shall have authority to make arrests, and to execute process in criminal cases; and in civil cases when specially directed by the judge of a court of record; and in all cases shall be governed by the laws regulating and defining the powers and duties of sheriffs when in the discharge of similar duties; except that they shall have the power and shall be authorized to make arrests and to execute all process in criminal cases in any county in the State. All officers operating by virtue of this Act shall have the authority to make arrests, as directed by warrants, and without a warrant under the conditions now authorized by law, and also in all cases when the alleged offender is traveling on a railroad, in a motor vehicle, aeroplane or boat. When any of said force shall arrest any person charged with a criminal offense, they shall forthwith convey said person to the county where he so stands charged, and shall deliver him to the proper officer, taking his receipt therefore. All necessary expenses thus incurred shall be paid by the State.

(5) SPECIAL RANGERS: The Commission shall have authority to appoint such number of special rangers as may be deemed advisable, not to exceed Three Hundred (300) in number; such rangers shall not have any connection with any Ranger Company or Highway Motor Patrol, but they shall at all times be subject to the orders of the Commission and the Governor for special duty to the same extent as the other law enforcing officers provided for in this Act; such special rangers, however, shall not have the authority to enforce any laws except those designed to protect life and property, and such rangers are especially denied the authority to enforce any laws regulating the use of the State highways by motor truck and motor buses and other motor vehicles. Such rangers shall not receive any compensation from the State for their services, and before the issuance of the commission each such ranger shall enter into a good and sufficient bond executed by a Surety Company authorized to do business in Texas in the sum of Twenty-five Hundred ($2,500.00) Dollars, approved by the Director, indemnifying all persons against damages accruing as the result of any illegal or unlawful acts on the part of such special ranger. All special ranger commissions shall expire on January 1st of the odd year after appointment, and the Director can revoke any special ranger commission at any time for cause, and such officer shall be designated in the Commission as Special Ranger.

Provided further that the Commission shall not issue more than ten commissions to special rangers for employment by any one persons, firm or corporation at any one time, except during an emergency, when in the opinion of the Commission it is necessary in the interest of the public justice to permit the employment of more than ten.

(6) In the execution of the laws of the State under the Department of Public Safety, the officials shall in all cases where it becomes necessary to seize property and destroy the same, to proceed as now provided by law; and all property so seized shall be stored and a list thereof presented to a District Judge in the District where such property is seized, who shall dispose of same in the mode and manner now provided by Articles Nos. 5112, 5113 and 5114, Revised Civil Statutes 1925.

Any official disregarding these provisions shall by virtue thereof be subject to removal from office.

*The remainder of the Bill discusses details of the Texas Highway Patrol, the Headquarters Division, the Bureau of Identification and Records, the Bureau of Communications, the Bureau of Intelligence and the Bureau of Education, and various other organizational items that are found in the preamble and are not germane to this historical register.*

[NOTE.— S. B. No. 146 passed the Senate, February 18, 1935, by a vote of 27 yeas, 1 nay; Senate refused to concur in House amendments, April 17, 1935, and Conference Committee was appointed, April 23, 1935; Senate adopted Conference Report, May 3, 1935, by a vote of 29 yeas, 1 nay; passed the House, with amendments, April 17, 1935, by a vote of 94 yeas, 34 nays; House adopted Conference Report, May 7, 1935, by a vote of 85 yeas, 44 nays.]

Approved May 8, 1935.
Effective 90 days after adjournment.

---

## FORTY-FIFTH LEGISLATURE — REGULAR SESSION.
## GENERAL AND SPECIAL LAWS.
## REVISING ADMINISTRATIVE DUTIES WITHIN
## TEXAS PUBLIC SAFETY COMMISSION.

H. B. No. 774.]                              CHAPTER 373.

An Act amending certain Sections of Senate Bill No. 146, passed by the Regular Session of the Forty-fourth Legislature of the State of Texas. to wit: Sections 5, 8, 11, 12, 15, 16, and 17; providing for the Public Safety Commission to appoint a Director and an Assistant Director whose salaries shall be fixed by the Legislature; providing for the Director with the advice and consent of the Commission to appoint Chiefs of the several Bureaus; providing for the Texas Ranger captains, headquarters sergeant, and privates; providing for the Texas Highway Patrol Division shall consist of the Chief Patrol officer, captains, sergeants, and privates as may be authorized by the Legislature, and such administrative and clerical help as determined by the Commission; providing for the Director with the advice and consent of the Commission to name the Chief of the Bureau of Communications; providing for the Director with the advice and consent of the Commission to name the Chief of the Bureau of Intelligence; providing for the Director with the advice and consent of the Commission to name the Chief of the Bureau of Education, and providing for the Chief of said Bureau to organize schools and give instruction; and declaring an emergency.

*Be it enacted by the legislature of the State of Texas*:

SECTION 1. Amend Section 5 of Senate Bill No. 146, passed by the Regular Session of the Forty-fourth Legislature of the State of Texas, to read as follows:

"Section 5. The Commission shall appoint a Public Safety Director herein designated as the 'Director,' who shall be a citizen of this State and who shall hold his position until removed by the Commission. The Commission shall also appoint an Assistant Director who shall perform such duties as may be designated by the Director. The Director and Assistant Director shall be selected on the basis of training, experience, and qualifications for said positions, and shall have at least five (5) years experience, preferably police or public administration. The Director and Assistant Director shall draw annual salaries as fixed by the Legislature. The Director shall be directly responsible to the Commission for the conduct for all the affairs of the Department."

SEC. 2. Amend Section 8 of Senate Bill No. 146, passed by the Regular Session of the Forty-fourth Legislature of the State of Texas, to read as follows:

"Section 8. It shall be the duty of the Director with the advice and consent of the Commission to appoint the Chiefs of the several Bureaus provided for in this Act."

SEC. 3. Amend Section 11, Paragraph 2, of Senate Bill No. 146, passed by the Regular Session of the Forty-fourth Legislature of the State of Texas, to read as follows:

"Section 11. (2) The Texas Rangers shall consist of six (6) captains, one headquarters sergeant, and such number of privates as may be authorized by the Legislature, except in cases of emergency when the Commission, with the consent of the Governor, shall have the authority to increase the force to meet extraordinary conditions."

*The remainder of the Bill discusses amendments concerning the Texas Highway Patrol, the Bureau of Identification and Records, the Bureau of Communications, the Bureau of Intelligence and the Bureau of Education, and declares an emergency, all of which are found in the preamble and are not germane to this historical register.*

[NOTE.— H. B. No. 774 passed the House, April 22, 1937, by a vote of 110 yeas, 0 nay; passed the Senate, with amendments, April 28, 1937, House refused to concur in Senate amendments, April 29, 1937, and Conference Committee appointed; House adopted Conference Committee report, May 18, 1937, by a vote of 132 yeas, 0 nay; Senate adopted Conference Committee report, May 18, 1937, by a vote of 28 yeas, 0 nays.]

Approved May 19, 1937.
Effective May 19, 1937.

---

## Government Code.
SUBTITLE B. LAW ENFORCEMENT AND PUBLIC PROTECTION.
CHAPTER 411. DEPARTMENT OF PUBLIC SAFETY OF THE STATE OF TEXAS.

### SUBCHAPTER A. GENERAL PROVISIONS AND ADMINISTRATION

Sec. 411.015. ORGANIZATION. (a) Except as provided by Subsection (b), the designation by this chapter of certain divisions and division chiefs is not mandatory and this chapter does not prevent the commission from reorganization or consolidation within the department in the interest of more efficient and economical management and direction of the department. The director, with the commission's approval, may organize and maintain within the department divisions of service considered necessary for the efficient conduct of the department's work.

(b) The number of divisions may not exceed the number of divisions existing on August 22, 1957. The division relating to the Texas Rangers may not be abolished.

Acts 1987, 70th Leg., ch. 147, Sec. 1, eff. Sept. 1, 1987.

### SUBCHAPTER B. TEXAS RANGERS.

Sec. 411.021. COMPOSITION. The Texas Rangers are a major division of the department consisting of the number of rangers authorized by the legislature. The highest ranking officer of the Texas Rangers is responsible to and reports directly to the director. Officers are entitled to compensation as provided by the legislature.

Acts 1987, 70th Leg., ch. 147, Sec. 1, eff. Sept. 1, 1987. Amended by Acts 1993, 73rd Leg., ch. 790, Sec. 11, eff. Sept. 1, 1993.

Sec. 411.022. AUTHORITY OF OFFICERS. (a) An officer of the Texas Rangers is governed by the law regulating and defining the powers and duties of sheriffs performing similar duties, except that the officer may make arrests, execute process in a criminal case in any county and, if specially directed by the judge of a court of record, execute process in a civil case.

(b) An officer of the Texas Rangers who arrests a person charged with a criminal offense shall immediately convey the person to the proper officer of the county where the person is charged and shall obtain a receipt. The state shall pay all necessary expenses incurred under this subsection.

Acts 1987, 70th Leg., ch. 147, Sec. 1, eff. Sept. 1, 1987.

Sec. 411.0221. QUALIFICATIONS. (a) To be commissioned as an officer of the Texas Rangers, a person must:

(1) have at least eight years of experience as a full-time, paid peace officer, including at least four years of experience in the department; and

(2) be a commissioned member of the department.

(b) The Texas Rangers is an equal employment opportunity employer; all personnel decisions shall be made without regard to race, color, sex, national origin, or religion.

Added by Acts 1993, 73rd Leg., ch. 790, Sec. 12, eff. Sept. 1, 1993.

Sec. 411.0222. ELIGIBILITY FOR PROMOTION. Except as provided by Section 411.0223, an officer of the Texas Rangers is eligible for promotion only if the officer has served in the next lower position for at least two years before the date of promotion.

Added by Acts 1993, 73rd Leg., ch. 790, Sec. 12, eff. Sept. 1, 1993.

Sec. 411.0223. APPOINTMENT OF HIGHEST-RANKING OFFICERS. (a) Except as provided by Subsection (c), an officer is eligible for appointment by the director to the highest rank of the Texas Rangers only if the officer has at least five years of supervisory experience as a commissioned member of the Texas Rangers.

(b) Except as provided by Subsection (c), an officer is eligible for appointment by the director to the second highest rank of the Texas Rangers only if the officer has at least four years of supervisory experience as a commissioned member of the Texas Rangers.

(c) If there are less than two qualified officers for appointment to the highest rank or the second highest rank of the Texas Rangers, the director may appoint an officer to the highest rank or the second highest rank only if the officer has at least two years of supervisory experience as a commissioned member of the Texas Rangers.

Added by Acts 1993, 73rd Leg., ch. 790, Sec. 12, eff. Sept. 1, 1993.

Sec. 411.023. SPECIAL RANGERS. (a) The commission may appoint as special rangers honorably retired commissioned officers of the department and not more than 300 other persons.

(b) A special ranger is subject to the orders of the commission and the governor for special duty to the same extent as other law enforcement officers provided for by this chapter, except that a special ranger may not enforce a law except one designed to protect life and property and may not enforce a law regulating the use of a state highway by a motor vehicle. A special ranger is not connected with a ranger company or uniformed unit of the department.

(c) Before issuance of a commission to a special ranger the person shall enter into a good and sufficient bond executed by a surety company authorized to do business in the state in the amount of $2,500, approved by the director, and indemnifying all persons against damages resulting from an unlawful act of the special ranger.

(d) A special ranger is not entitled to compensation from the state for service as a special ranger.

(e) A special ranger commission expires January 1 of the first odd-numbered year after appointment. The director may revoke a special ranger commission at any time for cause.

(f) The commission shall authorize a badge for persons appointed as special rangers under this section that is distinct in appearance from the badge authorized for special Texas Rangers under Section 411.024 and from any badge issued to a Texas Ranger.

Acts 1987, 70th Leg., ch. 147, Sec. 1, eff. Sept. 1, 1987. Amended by Acts 1999, 76th Leg., ch. 1189, Sec. 9, eff. Sept. 1, 1999.

Sec. 411.024. SPECIAL TEXAS RANGERS. (a) The commission may appoint as a special Texas Ranger an honorably retired or retiring commissioned officer of the department whose position immediately preceding retirement is an officer of the Texas Rangers.

(b) A special Texas Ranger is subject to the orders of the commission and the governor for special duty to the same extent as other law enforcement officers provided for by this chapter, except that a special Texas Ranger may not enforce a law except one designed to protect life and property and may not enforce a law regulating the use of a state highway by a motor vehicle. A special Texas Ranger is not connected with a ranger company or uniformed unit of the department.

(c) Before issuance of a commission to a special Texas Ranger the person shall enter into a good and sufficient bond executed by a surety company authorized to do business in the state in the amount of $2,500, approved by the director, and indemnifying all persons against damages resulting from an unlawful act of the special Texas Ranger.

(d) A special Texas Ranger is not entitled to compensation from the state for service as a special Texas Ranger.

(e) A special Texas Ranger commission expires January 1 of the first odd-numbered year after appointment. The commission may revoke the commission of a special Texas Ranger who commits a violation of a rule of the department for which an active officer of the Texas Rangers would be discharged.

(f) The commission shall authorize a badge for persons appointed as special Texas Rangers under this section that is distinct in appearance from the badge authorized for special rangers under Section 411.023.

Added by Acts 1999, 76th Leg., ch. 1189, Sec. 10, eff. Sept. 1, 1999.

## SUBCHAPTER J. UNSOLVED CRIMES INVESTIGATION TEAM

Sec. 411.261. DEFINITIONS. In this subchapter: (1) "Attorney representing the state" means a district attorney, criminal district attorney, or county attorney performing the duties of a district attorney.

(2) "Unsolved crime" means a criminal offense:

(a) that is an unsolved homicide or an unsolved felony that is one offense arising out of the same criminal episode as other unsolved felonies; and

(b) the investigation of which requires a level of expertise that is not readily available to local law enforcement agencies.

Added by Acts 2001, 77th Leg., ch. 1043, Sec. 1, eff. Sept. 1, 2001.

Sec. 411.262. UNSOLVED CRIMES INVESTIGATION TEAM. (a) The unsolved crimes investigation team is an investigatory unit within the department.

(b) The team will be located at the headquarters of the Texas Rangers in Austin, Texas, and will be commanded by the chief of the Texas Rangers.

(c) The director may employ commissioned peace officers and noncommissioned employees to perform duties required of the team.

(d) To be eligible for employment under this section, a peace officer must have not less than four years of experience as a peace officer and:

(1) a degree from an accredited institution of higher education in law, accounting, or computer science; or

(2) two or more years of experience in the investigation of homicides or other major felonies.

(e) To be eligible for employment under this section, a noncommissioned employee must meet the experience, training, and educational qualifications set by the director as requirements for investigating or assisting in the investigation of an unsolved crime.

Added by Acts 2001, 77th Leg., ch. 1043, Sec. 1, eff. Sept. 1, 2001.

Sec. 411.263. ASSISTANCE ON REQUEST. On the request of an attorney representing the state and with the approval of the director, the unsolved crimes investigation team of the department may assist local law enforcement in the investigation of crime.

Added by Acts 2001, 77th Leg., ch. 1043, Sec. 1, eff. Sept. 1, 2001

# Appendix F: The History of the Badge

One of the most enduring symbols concerning peace officers of the Old West is the Texas Ranger badge. Despite its presence in movies, TV shows, and books, this token of the Rangers' office was adopted relatively recently in their history. Until 1874, the Rangers were citizen-soldiers who had no desire or need for badges. Years after they became a permanent body of lawmen, warrants of authority—formal identifying documents—were issued to Frontier

Descriptive List of E. M. Dubose, 1899. Courtesy of the Archives and Information Services Division, Texas State Library and Archives Commission, Austin, TX.

# THE STATE  OF TEXAS

## ADJUTANT GENERAL'S DEPARTMENT
### *Warrant of Authority and Descriptive List*

THIS IS TO CERTIFY, That the bearer __Robert G. Goss__ is a __Texas Ranger__ in Company __"B"__ Ranger Force, State of Texas, and this is his Warrant of Authority as a Ranger, under an Act of the 36th Legislature of the State of Texas, Approved March 31, 1919, and Descriptive List for identification, and will be exhibited as his authority to Act as a Ranger when called upon for his credentials. This warrant must be surrendered to Company Commander by bearer when discharged. This Warrant of Authority and Descriptive List is signed by The Adjutant General under seal of office and attested by Company Commander.

Name __Robert G. Goss.__    Rank __Ranger.__
Age __33 yrs. 9 mo.__    Where born __Honey Grove, Texas.__
Height __5 ft. 11 in.__    Occupation __Texas Ranger.__
Weight __195 lbs.__    Residence __Honey Grove, Texas.__
Hair __Brown.__    Enlisted Where __Austin, Texas.__
Eyes __Grey.__    Enlisted When __April 28, 1932.__
Complexion __Fair.__    Enlisted by Whom __W. W. Sterling, The Adjutant General.__

This warrant of authority is void after __April 27, 1934.__ and must be returned to this Department for Cancellation.

Given under my hand and seal of office, this __28th__ day of __April__, __1932.__

The Adjutant General

Attest

Captain Ranger Force
Commanding Co. __"B"__

Warrant of Authority and Descriptive List of Robert G. Goss, 1932. Courtesy of the Archives and Information Services Division, Texas State Library and Archives Commission, Austin, TX.

Battalion officers, while the rank and file carried descriptive lists that merely detailed their physical appearance. Often, neither carried their credentials into the field so as not to lose them. Later, both captains and enlisted men in the Ranger Force possessed a single sheet that served as both warrant and descriptive list. This type of documentation continued in official use until 1935.

The earliest authenticated Texas Ranger badge, dating from 1889, is the "star-in-the-circle" (or "wagon wheel") version carried by Ira Aten. Currently, it is on display at the Texas Ranger Hall of Fame and Museum in Waco. Apocryphal legend states that badges were carved from silver Mexican eight-real or one peso coins by individual Rangers while in camp. More likely, a small number of Rangers or grateful citizens commissioned jewelers or silversmiths to custom-make a variety of badges from the coins. These original devices were fashioned in order to distinguish accredited Rangers from armed feudists or other gunmen. Another example is the variety worn by Curren L. "Kid" Rogers (younger brother of Captain J. H. Rogers), which was a favorite design around the turn of the century.

Badge of Ira Aten, 1889. Courtesy of the Texas Ranger Hall of Fame and Museum, Waco, TX.

In 1938, following their transfer to the Department of Public Safety, the State issued a new design to Rangers. The oval-shaped badge had "Dept. of Public Safety" on the top, "Texas Rangers" on the bottom, and the letters T-E-X-A-S surrounding a five-pointed star with the wearer's rank in the center. Gold badges were issued to captains, while the other ranks received silver.

In July 1957, the Department of Public Safety issued a new version of the old-style badges. The revised insignia featured a star upon a royal blue background with T-E-X-A-S in gold or silver letters. The outer circle was gold or silver, again depending upon the wearer's rank, with royal blue lettering. They proved to be very unpopular, and were known as the "bottle cap badges."

Badge of C. L. "Kid" Rogers, c. 1900. Courtesy of the Texas Ranger Hall of Fame and Museum, Waco, TX.

Author James M. Day credited Senior Captain Clint Peoples with conceiving the appearance of the current badges, but according to retired Ranger Glenn Elliott, Captain G. W. Burks of Company B was the one responsible. In the early 1960s, Burks, then a private, was a student of Ranger history and wanted to revive the old tradition of badges being fashioned from Mex-

Texas Ranger badge, 1938–1957. Courtesy of the Texas Ranger Hall of Fame and Museum, Waco, TX.

*Left:* Texas Ranger badge, 1957–1962. Courtesy of the Texas Ranger Hall of Fame and Museum, Waco, TX. *Right:* Texas Ranger badge, 1962–present. Courtesy of the Texas Ranger Hall of Fame and Museum, Waco, TX.

ican coins. Receiving permission from his captain, Bob Crowder, Burks went to Halton's Jewelry store in Fort Worth and ordered a custom-made badge. Burks' colleagues loved the design he chose and many began to order their own — including Colonel Homer Garrison. In October 1962, the colonel announced that Burks' design would become the new model for the official issue badge. Again, privates and sergeants (currently sergeants and lieutenants) received silver badges, this time fashioned from silver 1947 or 1948 *cinco peso* coins of 99.9-percent purity, while captains used either the *cinco peso* plated in gold or the 1947 *cincuenta peso* of 90-percent pure gold. Two symbols found on the Texas Great Seal are included on the current badge. The oak leaves on the left side signify strength and the olive branch on the right represents peace. The engraved cutout star in the center is inscribed with the company designation or rank of the wearer. The original coin markings are still visible on the reverse of the badge and on the edges.

# Bibliography

## Archive and Manuscript Collections

*Anson Jones to Zachary Taylor, August 23, 1845.* Texas Secretary of State Records, U.S. Diplomatic Correspondence, Archives and Information Services Division, Texas State Library and Archives Commission, Austin, Texas.

"B. F. Gholson Reminiscences, 1832–1860." Research and Collections Division, Dolph Briscoe Center for American History, the University of Texas at Austin.

*Barry, James Buckner, Papers, 1847–1917.* Research and Collections Division, Dolph Briscoe Center for American History, the University of Texas at Austin.

*Bourland, James A., Papers.* Manuscript Division, Library of Congress, Washington, D.C.

*Compiled Service Records of Confederate Soldiers Who Served in Organizations from the State of Texas.* War Department Collection of Confederate Records, Record Group 109, Microcopy No. 323. National Archives and Records Service, Washington, D. C. (Material accessed at the Historical Research Center, Texas Heritage Museum, Hill College, Hillsboro, Texas).

*Confederate Abstract File.* Archives and Information Services Division, Texas State Library and Archives Commission, Austin, Texas.

*Governor Edward Clark, March 29–October 22, 1861. Texas Secretary of State executive record books.* Archives and Information Services Division, Texas State Library and Archives Commission, Austin, Texas.

*Governor E. M. Pease, December 21, 1853–December 15, 1857. Texas Secretary of State executive record books.* Archives and Information Services Division, Texas State Library and Archives Commission, Austin, Texas.

*Governor Francis R. Lubbock, November 7, 1861–January 24, 1863. Texas Secretary of State executive record books.* Archives and Information Services Division, Texas State Library and Archives Commission, Austin, Texas.

*Governor H. R. Runnels, December 21, 1857–December 20, 1859. Texas Secretary of State executive record books.* Archives and Information Services Division, Texas State Library and Archives Commission, Austin, Texas.

*Governor Sam Houston, December 21, 1859–December 26, 1860. Texas Secretary of State executive record books.* Archives and Information Services Division, Texas State Library and Archives Commission, Austin, Texas.

*Governors Sam Houston and Edward Clark, December 27, 1859–November 1, 1861. Texas Secretary of State executive record books.* Archives and Information Services Division, Texas State Library and Archives Commission, Austin, Texas.

*Maj. Gen. Brooke, military orders #53, August 11, 1849, and #57, August 19, 1849.* Records of George T. Wood, Texas Office of the Governor. Archives and Information Services Division, Texas State Library and Archives Commission, Austin, Texas.

*Military orders, Texas State Troops records, Civil War records, Texas Adjutant General's Department.* Archives and Information Services Division, Texas State Library and Archives Commission, Austin, Texas.

*Ranger records, Texas State Troops records, Civil War records, Texas Adjutant General's Department.* Archives and Information Services Division, Texas State Library and Archives Commission, Austin, Texas.

*Texas Governor Sam Houston Records.* Archives and Information Services Division, Texas State Library and Archives Commission, Austin, Texas.

*Vertical Files.* Texas Ranger Research Center, Texas Ranger Hall of Fame and Museum, Waco, Texas.

"Willis Lang Diary, 1860." Research and Collections Division, Dolph Briscoe Center for American History, the University of Texas at Austin.

## Articles

Barker, Eugene C. "Journal of the Permanent Council (October 11–27, 1835)." *Southwestern Historical Quarterly* 7, No. 4 (April 1904).

Barton, Henry W. "Five Texas Frontier Companies During the Mexican War." *Southwestern Historical Quarterly* 66, No. 1 (July 1962).

———. "The United States Cavalry and the Texas Rangers." *Southwestern Historical Quarterly* 63, No. 4 (April 1960).

Cumberland, Charles C. "Border Raids in the Lower Rio Grande Valley—1915." *Southwestern Historical Quarterly* 57, No. 3 (January 1954).

Holden, William C. "Frontier Defense, 1846–1860." *West Texas Historical Association Yearbook* 6 (June 1930).

———. "Frontier Defense in Texas During the Civil War." *West Texas Historical Association Yearbook* 4 (July 1928).

Kinney, Harrison. "Frank Hamer: Texas Ranger." *American Gun* 1, No. 2 (Spring 1961).

Koch, Lena Clara. "The Federal Indian Policy in Texas, 1845–1860." Chapters II-IV. *Southwestern Historical Quarterly* 28, No. 4 (April 1925); 29, No. 1 (July 1925); 29, No. 2 (October 1925).

Pool, William C. "The Battle of Dove Creek." *Southwestern Historical Quarterly* 53, No. 4 (April 1950).

Reeve, Frank D. "The Apache Indians in Texas." *Southwestern Historical Quarterly* 50, No. 2 (October 1946).

Rippy, J. Fred. "Border Troubles Along the Rio Grande, 1848–1860." *Southwestern Historical Quarterly* 23, No. 2 (October 1919).

Rutledge, Lee A. "That Grand G. I. .45 Auto." *Guns and Ammo's Complete Guide to the .45 Auto. Guns and Ammo's Action Series*, Vol. 7, No. 1 (1989).

Weiss, Harold J., Jr. "The Texas Rangers Revisited: Old Themes and New Viewpoints." *Southwestern Historical Quarterly* 97, No. 4 (April 1994).

## Books

Adkins-Rochette, Patricia. *Bourland in North Texas and Indian Territory During the Civil War: Fort Cobb, Fort Arbuckle, and the Wichita Mountains*. 2 vols. Broken Arrow: www.Bourlandcivilwar.com, 2004.

Arnold, James R. *Jeff Davis's Own: Cavalry, Comanches, and the Battle for the Texas Frontier*. New York: John Wiley & Sons, Inc., 2000.

Barker, Eugene C. *The Austin Papers, Vol. II. Annual Report of the American Historical Association for the Year 1919*. Washington, D. C.: Government Printing Office, 1924.

Barry, James Buckner, edited by James Kimmins Greer. *Buck Barry, Texas Ranger and Frontiersman*. Waco: Friends of the Moody Texas Ranger Library, 1978; Lincoln: University of Nebraska Press, 1984.

Barton, Henry W. *Texas Volunteers in the Mexican War*. Waco: Texian Press, 1970.

Benner, Judith Ann. *Sul Ross: Soldier, Statesman, Educator*. College Station: Texas A&M University Press, 1983.

Brice, Donaly E. *The Great Comanche Raid: The Boldest Indian Attack of the Texas Republic*. Austin: Eakin Press, 1987.

Brown, John Henry. *Indian Wars and Pioneers of Texas*. Austin: L. E. Daniell Co., 1896(?).

Chabot, Frederick C. *Corpus Christi and Lipantitlan: A Story of the Army of Texas Volunteers, 1842*. San Antonio: Artes Graficas, 1942.

Chalfant, William Y. *Without Quarter: The Wichita Expedition and the Fight on Crooked Creek*. Norman: University of Oklahoma Press, 1991.

Cox, Mike. *Texas Ranger Tales: Stories That Need Telling*. Plano: Republic of Texas Press, 1997.

———. *Texas Ranger Tales II*. Plano: Republic of Texas Press, 1999.

———. *The Texas Rangers: Wearing the Cinco Peso, 1821–1900*. New York: Tom Doherty Associates, 2008.

Cozzens, Peter. *Eyewitnesses to the Indian Wars. Vol. III: Conquering the Southern Plains*. Mechanicsburg: Stackpole Books, 2003.

Davis, William C. *Lone Star Rising: The Revolutionary Birth of the Texas Republic*. New York: Free Press, 2004.

DeShields, James T. *Border Wars of Texas*. Tioga: The Herald Co., 1912.

———. *Cynthia Ann Parker: The Story of Her Capture*. St. Louis: Charles B. Woodward Printing and Book Manufacturing Co., 1886.

Durham, George, and Clyde Wantland. *Taming the Nueces Strip: The Story of McNelly's Rangers*. Austin: University of Texas Press, 1962.

Elliott, Glenn, with Robert Nieman. *A Ranger's Ranger*. Waco: Texian Press, 1999.

———. *Still a Ranger's Ranger*. Longview: Ranger Publishing, 2002.

Fehrenbach, T. R. *Comanches: The Destruction of a People*. New York: Alfred A. Knopf, 1974; New York: Da Capo Press, 1994.

Ford, John Salmon, edited by Stephen B. Oates. *Rip Ford's Texas*. 2nd ed. Austin: University of Texas Press, 1987.

Gammel, Hans Peter Nielson, Compiler. *The Laws of Texas 1822–1897*. 10 vols. Austin: The Gammel Book Co., 1898.

_____, Creator. *The Laws of Texas 1897–1902, Volume 11*. Austin: The Gammel Book Co., 1902.

_____, Creator. *The Laws of Texas 1917–1918, Volume 17*. Austin: The Gammel Book Co., 1917.

_____, Creator. *The Laws of Texas 1919, Volume 19*. Austin: The Gammel Book Co., 1919.

_____, Creator. *The Laws of Texas 1934–1935, Volume 29*. Austin: The Gammel Book Co., 1935.

Gillett, James B., edited by Milo Milton Quaife. *Six Years with the Texas Rangers, 1875 to 1881*. James B. Gillett, 1921; New Haven: Yale University Press, 1925; Chicago: The Lakeside Press (R. R. Donnelley & Sons Co.), 1943.

Greer, James Kimmins. *Texas Ranger: Jack Hays in the Frontier Southwest*. College Station: Texas A&M University Press, 1993. (Originally published as *Colonel Jack Hays: Texas Frontier Leader and California Builder*. New York: E. P. Dutton and Co., Inc., 1952.)

Hardin, Stephen L. *The Texas Rangers*. London: Osprey Publishing Ltd., 2000.

_____. *Texian Iliad: A Military History of the Texas Revolution*. Austin: University of Texas Press, 1994.

Harris, Charles H., III, and Louis R. Sadler. *The Texas Rangers and the Mexican Revolution: The Bloodiest Decade, 1910–1920*. Albuquerque: University of New Mexico Press, 2004.

Hatley, Allen G. *The Indian Wars in Stephen F. Austin's Texas Colony, 1823–1835*. Austin: Eakin Press, 2001.

Havins, Thomas Robert. *Camp Colorado: A Decade of Frontier Defense*. Brownwood: Brown Press, 1964.

Haynes, Samuel W. *Soldiers of Misfortune: The Somervell and Mier Expeditions*. Austin: University of Texas Press, 1990.

Henshaw, Thomas, Editor. *The History of Winchester Firearms 1866–1992*. Clinton: Winchester Press, 1993.

Hewett, Janet B., Editor. *Supplement to the Official Records of the Union and Confederate Armies. Part II—Record of Events*. Vols. LXVII and LXVIII—Serial No. 79. Wilmington: Broadfoot Publishing Co., 1998.

Houston, Sam, edited by Amelia W. Williams and Eugene C. Barker. *The Writings of Sam Houston, 1813–1863*. Vols. III, VII and VIII. Austin: University of Texas Press, 1940–1943.

Hughes, William J. *Rebellious Ranger: Rip Ford and the Old Southwest*. Norman: University of Oklahoma Press, 1964.

Ingmire, Frances Terry. *Texas Frontiersman, 1839–1860: Minute Men, Militia, Home Guard, Indian Fighter*. St. Louis: Ingmire Publications, 1982; Signal Mountain: Mountain Press, 2001.

_____. *Texas Ranger Service Records 1830–1846*. St. Louis: Ingmire Publications, 1982.

_____. *Texas Ranger Service Records 1847–1900*. 6 vols. St. Louis: Ingmire Publications, 1982; Signal Mountain: Mountain Press, 2001.

Jackson, H. Joaquin, and David Marion Wilkinson. *One Ranger: A Memoir*. Austin: University of Texas Press, 2005.

Jackson, H. Joaquin, with James L. Haley. *One Ranger Returns*. Austin: University of Texas Press, 2008.

Jenkins, John Holmes, and Kenneth Kesselus. *Edward Burleson: Texas Frontier Leader*. Austin: Jenkins Publishing Press Co., 1990.

Jennings, N. A. *A Texas Ranger*. New York: Charles Scribner's Sons, 1899; Dallas: Southwest Press, 1930; Norman: University of Oklahoma Press, 1997.

Johnson, David. *The Mason County "Hoo Doo" War, 1874–1902*. Denton: University of North Texas Press, 2006.

Katcher, Philip, and G. A. Embleton. *The Mexican-American War 1846–1848*. London: Osprey Publishing Ltd., 1976.

Knowles, Thomas W. *They Rode for the Lone Star: The Birth of Texas-The Civil War*. Dallas: Taylor Publishing Co., 1999.

Lambert, Joseph I. *One Hundred Years with the Second Cavalry: By the Commanding Officer, Second Cavalry*. Fort Riley: Capper Printing Co., 1939.

Lane, Walter P. *The Adventures and Recollections of General Walter P. Lane*. Marshall: Tri-Weekly Herald Job Print, 1887; Austin: Pemberton Press, 1970.

Malsch, Brownson. *"Lone Wolf" Gonzaullas, Texas Ranger*. Austin: Shoal Creek Publishers Inc., 1980; Norman: University of Oklahoma Press, 1998.

Martin, Jack. *Border Boss: Captain John R. Hughes—Texas Ranger*. San Antonio: Naylor Co., 1942; Austin: State House Press, 1990.

McConnell, Joseph Carroll. *The West Texas Frontier: Or, a Descriptive History of Early Times in Western Texas*. Vol. I. Jacksboro: Gazette Print, 1933.

McGowen, Stanley S. *Horse Sweat and Powder Smoke: The First Texas Cavalry in the Civil War*. College Station: Texas A&M University Press, 1999.

Meed, Douglas V. *Texas Ranger Johnny Klevenhagen*. Plano: Republic of Texas, 2000.

Michno, Gregory F. *Encyclopedia of Indian Wars: Western Battles and Skirmishes, 1850–1890*. Missoula: Mountain Press Publishing Co., 2003.

Moore, Stephen L. *Savage Frontier: Rangers, Rifle-*

men, and Indian Wars in Texas. Vol. I: 1835–1837. Plano: Republic of Texas Press, 2002.

_____. *Savage Frontier: Rangers, Riflemen, and Indian Wars in Texas. Vol. II: 1838–1839*. Denton: University of North Texas Press, 2006.

_____. *Savage Frontier: Rangers, Riflemen, and Indian Wars in Texas. Vol. III: 1840–1841*. Denton: University of North Texas Press, 2007.

Nance, Joseph Milton. *After San Jacinto: The Texas-Mexican Frontier, 1836–1841*. Austin: University of Texas Press, 1963.

_____. *Attack and Counterattack: The Texas-Mexican Frontier, 1842*. Austin: University of Texas Press, 1964.

O'Neal, Bill. *Encyclopedia of Western Gunfighters*. Norman: University of Oklahoma Press, 1979.

_____. *Fighting Men of the Indian Wars: A Biographical Encyclopedia*. Stillwater: Barbed Wire Press, 1991.

Paine, Albert Bigelow. *Captain Bill McDonald, Texas Ranger: A Story of Frontier Reform*. New York: J. J. Little & Ives Co., 1909.

Parsons, Chuck. *John B. Armstrong, Texas Ranger and Pioneer Ranchman*. College Station: Texas A&M University Press, 2007.

Parsons, Chuck, and Gary P. Fitterer. *Captain C. B. McKinney: The Law in South Texas*. Wolfe City: Henington Publishing Co., 1993.

Parsons, Chuck, and Marianne E. Hall Little. *Captain L. H. McNelly — Texas Ranger: The Life and Times of a Fighting Man*. Austin: State House Press, 2001.

Preece, Harold. *Lone Star Man: Ira Aten, Last of the Old Texas Rangers*. New York: Hastings House Publishers, 1960.

Price, George F. *Across the Continent with the Fifth Cavalry*. New York: Van Nostrand, 1883; New York: Antiquarian Press Ltd., 1959.

Proctor, Ben. *Just One Riot: Episodes of Texas Rangers in the 20th Century*. Austin: Eakin Press, 1991.

Raymond, Dora Neill. *Captain Lee Hall of Texas*. Norman: University of Oklahoma Press, 1940.

Richardson, Rupert Norval. *The Frontier of Northwest Texas, 1846 to 1876*. Glendale: The Arthur H. Clark Co., 1963.

Rigler, Lewis C., and Judyth W. Rigler. *In the Line of Duty: Reflections of a Texas Ranger Private*. Denton: University of North Texas Press, 1995.

Robarts, William Hugh. *Mexican War Veterans: A Complete Roster of the Regular and Volunteers Troops in the War between the United States and Mexico, from 1846 to 1848*. Washington, D. C.: Brentano's (A. S. Witherbee and Co., Proprietors), 1887.

Roberts, Dan W. *Rangers and Sovereignty*. San Antonio: Wood Printing and Engraving Co., 1914.

Robinson, Charles M., III. *The Men Who Wear the Star: The Story of the Texas Rangers*. New York: Random House, 2000.

Rosa, Joseph G. *Guns of the American West*. New York: Crown Publishers Inc., 1985.

Smith, David Paul. *Frontier Defense in the Civil War: Texas Rangers and Rebels*. College Station: Texas A&M University Press, 1992.

Sowell, A. J. *Early Settlers and Indian Fighters of Southwest Texas*. Austin: Ben Jones and Co., 1900; New York: Argosy-Antiquarian Ltd., 1964.

_____. *Rangers and Pioneers of Texas*. San Antonio: Shepard Bros. and Co., 1884; New York: Argosy-Antiquarian Ltd., 1964; Austin: State House Press, 1991.

Spellman, Paul N. *Captain J. A. Brooks, Texas Ranger*. Denton: University of North Texas Press, 2007.

_____. *Captain John H. Rogers, Texas Ranger*. Denton: University of North Texas Press, 2003.

Spurlin, Charles D., Compiler. *Texas Veterans in the Mexican War: Muster Rolls of Texas Military Units*. Victoria: Charles D. Spurlin, 1984.

_____. *Texas Volunteers in the Mexican War*. Austin: Eakin Press, 1998.

Stephens, Robert W. *Texas Rangers Indian War Pensions*. Quanah: Nortex Press, 1975.

Sterling, William Warren. *Trails and Trials of a Texas Ranger*. William Warren Sterling, 1959; Norman: University of Oklahoma Press, 1968.

Sullivan, W. John L. *Twelve Years in the Saddle for Law and Order on the Frontiers of Texas*. Austin: Von Boeckmann-Jones Co., Printers, 1909.

Thompson, Jerry. *Cortina: Defending the Mexican Name in Texas*. College Station: Texas A&M University Press, 2007.

Utley, Robert M. *Frontier Regulars: The United States Army and the Indian, 1866–1891*. Lincoln: University of Nebraska, 1973.

_____. *Frontiersmen in Blue: The United States Army and the Indian, 1848–1865*. Lincoln: University of Nebraska, 1967.

_____. *Lone Star Justice: The First Century of the Texas Rangers*. New York: Oxford University Press, 2002.

_____. *Lone Star Lawmen: The Second Century of the Texas Rangers*. New York: Oxford University Press, 2007.

Webb, Walter P. *The Texas Rangers: A Century of Frontier Defense*. Boston: Houghton Mifflin, 1935; Austin: University of Texas Press, 1965.

Wharton, Clarence R. *History of Texas*. Dallas: Turner Co., 1935.

Wilbarger, John Wesley. *Indian Depredations in Texas*. Austin: Hutchings Printing House, 1889.

Wilkins, Frederick. *Defending the Borders: The Texas Rangers, 1849–1861*. Austin: State House Press, 2001.

_____. *The Highly Irregular Irregulars: The Texas*

*Rangers in the Mexican War.* Austin: Eakin Press, 1990.
———. *The Law Comes to Texas: The Texas Rangers, 1870–1901.* Austin: State House Press, 1999.
———. *The Legend Begins: The Texas Rangers, 1823–1845.* Austin: State House Press, 1996.
Wilson, R. L. *Colt: An American Legend.* New York: Abbeville Press, 1985.
———. *Winchester: An American Legend.* New York: Random House, 1991.
Winfrey, Dorman H., and James M. Day. *The Indian Papers of Texas and the Southwest, 1825–1916.* 5 vols. Austin: Pemberton Press, 1966; Austin: Texas State Historical Association, 1995.

## Correspondence

Adkins-Rochette, Patricia. "McCord's Regt." E-mail to the author. 18 February 2009.
Brice, Donaly. "Re: Question for Donaly Brice." E-mails to the author. 7 August 2007; 22 August 2007.
Cawthon, Matt, Sergeant. "Hello." E-mail to the author. 9 July 2009.
De Los Santos, Gary, Captain. "Re: Commanders of UCIT." E-mails to the author. 24 August 2007; 27 August 2007.
Evans, Tracie. "Re: Artwork Request." E-mail to the author. 5 November 2007.
Evans, Tracie. "Re: Questions." E-mails to the author. 16 January 2008; 22 January 2008.
Evans, Tracie. "Re: Another Gun Question." E-mail to the author. 6 February 2008.
Hall, Jennifer. "Re: Ranger Captains." E-mails to the author. 16 August 2007; 17 August 2007.
Hall, Jennifer. "Re: More questions." E-mail to the author. 3 December 2008.
Hall, Jennifer. "Re: Ranger promotions, etc." E-mail to the author. 30 December 2008.
Hall, Jennifer. "Re: More questions." E-mail to the author. 8 January 2009.
Hall, Jennifer. "Re: New promotions." E-mail to the author. 3 March 2009.
Hall, Jennifer. "Re: Yet Another Question." E-mail to the author. 27 May 2009.
Hall, Jennifer. "Re: Most Recent Personnel Changes." E-mails to the author. 29 September 2009; 30 September 2009.
Henderson, H. D., Captain. "Re: Questions." E-mail to the author. 16 April 2008.
McLoughlin, Debi. "FW: Ranger Captains." E-mails to the author. 22 August 2007; 23 August 2007.
Moore, Stephen L. "Plum Creek." E-mail to the author. 6 October 2007.
Moore, Stephen L. "Re: Plum Creek." E-mail to the author. 9 October 2007; 12 October 2007.
Moore, Stephen L. "Re: 1st Two Chapters." E-mails to the author. 12 June 2009; 18 June 2009.
Moore, Stephen L. "Ranger List Notes." E-mail to the author. 23 June 2009.
Moore, Stephen L. "Ranger List Additional." E-mail to the author. 23 June 2009.
Moore, Stephen L. "Re: 1st Two Chapters." E-mails to the author. 25 June 2009; 7 July 2009.
Peers, Gary. "Re: Winchester Model 1895." E-mail to the author. 18 February 2008.
Shofner, Judy. "Re: DPS Texas Rangers." E-mail to the author. 14 November 2005.
Stopka, Christina. "Re: Sr. Capt." E-mail to the author. 11 June 2007.
Stopka, Christina. "Re: Question." E-mails to the author. 22 April 2008; 22 May 2008.
Stopka, Christina. "Re: Lt. Morrison's unit." E-mail to the author. 5 June 2008.
Stopka, Christina. "Re: 'Chief of Texas Rangers' title." E-mail to the author. 8 December 2008.
Texas Rangers. "Re: Sr. Capt." E-mail to the author. 27 June 2007.
Texas Rangers. "Re: Miscellaneous Questions" E-mails to the author. 12 January 2009; 9 March 2009; 26 March 2009; 31 March 2009.
Texas Rangers. "Re: Company A." E-mail to the author. 28 May 2009.

## Government Documents

Heitman, Francis Bernard. *Historical Register and Dictionary of the United States Army, from Its Organization, September 29, 1789, to March 2, 1903.* 2 vols. Washington, D.C.: Government Printing Office, 1903.
*Inactive Personnel Records.* Texas Department of Public Safety, Austin, Texas.
Smither, Harriet, Editor. *Journals of the Fourth Congress of the Republic of Texas, 1839–1840.* Vol. 1: The Senate Journal. Austin: Von Boeckmann-Jones Co., 1929.
United States Adjutant General's Office. *Register of the Army of the United States, for 1853.* Washington, D. C.: Government Printing Office, 1853.
United States War Department. *The War of the Rebellion: A Compilation of the Official Records of the Union and Confederate Armies.* Series I—Vols. I, IV, XV, XXII, XXVI, XXXIV, XLI, XLVIII, and LIII. Washington, D. C.: Government Printing Office, 1880–1901.
Winkler, Ernest William, Editor. *Journal of the Secession Convention of Texas, 1861.* Austin: Austin Printing Company, 1912.

## Internet Sites

Baker, Terry. "Fannin County Sheriffs Past and Present." 5 May 2005. Fannin County Sheriff's Office. 27 October 2007. <http://www.fanninso.org/fannincountysheriffs.html>.

Bauer, Esther M. "Oldest Texas Ranger: A Texas Lawman Rules His Range." 16 August 2000. *The Washington Post*. 10 April 2009. E. B. Writers of Dallas. <http://ebwriters.com/oldest_texas_ranger_18834.htm>.

Black, Tony. "Texas Adjutant General's Department: An Inventory of Ranger Military Rolls at the Texas State Archives, 1846–1861, 1874–1910, 1913–1914, undated." *Texas Archival Resources Online*. September 1998. University of Texas Libraries. 20 March 2005 <http://www.lib.utexas.edu/taro/tslac/30075/tsl-30075.html>.

———. "Texas Adjutant General's Department: An Inventory of Reconstruction Military Rolls at the Texas State Archives, 1865–1866, 1870–1877, undated (bulk 1870–1874)." *Texas State Archival Resources Online*. July 1986. University of Texas Libraries. 24 October 2007. <http://www.lib.utexas.edu/taro/tslac/30074/tsl-30074.html

Caver, Captain Barry. "Captain Barry Caver on the Republic of Texas Standoff." *The Texas Ranger Dispatch* 15 (Winter 2004). The Texas Ranger Hall of Fame and Museum. 13 January 2008. <http://www.texasranger.org/dispatch/MasterIndex/dispatch%20Index%202005.htm>.

———. "Guns of the Texas Rangers: Rifle Training with the New M4 Carbine." *The Texas Ranger Dispatch* 20 (Summer 2006). The Texas Ranger Hall of Fame and Museum. 13 January 2008. <http://www.texasranger.org/dispatch/20/M-4/M-4.htm>.

Cawthon, Sergeant Matt, and Captain Clete Buckaloo. "Standard Issue Field Equipment." *Rangers Today*. 2005. Texas Ranger Hall of Fame and Museum. 6 January 2008. <http://www.texasranger.org/today/Equipment.htm>.

Cool, Paul. "My Men Are All Frontiersmen: El Paso's Tejano Texas Rangers in the 1870s." *The Texas Ranger Dispatch* 26 (Summer 2008). Texas Ranger Hall of Fame and Museum. 23 November 2008. <http://www.texasranger.org/dispatch/26/Dispatch%2026 %204mg.pdf>.

Cox, Mike. "The Texas Rangers: From Horses to Helicopters." *Texas Almanac 2000–2001*. 2008. Dallas: Belo Communications. 16 March 2008. <http://www.texasalmanac.com/history/highlights/rangers/>.

Cutrer, Thomas W. "Smith, Thomas Ingles." *Handbook of Texas Online*. 6 June 2001. The Texas State Historical Association. 24 July 2007. <http://www.tsha.utexas.edu/handbook/online/articles/SS/fsm43.html>.

"Department of Public Safety of the State of Texas." *Texas Legislature Online*. 29 February 2008. State of Texas Legislature. 29 February 2008. <http://www.capitol.state.tx.us/>. Path: Statutes, Government Code, Title 4. Executive Branch Chapter 411.

Elliott, Glenn. "Now You Know: The Cinco Peso Badge." *The Texas Ranger Dispatch* 5 (Fall 2001). The Texas Ranger Hall of Fame and Museum. 11 December 2008. <http://www.texasranger.org/dispatch/5/NowunoBadge.htm>.

Emison, Celinda. "Mystery of babies solved? Mummified remains of 3 infants found in Bangs in 2003." *Reporter News*. 22 September 2007. Scripps Newspaper Group—Online. 27 March 2009. <http://m.reporternews.com/news/2007/Sep/22/mystery-of-babies-solved-mummified-remains-of-3/>.

"Historic Badges of the Texas Rangers." *Texas Ranger History*. 2003. The Texas Ranger Hall of Fame and Museum. 11 December 2007. <http://www.texasranger.org/history/HistoricBadges.htm>.

Krajicek, David. "Tommy Lynn Sells." *Crime Library*. 2008. truTV.com. 27 March 2009. <http://www.trutv.com/library/crime/serial_killers/predators/tommy_sells/index.html>.

"Krystal's Courage: The Trial." *48 Hours Mystery*. 16 August 2002. CBS News.com. 27 March 2009. <http://www.cbsnews.com/stories/2001/02/06/48hours/main269790.shtml>.

Matney, Eddie R. "Charges Against Captain G. W. Stevens." *The Texas Ranger Dispatch* 25 (Winter 2008). The Texas Ranger Hall of Fame and Museum. 23 November 2008. <http://www.texasranger.org/dispatch/25/Dispatch25.pdf>.

———. "The Keep Ranch Fight." *The Texas Ranger Dispatch* 20 (Summer 2006). The Texas Ranger Hall of Fame and Museum. 31 December 2007. <http://www.texasranger.org/dispatch/20/Keep%20Ranch%20Fight/Keep_Ranch_Fight.htm >.

Maxey, H. David. "Army of the Republic 1836–1841." 26 January 1999. Index to Military Rolls of the Republic of Texas, 1835–1845. 25 February 2005. <http://www.mindspring.com/~dmaxey/rep_cont.htm>. Path: Browse Groups of Rolls.

———. "Campaigns of 1842." 2 February 1999. Index to Military Rolls of the Republic of Texas, 1835–1845. 25 February 2005. <http://www.mindspring.com/~dmaxey/rep_cont.htm>. Path: Browse Groups of Rolls.

———. "Republic of Texas Militia 1836–1845." 2 February 1999. Index to Military Rolls of the Republic of Texas, 1835–1845. 25 February 2005. <http://www.mindspring.com/~dmaxey/rep_cont.htm>. Path: Browse Groups of Rolls.

"Model 1895." 17 January 2005. Winchester Arms

Collectors Association. 6 December 2008. <http://www.winchestercollector.org/guns/1895.shtml>.

"Officials are still uncertain how long the 3 infants discovered in Brownwood home have been dead." *PIO News*. 19 November 2003. Texas Department of Public Safety. 27 March 2009. <http://www.txdps.state.tx.us/director_staff/public_information/clips/ clips1117.pdf>.

Ramsland, Katherine. "Henry Lee Lucas." *Crime Library*. 2008. truTV.com. 30 March 2009. <http://www.trutv.com/library/crime/serial_killers/notorious/henry_lee_lucas/2.html>.

"Republic Claims." *Archives and Manuscripts*. 15 February 2009. Texas State Library and Archives Commission. 15 February 2009. <http://www2.tsl.state.tx.us/trail/Republic Search. jsp>.

Silvey, Stefanie, and Nick Storm. "Unsolved murder still haunts Tri-State family two decades later." 27 November 2007. 14 WFIE.com. 27 March 2009. <http://www.nbc14.com/global/story. asp?s=7372700&ClientType=Printable>.

Stopka, Christina, and Tony Black. "Partial Roster of Texas Ranger Unit Commanders." *Texas Ranger Research Center*. 2005. Texas Ranger Hall of Fame and Museum. 19 December 2007. <http://www.texasranger.org/ReCenter/commanders.htm>.

Stowers, Carlton. "Haunted House." *Dallas News*. 27 November 2003. Dallas Observer.com. 27 March 2009. <http://www.dallasobserver.com/2003–1127/news/ haunted-house/4>.

Stroud, David. "Guns of the Texas Rangers: Colt Model 1911 Automatic." *The Texas Ranger Dispatch* 3 (Spring 2001). 6 December 2007. Texas Ranger Hall of Fame and Museum. <http://www.texasranger.org/dispatch/3/1911Auto.htm>.

_____. "The Winchester Model 1895: The Gun That Shoots Two Miles." *The Texas Ranger Dispatch* 19 (Winter 2006). 6 December 2007. Texas Ranger Hall of Fame and Museum. <http://www.texasranger.org/dispatch/19/Winchester_Model%201895/ Winchester.htm>.

"Texas Rangers." 2000. Texas Department of Public Safety. 12 January 2008. <http://www. txdps.state.tx.us/director_staff/texas_rangers/index.htm>.

"Texas Adjutant General Service Records 1836–1935." *Archives and Manuscripts*. 26 March 2009. Texas State Library and Archives Commission. 26 March 2009. <http://www2.tsl.state.tx.us/trail/Service Search.jsp>.

"Two men plead guilty in Waco pedophile ring." 28 June 1998. Laredo Morning Times Online. 28 December 2008. <http://lmtonline.com/news/archive/062898/pagea6.pdf>.

Villafranca, Armando. "Officer's efforts helped put investigators on killer's trail." *Houston Chronicle.com*. 30 June 2000. CNN.com. 5 February 2008. <http://archives.cnn.com/2000/LOCAL/southwest/06/30/hci.railroad.killer/>.

## Interviews

Brandt, Jerry. Telephone interview with author. 2 April 2009.

Nieman, Robert. "Interview with Captain David Byrnes, Texas Ranger, Retired." *Texas Ranger Hall of Fame E-Book*. 7 January 2006. Texas Ranger Hall of Fame & Museum. 27 December 2008. <http://www.texasranger.org/E-Books/Oral%20History%20%20 Byrnes,%20 David.pdf>.

Thomasson, Michael R. Telephone interview with author. 15 July 2009.

## Newspapers

*Texas State Gazette* (Austin), August 25, 1849; March 2, 1850; and March 9, 1850.

## Speeches

Moore, Steven L. "The Unsung Heroes of San Jacinto." *San Jacinto Symposium 2007*. San Jacinto Museum of History. La Porte, Texas. 14 April 2007

## Theses and Dissertations

McClung, John Busby. *Texas Rangers Along the Rio Grande, 1910–1919*. Ph.D. dissertation. Fort Worth: Texas Christian University, 1981.

Smith, David Paul. *Frontier Defense in Texas: 1861–1865*. Ph.D. dissertation. Denton: North Texas State University, 1987.

_____. *In Defense of Texas: The Life of Henry E. McCulloch*. M.A. thesis. Nacogdoches: Stephen F. Austin State University, 1975.

Thomasson, Michael Reagan. *James E. McCord and the Texas Frontier Regiment*. M.A. thesis. Nacogdoches: Stephen F. Austin State University, 1965.

Ward, James Randolph. *The Texas Rangers, 1919–1935: A Study in Law Enforcement*. Ph.D. dissertation. Fort Worth: Texas Christian University, 1972.

## Unpublished Material

"The Ledger of Samuel Coleman Lockett: Texas Ranger Service Extract." Transcribed by Christina Stopka. Texas Ranger Hall of Fame and Museum, Waco, Texas.

Walter, John F. "Border Texas Cavalry." Capsule Histories of Texas Units. Typescript. Historical Research Center. Texas Heritage Museum, Hill College, Hillsboro, Texas.

———. "First (McCulloch's) Texas Cavalry." Capsule Histories of Texas Units. Typescript. Historical Research Center. Hill College, Hillsboro, Texas.

———. "Frontier Texas Cavalry." Capsule Histories of Texas Units. Typescript. Historical Research Center. Texas Heritage Museum, Hill College, Hillsboro, Texas.

———. "Ladies Rangers Texas Cavalry Company." Capsule Histories of Texas Units. Typescript. Historical Research Center. Texas Heritage Museum, Hill College, Hillsboro, Texas.

# Index

Abbott, Benjamin F. 230
Abilene, Tex. 168, 171, 187, 205, 208
Acklin, Christopher B. "Kit" 67
Adams, George F. 130
Adams, George H. 145
Adams, George W. 69
Adams, S. 220
Adams, Solomon 42, 43
Adams, William Wirt 41
Adobe Walls, battle of 158
Agua Dulce Creek, battle of 15
Agua Dulce River 54, 85
Alamo, siege of the 15, 30, 211
Alavarado, Tex. 195
Albers, E.G. "Butch," Jr. 208
Aldrich, Roy W. 181, 182, 184, 185, 188, 203
Aldridge, Marrie García 198
Alexander, Edward M. 113
Alexander, James M. 66
Alexander, John 146
Alexander, William J. 106, 107, 118, 120, 123
Alexis, Alvin A. "Al" 204
Alfred, Howard B. "Slick" 225
Alice, Tex. 171, 172, 185, 186, 187, 206, 244
Allee, Alfred Y., Jr. 225
Allee, Alfred Y., Sr. 194, 206, 225
Allen, Johnny 198
Allen, William W. 230
Alley, Rawson 9
Allison, Walter C. 230
Allred, James V. 184, 190
Alsans, Adam 64, 230
Alsobrook, William M. 244
Alston, Fielding 230
Amarillo, Tex. 169, 185, 186, 187, 205, 206, 222, 244
Anadarko (Ah-mau-dah-ka) Indians 61, 78, 90
Anahuac, Tex. 12, 172
Anders, Joseph L. 187, 188, 223
Anderson, C. Columbus 211
Anderson, J.B. 125

Anderson, Joseph S. 226
Anderson, William H. 230
Anderson Co., Tex. 85, 107, 204, 208
Andrews, Micah 33, 44
Andrews Co., Tex. 205, 207, 208
Angelina Co., Tex. 204
Angelina River 22
Angelina, Tex. 46
Anglin, Abram 211
Anglin, William B. 243
Apache Indians 7; Gila 80; Lipan 10, 20, 21, 50, 53, 79, 110, 137; Mescalero 137, 163
Aransas Co., Tex. 204, 207
Archer Co., Tex. 105, 107, 111, 122, 125, 130, 163, 169, 204, 205, 206
Arenosa Creek 49
Arkansas River 18, 82
Armstrong, Gabriel M. 71
Armstrong, John B. 154, 156, 219, 246
Armstrong Co., Tex. 205, 206
Army of the Republic of Texas *see* Texas Army
Arnold, Robert M. "Red" 225
Arnold, Thomas E. 225
Arrington, George W. 169
Arrington, William H. 15, 29
Arroyo Hondo, Hays' skirmish at 26, 213
Arroyo Seco 69; Karnes' skirmish at 20, 27, 212
Ashburn, H.T. 219
Ashby, Travis H. 115
Ashton, Chaucer 71, 230
Askins, Wesley 50
Atascosa Co., Tex. 83, 105, 117, 118, 133, 134, 172, 203, 206, 207
Aten, Ira 163, 167, 170, 220, 246, 310
Athens, Tex. 169, 209
Atkisson, Newt 146
Augustine, Henry W. 36
Austin Co., Tex. 204, 208
Austin, Stephen F. 7, 8, 9, 10, 12, 13, 14, 246

Austin, W.J.D. 230
Austin, Tex. 15, 44, 45, 48, 52, 56, 57, 61, 66, 68, 69, 79, 100, 105, 111, 142, 144, 156, 157, 162, 171, 181, 184, 185, 187, 188, 199, 202, 203, 209
Avriett, Hall 222
Aycock, John E. "Johnnie" 195, 225, 248

Badgett, R.L. "Bob" 225
Bagby, James D. 86
Bailey, David W.H. 243
Bailey, Jesse 226
Bailey, Marvin E. 185, 222
Bailey Co., Tex. 205, 206
Baird, P.C. 220
Baker, Anderson Yancey 222
Baker, David P. 139, 143
Baker, Isaac G. 226
Baker, John R. 55
Baker, Moseley 17
Baldwin, Berk C. 188
Ballantyne, Robert 87, 145
Ballinger, Tex. 172
Ballowe, Samuel L.S. 67
Bandera Co., Tex. 84, 97, 105, 121, 134, 143, 145, 168, 172, 203, 206, 207, 208
Bandera Pass 28
Bandera, Tex. 88, 145
"Bandit War" 177–179, 192
Banks, E.J. "Jay" 193, 204, 225
Banta, William 119
Banton, John D. 230
Barbee, James G. 119
Barber, William 230
Barker, D.S. "Dud" 221
Barkley, Robert 49
Barksdale, Tex. 170
Barler, W.L. 188, 223
Barnes, R.S. "Sam" 131, 217, 240
Barnett, George W. 12, 13
Barron, Thomas H. 30, 32, 33
Barrow, Clyde 184

321

Barrow, James C. 230
Barry, Augustus 134
Barry, James B. "Buck" 85, 99, 106, 109, 110, 111, 112, 114, 115, 116, 118, 123, 136, 216
Bartley, A. 119
Barton, Hale 226
Barton, John 132
Barton, Lewis 230
Barton, Samuel Baker 239
Bartrane, John 230
Bass, Sam 162
Bastrop Co., Tex. 21, 25, 41, 45, 172, 203, 208, 209
Bastrop, Tex. 14, 15, 29, 30, 31, 32, 41, 44, 209
Bates, Carroll 188
Bates, D.A. 146
Bates, W.B. 222
Bates, Winfred F. 223
Bau, Manuel 146
Bay City, Tex. 204
Baylor, George W. 163, 167, 168, 169, 219, 246
Baylor, Henry W. 50, 66, 69
Baylor, John R. 78, 82, 126
Baylor Co., Tex. 110, 130, 204, 205, 206
Bayne, Griffin 16, 30
Beall, Charles P. 223
Bean, J.B. 222
Bear Creek 170, 171
Beaumont, Tex. 180, 204
Beaver Camp, Tex. 94
Beaver Creek 120
Beavert, L.P. 169, 218
Beck, B.F. 218
Becknell, William A. 30, 40
Bee Co., Tex. 105, 133, 134, 170, 172, 206, 207
Beeville, Tex. 156, 207
Belknap, William W. 139
Bell, Peter Hansbrough 49, 57, 59, 65, 70, 71, 74, 76, 82, 84
Bell, William H. 230
Bell Co., Tex. 91, 96, 101, 203, 208
Bellville, Tex. 204
Belton, Tex. 91, 208
Benavides, Refugio 156
Bennett, Joseph L. 16–17, 34, 46
Benton, Jesse, Sr. 15, 16, 30
Benton, Nathaniel 79, 88
Bernard, A. 67
Berry, Henry W. 92, 216
Best, B.F. 171, 218
Best, Stephen Ernest, Sr. 206, 207
Bettinger, Francis 67
Bettis, William M., Sr. 125
Bexar Co., Tex. 25, 28, 48, 53, 57, 66, 74, 79, 83, 84, 88, 89, 97, 101, 105, 171, 203, 206, 207
Biberstein, Herman R. von 117, 131, 144
Bible, Noah 240
Biediger, Lorenz 242

Big Bend 139, 165, 180, 182
Big Spring (Hays County) 29
Big Spring, Tex. 168
Bigford, George 221
Billingsley, Jesse 31, 44, 45
Bingham, George R. "Red" 243
Bird, James (1) 23, 50, 226
Bird, James (2) 230
Bird, John 45
Bird's Fort, Tex. 54
Birdwell, George 117
Birdwell, Thomas G. 240
Bittick, G.C. 133
Black, Frank A. 223
Black, George K. 47
Black, Reading W. 89
Blackwell, Charles 76, 86, 268
Blackwell, Charles J. 182, 189
Blackwell, James 230
Blair, Jesse 226
Blakemore, Thomas M. 119
Blanco Canyon 141
Blanco Co., Tex. 74, 80, 84, 96, 97, 105, 133, 134, 143, 144, 203, 209
Blanco River 88, 89, 91
Blanco, Tex. 144
Block, H.R. "Lefty" 202, 203, 225
Blocker, A.P. 167
Blocker Station, Tex. 145
Bloxman, John R., Jr. 224
Blue, Erastus 240
Blythe, Champion 36
Boales, Calvin 32
Boerne, Tex. 145
Bogart, Samuel 56
Boggess, Giles S. 87, 88
Boggess, Milton M. 115, 216
Bohannon, William M. 243
Bois d'Arc Creek 37
Bone, John W. 126
Bonnell, George W. 39
Borden Co., Tex. 205, 207, 208
Border Regiment 100, 106, 107, 108, 110–111, 112, 124–126
Borgas, John 230
Borger, Tex. 182, 185, 186, 187, 188
Boring, Jesse 114
Bosque Co., Tex. 80, 84, 85, 94, 95, 99, 101, 105, 107, 111, 130, 131, 132, 135, 204, 208
Bosque River 48
Bostwick, Alexander 226
Bourland, James 52, 90, 106, 108, 111, 112, 124
Bourland, James S. 133
Bourland, William H. 70
Bourland's Texas Cavalry Regiment see Border Regiment
Boutwell, Alexander 135
Bowen, Thomas J. 35
Bowie Co., Tex. 25, 107, 182, 204, 205
Bowles, Duwa'li (Cherokee) 23
Bowling family 199–200
Bowyer, John M. 17, 20, 34

Box, James E. 38, 41, 42, 43
Brackett City, Tex. 147
Bradford, Cy 224
Bradshaw, James 36
Brady City, Tex. 187
Branch Davidians 196
Bravo, Calixto 18
Brazoria Co., Tex. 204
Brazoria, Tex. 12
Brazos Co., Tex. 204, 208
Brazos Reservation 78, 80, 82, 90, 91, 99
Brazos River 7, 8, 9, 10, 12, 13, 15, 16, 17, 20, 21, 28, 29, 30, 31, 32, 33, 34, 39, 41, 42, 45, 47, 48, 51, 52, 57, 65, 68, 69, 72, 73, 74, 77, 79, 96, 107, 110, 111, 118, 143, 168
Breazeale, F. 133
Breckenridge, Tex. 185, 189
Brennan, Thomas H. 47
Brewster Co., Tex. 170, 171, 207, 208
Briscoe, George C. 39
Briscoe Co., Tex. 205, 206
Brite Raid 180
Brittain, Jabez L. 98
Broadwater, G.B. 168
Brooke, George M. 74, 75, 76, 77
Brookfield, Walter 230
Brookfield, William C. 38, 53
Brooks, Augustus 231
Brooks, James A. 165, 166, 172, 185, 220, 246
Brooks, Joe B. 184, 189, 223
Brooks Co., Tex. 177, 206, 207
Brookshire, Nathaniel 45
Brown, Caleb S. 49
Brown, Edward 231
Brown, Henry S. 11
Brown, J.M. 216
Brown, James H. 97
Brown, John Henry 23, 82, 91, 111, 131, 132
Brown, P.P. (or J.) 217
Brown, Squire 36
Brown, William S. 124
Brown Co., Tex. 84, 89, 90, 93, 94, 105, 110, 111, 118, 122, 131, 132, 145, 148, 154, 163, 168, 170, 171, 172, 199, 207, 208
Browning, George W. 34, 36
Browning, J.E. 231
Brown's Fort 43
Brownsville, Tex. 75, 82, 83, 84, 87, 92, 93, 113, 151, 152, 172, 185, 186, 187, 188, 206, 209
Brownwood, Tex. 145, 148, 170, 171, 172, 187, 207, 208
Brune, Charles R. "Charlie" 203
Brunson, Allen 120
Brush, Gilbert 71
Bryant, Benjamin F. 42, 212
Bryant, R.E. 221
Bryant's Station, Tex. 42, 69, 51

Buchanan, John 231
Buchanan, Joseph B. 244
Buchanan Co., Tex. 90, 91
Buckaloo, Cleatis R. "Clete" 203, 206
Buckner, Aylett C. 10
Buena Vista, battle of 62, 214
Buffalo Gap, Tex. 168
Buffalo Station, Tex. 112, 125
Bugg, William 42, 52
Bullis, John 141, 155
Bullock, Julius 226
Bullock, Robert J. "Bob" 203
Burdett, Robert Lee 244
Bureau of Alcohol, Tobacco, and Firearms (ATF) 196
Burke, John 240
Burks, G.W. 195, 204, 225, 310–311
Burleson, Aaron B. 85, 97, 98, 113, 117
Burleson, Edward "Ed," Jr. 84, 94, 95, 102, 105, 114, 116, 136, 142
Burleson, Edward "Ned," Sr. 14, 16, 17, 20, 23, 31–32, 44, 50, 56
Burleson, Jacob 43
Burleson Co., Tex. 101, 203, 208
Burnam, Jesse 9
Burnet Co., Tex. 74, 84, 94, 105, 118, 132, 133, 134, 146, 161, 171, 203, 208
Burt, Harrison 231
Burton, Isaac W. 15, 16, 19, 29, 30, 31
Burton, Marvin "Red" 182, 186, 224, 246
Burton, Tex. 204
Bushong, George E. 115
Bustamante, Anastasia 12
Butler, Charles 231
Byars, W.S. 224
Byers, Benjamin F. 231
Byrne, Jerry, Jr. 207
Byrnes, David A. 196, 204

Caddo Indians 9, 20, 21, 61, 78, 80, 82, 90
Caddo Peak 147
Caddo Spring 91
Cady, David C. 57, 59, 66
Cain, John 226
Cairns, William J. 17, 54, 55
Caldwell, Mathew 11, 21, 23, 24, 26, 44, 47, 49, 50, 51
Caldwell Co., Tex. 105, 171, 203, 206, 207, 208, 209
Calhoun Co., Tex. 204, 206, 207
Callahan, James H. 53, 79, 88, 177
Callahan Co., Tex. 105, 110, 120, 121, 132, 147, 168, 171, 172, 204, 207, 208
Callan, James J. 118, 119, 121, 122
Calloway, William P. 147
Calvert, James 231
Camargo, Mexico 64, 67, 69, 82
Cameron, Ewen (1) 17, 27, 56, 177

Cameron, Ewen (2) 116
Cameron Co., Tex. 83, 105, 172, 177, 206, 207, 209
Cameron, Tex. 185
Camp Co., Tex. 204, 205
Camp Anderson, Tex. 120, 122
Camp Arbuckle, I.T. 124
Camp Arbuckle, Tex. 72
Camp Austin, Tex. 41
Camp Bee, Tex. 86
Camp Belknap, Tex. 122
Camp Blanco, Tex. 94
Camp Brazos, Tex. 45
Camp Breckenridge, Tex. 105, 120, 122
Camp Briscoe, Tex. 147
Camp Brown, Tex. 90
Camp Brunson, Tex. see Red River Station, Tex.
Camp Burgess, Tex. 171
Camp Burnet, Tex. 171
Camp Caldwell, Tex. 45, 47
Camp Carnes, Tex. 96
Camp Carrizo Springs, Tex. 168
Camp Cave, Tex. 93
Camp Charco del Monte, Tex. 87
Camp Cleveland, Tex. 147
Camp Coleman, Tex. 33; see also Fort Colorado, Tex.
Camp Collier, Tex. 105, 122, 123
Camp Colorado, Tex. (Republic of Texas post) see Fort Colorado, Tex.
Camp Colorado, Tex. (U.S. post) 79, 101, 102, 106, 109, 112, 113, 114, 115, 116, 117, 122, 123, 134, 144, 145
Camp Concho, Tex. 102, 114, 115
Camp Contrary, Tex. 171
Camp Cooke, Tex. 57
Camp Cooper, Tex. 79, 98, 99, 101, 102, 106, 112, 113, 115, 116, 122
Camp Corner, Tex. 94
Camp Crawford, Tex. see Fort McIntosh, Tex.
Camp Creek 115
Camp Cureton, Tex. 105, 122
Camp Davidson, Tex. 143
Camp Davis, Tex. (1) 48
Camp Davis, Tex. (2) 105, 120, 121
Camp Degener, Tex. 144
Camp DeKalb, Tex. 48; see also Fort DeKalb, Tex.
Camp Dix, Tex. 105, 121, 122
Camp Eagle Pass, Tex. 172
Camp Elm, Tex. 171
Camp Elm Creek, Tex. 144
Camp Eureka, Tex. 168
Camp Felder, Tex. 121, 123
Camp Franklin, Tex. 51
Camp Giles, Tex. 93
Camp Gillespie, Tex. 105, 120, 121, 122, 123
Camp Groce, Tex. (1) 31

Camp Groce, Tex. (2) 120, 121, 122, 123
Camp Grove, Tex. 126
Camp Harris, Tex. 45
Camp Hogg, Tex. 170
Camp Houston, Tex. 94, 97
Camp Hubbard, Tex. 168
Camp Hudson, Tex. 79
Camp Independence, Tex. 53
Camp Jackson, Tex. see Red River Station, Tex.
Camp Jim Bourland, Tex. 125
Camp Johnson, Tex. 171
Camp Journey, Tex. 37
Camp King, Tex. 170, 171
Camp Laguna Seco, Tex. 113
Camp Las Moras, Tex. 170
Camp Leon, Tex. 91
Camp Llano, Tex. 105, 121
Camp Logan, Tex. 125
Camp Loma Vista, Tex. 169
Camp Louise, Tex. 96
Camp Mabry, Tex. 171, 184, 185
Camp McCord, Tex. see Camp Salmon, Tex.
Camp McCulloch, Tex. 170
Camp McMillin, Tex. 105, 121, 123
Camp Menite, Tex. 172
Camp Montel, Tex. 105, 121
Camp Mousquie Cañon, Tex. 171
Camp Nashville, Tex. 45
Camp Nicholson, I.T. 124
Camp Nueces, Tex. 105, 122, 123
Camp Oakes, Tex. 86
Camp Pecan, Tex. 105, 122
Camp Point Lookout, I.T. 125
Camp Preston, Tex. 17
Camp Rabb, Tex. 105, 120
Camp Radziminski, I.T. 81, 93, 94, 96
Camp Rio Frio, Tex. 144
Camp Roberts, Tex. 168
Camp Roff, I.T. 124
Camp Rowland, Tex 122
Camp Runnels, Tex. 90, 91
Camp Russell, Tex. 144
Camp Salmon, Tex. 105, 120, 121, 122
Camp San Antonio Viejo, Tex. 85
Camp Sandy, Tex. 147
Camp San Francisco, Tex. 86
Camp San Saba, Tex. 105, 109, 121, 123, 134
Camp Sherman, Tex. 48
Camp Simons, I.T. 124
Camp Simpson, Tex. 171
Camp Steele, I.T. 124
Camp Steele, Tex. 171
Camp Stockbridge, Tex. 171
Camp Stroud, Tex. 51
Camp Swenson, Tex. 171
Camp Twitty, Tex. 125
Camp Verde, Tex. 79, 105, 108, 113, 114, 115, 116, 120, 121, 122, 123, 139, 143

Camp Vinton, Tex. 168
Camp Warren, Tex. 42, 45, 46
Camp Wehranz, Tex. 97
Camp Wichita, Tex. 93, 96, 126
Camp Williams, Tex. 41
Camp Wood, Tex. (1) 79
Camp Wood, Tex. (2) 143, 170, 172
Campbell, Charles A. 231
Campbell, G.W. 147, 168
Campbell, Tex. 170
Camy's Creek 91
Canadian River 80, 84, 90, 93, 94, 96, 158
Canales, José Tomás 180
Cañon de Uvalde *see* Uvalde Canyon
"Captain James Kerr" (Tonkawa) 44
Carder, Christian C. 231
Carder, Elijah 231
Cardis, Louis 162
Cardwell, P.A. 184
Cargile, I.D. 231
Carmack, Thomas K. 89
Carmichael, Jim 220
Carnes, Quirl Bailey 222, 244
Carothers, J.H. 146
Carpenter, John W. 226
Carranza, Venustiano 175, 177, 179, 181
Carrizo Springs, Tex. 156, 168, 170, 172, 185, 186, 206
Carroll, Nathaniel H. 47
Carson, N. 110–111
Carson Co., Tex. 205, 206
Carter, Andrew "Drew" 197
Carter, J.J. 145
Cartersville, Tex. 146
Cartwright, L.F. 221
Caruthers, L.B. 220
Casey, B.F. 145
Cass Co., Tex. 107, 182, 204, 205
Casteel, Bruce M. 202, 203, 205
Castile (Tonkawa) 129
Castro, Cuelgas de (Lipan Apache) 20, 21, 42
Castro, Juan (Lipan Apache) 50
Castro Co., Tex. 205, 206
Castroville, Tex. 61, 68, 86, 146, 155, 156
Cathey, William H. 132
Cathey, William J. 216
Cattle industry 137–138, 163
Caver, Barry K. 197, 207
Cawthon, William M. "Matt" 225, 197
Cedar Creek 47
Center, Tex. 204
Chaffner, Michael 71
Chalmers, William L. 95
Chamberlain, Bland 139, 144
Chambers Co., Tex. 172, 204
Chambers Creek 72
Chambliss, Simon 231
Chance, Joseph B. 29

Chandler, Benjamin T. 231
Chandler, Eli 52, 67
Chano, A. 231
Chase, W.R. 119
Chenoweth, B.D. 95
Cherokee Co., Tex.107, 204, 208
Cherokee Indians 21; and war with Texians 22
"Cherokee Line" 22, 35, 36, 37, 38, 40, 41, 43, 45, 47
Cherry, Henry G. 231
Chevallie, Michael H. 63, 66, 68
Chihuahua 18, 79, 179, 180
Childers, Francis 226
Childress Co., Tex. 172, 203, 205, 206
Chisum, Claiborne 35
Chriesman, Horatio 9
Christian, James 226
Churchill, Sylvester 61
Cisco, Tex. 172
Clapp, Elisha 34
Clark, Alvin A. 242
Clark, David 227
Clark, Edward 101
Clark, John 35
Clark, R. 231
Clark, Thomas W. 70
Clarksville, Tex. 30, 46, 51, 186, 204
Clay Co., Tex. 103, 105, 106, 107, 111, 116, 120, 125, 127, 130, 135, 143, 163, 169, 204, 205, 206
Clayton, William C. 128
Clear Fork Reservation 78, 79, 82, 85, 90, 91, 99
Cleburne, Tex. 188, 209
Cleveland, D.B. 116
Cleveland, John W. 40
Cline, Ira W. 223
Clinton, Tex. 149
Clopton, William H. 239
Clubb, David 227
Cobb, Edward H. 139–140
Cochran, John H. 96
Cochran Co., Tex. 205, 206
Cocke, James D. 39, 48
Cody, Matthew W. 55
Coe, Philip H. 12, 13
Coffman, Raymond L. "Ray" 202, 203, 206
Coke, Richard 142, 149, 161
Coke Co., Tex. 77, 207, 208
Coker, A. 217
Coldwell, Cornelius V. "Neal" 167, 168, 171
Coleman, Alexander 57
Coleman, Robert M. 12, 13, 14, 15, 16, 32
Coleman Co., Tex. 79, 90, 94, 102, 110, 118, 122, 131, 132, 144, 145, 150, 163, 168, 169, 170, 171, 207, 208
Coleto Creek 15, 32
Collier, Frank M. 121

Collin Co., Tex. 107, 204, 205
Collingsworth Co., Tex. 169, 205, 206
Collins, — 240
Collins Station, Tex. 156
Collinsworth, James 29
Colorado City, Tex. (Fayette Co.) 31
Colorado City, Tex. (Mitchell Co.) 168, 185, 186, 187
Colorado Co., Tex. 105, 204
Colorado River 7, 8, 9, 10, 11, 13, 15, 16, 20, 21, 22, 29, 30, 31, 32, 33, 41, 42, 43, 44, 45, 47, 48, 50, 52, 56, 69, 74, 77, 86, 98, 99, 110; Moore's attack at the Red Fork of 24
Colquitt, Oscar B. 175
Colt, Samuel 64
Columbus, Tex. 10, 14, 120, 121, 122, 123, 169, 171
Comal Co., Tex. 203, 206, 207
Comanche Co., Tex. 80, 84, 101, 105, 110, 115, 131, 132, 145, 148, 168, 207, 208
Comanche Indians 7, 11, 18, 20, 21, 27, 28, 61, 80–81, 82, 85, 107–108, 110–111, 112, 135, 137, 139, 140, 158, 159, 162; Comanche Moon 11, 84, 162; Comanche war trails 11, 82; *Comanchería* 11, 22, 80, 106, 137, 158; Kotsoteka 11, 80, 159, 141; Kwahadi 11, 160, 137, 141; Nakoni 11, 85, 141; Penateka 11, 21, 22–24, 78, 80; Yamparika 11
Comanche Reserve *see* Clear Fork Reservation
Comanche, Tex. 154, 203
Combs, C.R. 92
Comfort, Tex. 145, 148
Committee of Public Safety 100–101
Comstock, Tex. 168, 171, 186, 188, 189
Concepción, Tex. 156, 171; battle at 15
Concho Co., Tex. 207, 208
Concho Junction *see* Camp Concho
Concho River 52, 98, 11, 116, 137, 162, 168, 172
Confederate Congress 105, 108
Confederate States Army 106, 108; Confederate Central Sub-District of Texas 110; Confederate Eastern Sub-District of Texas 107; Confederate frontier strategy 101, 107, 112; Confederate Northern Sub-District of Texas 107, 108, 109, 110, 112; Confederate Western Sub-District of Texas 107, 108; conscription 109; deserters 107; surrenders of 112; Trans-Mississippi Department 112

Congress of the Republic of Texas 16, 17, 20, 21, 24, 25
Connell, J.G. 148
Connell, Richard 231
Connelly, Harrison R. "Tips" 240
Conner, John H. 61, 62, 68, 69, 73, 84, 89, 91, 93
Connor, Chris R. 162, 219
Connor, William 231
Conroe, Tex. 204
Conway, Samuel D. 231
Cook, Maurice C. 198, 202, 203, 207
Cook, Thalis T. 221
Cooke Co., Tex. 74, 93, 102, 103, 105, 107, 110, 111, 125, 128, 129, 130, 135, 137, 145, 204, 205; Indian raid in 107–108
Cooke, C.T.C. 231
Cooke, George B. 134
Cooke, Hiram W. 117, 118
Cook's Fort, Tex. 47
Coonrod, Stephen 231
Coonrod, William J. 231
Cooper, Joseph 227
Cora, Tex. 89
Corbin, Albert G. 43
Córdova, Vicente 21, 26
Corlew, Alney M. 231
Corley, Samuel 70
Corning, A.F. 129
Corps of Rangers 15, 15–16, 29–30
Corpus Christi, Tex. 18, 56, 57, 59, 65, 67, 72, 85, 151, 152, 156, 172, 182, 185, 186, 191, 199, 206, 207
Corrigan, James 231
Cortina, Juan N. 82–83, 150–151; and the "Cortina War" 83–84, 101
Coryell, James 227
Coryell Co., Tex. 74, 80, 84, 89, 95, 105, 111, 117, 130, 131, 132, 203, 208
Costley, Michael 34
Cottle, George W. 227
Cottle Co., Tex. 205, 206
Cotulla, Tex. 169, 170, 171, 172, 206
Council House Fight 22
Coushatta Indians 10
Couzens, Thomas 231
Cowan, David C. 90, 113
Cowan, Gideon P. 97
Cowsert, Gully, Sr. 206, 207
Cox, A.H. 143
Cox, Abner 231
Cox, H.M. 231
Cox, Jesse 231
Cox, M. 240
Crabtree, Job 231
Craddock, John R. 35
Craighead, J.P.N. "Pat" 222
Crane, John 227
Crane Co., Tex. 207, 208
Crayton, James 232
Creaner, Charles M. 53
Creery, John A. 41

Crockett Co., Tex. 207, 208
Crockett, Tex. 42
Crooked Creek, battle at 81
Crosby Co., Tex. 205, 206
Cross Timbers 18, 54, 139
Crowder, Robert A. "Bob" 193, 202, 204, 205, 225, 246, 311
Crowson, Henry P. 227
Crump, William G. 70, 72
Crutchfield, J.P. 127
Cuero, Tex. 156, 172
"Las Cuevas War" 152
Culberson, Charles A. 165
Culberson Co., Tex. 207, 208
Cullins, Aaron 227
Culver, William H. 130, 240
Culwell, Jonah S. 127
Cummings, A.P. "Sugg" 223
Cummings, David P. 227
Cummings, Wiley 232
Cundiff, Charles E. 232
Cunningham, Aaron W. 187
Cunningham, James 117, 131
Cunningham, John R. 49
Cunningham, K.F. 189, 224
Cureton, J.J. "Jack" 85, 98, 111, 122, 127, 129
Curtis, Charles 32, 33
Curtis, J.W. 110, 129
Cutler, F.L. 124

Daggett, Charles 71
Daggett, Ephraim 71
Daingerfield, Tex. 53, 191
Dallam Co., Tex. 205, 206
Dallas Co., Tex. 64, 107, 204, 205
Dallas, Tex. 58, 154, 182, 186, 204
Dalrymple, William C. 84, 85, 93, 95, 98, 101
Daniels, Joseph 39
Darnell, Dewitt C. 232
Darnell, Nicholas H. 95
Darst, Jacob C. 227
Davenport, James B. 91
Davenport, John M. 89
Davidson, James 138, 139, 142
Davidson, Jesse J. 232
Davidson, John W. 159
Davidson, S.G. 96
Davidson, Sidney Green 115, 240
Davis, Edmund J. 138, 139, 142, 179
Davis, George W. 14, 29
Davis, Henry Clay 57, 77, 87
Davis, Henry T. 121
Davis, Jefferson 105, 106, 108
Davis, John 227
Davis, Samuel 47
Davis, Will W. 188, 189
Dawson, Nicholas M. 26, 34, 50
Dawson, Tolliver "Tol" 195, 225
Dawson Co., Tex. 134, 205, 207, 208
Day, James M. 310
Day, Samuel 124
Daymon, Squire 227

Deaf Smith Co., Tex. 205, 206
Dean, Jack O. 195, 206
Dearduff, William 227
Dearing, Jacob 132
DeArmond, Russell 132
Decatur, Tex. 108, 117, 127, 128, 129, 130, 142, 206
Deckert, John 232
DeCourcy, James A. 95
Deggs, T.W. 218
DeJarnette, Frank W. 220
Delony, L.S. 220
De Los Santos, Gerardo J. "Gary" 203, 205, 206, 209
Del Rio, Tex. 171, 181, 185, 186, 187, 188, 189, 198, 200, 208, 209
Delta Co., Tex. 107, 204, 205
DeMay, Charles 232
Dendy, John 225
Dendy, Kirby W. 208
Denison, Tex. 182, 186
Denton, J.M. 167
Denton, John B. 227
Denton Co., Tex. 74, 107, 111, 125, 135, 140, 143, 204, 205
Denton, Tex. 143
Department of Public Safety, Texas (DPS) 190, 191, 193, 194, 196, 198, 200; Criminal Law Enforcement (CLE) Division 194, 198; Highway Patrol 190, 191, 193
Dereson, Jesse A. 114
Desdemona, Tex. 182, 185
Despallier, Charles 227
De Witt, Green 11
De Witt Co., Tex. 105, 149, 150, 152, 154, 156, 172, 204, 206, 207
Dial, Asa 232
Diamond, James J. 124
Diamond, John R. 112, 124, 126
Díaz, Porfirio 155, 165, 175
Dickens Co., Tex. 205, 206
Dickens, Tex. 185
Dickerson, Alamaron 11, 15
Dier, Wesley 232
Dillahunty, J.H. 127
Dimmit Co., Tex. 206, 207, 209
Dix, John J. 122
Doaty, Robert E. 243
Dog Cañon 144
Doherty, Bobby Paul 225, 245, 246
Dolan, Patrick 172
Dolson, George M. 52
Donelson, John 92, 113
Donley Co., Tex. 205, 206
Donna, Tex. 188
Dorbant, Christian 118
Dorsey, C.W. 117
Dorsey, L. 227
Douglass, Kelsey H. 17, 22
Douglass, Y. 162
Douthit, Benjamin W. 211
Dove Creek, Totten's battle at 100, 111–112, 217
Doyle, Nimrod 21, 44

Drennan, Thomas 239
Dressler, Charles F. 232
Dryden, Robert H. 114
Dublin, Tex. 147
Dubose, Harry G. 168, 171, 222
Duffinger, George 232
Duke, William A. 115
Dumas, Tex. 206
Dunaway, J.D. 185
Duncan, John R. "Jack" 154
Dunn, James 52
Durbin, J.W. 220
Durst, James H. 36, 39, 40, 48
Durst, John M. 38, 39
Durst, Joseph 46
Duval Co., Tex. 169, 170, 171, 172, 177, 181, 206, 207
Duvalt, Andrew 227
Dyches, P.F. 224
Dyer, Jake B. 240
Dyer, John H. 17, 31, 35

Eagle Pass, Tex. 74, 79, 88, 146, 152, 154, 156, 165, 186, 188, 189
Earbee, William 239
Earhart, J.B. 127, 129
Earle, John J. 227
Early, Frank S. 67
Earp, B.P. 117
Eastin, S.W. 147
Eastland, C.C. 232
Eastland, William M. 20, 21, 32, 33, 42
Eastland Co., Tex. 84, 103, 105, 110, 130, 132, 168, 172, 189, 204, 207, 208
Eaton, Alfred P. 227
Ector Co., Tex. 207, 208
Edds, John J. 223, 224
Edens, Balis 43
Edgar, Hyman T. 121
Edinburg, Tex. 156, 172, 187, 188
Edwards, John H. 232
Edwards, S.V. 220
Edwards Co., Tex. 134, 143, 170, 172, 207, 209
18th U.S. Infantry 165
8th U.S. Cavalry 158
8th U.S. Infantry 77
Eldridge, John T. 93
El Ebano, Tex. 188
11th U.S. Infantry 159
Elkins, John M. 145
Elliott, Glenn 195, 225, 310
Ellis, John 72
Ellis Co., Tex. 74, 107, 204, 208
Ellison Springs, Gilbert's battle at 110, 217
Elm Creek 19, 73, 98, 110, 168, 170
Elm Creek Raid 110–111
Elm Creek Station, Tex. 98
Elm Station, Tex. 68
El Olmito, Tex. 143
El Paso Co., Tex. 105, 139, 144, 149, 154, 156, 165, 168, 169, 170, 171, 172, 175, 207, 208; salt war in 161–162, 219
El Paso, Tex. 137, 172, 175, 181, 185, 186, 187, 200, 208
Emberson, John 44, 54
Encarnacíon, Mexico 62, 68
Enchanted Rock, Tex. 72
Encinal Co., Tex. 171, 172
Encinal, Tex. 172
English, George 35, 36, 38
English, James 131
English, Levi 88, 89
English, William T. 232
Epperson, G.M. 240
Erath, Anthony 232
Erath, George B. 19, 21, 32, 33, 44, 48, 51, 108, 110, 111, 116, 130
Erath Co., Tex. 80, 84, 89, 94, 96, 105, 110, 111, 117, 130, 131, 132, 204, 208
Estes, Smith 239
Estrange, Frank L. 93
Evans, Alfred 71
Evans, William G. 45
Everett, Alfred E. 240
Ewing, John 227
Ezell, C.M. 224

Fairfield, Tex. 208
Falcón, Cesario G. 139, 143
Falfurrias, Tex. 185, 187, 188, 206
Falls Co., Tex. 107, 204, 208
Falls of the Brazos 30, 33, 39, 51
Fannin Co., Tex. 35, 39, 40, 42, 45, 46, 48, 51, 54, 55, 58, 107, 204, 205
Farmer, David M. 227
Farr, D.H. 133
Farrar, Henry G. 132
Faulkenberry, David 211
Faulkenberry, Evan W. 211
Fauntleroy, F.W. 95
Fauntleroy, Thomas T. 31
Favor, Robert C. "Bob" 225
Fayette Co., Tex. 11, 21, 32, 105, 203
Federal Bureau of Investigation (FBI) 195, 196, 198
Ferguson, Isaac 71
Ferguson, James E. 177, 179, 182–183, 183–184
Ferguson, Joseph 40
Ferguson, Miriam A. "Ma" 182–183, 183–184
Field, Henry H. 232
Fields, Smallwood S.B. 50
5th U.S. Infantry 77, 158
Fink, Leopold 232
Fink, Napoleon 232
1st Regiment of Infantry 20, 22, 24
1st Texas Cavalry see 1st Texas Mounted Rifles (C.S. Army)
1st Texas Mounted Rifles (C.S. Army) 100, 101–103, 114–116
1st Texas Mounted Rifles (U.S. Army) 59–61, 66–67, 80
1st Texas Mounted Volunteers 64, 70–71
1st U.S. Artillery 83
1st U.S. Infantry 77, 83
1st U.S. Mounted Rifles 64–65, 77
Fishbaugh, William 227
Fisher, Israel P. 232
Fisher, James 37
Fisher, John King 154–155
Fisher, William S. 11, 26, 27
Fisher Co., Tex. 205, 207, 208
Fitzhugh, Gabe S. 95
Fitzhugh, William F. 73, 87, 88, 95
Flacco (Lipan Apache) 52, 53
Flanagan, Joshua 232
Flanders, John 227
Flat Creek 94
Flat Top Mountain 168
Flores, Juan 64
Flores, Manuel 22, 23
Floresville, Tex. 187, 188, 207
Floyd, Dolphin W. 227
Floyd, William F. 232
Floyd Co., Tex. 205, 206
Foard Co., Tex. 110, 205, 206
Fohr, Peter 227
Ford, — 240
Ford, David 119
Ford, John S. "Rip" 70, 75, 80, 82, 83–84, 90, 91, 92, 93, 100, 101, 113, 177, 246
Ford, Silas 232
Forney, Tex. 205
Fort Arbuckle, I.T. 106, 112, 124, 126
Fort Belknap, Tex. 77, 78, 80, 84, 96, 98, 99, 101, 102, 103, 105, 108, 109, 110, 111, 112, 116, 120, 121, 122, 123, 125, 126, 129, 132, 168
Fort Bend Co., Tex. 165, 170, 204
Fort Boggy, Tex. 48
Fort Brown, Tex. 59, 66, 80, 83, 113, 179
Fort Burleson, Tex. see new Fort Milam, Tex.
Fort Chadbourne, Tex. 77, 87, 102, 106, 111, 113, 115, 116, 117
Fort Clark, Tex. 77, 87, 89, 110, 137, 141
Fort Cobb, I.T. 106
Fort Coffee, Tex. 48
Fort Colorado, Tex. 33, 16, 20; see also new Fort Houston, Tex.
Fort Concho, Tex. 137, 158, 168
Fort Croghan, Tex. 74, 106
Fort Davis, Tex. 88, 137, 170, 171, 200
Fort DeKalb, Tex. 37, 39
Fort Dodge, Kan. 158
Fort Duncan, Tex. 74, 88, 108, 113, 120, 123, 137, 155
Fort Elliott, Tex. 162
Fort Ewell, Tex. 156, 172
Fort Fisher, Tex. 33

Fort Franklin, Tex. 52
Fort Gates, Tex. 74
Fort Graham, Tex. 74, 132
Fort Griffin, Tex. 137, 143, 158, 169
Fort Hancock, Tex. 185, 186, 187
Fort Henderson, Tex. 33
Fort Houston, Tex.: new post on the Colorado 29, 33, 36, 37, 38, 39, 40, 42, 43, 46; old post on the Trinity 21, 34
"Fort Iceberg," Tex. 170
Fort Inge, Tex. 74, 86, 108, 115, 121, 139, 143
Fort Inglish, Tex. 39, 40, 54
Fort Jesup, La. 59
Fort Johnson, Tex. 52
Fort Kickapoo, Tex. 22, 41, 43, 45
Fort Lacy, Tex. 46
Fort Lincoln, Tex. 74
Fort Lipantitlán, Tex. 15
Fort Lyday, Tex. see Fort DeKalb, Tex.
Fort Martin Scott, Tex. 74, 86
Fort Mason, Tex. 77, 79, 102, 106, 114, 115, 116, 143, 144
Fort McIntosh, Tex. 74, 113
Fort McKavett, Tex. 77, 102, 106, 114, 115, 116, 137, 170, 186
Fort Merrill, Tex. 86
Fort Milam, Tex.: new post on the east bank of the Brazos 39, 45; old post on the west bank of the Brazos 29, 33, 39
Fort Murrah, Tex. 110
Fort Parker, Tex. see Parker's Fort, Tex.
Fort Phantom Hill, Tex. 77, 102, 106, 111, 115, 116
Fort Quitman, Tex. 137, 144
Fort Richardson, Tex. 141
Fort Rusk, Tex. 39
Fort Saline, Tex. 40, 43
Fort Shelton, Tex. see Fort Rusk, Tex.
Fort Sill, I.T. 137, 140, 159, 160, 162
Fort Smith, Tex. 20, 33, 34, 45, 48
Fort Sterling, Tex. see Parker's Fort, Tex.
Fort Stockton, Tex. 18, 137, 185, 208
Fort Terrett, Tex. 77, 144
Fort Texas, Tex. see Fort Brown, Tex.
Fort Union, N.M. 158
Fort Viesca, Tex. see old Fort Milam, Tex.
Fort Warren, Tex. 54
Fort Washita, Tex. 68
Fort Wells, Tex. 48
Fort Worth, Tex. (military post) 74
Fort Worth, Tex. (town) 142, 168, 169–170, 182, 186, 188, 191, 204
Fossett, Henry S. 108, 109, 11, 112, 134
Foster, B.S. 171

Foster, James 232
"Four Great Captains" see James A. Brooks, John R. Hughes, William J. McDonald, and John H. Rogers
4th U.S. Artillery 77
4th U.S. Cavalry 141, 155, 159
Fox, J. Monroe 177, 178, 180, 183, 185, 186
Fox, John 239
Frandtzen, Erasmus 96
Franklin, John R. 132
Franklin, R.H. 124
Franklin Co., Tex. 107, 204, 205
Franks, Louis B. 30, 42
Frasch, Gustave 132
Fredericksburg, Tex. 108, 134, 147
Freeman, Charles T. 119
Freestone Co., Tex. 107, 204, 208
French, Hiram 232
Friar, Daniel B. 14, 23, 28–29
Friend, Samuel 117
Frio Canyon 144
Frio Co., Tex. 84, 97, 134, 168, 169, 172, 105, 206, 207
Frio River 49, 50, 72, 91, 105
Frontier Battalion (CSA) 108, 109, 111, 134
Frontier Battalion (TST) 151, 155, 157, 160, 161, 162, 163, 164, 165, 167; Co. A 160, 161, 163, 167–168; Co. B 158, 160, 162, 168–169; Co. C 160, 162, 169–170; Co. D 160, 161, 163, 170; Co. E 160, 163, 165, 171; Co. F 160, 165, 171–172
Frontier Forces 138, 139, 141, 143–144; Co. N 139
Frontier Men 142, 147–148
Frontier Organization (TST) 100, 108, 112; First Frontier District 108, 110, 111, 126–130; Second Frontier District 108, 110, 111, 130–132; Third Frontier District 108, 109–110, 111, 132–134
Frontier Regiment (Texas Army) see 1st Regiment of Infantry
Frontier Regiment (TST/CSA) 100, 104, 105, 106, 107, 108, 109, 110, 118–124; Co. A 108, 119–120; Co. B 108, 120; Co. C 109, 120; Co. D 109, 111, 120–121; Co. E 108, 121; Co. F 108, 121; Co. G 109, 111, 121–122; Co. H 109, 111, 122; Co. I 108, 122, 123–124; Co. K 108, 124
Frost, Thomas C. 89, 102, 104, 112, 114, 115, 116
Fry, James H. 93, 114
Fulcher, Simon F. 232
Fuller, Thomas L. 222, 243
Fullerton, John M. 232
Fullerton, William 227
Fuqua, Galba 227
Fusselman, Charles H. 220, 221, 243

Gage, David 52
Gaines Co., Tex. 205, 207, 208
Gainesville, Tex. 90, 124, 125, 126, 160, 205
Gaither, Carlos S. 232
Galaxa Pass, Hays' skirmish at 64, 214
Galbreath, Jo F. 119
Galveston Co., Tex. 172, 204
Galveston, Tex. 17, 84, 181, 182, 187, 189, 191
Garcia, Gregorio N. 139, 144
García, Ignacio 25
Garcitas Creek, Tumlinson's skirmish at 23, 212
Garcitas River 49
Garland, Tex. 202, 205
Garrett, J.F. 46
Garrett, John 41
Garvin, John E. 227
Garza Co., Tex. 205, 206
Garza Rodriguez, Catarino Erasmo 65
Gaston, John E. 228
Gates, Amos H. 36
Gatesville, Tex. 108, 132, 185, 204
Gault, Benjamin M. "Manny" 184, 205
Gay, Thomas 228
Geer, James "Jim" 225
Gentry, Frederick B. 96
George, James 228
Georgetown, Tex. 187
Gerth, William R. 225, 247
Gholson, Albert G. 30
Gholson, Benjamin F. 216
Gholson, Samuel S. 216
Giddens, James R. 111, 240
Gilam, Dudley 233
Gilbert, Richard S. 233
Gilbert, Singleton 110, 130, 240
Gill, John P. 46, 56
Gillespie, J.T. 171
Gillespie, James H. 67
Gillespie, Robert A. "Ad" 59, 60, 66, 67, 233
Gillespie, William M. 239
Gillespie Co., Tex. 74, 84, 88, 96, 102, 105, 110, 116, 120, 121, 132, 133, 134, 144, 145, 147, 161, 203, 208
Gillett, James B. 246
Gillett, James S. 70, 71, 72
Gilliland, J.C. 146
Gillintine, John O. 240
Gillintine, Nick W. 111, 131, 240
Gillintine, William M. 240
Gipson, Francis 240
Glass, William A. 243
Glasscock, Henry D. 224
Glasscock Co., Tex. 207, 208
Goff, Thomas J. 244
Goheen, Michael R. 13
Goliad Co., Tex. 21, 25, 57, 64, 86, 105, 204, 206, 207

Goliad Massacre 15, 79
Goliad, Tex. 7, 12, 18, 56, 85, 156
Gonzales, José María 47
Gonzales Co., Tex. 21, 25, 53, 101, 105, 154, 204, 206, 207
Gonzales, Tex. 11, 14, 15, 29, 44, 154
Gonzaullas, Manuel T. "Lone Wolf" 186, 191, 204, 224, 225, 246
Gooch, William J. 233
Good, Hannibal 35
Goodall, James P. 69
Gooding, Edgar D. "Ed" 192–193, 225
Goodlet, Patrick 242
Goodrich, Levi W. 114
Goodrich, O.W. 244
Gorhmly, James S. 233
Graham, Gideon "Ged" 131
Graham, James 128
Graham, John F. 48
Graham, Tex. 168, 204, 206
Grant, Ulysses S. 137, 142
Grape Creek 115
"Grass Fight" 15
Graves, Ransom 240
Graves, William 233
Gravis, John F. 221, 243
Gray, Jerry 183, 185, 186, 187
Gray, Mabry B. "Mustang" 63, 67, 177
Gray, S.B. 144
Gray Co., Tex. 169, 205, 206
Grayham, J.G. 40
Grayson Co., Tex. 107, 204, 205
Great Comanche Raid 22–24
Green, Jameson 233
Green, M.R. 148
Green, Samuel 116, 143
Green, Thomas 52, 60, 67
Greenville, Tex 204, 205
Greenwood, E.W. 145
Greenwood, Garrison 14, 29
Greer, Thomas N.B. 48, 52
Greer Co., Tex. 169
Gregg, Ellis 233
Gregg Co., Tex. 107, 182, 204, 205
Greggory, J.B. 233
Gregory, Thomas W. 233
Grier, Thomas 239
Griffin, C.W. 220
Griffin, John 233
Griffin, Joseph 233
Grimes, Albert C. 220
Grimes Co., Tex. 204
Grumbles, John J. 61, 62, 68, 69, 75, 85
Guadalupe Co., Tex. 203, 206, 207
Guadalupe Hidalgo, treaty of 64, 74, 82
Guadalupe Mountains, Tex. 161
Guadalupe River 11, 21, 22, 26, 28, 31, 32, 33, 44, 45, 47, 51, 56, 74, 79, 87, 89, 91, 168

Guerrero, Mexico 17, 26, 57
Guffey, Stanley Keith 195, 225, 245, 246, 247–248
Guinn, J.P. 127
Gunter, R.H. 233
Gussett, Norwick 133
Guthrie, W.A. 233
Gutierrez, José Angel 194

Haby, George 146
Hack, Isaac 233
Hackberry Springs, Tex. 168
Haggard, Squire 34
Hagler, James F. 124
Haigwood, Henry 228
Hale, Thomas J. 92
Hale, W.F. 224
Hale Co., Tex. 205, 206
Haley, G.W. 130
Haley, Richard 38
Hall, A.P. 145
Hall, H.M.C. 228
Hall, James 228
Hall, James M.W. 71
Hall, Jesse L. "Lee" 152–153, 154, 155, 156, 246
Hall, John 233
Hall, John L. 54
Hall, William 9
Hall Co., Tex. 169, 205, 206
Hallund, William V.R. 47
Halton, Reuben B. 233
Hamer, D. Estill 184
Hamer, Francis A. "Frank" 181, 183, 184, 185, 187, 188, 222, 223, 246
Hamilton, Alexander J. 135
Hamilton, C.H. 168
Hamilton, Jacob E. 45
Hamilton Co., Tex. 84, 94, 96, 105, 110, 131, 132, 163, 207, 208
Hamilton Creek 74
Hamm, Seabren O. 204, 206
Hammond, E.H. 187
Hamner, H.A. 93, 113
Hampton, G.J. 92
Handley, Alexander E. 71
Haney, B.B. 127
Hanks, J.M. 128
Hanna, Nick 199
Hannah, Leon P. 186
Hansford, John L. 119
Hansford Co., Tex. 205, 206
Hanson, William M. 180, 184, 187, 189
Harbour, William T. 116
Hardaway, James M. 233
Hardeman, Thomas 24
Hardeman Co., Tex. 110, 130, 169, 172, 205, 206
Hardin, Bud 221
Hardin, John Wesley 153–154, 154
Hardin Co., Tex. 204
Harknep, — 92

Harlingen, Tex. 185, 186, 187, 188, 206
Harney, John 233
Harney, William S. 61
Harper, Charles A. 66, 70
Harrell, Garrett 228
Harrell, George 162, 219
Harrell, Jacob M. 144
Harris, Charles H., III 177
Harris, E. 233
Harris, George 241
Harris, Hannibal 114
Harris, Kaylene "Katy" 198, 199
Harris, Tupper 221
Harris Co., Tex. 171, 204
Harrisburg, Tex. 15, 31, 109, 120, 121, 122, 123
Harrison, Charles A. 72
Harrison, Greenberry H. 21, 41, 43
Harrison, Joe 225
Harrison, Robert B. 114
Harrison, Thomas L. 85, 98
Harrison, W.B. 233
Harrison, William R. 124
Harrison Co., Tex. 25, 107, 172, 204, 205
Hart, Henry A. 233
Hart, James 233
Hart, John 39
Hart, Silas B. 66
Hartley Co., Tex. 205
Hartley, Tex. 169
Harwell, Jack 221
Haskell Co., Tex. 107, 130, 205, 206
Hasroot, Gus 140
Hastings, H.H. 233
Havrda, Charlie J. 202, 206
Hawes, Prince B. 233
Hawkins, Richard C. "Red" 184, 205, 222
Haynie, George E. 145
Hays, John C. "Jack" 23, 25, 25–26, 27, 28, 51, 53, 55, 56, 57, 60, 63, 64, 65, 66, 70, 77, 100, 157, 177, 213, 246
Hays Co., Tex. 105, 145, 203, 208, 209
Head, James A. 28
Heard, George W. 228
Heard, William J.E. 56
Hearn, Skylor D. 209
Hebbronville, Tex. 172, 185, 188, 206
Heintzelman, Samuel P. 83
Helena, Tex. 170
Hembree, J.H. 119
Hemphill Co., Tex. 205
Hemphill, Tex. 172
Hempstead, Tex. 109, 110, 120, 121, 122, 123, 171
Henderson, H.D. "Dino" 203, 209
Henderson Co., Tex. 107, 204, 208
Henderson, Tex. 186
Henry, William R. 79, 87, 88, 89, 91

## Index

Hensey, Hugh 70
Herbert, Claibourne C. 67
Hereford, Tex. 206
Herman, David 239
Herrill, Charles W. 233
Herrill, William 233
Herring, Curtis 133
Herron, Andrew 92
Herster, Daniel 146
Hewett, Ezekiel T. 233
Hewett, William M. 71
Hibbert, Charles 124
Hickman, Leo 198
Hickman, Thomas R. 181, 184, 185, 186, 189, 202, 224, 246
Hickory Creek 73; Cobb's battle at 139–140, 218
Hidalgo Co., Tex. 171, 172, 177, 206, 207, 209
Hidalgo, Tex. 188
Higgins, Peter 233
Highsmith, Samuel 71, 72
Hill, Alexander C. 83, 93
Hill, Benjamin F. 70, 73, 76, 86
Hill, James O. 129
Hill, John P. 127
Hill, Pierre Bernard 185
Hill, Washington L. 114
Hill, William W. 32
Hill Co., Tex. 74, 107, 204, 208
Hillhouse, Eli 28
Hines, Dan 186, 203
Hispanics 9, 11, 12, 83, 139; in the Lower Valley 82, 177; as majority population 82, 177; and the Plan of San Diego 177, 178; Rangers 194, 201; relations with Texas Rangers 175, 177, 193; struggle for equality 193–194; *see also* Cortina, Juan N.; the Mexican Revolution; Rodriguez, Catarino Erasmo Garza
Hobby, William P. 179, 180
Hockley Co., Tex. 205, 206
Hodges, John Seaborn 89
Hoffar, John 169
Hogg, Dickson H.L. 114
Holland, H.K. 239
Holly, R.B. 113
Holmes, Frank 242
Holmes, Peter W. 233
Holmork, Ansbury 234
Home Creek 94, 113, 117, 144, 171
Homsley, James M. 115
Hood Co., Tex. 107, 204, 208
Hooker, W.L. 243
Hopkins, C.A. 119
Hopkins Co., Tex. 107, 204, 205
Hord, William D. 118
Hord, William I. 234
Horne, Jacob 234
Hornsby, Moses S. 226
Hornsby's Station, Tex. 15, 29

Horrell-Higgins Feud 161
Horton, Albert C. 55, 56, 61
Horton, Alexander 34
Hosly, David V. 234
Houston, Samuel 15, 16, 17, 24, 25, 26, 27, 83, 84, 85, 101
Houston Co., Tex. 25, 36, 203, 204, 208
Houston, Tex. 18, 20, 34, 39, 177, 182, 187, 191, 202, 203, 204
Howard, Charles H. 161–162
Howard, George T. 49, 52
Howard, Harteford 142
Howard, Henry P. 114
Howard, William 93
Howard Co., Tex. 18, 39, 42, 43, 46, 53, 168, 205, 207, 208
Howell, D.S. 217
Hubbard Creek 98, 99, 123
Hubbard Creek Station, Tex. 116
Hudson, David 234
Hudson, R.M. "Duke" 222
Hudson, W.A. 133
Hudson, William 234
Hudson, William E. 145
Hudspeth Co., Tex. 137, 163, 207, 208
Huerta, Victoriano 175, 176
Hughes, John 228
Hughes, John R. 165, 166, 170, 175, 185, 187, 221, 246
Hughes, Moses 96
Hughes, W.S. 220
Hughes, William S. 68
Hulen, Eugene B. 223, 244
Hunt, Robert E. 244
Hunt Co., Tex. 107, 204, 205
Hunter, Alf 130
Hunter, James M. 108, 109–110, 119, 132, 144
Hunter, James S. 211
Hunter, Willis L. 147
Huntsville, Tex. 197, 204; state penitentiary at 154, 195
Hurst, Tex. 205
Huston, Felix 17, 22, 23, 49
Hutchison, Sidney S. 223
Hutchinson Co., Tex. 205
Hyde, Thomas C. 244
Hynes, John 133

Ikard, E.F. 169
Indian Territory *see* Oklahoma
Indio Cattle Company 188, 189
Inge, John J. 118
Ingram, James 144
Ingram, John 11
Ioni (Hainai) Indians 61
Irion Co., Tex. 207, 208
"Iron Jacket" (Comanche) 80
Irving, R.J. 133
Isbell, George 94, 127
Izod, James 49
Izúcar de Matamoros, Mexico, Hays' skirmish at 64, 214

Jack Co., Tex. 80, 85, 93, 99, 105, 107, 111, 118, 125, 127, 128, 129, 130, 137, 146, 147, 163, 168, 169, 204, 205, 206
Jacksboro, Tex. 93, 118, 128, 168, 205
Jackson, Daniel R. 48
Jackson, H. Joaquin 190, 191, 225
Jackson, Samuel 239
Jackson, Thomas 228
Jackson Co., Tex. 105, 204, 206, 207
January, James P.B. 54
Jaruata, Caledonio de 64
Jasper Co., Tex. 204
Jasper, Tex. 204
Jeff Davis Co., Tex. 137, 170, 207, 208
Jefferson Co., Tex. 204
Jenkins, Joe J. 222
Jennings, Henry L. 234
Jester, Sue M. "Mack" 223
Jett, Stephen 228
Jett, William G. 69
Jewell, George W. 34, 40
Jim Hogg Co., Tex. 206, 207, 209
Jim Ned Creek 171
Jim Wells Co., Tex. 206
Jobe, James L. 234
Johnson, Asa 145
Johnson, Francis N. "Frank" 185
Johnson, George H. 187
Johnson, Isaac W. 76, 85, 239
Johnson, John O. 167
Johnson, Middleton T. 71, 72, 84, 95
Johnson, Nathaniel 234
Johnson, Patrick H. 114
Johnson, T.J. 129
Johnson, Thomas J. 95
Johnson Co., Tex. 107, 111, 130, 131, 132, 204, 208
Johnson's Station, Tex. 68, 96
Johnston, Albert Sidney 17, 21, 79
Johnston, Alexander 95
Johnston, Harry M. 184
Johnston, Joshua W. 234
Jones, Frank D. 170, 243
Jones, Franklin 143
Jones, Gus T. "Buster" 222
Jones, Henry (1) 50
Jones, Henry (2) 242
Jones, Henry M. 114
Jones, James 241
Jones, John A. 234
Jones, John B. 151, 157, 158, 161, 162, 163, 167, 170, 172, 191, 218, 246
Jones, John W. 147
Jones, Nat B. "Kiowa" 224
Jones, Oliver 11
Jones, Randall 10
Jones, Richard 172
Jones, Sim 241
Jones, Stephen F. 96
Jones, William E. 134
Jones, William Jefferson 21, 41

Jones, Williamson 118
Jones, Willis E. 239
Jones Co., Tex. 77, 84, 102, 110, 130, 205, 206, 207, 208
Jordan, A. 35
Jordan, Alexander 45
Jordan, Powhatan 90, 92
Joslen, James 228
Jourdanton, Tex. 206, 207
Journey, Nathaniel T. 37
Jowers, William G.W. 43
Junction, Tex. 161, 168, 170, 206, 207
Juthan, Pope 234

Karankawa (Carancahua) Indians 9, 10
Karnes, Henry W. 20, 21, 22, 27, 35, 41, 47
Karnes Co., Tex. 83, 89, 105, 134, 170, 172, 203, 206, 207
Kaufman Co., Tex. 107, 204, 205
Kaufman Station, Tex. 72
Kea, Gene 225
Keechi, Tex. 146
Keese, William W. 234
Kegans, Benjamin H. 241
Keith, John J. 117
Keith, N. 147
Keith, Stephen P. 146
Kellogg, John B. 228
Kelly, William B. 241
Kelso, John R. 143
Kelso, Sid 185
Kemp, S.J. 216
Kendall Co., Tex. 74, 110, 134, 143, 145, 203, 208, 209
Kenedy Co., Tex. 206, 207
Kenedy, Tex. 186
Kennedy, J.H. 147
Kennedy, John 97
Kenney, Martin M. 167
Kent, Andrew 228
Kent Co., Tex. 205, 206
Kerr Co., Tex. 79, 84, 94, 105, 116, 120, 121, 133, 134, 143, 145, 147, 148, 156, 168, 171, 172, 203, 208, 209
Kerrville, Tex. 147, 203, 209
Kichai (Keechi) Indians 11, 20, 21, 61, 78
Kickapoo Indians 61, 79, 112, 137, 139, 141
Kilgore, Tex. 182, 185, 186, 187, 188
Killeen, Tex. 203, 208
Killough, Samuel B. 51
Kimbell, George C. 15, 30, 228
Kimble Co., Tex. 131, 132, 161, 168, 170, 171, 172, 207, 208; Jones' clean-up of 61
King, James P. 134
King, John R. 114
King, Richard 151
King, Wilburn H. 163
King, William P. 228

King Co., Tex. 205, 206
King Ranch 151, 177
King's Fort, Tex. 54
Kingsville, Tex. 206, 207
Kinney Co., Tex. 77, 79, 134, 143, 147, 172, 2087, 208, 209
Kinney Ranch & Trading Post 57, 85
Kinnion, H.H. 71, 234
Kinsey, Stephen 71
Kleberg Co., Tex. 206, 207
Kleid, Peter 144
Klevenhagen, John J. "Johnny," Sr. 192, 193, 225, 246
Knight, Dan G. 189
Knight, Richard 234
Knox Co., Tex. 110, 130, 205, 206
Koch, Henry 234
Koonsman, Martin N. 224
Koresh, David 196
Krauskopf, E. 132
Krueger, Glenn B. 225
Krumnow, John 225
Kuchler, Jacob 121
Kutch, B.F. 148
Kuykendall, Abner 9, 11, 13
Kuykendall, Matthew J. 115
Kuykendall, Robert H. 7, 10

La Bolsa, Ford's skirmish at 84, 216
Lacey, J.C. 145
Lackey, William 239
La Ebonal, Ford's skirmish at 83, 216
Lafayette, Tex. 53
La Grange, Tex. 203
LaGrulla, Tex. 181
Laguna de Las Flores, Tex. 156
Lamar, Mirabeau B. 16, 20, 21, 22, 24, 68, 73
Lamar Co., Tex. 25, 48, 53, 101, 107, 204, 205
Lamb, Mark 234
Lamb Co., Tex. 205, 206
Lamesa, Tex. 205
Lampasas Co., Tex. 84, 91, 96, 105, 118, 130, 132, 144, 145, 161, 163, 168, 169, 171, 172, 203, 208
Lampasas River 47
Lampasas, Tex. 96, 99, 130, 145, 161, 169, 209
Lane, Edwin D. 119
Lane, James 239
Lane, John W. 127
Lane, John William 46, 54
Lane, Joseph 64
Lane, Walter P. 63, 64, 67, 68, 69
Langtry, Tex. 165, 169, 170, 171, 172, 188
Lanham, B. 131
La Raza Unida (political party) 194
Laredo, Tex. 17, 19, 25, 26, 65, 68, 69, 73, 74, 85, 86, 139, 146, 151, 156, 169, 170, 171, 172, 181, 185, 186, 187, 188, 206, 209

Larremore, George W. 147
La Salle Co., Tex. 134, 169, 170, 171, 172, 206, 207
Latham, B.D. 241
Latharp, Oliver 234
Lavaca Co., Tex. 52, 105, 204, 206, 207
Lavaca River 49
Lawhon, John 120
Lawler, James W. 125
Layne, William 234
Layton, Floyd 222
Leal, Antonio "Tony," III 194, 202, 203, 209
Leal, Manuel 18
Ledbetter, William H. 145
Lee, R.J. 98
Lee Co., Tex. 203, 208, 209
Leon Co., Tex. 204, 208
Leon River 72, 74, 94
Leona River 49, 57, 72, 74, 86, 88
Lewis, George K. 69
Lewis, Gideon K. 77, 87
Lewis, Mark B. 21, 25, 41, 51
Lewis, Robert C. 221
Lewis, W. Charles 97
Liberty Co., Tex. 17, 204
Liberty, Tex. 204
*El Libre Pensador* (newspaper) 165
Liedtke, Franklin 124
Lilly, Joseph D. 53
Limestone Co., Tex. 107, 204, 208
Lincecum, Lycurgus 234
Lindley, Jonathan L. 228
Lindsey, A.M. 119
Lindsey, Ben D. 220
Lindsey, David E. 186
Linnville, Tex. 23
Lipscomb Co., Tex. 205, 206
Little, H.L. 112
Little River 30, 33, 45, 67, 69
Little River Fort, Tex. *see* Fort Smith, Tex.
Little Robe Creek, Ford's battle at 80, 215
Little Saline Creek 170
Little Wichita River 126, 147
Littleton, John 92, 93, 113
Live Oak Co., Tex. 83, 105, 133, 134, 206, 207
Live Oak, Tex. 144, 156
Livingston, Alonzo W. "Lonnie" 222
Livingston, Tex. 199, 204
Llano Co., Tex. 84, 90, 93, 94, 97, 105, 116, 117, 133, 134, 143, 146, 161, 169, 171, 195, 203, 208, 209
Llano Estacado 18, 141, 158, 159
Llano River 51, 52, 69, 72, 77
Llano, Tex. 146, 169
Locke, W.J. 132
Lockhart, Byrd B., Sr. 32
Lodge Creek 168
Lomo Blanco, Tex. 143
Long, G.D. 46
Long, Gabriel 32

Long, George W. 47
Long, Ira 167, 168
Long, James D. 36
Long, John 70
Longview, Tex. 186, 205
Longwa Indians 61
Lost Valley 99, 122; Jones' battle in 158, 218
Lost Valley Creek 99
Love, W.M. 241
Loving, James C. 128
Loving Co., Tex. 207, 208
Lowe, John C. 96
Loyd, Elijah 234
Loyd, M.B. 121
Lubbock, Francis R. 105, 106, 107
Lubbock Co., Tex. 205, 206
Lubbock, Tex. 202, 204, 205
Lucas, Henry Lee 195–196, 198
Luck, Adolphus G. 119
Luckey, James M. 128
Lufkin, Tex. 187, 203, 204
Lyday, Isaac 37
Lynch, J.P. 207
Lynch, John L. 33, 228
Lynn, Jerome C. "Bud" 241
Lynn Co., Tex. 205, 206
Lyon, Henry P. 234
Lyons, J.H. 71

Mabbitt, Leonard H. 36, 57
Mabray, James S. 241
Mabry, Woodford H. 165
Mace, Albert R. 187
Mack, Jesse 197
Mackenzie, Ranald S. 141, 155, 158, 159, 160
Madero, Francisco I. 175
Madison Co., Tex. 204, 208
Magill, James P. 134
Magruder, John B. 107
Mains, Samuel F. 125
Mallet, Nicholas R. 239
Malpass, William 235
Maltby, William J. "Jeff" 171
Mangum, Nathaniel H. 235
Manning, Richard P. 235
Marathon, Tex. 170, 171, 188
Marfa, Tex. 185, 186, 187
Marion Co., Tex. 107, 204, 205
Marlin, William N.P. 90, 91, 228
Marlin, Tex. 187
Maroney, P. Nelson 241
Marsh, Bryan 168, 246
Marshall, Tex. 187, 205
Martin, J.B.B. 130
Martin, Joseph S. 228
Martin, Philip 228
Martin Co., Tex. 205, 207, 208
Martinez, J.D. 146
Martinez, Ramiro "Ray" 194
Martinez, Tiophilo 239
Mason Co., Tex. 77, 84, 93, 97, 117, 121, 130, 131, 132, 143, 144, 146, 168, 170, 171, 105, 207, 208; range war in 161
Mason, Tex. 97, 117, 146, 168, 170, 208
Masters, James 235
Matagorda Co., Tex. 172, 204
Matagorda, Tex. 10, 18
Matamoros, Mexico 17, 27, 59, 66, 67, 82, 151
Mather, Joseph 33
Mathews, Olin 235
Matthews, James D. 21, 44
Matthews, Mansell W. 53
Maupin, Perry 241
Maverick Co., Tex. 105, 120, 134, 146, 154, 172, 206, 207, 208, 209
Maxwell, David 197
Maxwell, R.H. 241
Maynard, W.G. 119
Mayes, James N. 241
Mays, Curtis 85, 98
McAdoo, John D. 110, 111, 132
McAllen, Tex. 202, 209
McBride, John E. 243
McCain, Abraham K. 118
McCaleb, William B. 234
McCamant, A.S. 130
McCamey, Tex. 185
McCarty, Andrew J. 241
McCarty, Daniel 234
McCarty, Timothy J. 243
McCarver, W.P. 241
McCauley, William J. 169, 185, 221
McClure, Bartlett D. 11, 221
McClure, D.H. 146
McClure, Elmer B. 224
McClure, Robert B. 221
McCommas, Burk 234
McCommas, Stephen B. 234
McConnell, David D. 234
McCord, — 119
McCord, James E. 98, 105, 106, 108, 110, 123
McCormick, James W. 187, 202, 203, 207, 224
McCown, Jerome B. 67, 86
McCoy, Jesse 228
McCulloch, Benjamin 23, 26, 27, 44, 49, 52, 60, 62, 63, 66, 67, 68, 101, 246
McCulloch, Henry E. 23, 62, 69, 72, 75–76, 76, 85, 86, 101, 102, 103, 104, 107, 108, 110, 112, 114
McCulloch Co., Tex. 93, 105, 121, 123, 132, 144, 148, 170, 172, 207, 208
McCulloch's Station, Tex. 72
McDaniel, Fred L. 186, 204
McDaniel, John M. 55
McDonald, A.S. 55
McDonald, William J. "Bill" 165, 166, 168, 169, 185, 221, 222, 246
McDuffie, Dan L. 224, 244
McFadden, E.A. 94
McFarland, Andrew J. 125
McFarland, James D. 241
McGarrah, John "Jack" 58
McGee, William H. 46
McGehee, John G. 31
McGehee, Thomas G. 30
McGinnis, James 235
McGrew, G. Washington 228
McKamy, William C. 125
McKay, Francis 66, 235
McKay, William 239
McKee, James 241
McKeen, J.F. 132
McKenzie, Sam 186
McKidrict, Joseph W. "Joe" 221, 243
McKinney, Charles B. 172, 220
McKinney, John 235
McKinney, Tex. 88, 205
McKnight, David 114
McLaren, Richard 196–197
McLean, Ephraim W. 47, 56
McLennan Co., Tex. 74, 107, 116, 204, 208
McLeod, Hugh 17
McMillin, Newton D. 121
McMullen Co., Tex. 105, 133, 134, 172, 206, 207
McMurrey, William W. "Bill" 187, 206
McMurry, Samuel A. 156, 168
McNabb, A. 221
McNeel, James S., Sr. 171
McNelly, John 156
McNelly, Leander H. 149–150, 151, 152, 155, 156, 160, 177, 246
McPhail, Robert 235
McPherson, James 228
McRae, Colin D. 92
McReynolds, J.M. 130
Mechling, W.T. 113
Medina Co., Tex. 74, 79, 84, 86, 88, 92, 94, 105, 113, 133, 134, 146, 168, 171, 203, 206, 207
Medina River 34, 35, 42, 56, 57, 72
Memphis, Tex. 205
Menard Co., Tex. 77, 102, 132, 144, 147, 170, 171, 172, 207, 208
Menardville, Tex. 147, 161, 170
Menchaca, José Antonio 56
Medicine Lodge Treaty 137, 158
Menefee, John S. 55
Mercedes, Tex. 188
Merchant, James W.S. 124, 126
Meridian, Tex. 195
Merram, Edgar 235
Merrill, Nelson 45
Merritt, J.R. 156
Mexia, Tex. 182, 185, 186
Mexico 8, 9, 12, 16, 18, 21, 22, 26, 59, 61, 62, 63, 64, 65, 74, 79, 82, 109, 112, 141, 150, 151, 154, 155, 176, 177, 179, 180, 181; French Intervention in 138, 151; Mexican Revolution in 175, 179, 181; U.S. relations with 59, 138, 151, 152,

155, 176, 179; *see also* Chihuahua; Coahuila; Nuevo León; Tamaulipas
Mexico City  9, 12, 59, 64, 71, 151, 179
Meyers, J.  216
Middle Town, Tex.  89
Middleton, John W.  45
Midland Co., Tex.  207, 208
Midland, Tex.  168, 202, 207, 208
Mier Expedition  26–27, 61
Milam Co., Tex.  21, 25, 44, 51, 57, 58, 182, 203, 208
Miles, Alanson T.  17, 25, 53, 54
Miles, Alfred L.  228
Miles, Nelson A.  158, 159
Miles Co., Tex.  207
Miller, A.D.  110
Miller, Antonio  46
Miller, Charles E.  246
Miller, James L. "Jim"  203, 205
Miller, John  235
Miller, John A. "Arch"  222, 224
Miller, Ray "Pinochle"  224
Miller, Thomas R.  228
Millican, James W.  167
Milligan, Little  235
Mills, M.J.  235
Mills Co., Tex.  110, 172, 208
Millsaps, Isaac  229
Milton, Jefferson Davis "Jeff"  220
Mimms, Jefferson  235
Mina, Tex. *see* Bastrop, Tex.
Mindiola, Marino  229
Mineral Wells, Tex.  206
Minute Men: in antebellum Texas 84, 94, 95, 96–97; in Civil War Texas 100, 101, 108, 111, 116, 117–118; in post–Civil War Texas 141, 144–147, 149, 150, 156; in Texas Republic 25, 51, 52, 53, 54, 55
Mires, P.J.  147
Mission Concepción, Tex.  48
Mission San Jose, Tex.  48
Mission, Tex.  188
Mitchell, Bladen  134
Mitchell, Robert K. "Bob"  195, 208, 225
Mitchell Co., Tex.  168, 205, 207, 208
Mobeetie, Tex.  169
Molina, Melba  198
Moniere, Daniel M.  235
Monroe, Daniel  33
Montague Co., Tex.  84, 93, 97, 102, 104, 107, 108, 111, 117, 120, 121, 122, 125, 127, 128, 130, 135, 139, 143, 146, 147, 204, 205
Montague, Tex.  125, 127, 128, 146
Montel, Charles S. de  120
Monterey, Mexico  64, 67, 69; battle of 61, 214
Montes, Telesforro  156
Montgomery, A.D.  235
Montgomery, Robert  32
Montgomery Co., Tex.  25, 52, 204

Moody, Daniel J., Jr.  183
Moore, Azariah G.  32
Moore, Charles, Jr.  205
Moore, Charles O.  184
Moore, Charles R.  222
Moore, Edward H.  98
Moore, Elisha H.  235
Moore, Frank M.  170
Moore, J.W.  127
Moore, James H.  220, 243
Moore, James S.  125
Moore, John H.  12, 13, 14, 15, 21, 24, 42, 50
Moore, John W.  221
Moore, L.P.  124
Moore, William  235
Moore, William H.  32, 33
Moore Co., Tex.  205, 206
Morales, Pedro F.  229
Moran, John A.  244
Mordica, Benjamin H.  229
Morgan Creek  146
Morris Co., Tex.  107, 205, 206
Morrison, Moses  7, 13, 15, 150
Mortimer, C.E.  243
Morton, Russian  235
Morton, William A.  111
Moseley, D.H.  131
Moseley, W.T.  223
Mosley, W.T.  129
Motley Co., Tex.  205, 206
Mott, —  229
Mount Pleasant, Tex.  185, 205
Mountain City, Tex.  145
Mounted Regiment *see* Frontier Regiment (TST/CSA)
Muckelroy, David  70
Mullens, Isaac  131
Munson, Ira  43
Murchison's Camp, Tex.  38
Murphree, David  55
Murphy, Benjamin W.  235
Murphysville, Tex.  171
Murtry, W.S.  68
Musgrave, D.L.  221
Myers, Robert A.  115

Nacogdoches Co., Tex.  25, 39, 49, 52, 205
Nacogdoches, Tex.  7, 9, 12, 35, 36, 37, 38, 46, 49, 52
Nalls, J. Berry  224
Nash, Jesse E.  229
Nash Springs  130
Nashville-on-the-Brazos, Tex.  33, 51
Natus, John  221
Navarro Co., Tex.  74, 163, 107, 204, 208
Neal, Alpheus D.  215
Neal, Claiborne  229
Neatherey, Robert  241
Neches River  22, 29, 34, 36
Neches Saline  22, 37, 41
Neely, Doc  221

Neggan, George  229
Neil, Perry  235
Neill, Andrew  49
Neill, James C.  13
Neill, John C.  17, 41, 46, 55
Nelson, Albert A.  40
Nelson, Allison  90, 95
Nelson, Governeur H.  69, 89, 115
Neuhans, Charles  128
Nevill, Charles L.  163, 171
Newcomb, James W.  52
Newton, James R.  235
Newton Co., Tex.  204
Nichols, Ebenezer B.  48, 50
Nichols, John W.  212
Nichols, Roy C.  184, 187
Nichols, Thomas R.  212
Nichols, William  235
Nicholson, Andrew J.  124
Nicholson, S.G.  167
Nicholson, Wesley  229
Nicholson, William  229
Nickles, Robert  239
Nigh, Thomas P.  243
9th U.S. Cavalry  159
Nix, Christine  198
Nolan, Christian  235
Nolan, Mat  113
Nolan Co., Tex.  205, 207, 208
Nordyke, Clarence R.  245
Norias Raid  177
Norias, Tex.  185
Norris, James M.  105, 106, 118
North, Dan H.  203, 225
North Palo Pinto Creek  94
Norton, David O.  129
Nowlin, James C.  145
Nueces Canyon  144, 156, 172
Nueces Co., Tex.  56, 57, 65, 67, 149, 171, 172, 206, 207
Nueces River  17, 18, 21, 25, 44, 52, 53, 54, 55, 56, 59, 72, 74, 79, 83, 85, 86, 94, 137, 157
"Nueces Strip"  17, 25, 51, 53, 63, 82, 85, 86, 156; lawlessness in 17–18, 25, 83, 139, 150–151
Nuevo León  18, 20, 83, 151

Oakville, Tex.  156
Oatte, Charles  235
Obenchain, Alfred T.  105, 118, 123
O'Brien, William G.  123
O'Bryant, C.P.  235
Ochiltree Co., Tex.  205, 206
Oden, A.V.  221
Odneal, Harry T.  186
O'Doherty, Anthony  118
Oglesby, Thomas L.  155, 156, 168, 172
O'Hair, Michael  234
O'Hair, William  94
Oklahoma  22, 80, 82, 84, 96, 106, 107, 112, 125, 137, 153, 177
Old, A.Y.  222
Old, W.A.  222

Oldham, Richard "Dick" 225
Oldham, William 11
Oldham Co., Tex. 205, 206
Oliver, Eddie L. 203, 225
Olson, Fred C. 202
O'Neal, C.M. 146
O'Neal, James R. 35
O'Neal, William 235
O'Neill, John Q. 117
Orange Co., Tex. 169, 171, 204
Orange, Tex. 169, 171
Orrick, E.M. 128
Osgood, Joseph F. 242
Oska Horseback (Comanche) 140
Ouchaco, Tex. (Waco village) 30, 69, 72
Outlaw, Bass L. 221
Owen, Clark L. 49, 50, 55
Owen, Solomon H. 241
Owen, W.H. 167
Owens, Patrick 236
Ownby, James P. 17, 21, 25, 41, 53

Pace, W.B. 130
Packer, A. 70
"Paddy" 229
Palestine, Tex 185, 209
Palo Alto Prairie, Mexican War battle of 59, 214; McNelly's skirmish at 151, 218
Palo Pinto Co., Tex. 80, 84, 85, 89, 90, 91, 96, 99, 105, 107, 111, 116, 122, 125, 127, 128, 130, 146, 147, 168, 204, 205, 206
Palo Pinto, Tex. 146, 147
Pampa, Tex. 206
Pancoast, Josiah 70
Panhandle 164, 169, 182
Panola Co., Tex. 25, 107, 203, 205
Panther (Shawnee) 39
Parker, Benjamin 229
Parker, Cynthia Ann 18, 85
Parker, Daniel 14
Parker, James W., Sr. 28
Parker, Silas M., Sr. 14, 18, 28, 229
Parker, Tom 241
Parker Co., Tex. 85, 93, 105, 107, 111, 117, 125, 127, 128, 129, 135, 142, 146, 147, 168, 204, 205, 206
Parker's Fort 12, 13, 18, 28, 85
Parmer, Fletcher 236
Parmer Co., Tex. 205, 206
Paschal Co., Tex. 25, 53
Patterson, George W. 125
Patton, Charles A. 145
Patton, James M. 97
Patton, Samuel P.C. 108, 125
Paul, James 113
Payne, Morgan L. 66
Peace Policy 137, 141, 158
Peak, C.M. 95
Peak, Junius "June" 168
Pearce, J.C. 124
Pearsall, Tex. 169, 209
Pearson, Earl R. 197, 202, 203

Pease, Elisha M. 79, 80
Pease River 98, 99; Ross' battle at 85, 216
Pecan Bayou 20, 98, 99
Pecan Camp, Tex. 86
Pecan Springs, Tex. 169
Pecos Co., Tex. 137, 170, 171, 207, 208
Pecos River 18, 139, 170
Pecos, Tex. 207
Pedernales River 28, 51
Pelham, Thomas E. 236
Peltz, Otto 236
Pena, Tex. 169
Pendergrass, Nathaniel D. 236
Pennington, Ben L. 223, 244
Pensacola, Fla. 154
Peoples, Clinton T. "Clint" 202, 208, 225, 246, 310
Pérez, Antonio 25, 51
Pérez, Jesse, Sr. 224
Perkins, J.P. 223
Perkins, T.E.P. 223, 224, 244
Perry, Cicero Rufus "Rufe" 170
Perry, James 34
Perry, William 36
Perryman Station, Tex. 143
Pershing, John J. "Black Jack" 170
Peta Nocona (Comanche) 85
Peter, W.A. 124
Petit, R. 216
Petty, George M. 29
Peveler, William R. 122, 127, 241
Pharr, Tex. 185, 187
Philippine Insurrection 176, 177
Phillips, Royal B. 204
Phrene, Otto 236
Pickett, George B. 128
Piedras Negras, Mexico 79, 88
Pierce, John Constantinus 48
Pierson, John G.W. 31, 35
Pilkington, Samuel 39
Pitts, William A. 114
Place, Joe T. 224
Plácido (Tonkawa) 20, 21, 42, 50, 90, 96
Plainview, Tex. 189
Plan of San Diego 176–177, 177
Pleasanton, Tex. 117, 203
Plemons, Tex. 187
Plum Creek, battle of 23–24, 27, 50, 140, 212
Plummer, Jacob 229
Poe, Thomas C. 70
Point Isabel, Tex. 66
Polk, James K. 59
Polk Co., Tex. 204
Pollett, George 40
Poore, David N. 212
Porvenir Massacre
Post Davidson, Tex. 144
Post McCulloch, Tex. see McCulloch's Station, Tex.
Post Oak Springs 170
Post Washington, Tex. 31

Potter, Cincinnatus 108, 128, 129
Potter Co., Tex. 205, 206
Pound, J.M. 114
Powell, George E. "Gene" 203, 207
Powers, Andrew J. 229
Presidio Co., Tex. 105, 168, 170, 171, 180, 189, 207, 208
Presidio del Rio Grande, Tex. 72
Presidio La Bahía, massacre at 15
Presidio, Tex. 18, 185, 186
Preston, David 236
Preston, William G. 90
Price, Charles W. 223
Price, Harley 46
Price, James H. 112
Price, John T. 17, 25, 51, 53, 55, 57, 59, 66
Price, Leonidas "Lon" 96
Price, William R. 158
Prince, Bob G. 195, 196, 203, 208
Prince, John H. 119
Prince, Randy 205
Pritchett, Edley 236
Probst, Frank J. 205, 207
Prostoski, Joseph 236
Pue, Arthur 92, 93
Puebla, Mexico 64, 71
Pugh, E.B. 131
Pullin, T.N. 223
Purvis, Hardy B., Jr. 192, 203
Putman, J.M. 221
Putnam, Dickinson 31
Putz, Henry 220

Quanah Parker 85, 137, 160
Quanah, Tex. 169
Quayle, William 108, 110, 111, 126, 127
Queen, Lee 221
Quiñones, Agatón 18, 25

Rabb, Thomas 119
Rabb, Thomas J. 50
Radcliffe, Edward S. 236
Ragland, Thomas 222
Ragsdale, D.H. 97
"Railway Killer" see Angel Maturino Resendez
Rain, D.W.C. 116
Rainbolt, John P. 236
Rains Co., Tex. 107, 204, 205
Ralston, J.H. 71
Ramsey, Alexander 32
Ramsey's Creek 89
Rancho La Mesa, Ford's skirmish at 84, 216
Rancho Nuevo, Tex. 143
Randall Co., Tex. 205, 206
"Ranger Conviction" 151, 178
Ranger, Tex. 182, 188, 189
Ransom, Henry L. 117, 178, 186, 187, 233, 244
Rattan, Wade H. 229
Ratton, Littleton 236
Rawls, Amos 9

# INDEX

Ray, James E. "Jimmie"  225
Ray, James M. "Jim"  205
Raymondville, Tex.  185, 188, 206
Reagan Co., Tex.  207, 208
Real Co., Tex.  79, 203, 206, 207
Realitos, Tex.  171, 172
Red River  16, 17, 18, 21, 22, 37, 82, 84, 90, 98, 101, 105, 106, 108, 109, 110, 111, 113, 116, 137, 139, 157; Mackenzie's attack at the North Fork of 141
Red River Co., Tex.  25, 35, 37, 40, 45, 46, 48, 50, 51, 53, 107, 182, 204, 205
Red River Station, Tex.  102, 105, 108, 115, 116, 120, 121, 122, 123, 125
Red River War  158–160, 162
Reed, Henry  47
Reed, James B.  69
Reed, John A.  239
Reed, Thompson  236
Rees, Peter O.A. "Alonzo," Jr.  119
Reeves, R.O. (or R.P.)  124
Reeves Co., Tex.  168, 170, 172, 207, 208
Refugio Co., Tex.  21, 25, 55, 57, 204, 206, 207
Refugio, Tex.  15, 18, 55, 56, 156
Regency, Tex.  169
Remolino, Mexico  141
Renfro, David  37, 38
Republic of Texas (militia group)  196–197
Resaca de la Palma, battle of  59, 214
Resendez, Angel Maturino  197
Retama, Tex.  156
Reynolds, David  212
Reynolds, Joseph J.  138, 139
Reynolds, Nelson O. "Mage"  171
Reynolds, W.W.  118
Rhea, Danny V.  225
Rhew, William  236
Rice, James M.  131
Richarz, Henry Jones  139, 143
Richarz, Walter  217, 242
Richland Creek  57, 65, 73, 90
Richmond, Tex.  46, 170, 204
Richmond, Va.  101, 105
Riddles, James E.  207, 246
Rieger, R.T.  144
Riff, Joseph R.  217, 243
Riley, Ben C.  220
Ringgold Barracks, Tex.  168, 171
Río Escondido, Callahan's battle at  79, 215
Rio Grande  16, 17, 18, 26, 27, 51, 55, 56, 59, 65, 68, 72, 73, 74, 75, 77, 79, 82, 83, 84, 86, 87, 88, 89, 91, 92, 93, 105, 107, 112, 113, 137, 138, 139, 141, 149, 151, 152, 155, 162, 165, 168, 170, 175, 176, 177, 179, 180, 181, 183, 200, 209
Rio Grande City, Tex.  83, 84, 87, 87, 93, 151, 156, 169, 170, 172, 181, 185, 186, 187, 209
Rio Grande Station, Tex.  120, 123
Roane, —  68
Robinett, —  229
Robbins, George W.  134
Robbins, James  187
Robbins, John R.  236
Robbins, Thomas  31
Robbins' Ferry  31, 34
Robbless, Alexander  32
Roberson, H.L. "Hod"  222, 223, 224
Roberts, Alexander "Buck"  143
Roberts, Daniel W.  170, 218
Roberts, Jacob  71, 73, 76, 86
Roberts, James  236
Roberts, Joseph  236
Roberts, Mark R.  42, 45
Roberts, T.F.  12
Roberts, Thomas  236
Roberts Co., Tex.  205
Robertson, A.T.  46, 57, 127
Robertson, Sterling C.  30, 32
Robertson Co., Tex.  21, 25, 44, 46, 57, 203, 208
Robertson's Colony  29, 30
Robinson, J.  236
Robinson, Thomas J.  229
Robinson, William F.  131
Robinson, William H.  119
Robuck, W. Emmett  222, 244
Rock Creek Station, Tex.  128
Rocksprings, Tex.  207
Rockwall Co., Tex.  107, 204, 205
Roff, Charles L.  111, 124
Rogers, Curren L. "Kid"  221, 310
Rogers, Edward W.  85, 98, 101
Rogers, J.L.  225
Rogers, James  43
Rogers, James F. "Pete"  195, 203, 205, 225
Rogers, John A.  55
Rogers, John H.  165, 166, 171, 173, 174, 183, 186, 187, 220, 221, 222, 246, 310
Rogers, Joseph H.  52
Rogers, Patrick H.  87
Roma, Tex.  170, 181
Romaine, William C.  236
Roman, Richard  17, 66
Ross, Angus  236
Ross, James J.  10
Ross, Lawrence Sullivan "Sul"  80, 81, 84, 85, 86, 95, 97, 246
Ross, Peter F.  95, 136
Ross, Rueben  35, 46
Ross, Shapley P.  61, 62, 67, 69, 72, 76, 78, 80, 90
Ross, Tom M.  185
Round Mountain  144
Rowland, John T.  108, 120, 143
Rowland, Tex.  98
Rudd, William L.  156, 172, 220
Rugeley, John  55
Rundell, James L. "Skippy"  203, 205
Runnels, Hal G.  70
Runnels, Hardin R.  80, 83
Runnels Co., Tex.  102, 110, 132, 168, 172, 207
Runnolds, B.F.  236
Rush Springs, battle of  80–81
Rusk, Thomas J.  17, 22
Rusk Co., Tex.  101, 107, 204, 205
Russell, Eli  37
Russell, Grover Scott  222, 244
Russell, Walter  225
Ruzin, A.A.  243
Ryan, Hilary  91
Ryan, Phil  195
Ryan, William M.  187, 188

Sabinal Co., Tex.  96
Sabinal River  72, 88, 89, 91, 170
Sabinal, Tex.  96
Sabine Co., Tex.  172, 204
Sabine River  17, 20, 22, 29, 30, 37, 38, 40, 45, 46
Sadler, John W.  224
Sadler, Leonard T.  244
Sadler, Louis R.  177
Sadler, William T.  29, 36
Sageser, J.A.  241
St. Leon, Ernest  243
Salado Creek, Caldwell's battle at  26, 213
Salinas, Juan Flores  152
Salmon, John  84, 94, 120
Salt Creek  93, 168
Salt Creek Station, Tex.  125, 126
Saltillo, Mexico  9, 61, 68, 69
Sam Fordyce, Tex.  187
San Angelo, Tex.  170, 172, 185, 187, 188, 199, 205, 207, 208
San Antonio (San Antonio de Béxar) Tex.  7, 15, 17, 18, 22, 25, 26, 28, 30, 32, 34, 42, 47, 51, 53, 55, 56, 57, 61, 65, 66, 68, 69, 72, 75, 79, 85, 88, 113, 114, 115, 116, 137, 152, 155, 156, 181, 182, 185, 187, 188, 189, 191, 199, 200, 202, 203, 206, 207, 209
San Antonio River  31, 32, 34, 46, 55, 56, 134
San Antonio Road  9, 13, 22, 46, 48, 49, 53
San Augustine Co., Tex.  172, 204
San Augustine, Tex.  187, 204
San Benito, Tex.  185, 186
Sánchez, Lewis  36, 40, 45
Sanders, John J.  185, 186, 188, 222
Sanders, Joseph D.  236
Sanders, William  229
Sanderson, Tex.  186, 207
San Diego, Tex.  156, 172, 181
Sands, William B.  223
Sandy Creek  168
San Elizario, Tex.  144, 156, 162, 169
San Felipe, Tex.  8, 12, 14, 15

San Fernandez River 54
San Gabriel River 21, 42, 47, 67, 69
San Jacinto, battle of 16
San Jacinto Co., Tex. 204
San Jacinto River 8, 31
San Juan Teotihuacan, Hays' skirmish at 64, 215
San Marcos River 22, 29, 30
San Marcos, Tex. 208
San Patricio Co., Tex. 31, 53, 54, 156
San Patricio, Tex. 21, 25, 206, 207
San Pedro Creek 43, 79
San Saba Co., Tex. 84, 89, 93, 93, 94, 105, 116, 131, 131, 132, 145, 148, 165, 169, 171, 172, 207, 208
San Saba River 11, 21, 22, 42, 47, 52, 72, 77, 84, 97, 98, 170, 171, 172
San Saba, Tex. 89, 90, 93, 94, 116, 145, 169
Sansom, John W. 89, 91, 139, 143
Santa Anna, Antonio López de 12, 16, 62, 65
Santa Gertrudis Ranch *see* King Ranch
Santa María, Tex. 156, 172, 188
San Ygnacio, Tex. 181
Sauls, Charles 229
Sayers, Joseph D. 167
Scanland, John 97
Scheuster, Lewis P. 229
Schleicher Co., Tex. 207, 208
Schmid, Frank L., Jr. 221, 243
Schmitt, George H. 169, 220
Schuetze, L. 132
Schwethelm, Henry 145, 148
Scott, George L. 124
Scott, M.J. 130
Scott, Thomas M. 229
Scott, William 172, 220
Scott, Winfield 64, 65, 81
Scurlock, William 32
Scurry Co., Tex. 205, 207, 208
Seale, Eli 28
Seco Creek 74
2nd U.S. Cavalry 79, 80, 81, 83, 85
2nd U.S. Dragoons 61, 64, 77, 79
Sedberry, J.M. 220
See, Abraham H. 118, 119
Seguín, Juan N. 42
Seguin, Tex. 44, 53, 79, 206, 207
Self, William 71
Self, William B. 142
Sellers, Isaac 236
Sells, Tommy Lynn 198–199
Seminole Indians 79, 159; Seminole-Negro scouts 141, 155
Sessum, Jacob 236
Sessums, Grady 203
7th U.S. Infantry 77
Sevier, Charles 236
Sewell, Marcus L. 229
Shackelford Co., Tex. 98, 110, 137, 180, 204, 207, 208

Shackhart, Adolph 236
Shafter, William R. "Pecos Bill" 155
Shafter, Tex. 186
Shahan, William P. 236
Shannon, Sevier 128
Shaw, Joe R. 223, 244
Shaw, Owen 77, 86
Shawnee Indians 22, 90
Shawnee Town, Tex. 40
Shelby Co., Tex. 57, 182, 204
Shelbyville, Tex. 57
Shely, A.L. 220
Shely, Joseph 172
Sheridan, Philip H. 135
Sherman, S.F. 244
Sherman, Sidney 22
Sherman, William T. 141
Sherman Co., Tex. 205, 206
Sherman, Tex. 185, 186, 205, 206
Shields, James M. 237
Shipman, J.R. 132
Shipp, A.A. 119
Shoemake, William H. 129
Shoemaker, David H. 237
Shuffield, J.L.S. 127
Shults, Robert 237
Sieker, Frank E. 243, 220
Sieker, Lamartine P. "Lam" 167, 170, 184
Sierra Blanca, Tex. 186, 207
Sierra Diablo, Baylor's skirmish in the 162–163, 220
Silver Creek 172
Simmerman, G. 119
Simmons, James W. 39
Simmons, Laura 198
Simons, Thomas 237
Simpson, T.R. 217
Sims, Barlett 11
Sims, James W. 46
Sims, Samuel W. 70
Sims, W.H. 146
Sinton, Tex. 186, 206, 207
Sipe Springs 145
Sish, Alfred 237
Sisty, William R. 229
Sittanke (Kiowa) 141
6th U.S. Cavalry 158
Skaggs, D. 132
Slaughter, Benjamin 118
Slaughter, Christopher Columbus 99
Slein, John 229
Sloan, Robert 37
Smith, Abram T. 229
Smith, Augustus 239
Smith, Ben P. 237
Smith, Benjamin F. 46
Smith, C.C. 146
Smith, Edward H. 186, 187
Smith, Elisha 237
Smith, Erastus "Deaf" 19–20, 34
Smith, Focke 237
Smith, Francis M. 237

Smith, Henry M. 43
Smith, James 16, 22, 25, 34, 37, 70
Smith, James W. 224
Smith, John M. (1) 55
Smith, John M. (2) 92, 146
Smith, Joseph M. 72, 76, 86, 95
Smith, L. Berry "Sonny" 243
Smith, Lee C. 33
Smith, Persifor F. 77, 79
Smith, Robert W. 38
Smith, Samuel 31
Smith, Thomas 129
Smith, Thomas I. 57, 61, 62, 65, 68, 69
Smith, Thomas S. 167
Smith, W.J. 119
Smith, William 186, 187
Smith, William H. 16, 20, 31, 32
Smith, Zeno A. 192, 193
Smith Co., Tex. 107, 204, 205
Smith's Station, Tex. 69
Smithville, Tex. 203
Smithwick, Noah 21, 22, 42
Smock, — 75
Smock, Henry 70
Smythe, David P. 114
Snee, James 237
Snell, Martin K. 70
Snively, Jacob 36, 40
Snodgrass, Henry I. 241
Snyder, Tex. 208
Soleus, Charles B. 237
Somervell, Alexander 22, 26, 46; and the Somervell Expedition 26
Somervell Co., Tex. 107, 204, 208
Sonora, Tex. 207
Sowell, Andrew Jackson (1) 23
Sowell, Andrew Jackson (2) 140
Sowell, Joseph 46, 54
Spangler, John W. 81, 85
Spanish Fort, I.T. 125
Sparks, John C. 169
Sparks, Thomas M. 219
Spear, J.A. 128
Specht, Fred 146
Special Force 150, 152, 155
Special State Troops *see* Special Force
Speed, Robert E. 222
Speir, Wilson E. 194
Spofford Junction, Tex. 169
Spring Creek 39, 144, 145
Spy Buck (Shawnee) 39, 40
Staked Plains *see* Llano Estacado
Standifer, William J. 133
Stapp, Andrew 61, 68
Starr Co., Tex. 139, 143, 194, 206, 207, 209
State Ranger Force 173, 175, 177, 179, 180, 182, 183; Co. A 185; Co. A Volunteers 189; Co. B 182, 185–186; Co. B Volunteers 189; Co. C 173, 182, 186–187; Co. C Volunteers 189; Co. D 177, 187–188; Co. E 188; Co. F 188;

Co. G 188; Co. H 188; Co. K 188; Co. L 189; Co. M 189; Co. N 189; Emergency Co. #1 182, 189; Emergency Co. #2 189; Headquarters Co. 181, 182, 184–185
Steadman, Cheryl 198
Steen, Richard 237
Steene, John D. 242
Stein, John 229
Stephens, Hiram B. 35
Stephens, William F. 97
Stephens Co., Tex. 80, 90, 91, 98, 103, 105, 111, 120, 122, 127, 125, 129, 130, 131, 168, 189, 204, 207, 208
Stephenville, Tex. 96, 130, 143, 148, 204, 208, 209
Sterling, Ross S. 183
Sterling, William W. 183, 186, 187
Sterling Co., Tex. 207, 208
Sterne, Aldophus 49
Stevens, Charles F. 186, 188
Stevens, George W. 144, 147, 168
Stewart, F.C. 146
Stewart, Thomas 119
Stiff, James M. 237
Stiff, Jesse 40, 55
Still, Washington 242
Stillwell, William B. 244
Stockman, Reason P. 244
Stockton, James T. 184
Stone, James 237
"Stone Houses Fight" 20, 212
Stonewall Co., Tex. 205, 206
Story, Ephraim 237
Stout, Henry B. 48, 54
Stout, William B. 39, 48
Strong, J.R. 242
Strong, Lewis P. 119
Stroud, Ethan A. 42
Struhan, A. 237
Stuart, J. 242
Sublett, David L. 99
Sullivan, D.C. "Doc" 215, 239
Sullivan, W. John L. 221
Summers, William E. 229
Surles, Krystal 198, 199
Sutton, Charles F. 327
Sutton, James S. 72, 76, 86
Sutton, R.E. 85
Sutton Co., Tex. 77, 207, 208
Sutton-Taylor Feud 149, 150, 152–153
Sweaney, Richard H. 204
Sweetwater, Tex. 187, 207
Swift, Albert M. 243
Swift, John B. "Beak" 223
Swindells, James H. 95
Swisher, James M. 144
Swisher Co., Tex. 205, 206

Tacker, — 70
Tackett, Andrew C. 147
Tackett, Marion D. 117
Tackitt, Lewis Lycurgus "Like" 142

Tait, Charles W. 66
Talbot, William 327
Tamaulipas 18, 83, 151
Tankersly, James H. 90
Tanner, Harris T. 327
Tarish, Joseph D. 98
Tarrant, Edward H. 22, 25, 37
Tarrant Co., Tex. 74, 105, 107, 110, 142, 169, 170, 172, 204, 205
Tarver, Thad 224
Tawakoni (Tehuacana) Indians 9, 12, 15, 20, 21, 61, 78, 80, 90
Taylor, Brian 197
Taylor, Creed 222
Taylor, John 128
Taylor, Joseph 114, 223
Taylor, N.A. 216
Taylor, Robert H. 69
Taylor, William W. 188, 223
Taylor, Zachery 59, 60, 61, 62, 63
Taylor Co., Tex. 110, 132, 168, 171, 205, 207, 208
Taylor, Tex. 187
Tays, John B. 162, 169
Teague, John 142, 148
Teal, Richard S. 57
Tehuacana Creek 57, 65, 68
Tehuacana Springs, Coleman's skirmish at 12, 211
Tejanos see Hispanics
Temple, William B. 237
Temple, Tex. 209
Tenoxtitlan, Tex. 12, 30, 32, 33
10th U.S. Cavalry 159
10th U.S. Infantry 159
Terlingua, Tex. 185
Terrell Co., Tex. 207, 208
Terry Co., Tex. 205, 206
Texarkana, Tex. 192, 199, 205
Texas: annexation 12, 22, 59, 74, 77, 196; colonization 7–9, 9, 11; crime 17–18, 25, 75, 83, 107, 109–110, 138, 139, 149, 151, 153, 155, 164–165, 173, 175, 180, 183, 184, 191, 201; the frontier of 17, 19–20, 74, 77, 79, 84, 101, 102–103, 108; Reconstruction 135, 136, 138, 139, 142, 149; Republic of 15, 16; secession 100, 101, 107, 109; Texas Revolution 14–16, 17
Texas Army, in the revolution 15, 16, 17; Army of the Republic of Texas 17, 20, 24; Provisional Army of Texas 101
Texas City, Tex. 204
Texas Indian Reservations see Brazos Reservation and Clear Fork Reservation
Texas Legislature 76, 77, 79, 80, 100, 104, 105, 108, 135, 138, 141, 142, 149, 152, 165, 167, 175, 179, 181, 183, 190, 198, 200
Texas Militia 7, 9–11, 12, 17, 21, 22, 25, 26, 100, 111, 136, 138, 160
Texas Ranger Division 190, 194, 198, 199, 201; authorized strength 191, 194, 198, 201; caseloads 192, 201; Co. A 195, 198, 202; Co. B 195, 196, 198, 202; Co. C 195, 202; Co. D 200, 202; Co. E 197, 199, 202; Co. F 195, 196, 202; Co. G 198, 200, 202; duties 191, 201; Headquarters Co. 190, 202; Joint Operations Intelligence Centers (JOIC) 200; professional qualifications 190, 194–195, 201; Unsolved Crimes Investigation Team (UCIT) 200
Texas Rangers: badges 158, 191, 201, 308–111; and civil rights movement 193; and labor strikes 165, 175, 182, 191, 194; Loyalty Rangers 180, 189; and Mexican relations 61, 62–63, 63, 64–65, 82, 177, 178, 193–194; and oil towns 182; as peace officers 82, 110, 139, 149, 153, 157, 160, 163; as permanent force 80, 105, 157; and Prohibition 181–182; Railroad Rangers 182; Ranger Home Guard 180; as soldiers 82, 105, 138; Special Rangers 163–164, 175, 179, 183, 190; tactics 25, 27, 64, 103, 106, 108; wages 15, 79, 108, 138, 141, 155, 157–158, 175, 160, 173, 181, 183, 190, 191; weapons and equipment 27–28, 64, 76–77, 138, 140, 151–152, 154, 160, 175–176, 200–201; see also Frontier Battalion (TST); Frontier Battalion (TST/CSA); Frontier Regiment (TST) Special Force; State Ranger Force; Texas Ranger Division
*Texas State Gazette* (newspaper) 75, 76
Texas State Police 138, 139, 142, 149
3rd U.S. Cavalry 165
Thomas, Benjamin R. 33
Thomas, H.M. "Doc" 244
Thomas, Herman S. 327
Thomas, Jefferson 327
Thomas, John C. 46
Thomas, Robert 327
Thompson, David 327
Thompson, Henry J. 117, 127
Thompson, John S. 229
Thompson, Jonathan (1) 229
Thompson, Jonathan (2) 239
Thompson, S.G. 120
Thompsonville Station, Tex. 143
Throckmorton Co., Tex. 78, 98, 99, 122, 130, 168, 102, 110, 204, 205, 206
Throckmorton, James W. 111, 127, 135, 136
Thurber, Tex. 169, 187
Tidwell, Peter 327
Timberlake, Delbert "Tim" 223, 244
Timmins, James F. 40

Tinnin's Crossing 47
Tipps, Peter 40
Titus Co., Tex. 107, 204, 205
Tobin, William G. 83, 84, 88, 92, 115
Tolbert, John F. 327
Tom, John Files 133
Tom, William 88
Tom Green Co., Tex. 102, 111, 137, 170, 171, 207, 208
Tompkins, W.O. 220
Tonkawa (Toncahua) Indians 10, 20, 21, 44, 50, 53, 61, 78, 80, 90, 96, 159
Torrey's Trading House, Tex. 57, 65, 68
Totten, Silas S. 111, 130
Totty, F.M. 125
Townsend, Light 187
Townsend, Stephen 30
Townsend, Woody T. 189
Toyah, Tex. 168, 171
Trammel, Benjamin 327
Trans-Pecos region see Big Bend
Travis, Charles E. 87
Travis Co., Tex. 25, 41, 45, 48, 52, 57, 66, 68, 69, 74, 101, 105, 142, 154, 168, 199, 203, 208, 209
Treadwell, William 220
Trespalacios, José Felix 7
Trimmer, Beverly 328
Trinity Co., Tex. 204
Trinity River 11, 13, 16, 17, 20, 21, 28, 29, 30, 31, 34, 35, 36, 37, 38, 40, 48, 52, 54, 55, 57, 58, 61, 65, 68, 72, 73, 74, 90
Trinity, Tex. 186
Trollinger, Harris C. "Harry" 223
Truitt, Alfred 70, 71
Tufts, Charles W. 328
Tuggle, Ransom 112, 114
Tumlinson, George W. 230
Tumlinson, James 10
Tumlinson, John J., Jr. 10, 15, 16, 23, 29, 31, 47, 49, 54
Tumlinson, John J., Sr. 7
Tumlinson, Josiah 328
Tumlinson, Lott 222
Tumlinson, Peter 84, 92, 96
Tumlinson's Fort, Tex. 29
Turley, Elisha 238
Turnbo, L.S. 220
Turner, H.R. 244
12th U.S. Cavalry 177
Twitty, William C. 124
Tyler, John 59
Tyler Co., Tex. 204
Tyler, Tex. 204, 205

Underhill Springs 146
U.S. Army 64, 160, 175, 176, 180; and frontier defense policies 74, 77, 79, 80, 136–137, 139, 141, 155, 158, 177, 179; posts 74, 77, 79, 137
U.S. Congress 59, 135, 158, 179, 181

U.S.-Mexican War 59; frontier protection during 61, 65; and Mexican guerrillas 61, 63–64, 64; Texas Ranger behavior 61, 63, 64–65
Upshur Co., Tex. 107, 204, 205
Upton, Monroe 128
Upton Co., Tex. 207, 208
Utley, Robert M. 12, 28, 161
Uvalde Canyon 42
Uvalde Co., Tex. 74, 84, 89, 92, 96, 97, 105, 116, 121, 122, 123, 133, 134, 137, 143, 146, 155, 170, 171, 172, 206, 207
Uvalde, Tex. 91, 92, 146, 155, 170, 172, 185, 188, 205, 206, 207

Valentine, Tex. 185, 186, 189
Val Verde Co., Tex. 79, 168, 171, 172, 198, 207, 208, 209
Van Benthuysen, A.B. 20, 33, 34
Van Dorn, Earl 80, 81
Van Riper, J.E. 168
Vansickle, Benjamin A. 43
Vanslike, Andrew H. 238
Van Zandt Co., Tex. 107, 204, 205
Vásquez Raid 25–26, 61
Vatch, T.J. 238
Vaughan, Jefferson Eagle "Jeff" 185, 222
Vaughan, Richard 238
Veale, Bert C. 224, 244
Veal's Station, Tex. 117
Veatch, John A. 72
Velasco, Tex. 12, 21, 122, 123
Vera Cruz, Mexico 21, 64, 65, 71, 176
Verde Creek 79
Vergara, Mexico 71
Vernon, Thomas 238
Vernon, Tex. 169, 172, 204, 205
Vickers, W.D. 203, 204
Victoria Co., Tex. 25, 53, 54, 55, 56, 66, 105, 203, 206, 207
Victoria Peak 125
Victoria, Tex. 18, 23, 25, 31, 32, 51, 53, 54, 55, 156, 204, 209
Viesca, Tex. 12
Villa, Francisco "Pancho" 179, 181
Vining, W.W. 238
Vinson, Milton 238
Viveon, Thacker 238

Waco (Huaco) Indians 9, 10, 11, 12, 20, 21, 61, 78, 80, 90
Waco, Tex. 186, 196, 197, 202, 203, 204, 208, 209
Wade, Peter F. 238
Wahrmund, William 132
Waide, J.M. 145
Wakeman, Wende 198
Walden, Albert P.
Waldrip, Johnny L. 225
Waldrup, P. 134
Walker, Dixon 84, 94

Walker, Edward 117
Walker, J.G. 242
Walker, John G. 87
Walker, Joseph 92, 98
Walker, Leroy 101
Walker, Samuel H. 26, 27, 28, 59, 60, 64, 66, 176, 246
Walker Co., Tex. 204
Walker's Creek, Hays' battle at 28, 213
Walker's Station, Tex. 39
Wallace, Joseph W.E. 14, 50
Wallace, Warren 156
Wallace, William A.A. "Bigfoot" 26, 27, 60, 67, 76, 86, 246
Wallace Creek, Moore's battle at 21, 212
Waller, John R. 167
Waller Co., Tex. 172, 204
Wallis, Hayes 222
Walters, Baley C. 22, 39, 43
Walthersdorff, Albert 133
Ward, Cyrus L. 230
Ward, Henry 118, 128, 129
Ward, Joseph 120
Ward, Lafayette 23, 50, 56
Ward, Richard 95
Ward Co., Tex. 207, 208
Ware, Richard C. "Dick" 162, 219
Warfield, Hiram 72
Warnell, John 238
Warren, Benjamin G. 243
Warren Wagon Train Massacre 141
Warren's Trading Post 126
Warring, Thomas 238
Washington Co., Tex. 150, 152, 171, 204
Washington Co. Volunteer Militia see Special Force
Washington, D.C. 80, 137, 151, 176, 179
Washington-on-the-Brazos, Tex. 15, 30, 58
Waterloo, Tex. see Austin, Tex.
Waters, Raymond 205
Waters, Robert G. 238
Waters, William 238
Watkins, Theopilus 133
Watkins, W.C. 145
Watkins, William M. 94
Watson, — 219
Weatherby, Thomas C. 242
Weatherford, John 238
Weatherford, Tex. 127, 128, 142, 172, 185
Weathers, Carl F. 205
Weaver, Bud 180, 223
Weaver, J.G. 119
Weaver, William H. 230
Webb, Alexander W. 54
Webb, Andrew J. 230
Webb, Charles 154
Webb, Grover Cleveland 223
Webb, Milton 98, 116

Webb, Walter Prescott 28, 100, 138, 190–191
Webb Co., Tex. 146, 149, 156, 169, 170, 171, 172, 177, 206, 207, 209
Weber, Augustine 134
Webster, Booker 238
Webster, Charles H. 222
Wells, Joseph 238
Wells, Joseph P. 66
Wells, L.B. 220
Wells, Moses 48
Wells, Munroe 223
Wells, Wright C. 223
Werner, Walter 205
West, Jackson 238
West, Richard 55
West, William 238
Wethers, James W. 238
Whaley, Henry A. 124
Whaley, Thomas F. 129
Wharton Co., Tex. 171, 172, 204
Wheatley, J.B. 187
Wheatly, George A. 167
Wheeler, Royal T., Jr. 118
Wheeler Co., Tex. 162, 205, 206
Wheelock, E.L. Ripley 31
Whelan, D.M. 171
Whepler, Phillip 230
Whitaker, Madison G. 38
White, Ambrose B. 124, 125
White, Emmett 244
White, Goff 222
White, H.A. 245
White, Homer 222, 244
White, John Dudley, Sr. 244
White, John L. 114
White, Joseph S. 238
White, Newton 122
White, Robert 230
White, Robert M. 84, 94
Whiteside, Robert M. 122
Whitman, Henry L. "Hank," Jr. 206
Wichita Agency, I.T. 82, 96
Wichita Co., Tex. 107, 120, 125, 130, 169, 189, 204, 206
Wichita Expedition 80–81, 84
Wichita Falls, Tex. 169, 185, 186, 204, 205, 207
Wichita Indians 10, 61, 80
Wichita Mountains 80, 91, 106
Wichita River 93, 99, 116, 120, 125, 126, 147
Wiggs, William W. 114
Wilbarger, John L. 239
Wilbarger Co., Tex. 110, 130, 169, 172, 204, 205, 206

Wilbarger's Fort, Tex. 43
Wilie, Joe F. 205, 208, 225
Wilkerson, James A. 34
Willacy Co., Tex. 177, 206, 207, 209
Willard, Timothy S. 224, 244
Willhyte, William 238
Williams, J.N.B. 98
Williams, John (1) 226
Williams, John (2) 20
Williams, Joseph 38
Williams, R.C. 216
Williams, R.H. 134
Williams, Samuel 46
Williams, Thomas 238
Williams, William M. 54
Williamson, Robert M. 12, 13, 15, 29, 150
Williamson Co., Tex. 74, 203, 208
Willingham, Eli 238
Willingham, John J. 146
Willis, Henry J. 239
Willis, Lon L. 189
Willis, S.M. 242
Willow Springs 115
Wilson, J. Thomas 167
Wilson, Jason 35, 51
Wilson, John 230
Wilson, Levy C. 203, 207
Wilson, Samuel 238
Wilson, William A. 238
Wilson, William C. 31
Wilson, William D. "Bill" 202, 204
Wilson, William F. 47
Wilson, Woodrow 179
Wilson Co., Tex. 203, 206, 027
Winkler Co., Tex. 207, 208
Wise, J.M. 221
Wise Co., Tex. 84, 85, 93, 94, 105, 107, 111, 117, 125, 127, 128, 129, 130, 135, 138, 140, 142, 143, 144, 147, 148, 168, 204, 205
Witt, Pleasant 27
Witt, Preston 71
Witter, John L. 40
Woelber, A.H. 223
Wolf [deWolf], Gottip 230
Wolfenberger, Samuel 32
Wolfscroner, Augustus 238
Woll Raid 26
Woll's Crossing 72
Womack, Max V. 225
Wood, George T. 75
Wood, Hanna 99
Wood, J.G. 243
Wood, John M. 206
Wood, William Riley 94, 116

Wood Co., Tex. 107, 204, 205
Woodlan, Daniel 49
Woodland, Ben H. 224
Woodlief, Devereaux Jerome 21, 41
Woodruff, Fountain B. 240
Woods, D.R. 119
Woods, J.W. 244
Woods, William M. 95
Woodville, Tex. 204
Wool, John E. 61
Woolfolk, John A. 122
Worrall, J.R. 119
Worth, William J. 61
Wortham, John 39, 40, 42
Wray, S.M. 242
Wren, Nicholas 33
Wright, Claiborne 230
Wright, George W. 239
Wright, J.A. 145
Wright, J.M. 85, 99
Wright, James A. 209
Wright, L.B. 151
Wright, O.N. 222
Wright, Thomas C. 122
Wright, William L. "Will" 181, 183, 185, 187, 188, 222, 223, 224, 246
Wyche, William P. 38
Wylie, W.L. 242
Wyman, E.S. 62, 69

Yeager, William O. 104, 114
Yeary, David 128
Yoakum Co., Tex. 205, 206
York, John 11, 32
Young, Harve F. 242
Young, J.M. 119
Young, Lee Roy, Jr. 197
Young, William F. 46, 47
Young Co., Tex. 77, 80, 84, 85, 93, 96, 99, 102, 103, 105, 107, 111, 122, 125, 127, 128, 130, 135, 147, 148, 168, 169, 204, 205, 206
Yount, Andrew J. 98, 143
Ysleta, Tex. 168, 169, 170, 185, 186, 187, 188, 189

Zacualtipán, Mexico, Hays' skirmish at 64, 215
Zapata Co., Tex. 139, 144, 177, 181, 206, 207, 209
Zarragosa, Mexico 155
Zavala Co., Tex. 134, 170, 172, 194, 206, 209
Zimmerman Telegraph 179
Zumwalt, Adam 49, 52

www.ingramcontent.com/pod-product-compliance
Ingram Content Group UK Ltd.
Pitfield, Milton Keynes, MK11 3LW, UK
UKHW050543150426
5217IPUK00026B/2052